The Company of the Preachers

A History of Biblical Preaching from the Old Testament to the Modern Era

Volume 2

The Company of the Preachers

A History of Biblical Preaching from the Old Testament to the Modern Era

Volume 2

David L. Larsen

The Company of the Preachers: A History of Biblical Preaching from the Old Testament to the Modern Era, Vol. 2

Published by Kregel Publications, a division of Kregel, Inc., P.O. Box 2607, Grand Rapids, MI 49501. Kregel Publications provides trusted, biblical publications for Christian growth and service. Your comments and suggestions are valued.

Cover illustration: Patrick Kelley

ISBN 0-8254-3086-0

Printed in the United States of America

Contents

Chapter Nine:	Starbursts and Sidetracks of the Victorian Pulpit Part One: The Headwaters	415
Chapter Ten:	Starbursts and Sidetracks of the Victorian Pulpit Part Two: The Raging River	497
Chapter Eleven:	The Glory and Agony of Twentieth-Century Preaching Part One: Vitality or Entropy?	599
Chapter Twelve:	The Glory and Agony of Twentieth-Century Preaching Part Two: Resurgence or Senescence?	713
Epilogue:	The Prospects for Preaching	847
	Appendixes	853
	Indexes	859

CHAPTER NINE

Starbursts and Sidetracks of the Victorian Pulpit

Part One: The Headwaters

Our gospel came to you not simply with words, but also with power, with the Holy Spirit and with deep conviction. . . . The Lord's message rang out from you . . .

—1 Thessalonians 1:5, 8

With the help of our God we dared to tell you his gospel in spite of strong opposition. . . . We speak as men approved by God to be entrusted with the gospel. We are not trying to please men but God, who tests our hearts . . . And we also thank God continually because, when you received the word of God, which you heard from us, you accepted it not as the word of men, but as it actually is, the word of God, which is at work in you who believe.

—1 Thessalonians 2:2b, 4, 13

Beyond all question, the mystery of godliness is great: He appeared in a body, was vindicated by the Spirit, was seen by angels, was preached among the nations, was believed on in the world, was taken up in glory.

—1 Timothy 3:16

This is my gospel, for which I am suffering even to the point of being chained like a criminal. But God's word is not chained. Therefore I endure everything . . .

—2 Timothy 2:8b–10a

> But the Lord stood at my side and gave me strength, so that through me the message might be fully proclaimed and all the Gentiles might hear it.
>
> —2 Timothy 4:17

> The office of the preacher is to smite the rock, that the living waters may gush forth to satisfy the thirst of the age.
>
> —Archbishop of York, W. C. Magee (1821–1891), considered second only to Prime Minister William E. Gladstone as an orator

> Good expository preaching does not impress the congregation; it feeds them.
>
> —Walter L. Liefeld

As the eighteenth century closed with the American Revolution and the barbarism of the French Revolution,[1] the nineteenth century loomed with promise and change. The convulsions of the Napoleonic Wars,[2] the agricultural and industrial revolutions, immigration, the era of colonial expansion, and Victorianism created a milieu for heroic preaching. Here we shall see much maturity and pulpit potency, but here we shall also see the seeds of apostasy and a disappointing hesitancy.

In his monumental work *The Birth of the Modern: World Society 1815–1830,* Paul Johnson advances the thesis that the foundations were laid in these years for the new ideas, inventions, and technological progress that would shape the new world order to come.[3] Evangelical stalwarts like Wilberforce, Shaftesbury, John Bright, and Prime Minister William E. Gladstone (a lay preacher in his own right)[4] were front and center in England. James Madison, the fourth president of the United States, must be seen as "America's most theologically knowledgeable president." Madison graduated from the College of New Jersey (later to become Princeton), and stayed an additional year to study Hebrew with President John Witherspoon. His political ideas were largely derived from New-Side Presbyterians.[5]

Certainly the much maligned Victorians had inconsistencies and hypocrisies, but their overall commitment was to virtue. Marriage and the family were important to them. Gertrude Himmelfarb has ably shown that the Victorians did not take sin lightly.[6] She quotes the French historian Halevy to show how Wesleyanism stimulated family values in part through its fostering of worshiping together as a family unit.[7]

Peter Gay's multivolume series, *The Bourgeois Experience: Victoria to Freud,* shows the surviving influence of the Enlightenment on the nineteenth-century bourgeois, but cannot dispute the continuing impact of revival and preaching upon society in every echelon.[8] This is the context for our consideration of the promise that emanated from the Victorian pulpit.

---

1. For an important interpretation of the American Revolution, see Barbara Tuchman, *The First Salute: A View of the American Revolution* (New York: Knopf, 1988 see

also Howard Fast, *Seven Days in June: A Novel of the American Revolution* (New York: Brick Lane Press, 1994). This focuses on the first military encounter of the Revolution in Lexington and Concord on April 19, 1775. The best background of the French Revolution on a modest scale is R. R. Palmer, *The World of the French Revolution* (New York: Harper and Row, 1971). An estimated two million Frenchmen died (cf. Rene Sedillot).

2. For a significant newer study, see David Hamilton-Williams, *The Fall of Napoleon: The Final Betrayal* (New York: John Wiley, 1994). Hamilton-Williams argues that Napoleon was overthrown not in battle but by treason, and was murdered by his friend Montchenu.
3. Paul Johnson, *The Birth of the Modern: World Society 1815–1830* (New York: Harper/Collins, 1991).
4. David W. Bebbington, *William Ewart Gladstone: Faith and Politics in Victorian Britain* (Grand Rapids: Eerdmans, 1993). Contains an important treatment of Gladstone's spirituality and his sermons, 68ff.
5. William Lee Miller, *James Madison: The Business of May Next and the Founding* (Charlottesville: University of Virginia Press, 1992). Miller shows how Madison got many of his political ideas from the New-Side Presbyterians.
6. Gertrude Himmelfarb, *The De-Moralization of Society: From Victorian Virtues to Modern Values* (New York: Knopf, 1994), 26. In a remarkable article, "Is America's Moral Crisis Irreparable?" in *Human Events* (December 1, 1995): 10ff., Himmelfarb argues that Puritan and Wesleyan spirituality caused a moral order to flourish in England.
7. Ibid., 55.
8. Peter Gay, *The Naked Heart: The Bourgeois Experience: Victoria to Freud,* vol. 4 (New York: Norton, 1995).

9.1 THE SCOTTISH TORRENT

> How beautiful on the mountains are the feet of those who bring good news, who proclaim peace, who bring good tidings, who proclaim salvation, who say to Zion, "Your God reigns!"
>
> —Isaiah 52:7

Again we must visit Scotland to find the red-hot core of great preaching. Considering the relative smallness of her scattered population, the preaching phenomenon is all the more astounding. The vitality of evangelicalism at the time must be seen as the product of the Cambuslang Revival of 1742 and the ministry of the American evangelists. But the Church of Scotland was becoming increasingly divided between the moderates and the children of the revivals, the evangelicals.

9.1.1 THE HALDANE BROTHERS—LAYING THE FOUNDATION

> Disputes about election and predestination, or the extent of the atonement, are, amongst true disciples, generally little more than strifes of words, arising out of the partial restoration of spiritual eye-sight.

> The Scriptures contain a plain warrant to preach the Gospel to every creature. There is no exception. "Whosoever believes" this testimony, may conclude with certainty that for him Christ died.
>
> —Alexander Haldane (representing the thoughts and convictions of Robert Haldane, his uncle, and James Alexander Haldane, his father)

Nonordained servants of Christ loom large throughout this narrative. **Hannah More** (1745–1833), the poetess and friend of Samuel Johnson, was one such layperson. **David Garrick,** converted through John Newton's preaching and who established schools in Cheddar near Bristol in which twenty-five thousand students matriculated, was another.

The Haldane brothers provide us with a third example of effective lay preachers. They spent their fortune on evangelism and missions, only to be put out by the Kirk of Scotland. **Robert Haldane** (1764–1842) and **James Haldane** (1768–1851) were descendants of Danish chiefs and of the barony of Grayeagles. Their father was a wealthy sea captain and their mother a devout Christian who taught her sons to love Scripture. The two sons each pursued naval careers after schooling in Edinburgh. James sailed in and out of Macao and read Doddridge. Both were gloriously converted but were blocked in their aspirations to go to India as missionaries.

The Haldanes gave themselves to the study of Christian evidences at a time when the assaults of unbelief and the compromises of the moderates had left the Kirk of Scotland weak. When moderates opposed bringing the gospel to the heathen, old **John Erskine** (cf. 8.3.7) electrified evangelicals in the Assembly by demanding, "Moderator, rax me that Bible!" ("Reach me that Bible!"), and he read the Word to the abashed commissioners.[1]

The brothers were tireless in their preaching. Networking with John Newton, Charles Simeon, and Rowland Hill, they gave themselves to tract publication, the establishment of Sabbath schools, and a great preaching crusade in the Circus in Edinburgh. James traveled with Simeon on riding tours in 1794 and 1795 with revival breaking out here and there.

James made a memorable preaching tour of the Hebrides and the Orkneys.[2] Soon after, Robert sold the ancestral estate and was established as pastor of a tabernacle seating three thousand in Edinburgh. Tabernacles were also constructed in Glasgow, Dundee, and Perth. Training schools were held for young preachers. More than three hundred men known as Haldane preachers, several of whom were Gaelic-speaking, were sent forth.

In 1808, the brothers were immersed, and their followers became Baptists. "The church is in the wilderness," became their theme. Robert went to Geneva, Switzerland, and was followed by the English banker, Henry Drummond. There Haldane taught the Book of Romans with a great response among university students, and young pastors like d'Aubigne, Frederic Monod, Cesar Malan, Gaussen, and others (cf. 9.6) were converted.[3] This was the beginning of revival in both Switzerland and France. Wilberforce paid tribute to Robert and the "charms of his melodious eloquence." Chalmers himself used Robert Haldane on inspiration, which accounts in part for David Bebbington's irritation with

Haldane.[4] Meanwhile, James was itinerating extensively in Scotland and brought Andrew Fuller up for services.

The Haldanes' preaching was biblical and evangelistic, as an extract from Robert's commentary indicates:

> In the resurrection and exaltation of Jesus Christ, believers are taught the certainty of their immortality and future blessedness. Lazarus, and others who were raised up, received their life in the same state as they possessed it before; and after they arose they died a second time; but Jesus Christ in His resurrection, obtained a life entirely different. In his birth a life was communicated to Him which was soon to terminate on the cross. His resurrection communicated a life imperishable and immortal. Jesus Christ being raised from the dead, death hath no more dominion over Him . . .[5]

The Haldanes were also in touch with Bishop Edward Bickersteth, an outstanding evangelical, Andrew Thompson, the Scottish champion of plenary inspiration, and John Brown, the grandson of John Brown of Haddington in a delightful camaraderie of Bible preachers. How mightily God used the lives and utterances of the Haldane brothers.[6]

---

1. Alexander Haldane, *Memoirs of Robert Haldane and James Alexander Haldane* (Edinburgh: Hamilton, Adams, 1852), 131.
2. Ibid., 151.
3. Robert Haldane, *Exposition of the Epistle to the Romans* (Edinburgh: Banner of Truth, 1958). D. Martyn Lloyd-Jones regarded this commentary as one of his very favorite on Romans, so "warm in spirit and practical in application."
4. D. W. Bebbington, *Evangelicalism in Modern Britain* (London: Allen and Unwin, 1989), 87ff.
5. Ibid., 275.
6. A. T. Olson, *Believers Only* (Minneapolis: Free Church Press, 1964), 270. Olson shows how the Haldanes made an impact on Denmark and Sweden as well as Canada. The restoration movement in the U.S. reflects some Haldane features. In Gunnar Westin's *The Free Church Through the Ages* (Nashville: Broadman, 1958), we have frequent references to the Haldanes and their influence, as on 243, 265, 280, 285, 295, 329.

9.1.2 The Bonar Brothers—Looking to the Hills

> I find myself in the cleft of the rock and preach about it every Sunday.
>
> Very few ministers keep to the end the spark that was in their ministry at the beginning.
>
> Make my sermons like quivers full of arrows dipped in love.
>
> —Andrew Bonar

Of the seven sons in the Bonar family, three were outstanding preachers: **John Bonar** (1803–1891), **Horatius Bonar** (1808–1889), and the youngest, **Andrew Bonar** (1810–1892). All three graduated from the University of Edinburgh, in the city of their birth. John's ministry was largely at Greenock and then in the Free Church in 1843 at the Disruption. Horatius is best known as the writer of six hundred hymns, including "I Heard the Voice of Jesus Say," "I Lay My Sins on Jesus," and "Here, O My Lord, I See Thee Face to Face." He served with distinction at Kelso and then at Chalmers Memorial in Edinburgh. His was rich in the Scriptures and his preaching appealed especially to children.[1]

Both Horatius and Andrew served as moderators of the General Assembly. Andrew ministered first in Perthshire, and after the disruption pastored the Finnieston Free Church in Glasgow until his death. Like his brothers, Andrew was a fervent premillenarian and was part of the group that traveled to Palestine. The group, which included Robert Murray McCheyne, worked on behalf of the Church Mission to the Jews (1839). As a dear friend of McCheyne, Andrew wrote the highly charged *Memoirs and Remains of McCheyne*. He also edited Rutherford's letters (cf. 7.5.3).

Andrew was part of the so-called saints' school among Scottish evangelicals, explaining in part the vigorous upsurgence in Scottish preaching at the time. He was a warm, passionately revivalistic preacher who welcomed D. L. Moody to Scotland and visited Moody's Northfield Conference in the U.S. Andrew's confidence in the integrity of Scripture knew no bounds—while in his eighties he became deeply troubled over Marcus Dods' theological slippage. The depth of his exegesis can be seen in the *Book of Psalms* (1859), a choice example of what Bonar called "a dropping of the honeycomb."[2]

In his *Life and Letters,* Andrew pleads for "the necessity of preaching Christ in every sermon."[3] Indeed, he loved his calling so much that he asked the Lord to help him be "weaned from being too fond of preaching." With respect to his delivery style he testified: "I do not like paper."

Andrew always referred to his dear wife as "the desire of my eyes" in any public reference. W. Robertson Nicoll calls Andrew Bonar a "Prince of the Church" because his power was the power of prayer. "May every sermon be laid on the altar of incense," Bonar prayed. He reported of one Lord's Supper, "Every part of the Communion Service seemed to be under His smile . . . our objective being 'reclining on Christ's bosom.'"

---

1. Horatius Bonar, *God's Way of Holiness* (Chicago: Moody, n.d.).
2. Andrew Bonar, *Christ and His Church in the Book of Psalms* (London: Nisbet, 1859). A rich repository of exegetical and devotional thoughts.
3. Marjory Bonar, ed., *The Diary and Life of Andrew Bonar* (London: Hodder and Stoughton, 1894), 43.

9.1.3 Robert Murray McCheyne—Lifting the Tone

> A man cannot be a faithful minister unless he preaches Christ for Christ's sake.

> What would my people do if I were not to pray?
>
> Nothing is more needful for making a sermon memorable and impressive than a logical arrangement.
>
> —Robert Murray McCheyne

He stands as one of Scotland's most brilliant and able preachers. Believing that every sermon represented "an inch of time in which to stand and preach Christ . . . and then the endless roll of eternal years follows," **Robert Murray McCheyne** (1813–1843) packed as much into his thirty short years as any man ever did.

Born in Edinburgh, he was so precocious he learned the Greek alphabet at age four and enrolled in the University of Edinburgh at fourteen. He studied divinity under Chalmers but was not converted until the death of his brother, David. With the prayer "less like myself, more like my Master," and "Lord, purify me,"[1] the writings of both Jonathan Edwards and David Brainerd, as well as the letters of Samuel Rutherford shaped him. McCheyne soon developed a profound desire to please God. He once criticized another's sermons, saying, "Some things are powerful, but I long to hear more of Christ."

McCheyne served with John Bonar in Larbert and Duniplace and there imbibed Bonar's premillennial insistence on the restoration of the Jews. "Regenerated Israel will be as a dew from the Lord." His eschatological orientation was reflected in the signature he attached to his letters, "Yours in Jesus our Hope."[2]

In 1836 he took the call to St. Peter's, Dundee, a newly organized congregation of some 1,100 members. His sermons tended to be lengthy but greatly supported by prayer. "What would my people do if I were not to pray?" he asked. He confessed of his own preaching, "I am just an interpreter of Scripture; and when the Bible runs dry, then I shall."[3]

Because of his missionary spirit he was asked by Dr. Candlish to accompany three other ministers on a mission of inquiry to Palestine in the interest of Jewish evangelism. He regretted he could not speak Arabic and witness to the Muslims. On this epochal trip, he studied Bonar on Leviticus. On the way home they established a ministry to the Jews in Budapest (to which John Duncan was later called).[4]

Never physically hardy, McCheyne became deathly sick in Bouja near Smyrna on the way back. In praying for their pastor, the folk in Dundee experienced a special visit of the Holy Spirit at the same time of the stirring at Kilsyth, where **William C. Burns** was the pastor and where thousands were gathering for renewal and salvation. Burns (called by Hudson Taylor "the man of the Book," and the first English Presbyterian missionary to China) filled the pulpit in Dundee while McCheyne was abroad. Revival fires began to burn, and when the pastor returned he found his congregation in the ferment of awakening. He preached extensively and lived in the flame of revival in his own church where thirty-five prayer meetings were held every week, five of which were children's prayer meetings. He wrote several hymns still sung today, such as "Jehovah Tsidkenu," with the marvelous opening line, "I once was a stranger to grace and to God."

Like all of these Scottish divines, he seemed to confess sin more and more and practice it less and less. He was known for his "communion sessions" when "the Lord gave tokens."

McCheyne inscribed on his letters, "The night cometh." "Live so as to be missed," he advised, and so he was when after a sudden fever he parted from this life just short of his thirtieth birthday. His printed sermons remain a fragrant memorial to his faithful preaching.[5] We have the notes of three hundred or so of his sermons preached to the weavers of Dundee. Notes taken by a parishioner on his messages from Revelation 2–3 were published as *Expositions of the Epistles to the Seven Churches* (1838). "His preaching was a giving out of his inward life," one observer noted. Almost always textual, crisply outlined, pulsating with spiritual power, they merit reading yet today. Of particular worth are "Time Is Short," from 1 Corinthians 7:29–31, and "A Time of Refreshing," from Isaiah 44:3–4. Blaikie wrote of McCheyne's style:

> McCheyne brought into the pulpit all the reverence for Scripture of the Reformation period; all the honor for the Headship of Christ of the Covenanter struggle; all the freeness of the Gospel offer of the Marrow theology; all the bright imagery of Samuel Rutherford; all the delight of the Erskines in the fullness of Christ. In McCheyne the effect of a cultured taste was apparent in the chastened beauty and simplicity of his style, if you can call it a style—in a sense he has no style, or rather it was the perfection of style, for it was transparent as glass. The new element he brought to the pulpit, or rather which he revived and used so much that it appeared new, was winsomeness . . .[6]

McCheyne's own counsel was:

> Get your texts from God—your thoughts, your words, from God . . . It is not great talents God blessed so much as great likeness to Jesus. A holy minister is an awful weapon in the hand of God. A word spoken by you when your conscience is clear, and your heart full of God's Spirit, is worth ten thousand words spoken in unbelief and sin.

---

1. Andrew Bonar, *The Life of Robert Murray McCheyne* (Edinburgh: Banner of Truth, 1844, 1962), 16ff.
2. Ibid., 78.
3. Alexander Smellie, *Robert Murray McCheyne* (London: National Council of Evangelical Free Churches, 1913). A rich resource!
4. Robert A. Peterson, "An Early Scottish Mission to the Jews," *Israel My Glory* (June–July 1989): 22ff. McCheyne's and Bonar's journal on this trip is now available, cf. ed. Allan Harman, *Mission of Discovery: The Beginnings of Modern Jewish Evangelism* (Fearne, Ross-shire, Scotland: Christian Focus, 1996). Very rich.
5. Robert Murray McCheyne, *Sermons of Robert Murray McCheyne* (Edinburgh: Banner of Truth, 1961).

6. W. G. Blaikie in F. R. Webber, *A History of Preaching in Britain and America* (Milwaukee: Northwestern, 1955), 2:392.

9.1.4 Thomas Chalmers—Leading the Way

> Enthusiasm is a virtue rarely produced in a state of calm and unruffled repose. It flourishes in adversity. It kindles in the hour of danger and rises to deeds of renown. The terrors of persecution only serve to awaken the energy of its purposes. It swells in the pride of integrity, and great in the purity of its cause, it can scatter defiance amid a host of enemies.
>
> —Thomas Chalmers to four hundred or five hundred brethren in 1842 on the eve of the Disruption

> It would be difficult not to congratulate you on the unrivaled and unbounded popularity which attended you in the metropolis . . . The attention which your sermons have excited is probably unequaled in modern literature.
>
> —Robert Hall ("the greatest pulpit orator in England," cf. 8.5.7) when Chalmers came to London

> I suppose there will never again be such a preacher in any Christian Church.
>
> —Thomas Carlyle

What Smellie calls "the long reign of moderatism" (both a theological and a political problem) was moving toward a necessary confrontation. McCheyne, who died before this denouement, had said in a letter: "You don't know what Moderatism is. It is a plant that our Heavenly Father never planted, and I trust it is now to be rooted out."[1]

The leader who moved more than four hundred clergy to leave the established church and form the Free Church in 1843 was **Thomas Chalmers** (1780–1847).[2] Born in Fifeshire, Chalmers was probably the most gifted and powerful preacher since John Knox in Scotland. The sixth of fourteen children, he was the son of a shipowner and merchant.

Early in life Chalmers was much exposed to the Bible and *Pilgrim's Progress*. He began studies at St. Andrews, the oldest university in Scotland, when he was twelve. He was raised among moderates, and his mind soon clouded with doubt. He pursued studies in mathematics and physics, and tutored until he was old enough to become a probationer, finally taking a charge in Kilmany, where he served from 1803 to 1815. His preaching was, as he described it, "blanched morality."

At thirty, after reading Jonathan Edwards and William Wilberforce and after experiencing a severe illness, he wrote an article on Christianity for an encyclopedia. Soon he was wondrously converted, some say while preaching in his own pulpit.[3] Immediately he turned to preach the Bible, was married (1812), and soon gained acclaim as a pulpiteer of excellence. Now, "he has seen the reality of

Christ's atonement, and of the work of the Holy Spirit, and found a new value in prayer, and a new use of the sacred Scriptures."[4]

In 1815, Chalmers accepted a call to the Tron Church in Glasgow (with a parish of eleven or twelve thousand people) and took the teeming masses of the great city by storm. After four years he transferred to St. John's, where **Edward Irving** was his gifted associate in a great ministry of outreach, evangelism, and work among the poor. He gave himself totally to house-to-house visitation and to the establishment of Sabbath schools, including a Sabbath evening school of two thousand children. The impression he made in preaching was described as follows:

> The eyes are light in color and have a strange dreamy heaviness which contrasts [when] expanded in their sockets and illuminated into all their flame and fervor in some moment of high entranced enthusiasm . . . but the shape of the forehead is perhaps the most singular part of the whole visage . . . wide across the eyebrows . . . immediately above the extraordinary breadth of this region . . . an arch carrying out the summit boldly and roundly . . . unquestionably I have never heard, whether in England or in Scotland, any preacher whose eloquence is capable of producing an effect so strong and irresistible as his . . .[5]

In time he moved on to the chair of moral philosophy at St. Andrews (1823–1828), where he influenced students such as Alexander Duff (cf. 8.4.5). He preached at Edward Irving's opening at the Scottish Church in London (1827). Uncommonly nervous before speaking, Chalmers continued his battle for principles even against opposing faculty colleagues. In 1828 he took the chair of theology at the University of Edinburgh and sat as chair of the General Assembly in 1832. He poured out such writings as his four volumes on Romans. He epitomized the evangelical move that culminated in the Disruption in 1843 and the formation of seven hundred Free Churches, and his own assumption of the principalship at New College, Edinburgh, where he finished out his ministry.

Chalmers has been called a solar man, he was like the sun in prominence and power. He had a marked affection for the Scripture and a great dedication to study.[6] He counted as his friends Sir Walter Scott, Prime Minister Gladstone, Thomas Carlyle, and many such others. But his preaching of the Word was his forte. He testified, "There is no continuous passage which I read with greater delight than Isaiah 53. I can remember when I made at least one perusal of it a daily task. The very cadence of its sentence is dear to me."[7]

He was not without his critics. Hazlitt said, he "catches at truth with his fists like a monkey catching an apple." His voice was husky and his Scottish brogue heavy. Yet he used words so magnificently and with such intensity, his audience had to listen. People of all classes waited with bated breath for his preaching. His sermons were best-sellers. Chalmers was yielded to the supremacy of Scripture, claiming "I give myself over in my whole mind and whole person to the authority of a whole Bible."[8]

Both Pascal and Jonathan Edwards influenced Chalmers, but he was the quintessential Puritan in preaching sin and grace. He appealed to would-be preachers,

"Close with Christ, and accept of Him as he is offered to you in the Gospel," and warned of the danger that "the invitations of God's tenderness will give place and that speedily to the terrors of a vengeance which will burn all the more fiercely because of a slighted gospel and a rejected Saviour."[9]

Chalmers skillfully used rhetorical questions. His great sermon "The Expulsive Power of a New Affection" is typical, with both very short and very long sentences. This sermon is not like "a mighty maze and quite without a plan," but the classic example of a one-point sermon. Robert Hall suggested it was like a rocking horse, it "moves but does not go on." The congregation was "like a forest bending under the power of a hurricane."[10] Said one listener, "We went home quieter than we came."

---

1. Nigel M. de S. Cameron, ed., *Dictionary of Scottish Church History and Theology* (Downers Grove, Ill.: InterVarsity Press, 1993), 505.
2. Hugh Watt, *Thomas Chalmers and the Disruption* (Edinburgh: Thomas Nelson, 1943). An excellent study.
3. W. G. Blaikie, *Thomas Chalmers* (Edinburgh: Oliphant Anderson, 1896), 33. The definitive biography with complete bibliography is Stewart J. Brown, *Thomas Chalmers and the Godly Commonwealth in Scotland* (Oxford: Oxford, 1982).
4. Ibid., 41. Karl Marx dubbed Chalmers "the arch-parson Chalmers."
5. Ibid., 77.
6. Adam Philip, *Thomas Chalmers: Apostle of Union* (London: James Clarke, 1929), 36.
7. Ibid., 111.
8. G. D. Henderson, *The Burning Bush: Studies in Scottish Church History* (Edinburgh: St. Andrew, 1957), 201.
9. Ibid., 202. For an assessment of Chalmers' impact upon the politics and economics of his time, see Boyd Hilton, *The Age of Atonement: The Influence of Evangelicalism on Social and Economic Thought, 1795–1865* (Oxford: Clarendon, 1988), 55ff.
10. T. Harwood Pattison, *The History of Christian Preaching* (Philadelphia: American Baptist Publication Society, 1903), 297.

9.1.5 ANDREW THOMSON—LEANING ON THE SHEPHERD

> The framework of our Church may be better moulded, and its parts put into goodlier adjustment than before; but, like the dry bones in the vision of Ezekiel, even when reassembled into the perfect skeleton, and invested by a covering of flesh and skin, with the perfect semblance and beauty of a man—so our Church, even when moulded into legal and external perfection by human hands, may have all the inertness of a statue, and with the monumental coldness of death upon it, till the Spirit of God shall blow into it that it may live.
>
> —Thomas Chalmers

In the succession of those who believed that prayer and revival were the remedies above all others, Thomas Chalmers stepped into the leadership role which had been long carried by **Andrew Thomson** (1779–1831). Chalmers described Thomson as a man of "colossal mind, wielding the weapons of spiritual warfare" with "an arm of might and voice of resistless energy," carrying "as if by storm the convictions of his people."[1] When William Cunningham first spoke to the Assembly, "It was said of him that it was Andrew Thomson come again to hammer the Moderates."[2]

Thomson was born in a pastor's home in Dumfriesshire and educated at Edinburgh. After serving in Kelso and Roxburghshire, he ministered in Perth. He became known for his scintillating expositions of Scripture, and in 1814 he was called to the new St. George's on Shandwicke Place in Edinburgh. He won the hearts of his people, visited and catechized among them, and edited the controversial *Edinburgh Christian Instructor* (which greatly aided the evangelical cause). He also led the battle against inclusion of the Apocrypha in editions of the Bible and against slavery. His boldness turned the tide in favor of evangelism. When he died, his friend and admirer Chalmers stated in his funeral message:

> If our next war is to be a war of principles, then before the battle has begun, the noblest of our champions has fallen. Yet we dare not give up to despondency a cause which has truth for its basis and the guarantee of heaven's omnipotence for its complete and everlasting triumph.[3]

Thomson died of a heart attack on his own doorstep after a church meeting, but the set of the sail had been made. He was known for his love of music and arrangements of the Psalms, and he took up the cudgel willingly against the universalism of **Thomas Erskine** of Linlathen[4] and **John McLeod Campbell.** He maintained solid ties with some in the Secession Church and used their writers in his publication. The implosion of his preaching was characterized by Maclagan:

> But the preaching of Dr. Thomson was like a bombshell falling among the people. Not only did he give constant prominence to the distinctive gospel doctrines of grace and redemption by an atonement, but in terms of great directness and plainness of speech he denounced the customs of a society calling itself Christian; and in a marvelously short time, by his zeal and faithfulness under God, a remarkable change was effected in the habits and pursuits of many of his people . . .
>
> —from the history of St. George's[5]

Thomson was called by some "the gladiator of the intellect."[6] One analysis of his preaching concluded, "He brought culture back into the pulpit without in the least degree obscuring the cross." Perhaps something of the charm and vigor of the man is seen in his retort to the fellow minister who wondered why with his gifts of ready speech he spent so much time preparing his sermons. The minister said that he had on many occasions prepared a sermon and killed a salmon before breakfast. Thomson replied, "Well, sir, I would rather have eaten your salmon than listened to your sermon."[7]

1. Nigel M. de S. Cameron, ed., *Dictionary of Scottish Church History and Theology* (Downers Grove, Ill.: InterVarsity Press, 1993), 820.
2. Ibid.
3. Adam Philip, *Thomas Chalmers: Apostle of Union* (London: James Clarke, 1929), 55.
4. Nicholas R. Needham, *Thomas Erskine of Linlathen: His Life and Theology, 1788–1837* (Edinburgh: Rutherford House, 1990). A nephew of John Erskine (cf. 8.3.7), he drifted away from the center and denied any reprobating purpose in God. Robertson said to him, "The God whom you have chosen is agreeable to your feelings, but has it never occurred to you that you may not have chosen the God of the Bible?" (458).
5. A. E. Garvie, *The Christian Preacher* (New York: Scribner's, 1923), 224.
6. For a general overview, see Henry F. Henderson, *The Religious Controversies of Scotland* (London: T & T Clark, 1905).
7. T. Harwood Pattison, *The History of Christian Preaching* (Philadelphia: American Baptist Publication Society, 1903), 289.

9.1.6 John Duncan—Learning the Basics

> We must observe this enclosing language of Holy Scripture; we must not look beyond, but in the Scripture, and we will find that every passage either proves itself or is proved by parallelism. Hereby we know that we know him, by his Spirit that he hath given to us; the things revealed by the Spirit the Apostles spake. God employs human speech, but he himself selects the words that are to express his thoughts. He leaves not man to put words on them; the words are as much the Spirit's as the ideas, and the Apostle Paul studiously avoids other words.
>
> Oh, it is a pitiable thing for a poor silly puppy of a scilist to stand up in the pulpit vexing the people by shaking their confidence in our good English translation.
>
> I was a very popular preacher till I began to preach on the work of the Spirit, then the church grew thin.
>
> —John Duncan

Bolstering the outbreak of so much solid, Spirit-anointed preaching in Scotland were gifted and godly scholars like **John Duncan** (1796–1870). Duncan was a conscientious conservator of the Bible, who came out of an Original Secession background in Aberdeen. He was born the son of a shoemaker, and lapsed into infidelity and Sabellian and Socinian errors (unsound views of the Trinity and the deity of Christ) early in his life. Duncan was converted at Divinity Hall when Dr. Cesar Malan of Geneva (converted under the ministry of Robert Haldane) visited and preached. When Malan left he said of the young Duncan, "That man will soon be before you all; he believes the Word of God."[1]

Duncan preached in a rural chapel in Perthshire before moving on to lectureships in English at the Duke Street Gaelic Chapel. He was called *rabbi* by his students because of his long white beard. Elsewhere he drew notice as a gifted but absentminded preacher. Because of his brilliance in Hebrew, he was commissioned to a ministry among the Jews in Buda and Pesth in Hungary.[2] In 1843 he was invited to take the chair of Old Testament and Hebrew in New College in the wake of the Disruption. Duncan accepted and brought with him a recent convert, Alfred Edersheim, who went on to become author of the popular *Life and Times of Jesus the Messiah.*

Duncan exerted a powerful influence through his teaching and preaching and touched McCheyne, William Burns, A. Moody Stuart, and an entire generation of preachers-to-be. He loved evangelism and delighted to preach. "Preaching is the delivery of a message," he insisted.[3] Suffused with a deep personal piety and dedication to prayer (on occasion his opening prayer in class consumed half the period), he battled depression all his life. Fond of anecdote, he was in great demand as a visiting preacher, particularly in communion seasons. Dr. John Kennedy of Dingwall reported of a sermon:

> I stole quietly into the church, and heard a sermon that did not seem to have been prepared on earth, but felt as if one of the old Prophets had come from within the veil to tell us what was going on there. Nothing more heavenly did I ever hear from human lips.[4]

Duncan once stated, "Hyper-Calvinism is all house and no door: Arminianism all door and no house."[5] Liberalizing young theologues fresh from nests of skepticism on the Continent sought to deprecate him and his scholarship. When some of his students began to move toward higher criticism, the lifeline of biblical preaching was cut and preaching began to decline.[6] But Duncan's authenticity and obvious mastery of Hebrew made an immeasurable impact.

---

1. A. Moody Stuart, *The Life of John Duncan* (Edinburgh: Banner of Truth, 1872), 23.
2. For a sketch of Duncan's ministry in Hungary, see John S. Ross, "A Pioneer in Jewish Mission: Rabbi Duncan," *Christian Witness/Israel Herald* (June–August 1991): 10ff. Shows his great linguistic skills and movingly describes the conversion of Adolph Saphir, who became a leading Presbyterian minister in Scotland.
3. Ibid., 210.
4. F. R. Webber, *A History of Preaching in Britain and America* (Milwaukee: Northwestern, 1955), 2:322.
5. Ibid., 2:323.
6. Richard Allan Riesen, *Criticism and Faith in Late Victorian Scotland* (Lanham, Md.: University Press of America, 1985).

9.1.7 *EDWARD IRVING—LED ASTRAY*

> No man that I have known had a sunnier type of character or so little hatred toward any man or thing. Noble Irving! He was the faithful elder

> brother of my life in those years—generous, wise, beneficent all his dealings and discoursings were.
>
> —Thomas Carlyle after Irving's death

> He was unquestionably, by many degrees, the greatest orator of our times. Of him indeed, more than any man whom I have seen throughout my whole experience, it might be said with truth and emphasis, that he was a Boanerges, a son of thunder.
>
> —Thomas De Quincy

> He put me in mind of the devil disguised as an angel of light.
>
> —Sir Walter Scott

The path to preaching prowess is a slippery slope, and dangers lurk on every side. **Edward Irving** (1792–1834) exemplified the amazingly gifted preacher who stumbles and falls down that slope. Irving was born in Annan near Dumfries and studied at Edinburgh, supporting his work in divinity by teaching school in Haddington and Kirkaldy. He had decided to go to America when Thomas Chalmers asked him to assist him in ministry in the slums of Glasgow.

Mrs. Oliphant's *Life of Edward Irving* is particularly moving in its depiction of Irving's compassion and his marked influence among the disenfranchised of society. His millennialism was contagious. In 1822 he took a call to London to serve a small group of Scots living there. The ministry was so successful that the beautiful National Scottish Church at Regent Square was built for him in 1827.

Tall and strapping, handsome and willowy, Irving took London by storm. A vast influx of hearers came to hear his brilliant rhetoric: "Statesmen, philosophers, poets, painters, and literary men; peers, merchants and fashionable ladies in abundance."[1] Stoughton opined:

> Never since George Whitefield had anyone so arrested attention; and Irving went far beyond Whitefield in attracting the respectful, even the admiring, notice of lords, ladies and commons. His name was on every lip. Newspapers, magazines and reviews discussed his merits; a caricature in shop windows hit off his eccentricities.[2]

Another had the impression that "He has a powerful voice, feels always warmly, is prompt in his expression, and not very careful of his words."[3] In the first quarter of Irving's ministry in London, seatholders increased from fifty to fifteen hundred.

This was indeed gratifying to an ambitious man but exceedingly dangerous. His sermons became long and ranting. He expressed heterodox views on the sinless humanity of our Lord. Wilks says he fed his soul on Chrysostom, Jeremy Taylor, and Hooker but regarded no contemporary as able except for Chalmers.[4] He was impatient with the old paths, and espoused extreme views on prophesying and on speaking in tongues, although he himself never used the gifts publicly.

Irving's views became highly sacramentarian, and he established the Catholic

Apostolic Church. Warfield attributed his subsequent defrocking and collapse to "his over-weening confidence in himself."[5] His earlier sermons are worthy of emulation, but he soon moved "beyond the sermon" to the "oration," so much better suited to the higher class of person he was reaching. He flaunted his success shamelessly.[6]

Something seemed to have snapped inside of Irving. The influence of the romantic Samuel Taylor Coleridge did not help (cf. 8.2), and his disappointment in love (Jane, for whom he cherished a great affection, married Thomas Carlyle) fueled his instability. Dallimore bemoans that Irving began using a text as a peg for speculative ideas rather than opening the text expositorily.[7] He died at forty-two without ever fulfilling the exciting promise his gifts seemed to portend. McCheyne eulogized him at his passing:

> I look back upon him with awe, as on the saints and martyrs of old. A holy man in spite of all his delusions and errors. He is now with his God and Saviour whom he wronged so much, yet I am persuaded, loved so sincerely.[8]

---

1. Nigel M. de S. Cameron, ed., *Dictionary of Scottish Church History and Theology* (Downers Grove, Ill.: InterVarsity Press, 1993), 436.
2. A. E. Garvie, *The Christian Preacher* (New York: Scribner's, 1923), 227.
3. T. Harwood Pattison, *The History of Christian Preaching* (Philadelphia: American Baptist Publication Society, 1903), 299.
4. Arnold Dallimore, *Forerunner of the Charismatic Movement: The Life of Edward Irving* (Chicago: Moody, 1983), 28.
5. Ibid., 52.
6. Ibid., 54. An important analysis is found in Gordon Strachan, *The Pentecostal Theology of Edward Irving* (Peabody, Mass.: Hendrickson, 1973), who points out that Karl Barth acknowledges Irving as the forerunner of those holding to a radical Christology, in this case believing Christ has a fallen nature; see *Church Dogmatics,* 1.2 (153–54).
7. Ibid., 74.
8. Cameron, *Dictionary of Scottish Church History and Theology,* 437.

9.2 THE AMERICAN WHIRLPOOL

> The great engine for maintaining the effectiveness of religion in national life was not dogma at all but revivalism, intense, immediate and personal.
> —Robert Bellah in *The Broken Covenant*

The Second Great Awakening (1776–1810) touched both America and Europe. Bebbington correctly remarks, "Preaching the gospel was the chief method of winning converts."[1] We see this in the itinerations of **Henry Alline** (1748–1784) in Nova Scotia (although Alline stumbled toward the end of his ministry).

The powerful tides of deism and skepticism washed in on the newly independent colonies through the speeches and writings of **Thomas Paine** (1737–1809). Paine was a Methodist lay preacher at one time. Born in Thetford in England, he is mentioned in the journals of John Wesley as ministering in Sandwich.[2] Yet he became hostile toward all doctrine, and developed a particular contempt for the Bible and the cross of Christ. His every effort was bent toward the demolition of "the Christian view of revelation."[3]

But the resurgence of the Second Awakening counteracted his efforts and greatly Christianized the United States.[4] Indeed, democracy owes a great debt to Colonial preaching. It is our purpose to explore this relationship and its concomitants.[5] Of course there was transatlantic dialogue. Chalmers was indebted to Thomas Reid's commonsense realism, whose influence filtered across the ocean and helped shape Princeton Seminary.

---

1. D. W. Bebbington, *Evangelicalism in Modern Britain* (London: Allen and Unwin, 1989), 5.
2. John Keane, *Thomas Paine: A Political Life* (Boston: Little, Brown, 1995), 46.
3. Ibid., 498.
4. Ibid., 500ff.
5. George Mecklenburg, *Bowing the Preacher Out of Politics* (New York: Revell, 1928), N.B. chapter 6, "The Debt of Democracy to Colonial Preaching," 48–60; also Ellis Sandoz, ed., *Political Sermons of the American Founding Era: 1730–1805* (Indianapolis: Liberty Press, 1991). The concern is that the new nation be "under God."

9.2.1 Timothy Dwight—Brightening the Horizon

The plain meaning is the true meaning.

The trophies of the Cross are being multiplied.

—Timothy Dwight

Siren voices sought to lure spiritual leaders in the new republic away from their biblical roots. Among those who succumbed were the Unitarians, who repudiated core doctrines such as inerrant biblical authority,[1] or offbeat movements like the Shakers of Ann Lee with their eschatological proclamation that "Christ has come a second time" and who paid scant attention to preaching.[2]

Against these threats stood **Timothy Dwight** (1752–1817), the son of Jonathan Edwards' daughter. Young Timothy read Scripture with ease at four years of age and was studying Latin at six. Entering Yale at thirteen, he gave himself to revelry and card playing, but soon grew serious in his studies and became a tutor at Yale. At the time, homiletical training was largely an indoctrination in classical rhetoric. This was helpful for Dwight because he was hesitant in his speech. He became accomplished at style and composition, using Ward's *System of Oratory*.

In 1774 Dwight was converted. He joined the church and shortly after was married. For thirteen months he served as a chaplain in the Continental Army. After his ordination he took a congregation in Greenfield, Connecticut, and inveighed strongly against the Half-Way Covenant. He gave himself to preaching for the salvation of men "in a way that is subservient to the divine glory."[3] Eventually Dwight ministered in Greenfield for twelve years and established Dwight's Academy to supplement his annual income of five-hundred dollars. He also wrote hymns. His "I Love Thy Kingdom, Lord" is still one of the richest we have.

Tall, with an impressive appearance and voice, Timothy Dwight was elected president of Yale in 1795. Spirituality was at low ebb when he came and found, as he said, "a most ungodly state." His objective was to break the enemy's grip on Yale even though there were few Christians there. Lyman Beecher, who was converted in those years, describes the situation:

> Most of the class before me were infidels. They thought the faculty was afraid of free discussion; but when they handed Doctor Dwight a list of subjects for class disputation, to their surprise he selected this: "Is the Bible the Word of God?" and told them to do their best. He heard all they had to say, answered them, and there was an end. He preached incessantly for six months on the subject and all infidelity skulked and hid its head.[4]

A great outpouring of the Holy Spirit came and infidelity was routed. "No weeds of infidelity throve there," he noted. Beecher reported hearing him preach from Jeremiah 8:20. To use his words, "A whole avalanche rolled down on my mind. I went home weeping every step."[5] The series of sermons he preached to the class remain in his *Theology*.

Revivals came to Yale in 1808, 1812 to 1813, and 1814 to 1815. On one day fifty-two students came for prayer, and one hundred students were converted in the last visit. The revival spread to Princeton, where eighty of the one hundred five students there were converted and twenty-five went into the ministry.

Dwight's health collapsed in 1816. He died the following year of cancer of the bladder. His eloquent and forceful preaching challenged the fashionable infidelity and skepticism and caused "these things to lose their influence."[6]

---

1. John Fea, "Theodore Parker and the Nineteenth-Century Assault on Biblical Authority," *Michigan Theological Journal* 3 (1992): 65–80. Fea argues: "Parker's understanding of orthodoxy not only supports the fact that the infallibility of Scripture was dominant in the nineteenth century, but that this conservative position on the Bible was operative throughout all of church history. Parker's description of nineteenth-century bibliology seems not only to refute Sandeen's understanding of the history of this doctrine, but also makes a dent in the proposal expounded by those who would argue that the entire Christian Church never held to a view of infallibility in areas of science and history" (78).
2. Stephen J. Stein, *The Shaker Experience in America* (New Haven, Conn.: Yale University Press, 1992). Although later under the influence of American revivalism, Shakers began to pay attention to the Bible, and in their Shaker Manifesto have a column on the Bible and using expository methods (329). Shakers went to hear both Henry Ward Beecher and D. L. Moody.

3. Charles Cunningham, *Timothy Dwight: 1752–1817* (New York: Macmillan, 1942), 110.
4. T. Harwood Pattison, *A History of Christian Preaching* (Philadelphia: American Baptist Publication Society, 1903), 364.
5. Cunningham, *Timothy Dwight,* 334.
6. F. R. Webber, *A History of Preaching in Britain and America* (Milwaukee: Northwestern, 1957), 3:153. For important insights on the theological struggle at this time, cf. Joseph Conforti, *Samuel Hopkins and the New Divinity Movement: Calvinism, the Congregational Ministry and Reform in New England Between the Great Awakenings* (New York: Christian University Press, 1981).

9.2.2 John Witherspoon—Building the Body

> So very sacred a thing indeed is truth, that the very shadow of departure from it is to be avoided. . . . Let me therefore recommend to you a strict universal and scrupulous regard to truth; it will give dignity to your character, it will put power into your affairs, it will excite the most unbounded confidence, so that whether your view be your own interest, or the service of others, it promises you the most assured success.
>
> —John Witherspoon

> Dr. Witherspoon is a character well known. He is a man of considerable abilities, a little tinctured with fanaticism of the Whitefieldian complexion. Some years ago we had frequent occasion of mentioning his writings published while he was a minister in Scotland, his native country. He is now become an eminent preacher among the Americans . . . his doctrines breathe a spirit so candid and so agreeable to the moderation of the Christian character that, excepting a few passages tending to encourage the Americans in their scheme of independency, this animated and pious discourse might have been delivered with great acceptance and possibly with good effect before any Fast Day audience in the Kingdom without subjecting the preacher to the imputation of disloyalty or disaffection to the government.
>
> —*The Monthly Review*

The formative influence of preachers and preaching on the American Revolution and the subsequent emergence of the republic is generally acknowledged.[1] Such a shaper of men—and the only clergyman to sign the Declaration of Independence in 1776—was the illustrious preacher and longtime president of the College of New Jersey (later Princeton), **John Witherspoon** (1723–1794).

Witherspoon was born in a devout minister's home in Gifford, four miles southeast of Haddington. He entered Edinburgh at age thirteen. Ordained in 1743, he began his ministry in Beith in Ayrshire. Imprisoned briefly by the forces of the Pretender, he moved on to Paisley. A champion of orthodoxy and a preacher of the fundamental core of the gospel, he enjoyed twenty-four years of ministry and publishing. His *Essay on Justification* had wide circulation in Scotland. Through the influence of John Erskine, Witherspoon made contact with the board of the College of New Jersey. The emissary from America had difficulty in persuading Mrs. Witherspoon, but finally Witherspoon accepted the call to the presidency in 1768.

Just as Timothy Dwight was an archfederalist, Witherspoon rapidly became an American. None doubted he stood on the Colonial side. His celebrated sermon on "Christian Magnanimity," preached from 1 Thessalonians 2:12 on the occasion of commencement in 1775, was a defining moment.[2] Another sermon preached on the fast day in May 1776 was widely heralded. He was appointed as a delegate to the Continental Congress and presented his credentials on June 28, 1976.

The College of New Jersey grew rapidly. Nine of its graduates were delegates to the Constitutional Convention—fully one-sixth of the entire delegation. Aaron Burr and James Madison were both among the alumni.[3]

During debate in the Continental Congress, a dissenter ventured that the colonies were not ripe for independence, "Dr. Witherspoon rose to his great height and retorted in his strong Scottish brogue, 'In my judgment, sir, we are not only ripe but rotting.'"[4] When the British soldiers neared Princeton, Witherspoon closed the college. The Redcoats billeted in Nassau Hall and destroyed the college library. The college suffered abysmally from neglect during these years.[5]

During the war, Witherspoon was returned to Congress year after year and sat on the war board in some of the most critical phases of the rebellion. He sat on several committees with his former student, James Madison, whose gifts and convictions were increasingly decisive in deliberations. He regularly preached in Philadelphia and, on one occasion, expounded the text "redeeming the time" with a number of his fellow members of Congress present.[6]

After retiring from Congress, Witherspoon devoted his life to recouping the fortunes of the college. He made one bold trip back to Scotland and England, where he did some preaching but could raise no funds. At commencement in 1783, virtually the whole Congress and General George Washington were present. Washington presented a gift of fifty guineas to the college and sat for a portrait which still hangs at Princeton.[7]

When Witherspoon's daughter died, he preached a series of sixteen sermons on submission to God's will from Luke 22:42. He died in 1794 in his seventy-second year.

How significant that a stalwart champion of the Bible as "the unerring standard" and the gospel as the solution to the human predicament should have such opportunity to influence the founding days of our country. Here indeed is a light set upon a hill.

---

1. Bernard Bailyn, *Faces of Revolution: Personalities and Themes in the Struggle for American Independence* (New York: Knopf, 1990). In a poignant section Bailyn shows an obscure Connecticut minister, Stephen Johnson, who in 1765 published six newspaper articles and a sermon that anticipate "almost the entire range of arguments that would be debated in the coming decade."

2. Varnum Lansing Collins, *President Witherspoon* (Princeton, N.J.: Princeton University Press, 1925), 1:178.
3. John Eidsmoe, *Christianity and the Constitution: The Faith of Our Founding Fathers* (Grand Rapids: Baker, 1987), 83.
4. Merle Sinclair and Annabel Douglas McArthur, *They Signed for Us* (New York: Hawthorne, 1957), 43.
5. Collins, *President Witherspoon,* 118. A choice sermon by John Witherspoon is "On Ministerial Character and Duty" from 2 Corinthians 4:13, "We also believe and therefore speak" in *Sermons by the Late John Witherspoon* (Edinburgh, 1798), 1–19.
6. Ibid., 22.
7. Ibid., 135–36.

9.2.3 Francis Asbury—Emblazoning the Gospel

> July 28: Arose, as I commonly do, before five o'clock to study the Bible. I find none like it; and find it of more consequence for a preacher to know his Bible well than all the books and languages in the world—for he is not to preach these, but the Word of God.
>
> Sunday, July 20, 1880, Lynn, Massachusetts: There had been a long drought here, and nature seemed as if she were about to droop and die. We addressed the throne of Grace most fervently and solemnly, and had showers of blessings. Whilst I was preaching, the wind came up and appeared to whirl around every point, and most gracious rain came on; this I considered as a most signal instance of divine goodness.
>
> —from Francis Asbury's journal

In his stimulating *The Democratization of American Christianity,* Nathan Hatch argues that the Second Great Awakening tended to be antielitist, anticlerical, and in many cases anti-Calvinistic. As the population surged over the Alleghenies, the tilt was away from Episcopal, Congregational, and Presbyterian toward Methodist, Baptist, and Christian (Campbellite) expressions of spiritual fervor.

Methodist strength was minimal at the time of the Revolution, but by 1820 membership had reached a quarter of a million and by 1830 was twice that. Baptists multiplied ten times in the three decades following the revolution.[1] In all of this, Hatch sees the inversion of authority, the "withering of establishments," and "the triumph of vernacular preaching" in a climate that saw the "birth of American gospel music."[2] At the very forefront of this magnificent advance was what Hatch calls "the spartan mission of Francis Asbury."[3]

Francis Asbury (1745–1816) was born in Hamsted Bridge near Birmingham in England in modest circumstances. As a youth he was apprenticed to a blacksmith. His Welsh mother taught him the Scriptures and encouraged him to hear the itinerant Methodist preacher who visited their town. Praying in his father's barn at the age of fourteen, Asbury was converted and almost at once began to preach three, four, or five times a week.[4] He took his first circuit in 1766 and ultimately volunteered to go to America, sailing in 1771.

At his first conference, there were ten preachers representing about six hundred Methodists in America; at his last conference seven hundred preachers represented 218,000 registered communicants. He was first cosuperintendent with **Thomas Coke** (1747–1814). When Coke returned to England in 1784, Asbury was elected bishop.

Asbury embodied what Hatch calls "an ethic of sacrifice." He worked indefatigably and preached in excess of 16,500 sermons until he died at Spotsylvania in 1816.

Asbury was a school dropout and a simple gardener's son, yet he had more power than any other figure in religion in his time. A plain preacher, Asbury was poor, unworldly, and celibate all his life. He feared those who wanted to become great without work and sacrifice. "Don't be a gentleman," he urged, "be a common man." His heart's longing was "Lord, keep me from all superfluity of dress, and from preaching empty stuff to please the ear, instead of changing the heart." He discarded Wesley's liturgical and sacramental style, even doing away with clerical dress.

Revival fires began to burn after 1800 and camp meetings proliferated.[5] Again Asbury took to the circuit. As he charged his preachers: "When you go into the pulpit, go from your closets . . . take with you your hearts full of fresh spring water from heaven, and preach Christ crucified and the resurrection, and that will conquer the world."[6]

Half of the circuit riders died before they were thirty. Yet Asbury rode on. Often in ill-health, he traveled on horseback twenty-five to fifty miles a day. His remarkable journal is an endless reiteration of "I preached" and "I preached."

> Wednesday, June 6: We had twelve miles to R.'s, along a busy, hilly road. A poor woman with a little horse, without a saddle, outwent us up and down the hills, and, when we came to the place appointed, the Lord met with and blessed her soul. . . . [Later he preached to three hundred people] but there were so many wicked whiskey-drinkers, who brought with them so much of the devil, that I had little satisfaction in preaching.[7]

In his journal we have outlines of two hundred sermons and texts for another seven hundred. He did not aspire to be nor was he ever an orator, but steeped in Scripture as he was, he would always take a text and preach it with authority. He preached on Galatians 6:14, endeavoring to show:

1. What it is for a man to glory in a thing;
2. What men glory in, which is not the cross of Christ;
3. What is glory in the cross of Christ;
4. How a person may know when he glories in the cross of Christ—namely, by the world being crucified to him and he to the world.[8]

One contemporary wrote that Asbury's sermons were the result of sound wisdom and good common sense and were "delivered with great authority and gravity, often attended with divine unction, which made them as refreshing as the dew of heaven."[9] Usually he preached an hour even when he was old and frail and had to be literally carried to the pulpit. He wrote:

> I preached at the chapel, to about four hundred serious people, from John 4:48: I spoke for two hours; perhaps it is the last time . . .[10]

He delighted in preaching on the beauties of the Book of Revelation. He read the Scripture effectively, and people were moved in its presentation by itself.[11] He had haunting dreams of heaven and hell. In his notes to the Discipline, he urges his preachers "to convince sinners of their danger, to set forth the atoning blood, to keep engagements and that on time, to be deeply serious, to be cautious of allegorizing, to avoid awkward gestures, to beware of writing for the press on the advice of a few enthusiastic friends."[12] He used vivid illustrations and was particularly effective in ordination sermons and at funerals.

The memorial statue of Asbury in Washington, D.C. is that of a weary old man and a tired horse with a drooping head. Yet the statue breathes "dogged determination." In dedicating the monument in 1924, President Coolidge paid tribute to Asbury as "one of the builders of our nation, this circuit rider who spent his life making strong the foundation on which our Government rests."

---

1. Nathan O. Hatch, *The Democratization of American Christianity* (New Haven, Conn.: Yale University Press, 1989), 3. Note also Hatch's important redefinition of the Second Great Awakening, Appendix 1.
2. Ibid., 125.
3. Ibid., 81ff.
4. James Lewis, *Francis Asbury: Bishop of the Methodist Episcopal Church* (London: Epworth, 1927), 16.
5. A. K. Curtis, ed. "Spiritual Awakenings in North America," *Christian History* 8, no. 3, issue 23. An important source. In his disappointing *Revivals and Revivalism* (Edinburgh: Banner of Truth, 1994), Iain H. Murray is too dismissive of camp meetings, the altar call, and "decisionist evangelism." Where is evangelical catholicity?
6. Charles Ludwig, *Francis Asbury: God's Circuit Rider* (Milford, Mich.: Mott Media, 1984), 165.
7. Lewis, *Francis Asbury,* 87.
8. Ibid., 126.
9. Herbert Asbury, *A Methodist Saint: The Life of Bishop Asbury* (New York: Knopf, 1927), 281.
10. L. C. Rudolph, *Francis Asbury* (Nashville: Abingdon, 1966), 81.
11. Ibid., 93.
12. Ibid.

9.2.4 EDWARD GRIFFEN—BREATHING THE SPIRIT

> This pulpit was not erected to hurl anathemas against men who to their own master must stand or fall. . . . The business to be transacted here lies

> not between us and our brethren of different names or opinions, but between God and our own souls.
>
> —Sermon on the occasion of the dedication of Park Street Church

> But let any man continually carry about him a full and distinct image of God, exhibiting all the truths of His Word, all the strictness of His law, all the guilt and danger of sinners—carrying reproof to everything selfish, everything proud, everything vain, everything that does not make God the supreme object—and let him moreover be constituted by his age or office a reprover; and there is not a community of worldly men in Christendom who will not be offended . . . This must be true or the "carnal mind" is no longer "enmity against God."
>
> —Edward D. Griffin

While Nathan Hatch's thesis as to the democratization of Christianity in the burgeoning new nation has validity, there is yet the moving of the Spirit in the more traditional and establishment-type churches. The effective preaching ministry of **Edward D. Griffin** (1770–1837) surely demonstrates this. Griffin was born into a home of comfortable means and studied at Yale. His parents had no particular spiritual profession, but young Edward had "religious impressions" from very early in his life. After an illness at Yale, he sought the Bible and discovered the Sermon on the Mount in which "the whole character of Christ as a preacher opened to my view."[1] The upshot was "I chose to be a minister . . . I hugged the cross."

Griffin studied theology with **Jonathan Edwards Jr.** (1745–1801), who denied imputation and advanced the governmental view of the atonement. Griffin himself was thoroughly orthodox. Strikingly handsome, Griffin was tall, with a powerful voice and effective gesture. Initially he did supply preaching at Park Street, or "Brimstone Corner," as it was called. Henry James called it "the most interesting mass of brick and mortar in America."[2] He soon took a pastorate in New Hartford, followed by a charge in Newark, New Jersey. He served briefly as Bartlett Professor of Pulpit Eloquence at the new Andover Theological Seminary, founded to set forth orthodoxy more clearly and compellingly. Griffin went on to the pastorate of historic Park Street Church in Boston (1809–1815).

After some tensions over finances in Boston, Griffin went back to the strategic pulpit in Newark and then in 1821 on to the presidency of Williams College, where the famous Haystack Prayer Meetings took place. When his health failed in 1837, he returned to Newark where he died.

Griffin always had a strong missionary impulse. He was part of the American Board of Commissioners for Foreign Missions, which sent out Adoniram Judson, Samuel Newell, Samuel Nott, Gordon Hall, and Luther Rice, and was one of the founders of the American Bible Society.

His Park Street lectures on the theological issues of the day show him to be a strong, traditional Calvinist.[3] His method of pulpit preparation was unique. He wrote out numerous pages of content and text without any particular care for logical order. He would then organize the material.[4] His sermons show various patterns in structure, including the interrogative type outline as in the sermon he preached at the dedication of Park Street Church on the corner of Park and Tremont on the Commons on January 10, 1810, from 2 Chronicles 6:18: (1) Does the omnipresent God dwell in any one place? (2) Will God dwell with men on the earth? and (3) Can it be presumed that he will dwell in this house which we have built? His answer was in the affirmative.[5] The collected sermons are a rich repository, especially "Adam, Our Federal Head" from Romans 5:12–19,[6] "Returning from Crucifixion" from Luke 23:47–49,[7] and "The Brazen Serpent" from John 3:14–15.[8]

His ministry and preaching were always revivalistic. From his very first sermon, "His preaching was almost immediately attended by manifest tokens of the presence of the Holy Spirit."[9] The cross of Christ and the blood of the Savior were constant themes. His former view of the atonement (governmental) was abandoned: "God has declared that he will accept this sacrifice for men, and we must believe him, and must expect to discover the reality and glory of the atonement by faith and not by speculation."[10]

Griffin was a pastor who not only visited conscientiously but also preached passionately. He exhibited a warm and tender generosity to his flock and always preached for conversions. His biographer claims, "It would be difficult to name the individual in our country since the days of Whitefield who has been instrumental of an equal number of hopeful conversions."[11] In one stirring of the Spirit in Newark, ninety-seven people joined the church in one day.[12]

Strong biblical and doctrinal preaching built the nation and changed lives. They will still do so today.

---

1. William B. Sprague, *Sermons of Edward D. Griffin and a Memoir of His Life*, vol. 1 (Edinburgh: Banner of Truth, 1987), 5.
2. H. Crosby Englizian, *Brimstone Corner: Park Street Church Boston* (Chicago: Moody, 1968), 11.
3. Ibid., 59.
4. F. R. Webber, *A History of Preaching in Britain and America* (Milwaukee: Northwestern, 1957), 3:174.
5. Englizian, *Brimstone Corner*, 38.
6. Sprague, *Sermons of Edward D. Griffin*, 305.
7. Ibid., 597.
8. Ibid., 2:15.
9. Ibid., 8.
10. Ibid., 70.
11. Ibid., 259.
12. Ibid., 90.

9.2.5 *ARCHIBALD ALEXANDER—BRACING THE FOUNDATIONS*

> He appeared absolutely overpowered by the truths he was presenting and his every feature was illuminated and glowing with the fire within.
>
> —Comment by someone listening to Archibald Alexander preach

> The pulpit is no place for historical, philosophical or political discussions . . . Sometimes a preacher becomes so enveloped in criticism or metaphysics that plain people cannot understand him. The minister should be a critic and a metaphysician but carry only the result to the pulpit . . . Preaching the Gospel is not to gratify a refined taste . . . but the preacher should avoid disgusting men of taste . . . It is a grievous fault to speak nonsense in the name of the Lord . . . the main object is to make preaching useful to the souls of men.
>
> —Archibald Alexander

The first president of Princeton Theological Seminary, and the man who set the course for the school so dominant in theology and homiletics, was born in Valley of Virginia, Tidewater country, in 1772. **Archibald Alexander** (1772–1851) was the third of ten children in a prosperous farmer's home. He studied in Liberty Hall, which later became Washington College, but interrupted his schooling to serve as a private tutor for a while. He was converted at seventeen after studying with William Graham, reading John Flavel, and listening to Baptist preachers during what would be called "The Revival of 1789."[1]

Though ultimately a leader of the Old School, Alexander had known "great outpourings of the Holy Spirit" and "the internal evidences of Christianity."[2] Deeply tinctured with the Common Sense Realism of Thomas Reid from Scotland, he sought to set a course between the sterilities of the Enlightenment and the theological mushiness in vogue in much of Pietism. He believed with Edwards that the affections direct the will.

Alexander preached his trial sermon in 1791. Appropriately, the text was from Jeremiah 1:7. He soon served several smaller congregations and itinerated widely as an increasingly sought-after preacher.

He preached with great rapidity ("I ran on until I was perfectly out of breath") and had a habit of "looking steadily down upon the floor." His voice was powerful and clearly heard even in a large room, but "I was so conscious of my own defects that often after preaching, I was ashamed to come down from the pulpit."[3] Two great orators contemporary with Alexander influenced him: Patrick Henry, who lived just six miles away, and John Randolph of Roanoke.[4]

At twenty-five he became president of Hampden-Sidney College, but in a stringent shortage of ministers was called to the pastorate of Third Presbyterian Church in Philadelphia (Pine Street Church). The church flourished and grew 50 percent in his time there. He was elected Moderator of the General Assembly. Throughout his years in Philadelphia, Alexander's neighbor was the English nonconformist and chemist **Joseph Priestly,** who pastored the Universalist congregation where John Adams and other members of Congress attended.

Alexander took a preaching tour of New England. He preached for the eminent Dr. Emmons as well as in Dr. Hopkins' pulpit. (Both Alexander and his successor, Charles Hodge, were Hopkinsian postmillennialists and expected that missions would convert the world.[5]) Alexander's text was John 14:21: "Whoever has my commands and obeys them, he is one who loves me." His outline diverged from the Puritan model, reverting to the more classical type:

I. The foundation of love to Christ as it relates both to the object and subject of the affection;
II. The properties of love to Christ: sincerity, supremacy, constancy;
III. The evidences of love to Christ: a desire of pleasing and fear of offending; a desire of conforming to his character; a desire of communion and sorrow on account of absence; a desire to promote his glory.

Alexander related, "I insisted strongly on the position that love must terminate on the true character of the object beloved."[6]

In 1812 he accepted the call to establish Princeton Seminary. He also served as professor of didactic and polemical divinity. Here the foundations were laid for Princeton Theology, a vital response to the Scottish moderate Hugh Blair's sacred rhetoric at Harvard (which had a damaging impact on Ralph Waldo Emerson). Alexander's "less formal pulpit vitality" reigned at Princeton.[7]

For thirty-nine years Alexander presided over Princeton and the accompanying trend toward expounding larger passages of Scripture. Though short of stature, Alexander was commanding in the pulpit with his "crown of iron-gray hair, uncombed" and his old-fashioned rectangular glasses.[8] For his part, his sermons were not theological lectures but the opening of a text and the division of the same with theological and doctrinal integrity.[9] His evening sermons to students, preached from scraps of paper, were the occasion of many conversions and were typical of "all those qualities which made him eminently popular among the common people, who preferred his free and often irresistible invitations. His lively and penetrative voice was a welcome contrast to the more staid and scholastic addresses which smell of the lamp and sacrifice religious to literary merit."[10]

---

1. James A. Alexander, *The Life of Archibald Alexander* (New York: Scribner's, 1854), 39ff.
2. Lefferts A. Loetscher, *Facing the Enlightenment and Pietism: Archibald Alexander and the Founding of Princeton Theological Seminary* (Westport, Conn.: Greenwood, 1983), 21.
3. Ibid., 50.
4. One of the best studies of this incomparable orator is that of Russell Kirk, *John Randolph of Roanoke: A Study in American Politics* (Indianapolis: Liberty Press, 1951).
5. John Wheeler Auxier, "Princetonian Eschatology 1812–1878: The Neglect of the Apocalypse" (M.A. thesis, Trinity Evangelical Divinity School, 1986).
6. Alexander, *The Life of Archibald Alexander,* 247.
7. Loetscher, *Facing the Enlightenment and Pietism,* 237.
8. F. R. Webber, *A History of Preaching in Britain and America* (Milwaukee: Northwestern, 1957), 3:187.
9. Alexander, *The Life of Archibald Alexander,* 683. The breadth of Alexander's legacy is seen in his student, Charles Hodge, who spent 1826–1828 in Europe, where he was taught German by George Müller at Halle and contacted Tholuck, Hengstenberg, Olshausen, Krummacher, Neander, Monod, Ewald, and heard Charles Simeon preach in England (A. A. Hodge).
10. Ibid., 377.

9.2.6 *Lyman Beecher—Bequeathing the Legacy*

> When I've nothing to say I always holler.
>
> I went home expecting, and the word was sent up from the Springs that the Lord had come down on the previous Sunday, and that a meeting was appointed for Tuesday evening, and I must not disappoint them. I went and preached. I saw one young man with his head down. I wanted to know if it was an arrow of the Almighty. I came along after the sermon and laid my hand upon his head. He lifted his face, his eyes all full of tears; I saw it was God. Then I went up to the Northwest and the Lord was there; then to Ammigansett and the Lord was there; and the flood was rolling all around. Oh, what a time it was!
>
> I soon found myself harnessed to the Chariot of Christ, whose wheels of fire have rolled onward, high and dreadful to his foes, and glorious to his friends. I could not stop.
>
> —Lyman Beecher

The progenitor of the great house of preaching Beechers was **Lyman Beecher** (1775–1863). Beecher was born in New Haven to a line of blacksmiths and farmers. When his mother died in his third year, he was transplanted to Guilford in Connecticut, where he was raised, and then on to Yale, where he was converted during the presidency of Timothy Dwight (cf. 9.2.1). Already under conviction by thoughts of his hometown inebriate's destiny in hell, Beecher was "defenseless" before President Dwight's sermon on Jeremiah 8:20, "The harvest is past, the summer is ended and we are not saved."[1] "A whole avalanche rolled down," reported Beecher, and he went home "weeping every step." Throughout his ministry, Henry observes, "Hell was dreadfully important to Lyman Beecher."[2] He graduated from Yale in 1797 and studied theology with Dwight.

Beecher was a Calvinist but reacted against what he called "the sloughs of high-Calvinism." He was impatient for revival, and while serving in his first pastoral charge in East Hampton, Long Island (1800–1810), he suffered a total collapse that left him unable to preach for a year. Subsequently he moved to Litchfield, Connecticut, where his ministry was richly blessed.

Beecher was totally dedicated to the temperance cause and preached an epochal series of six sermons which are doubtless some of the strongest preaching on the use of beverage alcohol ever preached.[3] Interestingly, the Old Light Charles Hodge thought that both abolition and temperance were not movements in which Christian ministers should be involved because they were not authorized in the Scripture. But Lyman Beecher thundered out the message:

> Oh! were the sky over our heads one great whispering gallery, bringing down about us all the lamentation and woe which intemperance creates, and the form of earth one sonorous medium of sound, bringing up around us from beneath the wailings of the damned, whom the commerce in

> ardent spirit had sent thither—those tremendous realities assailing our senses would invigorate our conscience and give decision to our purpose of reformation.[4]

When Alexander Hamilton was killed in a duel with Aaron Burr, Beecher preached against dueling. His message helped lead to legislation outlawing dueling. He also preached a notable series at Park Street Church in Boston in 1823 with revival fires burning, and ultimately his son Edward came to serve that congregation as its pastor. His famous sermon on "The Bible as a Code of Laws" was preached first in Litchfield in segments, the final manuscript running to more than fifty pages.

From 1826 through 1832 he served the Hanover Street Church in Boston. Beecher led an overt challenge to the Unitarian tide sweeping New England. The Unitarians were led by the articulate and able **William Ellery Channing.** But Beecher, "in the prayer and in the sermon that seemed like the rolling in of the Atlantic upon the beach," raised a bulwark. His preaching was heavily doctrinal but extremely vital. One contemporary spoke of him "as a thunderbolt—you never knew where it would strike, but you never saw him rise to speak without feeling that so much electricity must strike."[5]

In 1832 Beecher moved west to take the presidency of Lane Seminary in Cincinnati and the pastorate of Second Presbyterian Church, the most distinguished in that city. The Albert Barnes heresy trial in 1831 (charging Barnes with taking up the New Theology and the governmental view of the atonement) ended with Barnes being "provisionally censured."[6] Beecher faced a heresy trial as well. The germs of New England theology lay in his drift from infant damnation and Calvinism toward "a more optimistic anthropology" and an insistence on man's moral ability. He clashed with Charles G. Finney on "the new measures," but agreed with Finney in terms of theological direction. With attorney Salmon P. Chase defending him, Beecher was vindicated. Chase, a member of Second Church, would later join Lincoln's cabinet.

The years at Lane were sometimes turbulent because of controversies over slavery. Theodore Weld, who had been converted by Finney, led debates on the issue. These were eventually banned by the trustees. Professor Asa Mahan led the students up to Oberlin where he became president and Finney Professor of Theology. During the schism between New School and Old School Presbyterians (1835–1846), Beecher desperately sought to save the school from financial ruin.

In 1851, Beecher walked away from Lane and moved to Maine, where his daughter Harriet and her husband, Calvin Stowe, were living. His children were one of his chief legacies, especially Harriet, "a genius in a family of eccentrics," whose *Uncle Tom's Cabin* was so influential in pre-Civil War America. Harriet testified, "I have sat under preaching which didn't hit and didn't warm and did not comfort."[7] It was not her father's "sledgehammer sermons" that she was describing. Son Henry Ward also gained preaching notoriety. His unfortunate leanings will come into focus in the next chapter.

Much in Beecher was modeled on Jonathan Edwards, including the stern stress on God's offended holiness. Beecher was a true revivalist and a hard preacher.

"Cut and thrust, hip and thigh, and [don't] ease off,"[8] he liked to say. He prepared his sermons shortly before the service time and would then rush to the church. On at least one occasion he dispensed with all hymns and prayers.[9] He would expound Scripture, face objections, and then make application. Out on the frontier he preached to thousands in camp meetings and outdoor services and was frequently the agent of multiplied conversions.

When someone asked him what the greatest pursuit was, he replied, "It is not theology; it is not controversy; but it is to save souls."[10] In his declining years Beecher moved to Boston. Once, when reference was made to his failing strength, he leaped up and preached an impassioned sermon as of old.

Lyman Beecher died before his son Henry's scandals blurred Beecher's remarkable legacy.

---

1. Stuart C. Henry, *Unvanquished Puritan: A Portrait of Lyman Beecher* (Grand Rapids: Eerdmans, 1973), 40.
2. Ibid., 41.
3. Ronald G. Walters, "Strong Drink," in *American Reformers, 1815–1860* (New York: Hill and Wang, 1978), 123–43.
4. T. Harwood Pattison, *The History of Christian Preaching* (Philadelphia: American Baptist Publication Society, 1903), 366.
5. Ibid., 367.
6. Henry, *Unvanquished Puritan,* 107.
7. Joan D. Hedrick, *Harriet Beecher Stowe* (New York: Oxford University Press, 1994), 370.
8. Edward F. Hayward, *Lyman Beecher* (Boston: Pilgrim, 1904), 26.
9. Milton Rugoff, *The Beechers: An American Family in the Nineteenth Century* (New York: Harper, 1981), 76.
10. Pattison, *The History of Christian Preaching,* 367.

9.2.7 Asahel Nettleton—Budding of Holiness

> It is no use to preach, if the church does not pray.
>
> —Asahel Nettleton

> I suppose no minister of his time was the means of so many conversions. . . . He . . . would sway an audience as the trees of the forest are moved by a mighty wind.
>
> —Francis Wayland, president of Brown University, 1827–1855

Often overlooked in the history of preaching is **Asahel Nettleton** (1783–1844), possibly the greatest evangelist New England saw since George Whitefield. Nettleton was God's instrument in bringing more than twenty-five thousand converts to Christ. He was born on a farm in Killingworth, Connecticut, near New Haven, at a time when the excesses of past revivals, the extreme behavior of the Davenportites, and the roving evangelists made most church people leery of revival. The "New Divinity" preachers did call for immediate repentance[1] (as opposed to the "Old," who maintained that God would do it in his own time).

At about eighteen, Nettleton had ominous thoughts of divine judgment after a Thanksgiving ball in his community. After hearing sermons by his pastor, Josiah Andrews, on regeneration and the danger of quenching the Spirit, he had a genuine conversion.[2] Soon after, he felt called to missionary service. Nettleton went on to Yale in 1805 and witnessed the moving of the Spirit there under President Dwight. Touched by the teaching that came out of Yale, Nettleton saw that "man has the power and duty to repent."[3] He was licensed and began to preach as an evangelist, experiencing remarkable visits from heaven in locales like Newington where converts swelled the membership from 64 to 132.

Stocky in build and ruddy in complexion, Nettleton was not the highly refined preacher that some of his compatriots were. Yet he had a dramatic flair, using a theatrical introduction and employing "the vacant people" to good effect, often likened to the rustic John Bunyan.[4] In all of the preaching by American-trained preachers at this time we see a marked move away from the Puritan style, influenced by the more classical rhetorical instruction, back to the modified form espoused by Hyperius and Henry Smith (cf. 6.1). Classical emphases were mixed with a religious intellectualism after the colonial period, and a marked English influence crept in.[5]

Nettleton's friend Bennet Tyler preserved specimens of Asa's preaching. His sermon on John 4:29, "Come, see a man which told me all things that ever I did," is a typical example:

I. The duty of preachers. It is to tell sinners their hearts. "He told me . . ."
II. Preaching which discloses the hearts of sinners is likely to be remembered. "He told me all things . . ."
III. The preacher who tells sinners their hearts is not likely to want for hearers. The invitation will be given, "Come, see the man which told me . . ."
IV. The conversion of one sinner is likely to be followed by the conversion of others. The invitation was complied with and a great spiritual harvest followed.[6]

Some of these messages are remarkably creative as "Some who are living, greater sinners than some who are in Hell," from Luke 13:1–5.[7] Dr. Wayland of Brown, who had heard Chalmers, gave Nettleton high marks for logical coherence, positive use of questions, and doctrinal thoroughness. His voice was "piercing," and his eyes are described by one thoughtful hearer:

> But his eye, after all, was the master power in his delivery. Full and clear and sharp, its glances, in the most animated parts of his discourses, were quick and penetrating, beyond almost anything I recollect ever to have witnessed. He seemed to look every hearer in the face, or rather to look into his soul, almost at one and the same moment.[8]

He pleaded and persuaded in such a manner that even Thornbury concedes that he scarcely sounded like a Calvinist. In fact, he introduced inquiry meetings and anxious services for those exercised in conviction.

In 1822 Nettleton was drastically limited for two years by typhus fever. During that confinement he produced his *Village Hymns,* which was sorely needed in New England, and introduced such jewels as Tappan's "Tis Midnight and on Olive's Brow" and many others. He never truly recovered from his illness but did resume itineration particularly in the South. In 1831 he visited Scotland and Europe, where no auspicious response attended his preaching but where he had excellent opportunity to network with such as John Angell James of Carr's Lane, Birmingham, William Jay, Robert Murray McCheyne, and Andrew Bonar. Both of the latter were divinity students at Edinburgh at the time.[9]

Not only was Nettleton dogged by ill health, but slanderous charges of immoral behavior dulled the luster of his last years, and he was constantly embroiled in controversy. He was troubled by reports of the Western revivals, particularly under Charles G. Finney, whose "new measures" greatly perturbed him. Nettleton's concerns included the anxious seat, women praying in public in mixed assemblies, praying for individuals specifically by name, hasty recognition of individuals as converted, and severe language in preaching.[10] The two antagonists met several times without resolving their differences, but both made clear they doubted neither the converts nor the sincerity of the other.

Deepening tensions over the New England Theology of Nathaniel Taylor were foreshadowing the tragic American denial of sin and depravity as well as imputation. This would all have a negative effect on Phillips Brooks and Henry Ward Beecher, and indeed persists to our own time. Oddly enough, both Samuel Hopkins and Charles Finney denied imputation, and poor Lyman Beecher tried to bridge all parties. Even Nettleton was veering toward the governmental view of the atonement and denying that a price had to be paid, though he stood against Beecher and Taylor in the crucial encounters. New England theology was in crisis.

In 1834, Bennet Tyler established a training school in protest against New England Theology which later became the Hartford Seminary. Tyler became the first president, and Nettleton became professor of pastoral duty. As a tribute to his biblical learning, the Nettleton Rhetorical Society was founded. The Society served as a memorial to "his defense of the faith and dedication to a style and vivacity of thought which was able to arrest, interest and instruct."[11]

We have just the skeletons of Nettleton's sermons, but sufficient testimony remains of the rich illustrative material and vocabulary employed by this precious servant of Christ. Nettleton finally succumbed to his physical ailments and died in 1844.

---

1. Sherry Pierpont May, "Asahel Nettleton: Nineteenth-Century American Revivalist" (Ph.D. dissertation, Drew University, 1969), 23.
2. Bennet Tyler, ed., Andrew A. Bonar, *Nettleton and His Labours* (Edinburgh: Banner of Truth, 1854), 23ff.
3. May, "Asahel Nettleton," 48.
4. J. F. Thornbury, *God-Sent Revival: The Story of Asahel Nettleton and the Second Great Awakening* (Welwyn, Herts, England: Evangelical Press, 1977), 19, 73.

5. Warren Wiersbe and Lloyd M. Perry, *The Wycliffe Handbook of Preachers and Preaching* (Chicago: Moody, 1984), 118ff.
6. Tyler, *Nettleton and His Labours,* 176.
7. Ibid., 185.
8. Thornbury, *God-Sent Revival,* 106.
9. Ibid., 206.
10. May, "Asahel Nettleton," 106.
11. Thornbury, *God-Sent Revival,* 222.

9.2.8 Gardiner Spring—Battling for the Truth

> Few know how much they are under obligations to the pulpit. They boast of other influences but overlook this simple institution of heavenly wisdom. But for this single institution, what a world would this earth of ours have been! Blessed are the people that "know the joyful sound." Favored is the man who bears even nothing more than the mark of the pulpit upon his conscience, exciting his fears, restraining his vices, and reaching forth its hand to keep him from the gulf of perdition before the time!
>
> Different ages of the world and different lands and different departments of the Christian church are a sort of transcript of the pulpits that have instructed them, and bear their peculiarities to the present hour.
>
> Oh, if ministers only saw the inconceivable glory that is before them, and the preciousness of Christ, they would not be able to refrain from going about, leaping and clapping their hands for joy, and exclaiming, I am a minister of Christ! I am a minister of Christ!
>
> —Gardiner Spring

Gardiner Spring (1785–1872) was born into the home of a prominent clergyman, Samuel Spring, in Newburyport, Massachusetts, the town in which George Whitefield died. The elder Spring had been a chaplain in the Continental Army. Gardiner Spring was raised in this godly environment and went on to Yale and then to Bermuda briefly while studying for the law. He was admitted to the bar. Yet he felt God's call to ministry and went on to Andover Seminary (of which his father was a founder). He was ordained to the ministry in 1810 as he began his ministry at the Brick Presbyterian Church in New York City. He remained in that charge for sixty-two years until his death.

Spring was a staunch Calvinist with a slight Hopkinsian tinge. He was a critic of what he called "spurious revivals." Indeed we have the spurious and the genuine described in Scripture, an example of a spurious revival under Joash (2 Chron. 24), and a genuine revival under Hezekiah (2 Chron. 29ff.). A close friend of Nettleton, he was in the middle of much of the turmoil in the nineteenth century. His first four years in New York City were uneventful, but then waves of revival swept over pastor and people. He wrote widely and was active in many missionary endeavors. One of his choice volumes, *The Power of the Pulpit,* is an example of an able preacher's serious reflection on the craft. He believed preaching to be the preeminent task of the pastor.[1]

Here is a capable preacher who pondered everything from the indispensable message to the urgent necessity of "feeling his subject." He pleaded for integrity, and urged that the preacher's heart "be a transcript of his sermons, and then he will be a chosen vessel to carry to lost men his name who was crucified."[2] Preaching is what angels wished to do, he alleged, and insisted that those who train preachers be deeply versed in the pastoral office. Preachers have a duty to enjoy their office, for indeed:

> It is the Saviour's voice by whom this message is uttered. He bows the heavens and comes down. He walks amidst the golden candlesticks. When his ministers speak in his name, he is with them; when his people meet together, he is there. He will be sanctified in them that come nigh him, and before all the people will he be glorified.[3]

Spring was of the conviction that the preacher should "preach as though he were in sight of the cross and heard the groans of the Mighty Sufferer of Calvary." The centrality of the cross and samples of his style may be examined in his priceless volume *The Attraction of the Cross.*[4]

Spring held that all things are tributary to the cross and that "the cross was designed to be the most compendious and vivid expression of all religious truth."[5] In a time when many were slipping from the penal and forensic view of the sacrifice at Calvary, Spring stood steadfastly for propitiation. The wave of the future would be New England Theology and the governmental view, but Spring pointed out the intertwining of sin, repentance, and substitutionary atonement. He trumpeted the cross as "the only propitiation," a transaction by which Christ bore our sins in his own body. In his W. H. Griffith Thomas Lectures at Dallas Theological Seminary in 1987, David Wells aptly demonstrates how crucial the debate over the atonement was in the nineteenth century. He quotes A. A. Hodge on the point at hand:

> The two great doctrines just at present most generally brought into question, and which have suffered most at the hands of Rationalistic criticism, are those concerning the nature and extent of biblical Inspiration, and the nature of the redemptive work of Christ. These naturally stand or fall together. For if the inspiration of the Scriptures is plenary, then the church doctrine as to the nature of the Redemption remains impregnable. But if the authority of the Scriptures may be abated, the way is open, of course, in due proportion, to theories of Redemption adjusted to "the finer feeling," the "moral intuitions," and the administrative experiences of mankind.[6]

Gardiner Spring was a strong and discerning champion of theological orthodoxy in a time of considerable erosion and declension, and one who magnified the preaching office in a time of mediocrity.

1. Gardiner Spring, *The Power of the Pulpit: Thoughts Addressed to Christian Ministers and Those Who Hear Them* (Edinburgh: Banner of Truth, 1848, 1986), 109.
2. Ibid., 154.
3. Ibid., 239.
4. Gardiner Spring, *The Attraction of the Cross* (New York: M. W. Dodd, 1859).
5. Ibid., 35.
6. David F. Wells, "The Debate over the Atonement in Nineteenth-Century America," *Bibliotheca Sacra* 144, no. 575 (July–September 1987): 247. These four lectures are of extraordinary importance. The diminution of clarity with respect to scriptural authority or the atoning work of Christ is disastrous for preaching as later events would show in Scotland. Biblical authority and the blood atonement are the special objects of satanic fury and hostility.

9.3 THE ENGLISH WATERFALL

> . . . the age was one of religious seriousness.
>
> —A. R. Vidler

> Not only a modified Sunday observance, but Bible reading and family prayers were common until near the end of the century.
>
> —G. M. Trevelyan

> If one asks how nineteenth-century English merchants earned the reputation of being the most honest in the world (a very real factor in the nineteenth-century primacy of English trade), the answer is: because hell and heaven seemed as certain to them as tomorrow's sunrise, and the Last Judgment as real as the week's balance-sheet. This keen sense of moral accountancy had also much to do with the success of self-government in the political sphere.
>
> —R. C. K. Ensor

The post-Napoleonic years were commonly called the Victorian Age, although Queen Victoria did not ascend the throne until 1837. It was a time of expanding empire, an era of immense literary productivity (with the likes of Dickens, Jane Austen, Thomas Carlyle, Thomas and Matthew Arnold, Lord Tennyson, Robert Browning, and Anthony Trollope). Frederick Karl's magisterial biography of George Eliot (Mary Ann Evans) speaks of her as the "voice of a century."[1] Profoundly religious and even evangelical early on, Eliot moved to secular humanism and a morally deficient life. She slowly defected from her evangelical reading, church attendance, and old friends. In the face of a tradition-driven society, she found her own way. Eliot exemplifies the trend of the times.

---

1. Frederick R. Karl, *George Eliot: Voice of a Century* (New York: Norton, 1995). A treasury of Victoriana.

9.3.1 *John Angell James—Raising the Standard*

> Oh . . . how delightful is it, notwithstanding the humbling and sorrowful consciousness of defects and sins, to look back upon a life spent for Christ.
>
> Preach as in full view of all the wonders of Calvary, and let it be as if, while you spoke, you felt the Saviour's grace flowing into, and filling your soul, and as if at that moment you were sympathizing with the apostle in his sublime raptures—"God forbid I should glory, save in the cross of our Lord Jesus Christ."
>
> While yet a youth engaged in secular concerns, I had been deeply susceptible of the power of an awakening style of preaching, which was strengthened by the perusal of the rousing sermons of Dr. Davies of New Jersey. From that time to the present I have made the conversion of the impenitent the great end of my ministry.
>
> —John Angell James

One of the honored deans of nonconformity in early Victorian England and first in the noble succession of James, R. W. Dale, and J. H. Jowett at Carr's Lane Chapel in Birmingham was **John Angell James** (1785–1859). Birmingham came to prominence with a great influx of nonconformists after the Restoration, and Carr's Lane came into existence as a protest against Unitarianism. Arthur Porritt, Jowett's biographer, argued that "the position occupied by Carr's Lane Church in the life of Birmingham has perhaps no parallel in any other English city."[1] During the tenure of James, which began in 1804 and lasted until 1859, the church became a powerful center of biblical preaching and missionary outreach and vision.

The man who entered such large responsibility at age nineteen was born in Dorset. Apprenticed to a draper for several years, James converted under strong gospel preaching. He began to teach Sunday school and then attended Dr. Bogue's school at Gosport, which had been established under the auspices of the Haldanes. Carr's Lane was small when he commenced his labors, and for the first seven years not much seemed to happen. James testified that first he learned to preach and then he began to learn to pray and in the eighth year there came a turn. Soon a new church edifice was needed to seat eighteen hundred people.

When asked why he didn't preach his Calvinism, James responded, "Because I do not seem to find much about Calvinism in the Bible."[2] He prepared thoroughly for his preaching with great attention to the text. Composed and serious in his delivery, he wanted to avoid both "the contortions of an epileptic zeal" and "the numbness of a paralytic one." "He attached the utmost importance to the proper reading of the Holy Scriptures . . . it was quite a feast to hear him."[3] James stressed Christian character as the outcome of Christian conversion, and indeed, "The motto of all his discourses, as of all his works was 'Holiness to the Lord!'"[4] His preaching was not eloquent in the learned sense but good old Anglo-Saxon, as when he made three prescriptions for preachers: (1) brains, (2) bowels (compassion), and (3) bellows (lungs).[5]

James' written legacy goes to seventeen volumes, including his influential *The Anxious Inquirer after Salvation* (600,000 copies!) where he quotes widely from bishops and Adam Clarke. He read widely and had broad interests. One significant piece from his hand and heart is a "Review of the Character" of Richard Knill, whose ministry in India but particularly in St. Petersburg was outstanding, in which he was the forerunner of the great Lord Radstock.[6] James was determined to preach law first and was convinced that exegesis should be augmented by persuasion and pleading. As he so characteristically put it:

> It is delicious, I know, to hear a fine, eloquent and richly theological descant upon a redeeming love and pardoning mercy—to have the imagination and heart regaled with rhetoric, radiant with the glories of the cross and redolent with the odour of that Name which is above every name: it is gratifying to the thinking mind to have the intellect pleased with logical dexterity, and the fine abstractions of clear and strong thinking: it will be well enough also to have the subjects of moral obligation discussed in vague generalities and by elegant composition—but it is not so acceptable to have all the special and difficult duties of the Christian's life, or man's conduct to his fellows, set clearly before the understanding and enforced upon the conscience. Men do not so well like to be followed through all the labyrinths of the heart's deceitfulness, beaten out of every refuge of lies, and made to feel the obligations to love where they are inclined to hate and to forgive where they desire to revenge. And we ministers pander too much to this taste.[7]

James was known for finishing his sermons well. He initiated his successor, Robert W. Dale, into the work and saw many conversions attending his ministry. Years later, Joseph Parker observed that "a kind of Pentecostal effect" was part of his ministry and that "he reaped a harvest second to none."[8] In advanced age, James reflected:

> Ministers may think too little of this now, and the work of conversion be lost sight of too much, in their eager desires and ardent ambition after popularity and applause; but the time is coming when these, except as they give a man a wider sphere for his converting work, will be thought worthless and vain. Amidst the gathering infirmities of old age, and the anticipations of eternity—much more at the bar of Christ, and in the celestial world—it will be deemed a poor and meagre reflection to a minister of Christ, that he was once followed and applauded by admiring crowds.[9]

---

1. Arthur Porritt, *John Henry Jowett* (London: Hodder and Stoughton, 1924), 70.
2. F. R. Webber, *A History of Preaching in Britain and America* (Milwaukee: Northwestern, 1952), 3:467.

3. John Campbell, *John Angell James* (London: John Snow, 1860), 45.
4. Ibid., 51.
5. Ibid., 77.
6. James' chapter is in C. M. Birrell, *The Life of Rev. Richard Knill of St. Petersburg* (London: Religious Tract Society, 1859), 255–70. Knill knew Carey and Judson and preached widely abroad. He was close to William Jay in Bath. He ultimately served the church in Chester earlier served by Matthew Henry.
7. Campbell, *John Angell James,* 188.
8. Webber, *A History of Preaching,* 3:468.
9. Campbell, *John Angell James,* 240.

9.3.2 Thomas Binney—Affirming the Basics

> Truth cannot be injured by fair and full discussion, and by open and uncompromising statements. I have no hesitation about saying that I am an enemy to the Establishment . . . I confess as a matter of deep serious religious conviction that the Established Church is a great national evil . . . that it destroys more souls than it saves.
>
> That there is a grandeur investing our position, may be further felt by adverting to the fact of our aim and solicitude being precisely those of the Saviour himself . . . we sustain that office which He sustained and are discharging its functions as representatives of Him.
>
> It is an inestimable blessing to possess these "writings;" to draw near to them as to a "holy oracle;" and to learn, immediately and directly from themselves what the Lord God has "made known" to man or "requires" of him. Still, a living agency, official teaching, a ministerial "stewardship of the mysteries of God," is a necessary and permanent institution. It is necessary for the preservation, improvement and perseverance of Christians themselves, for it is "the gift" of Christ for the "edifying of his body," and "the perfecting of the saints;" for far more is it necessary for the promulgation of the Truth, and through that, for the extension, enlargement and triumph of the Church.
>
> —Thomas Binney

Another of the defining mentors of Victorian dissent was **Thomas Binney** (1798–1874), who modeled a straightforward style of preaching for many nonconformists. Binney initially considered Spurgeon an upstart, but he came to admire and commend the younger man.[1] Born in Newcastle-on-Tyne in Northumbria, Binney was instructed in Latin and Greek by an old Presbyterian minister. He developed a great love for books while working in a book store. He attended Coward College (the Congregational seminary) in Wymondly, which was maintained by the Reverend Thomas Morell.

After serving briefly in Bedford and on the Isle of Wight, in 1829 he took the pastorate of the King's Weigh-House Chapel in London, where he served for over forty years. The chapel was in a sense the nonconformist cathedral in London and drew many persons of wealth and from the middle class. Like Isaac Watts in an earlier generation, Binney dedicated himself to raising the level of congregational worship and singing. A new sanctuary was necessary to accommodate the growing throngs which gathered to hear the forceful biblical preaching of Thomas Binney.

He was an early pamphleteer, putting his strong convictions into print for a widening audience. As a preacher, he was a master of accent and eloquent in his own way, with a great power to paint a picture and to be alternately "fiend or angel."[2] Browning, who had nonconformist roots, certainly would have found in Binney what he longed for in a chapel preacher, as reflected in his "Christmas Eve and Easter Day." He was criticized for lack of culture but adhered to the highest view of the authority of Holy Scripture. He had drunk deeply at the springs of Augustine, Calvin, Howe, Charnock, and Baxter.[3] Some of his noted sermons were his address to the London Missionary Society on "Messiah Suffering and Messiah Satisfied" and his memorable funeral sermon for Algernon Wells, "Light and Immortality Brought to Light by the Gospel."

The great Alexander Maclaren testified that it was Binney who taught him how to preach. Like South and Latimer before him, Binney was, according to Hood, "The most charming humorist in the pulpit of our time."[4] He always preached without notes and used humor effectively. Yet he tended to be nervous and was a man of considerable eccentricity. Some likened him to Lacordaire, the French preacher of consummate skill (cf. 6.3.2.3). Listeners occasionally had difficulty because of his habit of dropping his voice at the end of a sentence. We have a sterling example of good division of a text and skillful impartation of its truth in "The Ultimate Design of the Christian Ministry" delivered to the London Missionary Society, and then also in his brilliant "The Christian Ministry Not a Priesthood."[5] One hearer recorded his impression at Weigh-House:

> The moment we saw a gentleman ascending the pulpit stairs, we felt assured, from the description we had previously been favored with that he must be the minister of whom we had heard so much; he was tall and large-chested, but the head and face were the most strikingly intellectual in their developments we had ever looked upon. In a tone of voice so low as to be heard with great difficulty, even by us who were so near him, he read a chapter . . . there is no familiarity, no bawling, no hurry; all is calmness, earnestness and quiet supplication . . . that he is excessively nervous is easily perceptible from the anxious look which he directs to some part of the chapel, whence a slight noise proceeds, and by the occasional twitching of his facial muscles . . . we listen with the utmost attention lest a word should escape us . . . in spite of his peculiarities, he is a very great preacher.[6]

---

1. G. Holden Pike, *The Life and Work of Charles Haddon Spurgeon* (Edinburgh: Banner of Truth, 1894, 1991), 1:134.

2. E. Paxton Hood, *Thomas Binney: His Mind, Life and Opinions* (London: James Clarke, 1874), 54.
3. Ibid., 84.
4. Ibid., 118.
5. Thomas Binney, *The Ultimate Design of the Christian Ministry* and *The Christian Ministry Not a Priesthood* (London: Jackson and Walford, 1849).
6. Hood, *Thomas Binney*, 148–50.

9.3.3 JOHN HENRY NEWMAN—RISKING ALL

> Definiteness is the life of preaching. Nothing that is anonymous will preach, nothing that is dead and gone.
>
> Lead, kindly Light, amid th' encircling gloom, Lead Thou me on! The night is dark, and I am far from home; Lead Thou me on! Keep Thou my feet; I do not ask to see. . . . The distant scene; one step enough for me.
>
> —John Henry Newman
>
> He was interested in everything that was going on . . . in science, in politics, in literature. Nothing was too large for him, nothing too trivial, if it threw light on the central question what man really was and what his destiny . . . He had read omnivorously, and studied modern thought in all its forms, and with all its many-colored passions.
>
> —J. A. Froude

In the front ranks of English preachers is **John Henry Newman** (1801–1890). The son of a London banker and a Huguenot mother, Newman came under evangelical influence while a student of fifteen at Ealing. One of his classics teachers, the Reverend Walter Mayers, "an ardent Evangelical and a Calvinist," influenced both John Henry and his brother Francis. Mayers encouraged the Newmans to read Thomas Scott, Philip Doddridge, and Beveridge's *Private Thoughts*.[1]

Francis joined the Plymouth Brethren[2] but lost his faith on the mission field under the corrupting influence of Bishop Colenso and his higher critical extremism.[3] John Henry often spoke of his conversion in this time-frame. It was a time of some uneasiness in the Church of England with evangelicalism evincing unexpected strength. Could evangelicalism hold the ground for orthodoxy in the face of mounting antisupernaturalistic influence from Germany, or would the Bible become a casualty, with the authority of Rome offering ecclesiastical security in the raging storms?

John Henry went on to Oriel College at Oxford, where his own evangelicalism gradually faded. He followed E. B. Pusey, Keble (the preacher and hymnwriter), and his friend Froude into the Oxford Movement, or Tractarianism. The Oxford Group was largely an offshoot from evangelicalism. In the British Isles as well as America, preaching drifted away from the Puritan and post-Puritan models.[4] Newman would eventually go with Henry Manning into the Roman Catholic Church itself (his friend F. W. Faber, who wrote "Faith of our Fathers," went with him).

Newman was a remarkably serious follower of Christ and student of the Bible early on. His prayer was "Give me grace—make me holy."[5] He felt called to the ministry and began to preach at St. Clement's in Oxford. While at Oxford he came under the spell of **Richard Whatley** (1787–1863), his principal at Merton College and an expert in logic and mathematics. Whatley was also a Broad churchman, and later became archbishop of Dublin. His rhetorical theory advanced the notion that reasonable and logical proof consists not of "invention" but rather pursuing a proposition with the support of varying kinds of testimony. Both Newman and F. W. Robertson were molded to some degree by Whatley. Newman assisted Whatley in the preparation of *Elements of Logic* in 1826.[6] In 1828 he was appointed Vicar of St. Mary's, Oxford, the university church, where his outstanding preaching became increasingly well known. While on a Mediterranean trip he became ill, and on board ship wrote his stately hymn "Lead, Kindly Light."

His earlier preaching in St. Mary's was strongly biblical and focused on Christ and his cross:

> The doctrine of Christ crucified is the only spring of real virtue and piety, and the only foundation of peace and comfort . . . Comfort is a cordial, but no one drinks cordials from morning to night. . . . [7]

For twenty years Newman drifted toward Rome. When he finally converted in October of 1845, he took over the Oratory in Birmingham. His last sermon in St. Mary's, "The Parting of Friends," left his friends and his church stunned. The defection of such a prince to Rome shook the foundations. He worked in Ireland from 1854 to 1862 in order to establish a national Catholic university. Thereafter he was made a cardinal in 1879, and he preached and wrote until his death.

The sermons of Newman, particularly his earlier efforts, have an extraordinary power and beauty. All of the sermons in his famous *Parochial and Plain Sermons* come prior to 1843. Dean Lake described the preaching and its effect:

> There was first the style, always simple, refined and unpretending, and without a touch of any thing which could be called rhetoric, but always marked by a depth of feeling which evidently sprang from the heart and experience of the preacher, and penetrated by a suppressed vein of the poetry which was so strong a feature in Newman's mind and which appealed at once to the hearts and the highest feelings of his hearers . . .[8]

In the succeeding days he often preached on the Second Coming and the challenge of the Antichrist as did the Tractarians generally. After preaching once on "The Incarnate Son, a Sufferer and Sacrifice,"[9] Newman's magnetism is described:

> Newman had described closely some of the incidents of our Lord's Passion; he then paused. For a few moments there was a breathless silence. Then in a low, clear voice, of which the faintest vibration was audible in

> the farthest corner of St. Mary's, he said: "Now I bid you recollect that He to whom these things were done was Almighty God." It was as if an electric stroke had gone through the church, as if every person present understood for the first time the meaning of what he had all his life been saying. I suppose it was an epoch in the mental history of more than one of my Oxford contemporaries.[10]

In growing increasingly high church, Newman became harder and more vehement in his preaching with "an under-current of pessimism and gloom." We see this in his famous sermons "Christian Nobleness" and "Feasting in Captivity."[11] Samuel Wilberforce spoke of "the general tone of the Sermons is that of requisition."[12] Always veering toward the severe and the ascetic, Newman's listeners heard less and less of the joyful sound. He was a gifted and great preacher but he lost something essential: "The glorious gospel of our Blessed God!"

---

1. David Newsome, "The Evangelical Sources of Newman's Power," in *The Recovery of Newman: An Oxford Symposium,* ed. John Coulson and A. M. Allchin (London: SPCK, 1967), 11, 13. A good overall treatment of the life and ministry of Newman is Brian Martin, *John Henry Newman: His Life and Work* (Oxford: Oxford University Press, 1982).
2. William Robbins, *The Newman Brothers* (Cambridge, Mass.: Harvard University Press, 1966), 30.
3. B. B. Warfield, "Some Perils of Missionary Life," in *Selected Shorter Writings* (Philipsburg, N.J.: Presbyterian and Reformed, 1973), 2:502ff.
4. O. C. Edwards, "Newman and Robertson," in *Concise Encyclopedia of Preaching* (Louisville: Westminster John Knox, 1995), 219. Newman always preached his proposition; see Lewis O. Brastow, *Representative Modern Preachers* (New York: Macmillan, 1904), 302.
5. Dr. Zeno, *John Henry Newman: His Inner Life* (San Francisco: Ignatius, 1987), 28.
6. R. D. Middleton, *Newman at Oxford: His Religious Development* (London: Oxford University Press, 1950), 44.
7. Zeno, *John Henry Newman,* 40.
8. Middleton, *Newman at Oxford,* 94.
9. John Henry Newman, *Parochial and Plain Sermons* (San Francisco: Ignatius, 1987), VI, 1220. Eight volumes of his sermons (169 sermons) beautifully bound together.
10. Middleton, *Newman at Oxford,* 96ff. Newman read his sermons, but Gladstone said his matter overcame his manner.
11. David Newsome, *The Parting of Friends: The Wilberforces and Henry Manning* (Grand Rapids: Eerdmans, 1966), 180–81.
12. Ibid., 202. In his *Newman: An Appreciation* (Edinburgh: Oliphant, 1901), Alexander Whyte shares his great fondness for Newman, with whom he spent some time, but also voices his regret that the gospel message doesn't sound clearly and authentically in Newman.

9.3.4 *SAMUEL WILBERFORCE—RELISHING THE FELLOWSHIP*

> My own belief is that things will grow worse and worse . . . I think that the Church will fall within fifty years entirely and the State will not survive it much longer.
>
> —Samuel Wilberforce

> Charles Simeon and Samuel's father-in-law, John Sargent, visited the Wilberforces on the Island of Wight, reporting a conversation after an evening service—Simeon, contrasting this time with Whitefield's and Wesley's, spoke of the coldness now: "Such men as Daniel Wilson, Marsh, etc. laboring, with little or no fruit. There's a dew everywhere but a shower nowhere."

Along with Simeon, the name of Wilberforce alone stands to the fore as we consider the pioneers of the evangelical renaissance in the early nineteenth century. **William Wilberforce** (1759–1833) was the gifted orator and spiritual leader of the Clapham Group, which spearheaded the abolition of slavery, improvement of prison conditions, and revocation of the Corn Laws.[1] William was a devout Anglican, and spent two hours daily before breakfast studying Scripture and praying. He served in a Parliament that from 1784 to 1832 boasted 112 evangelicals. Evangelicals also obtained their first bishops—Ryder in Gloucester, C. R. Sumner in Llandaff, and his brother J. B. Sumner in Chester, later archbishop of Canterbury (1848–1862).[2]

Yet the harsh winds of German rationalism[3] and Darwinian theories of origin were threatening the foundations of orthodoxy.[4] With fully one-third of the Anglican clergy being evangelical, the evangelical understanding of salvation was dominant until the 1840s. The coming collapse of evangelical orthodoxy would involve a move away from eternal punishment and the vicarious atonement, a move from Jesus the Lamb to Jesus the Man, what F. D. Maurice described as "a shift of the center of gravity from the atonement to the incarnation."[5] These are the views enshrined in the popular volume *Lux Mundi* edited by Charles Gore.

And how would the rising generation meet the challenge to orthodoxy? Some as we have seen opted for the trek to Rome; others became concessive Broad churchmen. Many remained evangelical. Some, like **Samuel Wilberforce** (1805–1873), son of William Wilberforce, were torn in various directions.

Raised in a pious home, Samuel went to Oxford. One of his dear friends there was Francis Lyte, who wrote "Abide with Me." Samuel was married in 1828 to a daughter of John Sargent, close friend and confident of Charles Simeon, who performed the marriage. After a curacy near Oxford, he moved to Brighstone on the Island of Wight, where his preaching soon gave him a widening reputation. Worried much about the antinomianism of the dissenters, Samuel preached vigorously and directly on smuggling and other sensitive topics on the island. His sermons were lengthy:

> Extra services and classes were at once begun, not only in the parish church, but the outlying hamlets; and to this day the villagers remember how no weather stopped him; while as to his preaching, a story is yet current how at evening service he would sometimes go on till it grew dark, so that you could not see him; but, it is added, "the people would have sat all night listening."[6]

Wilberforce was not an original thinker, but he was a reader and activist with an amazing capacity for work. He was out front on all of the critical issues of the day and close to Prime Minister Gladstone. He tended toward high church, and preached a series of sermons at the University Church in Oxford. He felt that Hook preached essays rather than sermons in that pulpit. Wilberforce preached without notes and with such adaptability that he was asked to explain his style:

> He replied that he owed his facility of speech mainly to the pains his father had taken with him. His father used to cause him to make himself well acquainted with a given subject, and then speak on it, without notes, and trusting to the inspiration of the moment for suitable words. Thus his memory and his power of mentally arranging and dividing his subjects were strengthened.[7]

In 1841 he was assigned Alverstoke and the archdeanery of Surrey. At this time he was made chaplain to Prince Albert, preaching in the Royal Chapel at Windsor.[8] Shortly after moving to Alverstoke, his beloved wife passed away. He never remarried. Wilberforce was deeply troubled over Maurice's views on the atonement,[9] and endured the debacle of a debate with T. H. Huxley.[10] He saw his daughter, his three brothers, his son-in-law, and four brothers and sisters-in-law leave the Church of England and take up spiritual residence in the Church of Rome. As the Oxford Group continued toward Rome, Samuel broke with Pusey, denying that the Eucharist had any salvific value.

Wilberforce's critics thought he was evasive and too adroit. They called him "sly Sam" or "soapy Sam," ostensibly because he would wring his hands as he spoke. He saw his brother-in-law Henry Manning and Newman become Catholic bishops.[11] He parted ways with Newman and declined to write for his publication.

We do not possess many of Wilberforce's sermons, but his writings suggest a direct manner with a clear concern to let the text speak.[12] The publication of his brother Robert's work on the incarnation of Christ demonstrates the basic soundness in theology inherited from their father, since the mediatorial work of Christ as sin-bearer and perfect sacrifice on the cross is made very clear.[13] Samuel Wilberforce faltered and wavered on many issues, but on balance he held the banner of biblical preaching high, as he reflects about a visit to Ryde and the curate there:

> He seems to me to be a sincere and humble Christian, but very slow indeed, and his sermons from all accounts are of just the lunar rainbow

> sort of inefficiency and generalization, which you would expect to find from an X superstructure upon so foggy a foundation. . . . The more I see the more I am convinced of the evil of general preaching, of the evil of cold preaching, and of the infinite superiority of the X's over the Z's (X being Evangelical and Z being High and Dry).[14]

Samuel Wilberforce was made dean of Westminster and then bishop of Oxford in 1845, serving in that capacity until 1870, when he was made bishop of Winchester. He died in 1873 when he fell from his horse.

---

1. William Wilberforce, *Real Christianity Contrasted with the Prevailing Religious System* (Portland, Oreg.: Multnomah, 1982). Note Charles W. Colson, "Standing Against All Odds," *Christianity Today* (September 6, 1985): 26ff.
2. G. R. Balleine, *A History of the Evangelical Party in the Church of England* (London: Longman, Greens, 1908), 196.
3. John Louis Haney, *The German Influence on Samuel Taylor Coleridge* (New York: Haskell House, 1966). A sample tracing of an important theological and cultural influence.
4. Charles Coulston Gillispie, *Genesis and Geology: The Impact of Scientific Discoveries Upon Religious Beliefs in the Decades Before Darwin* (New York: Harper Torchbooks, 1951). An important study of pre-Darwinian development.
5. Boyd Hilton, *The Age of Atonement: The Influence of Evangelicalism on Social and Economic Thought, 1795–1865* (Oxford: Clarendon, 1988), 5.
6. A. R. Ashwell and Reginald G. Wilberforce, *The Life of Samuel Wilberforce* (New York: Dutton, 1883), 18.
7. Ibid., 47.
8. Ibid., 70. For a moving description of Wilberforce's friendship with Richard Trench, whose studies on the miracles and the parables have been such an enrichment over the years, see Warren Wiersbe, *Living with the Giants* (Grand Rapids: Baker, 1993), 29. Trench followed Whatley as archbishop of Dublin at a difficult time.
9. Ibid., 228.
10. William Irvine, *Apes, Angels and Victorians: Darwin, Huxley and Evolution* (New York: McGraw-Hill, 1955), 5–8. This is a caustic but essentially accurate description of this unfortunate encounter, when Bishop Wilberforce turned to Huxley and "begged to know, was it through his grandfather or his grandmother that he claimed his descent from a monkey." Huxley slapped his knee and softly said to his neighbor, "The Lord has delivered him into my hand." Huxley saw that by using ridicule, Wilberforce opened himself up to the same.
11. David Newsome, *The Parting of Friends: The Wilberforces and Henry Manning* (Grand Rapids: Eerdmans, 1966). This book is a treasure, a most genteel and thoughtful tracing of complex relationships in a troubled time.
12. Samuel Wilberforce, *Heroes of Hebrew History* (London: W. H. Allen, 1896).
13. Archdeacon Robert Wilberforce, *The Doctrine of the Incarnation of Our Lord Jesus Christ* (London: Mozley and Smith, 1879).
14. Newsome, *The Parting of Friends,* 170.

9.3.5 *F. W. Robertson of Brighton—Reaching for the Idea*

> The preacher's preacher!
>
> —John Bishop

> The one great preacher in the history of the English Church.
>
> —Canon Charles Smith

> Save yourself from sectarianism; pledge yourself to no school; cut your life adrift from all party; be a slave to no maxims: stand fast, unfettered and free, servants only of the truth . . .
>
> I believe I could have become an orator, had I chosen to take pains. I see what rhetoric does and what it seems to do, and I thoroughly despise it . . . and yet perhaps I do it injustice; with an unworldly noble love to give it reality, what might it not do!
>
> —F. W. Robertson

There was much preaching in Victorian England and much boring preaching and indeed much boring evangelical preaching. Anthony Trollope wrote in *Barchester Towers*, "There is perhaps no greater hardship inflicted on mankind in civilized and free countries than the necessity of listening to sermons."[1] Trollope was not alone in deploring the "tedium of sermons," and what was among the evangelicals exceedingly dreary "if not subversive." His characters like Reverend Samuel Prong and Rev. Joseph Emilius (a wife-beater and a bigamist), to say nothing of Archdeacon Grantley, whose "frolics were of a cumbrous kind," reinforce Trollope's childhood impression of "trashy sermons in ludicrously theatrical manner."[2]

But there were exceptions, such as the brief but stellar ministry of **Frederick W. Robertson** (1816–1853), of whom Dean Church said, "He has become beyond question the greatest preacher of the nineteenth century." Robertson was born in a family that had long been in the military. His commission was delayed so long that his father urged him to enter the ministry. Five days later the commission came, but he was already at school.

Robertson was a frail and sensitive young man whose first brief charge was at Cheltenham, then for a short time at the English church in Heidelberg in Germany, then St. Ebbe's in Oxford, and then for six years at Trinity Chapel in the resort city of Brighton. Only one of his sermons was published before his death at age thirty-seven, but quickly his remarkable sermons began to circulate and his stature was recognized. On his monument in Brighton are written the words: "He awakened the holiest feelings in poor and in rich, in ignorant and in learned. There is he lamented as their guide and comforter."

Here is preaching that made a difference. Robertson was a staunch evangelical who had moved away from an earlier transcendentalism and Shelley's "atmosphere of profligacy" to the more Wordsworthian and Shakespearean tradition compatible with the evangelicals in the Church of England.[3] Poets like Tennyson and writers like Ruskin (with whom he debated in the Oxford Union) were his friends rather than the philosophers. Perhaps he overreacted against rationalism, but he treasured and memorized Scripture constantly.[4]

Robertson occasionally recoiled from evangelical cant. He walked a solitary path, and both liberals and hard-shell conservatives found fault with him. Yet he sustained a steady and conscientious course and could not tolerate the liberal vivisection of Scripture. The chapel in Brighton overflowed.

At an early stage, Robertson had been taken by Newman but he soon regained his poise. His preaching was always biblical and textual. His sermons, invariably with two divisions, were dedicated to saying what the text of Scripture says. He labored diligently in his preparation. He ordinarily preached forty-five minutes and spoke quite calmly, calling fluency the "fatal gift."[5] "To preach Christ," he said, "was to preach the doctrines of Christ, that men may be saved."[6] He eschewed emphasis on memory:

> All public speakers know the value of method. Persons not accustomed to it imagine that a speech is learnt by heart. Knowing a little about the matter, I will venture to say that if any one attempted that plan, either he must have a marvelous memory, or else he would break down three times out of five. It simply depends upon correct arrangement. The words and sentences are left to the moment; the thoughts methodised beforehand; and the words, if the thoughts are rightly arranged, will place themselves. But upon the truthfulness of arrangement all depends.[7]

He preached from a very small piece of paper and wrote up the sermon on the next day. Stopford Brook, his principal biographer, gathered six volumes of sermons.

Because he was a master of illustration and application, his sermons have a remarkable literary quality even in the abbreviated form in which we have them. His famous sermon on "The Loneliness of Jesus" from John 16:31–32 is almost autobiographical:

> There are two kinds of solitude; the first consisting of isolation in space; the other isolation of the spirit.

His first main division treats Christ's loneliness, and then he moves on to the loneliness of the obedient follower of Christ. He was a suffering soul, first from debilitating illness, then from misunderstanding and criticism which he did not handle well, and then from self-doubt and feelings that he was a failure. His deep melancholy was evident to the Swiss preacher Malan, who told him: "You will have a sorrowful life and a sorrowful ministry." Robertson chose his direction:

> I would rather live solitary on the most desolate and the most solitary crag, shivering, with all the warm wraps of falsehood stripped off, gazing after unfound truth . . . than sit comfortably on more inhabited spots,

> where others were warm in a faith which is true to them, but which is false to me.[8]

Every preacher should dip into Robertson's life and letters[9] and read some of his sermons. They are for the ages. The main volume of his sermons was published by Harpers in 1870 and has been continuously in print ever since. His exegesis was radioactive. A typical sermon is "The State of Nature and the State of Grace" from Ephesians 2:3–5 with two obvious divisions. An unusual sermon on "The Three Crosses on Calvary" from Luke 23:33 has three points with Christ on the cross being the first and then on to each of the malefactors.[10] Some have claimed him as the forerunner of the psychological preachers, but this is only to underscore the great pastoral instincts and applicatory skills that Robertson brought to the preaching task.[11] How sad that Anthony Trollope never got to hear the likes of F. W. Robertson.

---

1. Victoria Glendinning, *Anthony Trollope* (New York: Knopf, 1993), 230.
2. Ibid., 93.
3. Lewis O. Brastow, *Representative Modern Preachers* (New York: Macmillan, 1904), 51, 59.
4. James R. Blackwood, *The Soul of Frederick W. Robertson* (New York: Harpers, 1947), 14. Robertson discussed with Wilberforce his inability to hold to or preach baptismal regeneration when he was offered St. Ebbe's in Oxford on a permanent basis; see David Newsome, *The Parting of Friends* (Grand Rapids: Eerdmans, 1966), 333.
5. Ibid., 88.
6. Ibid., 107. For a fine study consult Gilbert E. Doan's introduction to *The Preaching of F. W. Robertson* (Philadelphia: Fortress, 1964).
7. Ibid., 113. For Robertson, obedience is the organ of spiritual knowledge.
8. Ibid., 142.
9. Stopford Brooke, ed., *Life and Letters of Frederick W. Robertson* (London: Henry S. King, 1872).
10. Frederick W. Robertson, *The Human Race and Other Sermons* (New York: Harper, 1870), 115.
11. Charles Smyth speaks of him as "the first and greatest psychological preacher in the Church of England," because he coupled with his "exact and extensive knowledge of the Bible" such a "deliberate referencing to modern conditions—so personal," cf. *The Art of Preaching: A Practical Survey of Preaching in the Church of England 747–1939* (London: SPCK, 1940), 230. Robertson's "passionate devotion to Christ" is also part of the mix.

9.3.6 *The Bickersteths—Reiterating the Advent*

> If ever a Church Missionary was filled with the Spirit, that secretary was Edward Bickersteth.
>
> —Eugene Stock

> The Scripture, in the Old and New Testament alike, detaches our ultimate confidence from man, the creature, and attaches it to God, the Creator. Scripture, in the Old and New Testament alike, requires us to repose our ultimate confidence in the Lord Jesus Christ.
>
> —Edward Henry Bickersteth

With the waning of Simeon and Wilberforce, leadership among evangelicals largely fell to **Edward Bickersteth** (1786–1850), the son of a doctor, whose remarkable family was so squarely evangelical and who provided the Church of England with two bishops, an archdeacon, and a son-in-law, Thomas Birks, who was the first secretary of the Evangelical Alliance. Evangelicalism was not strong in scholarship, although it was represented by Bishop Ellicott of Gloucester and Bristol, who wrote significant Bible commentaries, Alexander M'Caul, who was Hebrew professor at King's College in London, Cyril Garbett, who edited the *Record* and refuted Darwin, and John William Burgon (1813–1888), the champion of the Textus Receptus and later dean of Chichester, all of whom were solid biblical preachers of note and effect.

Edward Bickersteth came from old Lancashire stock tracing back to Bickerstaffe in the twelfth century. He became secretary of the Church Missionary Society in 1824 and is described by Professor Chadwick as "the most colorful and godly of the Evangelical clergy."[1] He traveled widely abroad (especially in Africa) and preached constantly in the homelands and always at Wheler Chapel, Spitalfields, when not otherwise engaged. In 1830 he became rector of Watton near Hertford, where he had an outstanding ministry of systematic biblical exposition although still traveling extensively for the CMS. He also published *Christian Hymnody* in 1830 and was known as the evangelical Keble. He wrote four books on Bible prophecy reflecting the view of the imminent return of Jesus Christ for his church:

> He was led to believe that the second coming of Christ will precede the Millennium; that the first resurrection is literal, and that Christ will establish a kingdom of righteousness on earth at His return, before the resurrection of the wicked and their final judgment.[2]

He believed the Jews would return to Palestine in the complex of end-time events. He joined with John Angell James in establishing the Evangelical Alliance in 1845.

Anthony Ashley Cooper, later Lord Shaftesbury (1801–1885), successor to William Wilberforce as lay leader of the evangelicals and the great Christian philanthropist, resided near Watton and studied prophecy with Bickersteth, who convinced him that "Christ would come suddenly and soon."[3] Together they became early advocates of Christian Zionism in Britain. His buoyancy and warmth infused his preaching and it was said that "the waves of vehement argument were often calmed down by the oil of Mr. Bickersteth's affection."[4]

Bickersteth's only son, **Edward Henry Bickersteth** (1824–1906), early on took a living on Shaftesbury's estate, where he was known for his pastoral and evangelistic zeal.[5] He labored then for thirty years as Vicar of Christ Church, Hampstead, went on to be dean of Gloucester in 1885, and then bishop of Exeter. Like his father, he wrote hymns and published a hymnal called *Hymnal Companion to the Book of Common Prayer* (1870), of which Dr. Julian in the *Dictionary of Hymnology* says: "Bishop Bickersteth's work is at the head of all hymnals in the Church of England, and in keeping with this unique position it has also the purest texts."[6] His own hymns include "Peace, Perfect Peace," "Till He Comes," "Not Worthy, Lord, to Gather Up the Crumbs," and "O Brothers, Lift Your Voices." He was also known for his effective outdoor preaching.

The high quality and richly biblical and doctrinal content of Bickersteth's sermons are also reflected in the several volumes that he wrote on the inspiration of Scripture and his superb piece on the Holy Trinity.[7] Evangelical churchmanship was also upheld by his cousin Robert, who was bishop of Ripon,[8] and by another cousin Edward, who was dean of Lichfield. Other worthy successors in following generations carried the torch of truth ignited early in the Bickersteth lineage.

---

1. Michael Hennell, *Sons of the Prophets: Evangelical Leaders of the Victorian Church* (London: SPCK, 1979), 29.
2. Ibid., 44.
3. John Pollock, *Shaftesbury: The Poor Man's Earl* (London: Hodder and Stoughton, 1985), 53. For a significant treatment of one of Shaftesbury's ardent sympathizers, see Cecil Woodham-Smith, *Florence Nightingale* (New York: McGraw-Hill, 1951). For consideration of the place of Bible prophecy at this time, see J. F. C. Harrison, *The Second Coming: Popular Millenarianism 1780–1850* (New Brunswick, N.J.: Rutgers University Press, 1979); also W. H. Oliver, *Prophets and Millennialists: The Uses of Biblical Prophecy in England from the 1790s to the 1840s* (Auckland, New Zealand: Auckland University Press, 1978). Herein is traced the influence of the famous Albury Conferences sponsored by the banker Henry Drummond starting in 1826. Edward Irving was involved early but was destroyed by his excesses. Hugh McNeile, later dean of Ripon, was a leader in the movement, as was Edward Bickersteth. Keble and Newman were as concerned about the last days as was Bickersteth (142). Newman argued: "He will very soon be here, that is quite certain and He has given us all notice." He has sermons on "Watching" and "Waiting for Christ."
4. D. N. Samuel, ed., *The Evangelical Succession in the Church of England* (Cambridge, Mass.: James Clarke, 1979), 73.
5. Pollock, *Shaftesbury,* 102. Shaftesbury was aroused about the poor after viewing a pauper's funeral.
6. G. R. Balleine, *A History of the Evangelical Party in the Church of England* (London: Longmans, Green, 1908), 282.
7. Edward Henry Bickersteth, *The Rock of Ages* (New York: The Bible Scholar, n.d.). A very rich study.
8. Montagu Cyril Bickersteth, *Robert Bickersteth* (New York: Dutton, 1887). Interestingly, Robert was saved from drowning by Dean Henry Alford of Canterbury, a venerable name in evangelical scholarship (21).

9.3.7 *Charles Kingsley—Assessing the Emphasis*

> Let us read the Bible as we never read it before. Let us read every word, ponder every word; first in its plain human sense. . . . In the present day a struggle is coming . . . a question must be tried—is intellectual Science or the Bible, truth; and All Truth?
>
> If, however, I found it in Scripture, I should believe it: what I want is—plain, inductive proof from texts.
>
> For if we once lose our faith in the Old Testament, our faith in the New will soon dwindle to the impersonal "spiritualism" of Frank Newman, and the German phosophasters [those who turned to salt].
>
> The value of the Bible teaching depends on the truth of the Bible story. That is my belief. Any criticism which tries to rob me of that, I shall look at fairly, but very severely indeed."
>
> —Charles Kingsley

Evangelicals were filling the land with a rhapsodic diversity of preaching. They ranged from the perennially popular convert from Catholicism **William Blake Kirwan** (1754–1805) to **Henry Melvill** (1800–1871), who particularly influenced Ruskin and Browning and whom Spurgeon called "a Demosthenes among preachers."[1] The Broad church preachers (comparable to the mediating school in Germany) were often reared as evangelicals, like **Frederick Denison Maurice** (1805–1872), who was always at the center of controversy. Coleridge and the German school of Schleiermacher exerted much influence on these thinkers, although Maurice was electrifying in his preaching. One listener said of him, "He seemed to be the channel of communication, not the source of it." A close friend of Maurice was the irrepressibly robust **Charles Kingsley** (1819–1875), who one day walked fifty-two miles.

Kingsley was born into an evangelical minister's home. He was something of a prodigy, preaching a sermon on "Following God" at the age of four. The sermon was transcribed by his mother.[2] She sent it to the bishop of Peterborough, who predicted a bright future for its author. Quite shy and never popular while growing up, he had a cumbersome hesitation in his speech, yet it never manifested itself while he preached.[3] After his studies at Cambridge, he took the curacy at Eversley near Hampshire, a neglected rural parish where he spent the next thirty-three years. Like Baxter at Kidderminster, Kingsley made the parish. When he arrived, the alehouses were full and the church was empty, but Kingsley set himself to a vigorous ministry that changed the whole community.

A glutton for work, Kingsley tended to wear himself out until he needed a leave of absence. He served first as professor of English literature and composition at Queen's College and then filled the chair of modern history at Cambridge vacated by William Wilberforce's son-in-law, **Sir James Stephen.**[4] He would teach one day per week. He introduced an evening service at Eversley, as Samuel

Wilberforce had done on the Isle of Wight. Kingsley was a great lover of the Bible, and was deeply committed to preaching the text. He regarded David Strauss, whose *Leben Jesu* went so far as to deny the historicity of Jesus, as "the great false prophet of the day, who must be faced and fought by the clergy."[5] Through all of his hyperactivity, he kept his focus: "One thing I do know, that I have to preach Jesus Christ and Him crucified."

Kingsley identified with the impoverished rural folk in his parish and led the Chartist charge for social reform. He was a prolific writer of novels, poetry, and drama. Although prolix in style, his great sea story *Westward Ho* is one of the best. *The Water Babies* and the plight of Tom, the little chimney-sweep, deeply moved Lord Shaftesbury, and *Alton Locke* was heralded by Thomas Carlyle as "a new explosive or red-hot shell against the devil's dung-heap."[6] His novel *Hypatia* concerns the conflict between the early Christians and Alexandrian philosophy. His description of decadent religion as "the opiate of the people" was seized by Karl Marx as apt for his purposes.

Kingsley's literary feats led him to significant friendships with Frederica Bremer, who visited the Kingsleys, as well as Harriet Beecher Stowe and John Greenleaf Whittier. The Kingsleys on occasion vacationed with the Tennysons.[7] He fought the Tractarians, and his attack on Newman precipitated Newman's famous *Apologia Pro Vita Sua.* The Roman Catholic convert and poet Gerard Manley Hopkins said that Kingsley had "the air and spirit of a man bouncing up from the table with his mouth full of bread and cheese and saying that he meant to stand no blasted nonsense." He became one of the queen's favorite preachers and engaged in correspondence with **Adolph Saphir**, the Jewish convert who preached so magnificently and made clear his belief "as firmly as any modern interpreter of prophecy, that you are still the nation, and that you have a glorious, as I think a culminating part to play in the history of the race."[8] Doubtless to his physical disadvantage, he took on additional roles and assignments, first as canon of Chester in 1869 under the godly Dean Howson and then as canon of Westminster. He regularly preached in these famous cathedrals.

We are blessed with various collections of his preaching, including village sermons and sermons from Westminster. One observer commented:

> In preaching he would try to keep still and calm, and free from all gesticulation; but as he went on, he had to grip and clasp the cushion on which the sermon rested, in order to restrain the intensity of his own emotion; and when, in spite of himself, his hands would escape, they would be lifted up, the fingers of the right hand working with a peculiar hovering movement, of which he was quite unconscious; his eyes seemed on fire, his whole frame worked and vibrated. It was riveting to see him as well as hear him, as his eagle glance penetrated every corner of the church, and whether there were few or many there, it was enough for him that those who were present were human beings standing between two worlds, and that it was his terrible responsibility as well as high privilege, to deliver a message to each and all.[9]

Kingsley was a renaissance man with wide interests and love for nature. He was a wonderful father to his children and husband to his dear wife, Fanny. Unstinting in his preparation, he often talked about his next week's text on Sunday evening after a busy Lord's Day and started promptly on Tuesday in his work, allowing it to simmer through the week until providing the finishing touches on Friday. He traveled to the West Indies and later to America, where he had special joy in his visits with William Cullen Bryant. He was a man who could sleep at anytime or anywhere and derive much benefit from a brief rest.

Among his best sermons are those preached on "The Mystery of the Cross" and "The Word of God" from Psalm 119:89–96.[10] These are hearty, sound messages well applied. In the latter he begins by saying:

> This text is of infinite importance, to you, and me, and all mankind. For if the text is not true; if there is not a Word of God, who endures [and] is settled forever in heaven: then this world is a miserable and a made place; and the best thing, it seems to me, that poor ignorant human beings can do, is to eat and drink, for tomorrow we die.

He argues here for the indissoluble unity of the written and the living Word of God. In his "Good News of God" he shared his typical preaching, simply structured, and full of Christ and his cross. He ranged over the whole of Scripture and was concerned to expose the text and its meaning for all of his hearers. When asked the secret of his inner life, he responded: "I had a friend!" Charles Kingsley died at fifty-six after a full and energetic life lived for his Lord and Master.

---

1. T. Harwood Pattison, *The History of Christian Preaching* (Philadelphia: American Baptist Publication Society, 1903), 305ff.
2. Fanny Kingsley, ed., *Charles Kingsley: His Letters and Memories of His Life* (London: Kegan Paul, 1882), 1:5.
3. Ibid., 1:13, 245.
4. Ibid., 1:115, 2:107. A delightful sketch of Stephen may be found in Michael Hennell, *Sons of the Prophets: Evangelical Leaders of the Victorian Church* (London: SPCK, 1979), 91–103.
5. Kingsley, *Charles Kingsley,* 1:193.
6. Johnstone G. Patrick, "A Fighter for the Faith: Centenary Salute to Charles Kingsley," *Life of Faith* (January 25, 1975): 3–4. Kingsley would often say, "Never lose an opportunity to see something beautiful!"
7. Kingsley, *Charles Kingsley,* 1:89.
8. Ibid., 1:280.
9. Ibid., 1:283.
10. Charles Kingsley, *Westminster Sermons* (London: Macmillan, 1884); *The Good News of God* (London: Macmillan, 1908). We happily possess quite a battery of books containing the sermons of Charles Kingsley.

9.4 *THE CONTINENTAL CATARACT*

> And the whole nineteenth century was dominated by this apostasy from Christianity.
>
> —Kurt Aland

After the French Revolution and the Napoleonic era, all of central Europe was reorganized. Under the aegis of **Frederick William III** of Prussia (a devout Calvinist), the Lutheran and Reformed churches in Germany came into union in 1817. But as Germany moved to unification, unbelief and skepticism about the Bible swept through the universities. "Kant is our Moses," chortled Holderlin, as he heralded deliverance from orthodoxy via Kant's epistemological bifurcation. But Kant left Christian faith in the shifting realm of the subjective.[1] Burgeoning secularism deadened the churches. Hegel and his disciple Karl Marx lost God in the dialectic of history, and Ludwig Feuerbach's *The Essence of Christianity* in 1841 concluded that God was only the projection of the human mind.

As we have seen, there were those particularly in the Broad church party in England who were taken with the new styles in thinking. George Eliot, Frank Newman (the cardinal's brother), and J. A. Froude hustled into the vanguard of those who took their signals from the Continent. F. D. Maurice and Benjamin Jowett, the great Oxford don, couldn't jettison the categories of orthodoxy fast enough. When the notorious *Essays and Reviews* of 1860 were published, Samuel Wilberforce observed, "Trains of German doubt intended to blow up the Church."[2]

Yet there were champions of historic Christianity who came to the fore, such as the redoubtable **E. W. Hengstenberg,** the Berlin professor, editor, and prolific writer joined more traditional and pietistic forces to do battle for orthodoxy.[3] (Hengstenberg's massive *The Christology of the Old Testament* and his commentaries continue to be a great blessing today.) A powerful revival of confessionalism rose to counteract the tidal waves of infidelity pouring out of the universities. Bible societies, the Inner Mission, and foreign missionary societies began to proliferate. Movements like the Basel Mission Society, founded in 1815, and the Rhenish Mission Society, founded in 1828, were committed to the propagation of the gospel of Christ.[4] God was not without his witnesses in this tempestuous time.

---

1. James J. Sheehan, *German History* (Oxford: Clarendon, 1989), 242. The best recent survey.
2. M. A. Crowther, *Church Embattled: Religious Controversy in Mid-Victorian England* (London: David and Charles, 1970). Shows the negative but also the positive under men like Olshausen, Stier, Dorner, and those who came together in the Evangelical Alliance where Krummacher gave one of his most memorable addresses.
3. Sheehan, *German History,* 561.
4. Kurt Aland, *A History of Christianity* (Philadelphia: Fortress, 1986), 2:352.

9.4.1 F. W. Krummacher—The Dynamism of Preaching

> There have fallen again the tongues of fire which bear witness for Christ; from the pulpits there is heard more and more in new and distinct utterances the proclamation of the old good Word; there are flourishing mission schools under the shelter of the gentle royal scepter; Bible societies in full and unwearied activity; institutions aiming at the promotion of the welfare of the neglected and the criminal, and what is yet more than all this there are considerable bands of men continually increasing in number in all districts of the land who have sworn that they will never bow the knee to Baal; a company of praying men encompassing the land as a chain, diffusing blessings all around.
>
> —F. W. Krummacher

The leading preacher in this rekindling of evangelical zeal in an age of torpor was **Friedrich Wilhelm Krummacher** (1796–1868). Krummacher was born in a line of preachers from both his father's and mother's families. John Ker likens him to Thomas Guthrie "in appearance and in his pulpit manner, as well as in the tone of his mind."[1]

The Krummacher family must be recognized as pivotal in a spiritual awakening along the lower Rhine.[2] Krummacher later wrote of his father's sermons:

> I do not remember ever to have heard anyone preach the Gospel in a more loving tone and with a more dignified mien, or in a more heart-winning manner, than he did. Were I to give a motto to his sermons which would at once characterize their spirit and their general theme, I would present these words of the apostle, which naturally suggest themselves—"But after that the kindness and love of God our Saviour toward man appeared, not by works of righteousness which we have done, but according to His mercy He saved us, by the washing of regeneration, and renewing of the Holy Ghost." He discerned his commission as a preacher especially in these words of Isaiah—"Comfort ye, comfort ye my people, saith your God. Speak ye comfortably to Jerusalem, and cry unto her, that her warfare is accomplished, that her iniquity is pardoned." And he remained true to this commission to the end of his days, only with ever-increasing penetration into the mysterious ground on which the command rested.[3]

Young Krummacher studied at both Halle and Jena universities. By this time Semler and Gesenius were inducting students at Halle into a cold rationalism. Rationalism would not be countered until the ascendancy of Tholuck in 1827. Krummacher says of his seminary experience:

> We saw the Lord of Glory stripped of all His supernatural majesty, shrivelled into the rank of a mere Rabbi, noble indeed, and high gifted, but yet always entangled by the prejudices of his time. He had never performed a miracle, and had neither risen from the dead nor ascended up

> into heaven. We saw also the whole contents of the Gospel, after being stripped of its particularistic and mythic veilings, reduced to a mere moral system, for the manifestation of which no divine revelation was at all needed.[4]

Luther's works steadied Krummacher, and his family and friends upheld him. He survived what carried away thousands of students and "doomed many congregations to this day to spiritual famine because they have presented to them only the husks and chaff which were there gathered and stored up by his [Wegscheider's] students."[5] Krummacher went on to serve five fulfilling years as assistant in Frankfort-on-Main and then to several happy years as pastor of the Reformed congregation at Ruhrort, of which he later spoke:

> Oh, how incomparably happy was the time which was granted to me in dear Ruhrort. I not only preached to a congregation hungering for the Word of God, which received from my lips with eyes beaming with delight whatever I had to offer them from the treasury of the gospel; but I also felt myself as if borne up by the affections and by the prayers of considerable circles of experienced and well-informed Christians who gathered around me. . . .[6]

He spent nine fruitful years at Barmen and then went on to Elbersfeld, where the blessing of God was poured out most lavishly upon his preaching. While there he preached the sermon on Galatians 1:8–9 which he called "the torch of war into the midst of the church life." It was a sermon that raised a clarion call against rationalism and unbelief. At this time he declined the call to the faculty of the Mercersburg Seminary in Philadelphia. Instead he recommended Dr. Philip Schaff, who accepted the position and went on to a noteworthy career in the United States. Schaff described Krummacher's preaching:

> Krummacher does not make a pleasing impression at first sight. He is not good looking. He is built like a lion, and his eloquence corresponds with his build. An imposing, strong figure, massive facial features, a wild confused head of hair, gray eyes, the man vanishes, so to speak, in the pulpit orator. The solemn bass voice which itself sounds forth like thunder upon his congregation, the rushing torrent of his figures, the bold but controlled gestures, the tossing of the head from side to side, the contents of the sermon itself, which is always original and, clothed in splendid garb, unlocks the depths of sin and grace, now breaking to pieces the fabric of the old man and the pleasures of the world, now comforting and with magic softness wooing to the source of salvation . . .[7]

By this time his sermons and books were in widening circulation. His work with the Evangelical Alliance extended his influence around the world, and he was called to the great Trinity Church in Berlin. Schleiermacher had once preached in Trinity, and now the church was empty. Soon it was filled, but

Krummacher realized what devastation higher criticism had wrought. He spoke in terms of "a new fall of man" and used the Lamentations for his jeremiads of doom. In 1853 the king called him to be court preacher at Potsdam, where he ministered until his death. The king wrote him on one occasion, "That advent sermon which you preached surpassed all I have ever heard," and ordered copies. But when warned of the king's displeasure if he did not conform to a certain controversial edict, Krummacher responded, "Tell his Imperial Majesty that I am ready at any time to lay my head on the block at His Majesty's command; but when His Imperial Majesty presumes to be lord of the gospel, I despise His Imperial Majesty!" (M. Niemoller, cf. 12.6.1).

Krummacher's introductions were brief and his divisions of the text were clear. Ker likens his sermons to "a gallery of paintings." He was so graphic and detailed in sketching the death of John the Baptist that some in the audience shrieked and fainted.[8] Sterling examples of his expositions are his popular sermons on Elijah and Elisha.[9] Good samples of his prose style include his peerless meditations on the last days of Christ, of which the eminent evangelical bibliographer, Wilbur Smith, once said: "I believe that the greatest single volume written during the entire nineteenth century is *The Suffering Saviour*, by Friedrich Wilhelm Krummacher."[10] The organizational schema and his chapters on "Lord, Is It I?" and "It Is Finished" are without equal. Smith's work contains a complete listing of the works of Krummacher translated into English. His brief introduction to a sermon from 1 Kings 8:65 on "Solomon's Feast" displays some of his charm:

> The words we have read place us in one of the happiest times in the history of Israel. They introduce us to a feast. The joyful songs of these fair days have been silenced for thousands of years. But if we listen, they renew themselves in our hearts with loftier tones. Let us try to catch their echoes by thinking, first, of the object of the feast, and, secondly, of the feast itself.[11]

---

1. John Ker, *Lectures on Preaching* (New York: Armstrong, 1889), 357.
2. Kurt Aland, *A History of Christianity* (Philadelphia: Fortress, 1886), 2:339.
3. F. W. Krummacher, *Friedrich Wilhelm Krummacher: An Autobiography* (New York: Robert Carter, 1869), 29–30. Preface by John Cairns.
4. Ibid., 52.
5. Wilbur M. Smith, "Biographical Introduction" to F. W. Krummacher, *The Suffering Saviour* (Chicago: Moody, 1952), xv.
6. Ibid., xvii.
7. Ibid., xx.
8. Ker, *Lectures on Preaching*, 363.
9. F. W. Krummacher, *Elijah the Tishbite* (Grand Rapids: Zondervan, n.d.); *Elisha* (Grand Rapids: Zondervan, n.d.); of special delight and fragrance, *Cornelius the Centurion* (Edinburgh: Fraser and Crawford, 1839).
10. Smith, "Biographical Introduction," xi.
11. Ker, *Lectures on Preaching*, 367.

9.4.2 *Rudolf Stier—The Demands of the Text*

> I solemnly pledge myself to preach to you nothing else than what stands in the Bible; to derive everything from the sacred text; to make the Bible clear to you; to initiate you so into it that you may yourselves be able to see the only true and best preaching in the very text itself.
>
> —E. Rudolph Stier at his installation at Frankleben, 1829

> Preserve unto us, above all things, thy Holy Word and Gospel, and may they ever be preached more fruitfully among us, that our devotion and true knowledge may ever grow hand in hand! Constantly accompany our music and song with the power of thy Spirit upon all hearts, and may we also be ever consecrated to thee. Let whoever shall hear this organ be reminded thereby of thee, and of the eternal glory to which thou invitest us all! And let whoever shall pass by this house of God on worldly business be exhorted, by the tones he shall hear, to give heed to thy word, and to humble himself before thee that he may be saved!
>
> —E. Rudolph Stier's prayer at the organ dedication in Frankleben

A peasant said to his pastor that the people could understand him because he preached "just as it was in the Bible, and if they did not do right now, the fault could not be his."[1] That pastor was **Ewald Rudolf Stier** (1800–1862), well known for his Bible commentaries and biblical preaching. He was born the second child in a Lutheran Prussian family and early made quite a record for himself in school. He began to study law at the University of Berlin but decided against a legal career because of his love for poetry. Then he shifted to theology under the famous Neander, even in the face of his father's opposition.

From 1815 to 1818, Stier sat under Schleiermacher and DeWette. He studied also under Gesenius and Wegscheider, but was not swept into antisupernaturalism. The influence and example of his grandfather, who was an old-time preacher, and his uncle helped spare him from the poison of their rationalism. The death of his fiancée Pauline, along with his reading of Thomas à Kempis, also inclined him to spiritual things. At this time Tholuck became his good friend.

Further moved by the Bible exposition sponsored by Baron von Kottwitz,[2] Stier made "his full and radical self-consecration to God."[3] He became convinced "that Scripture cannot be holy Scripture and the norm of faith unless it have the character of strict inspiration."[4] Finishing his training at the University of Wittenberg, Stier preached his first sermon on the death of Christ for needy sinners.

For a while Stier taught in Lithuania and pursued a beautiful courtship with Ernestine, daughter of the venerable Dr. K. I. Nitszche of Bonn. Upon their marriage, he accepted a call to teach Old and New Testament in the original languages at the Mission Seminary in Basle, where he was associated with President Christian Gottlieb Blumhard. In that same year his first book, *Hints on the Believing Interpretation of the Scriptures,* was published; in it he argues that the Bible is the source of all true knowledge.

The school was a beehive of activity for evangelical missionaries, but after four years Stier's health collapsed. He was virtually an invalid from the beginning of his clerical career and often preached sitting down. The death of his wife was a heavy blow to his already weakened frame, but he remarried and went on to produce his famous Polyglot Bible and a highly acclaimed series of sermons on Old Testament saints.

After a year's leave, he took a pastoral assignment in Frankleben (1829), where he wrote his *Keryktics* on the science of preaching. He then went on to Wichlinghausen (1838), where his penchant for the fusion of exegetical and practical became well known. His series of expository sermons on James was attended by large and appreciative crowds. He took the opposite of Luther's view on the importance of James.[5]

Ker says of his preaching:

> But Stier went to the Bible alone, and to all the Bible, and in approaching it he sought to strip himself of everything that would prevent him from receiving its full impression and from reflecting it in its rounded completeness on his fellow-men. This is why we have called him a biblical preacher . . . the Bible is one book with a pervading plan—the history of salvation—and with the living breath of the Holy Ghost through it all. No part, therefore, can be interpreted by itself; each part must be taken in the light of the whole, and has always some reference to the whole.[6]

His sermons implemented a brief introduction and a focus on the development of the main principle in the text which then must be applied. To Stier, all sermons were to be both scriptural and personal.[7] His classic works have widely influenced many, particularly his *Words of the Lord Jesus,*[8] *Words of the Apostles,*[9] and *Words of the Risen Saviour.*[10] All of these volumes were translated into English and circulated broadly. He was also known for the hymnbook he produced. He gathered ministers together for the purpose of digging into the Scripture.

From 1847 to 1850, Stier lived in retirement at Wittenberg, but subsequently took pastoral superintendencies in Schkeuditz near Magdeburg and at Eisleben, where he died. On his gravestone is inscribed: "But the Word of our God shall stand forever."[11]

Here was a preacher deeply rooted in the text of Scripture. God was yet at work, and even out of the world's hotbed of rationalism and skepticism came streams of living water.

---

1. John P. Lacroix, *The Life of Rudolf Stier* (New York: Nelson and Phillips, 1874), 211.
2. Ibid., 47ff.
3. Ibid., 55ff.
4. Ibid., 61.
5. Ibid., 279.
6. John Ker, *Lectures on the History of Preaching* (New York: Armstrong, 1889), 352.
7. Ibid., 356.

8. Rudolf Stier, *Words of the Lord Jesus* (Edinburgh: T & T Clark, 1872).
9. Rudolf Stier, *Words of the Apostles* (Edinburgh: T & T Clark, 1889).
10. Rudolf Stier, *Words of the Risen Saviour* (Edinburgh: T & T Clark, 1887). The translator is William B. Pope, the British Methodist from Manchester whose *A Higher Catechism of Theology* is a mature Wesleyan statement. All three of Stier's books are rich, careful exegetical treatments of key passages.
11. Lacroix, *The Life of Rudolf Stier,* 332.

9.4.3 THE BLUMHARDTS—THE DEVOTION OF THE PREACHER

> When Blumhardt preached, it was out of a vision . . . he himself lived in the powers of the kingdom which he proclaimed, and therefore he could say: "One needs to have experienced something of heaven, then one knows what the kingdom is."
>
> —R. Lejeune

> It was not ability, not art, not fluency of speech—it was a power of the Saviour that made my father a preacher . . . If only people had prayed with my father, we would have had a different theology a long time ago . . . to him the Kingdom of God was something immensely greater, more eternal and more effective for body and soul than anything he saw in Christianity.
>
> —Christoph Blumhardt

Even in the stygian darkness of unbelief, there were those who were watchers in the night. Among those who stood against "the bold mocking spirit of the age" were **Gerhard Tersteegen,** the sweet singer from the previous century whose great hymns John Wesley translated. "O Thou Hidden Love of God" was thought by Oliver Wendell Holmes to be the greatest hymn in the English language. **E. W. Hengstenberg** (1808–1869), was staunch in defense of Scripture at Berlin. **August Tholuck,** whom we have already seen spearheading a remarkable renaissance of pietism at Halle,[1] drew John Ker, Charles Hodge, and Calvin Stowe, husband of Harriet Beecher Stowe, to that university.[2] And **Julius Muller** (1801–1878) of Marburg was a champion of orthodox faith and biblical exposition.

In the vanguard of those who had a truly spiritual ministry in this dire time were **Johan Christoph Blumhardt** (1805–1880) and his son **Christoph Blumhardt** (1842–1919). The elder Pastor Blumhardt, as he was called, was born near Stuttgart and trained for ministry at Tubingen. He then served a brief vicarate, after which he taught at the Basle Mission Seminary for six years.[3] After serving another assistantship, he took the pastorate of the Mottlingen parish, where three phenomena took place:

1. Blumhardt experienced what he called "the battle," the confrontation with evil and the demonic that focused on one of his parishioners, Gotliebin Dittus, who had dabbled in magic arts when young and was now demon-possessed and suicidal;[4]

2. The movement of repentance and awakening that reached out to many in all parts of Germany;
3. The ministry of prayer and healing that led him ultimately to leave Mottlingen and purchase Bad Boll, to which the sick and hopeless of all classes resorted for the ministry of the Word and prayer.

At his death, his son Christoph became his successor in the ministry.[5]

Like his father, Christoph was a gifted and powerful preacher. After serving several parishes, he joined his father and went on extensive preaching missions throughout the nation. He preached twenty times to thousands in Berlin in 1888. He shared the "Jesus is Victor!" emphasis of his father and increasingly ministered outside traditional circles. "Die and Jesus will live" epitomized his thrust. He became involved in political affairs and strove for social justice, serving in the legislative assembly in Wurtemberg from 1900 to 1906.[6] Blumhardt focused on the Second Coming of Christ and proclaimed that "Jesus is on the way!" The fullness of his now/not yet tension came to be widely celebrated by Eduard Thurneysen, who introduced him to his appreciative friend Karl Barth. Barth affirmed the preaching on the "old texts" and wrote approvingly of Blumhardt in 1916.[7] Bonhoeffer, Moltmann, Jacques Ellul, and many others have acknowledged the positive influence of the Blumhardts. Their writings and sermons have been kept available through the efforts of Hutterian Brothers in New York and Connecticut.[8]

The sermonic style is simple and direct; the use of the text is striking and dominant. A passion and warmth are apparent. Such messages as "Jesus among the Wretched" from Romans 10:10[9] and "The Saviour Is Coming" from Matthew 24:36–42 are typical of the gripping nature of Blumardt's preaching.[10] We are very much reminded of what Jessie Penn-Lewis, Watchman Nee, and T. Austin-Sparks were to do later.

Above all, Blumhardt's Christocentricity and faithful commitment to biblical preaching kept the work from spilling over into the serious pathology often characteristic of experience-oriented movements.

---

1. We shall consider George Müller among the English Plymouth Brethren, but he came from the Halle circle in Germany, where he tutored Charles Hodge for a time; see A. T. Pierson, *George Muller of Bristol* (London: Pickering and Inglis, 1899). Franke's orphanages were Müller's. Again we see a fascinating networking.
2. Andrew L. Drummond, *German Protestantism Since Luther* (London: Epworth, 1951), 128.
3. Kenneth Scott Latourette describes the critical founding of the Basle Mission Society in *A History of the Expansion of Christianity* (Grand Rapids: Zondervan, 1941, 1969), 4:90–91; the theological course of the mission and its now defunct training schools are traced by Jacques Weber, "The Basel Mission: Its Historic Deviations from and/or Its Adherence to Its Founding Principles" (M.A. thesis, Trinity Evangelical Divinity School, 1982).
4. Frank S. Boshold, trans., *Blumhardt's Battle: A Conflict with Satan* (New York: Thomas E. Lowe, 1970).

5. Alo Munch, *Johan Christoph Blumhardt, ein Zeuge des gegenwartligen Gottes* (Basel, Switzerland: Brunnen-Verlag Giessen, 1949); Hans Fredrich Lavater, *Bad Boll durch 350 Jahre und Beide Blumhardt* (Basel, Switzerland: Brunnen-Verlag Giessen, 1951).
6. R. Lejeune, *Christoph Blumhardt and His Message* (Rifton, N.Y.: Plough, 1938, 1963), 71.
7. Karl Barth, *Action and Waiting* (Rifton, N.Y.: Plough, 1969).
8. Johan Christoph Blumhardt and Christoph Friedrich Blumhardt, *Now Is Eternity* (Rifton, N.Y.: Plough, 1976); Vernard Eller, ed., *Thy Kingdom Come: A Blumhardt Reader* (Grand Rapids: Eerdmans, 1980).
9. Lejeune, *Christoph Blumhardt and His Message,* 186.
10. Ibid., 220.

9.4.4 *JOHAN TOBIAS BECK—DARING IN THE PULPIT*

> It is Scripture, in union with nature and life, faithfully appropriated on all sides, and realized in a man's own experience, which makes the theologian and preacher, the teacher and pastor, capable of striking out a course for eternal truth amid the rocks and currents of opinion in his time, in every sphere both small and great, and fashioning men of God, characters meet for the kingdom of heaven.
>
> —J. T. Beck in *Pastoral Theology of the New Testament*

The curate in Charles Kingsley's novel *Yeast* observed from his standpoint that all Germans were pantheists. This was of course not true, but Hegel's influence made it seem that way at times. Radical scholarship seemed to be in the driver's seat in most of the universities. Names like Ewald, Wellhausen, and his successor Harnack, whose *What Is Christianity?* epitomized liberal thought, dominated the scene. Hermann and Ritschl, whose thinking on the atonement was anthropocentric,[1] all were part of a great swell of unbelief and skepticism.

Of course there were pockets of conservatism and orthodoxy such as at Leipzig, where the renowned Orientalist **Franz Delitzsch** (1813–1888), known as the Christian Talmudist, stood firmly for the supernatural and established the *Instituta Judaica.* His collaborator on the still widely-used Old Testament commentary series, **Karl Friedrich Keil,** a student of Hengstenberg, likewise took a firm stand on the miraculous.

Another orthodox wheelhorse important in the company of the preachers is **Johan Tobias Beck** (1804–1879), born near Stuttgart and educated at Tubingen, where Strauss and Baur carried the day with their advocacy of a purely historical study of the Bible. They acknowledged only Romans, Corinthians, and Galatians as genuine Pauline letters. His close friendship with **Wilhelm Hofacker** and others helped him fend off hypercritical views. He fed deeply on Bengel and Oetinger and served well in several smaller parishes where he gained quite a reputation for his biblical exposition.

Beck was called to teach as assistant professor and preacher in Basel, leaving us six volumes of his sermons from that time period. His plain, simple lifestyle and his dedication to the text made a great impression. His sermons were almost all homilies, and he always sustained a passionate emphasis on missions and evangelism.

In 1843, Beck took the appointment to Tubingen, where F. C. Baur favored him because of a long-standing feud with Ewald, who opposed Beck.[2] He stepped into the vacuum at Tubingen and served a noble purpose, enjoying popularity among the students. The impact upon Wurtemberg and southern Germany cannot be overstated. Ker reports of Beck's attractiveness:

> He had laid not only his understanding but his heart, conscience, his spirit, close to the Bible, having made it the unbroken study of his life. He knew it as a man knows the home in which he has lived for years, and was "a man of the Word," as few have been since the days of the Apostles.[3]

Beck had a reputation for preaching in the classroom and teaching from the pulpit. *Ideae Scripturariae* must be above *ideae academicae*. He saw Strauss, Baur, and Renan as "anatomists" who missed the life of the organism.[4] His classic *Pastoral Theology of the New Testament* represents his mature thinking. It is drenched with Scripture and points to Christ as the pattern. The models for ministry in the New Testament, according to Beck, are prescriptive in a principal sense. He explores the preaching of Jesus and the apostles for clues relevant to our preaching.[5] Beck also left major commentaries on Romans and the Pastorals. Here is a preacher-scholar blooming in an arid venue.

---

1. Andrew L. Drummond, *German Protestantism Since Luther* (London: Epworth, 1951), 143. It is worthwhile to peruse Albrecht Ritschl's *The Christian Doctrine of Justification and Reconciliation* (Edinburgh: T & T Clark, 1900) just to perceive the disastrous theological defection that had taken place.
2. Horton Harris, *The Tubingen School: A Historical and Theological Investigation of the School of F. C. Baur* (Grand Rapids: Baker, 1975, 1990), 43, 52.
3. John Ker, *Lectures on the History of Preaching* (New York: Armstrong, 1889), 384.
4. Ibid., 385.
5. J. T. Beck, *Pastoral Theology of the New Testament* (New York: Scribner and Welford, 1885). Old but choice.

9.4.5 C. E. Luthardt—Drive in the Pulpit

> A bridge must be thrown over the abyss that separates the holy God from sinful people. God must come to us, in order that we may come to him: "Where sin abounded, grace did much more abound" in Jesus who appeared as Mediator between God and us.
>
> —C. E. Luthardt

Beautiful Leipzig in Saxony claimed cultural distinction in musicians like Bach, Schumann, Mendelssohn, and Wagner, as well as the philosopher Leibniz and the poet Goethe. Its university, founded in 1409, maintained its strength in the onslaught of rationalism in the nineteenth century, not only in biblical studies with Delitzsch but also in systematics with **Christoph Ernst Luthardt** (1823–1902). Luthardt was born near Nuremberg and studied at Erlangen and Berlin. Not only was he a strong exegete—his commentary on the Gospel of John is still used—but he was an ecclesiastical statesman of repute, the author of a major dogmatics, and a powerful preacher. He taught at Erlangen and Marburg and went on to an illustrious career at Leipzig from 1856 to 1902.

Luthardt's exegetically oriented systematic theology has exerted a lasting influence on many Lutherans.[1] He took the position over against Schleiermacher and others that, while the material principle of dogmatics is fellowship with God through Christ's atonement, the normative principle is the Holy Scripture and "that Scripture is the authentic original record of divine revelation, and as such the Christian is sure of its truth."[2] What establishes the truth of Scripture above all else is the internal witness of the Spirit. Luthardt not only taught this but preached it eloquently and effectively. Dargan refers to his appeal to the emotions as he preached,[3] and Ker speaks of him as "a distinguished [preacher] who never fails to find an audience . . . his aim is to reach the heart and conscience, but his sermons are marked by a union of simplicity with elevation, and by thoughtfulness compressed often into short, sententious sentences."[4]

A recent issue of *Decision* carried the gist of a sermon on "Jesus Christ: the God-Man," which is a moving example of biblical preaching coupled with a strong sense of theological construct. What a tribute and testimony to God's gifted servant. "He being dead, yet speaks."[5]

---

1. R. F. Weidner, *An Introduction to Dogmatic Theology based on Luthardt* (New York: Revell, 1888).
2. Ibid., 82.
3. E. C. Dargan, *A History of Preaching* (New York: Hodder and Stoughton, 1912), 2:382.
4. John Ker, *Lectures on the History of Preaching* (New York: Armstrong, 1889), 385.
5. Christoph Ernst Luthardt, "Was Jesus Christ Really God and Man?" *Decision* (December 1995): 26–27.

9.4.6 *Theodor Christlieb—Designer of the Craft*

> The great work of the Christian preacher is not to be an orator but an interpreter, to teach the people how to read and use the Word of God. He is a conveyance-pipe to draw the water from the fountain and pour it on grass and flowers to make them grow, also on consuming fires of sin to extinguish them.
>
> —Dr. John Ker

Dr. John Ker, who lectured on preaching and practical theology for his United Presbyterian Church school in Glasgow, himself had served several congregations and was a preacher "of rare and manifold faculty."[1] He gave particular attention to German preaching, having spent time in Germany and seeing certain negatives:

> There are some preachers who cut down the tree of life, and deal it out in hard dry planks, sometimes even presenting hard knots and sawdust—abstract doctrines without sap or sympathy. Others give flowers from parasitical plants which they have attached to it, things which have no fruit and no healing leaves. The first is the deadly formal; the second, the equally deadly fanciful.[2]

Such was not the preaching of **Theodor Christlieb** (1833–1889). Born in Birkenfeld and trained at Tubingen under Beck and Baur, Christlieb was decisively influenced by the former. He always placed the strongest stress on conversion. Christlieb served the German church in London for a time. This exposure to the larger Christian family encouraged him to be active within the Evangelical Alliance. He opposed the sterile rationalism that permeated the churches and universities and served as university preacher and professor of theology at Bonn with great distinction. Christlieb believed so strongly in the unique endowment of evangelists for Christ's church that he led in the purchase of a redundant Presbyterian Chapel in Bonn that was used for the training of evangelists. The school later moved to Bremen.

The brilliance of Christlieb's scholarship is seen in his magisterial *Modern Doubt and Christian Belief*, a peerless apologetic address to the burning issues of his time.[3] No one faced Hegelian pantheism and deistic rationalism more boldly or deftly than did Christlieb. He waded into the battles over the bodily resurrection of Christ and the miracles of the Bible. But further, Christlieb lectured and wrote on the homiletical issues necessary for the communication of the historic gospel. Dargan uses twenty-four footnotes from Christlieb in his treatment of German preaching, and Christlieb's *Homiletic: Lectures on Preaching* is a classic summons to build the sermon on the text itself.[4] While recognizing that expository preaching can never be independent of rhetoric, he yet saw the sermon as *sui generis* (unique). His treatment of the special occasions for preaching such as baptism, confirmation, marriage, and the funeral are exceedingly rich. He also spoke to preaching in connection with the observance of the Lord's Supper.[5] His thinking on preaching was sound and influential and the example of his own evangelistic sermons is particularly striking.

---

1. John Edwards, *Nineteenth-Century Preachers and Their Methods* (London: Charles Kelly, 1902), 65.
2. Ibid., 73.
3. Theodor Christlieb, *Modern Doubt and Christian Belief* (New York: Scribner, Armstrong, 1874), 549 pages. The best biographical data are in *Theodor Christlieb of Bonn: Memoir by His Widow and Sermons* (Edinburgh: Hodder and Stoughton, 1892). Other strong commentaries from this era are by Johan Peter Lange (1802–1884) and H. A. W. Meyer (1800–1873). Conservatives produced a vital literature at this time of assault on faith.
4. Theodor Christlieb, *Homiletic: Lectures on Preaching* (Edinburgh: T & T Clark, 1897).
5. Ibid., 291–307.

9.4.7 *ABRAHAM KUYPER—THE DREAM OF THE KINGDOM OF GOD*

> In a sermon on Revelation 3:11 on Hold that fast which thou hast: Do not bury our glorious orthodoxy in the treacherous pit of a spurious conservatism.
>
> Everything depends, therefore, upon a true and certain knowledge that our Refuge and Mediator really poured out His blood for us.
>
> —Abraham Kuyper

The Netherlands, so often crushed between great powers, has seen a remarkable church life down through the centuries and has produced many significant preachers, not the least of whom is **Abraham Kuyper** (1837–1920). Radicals like Kuenen and moderates like Van Oosterzee, who himself was an able expositor of Scripture, seemed to be carrying the day. It was then that the poet Bilderdikj and two Jewish converts of his, Isaac da Costa and Cappadose, "denounced with glowing fury the general declension" from orthodoxy.[1]

Kuyper's pastor father stayed in the state church when the secession of conservatives took place in 1834, while the young Kuyper at the University of Leiden drifted away from his orthodox moorings.[2] He was moved spiritually by a mediocre English novel by Yonge titled *Heir of Redclyffe* and by an old peasant woman whose stubborn orthodoxy struck him with the strange persistency of orthodoxy in the face of all comers. He soon broke completely with modernism and served significant pastorates in Utrecht and in Amsterdam. His watchword was ever "God is absolutely sovereign."

Kuyper was acclaimed as a preacher who loved to open the Scripture in the ministry of the Word. His sermon "The Antithesis Between Symbolism and Revelation" left no doubt that he regarded ritualism and symbolism as replacing revelation and moving dangerously from conscious to unconscious religion. Indeed, he astutely saw such a move as taking the faithful along the road to Asia not Calvary.[3]

Kuyper entered politics and as early as 1874 took a seat in Parliament, where he spoke on behalf of the poor and disenfranchised.[4] In 1875 he attended one of the D. L. Moody meetings in Brighton. He founded the Free University of Amsterdam in 1880, where he sought to further the strength of orthodoxy and where he served as professor of theology. In 1892 a merger of the church of the secessionists (including Kampen and Bavinck) with the main body formed the Netherlands Reformed Church. In 1898 he gave the Stone Lectures at Princeton on Calvinism, and in the same year he issued his princely *Encyclopedia of Sacred Theology.*

Kuyper wrote two hundred volumes and for many years edited a daily newspaper and a religious journal. In 1899 his beloved wife of thirty-six years died, and he did not remarry. In 1901 he was invited by Queen Wilhelmina to become Prime Minister of the Netherlands, where he served until 1905.

Above all in his lustrous career, Kuyper wanted to be known as a preacher of the Word of God. Turnbull argues that his primary burden was the exposure of the text.[5] Kuyper's studies on women in the Scriptures and his masterful work on the Holy Spirit give us a sense of the genius and giftedness of this devoted servant of Christ for whom the very reading of the Scripture in public was an interpretation of the Scripture.

Kuyper repeatedly stressed the necessity of "drawing near to God."

> The fellowship of being near unto God must become reality, in the full and vigorous prosecution of our life. It must permeate and give color to our feeling, our perceptions, our sensations, our thinking, our imagining, our willing, our acting, our speaking. It must not stand as a foreign factor in our life, but it must be the passion that breathes throughout our whole existence. . . . Stress on creedal confession, without drinking of these waters, runs dry in barren orthodoxy, just as truly as spiritual emotion, without clearness in confession standards, makes one sink in the bog of sickly mysticism.[6]

---

1. E. C. Dargan, *A History of Preaching* (New York: Hodder and Stoughton, 1912), 2:420.
2. The best biography available is Frank Vandenberg, *Abraham Kuyper* (Grand Rapids: Eerdmans, 1960).
3. Abraham Kuyper, *The Antithesis Between Symbolism and Revelation* (Edinburgh: T & T Clark, n.d.).
4. James W. Skillen, ed., *Abraham Kuyper's The Problem of Poverty* (Grand Rapids: Baker, 1891, 1991).
5. Ralph G. Turnbull, *A History of Preaching* (Grand Rapids: Baker, 1974), 3:367–68.
6. Abraham Kuyper, *Near to God* (Grand Rapids: Eerdmans, 1961).

9.5 *THE SWISS-FRENCH BROOK*

> The gospel is believed when it has ceased to be to us an external and has become an internal truth, when it has become fact in our consciousness. Christianity is conscience raised to its highest exercise.
>
> —Alexandre Vinet

> Whoever speaks, let him speak, as it were, the utterances of God.
>
> —1 Peter 4:11a (NASB)

After the revocation of the Edict of Nantes in 1685, two hundred thousand of the approximately nine hundred thousand Huguenots fled France for more distant parts. Persecution began to abate after the death of Louis XIV, but life in the Church of the Desert was arduous. Outbursts of intolerance, the defection of the Camisards, and inner turmoil in the nation upended stable growth.[1] Then came the traumas of the French Revolution and the Napoleonic wars. As late as 1815 to 1816, a wave of terror was directed at French Protestants. Protestants were dwindling.

In the nineteenth century such pulpit giants as **Henri Dominique Lacordaire,** who stood in the tradition of the great court preachers of the seventeenth century (cf. 6.3.2.3), held forth in Notre Dame and elsewhere in widely acclaimed discourses on redemption and upright living.[2] Lacordaire was supported especially by the bishop of Orleans, **Felix Dupanloup** (1801–1878), whose book *The Ministry of Preaching* is one of the better homiletics of the time. Although there were proportionately few preachers of note, there always were some who espoused popular preaching of the Scriptures to the flock. Steeped in all the classical sources, Dupanloup pressed his preachers "to put into the preaching of the Word that fire and vividness which go direct to hearts because they come from the heart; which take hold of and penetrate souls, which enlighten, soften, win over and convert them."[3] The Bible was for him "the very Word of God," and he advanced the thesis that a good pastor must seek to be a good preacher. He wanted subjects that led to conversion.[4] Dupanloup urged that sermons be characterized by clearness, vivacity, directness, movement, warmth, simplicity, and "familiarity . . . but never to the point of vulgarity."[5] He spoke against the dogma of papal infallibility at the Vatican Council in 1870. Here is evidence of clear thinking in an unexpected place and time.

Another medium for the propagation of the Word was through the outreach of the British and Foreign Bible Society. The saga of **George Borrow** (1803–1881) was legendary. An uneducated man from Norwich, Borrow was exceptionally gifted in linguistics, reading the Bible in thirteen languages. He was hired to translate a Manchu-language Scripture, and from 1833 to 1835 was posted to St. Petersburg. For the next five years he traveled in Portugal and Spain with a special burden for the Gypsies and the desire to translate the Bible into Romany. His book *The Bible in Spain*[6] and his collected letters[7] tell an absorbing story of heroism in preaching and testifying for Christ. The Reverend **R. B. Girdlestone** paid tribute on behalf of the society for his translations and ministry.[8] Thus was the Word transmitted in even the dreariest of settings.

---

1. John D. Woodbridge, *Revolt in Pre-Revolutionary France: The Prince de Conti's Conspiracy Against Louis XV* (Baltimore: Johns Hopkins University Press, 1995).
2. H. L. Sidney Lear, *Henri Dominique Lacordaire* (London: Rivingtons, 1882), 186.
3. Felix Dupanloup, *The Ministry of Preaching* (London: Griffith Farran, 1893), liii.
4. Ibid., 121.
5. Ibid., xix.
6. George Borrow, *The Bible in Spain* (London: Thomas Nelson, 1893).
7. T. H. Darlow, ed., *Letters of George Borrow* (London: Hodder and Stoughton, 1911).
8. Ibid., 471. Girdlestone wrote *The Grammar of Prophecy* (Grand Rapids: Baker, 1955).

9.5.1 Cesar Malan—Spearheading the Revival

Thank God the gospel has been once more preached in Geneva!

—Robert Haldane to Malan in Geneva, 1817

Rationalism had left a significant residue of resistance to the supernatural gospel, but a movement of revival emanating from Switzerland called the Reveille surged in a dramatic renewal of biblical preaching between 1820 and 1850. The exposition of Romans by Robert Haldane (cf. 9.1.1) in early 1817 fanned "the dying embers of Moravian pietism into a new flame."[1] Several new congregations were formed, including one led by **Merle d'Aubigne** (1794–1872), whose writings on Calvin continue to be a mainstay, and another led by **Cesar Malan** (1787–1864). A descendant of the Waldenses and the great-grandson of Reformation martyrs, Malan was steeped in Voltaire and Rousseau but went on toward ordination in 1810 and did some teaching. In 1816, under the influence of the Moravian Brethren, he was converted, and in the following year came into contact with the teaching of Haldane. Immediately he dedicated his life to preaching justification by faith alone wherever he could—which did not ingratiate him with the Reformed church in the canton.

Malan traveled extensively in Europe and in England and Scotland preaching with large effect. In appearance he was "apostolic," it was said, "with his hair long, forehead bare, and on each side a few little curls."[2] His preaching was characterized by what was called winning sweetness. This really was the beginning of the Free Evangelical churches of Switzerland. In 1831, the Societe Evangelique was formed to unify adherents of the revival under the leadership of **Professor Louis Gaussen** (1790–1863) and d'Aubigne. Gaussen was known for his great work on the full inspiration of Scripture and for his strong biblical commentaries.[3] Malan gathered an anthology of hymns for worship in 1834 which was titled *Chants de Sion.*[4] When he was in England he met a young woman, Charlotte Elliott, who seemed unclear on the way to salvation. He told her "Come just as you are, Charlotte," and of course she then wrote the great gospel invitation hymn, "Just as I am, without one plea, but that Thy blood was shed for me."[5]

Even though violence was directed against Malan and his followers, his popularity as a preacher continued to grow. His son Salomon was a gifted linguist in the Indian missionary movement and also wrote a definitive work on Gregory the Illuminator (256–332) in old Armenia. Malan's sermon on "The Piety of the Young Daniel" is a model of simplicity, biblicality, and spiritual passion.[6]

---

1. Stuart Piggin and John Roxborogh, *The St. Andrews Seven* (Edinburgh: Banner of Truth, 1985), 19.
2. Ibid., 19.
3. S. R. L. Gaussen, *The Inspiration of the Holy Scriptures* (Chicago: Moody, 1949). Gaussen contends: "Not only was the Scripture inspired on the day when God caused it to be written, but that we possess this word inspired eighteen hundred years ago; and that we may still, while holding our sacred text in one hand, and in the other all the readings collected by the learned in seven hundred manuscripts, exclaim with thankfulness, 'I hold in my hands my Father's testament, the eternal word of my God!'" (197). See also S. R. L. Gaussen, *The Prophet Daniel Explained,* 2 vols. (London: J and C Mozley, 1873) and *The World's Birthday: A Book for the Young* (London: T. Nelson, 1891). Gaussen served as professor of systematic theology, Oratoire, Geneva.

4. H. Daniel-Rops, *Our Brothers in Christ 1870–1959* (London: J. M. Dent, 1965), 245.
5. E. C. Dargan, *A History of Preaching* (New York: Hodder and Stoughton, 1912), 2:452.
6. Ibid., 452.

9.5.2 *Alexandre Vinet—Speaking in the Revival*

> . . . that ugly man who becomes beautiful when he speaks.
> —the comment of a woman who listened to Alexandre Vinet

Preacher par excellence and homiletician of the revival was the celebrated **Alexandre Vinet** (1797–1847). Vinet was born near Lausanne, the son of descendants of Huguenot refugees. Early in life he was a connoisseur of literature and the arts. By age twenty he was a professor in a gymnasium and then at the University of Basel. He came to know Christ through the ministry of Cesar Malan and quickly took his place among the *momiers* or *mummers*, the epithet used to taunt the evangelicals. He gained notoriety in 1826 for his prize-winning essay calling for full religious freedom, titled "Memoir in Favor of Liberty of Cults."[1] He was consequently excluded from professorial chairs and served for ten years as professor of practical theology at Lausanne. He was highly respected and extended his significance beyond Switzerland to France.[2] Even the Roman Catholic Daniel-Rops pays him tribute:

> Beneath a calm exterior there lay a fiery soul. He followed in the steps of Pascal, with a stern conscience, a love for saintliness and a wide-ranging mind capable of seizing on essentials. He was prepared to sacrifice everything for his convictions. He demonstrated the painful void of the heart, which only the revelation of God incarnate and sacrifice can fill . . .[3]

Widely known for his *Treatise on Homiletics* and his *History of Preaching among the Reformed During the Seventeenth Century,* Vinet advocated careful biblical exposition and practiced it. He illustrated skillfully, and his view of speaking style was well expressed:

> Neither an anathema on art, nor art for art's sake, but art for God's sake, is what we insist upon. It results, as it seems to us, from what we have said, that good style is necessary, and that good style does not come of itself.

Significantly, America's two premier homileticians of the nineteenth century both show awareness of and indebtedness to Vinet. Austin Phelps of Andover makes eight references to Vinet,[4] and John Broadus of Southern Baptist makes twenty-six references.[5] As late as 1923 A. E. Garvie cites Vinet six times.[6]

Alexandre Vinet made a mark not only in his time but for eternity.

1. A. H. Newman, *A Manual of Church History* (Philadelphia: Judson, 1902), 2:572.
2. Paul T. Fuhrmann, *Extraordinary Christianity: The Life and Thought of Alexandre Vinet* (Philadelphia: Westminster, 1964).
3. H. Daniel-Rops, *Our Brothers in Christ 1870–1959* (London: J. M. Dent, 1965), 167.
4. Austin Phelps, *The Theory of Preaching* (London: Richard D. Dickinson, 1882).
5. John A. Broadus, *A Treatise on the Preparation and Delivery of Sermons* (New York: Armstrong, 1898).
6. A. E. Garvie, *The Christian Preacher* (New York: Scribner's, 1923).

9.5.3 Adolphe Monod—Strengthening the Revival

> Great artist by temperament, Monod was so also by conscience; for he considered it a duty to take all the literary care of which he was capable to convince and persuade men of the truth which saves.
>
> —Professor Paul Stapfer

Frederick L. Godet (1812–1900) provided sound exegesis to Francophones and to the world with commentaries on Romans, Luke, and the Gospel of John. Born in Neuchatel, Switzerland, but educated in Berlin and Bonn, Godet pastored churches, served as preceptor of the crown prince of Prussia for three years, and ultimately went on to professorships in his native land until his death. His *Commentary on Romans* has been immensely influential, with a strong insistence on the "moral liberty of man."[1] Godet was associated with the Free Evangelical movement and Pastor Otto Stockmeier.

The crowning expression of the Reveille in terms of preaching can be seen in **Adolphe Monod** (1802–1885). Four sons were born to Pastor Jean Monod: Frederick, Adolphe, William, and Horace. All four became preachers.

Adolphe was born in Copenhagen, where his father was serving the French Reformed Church. His brother Frederick was the prime mover in the formation of the Paris Evangelical Missionary Society in 1882.[2] Young Adolphe studied both in Paris and Geneva but was chilled by the rationalistic environment. He was converted in 1825 under the influence of Malan and d'Aubigne.[3] After pastoring briefly in Naples, he went to Lyons and lectured at the seminary in Montauban. Monod finished his ministry as pastor of the Church of the Oratory, the leading Reformed church in Paris until his demise. Christ-centered in his preaching, Monod was known for his humor and godly piety. Professor Stapfer considered Bossuet and Monod to represent French preaching at its apex.

In his widely noted lecture on "The Delivery of Sermons," Monod characteristically asserts:

> Take your position as the ambassador of Jesus Christ, sent by God to treat with sinful men; believe that He who sends you will not leave you to speak in vain; labor for the salvation of those whom you address, as if it were your own; so forget yourself to see only the glory of God and the

salvation of your hearers; you will then tremble more before God, but less before men.[4]

In a superb sermon on Luke 4:1–13 on "The Weapon in Christ's Conflict" (in which he acknowledges his indebtedness to Krummacher), Monod takes us through the temptations of Christ. This message is one in a series given to the seminary students at Mantauban and breathes a radiant confidence in the Scripture. One senses the nerve and the verve of the preacher.[5]

Another remarkable preacher is **Eugene Bersier** (1831–1889). Although he was born in Switzerland, Bersier served with enormous distinction in Paris. He nearly lost everything theologically while on an extended visit to the United States, but recovered while studying under d'Aubigne in Geneva. He led in building a great independent congregation that drew many in Paris and always had many visitors, and he saw the Eglise de l'Etoile build "a noble edifice near the Arc de Triomphe."[6] Yet another special ministry belonged to **Robert W. McAll** (1820–1893), an English preacher of ability, who left his pastorate and came to Paris for evangelistic work. He established the McAll Mission where his moving gospel preaching saw in one year "over one million hearers in its halls and 10,000 scholars in its Sunday Schools."[7] Thus even in a time of considerable spiritual sterility, the gospel message was heard.

---

1. Frederick L. Godet, *Commentary on the Epistle to the Romans* (Grand Rapids: Zondervan, 1883, 1956).
2. Kenneth Scott Latourette, *The Great Century: Europe and the United States* (Grand Rapids: Zondervan, 1969), 92.
3. E. C. Dargan, *A History of Preaching* (New York: Hodder and Stoughton, 1912), 2:457.
4. H. C. Fish and D. W. Poor, eds., *Select Discourses* (New York: Sheldon and Lincoln, 1860), 400.
5. Ibid., 150–79. Monod was a favorite at the Keswick Convention, where it was said of him: "Small of stature, with an aesthetic appearance and vivacious personality, he spoke fluently in English—but with many a quaint turn of phrase." The volume *Keswick's Authentic Voice* edited by Herbert F. Stevenson (London: Marshall, Morgan, and Scott, 1959) contains Monod's stirring message "With the Whole Heart" from Jeremiah 32:41, delivered in 1882 (248, 281–86).
6. Dargan, *A History of Preaching,* 2:469.
7. T. Harwood Pattison, *The History of Christian Preaching* (Philadelphia: American Baptist Publication Society, 1903), 222.

9.6 *THE SCANDINAVIAN STREAM*

May the Lord be praised! Gladdening news is reaching us from many areas of our land of an awakening of spiritual need and life. The long, cold, dark winter of indifference and security is yielding to the warm rays of the Sun of Righteousness.

—C. O. Rosenius of Sweden in *Pietisten,* 1850

> During the winter 1850–51 there was considerable expansion of the spiritual revival among us. It was felt everywhere. From many directions we heard that the "dead bones" were coming alive.
>
> —Matilda Foy

The Scandinavian countries followed Luther in the Reformation, but "the tidal waves caused by the revolt of Martin Luther had flattened out by the time they reached Scandinavian shores."[1] Olaus Petri, the great Swedish Reformer, studied at Wittenberg from 1516 to 1518. Awakened pastors like Nils Grubb (1681–1724) and Jacob Otto Hoof (1769–1839), who as a minister was dramatically converted out of drunkenness, were fiery preachers whose influence extended well beyond their home province.[2] The American Presbyterian Robert Baird visited Sweden in 1836 and launched a vigorous temperance movement, and George Scott the English Methodist spent ten years in Sweden stirring revival fires. Representatives of the Haldane brothers visited Scandinavia, and the translated pamphlets of Doddridge, Fuller, and Angell James had profound effect.[3] We have already noted the able preaching of Schartau (cf. 8.2.7), which had particular impact on southern Sweden. While Schartau shrank back from Herrnhuter emphasis, Moravian pietism was pervasive in the revival movement, particularly with its "The Spirit always answers to the blood" foundation. Professor Montgomery titled one of his books *The Wind from the Spirit in Sweden and Norway.* In this gracious time of visitation, preaching was pivotal.

---

1. Leslie Stannard Hunter, ed., *Scandinavian Churches: The Development and Life of the Churches of Denmark, Finland, Iceland, Norway, and Sweden* (Minneapolis: Augsburg, 1965), 15.
2. Karl A. Olsson, *By One Spirit* (Chicago: Covenant, 1962). This compendious study is most worthwhile.
3. Gunnar Westin, *The Free Church Through the Ages* (Nashville: Broadus, 1958), 280.

9.6.1 Hans Nielsen Hauge—The Irrepressible Preacher

> The worst temptation I have to resist is this that when I speak to those who have a desire to hear and a will to follow my admonitions, and who may by the power of God even amend their lives, then I am given the praise and thanks for it. This is bad for me as the evil spirit thereby fills my mind and corrupt flesh with thoughts that I am exceedingly good, have great reward with God, and am better than others. But God does not forbid me to speak and this gives me confidence.
>
> By the grace of God, nothing shall ever draw me away from the truth of the Holy Scriptures. After many trials, I have found that Scripture alone is able to give true peace, blessed joy, power to conquer sin, comfort in death, and a constant hope of eternal life. In this life it furnishes the mind with all Christian virtue.
>
> —Hans Nielsen Hauge

The revival in Norway was especially sweet and was contained almost entirely within the established state church. To this day the Free Church movement is relatively small. From 1536 Norway was part of Denmark until the Treaty of Kiel in 1814, when Denmark handed Norway over to Sweden. Independence was not achieved until 1905. Through this period, German rationalism and the fallout of the Enlightenment took a negative toll on the churches.[1]

The visit of the Spirit in the Norwegian revival was focalized in the ministry of **Hans Nielsen Hauge** (1771–1824), who was born on a farm near Thun in southeastern Norway. He had little formal schooling but was deeply imbued with the Bible and Luther's Catechism in his home, and as well was exposed in large doses to Arndt, Pontoppidan, and Kingo. Though often terrified by his violation of the law of God and almost perishing on occasion, Hauge was not converted until 1796 while at work in his father's field:

> My heart was so uplifted to God that I do not know nor can I express what really took place in my soul. As soon as my senses returned to normal, I regretted that I had not served the loving and all-gracious God; now I felt that no worldly thing was of importance. It was a glory which no tongue can express; my soul felt something supernatural, divine and blessed . . . I had a completely transformed mind, a sorrow over all sins, a burning desire to read the Scriptures, particularly Jesus' own teachings, as well as new light to understand them and the teachings of godly men; toward the one goal, that Jesus Christ has come to be our Savior, that we should be born again by his spirit, be converted and sanctified more and more in godliness to serve the triune God alone, in order to improve and prepare our souls for the eternal blessedness.[2]

Hauge then embarked on a series of preaching missions throughout Norway (1796–1804). He often encouraged trade activities among his converts. He loved to sing hymns and preach the Word. He wrote thirty-three books and supervised their printing and their distribution. He was imprisoned for breaking the Conventicle Act by preaching as a layman.[3] His health broken by conditions during his imprisonment from 1804 to 1814, he continued to preach and indeed preached from his deathbed to the salvation of lost souls.[4] The ecclesiastical authorities were scandalized by his success and his direct, simple message. "But," he testified, "I discovered that there was a power of God in the foolishness of preaching, as Paul says in 1 Corinthians 1:31."[5] He was a zealous soulwinner and could not obey the edicts to keep quiet about Jesus and the gospel.

Hauge's conversion was paradigmatic for him, and he never ceased to marvel how deep the well was from which he drew the water of salvation. He felt the fire burning in him to preach. He preached even to the bailiff's wife when he was on trial.[6] Several times he traveled to Copenhagen for ministry, and while many were eager to hear the Word, there were many who rebuffed him and his message. At Tromso both Norwegians and Finns wept "and were open to persuasion."[7] He explained to the dean of Stavanger, who came to hear him, that "I can only express those things that coming to my heart and mind from the text of the Bible I am convinced and believe are right."[8]

The Haugean movement in Norway and in this country would be described as "a Low-Church form of orthodox Lutheranism, conservative in matters of biblical criticism and once powerful enough to found the private Theological Faculty at Oslo in protest against the liberal school dominant at the University at the beginning of the century."[9] The long-time teacher and the founder of the school was the widely-read **Ole Hallesby** (1879–1961), whose books on prayer, conscience, and *Why I Am a Christian* remain part of the rich legacy of this movement. Other professors of note from this school, which still provides training for one-third of the ministers of the state church in Norway, are **Olaf Moe** (whose volumes on the apostle Paul are sterling),[10] and **Olav Valen-Sendstad** (whose *The Word That Can Never Die* is a scholarly refutation of modernistic incursions in today's theology).[11] The Haugean influence is also to be seen in the founding of missionary societies and the Bible society as well as in the Inner Mission lay movement which is still very strong in Norway. The scholarly ministry of **Gisle Johnson** at the University of Oslo and the Johnsonian revival of confessionalism in the last half of the century must be seen as a further impetus of the Haugean impulse. Norwegian pietism is a somber pietism (as we pick it up in the novels of Alexander Kielland) but is a vital and a strong spiritual movement.

---

1. T. K. Derry, *A History of Modern Norway* (Oxford: Clarendon, 1973).
2. G. Everett Arden, *Four Northern Lights: Men Who Shaped Scandinavian Churches* (Minneapolis: Augsburg, 1964), 57.
3. Joel M. Njus, trans., *Autobiographical Writings of Hans Nielsen Hauge* (Minneapolis: Augsburg, 1954), 12.
4. Ibid., 14.
5. Ibid., 47.
6. Ibid., 103.
7. Ibid., 118.
8. Ibid., 122.
9. Leslie Stannard Hunter, ed., *Scandinavian Churches* (Minneapolis: Augsburg, 1965), 177.
10. Olaf Edward Moe, *The Apostle Paul: His Life and Work* (Grand Rapids: Baker, 1923). Volume 2 is on the Epistles.
11. Olav Valen-Sendstad, *The Word That Can Never Die: A Scriptural Critique of Theological Trends* (St. Louis: Concordia, 1949). Argues that the humble form of Scripture is analogical to the perfect humanity of Christ.

9.6.2 Paavo Henrik Ruotsalainen—The Inextinguishable Preacher

> Let trouble and sorrow drive you to seek the revealed and despised Savior in his Word . . . No matter how cold and unresponsive you may feel yourself to be, diligently hear and use the Word whence comes the hidden light for those who yearn for light . . . The Word awakens in the heart a desire for Christ,

> and this desire moves the heart to pray and long for the well-spring of life, and ere you are conscious of it, the Christ-life has been born within you.
>
> —Paavo Henrik Ruotsalainen

Always considered a Scandinavian country but with a language and history so different (although 8 percent of the people are Swedish-Finns), Finland became Protestant in the Reformation, and in the Vasteros Edict of 1527 it was stipulated: "The pure Word of God is to be preached throughout the land."[1] Bishop Agricola in this time characterized most preaching as "both nasty and lazy."[2] To this day 92 percent of the Finns are Lutheran but not very spiritually lively. Most are nominal.[3] This deadness and formalism have been challenged from time to time by movements of revival but none quite like that led by **Paavo Ruotsalainen** (1777–1852). Other movements among the Swedish-Finns in the west joined forces with Ruotsalainen, while Henry Renqvist inclined more to a prayer movement and F. G. Hedberg turned from Ruotsalainen to follow Rosenius.[4] Some Finns followed the Swedish revivalist Laestadius in an emphasis on mutual confession and absolution. Theologically the Church of Finland was much influenced by J. T. Beck of Tubingen (cf. 9.4.4). After long union with Sweden, in 1809 Finland was seized by Russia and was a Russian duchy until 1917, when she declared her independence. The heroism of the Finnish people will long be remembered as they so stoutly resisted Russian incursion in 1939 in the Winter War under their gallant General Carl von Mannerheim.

Ruotsalainen was born into a poor peasant family and learned to read but never learned to write. All that we have from him in print was dictated. The revivals came sweeping through Finland as through Norway and Sweden. Young Paavo was gripped by what took place and began to read the Bible, Luther's Shorter Catechism, and the writings of John Bunyan, Pontoppidan, and other confessional Lutherans. He heard of a blacksmith, Jacob Hogman, who lived some distance away who had an authentic walk with the Lord, and he journeyed to meet him, begging food and lodging along the route. Hogman had a simple word of advice for him: "One thing you lack and therewith you lack all else: the inner awareness of Christ."[5] This was his tower experience, and it set the serious, almost grave tone for his subsequent life and ministry. When excesses of glossalalia threatened the movement, Ruotsalainen pulled things back to the center. He was a powerful preacher "who had the knack of communicating his thoughts so clearly and directly that the old Gospel truths of which he spoke were luminous with new light and meaning."[6] He was the architect of a spirituality which to this day represents an alternative to overinstitutionalized formalism. He placed great emphasis on the assurance of salvation and inner peace.

> To him whose conscience has been awakened you shall say that he must never think too highly of himself, but must not therefore doubt or hesitate. He must lay hold of God's gracious promises and with patience look unto Christ as his helper, until the Holy Spirit bears witness to him that he really possesses the righteousness of Christ.[7]

This peace is not spiritual euphoria and ecstasy chiefly, but the reality of the living Christ within and slow, patient learning in the school of the cross. He argued that "the objective reality of a gracious, redeeming, loving God is there at the center of life itself, quite apart from any tangible or palpable human experience."[8] In Ruotsalainen we have another revivalistic lay preacher whose message shook and shaped a nation.

---

1. John H. Wuorinen, *A History of Finland* (New York: Columbia University Press, 1965), 61.
2. Ibid., 65.
3. Leslie Stannard Hunter, ed., *Scandinavian Churches* (Minneapolis: Augsburg, 1965), 68–75.
4. Conrad Bergendoff, *The Church of the Lutheran Reformation* (St. Louis: Concordia, 1967), 222.
5. G. Everett Arden, *Four Northern Lights: Men Who Shaped Scandinavian Churches* (Minneapolis: Augsburg, 1964), 25.
6. Ibid., 25.
7. Ibid., 29.
8. Ibid., 39.

9.6.3 *Carl Olof Rosenius—The Indefatigable Preacher*

> When fruitlessly exerting all your powers in the desperate attempt to do the will of God, you shall ultimately be impelled to pray for the Spirit of God to help you. Then shall you in the school of experience receive the true light upon the Word of God—the light from heaven. Without this experience, the highbrows and scribes are blind as bats in things spiritual. Without the Holy Spirit, the Word of God is not understood. Luther says: "When God gave His Word, He said: I shall let it be plainly written and preached, but I shall so arrange matters, that it shall depend upon my Spirit as to who shall understand it. Hence we see that they who think that they are able to understand the saving doctrine of their own mental astuteness, remain in spiritual darkness."
>
> —Carl Olof Rosenius

The vapid rationalism that wasted the other Scandinavian countries had a similar impact upon Sweden. An intellectual like Emanuel Swedenborg (1688–1772), whose father was bishop of Skara, had attempted to fuse science and mysticism into a religious system that still has followers today, even though it is a cultic denial of the Christian faith. Under the influence of the Moravian Brethren and older Swedish Pietists like the gifted preacher **Anders Rutstrom** and **Peter Murbeck**, revival fires began to glow in Sweden as in Norway and Finland.

The embodiment of Pietistic orthodoxy is to be seen in **Carl Olof Rosenius** (1816–1868), born in a parsonage in Lulea in Norrland. His father was clearly in the camp of the evangelical revivalists, and young Carl was nurtured in the context of this life movement. He was converted at the age of fifteen and conducted his first Bible meeting shortly thereafter.[1] With the unrest and anxiety accompanying rapid industrialization and a changing society and economy, many were more open to the gospel. Rosenius studied for a while at Uppsala but became a private tutor until he joined with the English Methodist George Scott. Their ministry of evangelism and outreach "promoting the revival of pure Christianity" centered in the independent Bethlehem Chapel in Stockholm. Early in 1840 Rosenius "attempted his first Bible exposition," and Scott immediately recognized the rich gifts of his somewhat bewildered young friend.[2] The salary of Rosenius was paid by an American organization called the Foreign Evangelical Society of New York City. Rosenius was soon the preaching equal of Scott. In 1842 *Pietisten,* the immensely popular periodical, was established with Rosenius as its editor, and he became a household name in Sweden.[3] He preached in the dialect of the people and was dubbed by some as a mystical fanatic. He traveled widely and while always faithful to confessional Lutheranism, he ministered in a church within a church, existing to this day as Evangeliska Fosterlandsstiffelsen (the Evangelical Patriotic Society). His writings reflect his careful and meticulous biblical scholarship and his vigorous confidence in Scripture and insistence on conversion.[4] Colporteurs and criers moved through the countryside. Signs and wonders were not uncommon. "Preaching sickness" would come on children and youth and people of both sexes. One of my grandparents was converted when a dying boy in the parish preached law and gospel with prophetic vision.[5]

The sermons of Rosenius were fruitful and productive. In reaction against "the dull, deadening theological status in the universities," Rosenius trumped the condemnation of law and then the healing balm of "saved by grace through faith alone." Music by Ahnfelt, the Lutheran Sankey of Sweden, and others resounded through the land. Rosenius particularly loved Romans (and ran a six-year series on Romans in the paper). Professor Hult comments on his probing "into the interior of the text with astounding patience . . . such intense scanning of the inner heart and organism of the Word of God."[6] But all of this, we must be assured, was predicated on the premise: "The Church work of Rosenius was—to save souls!"[7] Analysis of his sermons shows them not to be highly structured but filled with Scripture and warm exhortation.

Following in the succession in Swedish revivalism must be **Lektor Paul Peter Waldenström** (1838–1917), a Ph.D. from Uppsala, who brought together most of the Free Church people into what was organized as the Swedish Mission Covenant in 1878. Unfortunately tinged with a Ritschlian view of the atonement, Waldenström was a preacher of considerable force and power.[8] "Where is it written?" became the watchword of the Mission Friends in Sweden and in America. He visited the United States five times and served in the Swedish Parliament from 1894 to 1905.[9] His sermons were biblical and forceful and he became more conservative as he grew older.[10] The biblically and theologically rich preaching of Waldenström did not characterize all of his successors in the pietistic institutionalization that he led.[11] Quite clearly biblical preaching is of the essence in the revivals in Sweden that have had such powerful impact on Scandinavian Free Church movements on this side of the Atlantic.

1. G. T. Rygh, Preface to C. O. Rosenius, *A Faithful Guide to Peace with God* (Minneapolis: Augsburg, 1923), 10.
2. Karl A. Olsson, *By One Spirit* (Chicago: Covenant, 1962), 50. For the impact of industrialization and the agricultural crisis that so upended society, see Ingvar Andersson, *A History of Sweden* (Westport, Conn.: Greenwood, 1968), 351–74.
3. G. Everett Arden, *Four Northern Lights: Men Who Shaped Scandinavian Churches* (Minneapolis: Augsburg, 1964), 124.
4. Carl Olof Rosenius, *A Faithful Guide to Peace with God.* Especially rewarding sections on law, conversion, the revelation of the mystery, etc.
5. Olsson, *By One Spirit,* 60.
6. Adolf Hult, trans., *C. O. Rosenius, The Believer Free from the Law* (Minneapolis: Lutheran Colportage, 1923), 16.
7. Ibid., 19.
8. John Wordsworth, *The National Church of Sweden* (London: Mowbray, 1911), 375.
9. Ragnar Tomson, *Den Radikale Waldenström* (Stockholm: Missionsforbundets Forlag, 1945).
10. P. P. Waldenström, *Biblisk Troslära* (Stockholm: Svenska Missionsforbundets Forlag, 1918).
11. J. G. Princell, trans., P. P. Waldenström, *The Lord Is Right: Meditations on the Twenty-fifth Psalm* (Chicago: John Martenson, 1889). Eric G. Hawkinson has a sensitive treatment on the centrality of preaching among the Scandinavian immigrant churches in *Images in Covenant Beginnings* (Chicago: Covenant, 1968) in which he observes: "Preaching was seen as the very heart of the mission of the fathers . . . the Bible was the trustworthy Word of God. Its message had to do with what God had done in Jesus Christ for man's salvation. It was for man—when he saw what God had done—to accept this grace and believe. The texts were as often chosen from the Old Testament as the New. The Bible was one book and spoke of one grace. The burden was to discover what the Bible had to say to man" (130). See also Herbert E. Palmquist, trans., *The Word Is Near You* (Chicago: Covenant, 1974).

9.6.4 Nikolai F. S. Grundtvig—The Incandescent Preacher

> Then it was brought home to them that faith itself is the work of the Holy Spirit, and they ceased from all righteousness in their own conceit, and denied themselves, and took up their cross and followed Jesus. That, my friend, is the way, the truth and the life. If we acknowledge our own impotence and unworthiness, and the necessity of becoming altogether new human beings through spiritual rebirth, of becoming members of Christ's body, having no life, no salvation apart from him, then we shall sigh until we learn to pray, think, until we learn to feel. We shall journey and rest with the thought that God sees us, that only Jesus can save us, that only the Holy Spirit can enlighten, move and strengthen us.
>
> —N. F. S. Grundtvig

Beautiful little Denmark, like the other Scandinavian countries, was in the grip of sweeping change in the nineteenth century, with her imperial possessions stripped away, the loss of Schleswig-Holstein to Germany, and the impact of new and high-powered economic change. Religiously Denmark was much affected by Enlightenment rationalism, and notwithstanding the new Danish Constitution of 1849 guaranteeing religious freedom, the Danish Folk-Church was in a state of abysmal torpor. The earlier Pietistic influence on the royal court, which resulted in sending out missionaries to India (cf. 8.4.1), had dissipated, and historic doctrines of the Trinity and the Atonement were abandoned in favor of a toothless religion of gentle Jesus and good deeds.[1] Of course there were exceptions, and beacon lights like the south Jutlander **Bishop Erik Pontoppidan** and **Hans Adolph Brorson** (who wrote "Behold the Host Arrayed in Light") were mighty preachers of conversion and sanctification.[2]

The mighty revivals that cascaded across the northern countries did not come in such force among the more sedate and self-sufficient Danes, but there was a little springtime led by **J. P. Mynster** (1775–1854) and **N. F. S. Grundtvig** (1793–1877). The latter was born and nurtured within a parsonage. He was something of a romantic in reaction against rationalism but quite critical of the Pietists for their individuality. He leveled devastating critiques against the Church of Denmark. He studied at the University of Copenhagen and afterwards tutored in a wealthy family until he went to be associate to his father. His first sermon in 1810 in this role was titled "Why Has the Word of the Lord Vanished in His House," which was a withering blast against the rationalism of the clergy.[3] His questioning of the spiritual status quo led to his own spiritual awakening. Grundtvig specifically attacked Professor H. N. Clausen and was sued and found guilty and subsequently fined. Many left him in "the Church Struggle," but in 1839 he took the pastorate in Vartov, which was really the chaplaincy of a home for aged women.[4] Here he preached and counseled and wrote until his death, becoming the center of a spiritual stirring that reached all of Denmark. He wrote one thousand hymns, including the classic "Built on the Rock the Church Doth Stand." He initiated popular education in Denmark. He was highly sacramental and because his followers stayed in the church they influenced the church greatly in this regard. At some theological points Grundtvig deviated from orthodoxy, being concerned at times overmuch to foster a happy Christianity. One secular historian speaks of Ansgar as the prophet of the north in the ninth century and Grundtvig as the prophet of the north in the nineteenth century.[5]

Also challenging the largely moribund state church was **Soren Kierkegaard** (1813–1855), who scathingly attacked the church in which he argued "Christianity has ceased to exist." In such strong reaction against Hegalian rationalism, he is one of the fathers of modern existentialism. He loved to read sermons aloud, and his *Edifying Discourses,* including the peerless *Purity of Heart Is to Will One Thing,* are really unpreached sermons.[6] He advocated a leap of faith in his brilliant treatment of the Abraham and Isaac story in *Fear and Trembling* and in his address to despair in *The Sickness Unto Death.* Kierkegaard savaged **Bishop H. L. Martensen** (1808–1884), denying that he could have been a "truth-witness." This was extreme because Martensen was an able preacher of Christ concerning whom he said late in his life, "Nothing is for me more certain than the risen, ascended Christ and the heavenly kingdom."[7] Kierkegaard also has significance in the history of preaching for his notion of indirect address, which Fred Craddock has picked up in his *Overhearing the Gospel.* In this a subtle, nondeclamatory approach is advocated for preaching.

Kierkegaard's assaults did inspire **Vilhelm Beck** (1829–1901) to join with others in founding the Inner Mission. He was stirred by Kierkegaard's scathing critique of the worldliness of the church. He was converted in 1859 and began to preach with great power and eloquence. He differed from Grundtvig with respect to biblical inerrancy, holding to a conservative formulation. He preached revivals through Jutland emphasizing "Conversion and Faith." He is seen by some as "the last of the great Danish preachers of the nineteenth century."[8] At the time of his death there were four hundred meeting houses in the movement, but they stayed within the state church.

A more separatistic stance was taken by **Niels Pedersen Grunnet** (1827–1897), who was influenced by a Moravian Pietist to go to Basle and study there at the Mission-Seminary. He married a Swiss woman, Maria Vatter, in 1856 and came back to Copenhagen to lead in founding the Evangelical Lutheran Free Church in 1855. Grunnet founded churches throughout the country and served and preached with effectiveness at Martin's Church on Martin's Road in Copenhagen. He wrote many treatises such as "Some Truths and Testimonies Against the Teaching of the Conversion after Death" (1857) and a collection of eighteen sermons titled "Come Jesus Christ to Mind" (1889). Only seven of these congregations remain, but Martinskirken is still well worth a visit in Copenhagen. This was a small come-out group, but in the main the evangelical movement was kept within the state church.

---

1. The classic delineation of this view is seen in Adolph Harnack, *What Is Christianity?* (New York: Putnam). Supernaturalism has been effectively surrendered.
2. Jens Christian Kjaer, *History of the Church of Denmark* (Blair, Neb.: Lutheran Publishing House, 1945), 68ff.
3. Ibid., 84.
4. G. Everett Arden, *Four Northern Lights: Men Who Shaped Scandinavian Churches* (Minneapolis: Augsburg, 1964), 95.
5. J. H. S. Birch, *Denmark in History* (Westport, Conn.: Greenwood, 1938, 1975), 358.
6. Douglas V. Steere, trans., Soren Kierkegaard, *Purity of Heart Is to Will One Thing* (New York: Harpers, 1938, 1948). For a choice analysis of Kierkegaard, see E. J. Carnell, *The Burden of Soren Kierkegaard* (Grand Rapids: Eerdmans, 1965). Neglected by his contemporaries Kierkegaard was rediscovered in our century and has profoundly shaped existential theology with its tragic denial of supernatural and metaphysical approaches to theology. The consequences of Kierkegaard's "truth is subjectivity" is painfully apparent in Catholic, Protestant, and atheistic varieties of existential theology. There is no "true principium" here for the construction of theology.
7. Kjaer, *History of the Church of Denmark,* 107. See Thomas Oden, ed., *Parables of Kierkegaard* (Princeton, N.J.: Princeton, 1979).
8. Ibid., 109.

CHAPTER TEN

Starbursts and Sidetracks of the Victorian Pulpit

Part Two: The Raging River

And at his appointed season he brought his word to light through the preaching entrusted to me by the command of God our Savior.

—Titus 1:3

You must teach what is in accord with sound doctrine. . . . so that no one will malign the word of God.

—Titus 2:1, 5b

For we also have had the gospel preached to us, just as they did; but the message they heard was of no value to them, because those who heard did not combine it with faith. . . . For the word of God is living and active. Sharper than any double-edged sword, it penetrates even to dividing soul and spirit, joints and marrow; it judges the thoughts and attitudes of the heart.

—Hebrews 4:2, 12

See to it that you do not refuse him who speaks. If they did not escape when they refused him who warned them on earth, how much less will we, if we turn away from him who warns us from heaven?

—Hebrews 12:25

> He chose to give us birth through the word of truth, that we might be a kind of firstfruits of all he created. . . . Therefore, get rid of all moral filth and the evil that is so prevalent and humbly accept the word planted in you, which can save you. Do not merely listen to the word, and so deceive yourselves. Do what it says.
>
> —James 1:18, 21–22

> Preaching is indispensable to Christianity. Without preaching, a necessary part of its authenticity has been lost. For Christianity is, in its very essence, a religion of the Word of God.
>
> —John R. W. Stott

> Apart from blunt truth, our lives sink decadently amid the perfume of hints and suggestions.
>
> —Alfred North Whitehead

> The Bible is not telling us about human preachers; it is telling us about preaching. Furthermore, the prior Greek history gives no specific meaning to *kerux* (to proclaim). The New Testament knows nothing of sacred personages who are inviolable in the world. . . . The messengers are like sheep delivered to wolves (Matthew 10:10). As the Lord was persecuted, so His servants will be persecuted (John 15:20). The servants of Christ are, as it were, dedicated to death (Revelation 12:11). But the message does not perish with the one who proclaims it. The message is irresistible (2 Timothy 2:9). It takes its victorious course through the world (2 Thessalonians 3:1). Hence *kerussein* (what is proclaimed) is more important then the *kerux* in the New Testament.
>
> —Kittel and Friedrich

The nineteenth century was a self-conscious time of transition. John Stuart Mill observed in 1831 that "mankind have outgrown old institutions and old doctrines, and have not yet acquired new ones."[1] Bulwer-Lytton moaned, "The age then is one of destruction! . . . Miserable would be our lot were it not also an age of preparation for restructuring."[2] Charles Kingsley offered the opinion that "few of us deeply believe anything."[3] The rationalism and the romanticism of the Enlightenment were making hash out of accepted orthodox belief.

The likes of David Hume and Herbert Spencer were drawing many to doubt and denial. Tennyson's *In Memoriam* is not belief or unbelief; it is doubt. Matthew Arnold's *Dover Beach* is a melancholy review of the recession of faith. George Eliot cut off her evangelical roots because of biblical criticism and went on to be an advocate of free love. Auguste Comte's religion of humanity tantalized many on the Continent. Ruskin tried desperately to hold on to theism in some sense. Thomas Carlyle in *Past and Present* celebrates his heroes but is "full of contradictory notions and beliefs." Once planning to study for the ministry, he became a teacher and then a writer, and in this 1843 volume becomes "the Victorian prophet of the great fight."[4] Lytton Strachey's *Eminent Victorians* is a mishmash.[5] Friedrich Wilhelm Nietzsche was the son of a German minister but developed doctrines of the superman and the will to power. Before dying of paresis, he conceded, "A man of spiritual depth needs friends, unless he still has God as a friend. But I have neither God nor friends."[6]

In her novel of a clergyman, *Robert Elsmere,* Mrs. Humphrey Ward, a niece of Thomas Arnold and editor of *Amiel's Journal,* depicts characters who "have a hunger for life and its satisfactions, which the will was more and more powerless to satisfy."[7] A vacuum was emerging. The optimisms of empire and the new age of science were doomed to disillusionment in the quagmire of suicidal war, the Holocaust, and the horrors of the atomic age. Meanwhile, the faithful preaching of the supernatural gospel and the exposition of Holy Scripture continued to make a significant impact in Europe and America and indeed around the world. The Christian church was becoming an international community of the blood-bought and the born-again.

---

1. Walter E. Houghton, *The Victorian Frame of Mind* (New Haven, Conn.: Yale University Press, 1957), 1.
2. Ibid., 3.
3. Ibid., 22.
4. Ibid., 206.
5. Lytton Strachey, *Eminent Victorians* (Garden City, N.Y.: Garden City Publishing, 1917).
6. Kurt F. Reinhardt, *The Existential Revolt: The Main Themes and Phases of Existentialism* (Milwaukee: Bruce, 1952), 59. See also Carl Pletsch, *The Young Nietzsche: Becoming a Genius* (New York: Free Press, 1991).
7. Houghton, *The Victorian Frame of Mind,* 65.

10.1 THE TRIBUTARY OF THE EVANGELISTS

> He who descended is the very one who ascended higher than all the heavens, in order to fill the whole universe. It was he who gave some to be . . . evangelists.
>
> —Ephesians 4:10–11

Evangelistic preaching is a special genre. During this complex time, the outburst of powerful evangelistic preaching on every continent was to become a vital part of history.

10.1.1 CHARLES G. FINNEY—THE LAWYER IN THE PULPIT

> The question of the inspiration of the Bible is of the highest importance to the Church and the world, and that those who have called in question the plenary [total] inspiration of the Bible, have, sooner or later, frittered away nearly all that is essential to the Christian religion.

> I gave myself to a great deal of prayer. After my evening services, I would retire as early as I could; but rose at four o'clock in the morning, because I could sleep no longer, and immediately went to the study, and engaged in prayer. And so deeply was my mind exercised, and so absorbed in prayer, that I frequently continued from the time I arose at four o'clock till the gong called for breakfast at eight o'clock. My days were spent, so long as I could get time, in searching the Scriptures. I read nothing else, all that winter, but my Bible; and a great deal of it seemed new to me . . . the whole Scriptures seemed to me all ablaze with light.
>
> —Charles G. Finney

Called the father of American revivalism and the originator of a new style of pulpit oratory, **Charles Grandison Finney** (1792–1875) saw five hundred thousand professions of Christ in his ministry. He played a crucial part in the western revivals that led to the Great Prayer Meeting Revival of 1857–58.[1] His "new measures" were innovative in evangelism. Perry Miller pays high tribute to Finney's *Lectures on Revivals of Religion* as the key exposition of the movement and to Finney himself. Miller wrote, "No religious leader in America since Edwards had commanded such attention; no one was to do it again until Dwight Moody."[2]

Finney was born in an old New England family in Connecticut but moved to New York. In time he studied law and led the choir in a Presbyterian church pastored by George Gale, a Princetonian of the Old School who later founded Knox College in Galesburg, Illinois, which is named after him.

Finney had been deeply moved by a man he heard praying, and this left a profound mark on him. For Finney, prayer was always uppermost, and he was unusually sensitive to what he called "an earnest spirit of prayer." After much reading of Scripture, he went out into the woods, declaring, "I will give my heart to God or I will never come down from there." What he called "waves of liquid love" flowed over him. He struggled with the Old School passivity and reluctance to invite sinners to come to Christ, and in 1824 he began to preach in the "burned-over district" in which he lived.[3]

His preaching was extempore and sometimes impromptu, "throwing manuscripts away."

> In delivering a sermon in this essay style of writing, the power of gesture and looks and attitude and emphasis is lost. We can never have the fullness of the gospel till we throw away our written sermons.

He remembered an old preacher who read his sermons and made no impression whatever on anyone's mind. Not so Finney! But even more controversial was his theology. Ever since the days of Solomon Stoddard, Calvinists had been torn by revivals—how did they fit into the scheme of things? Finney chose to build on Jonathan Edwards and the New England theology that grew out of his thinking.[4] Edwards' disciples went much farther than the master, as when Nathaniel Taylor denied original sin. Finney followed on this track and moved to a governmental view of the Atonement. His new measures created a furor, but the one most vociferously opposed was Finney's insistence that women participate in the prayer meetings. Warfield, while acknowledging that Finney "conducted the most spectacular evangelism activities the country has ever witnessed," was not unfair with respect to the serious nature of Finney's theological lapses.[5] Later accretions of perfectionism and the development of Oberlin perfectionism would come via J. H. Noyes and the Oneida Community in New York.

The climax of Finney's itinerant ministry was in the great Rochester Revival in 1830–31, which saw thousands come to Christ and the forces of evil put on the run. In 1831 he published his *Revival Lectures,* and in 1835 began to preach in the Broadway Tabernacle in New York City. He crossed the Atlantic several times and had a fruitful ministry, yet everywhere he went he fomented opposition. Samuel Tregelles, the Brethren New Testament scholar in Britain, spotted the chinks in his armor, and the Old School were against him. He and Lyman Beecher wrangled, but Beecher himself gave way to the new theology when all was said and done. The Universalists and Unitarians could not abide Finney's strong preaching on hell. Drummond argues that Finney "mellowed" on several of the theological matters, particularly regarding human ability.[6] Evidence for this claim is sparse at best.

Social and societal issues were always important for Finney, and he led in the abolitionist cause long before it was popular. He pushed temperance issues and anti-Masonry. Finally he became a professor at Oberlin, Ohio, and was eventually elevated to president of that school.

But as a preacher, Finney was rapierlike in his lawyerly logic and clarity. He had a resonant voice, yet not as powerful as Whitefield, and great dramatic ability. As he preached "an awful solemnity" would fall on the audience. People wilted before the preaching of the Word of God, which often went two hours in length. Many testified to his "unforgettable eyes . . ." "his prominent forehead and those remarkable, hypnotic eyes . . . large and blue, at times mild as an April sky and at others, cold and penetrating as polished steel."[7]

Many have argued that what Andrew Jackson was in politics, Finney was in religion. He could be denunciatory. He called for immediate response, and sometimes seekers started toward the mourner's bench or inquirer's room even before he finished the sermon.

Finney's language in preaching was spare, and he could outline a sermon well.[8] In a great sermon on Luke 16:2 simply titled "Stewardship," Finney launched from the text, "Give an account of your stewardship." He drew seven applications and fashioned a concluding section for hell-bound sinners from the clause, "You shall no longer be my steward." Finney always preached with "spiritual travail" and leaned on and expected the anointing of the Holy Spirit. As late as 1871 he preached a great sermon on "The Gift of the Holy Spirit" to the National Congregational Council meeting at Oberlin.[9] He reflected on his long years pastoring at First Congregational in Oberlin: "I ploughed my church up every year." He believed that the problem for sinners in coming to Christ was not "cannot" but "will not." He advised, "The Almighty God awaits your consent."

---

1. Though very critical, see William G. McLoughlin, *Modern Revivalism* (New York: Ronald Press, 1959).
2. Keith J. Hardman, *Charles Grandison Finney: Revivalist and Reformer* (Syracuse: Syracuse University Press, 1987), x. Finney's *Revivals of Religion* (Chicago: Moody, 1962) is available in paper and is most worthwhile—a stirring read.
3. James E. Johnson, "Father in American Revivalism," *Christian History* 7, no. 4, issue 20: 6ff. The entire issue is on Finney.
4. Allen C. Guelzo, *Edwards on the Will: A Century of Theological Debate* (Middletown, Conn.: Wesleyan, 1989). Charles Hambrick-Stowe argues that Finney sought evangelical consensus, cf. his *Charles G. Finney and the Spirit of American Evangelicalism* (Grand Rapids: Eerdmans, 1997). He overstresses Finney's Calvinistic ties.
5. B. B. Warfield, *Perfectionism* (Philadelphia: Presbyterian and Reformed, 1967), 166ff. Finney doubtless had an important influence on the higher life movement, but Warfield is unnecessarily severe on Keswick theology, which does not partake of the serious errors of Finney in his denial of original sin and imputation of righteousness. For an important analysis of Finney, see Jay E. Smith, "The Theology of Charles Finney: A System of Self-Reformation," *Trinity Journal,* 13 n.s. (1992): 61–93. A neglected dimension in Finney and others is excavated by Donald W. Dayton, *Discovering an Evangelical Heritage* (New York: Harper, 1976), 15–24.
6. Lewis A. Drummond, *The Life and Ministry of Charles G. Finney* (Minneapolis: Bethany House, 1983), 115.
7. Hardman, *Charles Grandison Finney,* 35. See V. Raymond Edman, *Finney Lives On* (New York: Revell, 1951).
8. Louis Gifford Parkhurst Jr., ed., *Charles G. Finney, Principles of Revival* (Minneapolis: Bethany House, 1987). We are in the debt of Bethany House and Parkhurst for republishing so many of Finney's sermons and articles.
9. J. Gilchrist Lawson, *Deeper Experiences of Famous Christians* (Anderson, Ind.: Warner, 1911), 243ff.

10.1.2 Peter Cartwright—A Frontiersman in the Pulpit

> Many nights, in early times, the itinerant had to camp out, without fire or food for man or beast. It is true we could not, many of us, conjugate a verb or parse a sentence, and murdered the king's English almost every lick. But there was a Divine unction attended the word preached and thousands fell under the mighty power of God, and thus the Methodist Episcopal Church was planted firmly in this western wilderness, and many glorious signs have followed, and will follow, to the end of time.
>
> —Peter Cartwright

In the great westward movement into and beyond the valley of the Mississippi, God too was moving mightily. This historic epoch was a time of great revival.[1]

One of the key preachers in this breakthrough was **Peter Cartwright** (1785–1872), who served as a presiding elder in the Methodist Episcopal Church for fifty years, preached more than fifteen thousand sermons, baptized twelve thousand persons, received ten thousand into the church, twice served in the Illinois State Legislature, and was defeated for the U.S. Congress in 1846 by Abraham Lincoln.[2] This thickset, muscular man was born in Virginia into the home of a soldier who had fought in the American Revolution. His family moved to Kentucky by packhorse into an area known "Rogue's Harbor." Here was born the camp meeting and an incendiary movement of the Holy Spirit.

Peter heard preaching in the family cabin when he was nine and later was converted out of a life of sin. Francis Asbury was a potent factor in the explosive growth of the Methodist church, and influenced the Gasper River and Cane Ridge Camp Meetings which were such a significant part of the Second Great Awakening.[3] This was known as the Cumberland Revival.

Called by some the Kentucky boy, Cartwright said, "I took my text and preached." First appointed as an exhorter and then put into "the traveling connection," Peter would preach up to three hours and sometimes two or three times a day as he traveled.[4] He was directed by his presiding bishop to a course of study, but his texts were usually one verse, as when he preached on Isaiah 26:4, "Trust ye in the Lord forever: for in the Lord Jehovah is everlasting strength." Cartwright reported that the Lord gave light, liberty, and power, and the congregation melted into tears with conversions.[5] Sometimes he would stay for protracted meetings, notwithstanding rowdies (whom he dealt with handily), denominational tensions, and critics. One learned preacher tried to humiliate him by using Greek words, which Cartwright did not understand. Cartwright responded in German, which this minister thought was Hebrew and commended Cartwright for his erudition.[6] The mighty power of God fell on the meetings with great regularity. He feared no one, not even the famous General Andrew Jackson, who appreciated Cartwright for his forthrightness.

Because of his aversion to slavery, Cartwright asked for transfer to Illinois, which was just beginning to break open. He settled his family in Sangamon County where his forty-mile days continued and the conversions multiplied. He faced Arians, deists, Universalists, skeptics, Shakers, and—at nearby Nauvoo—Mormons. One winter he led a five-month revival. "I preached, exhorted, sung, prayed and labored at the altar," said Cartwright. "I need not say several times a day or night, but almost day and night for months together."[7]

He also did extensive evangelism among the Indians. When he went back to General Conference in Boston in 1852, he expounded on great texts such as Hebrews 10:22 and Job 22:21. But none evoked as much stir as when he took Matthew 11:12 and was simply "the old pioneer of the west."[8] There was in his own style what he called "animal excitement." He attributed his immense physical strength to a simple regimen: "Keep your feet warm, your head cool, your bowels well regulated, rise early, go to bed early, eat temperately and drink no spirits." Peter Cartwright was a rough-hewn instrument, available and dispensable in God's hands.

1. Stephen E. Ambrose, *Undaunted Courage: Meriwether Lewis, Thomas Jefferson and the Opening of the American West* (New York: Simon and Schuster, 1995). Provides a feel for the burgeoning west and the movement to it.
2. F. R. Webber, *A History of Preaching in Britain and America* (Milwaukee: Northwestern, 1957), 3:217.
3. A. K. Curtis, ed. "Spiritual Awakenings in North America," *Christian History,* 8, no. 3, issue 23:24ff.
4. W. P. Strickland, ed., *Autobiography of Peter Cartwright: The Backwoods Preacher* (Cincinnati: Jennings and Graham, 1856), 54.
5. Ibid., 68.
6. Ibid., 80.
7. Ibid., 406.
8. Ibid., 477.

10.1.3 Lorenzo Dow—The Eccentric in the Pulpit

> The language of my heart is, "What is past, I know; what is to come, I know not. Lord, bless me in the business I am set out upon."
>
> Justification by faith is what God does for us, through the death of his Son; but regeneration or the new birth, also called sanctification, is what God does in us by the operation of his Holy Spirit. The first work is pardon, the latter is purity. One is to forgive, the other is to make holy.
>
> —Lorenzo Dow in *Babylon to Jerusalem*

The preacher called Crazy Dow was born **Lorenzo Dow** (1777–1834) in Coventry, Connecticut. He was part of the first surge from the East that spilled westward. Johnny Appleseed (born John Chapman in Massachusetts in the same time frame) went into the Ohio Valley spreading apple seeds and sprouts and the teachings of Swedenborg. Lorenzo Dow, eccentric but grippingly effective as a preacher, headed west spreading the gospel.

Asthmatic from childhood, through his whole life Dow had visions and dreams beyond the ordinary. He had a long beard and hair to his shoulders. His clothing was usually ragged and he was sometimes shoeless, yet he was heard widely, making three preaching tours to Ireland and England. In appearance he was "tall and fragile, stoop-shouldered with thin legs and arms, a thin nose and bright blue eyes in a pallid face. He was generally wrapped in a black cloak . . . his voice was harsh from continual use and he spoke in gasps with difficulty, his shoulders moving convulsively up and down, as he worked his vocal organs as laboriously as a man would work at a dry pump, although with a little more success."[1] He rode or walked many miles each day, usually preaching about noon daily in a meeting house, a bar, or the open air. Sometimes he preached without preliminaries, taking a text and always including his personal testimony. He carried and sold Methodist books and preached many one-week camp meetings. He introduced the camp meeting to English Methodists and thereby provoked a split between the Primitive Methodists and the main body.

Dow was converted under the preaching of Hope Hull, the Methodist evangelist. He was called to preach in a dream he had about John Wesley. In April of 1796, he preached his first sermon. He later wrote of it:

> I being both young in years and ministry, the expectations of many were raised, who did not bear with my weakness and strong doctrine, and would not consent that I should preach there again for some time.[2]

From 1799 to 1801, he ministered in Ireland with considerable effect, returning in 1802 to marry Peggy, whom he always affectionately called "my rib." He made a great swing down through Georgia and preached "the first Protestant sermon in Alabama." He did five hundred to eight hundred meetings a year. Because of his idiosyncratic ways, he was always in and out of acceptance in Methodist circles. He had the unfortunate tendency to pick peculiar texts and controversial titles like "Good News from Hell." It was Dow who preached against women's hairstyles from the text "Top-knot come down" (Matt. 24:17 actually says, "Let him who is on the housetop not come down"). He was known to have jumped out the window after a meeting just to move on a little more rapidly. Critics spoke of "the taint of vulgar popularity" which tended to adhere to "Lorenzo," or "the cosmopolite," as he called himself. The shaggy stranger was not only a pamphleteer but gave himself to peddling "Lorenzo Dow's Family Medicine."

Dow would occasionally stuff miscellaneous information into his sermons. His preaching became increasingly dominated by lurid prophecies of woe. Once when preaching about those "cast into hell" he heaved a young boy across the room.[3] He gave himself increasingly to the popularization of the "popish menace." But his famous "watch sermon" made effective visual use of the timepiece.

His dear Peggy died of consumption after fifteen years of marriage. Although he soon remarried, Dow himself died in 1834 at the age of fifty-six. He wrote twenty-five books and dreamed of establishing a city of peace, Loren, in western Wisconsin.

The heart of his conviction is reflected in words he wrote "On the Ministry":

> How shall one know whether it be his own duty to preach or not? There are but three evidences by which he may be able to judge and determine concerning him on that subject: (1) Divine evidence in his own soul; or (2) by the fruits of his labor; or (3) the witness of his word with power.[4]

Because of his strong dependence on the Holy Spirit he was accused of being "Quakerized."[5] But the truth of the matter was that his word was with great power. Despite his many eccentricities, Crazy Dow was part of that noble army who brought Christ to the farthest reaches of the frontier.

---

1. Charles Coleman Sellers, *Lorenzo Dow: The Bearer of the Word* (New York: Minton, Balch and Company, 1928), 5.
2. Lorenzo Dow, *The Life, Travels, Labors and Writings of Lorenzo Dow, Including*

His Singular and Erratic Wanderings in Europe and America (New York: R. Worthington, 1881), 27.

3. Sellers, *Lorenzo Dow,* 214.
4. Dow, *The Life, Travels, Labors and Writings,* 396. Earle E. Cairns gives Dow a prominent place in *An Endless Line of Splendor.*
5. J. Gilchrist Lawson, *Deeper Experience of Famous Christians* (Anderson, Ind.: Warner, 1911), 223.

10.1.4 Phoebe Palmer—A Sister in the Pulpit

> This Revelation—holy, just and true—
> Though oft I read, it seems forever new;
> While light from heaven upon its pages rest,
> I feel its power, and with it I am blest.
>
> —Phoebe Palmer, age eleven

Walter Palmer (1804–1890), himself a well-known physician, and his wife **Phoebe Palmer** (1807–1874) traveled much in churches and camp meetings and saw more than 25,000 persons receive pardon. Phoebe came to prominence in the spiritual stirring often called the Third Awakening. This great work sprang out of a vital prayer movement in New York City, as ten thousand people met daily for prayer from 1857 to 1859.

The Palmers ministered with powerful impact in Canada, the United States, and in the British Isles. Phoebe Palmer also established the Five Points Mission in the Bowery in New York City, reinforcing Timothy Smith's important thesis tying revivalism in with social and benevolent concerns.[1]

Phoebe Worrall Palmer was born in New York City in a devout home and converted at an early age. She married Dr. Palmer at age nineteen and was "quickened in the divine life" at a revival in the Allen Street Methodist Episcopal Church after the death of her firstborn son. With her sister she initiated "The Tuesday Meeting" in the interest of a deeper Christian life.[2] She began to probe the Scriptures and to develop an "altar theology" that became part of her enlarging Bible teaching ministry. She wrote extensively on sanctification and prophecy and on the return of the Jews to Palestine. Palmer had a marked influence on Bishop Matthew Simpson and William and Catherine Booth.

As one not ordained, it was quite a while before Phoebe acknowledged that her speaking was in fact preaching. Close inspection of her writings and sermons shows how much John Wesley and John Fletcher shaped her thinking and style. She was steeped in the biblical commentaries of Adam Clarke. She was indefatigable in her promotion of scriptural holiness, arguing that revival was "only a return to primitive Christianity untrammeled by mere human opinions and church conventionalisms."[3] She could discourse for an hour without her voice tiring. The fruit was gathered at the altar.

Palmer's sermonic structure was simple and direct, her content rich with a heavy overlay of exhortation. Her record of overseas itineration is particularly moving, and the richness of her work *The Way of Holiness* is wonderfully evident.[4] The Methodist church in the United States increased by more than two hundred thousand members from 1842 to 1850. God was working mightily, and Phoebe Palmer was undeniably one of his remarkable instruments.

---

1. Timothy L. Smith, *Revivalism and Social Reform: American Protestantism on the Eve of the Civil War* (Nashville: Abingdon, 1957; rev. 1980). A classic study in which the Palmers loom large.
2. Charles Edward White, *The Beauty of Holiness: Phoebe Palmer as Theologian, Revivalist, Feminist, and Humanitarian* (Grand Rapids: Francis Asbury/Zondervan, 1986), 9ff.
3. Ibid., 166. See John D. Hannah, "The Layman's Prayer Revival of 1858," in *Bibliotheca Sacra* 134, no. 533 (January–March 1977): 59.
4. Thomas Oden, ed., *Phoebe Palmer: Selected Writings* (Mahwah, N.J.: Paulist, 1988), 165ff.

10.1.5 Christmas Evans—Imagination in the Pulpit

> You will observe that some heavenly ornaments and power from on high are visible in many ministers when under the Divine irradiation, which you cannot approach by merely imitating their artistic excellence, without resembling them in their spiritual taste, fervency and zeal, which Christ and His Spirit "work in them." This will cause, not only your being like unto them in gracefulness of action and propriety of elocution, but will also induce prayer for the anointing of the Holy One, which worketh mightily in the inward man. This is the mystery of effective preaching. We must be endued with power from on high.
>
> —Christmas Evans

In his classic *Handbook of Revivals,* Henry C. Fish advanced the thesis that "foremost among the instumentalities for saving men is the pulpit."[1] Fish cites historical examples and Elder Jacob Knapp and A. B. Earle in his own time as corroboration. A sterling historical instance is certainly **Christmas Evans** (1766–1838), who was born on Christmas Day in South Wales. Evans was called the John Bunyan of Wales, "the one-eyed man from Anglesea," and the "prophet sent from God."

His father was a poor cobbler who died when Christmas was nine. Evans himself lived a rough life with several miraculous escapes from death before his conversion in 1783. At the time of his salvation experience he could neither read nor write. He taught himself to read both Hebrew and Greek so he could truly exegete a text. In 1787, he was waylaid by former carousing friends and lost one of his eyes. He was ordained in 1789 and served two years in North Wales, borrowing most of his sermons from Beveridge and Rowland. Evans then itinerated for several years, preaching five times on Sunday "and walking as far as twenty miles a day."[2] In 1791 he began an extended ministry on the Isle of Anglesea.

Although he was an Arminian Presbyterian early on, Evans became a Calvinistic Baptist. He was one of the greatest Welsh preachers ever. To speak Welsh, it is said that one must have a cold in the head, a knot in the tongue, and a husk of barley in the throat. Evans had to combat the Sandemanian heresy. A blessed filling of the Holy Spirit led to a great revival on the island, and Evans relates, "Thus the Lord delivered me and the people of Anglesea from being swept away by the evils of Sandemanianism."[3] Eventually Evans learned to preach in English and read theology voraciously. Reference to his sermons shows he organized and structured his messages with assiduous care.

Perusal of his remarkable sermons, even though some of the subtleties in the Welsh original cannot be translated, discloses some of the finest sermons ever. Eight of the twenty-two sermons in Joseph Cross' splendid selection treat the meaning of Jesus' death on Calvary. His "covenants" with God are models of entire consecration.[4] He was richly doctrinal and went right to justification by faith and the Christological issues as foundational for everything Christian. He frequently took two mains, as in his superb message on "One God and One Mediator" from 1 Timothy 2:5.[5] In "The Sufferings of Christ" from 1 Peter 2:24, Evans gave meticulous attention to the text and drew subs as well as mains from it.

He preached with unusual imagination, evoking both laughter and convulsive tears in his hearers. Above all, "Jesus Christ and him crucified" was "the alpha and the omega" of Christmas Evans' utterance.[6]

---

1. Henry C. Fish, *Handbook of Revivals* (Harrisonburg, Va.: Gano, 1874, 1988), 254.
2. Earle E. Cairns, *An Endless Line of Splendor: Revivals and Their Leaders from the Great Awakening to the Present* (Wheaton, Ill.: Tyndale House, 1986), 139.
3. J. Gilchrist Lawson, *Deeper Experiences of Famous Christians* (Anderson, Ind.: Warner, 1911), 206.
4. Christmas Evans, *Sermons and Memoirs of Christmas Evans* (Grand Rapids: Kregel, 1986), 265.
5. Ibid., 54.
6. Ibid., 299.

10.1.6 Billy Bray—Abounding Joy in the Pulpit

> You must know that the Devil is not deaf either, and yet his servants make a great noise. The Devil would rather see us doubting than hear us shouting . . . If they were to put me in a barrel, I would shout "glory" out through the bunghole. I can say glory, glory; I can sing glory, glory; I can dance glory, glory.
>
> —Billy Bray

God had his mouthpiece even in the far reaches and wilds of Cornwall, England. This was Methodist country after Wesley's escapades in quest of the tin miners, but **Billy Bray** (1794–1868) was the man God used to dot the landscape with chapels for the preaching of the Word of God. The area desperately needed his spiritual fervor.

The noted scholar and skeptic of this century, A. L. Rowse, has chronicled his own Cornish childhood and noted how the local rector had preached a particularly moralizing sermon one Sunday and then the next day decamped with the church organist. The successor was "intolerably tedious," with a penchant for the pyramids, British Israelism, and Christadelphianism.[1]

Small in stature but great in heart, Billy Bray was born in Twelveheads near Truro and became a drunken and dissolute man. Like the vast majority of his people, he was a tin miner and several times was nearly killed in his dangerous work.

Bray was soundly converted after reading Bunyan's *Visions of Heaven and Hell* and began to preach in chapels and in fields. He soon became one of Cornwall's "most illustrious sons."[2] Bray worked with the Wesleyans and the Primitive Methodists but was a part of the Bible Christian movement (Bryanites) that built chapels all over the countryside. This joyous, loving, trusting believer truly walked with the living Christ.[3] The remarkable answers to his prayers and his childhood confidence in the Lord made him a legend in his own time.

He never stopped working in the mines, but traveled weekends in his somber clerical black. He preached three times on a Sunday, singing loudly en route and back. Often he was joined by happy pilgrims.[4] The Bible was Bray's only textbook, and his sermons were simple explanations of Scripture with appropriate appeal. His illustrations were common but effective—"a farmer digging potatoes, the fall of a rock in a tin mine, an auction sale of household goods, the sight of a burning cottage, and even a woman caring tenderly for a sickly barnyard fowl."[5] In preaching to a group of miners on Jesus' words, "I am the Bread of Life," Bray said:

> Precious loaf this! The patriarchs and prophets ate of this loaf, and never found a bit of crust about it. The apostles and martyrs ate of this loaf, too, for many long years, and never found a bit of "vinny" in it. And bless the Lord! Poor old Billy Bray can eat it without teeth and get fat on it![6]

Bray was a man of such absorbing prayer and intercession "who set the Lord always before him." He had a strong influence on the Anglican minister **William Haslam** (1818–1905), who was converted and became a flaming preacher through the whole of England, "admonishing the people against a mere outward loyalty to externals rather than trust in the Lamb of God that taketh away the sin of the world."[7] When Haslam preached his fervent message on this theme in St. Paul's Cathedral in 1874, he nearly broke up the furniture in his zeal. The theme and thrust of Billy Bray lived again!

Billy Bray caught the fancy of both Spurgeon and Queen Victoria. Mark Guy Pearse maintained that "from one end of Cornwall to another, no name is so familiar as Billy Bray."[8]

1. A. L. Rowse, *A Cornish Childhood* (London: Clarkson L. Potter, 1942), 136.
2. F. R. Webber, *A History of Preaching in Britain and America* (Milwaukee: Northwestern, 1952), 1:727.

3. John Tallach, *God Made Them Great* (Edinburgh: Banner of Truth, 1974), 69ff.
4. Webber, *A History of Preaching,* 1:730.
5. Ibid., 1:731.
6. Ibid., 1:744.
7. F. W. Bourne, *Billy Bray: The King's Son* (London: Epworth, 1877), 29.
8. Ibid., 31.

10.1.7 Dwight Lyman Moody—Flaming Fire in the Pulpit

> I know perfectly well that, wherever I go and preach, there are many better preachers known and heard than I am; all that I can say about it is that the Lord uses me.
>
> —D. L. Moody

> If you will stop preaching your own words and preach God's Word, He will make you a power for good.
>
> —Henry Moorhouse to D. L. Moody

Dwight Lyman Moody (1837–1899) was known for murdering the king's English. He could pronounce Nebuchadnezzar in two syllables. Yet his evangelistic preaching missions in the United States and Britain were part of a virile spiritual quickening in the 1870s and afterward, which strongly defied the incursions of secularism and unbelief.

William G. McLoughlin is quick to dismiss Moody as "a young tycoon of the revival trade,"[1] as is Sidney Mead. And Iain Murray, from the standpoint of imperial Calvinism, looks askance at Moody as a mere promoter of "revivalism" (as he does to Wesley and Finney) rather than as a leader in "godly revival" because of the tilt toward Arminianism.[2] But serious historians like Gundry and Findlay see Moody's powerful impact as much more than "a backward look at a simpler America."

The fifth of nine children, Moody was born in Northfield, Massachusetts. His father was a heavy-drinking brickmason who died when Dwight was four. The impoverished family was aided by the Unitarian Congregational Church.[3] At seventeen, Moody went to Boston to sell shoes for his uncle, an arrangement contingent upon his attending church at the Mt. Vernon Congregational Church. His Sunday school teacher from that church, Edward Kimball, came to his shoe store and led him to Christ in 1855. Moody never before had heard of the new birth. His acceptance into membership was deferred a year because of his abysmal ignorance of the Scripture. In 1856 he moved to Chicago to sell shoes and met Emma Revell, who was to be his wife, at the Wells Street Mission of the First Baptist Church. In the swell of revival in the city, he organized the North Market Sabbath School. His amazing gifts as a soulwinner soon became evident. He became known as Crazy Moody because of his zeal, and soon built attendance to fifteen hundred boys and girls.

John Farwell of First Methodist Episcopal Church saw how Moody could tell a Bible story and influence these children. He cast his substantial resources into the cause that ultimately became the Moody Church. Henry Sloan Coffin heard Moody preach on "Dan'l" at Northfield and felt it so vividly that he later said, "He made us feel we were right on the spot." Abraham Lincoln was invited by Farwell to attend on one occasion and spoke briefly, protesting "I have never preached a sermon in my life."

Moody did Civil War duty working with Union soldiers in the border states, returning to Chicago to work with the YMCA and his Sunday school. In 1867 Moody visited Britain to meet and study the methods of Charles Spurgeon and George Müller. In England and Scotland, Spurgeon, the Bonars, and R. W. Dale were strong supporters, the latter testifying that what drew him to Moody was the fact that he never talked about lost souls without tears in his eyes. A convert in England was C. T. Studd's father. While in Dublin, Moody heard **Henry Varley** issue the challenge: "The world has yet to see what God will do with and for and through and in and by the man who is fully consecrated to him." Also formative in his influence was the English boy preacher **Henry Moorhouse** (1840–1880), who preached for Moody in Chicago and urged him to be more inductive in his study of Scripture and to give "Bible readings." Moorhouse preached night after night from John 3:16. Moody was moved.[4]

While raising funds in the East after the great Chicago fire of 1871 had destroyed the tabernacle and his home, Moody had a deepening touch and anointing of the Holy Spirit.[5] About this time **Ira D. Sankey** (1840–1908), whom Moody met at a YMCA convention in Indianapolis, began to travel the world with him. Moody traveled more than a million miles and preached to more than a million people with converts by the thousands.[6]

Moody's theology was simple and direct: ruined by the fall, redeemed by the blood, regenerated by the Spirit. His famous sermon on the new birth was preached 183 recorded times from 1881 to 1899.[7] Undoubtedly Plymouth Brethren preachers like John Nelson Darby, Henry Moorhouse, C. H. McIntosh, and George Müller influenced Moody theologically, especially in his eschatology.[8] While the campaigns around the world were always controversial, the great Chicago Revival of 1876 was typical. Out of a population of four hundred thousand people, half of the city was unchurched. In the three-and-one-half months of the campaign, a tabernacle seating eight thousand was built; more than nine hundred thousand attended with six thousand names added as converts. Moody spent the first two weeks of the campaign on the Christians. The song service linked the people together, and then Moody got up to preach in his "locomotive style of delivery."[9] No offering was taken until the end, and the offering was then given to the YMCA. At the last service four hundred converts sat together. He always used the inquiry room for seekers.

As the years passed, Moody added considerable weight to his bullish frame. Yet he was first of all a "muscular Christian" with an extraordinary sensitivity to his audience. His sermons were simply constructed and delivered without great emotional volatility. Sometimes he would preach from the wordless book with the black, red, white, and gold leaves. He would gather material for his sermons, which were more topical than textual, in envelopes. He used interleafed Bibles with his handwritten notes intercalated. He read Scripture slowly but accelerated as he preached to about 220 words per minute. He held unswervingly to biblical inerrancy but fellowshiped with believers who did not share his way of stating his conviction. He invited many of them to the great Northfield Conference he established. Both R. A. Torrey in his famous *Why God Used D. L. Moody* and Charles Erdman in his splendid study attribute a great part of Moody's success in ministry to the character and quality of his dedication to biblical preaching.[10] His great book of messages on heaven is peerless as an exposition of where heaven is, who its inhabitants will be, and how to get there.[11] In his classic message on "The Results of True Repentance," he draws out five specific consequences of genuine repentance, but he does not always have such a clear outline.[12] He often preached on the blood of Christ,[13] and many of his sermons are included in the Sword of the Lord series of *Great Sermons*.[14] After Moody's death, John R. Mott (himself a convert of Moody's meetings) observed:

> I can safely say that I have not visited a country in Europe, Asia or Africa, where the words of Mr. Moody are not bearing fruit. Next to the words of the Bible, and possibly those of Bunyan, his words have been translated into more tongues than those of any other man. Oh, the infinite possibilities of the surrendered, subjugated, consecrated tongue . . .[15]

---

1. William G. McLoughlin, *Modern Revivalism* (New York: Ronald Press, 1959), 216.
2. Iain H. Murray, *Revival and Revivalism: The Making and Marring of American Evangelicalism, 1750–1858* (Edinburgh: Banner of Truth, 1995). This unfortunate book is well reviewed by Mark Noll, "How We Remember Revivals," in *Christianity Today* (April 24, 1995): 31ff., in which Noll points out that such heroes of Murray as Charles Hodge were critical of all revivals, including those very dear to Murray. Such a matter is not mentioned in Murray.
3. The best Moody biography must still be that of John Pollock, *Moody: The Biography* (Chicago: Moody, 1963, 1983).
4. William R. Moody, *The Life of Dwight L. Moody* (New York: Revell, 1900), 137. Pollock's *Moody* shows Moody's adaptation of the "Bible Reading" from Moorhouse (90). In chapter 11 we shall deal at length with the development of the "Bible Reading" or renewal of the ancient homily among the Brethren.
5. J. Gilchrist Lawson, *Deeper Experiences of Famous Christians* (Anderson, Ind.: Warner, 1911), 348.
6. Ira D. Sankey, *My Life and the Story of the Gospel Hymns* (Philadelphia: Sunday School Times, 1906). The conversion of the noted medical missionary, Wilfred Grenfell, is chronicled in *A Labrador Doctor: Wilfred Thomas Grenfell,* in which he tells how he came to Christ in 1885 in a Moody-Sankey tent.
7. Stanley N. Gundry, *Love Them In: The Life and Theology of D. L. Moody* (Chicago: Moody, 1976).
8. James F. Findlay, *Dwight L. Moody: American Evangelist* (Chicago: University of Chicago, 1969), 125.

9. Darrel M. Robertson, *The Chicago Revival: 1876* (Metuchin, N.J.: Scarecrow, 1989). A rich study.
10. Charles R. Erdman, *D. L. Moody: His Message for Today* (New York: Revell, 1928).
11. D. L. Moody, *Heaven* (Chicago: Moody, 1880).
12. D. L. Moody, *The Overcoming Life* (Chicago: Moody, 1986, 1994), 40.
13. Wilbur M. Smith, ed., *Great Sermons on the Death of Christ* (Natick, Mass.: W. A. Wilde, 1965), 33ff.
14. Curtis Hutson, ed., *Great Sermons on the Holy Spirit* (Murfreesboro, Tenn.: Sword of the Lord, 1988), 49.
15. Smith, *Great Sermons on the Death of Christ,* 44.

10.1.8 Brownlow North—Gentleman in the Pulpit

> God helping me, I will stand or fall by the Lord Jesus Christ. I will put my trust in His truth, and in His teaching as I find it in the written Word of God; and doing that, so sure as the Lord Jesus Christ is the truth, I must be forgiven and saved.
>
> Don't think that I am intruding into the office of the holy ministry. I am not an authorized preacher, but I'll tell you what I am; I am a man who has been at the brink of the bottomless pit and has looked in, and as I see many of you going down to that pit, I am here to "hollo" you back and warn you of your danger. I am here, also, as the chief of sinners, saved by grace, to tell you that the grace that saved me can surely save you.
>
> —Brownlow North

As D. L. Moody was never formally ordained, neither was the gentleman evangelist **Brownlow North** (1810–1875). This was a time of great spiritual awakening. From 1762 to 1862 there were fifteen outstanding revivals in Wales alone. In these stirrings, 110,000 converts were added to the churches.[1]

Brownlow North was born into a Scottish noble family. He was a grandnephew of Lord North, who was Prime Minister under George III, and his grandfather was bishop of Winchester. North attended Eton and graduated from Magdalen College at Oxford. He had a wild spirit, but his godly mother prayed unceasingly for him. The death of a friend in a horseback riding accident sobered him. North spent some time in Ireland, married, and later settled in Aberdeenshire. In November of 1854 he fell under great conviction of sin while playing cards and was converted. The duchess of Gordon led him into a remarkable mastery of the Word and into ministry. He became a dedicated winner of souls and an evangelistic preacher of unusual power.

Called by some the John the Baptist of the revival of 1859, Brownlow North was known for his great earnestness. One newspaper in Stirling gave this account:

> The intense earnestness of his manner, indicative of the deepest feeling of compassion for the perishing, was obviously the grand secret of his

> tremendous moral power. The most common truths appear to be unheard-of-realities, because they are manifestly the utterance of a mind to which they are real, present, and momentous, and they enter many a startled ear because pronounced with burning lips as a message from the Majesty of heaven.[2]

He ministered through the British Isles with one object: "the preaching of the Word and gaining souls for the Master."[3] His intense reverence for the Scriptures and their plenary authority was foundational. Early in 1859 a great wave of the Spirit broke out in Northern Ireland (Ulster) in which one hundred thousand converts were added to the churches. His expositions from Luke 16:19–31 were often preached to thousands in the open air. Five thousand persons listened in the marketplace at Londonderry, eleven thousand at Ballymena, and twelve thousand at Newtonlimavady. Sermons on such engaging themes as "How the Beggar Became Rich," "How the Rich Man Became Poor," and the classic "Earnest, Heart-felt, Too-late Prayer" capitalized on the story line in the narrative as North argued that no one is lost because he is rich or saved because he is poor. "The cups of both were filled to the brim,"[4] he stated. His preaching was rooted deeply in the text and his confidence in the sufficiency of the Scriptures.

---

1. Efion Evans, *Revival Comes to Wales* (Cardiff: Evangelical Press of Wales, 1979), 97, 99.
2. K. Moody-Stuart, *Brownlow North: His Life and Work* (London: Banner of Truth, 1878, 1961), 57.
3. Ibid., 69. An important study: R. F. Foster, *Paddy and Mr. Punch: Connections in Irish and English History* (London: Penguin, 1995). An Irish historian dismantles "the romantic myth" of Irish enslavement.
4. Brownlow North, *The Rich Man and Lazarus* (London: Banner of Truth, 1960), 15.

10.2 THE SURGING FLOW OF THE MISSIONARIES

> Therefore go and make disciples of all nations, baptizing them in the name of the Father and of the Son and of the Holy Spirit, and teaching them to obey everything I have commanded you.
>
> —Matthew 28:19–20

> Go into all the world and preach the good news to all creation.
>
> —Mark 16:15

Spiritual awakening, biblical preaching, and the gracious visits of the Holy Spirit not only counteracted a flood-tide of error and unbelief but also quickened evangelization both at home and abroad. An inevitable concomitant of spiritual renewal was the fueling of missionary expansion on all fronts. In his massive treatment of the history of missions, Kenneth Scott Latourette calls the period from 1815 to 1914 "the great century." Volume 4 particularly zeroes in on the factors which ignited an unparalleled expansion of the Christian faith among the nations.[1] This was, as Ruth Tucker points out, "the Protestant Era," and commercial expansion and colonialism were interwoven with gospel extension in a complex mix. Nevertheless this was a period when preaching went global and the harvest was vast.[2]

1. Kenneth Scott Latourette, *The Great Century,* vol. 4 (Grand Rapids: Zondervan, 1941, 1969).
2. Ruth A. Tucker, *From Jerusalem to Irian Jaya* (Grand Rapids: Zondervan, 1983), 109ff.

10.2.1 Opening Up Africa—David Livingstone

> 19 March 1872—Birthday. My Jesus, my King, my life, my All; I again dedicate my whole self to Thee. Accept me and grant, O gracious Father, that ere this year is gone I may finish my task. In Jesus' Name I ask it. Amen, so let it be. David Livingstone.
>
> —written in his diary shortly before his death

Unduly lionized by some and unreasonably lambasted by others as an agent of imperialism, **David Livingstone** (1813–1873) was foremost a missionary of the cross and secondarily an explorer and an antagonist of the slave trade.[1] His ancestors came from the island of Ulva off Scotland and settled in Blantyre in the Scottish Highlands, where Livingstone was born. His father was a poor but devout man who sold tea from door to door. The elder Livingstone left the highly Calvinist kirk for an independent Congregational church in nearby Hamilton. He sent his son Charles to Finney's school at Oberlin in the U.S. because he agreed with Finney that "The Holy Spirit is given to all who ask."[2] A similar independency characterized his son David, who leaned more to the Church of England later in his life but never joined it.

David Livingstone started working at age ten as a cotton-spinner in a factory. He used to say his parental home was the mirror image of *The Cotter's Saturday Night,* and David knew considerable spiritual conviction early on. After reading Dick's *Philosophy of a Future State,* he was converted and sensed a call to missions overseas. "He could now see that all he needed to do was to seek God with all his heart, hand over to him the penitent soul, and accept the pardon purchased by Jesus' blood on Calvary."[3] Livingstone studied medicine in Glasgow and applied to serve under the London Missionary Society. He was strongly evangelical and decidedly influenced by the ideas of **Vinet** (cf. 9.6.4).[4] Trained as a preacher by Richard Cecil, who stressed memorization of the manuscript, Livingstone's first effort was a disaster. He began reading his text and then said abruptly, "Friends, I have forgotten all I had to say," and fled.[5] Yet he was ordained in 1840 and sailed for the Cape of Africa the next year. He commenced his mission work with **Robert Moffat** (cf. 8.4.7), whose daughter Mary he would marry.

Livingstone spent thirty years in Africa, returning home twice for only two years. While on his first furlough in 1857, he published his famous *Missionary Travels,* which built some of the myth around the man. He was five foot six inches tall—slender and sinewy. Once he was severely mauled by a lion and thereafter was unable to raise his right arm. He often knew great loneliness in the bush along with weakness through fever and hunger. One of his sons, Robert, served with the Union Army in the American Civil War and died in a prisoner-of-war camp in Atlanta in 1865. But truly he was an indefatigable servant of Christ. Blaikie describes Livingstone's preaching:

> Livingstone was in the habit of preaching to the natives and conversing seriously with them on religion, his favorite topics being the love of Christ, the Fatherhood of God, the resurrection, and the last judgment. His preaching to them, in Dr. Moffat's judgment, was highly effective. It was simple, scriptural, conversational, went straight to the point, was well fitted to arrest the attention, and remarkably adapted to the capacity of the people. To his father he writes (July 5, 1848): "For a long time I felt much depressed after preaching the unsearchable riches of Christ to apparently insensible hearts; but now I like to dwell on the love of the great Mediator, for it always warms my own heart, and I know that the gospel is the power of God—the great means which He employs for the regeneration of our ruined world."[6]

He loved to speak of Jesus but was often spurned and he felt it deeply. In traveling twenty-nine thousand miles—discovering Victoria Falls and many other key sites—he undoubtedly preached to more Africans than many missionaries ever dreamed. One of his early converts was Chief Sechele, who with Setefano was among the earliest baptized.

Livingstone said, "I am a missionary, heart and soul. God had an only Son, and He was a missionary and a physician. A poor, poor imitation of Him I am, or wish to be. In this service I hope to live, in it I wish to die." His wife died at Shapanga in 1862 and left him with motherless children.

Livingstone's second term out was not under the London Missionary Society but directly under the British government. In this term he was lost from all contact for two years, and the Welsh journalist, **Henry M. Stanley,** went out and found him. At that time Livingstone had no book but the Bible in his possession. Livingstone's life and testimony won Stanley to Christ in the heart of Africa.[7]

He was truly an evangelist, pleading with the townspeople of Blantyre on a visit home "to accept God's offers of mercy to them in Christ and give themselves wholly to Him. To bow down before God was not mean; it was manly. His one wish for them all was that they might have peace with God and rejoice in the hope of the eternal inheritance."[8]

Livingstone was always sound, differing from Bishop Colenso's liberal and critical views of Scripture.[9] "I cannot leave Africa with my work unfinished," he stated. His faithful valet Susi found him dead, kneeling in prayer by his bed, on

April 29, 1873. We possess few of his sermons, but we sense how his proclamation of the gospel remains as one of the most heroic chapters in the saga of the preaching of the grace of God.

---

1. The conclusion of "David Livingstone and Africa," a seminar at the Centre of African Studies at the University of Edinburgh held on the centenary of Livingstone's death, May 4–5, 1973, and published with the proceedings.
2. Tim Jeal, *Livingstone* (New York: Putnam, 1973), 12. The most solid recent treatment of Livingstone, but a work that does not truly understand his spiritual ministry. A lavishly illustrated study is Elspeth Huxley's *Livingstone and His African Journeys* (New York: Saturday Review Press, 1974).
3. Jessie Kleeberger, *David Livingstone: Missionary Explorer of Africa* (Anderson, Ind.: Gospel Trumpet, 1925), 10.
4. W. G. Blaikie, *The Personal Life of David Livingstone* (New York: Revell, 1880), 40.
5. Kleeberger, *David Livingstone,* 14.
6. Blaikie, *The Personal Life of David Livingstone,* 110. Blaikie's study is old but the most inwardly sensitive to the spirit of the man.
7. Charles J. Finger, *David Livingstone: Explorer and Prophet* (Garden City, N.Y.: Doubleday, 1927), 257.
8. Blaikie, *The Personal Life of David Livingstone,* 240. Of immense interest are *Livingstone's Family Letters* (Westport, Conn.: Greenwood, 1959), in 2 volumes.
9. Ibid., 362. Frank Boreham's great sermon on "David Livingstone's Text" on the Great Commission which contains his famous words, "It is the word of a gentleman," is to be found in *A Bunch of Everlastings* (New York: Abingdon, 1920), 129ff. Colenso was a radical missionary bishop who adversely effected John Henry Newman's brother (cf. 9.3.3).

10.2.2 Pioneer in China—J. Hudson Taylor

> Perishing China so filled my heart and mind that there was no rest by day and little sleep by night, till health gave way.
>
> The secret was that Jesus was satisfying the deep thirst of heart and soul.
>
> I did long to be able to tell them the Glad Tidings.
>
> —J. Hudson Taylor

Another cross-cultural crusader for Christ whose preaching was pivotal was **James Hudson Taylor** (1832–1905), the great pace-setting missionary who opened up the heart of China to the gospel. Born in Yorkshire to praying parents, he was reared as a Methodist. His father was a somewhat disaffected class leader who moved into the Methodist Free Church while young Taylor increasingly fellowshiped with the Plymouth Brethren. James was converted in 1849 when his mother was on her knees interceding for him as he read a booklet on the finished work of Christ.[1]

At an early age, Taylor spoke of God's call to go to China. China was a troubled country, with its Western influence confined to the treaty ports.[2] Taylor worked as a dispenser for Dr. Richard Hardey and began medical school with the help of the Chinese Evangelization Society founded by Dr. Gutzlaf of Hong Kong. While still in Hull in England he preached his first sermon. The call of God burned in his being. He wrote his sister of the experience:

> On Tuesday I went to preach at Royston. The room was crowded; there would be from fifty to sixty present. I never was so blessed in my life. We had a prayer-meeting afterwards in which ten or twelve took part. One little girl of about thirteen came to the penitent-form and professed to find peace. She is young, but Jesus can keep her.[3]

At age twenty-one he sailed for China on a five-and-a-half month voyage. During the trip he held sixty services on board, systematically opening Scripture beginning with Romans 4.[4] Arriving in China he first heard preaching in the Shanghai dialect and set himself to language study. We must bear in mind that most of these missionaries did their preaching in languages which were not easy to learn.

Dressing as a Chinese—to the disapproval of most of the other missionaries—Taylor began his preaching tours in 1855 and baptized his first convert.[5] Excited crowds gathered, and he gave himself to his itinerant vision of "preaching where Christ was not named."[6] On his fifth journey, Taylor recorded his search for an appropriate pulpit from which to preach and used a bronze incense vase. He described the response:

> At the lowest computation, five or six hundred persons must have been present, and I do not think it would be over the mark to say a thousand. As they quieted down, I addressed them at the top of my voice, and a more orderly, attentive audience in the open air one could not wish to see. It was most encouraging to hear one and another call out . . . pugh-ts's, pugh-ts's . . . not wrong, not wrong, as they frequently did when something said met with their approval.[7]

Taylor anguished over the death of his wife, Maria, and several of his children. He struggled for personal holiness, resolving his quest to a large degree with his discovery of the believer's union with Christ. Taylor exclaimed, "I am one with Christ." He endured conflict with other missionaries over such things as baptism. Taylor himself was eventually rebaptized among the Brethren in Hull. The Anglican leader, George Moule, was upset, but ultimately many Anglicans became part of the China Inland Mission founded by Taylor on his first furlough.

The China Inland Mission (OMF today) sprang out of the Great Revival of 1859 and "the hidden years" (1860–1864) when Taylor stayed in England. In all of this time he had great joy in preaching and was heard often at Keswick, where he enjoyed a lifelong association. It was at Keswick that he led F. B. Meyer into the truth of the Spirit-led life. Taylor held to the inerrancy of Scripture and the imminency of Christ's return involved with the return of the Jews to Palestine. He visited America and preached at both the Niagara Conference and at Northfield. He developed deep ties with Lord Radstock in the raising of funds for sending out personnel and rejoiced at Radstock's later revival ministry among Tsarist nobles in Russia.[8]

Taylor was associated with the young evangelist H. Grattan Guiness in meetings in Dublin. Good samples of his preaching in the Western world are to be found in his studies in the Song of Solomon titled *Union and Communion.*[9] These messages were widely heard and a trifle allegorical—not strange to Plymouth Brethren ears.

Yet his life and ministry were mainly in China, where he would often preach to workers in English on Sundays and then go on his journeys into the interior during the week. "I never made a sacrifice," he would say, but he faced bandits, uprisings, hostilities, and great dangers with his beloved Savior and his dear old harmonium to accompany singing. By 1900 the China Inland Mission had 750 missionaries under call. The summons was to men and women "to live and preach Christ openly!"[10]

---

1. Dr. and Mrs. Howard Taylor, *Hudson Taylor's Spiritual Secret* (London: China Inland Mission, 1932), 13–14.
2. J. C. Pollock, *Hudson Taylor and Maria* (Grand Rapids: Zondervan, 1962), 22. The best modern biography.
3. Dr. and Mrs. Howard Taylor, *Hudson Taylor: The Early Years—The Growth of a Soul* (London: China Inland Mission, 1911), 1:105. The large two-volume work is classic and every page brimming with blessing. The leader of the Assembly in Hull was Andrew Jukes, whose *The Law of the Offerings* (London: Lamp Press, 1954) is immensely helpful.
4. Ibid., 1:192.
5. Pollock, *Hudson Taylor and Maria,* 51.
6. Taylor, *Hudson Taylor,* 1:186.
7. Ibid., 1:279.
8. Pollock, *Hudson Taylor and Maria,* 130; also Taylor, *Spiritual Secret,* 83.
9. J. Hudson Taylor, *Union and Communion: Thoughts on the Song of Solomon Relating to Personal Fellowship with Christ* (Chicago: Moody, n.d.). Fifty thousand copies are in print; introduction by J. Stuart Holden.
10. Taylor, *Spiritual Secret,* 149.

10.2.3 BEACON IN SOUTHEAST ASIA—ADONIRAM JUDSON

> In the great country of America, we sustain the character of teachers and explainers of the contents of the sacred Scriptures of our religion. And since it is contained in those Scriptures, that, if we pass to other countries, and preach and propagate religion, great good will result, and both those who teach and those who receive the religion will be freed from future

> punishment, and enjoy, without decay or death, the eternal felicity of heaven—that royal permission be given, that we, taking refuge in the royal power, may preach our religion in these dominions, and that those who are pleased with our preaching and wish to listen to and be guided by it, whether foreigners or Burmans, may be exempt from government molestation, they present themselves to receive the favor of the excellent king.
>
> —Adoniram Judson in 1819 to the emperor of Burma at Ava

Another valiant emissary of the cross of Christ was **Adoniram Judson** (1788–1850). He was born the oldest of four children in Malden, Massachusetts, to an old-line Congregational minister who opposed New England theology. Adoniram means "Lord of Height," and very early in his life he excelled, learning to read the Bible at three and preaching to other children at four. His favorite childhood hymn was "Go preach my gospel, says the Lord."

Judson went to Brown University, where he graduated valedictorian of his class in 1807, but in the process lost his faith to French infidelity and deism. In 1808, while he was staying in a country inn after a raucous indulgence, he was deeply troubled over the agony of a man in the next room. The next day he was stunned to learn the man had died. That man was Jacob Eames, a compatriot of his in profligacy.[1] Shortly thereafter he was converted and matriculated at Andover Theological Seminary. There he found common cause with a group of young men who had been part of the Haystack Prayer Meetings at Williams College (cf. 9.2.4).

A sermon by Dr. Claudius Buchanan of Bristol inflamed him for missions and caused him to exclaim, "The New Testament is all missions!"[2] Rather than taking the call to be associate to Dr. Griffin at Park Street Church, Boston, Judson took his bride and sailed for India. His penchant for evangelistic preaching had been demonstrated earlier when he was imprisoned by a French privateer. In Bayonne, France, as a prisoner, he pleaded with his hearers to receive Christ with "just the sort of sermons he later preached in Burma."[3] Shortly thereafter they released him.

Although they were sent out by the American Board in 1812, Judson and his wife were moved to shift their views on baptism and were immersed in India. Still, William Carey was dubious about them and sent them on to the Isle of France in the Mauritius Islands, where Judson preached to the English soldiers. About to be sent home, he and his wife hopped on a ship to Rangoon and launched the American Baptist Missionary Union work in Burma.

The Judsons and the small band of workers who joined them worked seven years before their first convert was received. The "extravagant idealism and nihilism" of the Hinayana Buddhism of Burma presented "no God to save, no soul to be saved and no sin to be saved from." Progress was exceedingly slow.

Yet within the first year, the Judsons had commenced public worship and preaching. The Buddhists had zayats, which were covered areas where lay teachers could sit on a raised platform and where people could come to rest and talk. Judson built a Baptist zayat and there preached the gospel.[4] A primary objective in his life was to translate the Bible into Burmese, a task he finished in January 1834. Judson and his family endured brutal persecution, and he was cruelly imprisoned. He lost two wives and two children and was survived by his third wife only a few years in his own passing. He loved to preach, and his wife in *Wayside Preaching* describes his messages:

> His preaching was concrete. He did not deal in vague abstractions. Truth assumed in his mind statuesque forms . . . Behind his words when he preached lay the magnet of a great character.[5]

When Judson was home on furlough he preached biblical messages that sometimes disappointed the crowds, who wanted exciting stories of danger and heroism.[6] Yet his "vigorous sermons tinged with humor" always made a clear mark on the hearers.

Adoniram died after a long illness while out at sea off Burma in a French ship and was buried at sea. His wife, assisted by Dr. Francis Wayland, president of Brown University and a gifted preacher in his own right, developed his memoirs.[7] In tribute to him are Judson churches, Judson Press, Judson College—but more significantly, many souls which shine as stars in the heavens to the praise of our God. At the time of his death in 1850 there were seven thousand converts (both Burmans and Karens, a mountain people in Burma) with sixty-three different congregations and an outreach stretching into Siam and to the Jews.

---

1. L. Helen Percy, *Adoniram Judson: Apostle of Burma* (Anderson, Ind.: Gospel Trumpet, 1926), 19.
2. J. Mervin Hull, *Judson the Pioneer* (Philadelphia: American Baptist Publication Society, 1913), 25.
3. Ibid., 43.
4. Courtney Anderson, *To the Golden Shore: The Life of Adoniram Judson* (Boston: Little, Brown, 1956), 219.
5. Harlan P. Beach, *Knights of the Labarum* (New York: Student Volunteer Movement, 1898), 33.
6. Anderson, *To the Golden Shore,* 457, 462. For the rigor and romance of translation, see Eunice Pike, *Words Wanted* (Chicago: Moody, 1958).
7. Francis Wayland, ed., *Memoirs of Adoniram Judson,* 2 vols. (Boston: Sampson, 1855).

10.2.4 FINDING THE KEY—JOHN LIVINGSTONE NEVIUS

> The Holy Spirit was gradually but continually shedding light into my soul, and taking of the things of Christ and showing them to me. In a word, I am changed . . . I now feel my utter inability to take the first step in the Christian life without divine aid. Sinfulness and selfish motives are mixed with all I do. My only hope is in God's mercy through faith in the Lord Jesus Christ.

> What should be my gratitude to being able so soon to have the oversight of a flock of Christ's sheep in this far-off wilderness; to speak to them in their own tongue of the wonderful works of God; and to point inquiring souls "to the Lamb of God who taketh away the sins of the world"!
>
> —John Livingstone Nevius

John Livingstone Nevius (1829–1893) had two special joys—horses and street preaching. Born in Seneca County in western New York within a staunchly Presbyterian family, Nevius was of Dutch descent. His family possibly dates back to the French Huguenot refugees. His father died when he was two, but his hard-working mother helped him attend Union College in Schenectady. After graduating, he spent a year teaching in Georgia. At this time he came under deep conviction for sin and came to Christ.[1] Then, sensing God's call on his life, he went on to Princeton Theological Seminary in 1850.

During his seminary days he felt especially close to Charles Hodge and was profoundly moved by the preaching of Archibald Alexander.[2] He was always an avid Bible student and gave himself unstintingly to Scripture and to the mastery of "the cardinal doctrines of the Bible."[3] Teaching Sunday school and taking services in the neighboring communities, he felt keenly disappointed in his own preaching but preached on occasion before the president and faculty with increasing approbation.[4] After reading Mrs. Adoniram Judson's memoirs of missionary work in Burma, he responded to the call to China.

In 1853 Nevius sailed for China with his physically fragile bride. They were first stationed for language study at Ningpo, where the church consisted of one hundred disciples. Helen Nevius had to return home for a year and a half, and both of them suffered permanent debilitation from the strange fevers that vexed their bodies. Nevius was made pastor of the native church and preached the Word with facility in Chinese. While Hudson Taylor believed wearing Chinese native dress was advantageous, Nevius felt such effort was futile. Yet the Lord greatly blessed both men with real harvest despite their divergent convictions on this issue. Mrs. Nevius reported:

> My husband's sermons preached on these occasions were carefully prepared, and were listened to with deepest attention.[5]

Their ministry shifted to Hang-Chow and then north to Shantung province and the city of Tung-Chow. This is the area made famous by Langdon Gilkey's *Shantung Compound,* the story of World War II incarceration. Here Nevius continued to preach, travel, and write a systematic theology. The Neviuses made a voyage to England, where they fellowshiped with the Hudson Taylors, and then went on to the United States, where they spent three years before returning to China.

The work in China was growing significantly in spite of famines, rebellions, and the perennial shortage of workers. At this time he was writing his still classic study on demon possession. He translated Luke 8–23 and James 3 to Revelation

2 for the Chinese Bible. He was moderator of the Shanghai Missionary Conference in 1890, when more than four hundred missionaries gathered for prayer and strategizing.

John and Helen Nevius visited "the hermit kingdom" of Korea in 1890 as well as Japan. But it was in Korea that the Nevius Method of "self-governing, self-supporting and self-propagating" missions was most impressively implemented. The Korean revival (1904–1910), saw a 300 percent growth rate in the church.[6]

Nevius was known for his incisive and biblical missionary addresses at home and abroad. He and his wife sailed once again for China in 1892 on the *Empress of China,* and he died there in the following year at the age of sixty-four. He had been a stalwart preacher and a gifted man of vision.[7]

---

1. Helen S. Nevius, *The Life of John Livingstone Nevius* (New York: Revell, 1895), 56ff.
2. Ibid., 73.
3. Ibid., 97.
4. Ibid., 83, 107.
5. Ibid., 160.
6. Roy E. Shearer, *Wildfire: Church Growth in Korea* (Grand Rapids: Eerdmans, 1966); See also "The Koreans' Formula: Independence, Dependence," *The Presbyterian Journal* (February 19, 1969): 9ff.
7. Other significant statements of missionary strategization must include that of another North China missionary, Roland Allen, *Missionary Methods: St. Paul's or Ours* (Chicago: Moody, 1912, 1959) and the definitive work of Johannes Warneck of the Rhenish Mission, *The Living Christ and Dying Heathenism* (Grand Rapids: Baker, 1954), written over against the remarkable response of the Battaks of Sumatra.

10.2.5 Pressing the Parameters—Mary Slessor

> There is nothing small or trivial, for God is ready to take every act and motive and work through them to the formation of character and the development of holy and useful lives that will convey grace to the world.
>
> It was the dream of my childhood to be a missionary to Calabar.
>
> All is dark except above . . . Calvary stands safe and secure.
>
> —Mary M. Slessor

One of the most courageous chapters of missionary expansion was written by **Mary Slessor** (1848–1915), who carried the Word of God into situations of indescribable difficulty. Born in Aberdeen, Scotland, the second of seven children, she was reared by a godly mother who despite a cruel and drunken husband directed her children aright. The preaching of the fires of hell drove Mary to Christ,[1] and the reality of the Savior sustained her as from age eleven she toiled from six to six in the mills.

The mission of the United Presbyterian Church in Calabar (now Nigeria) early gripped her imagination, and the death of Livingstone clinched her call. At age twenty-eight she sailed for the field to work as a missionary teacher in "the white man's graveyard." Already on the coast there were 174 members and one thousand people meeting on the Lord's Day. Her personal text was "Learn of Me," and she opened Scripture with deftness and clarity. The menace of slavers and the darkness of witchcraft and sorcery pressed in upon her, but she visited the hovels and sought to win the respect of both the native chiefs and the governing authorities.

Slessor first learned to speak Efik, the trade language, and at her first opportunity preached on John 5:1–24. She spoke of "their need of healing and saving, of which they must be conscious through their dissatisfaction with this life, the promptings of their higher natures, the experience of suffering and sorrow, and the dark future beyond death, and asking the question 'Wilt thou be made whole?' pointed the way to peace."[2] Slessor developed a considerable ease with the language, conducting large Sunday school classes. "Preaching the love of Christ was her passion."[3] Her visits home were not easy. As she put it:

> I am pained often at home that there is so little of depth, and of God's Word, in the speeches and addresses I hear. It seems as if they thought anything will do for children, and that any kind of talk about coming to Christ and believing on Christ will feed and nourish immortal souls.[4]

Slessor remained convinced that the great need was for the systematic teaching of the Bible.

She almost married on one visit home, but chose to return to Africa when her fiancé was deemed not physically strong enough for service overseas. Upon returning to Calabar, her ministry moved inland to the Okoyongs, a people given to violence and unspeakable cruelty. "No man can do anything with such a people," she conceded, but she saw God perform the impossible. Dressed unlike the other Europeans and without shoes, Slessor marched into the bush to preach Christ. She presented the story of Jesus and persisted in the simple, direct gospel message.[5] She fought malarial fever and terrible boils, claiming Romans 8:11 as her life verse. She served as judge in the courts and as consul for her government, but her obsession was to share the Word wherever she went. Robert Glover in his classic survey of worldwide missions says:

> It is a question if the career of any other woman missionary has been marked by so many strange adventures, daring feats, signal providences, and wonderful achievements.[6]

---

1. W. P. Livingstone, *Mary Slessor of Calabar: Pioneer Missionary* (London: Hodder and Stoughton, 1917), 3.
2. Ibid., 26.

3. Ibid., 34.
4. Ibid., 46.
5. Ibid., 67, 112.
6. T. J. Bach, *Vision and Valor* (Grand Rapids: Baker, 1963), 81.

10.2.6 Into Peril—John G. Paton

> Nothing known to men under Heaven could have produced their new character and disposition except only the grace of God in Christ Jesus. Though still marred by many of the faults of heathenism, they were at the roots of their being really new creatures, trying, according to their best light, to live for and to please their new Master, Jesus Christ.
>
> What power in the gospel! O God, give me health and long life that I may teach the gospel to these people.
>
> —John G. Paton

> Those who are wise will shine like the brightness of the heavens, and those who lead many to righteousness, like the stars for ever and ever.
>
> —Daniel 12:3

The news of the martyrdom of **John Williams,** the apostle to Polynesia, stunned the Christian world, but such was the tidal wave of gospel advance that many sought to take his place or came forward as willing to pay the price wherever the Lord would send. Among these "of whom the world was not worthy" was **John G. Paton** (1824–1906), who came from the old covenanting Reformed Presbyterian Church of Scotland. Though poor—his father was a stocking weaver—family prayers were made morning and evening in his home and the Scripture was central.

For nine years, Paton served the Glasgow City Mission, reaching the lost through outdoor preaching and furthering the cause of total abstinence.[1] Sensing the call to preach the gospel, he sailed in 1828 with his new wife to the New Hebrides, thirty small islands northeast of Australia. "The wail of the perishing heathen in the south seas" was inescapable.[2] The environment was physically hostile. Both his wife and baby died the first year, and the darkness threatened to swallow him up as he stood between the warring inland people and the harbor people. The constant movement of armed men and the shrieks of women being sacrificed took a heavy toll. Nonetheless, he would not be deterred, and he held meetings in the villages to preach against idolatry.[3]

Returning with his second wife, Paton settled in Aniwa, where he established credibility by digging a well and obtaining much-needed water in this unheard-of way.[4] The missions ship *Dayspring* helped them move among the islands, and Paton went back and forth to both sides of the continuing conflict. Cannibals began to praise God—up to six thousand converts in number.[5] The first communion service on Aniwa was memorable. As always the Word was given, "a short and careful exposition of the Ten Commandments and the way of salvation according to the gospel."[6] Paton also translated the Gospel of Mark into the aboriginal tongue.

Itinerating in the homeland was an important opportunity for Paton, and he spoke to fourteen hundred different audiences in a two-year period. Sponsoring him were J. Oswald Dykes, the British Presbyterian, J. Hood Wilson of Edinburgh, Lord Radstock, F. B. Meyer in Leicester, and John Hall of Fifth Avenue Presbyterian in New York City. He was especially effective at the Mildmay Conference in England.

Spurgeon called John Paton the king of the cannibals. How many others there are who ought to be included in this narrative, who like Paton preached the everlasting gospel without fear or favor.

---

1. J. J. Ellis, *John G. Paton: The Story of a Noble Life* (London: Pickering and Inglis, n.d.), 20.
2. John G. Paton, *Autobiography* (New York: Revell, 1898), 85, 87. Appreciation by A. T. Pierson.
3. Bessie L. Byrum, *John G. Paton: Hero of the South Seas* (Anderson, Ind.: Gospel Trumpet, 1924), 96.
4. Ellis, *John G. Paton,* 90; Paton, *Autobiography,* 178–79.
5. Byrum, *John G. Paton,* 108.
6. Paton, *Autobiography,* 221. An extraordinary document.

10.2.7 Around the World—Fredrik Franson

> That which is biblical is everywhere appropriate, for all countries and all peoples.
>
> Fellowship with Jesus and work for Jesus are two preoccupations that we can never assess too highly.
>
> —F. Franson

"The crowds of listeners that streamed to Franson's meetings . . . can be counted in the tens of thousands, and thousands of people came to faith in Christ through his preaching."[1] That fiery preacher was **Fredrik Franson** (1852–1908), not known widely outside of Scandinavia. Yet he was the founder and strategist of a missionary movement of awesome power.

Franson was born into a godly home in Westmanland in Sweden. The revivals kindled by Rosenian pietism fostered an atmosphere of the awareness of sin and grace, but Franson was not converted until emigrating to Nebraska. After a bout with malarial fever, Franson came to Christ in a Swedish Baptist congregation in his community. Feeling God's call, he attached himself as an apprentice to D. L. Moody and joined the Moody Church in Chicago. Franson traveled as an evangelist working in Mormon country. Many Scandinavians had come to Utah under the aegis of the Mormons.

His motto was "Have faith in God," and he broke free from ethnic bonds and preached widely on all continents except Australia. He attended the Evangelical Alliance conference in Copenhagen in 1884; there he met Professor Christlieb (cf. 9.4.6) and heard his great message in German on "The Religious Indifference and the Best Means to Combat It."[2]

Franson's vision for outreach led to the formation of the Scandinavian Alliance Mission in Chicago, known now as the Evangelical Alliance Mission. He networked with both J. Hudson Taylor and A. B. Simpson.[3] He was a great lover of the truth of the Lord's return, but unfortunately in his book, *Himlauret, The Heavenly Clock,* he set a date for the rapture. Franson was close to Andrew Murray in South Africa.[4] He traveled widely in South America and planted churches there that still bear remarkable fruit.

Several societies still vital in Scandinavia trace their lineage to Franson. He must be seen as one of the premier missiologists of his time and a preacher who had great strength in presenting and applying the Scriptures. He said:

> What a difference between Stockholm and Copenhagen! It seems as if the true religion of Jesus has caught hold among both the higher and lower levels of society, and the Gospel is being preached . . . in a great many meeting places. Nevertheless, regardless of how much one works and preaches, it seems as if it is hard to meet the ever growing cravings of the people to hear the Word of God. One must adjust oneself to preach three to four times on Sunday. On coming Ascension Day, I expect to have to speak at five or six meetings.[5]

Fredrik Franson died at fifty-six in Idaho Springs, Colorado, after crossing over to the United States from Mexico to take a short rest from his evangelistic travels.

---

1. Edvard Torjesen, *Fredrik Franson: A Legacy* (Wheaton, Ill.: TEAM, n.d.), 11. Torjesen is *the* Franson scholar today.
2. O. C. Grauer, *Fredrik Franson* (Chicago: Scandinavian Alliance Mission, n.d.), 54.
3. Ibid., 75. To my knowledge, Mrs. J. G. Princell's excellent biography was never translated into English.
4. Ibid., 188. For the choicest on the Swedish situation, see David Nyvall, *My Father's Testament* (Chicago: Covenant, 1974), 197.
5. Edvard Torjesen, *Fredrik Franson: A Model for Worldwide Evangelism* (Pasadena, Calif.: William Carey, 1983), 54.

10.3 THE SWELL AND THE UNDERTOW OF AMERICAN PREACHING

> Two inestimable advantages Christianity has given us: first the Sabbath, the jubilee of the whole world; whose light dawns welcome alike into the closet of the philosopher, into the garret of toil, and into prison cells, and everywhere suggests, even to the vile, the dignity of spiritual being. . . . And secondly, the institution of preaching in the speech of man to man—essentially the most flexible of all organs, or all forms. What

> hinders that now, everywhere, in pulpits, in lecture rooms, in houses, in fields, wherever the invitation of men or your own occasion lead you, you speak the very truth, as your life and conscience teach it, and cheer the waiting, fainting hearts of men with new hope and new revelation.
>
> —Ralph Waldo Emerson's address to the senior class at Harvard Divinity School in 1838

As we turn to consider American preachers in the latter half of the nineteenth century, we must brace for some shock and disappointment. Certainly there were solidly biblical servants of the Word, and we shall note them with appreciation and gratitude. But there was an undertow that arose out of New England theology and its denial of original sin, its depreciation of imputation, and its devaluation of an Anselmian or substitutionary aspect of the atonement. As early as 1831, de Tocqueville, the inveterate French observer, said of American preachers:

> It is often difficult to ascertain from their discourse whether the principal object of religion is to procure eternal felicity in the other world or prosperity in this.

In his invaluable *Cosmos in the Chaos: Philip Schaff's Interpretation of Nineteenth-Century American Religion,* Stephen Graham shares the overview of the great church historian **Philip Schaff** (1819–1893). Schaff came from Germany to teach at Mercersburg Seminary in Pennsylvania and at Union in New York. He was trained at Halle, Tubingen, and Berlin, and took a pietistic stand against Enlightenment rationalism. Schaff also affirmed the authority of Scripture.[1] Yet he was inordinately critical of the Puritans and revivalists, although he liked D. L. Moody.[2] Schaff was antislavery but pro-evolution. He favored biblical revision and oversaw the translation of the Lange commentaries and the assembling of the great *Schaff-Herzog Encyclopedia.* He was a strong advocate of the total abstinence movement and Sabbath societies.

The anguish of the Civil War and the opening of the west must be thoroughly worked into our perspective on the American pulpit at this time.[3]

---

1. Stephen R. Graham, *Cosmos in the Chaos: Philip Schaff's Interpretation of Nineteenth-Century American Religion* (Grand Rapids: Eerdmans, 1995), 74.
2. Ibid., 154.
3. Schaff admired Lincoln's stand. Out of the vast literature, I believe one of the most helpful pieces for our purposes is Elton Trueblood, *Abraham Lincoln: Theologian of American Anguish* (New York: Harper, 1973). Not to be underestimated is Lincoln's own paradigm of communication, particularly the *Gettysburg Address,* 272 words "which remade America"; see Garry Wills, *Lincoln at Gettysburg* (New York: Simon and Schuster, 1992). Lincoln according to Wills was a student of the Word. His use of vernacular rhythms is striking.

10.3.1 Horace Bushnell—Rudderless in the Pulpit

> I have been greatly blessed in my doubtings.
>
> I really did not expect to remain in the ministry long. I thought if I could sometime be called to a professorship of moral philosophy, it would be a more satisfactory field of exertion.
>
> —Horace Bushnell

Without question a brilliant preacher and person of huge intellectual capacity, **Horace Bushnell** (1802–1876) must yet be seen as a tragic figure in American pulpit annals. He was born in Litchfield, Connecticut. His father was a Methodist and his mother an Episcopalian, but he was a member of the only local church, the Congregational.

Bushnell started at Yale in 1823, and after graduating did stints in teaching and in newspaper work in New York. He was not happy, nor was he ever healthy. He returned to Yale to attend law school and remained aloof when revival came to the campus in 1831.[1] His hero was Samuel Taylor Coleridge. Neither sin nor the cross were central in Bushnell's thinking. Nonetheless in 1833 he took the pastorate of North Church, Hartford, where he stayed until he was forced to retire for reasons of health in 1859.

Bushnell has been called the father of liberalism, and indeed in moving beyond New England theology he lurched very close to Unitarianism. Certainly in *God in Christ* he lapsed into Unitarian thinking, espousing a modal view of the Trinity. In his *Vicarious Sacrifice* and *Forgiveness and Law,* Bushnell jettisoned transactual and propitiatory aspects of the atonement. In a reaction against revivalism, he opted for gradualism rather than conversion in his book *Christian Nurture*. Neither did he believe a child to be depraved. He believed the child was to grow up never knowing that he or she is other than a Christian.

Charles Hodge spoke of his views as "less than Christian."[2] For Bushnell the Bible was essentially figurative. In 1866 he indicated his leaning toward understanding the fall in Eden as a myth. Jesus was teacher rather than the crucified and suffering God. His were "orthodox memories, Unitarian hopes."[3] The old wine had not survived being transferred to new bottles.[4] He scoffed at the idea of the Second Coming.[5] He was very theological but he did not preach sound doctrine.

Yet Bushnell was a preacher's preacher. There was a virility in his style and a fire inside him, but the common people were not drawn to his variety of naturalism. Early on, he gained a reputation as a public speaker of note, and his ability to title sermons is dramatic. Little wonder he was offered the presidency of the College of California (later the University of California at Berkeley), which he turned down.[6]

Bushnell's celebrated sermon on "Unconscious Influence" is based on John 20:8, "Then went in also that other disciple." But for Bushnell this had nothing to do with the resurrection or Jesus Christ. He did not do exegesis, and even Brastow speaks of his interpretations as often "fanciful" and lacking "the support of recognized exegetical canons."[7]

Bushnell may have been "a homiletical genius," but he was not a biblical preacher, and his influence upon successive generations has been unfortunate. His sermons were in fact "an essay in social psychology," as David Smith observes.[8] Bushnell's own reflections on preaching are unrelievedly horizontal.[9] If his sermons were on every preacher's shelves in Scotland, we can begin to grasp why Scotland was in such a theological tailspin in the nineteenth century.

---

1. Barbara M. Cross, *Horace Bushnell: Minister to a Changing America* (Chicago: University of Chicago Press, 1958), 10.
2. David L. Smith, *Symbolism and Growth: The Religious Thought of Horace Bushnell* (Chico, Calif.: Scholars Press, 1981), 78.
3. Ibid., 104. For a critique of Bushnell on the atonement, see H. D. McDonald, *The Atonement of the Death of Christ* (Grand Rapids: Baker, 1985), 299. "The penal doctrine was specially anathema."
4. Ibid., 140. On Bushnell's subjective view, see David Wells, "The Collision of Views on the Atonement," *Bibliotheca Sacra* 144, no. 574 (October–December 1987): 374ff.
5. Mary Bushnell Cheney, *Life and Letters of Horace Bushnell* (New York: Arno, 1969), 99.
6. Howard A. Barnes, *Horace Bushnell and the Virtuous Republic* (Metuchen, N.J.: Scarecrow, 1991), 10.
7. Lewis O. Brastow, *Representative Modern Preachers* (New York: Macmillan, 1904), 150.
8. Smith, *Symbolism and Growth*, 49.
9. Horace Bushnell, *Pulpit Talent: Training for the Pulpit Manward* (London: Richard Dickinson, 1882).

10.3.2 Henry Ward Beecher—The Pulpit with a Popular Showman

> I am, in the providence of God, so circumstanced in reference to public speaking, which seems to be my specialty, that I put my whole strength into that and give up everything else to it.
>
> —Henry Ward Beecher

> It was one of the most signal triumphs of oratory in the history of human speech . . . it was also one of the most significant exhibitions of the power of a great personality as the unofficial representative of a nation.
>
> —Lewis Brastow on Beecher's travels in Britain and on the Continent in 1863

Dubbed "the most eloquent preacher of his day" (O. C. Edwards), "the most popular preacher in the Greater New York metropolitan area" (F. R. Webber), and "the greatest preacher of America and of our century . . . the greatest preacher Protestantism has ever produced" (Phillips Brooks), **Henry Ward Beecher** (1813–1887) did indeed build America's largest church at the time and a national pulpit as have few others. However we assess him as a preacher, none will contest William McLoughlin's description of him as "the high priest of American religion."

Beecher was deeply indebted to and influenced by Horace Bushnell, putting Bushnell's message on the wings of a highly emotional oratory. But he was at bottom the exponent of an American religion that was, as Alan Bloom saw it, "a kind of Emersonian gnosticism." "His work was to secularize the American pulpit."[1] Listed by even the gentle Ralph Turnbull under those of "liberal convictions," we have a preacher over whom Spurgeon and Joseph Parker disagreed sharply, with Parker welcoming Beecher into the pulpit of the City Temple in London.[2]

Beecher was the seventh of eight living children in the Lyman Beecher manse (cf. 9.2.6). In a sense he continued on where his New School Presbyterian father left off. He created a romantic Christianity, becoming himself an "effective role model for liberal preachers in the early part of the twentieth century, especially for one like the Reverend Harry Emerson Fosdick."[3] His six brothers all became preachers. Little in Henry's early life indicated an orator was in process. He was so backward in his studies that he was not sent to Yale but to Amherst and then to Lane Seminary to study during his father's agonies there. He served two churches in Indiana, and in the Second Presbyterian Church of Indianapolis (1839–1847) he came into his own as a pulpiteer, publishing his famous *Lectures to Young Men* on issues such as gambling, cheating, and intemperance.

Beecher's successes in the West brought him to the attention of Henry Bowen and John Howard, who were establishing the first Congregational church in the growing New York suburb of Brooklyn. From the outset Beecher promised he would "wear no fetters" in his pulpit, and two years later he led in rebuilding after a fire destroyed the old building in Brooklyn Heights. The congregation built a new sanctuary seating thirty-two hundred with no pulpit but a small desk. The structure still stands in Brooklyn Heights.

While we must give Beecher credit for speaking against slavery when many were mute, we must also recognize that his secular agenda overshadowed spiritual priorities. He made his pulpit into a center of antislavery propaganda, using the mock auction of slaves as a technique. He was admittedly the P. T. Barnum of the pulpit. Numerous boats, called Beecher's barges, came over from Manhattan to hear him. The crowds that flocked to his services would vanish when he was not present.

Beecher's innovative delivery, powerful voice, fervent excoriation of the wealthy, and adept humor filled Plymouth twice every Sunday and brought seven or eight hundred back on Fridays for a lecture and questions. He became the most sought-after lecturer in America.[4] He spent forty years at Plymouth and was unquestionably the Shakespeare of the modern pulpit.[5]

Beecher preached "a new experimental Christianity with God as love" as the center.[6] This effectively did away with the "stern God of justice" and hell and conversion as such, substituting for it the gradual growth of character in the Bushnellian sense, as if the two were mutually exclusive. The Bible was the finger pointing to truth, but nature was an even more significant revelator of the majesty of God. This was a gospel of success, and as McLoughlin observes, Beecher became "a prophet of reassurance for a nation that wants to be loved and to love itself."

Strongly influenced by Herbert Spencer of England and enamored with the evolutionary vision, Beecher was "obsessed to add to his own popularity."[7] Webber opines that it was hard for him to be serious.[8] His was a message of "the fatherhood of God and the brotherhood of man,"[9] in which edification gave way to entertainment. Although his gift was not organization, he carried discourse through his great dramatic gifts, the concreteness of his illustrations, and his extraordinary phrasing.[10] Harriet reported that her brother lectured at Tremont Temple in Boston with "unreportable pyrotechnic splendors."

Beecher began preparing his morning sermon an hour before the service and did his evening sermon on Sunday afternoon. He preached virtually extemporaneously with much ad-libbing. He had the most unusual "verbal memory." Beecher published a novel, *Norwood,* which brought him money but much panning in the press. One of his last books, *Evolution and Religion* (1885), sums up everything: modified Socinian, very little Bible, derision of conversion, and the repudiation of any transactualism in the Atonement.[11]

In his years of ministry Beecher lived through many national crises. After the war, in an era of scandals and a major depression,[12] he himself knew the disaster of debt and a trial for adultery, demonstrating how dangerous the gospel of love and its theme of freedom can be. A series of reports and allegations did great damage to Beecher before the Tilton affair (the charge by one of Beecher's best friends that he had an adulterous affair with his wife), but his omission of the authority of Scripture in doctrinal statements and his watering down of scriptural authority were enhanced by his "role in the erosion of traditional authority."[13]

Henry Ward Beecher is a profound study in accommodation in message and method. Under his aegis the Lyman Beecher Lectures on preaching at Yale were inaugurated, and he himself gave the first three series. R. W. Dale of Birmingham spoke of Beecher as "the greatest preacher of the Christian Church," but such euphoria had lost touch with reality. We face the same issues today.

---

1. William G. McLoughlin, *The Meaning of Henry Ward Beecher: An Essay on the Shifting Values of Mid-America 1840–1870* (New York: Knopf, 1970), ix. See also *Henry Ward Beecher as His Friends Saw Him* (Boston: Pilgrim, 1904).
2. G. Holden Pike, *The Life and Work of Charles Haddon Spurgeon* (Edinburgh: Banner of Truth, 1894, 1991), 5:67, 337.
3. Halford R. Ryan, *Henry Ward Beecher: Peripatetic Preacher* (Westport, Conn.: Greenwood, 1990), 7. Volume 5 in the "Great American Orators Series." American presidents and world statesmen took the counsel of Beecher.
4. Ibid., 75.
5. Lewis O. Brastow, *Representative Modern Preachers* (New York: Macmillan, 1904), 137.
6. Clifford E. Clark Jr., *Henry Ward Beecher: Spokesman for Middle-Class America* (Urbana: University of Illinois, 1978), 4. Beecher's oration at the rededication of Ft. Sumter in 1865 must be seen as a classic.
7. Ibid., 254. Clark describes how Lyman Abbott took over Beecher's journalistic tasks. Abbott was to follow Beecher at Plymouth to a congregation reduced by half (1887–1899). His messages were largely secular, and like Beecher he was much into

evolutionary theology. He jettisoned a literal second advent and the resurrection of the body. He was uncertain about the virgin birth. Phillips Brooks attended his installation council. See Ira V. Brown, *Lyman Abbott: Christian Evolutionist—A Study in Religious Liberalism* (Westport, Conn.: Greenwood, 1953).

8. F. R. Webber, *A History of Preaching in Britain and America* (Milwaukee: Northwestern, 1957), 3:360.
9. Daniel Dulany Addison, *The Clergy in American Life and Letters* (London: Macmillan, 1900), 313.
10. Brastow, *Representative Modern Preachers,* 140.
11. See the multiple volume *Plymouth Pulpit* (New York: Ketcham, 1893). Also *Beecher in England* (London: Clark, 1886).
12. Ari Hoogenboom, *Rutherford B. Hayes: Warrior and President* (Lawrence: University Press of Kansas, 1995).
13. Altina L. Waller, *Reverend Beecher and Mrs. Tilton* (Amherst: University of Massachusetts Press, 1982), 70. Waller shows how Beecher "packaged ideas and style in response to the market" (27). Here we have an early version of the popular American "audience-centered preaching" intending to "mass-produce personal religion."

10.3.3 Phillips Brooks—The Pulpit with a Powerful Personality

> To be dead in earnest is to be eloquent.
>
> Preaching is the communication of truth by man to men. It has two essential elements, truth and personality . . . Preaching is the bringing of truth through personality.
>
> There must be a man behind every sermon.
> —from Phillips Brooks' Beecher Lectures, sixth in the series, 1877

If listening to Beecher was like trying to drink water from a fire hydrant, **Phillips Brooks** (1835–1893) was like a deft surgeon, a skilled artist, a refined craftsman. Brooks drew great audiences, and his thoughts on preaching as set forth in his Beecher Lectures are considered one of the highlights of that series.[1] He was born in Boston as the ninth generation of cultured Puritan stock. Brooks always had a kind of Puritan reserve, but was baptized a Unitarian and reared an Episcopalian by doting parents who moved increasingly to serious doctrinal definition. He graduated from Boston Latin School, Harvard, and Virginia Theological Seminary in Richmond, where he felt somewhat out of place, scorned "anti-intellectualism of the Evangelicals," and drank deeply of Schleiermacher.[2] Brooks' teaching experience at Boston Latin was a disaster, so he turned to pastoring. His pulpit prowess in Philadelphia and then at Trinity Church, Boston, began to attract considerable attention. Elected bishop of Massachusetts in 1891, after only fifteen months in office he died of a diphtheroid disease. He was fifty-seven.

Brooks traveled widely, and as he never married, he was unencumbered and financially independent. At six feet four inches tall and three hundred pounds, he was an imposing figure. His two most memorable sermons, "Our Mercies of Reoccupation" on Thanksgiving Day and "The Life and Death of Abraham Lincoln" in 1865, qualify as literature.[3] "Harvard Commemoration," from the end of the Civil War, is an oratorical tour de force.[4]

"He made an overwhelming impression" was the universal verdict. People went away saying "How good it is to be alive" and "How easy it seems to be heroic."[5] Brooks was a topical preacher, only very rarely textual. Yet he used the historic present to give a dramatic immediacy in his preaching. There was "no touch of self-consciousness."[6] He sought a principle in the text but did not feel controlled by it. The four rivers in Eden would give him occasion to speak of four aspects of any subject. He could preach at Christmas on John 1:14 and talk about shepherds but not about the angel's announcement of the redemption story.

Thus although all agree he was a great man and a great preacher, we are concerned about his impatience with theology. He held to the Thirty-nine Articles and the Creeds and he urged preaching of doctrine in his lectures,[7] yet he disparaged expository preaching and did not himself preach much doctrine. Those who influenced him were Schleiermacher, Maurice, Coleridge, Carlyle, and Ruskin. He loved Milton, Tennyson, and Browning but eschewed preaching a theological system. Barstow calls him "the Christian humanist" because he sensed his vocation to be "to interpret men to themselves."[8] Brooks loved the church because "it represented ideal humanity."[9] He saw the moral significance of Christ to be the completion of "the realization of the ideal in humanity."[10] Redemption was by revelation, and the Bible "is not authority but the record of authority."[11] Soteriology was in the Incarnation. His successor as bishop, William Lawrence, relates in his biography of Brooks his mother's concern:

> His mother had in the earlier years of his ministry feared for his faith, and she had prayed mightily that he might remain true. She warned him against a certain volume of sermons, "They tear the view of Christ's vicarious suffering all to pieces. I hope you do not own the book, but if you do, I want you to burn it with Frederick [his brother] present to witness and exult over it." No, my dear child; remember, you have promised to preach Christ and Him crucified in the true meaning of the words, and I charge you to stand firm.[12]

But T. J. Jackson Lears correctly perceives that rather "he blunted all the sharp edges in Protestant tradition and produced a bland religion of reassurance."[13] Woolverton is right that "The Bible did not dominate his idealism," nor did he "explore the singularity of the Scriptures."[14] His exquisite Bohlen Lectures on "The Influence of Jesus" are without any focus on redemption.[15] His preaching is artistic but disappointingly horizontal. Here in the succession of Bushnell and Beecher we have "feel-good theology" and "feel-good preaching" but little substance. Where is the Word of God?

A. B. Bruce and a vast horde pay lavish tribute to Brooks.[16] To be sure, he exerted a positive influence, but compare him with the other Episcopalian preacher of note in early America, George Whitefield. Brooks' sermons were carefully prepared and read without melodrama. Brooks' preaching voice was not strong,[17] and he took voice lessons to improve.[18]

Brooks' serious modification of theology, however, meant, as Hethcock remarks, that "He, more than any other of his century, integrated homiletics and preaching into the liberal project in America."[19] Roger Lundin argues that "his romanticism emasculated Christianity," and he laments, "If only Brooks had sided more with Edwards than with Channing."[20] George Marsden has recently described both Beecher and Brooks as liberals, citing the latter's "believe in yourself" approach and his view that "the ultimate fact of human life is goodness and not sin" as prima facie evidence of a grave deficiency.[21]

Phillips Brooks was a remarkable preacher, and before he was thirty-two he wrote the magnificent Christian hymn, "O Little Town of Bethlehem." But, like his preaching, even the hymn lacks strong Christological affirmation. The American pulpit was in serious danger of selling its birthright.

---

1. On the history of the Beecher Lectures, see Edgar Dewitt Jones, *The Royalty of the Pulpit* (New York: Harper, 1951), biographical analysis; Batsell B. Baxter, *The Heart of the Yale Lectures* (New York: Macmillan, 1947).
2. John V. Woolverton, *The Education of Phillips Brooks* (Urbana: University of Illinois Press, 1995), 70, 75.
3. Daniel Dulany Addison, *The Clergy in American Life and Letters* (London: Macmillan, 1900), 342.
4. Ibid., 350.
5. Ibid., 355.
6. Alexander V. G. Allen, *Phillips Brooks* (New York: Dutton, 1907), 581. Hagiographic but voluminous.
7. Phillips Brooks, *Lectures on Preaching* (Grand Rapids: Zondervan, n.d.), 129.
8. Lewis O. Brastow, *Representative Modern Preachers* (New York: Macmillan, 1904), 204.
9. Ibid., 198.
10. Ibid., 214.
11. Ibid., 229.
12. William Lawrence, *Life of Phillips Brooks* (New York: Harper, 1930), 125f.
13. Woolverton, *The Education of Phillips Brooks,* 6.
14. Ibid., 105.
15. Phillips Brooks, *The Influence of Jesus* (London: Allenson, 1879); see Brooks' *Addresses* (Chicago: Henneberry, n.d.). This collection contains the Lincoln sermon and other beautiful expressions.
16. Allen, *Phillips Brooks,* 580.
17. Raymond W. Albright, *Focus on Infinity: A Life of Phillips Brooks* (New York: Macmillan, 1961), 141.
18. Ralph M. Harper, "Phillips Brooks' Voice Lessons," *Church Management* (January 1947).
19. William Hethcock on "Phillips Brooks" in *Concise Encyclopedia of Preaching* (Louisville: Westminster/John Knox, 1995), 48.

20. Roger Lundin quoted in Woolverton, *The Education of Phillips Brooks,* 112–13.
21. George Marsden, *Understanding Fundamentalism and Evangelicalism* (Grand Rapids: Eerdmans, 1991), 19.

10.3.4 Matthew Simpson—The Pulpit with a Bible-Preaching Bishop

> The preacher—His throne is the pulpit; he stands in Christ's stead; his message is the Word of God; around him are immortal souls; the Savior, unseen is beside him; the Holy Spirit broods over the congregation; angels gaze upon the scene, and heaven and hell await the issue. What associations and what a vast responsibility!
>
> —Matthew Simpson

Many have preached in the tradition of the Enlightenment—anthropocentrically and horizontally—but **Matthew Simpson** (1811–1884) was a Methodist bishop who preached in the tradition of the Reformation: in God-centered and Christ-centered terms. The youngest and largest of America's denominations, Methodism at this time was preaching full and free salvation in a spiritual explosion on the frontiers. Simpson was born in Cadiz, Ohio, in a settler's home where he learned to read at the age of three. Educated at Madison College (later Allegheny College) near Pittsburgh, he read voraciously and learned to love Latin, Greek, and Hebrew. Simpson was a tall, gangling young man who was converted in a camp meeting in 1829. He studied medicine, and in 1834 felt the call to preach. Assigned to Pittsburgh, he preached two or three times each Sunday. His voice was never strong and his words suffered from that pious suffix, "uh."[1] He set out to improve, and even delivered a commencement address in Hebrew at Allegheny College. He successively served some brief pastorates, then professorships, and became founding president of Indiana Asbury University at Greencastle.

An example of his expository preaching was a great study of Ezekiel 47 given in his twenty-seventh year on the occasion of the one hundredth anniversary of John Wesley's founding of the Methodist Society.[2] How refreshing to follow the text of Scripture! Simpson then served as editor of the Western Christian Advocate out of Cincinnati, as his church was in the throes of agony over the slavery issue and ultimately was torn in two. This national trauma was undoubtedly a serious distraction for all of the preachers of the era, but Simpson was not to be diverted from preaching the gospel.

Simpson was elected a bishop in 1852 at the age of forty-two. Soon thereafter he preached his famous "King sermon" in Corvallis, Oregon, on Paul's great autobiographical "But none of these things move me" out of Acts 20:24.[3] He and his family successively moved to Chicago, Philadelphia, and Washington, D.C., where he preached before Congress and knew Secretary Chase and President Lincoln well. He preached in the House of Representatives after the second inaugural.[4] Bishop Simpson preached the funeral sermon for President Lincoln at Springfield, Illinois, having ministered to the Lincoln family after the assassination.

He was through and through an old-time Methodist preacher who could "put on the rousements." Frances E. Willard, founder of the Women's Christian Temperances Union, heard Simpson give his renowned sermon on "The Victory of Faith" from 1 John 5:4[5] to more than eight thousand at the Des Plaines Camp Meeting outside of Chicago. Willard was ecstatic in her endorsement:

> I have heard great preachers, Beecher, Talmage, Spurgeon in England, Pere Hyacynthe in France, but to my thought, no flight was ever so steady, so sustained, so lofty, as that of Bishop Simpson on that memorable day.[6]

In 1878, Simpson followed Beecher at the Opera House in San Francisco, and while he could not equal the old war horse in theatrics, his timely and logical message on "Is Christianity a Failure?" was reported in the *Chronicle* with glowing terms:

> In the outward graces of oratory, Beecher was "incomparably the superior"; but for "intellectual depth and grasp" the palm must be according to the Bishop. The tall, lean, thin-faced old man with the shrill, piping voice was extraordinarily moving. As he began to speak his face lighted up, his eyes flashed and he carried men away on a "sparkling stream of thought" that made them forget his ungainly figure and uncouth gesture. The great audience listened with deep attention, broken only by expressions of approval, sobs and shouts. He was the "old man eloquent."[7]

Simpson's Beecher Lectures at Yale in 1878 and 1879 developed the thesis that "Preaching is the chief work but not the only work of the Christian minister."[8] How delightful to hear his ringing call for Christ-centered preaching! He reiterated the centrality of the Scripture and the importance of preaching the biblical text.[9] While Simpson saw arrangement as critical, and while he urged preaching extempore,[10] he warned of the danger of "being drawn into the political canvass."[11] His two strongest lectures are "The Influence of the Pastorate Upon the Pulpit" and "Is the Modern Pulpit a Failure?"

In his collected sermons we relish especially his two magnificent sermons on Christ's resurrection. He skillfully divided the sermon in "Our Times in God's Hands" from Psalm 31:15 and others. He preached on "The Great Commission" and appealed to sinners to be converted.[12] He preached clearly on "Glorying in the Cross" and left no one in any doubt that he saw Christ as a sacrifice for our sin.[13] He pressed such a message as "What Think Ye of Christ?" and spoke of the eschaton and the Lord's return.[14]

Not all American preachers were given to the vagaries and vanities of pious platitudes. Matthew Simpson offered strong and convicting preaching for hungry souls.

---

1. Robert D. Clark, *The Life of Matthew Simpson* (New York: Macmillan, 1956), 36.
2. Ibid., 77.
3. Ibid., 188.

4. Ibid., 246.
5. George R. Crooks, ed., *Sermons of Bishop Matthew Simpson* (New York: Harper, 1885), 193ff.
6. Clark, *The Life of Matthew Simpson,* 272.
7. Ibid., 302.
8. Matthew Simpson, *Lectures on Preaching* (New York: Phillips and Hunt, 1879), 11.
9. Ibid., 73, 100, 108.
10. Ibid., 173.
11. Ibid., 306.
12. Crooks, *Sermons of Bishop Matthew Simpson,* 111.
13. Ibid., 253.
14. Ibid., 293.

10.3.5 John Hall—The Pulpit with a Gifted Ulsterman

> Remember, that the great business of your life is to be the exegesis of the holy Word.
>
> A verse rightly put and rightly repeated, will often fix a truth better than a whole sermon.
>
> If it please God to put you into the ministry, prepare your sermons from the Word, and order your work with a view to the conversion of men.
>
> The main thought of the text should be the main thought of the sermon.
>
> —John Hall in his Beecher Lectures, 1875

Upon a preaching scene awash with eloquent artifice but little scriptural substance, came a call from an Ulsterman located in New York City. "What prevents our ministers from adopting, more generally than they do, the practice of expository preaching?"[1] asked **John Hall** (1829–1898). Hall was the son of Scottish immigrants who settled in County Armagh, Northern Ireland. Also from Ulster came such preaching giants as **Alexander Carson** (1776–1844), who was called the Jonathan Edwards of Ireland and whose masterful studies on divine providence are classic.[2] Evangelist **William P. Nicholson** (1876–1959) hailed from Ulster as well. Despite his unorthodox methodology, he brought many to Christ.[3]

Reared on a farm in modest circumstances, John Hall studied at the Royal College in Belfast before attending seminary. He was classically educated, and throughout his life wrote Latin prayers for his notebooks and his sermon conclusions.[4] His first pastoral charge was in Connought, in the west of Ireland, during the potato famine. In 1852 he moved on to the First Presbyterian Church of Armagh and then to a tenure at Scott's Church, Mary's Abbey, Dublin. Eventually he took the successor post at Rutland Square Church, Dublin, where his strong biblical preaching drew great throngs and necessitated the building of a new church.

Hall was consumed with a great missionary zeal and was a participant in the powerful stirring of the Spirit in Ulster in 1859. Although he was a reserved Presbyterian, some thought he more closely resembled a Methodist because of the prayer meetings he led and the extra preaching services he conducted.[5] He was known for his careful and faithful pastoral visitation. He even preached aboard ship while traveling to America. Upon his arrival, he itinerated widely and was so appreciated that he was called to Fifth Avenue Presbyterian Church in New York City.

Hall was close to Charles Hodge and at the same time deeply involved with the American Sunday School Union.[6] He had tensions with Henry Ward Beecher over theology, as might be expected, but Hall was always a Christian gentleman in his defense of the faith. The heresy of Dr. Charles Briggs, who was brought finally to trial, deeply pained him.[7]

Hall preached strong biblical sermons at Fifth Avenue, a prestigious Old School congregation, and once again saw the congregation grow until a new church was built to accommodate the crowds. He ministered for thirty years in his increasingly famous pulpit, but his last years were clouded somewhat by controversy over his loyalty to a Jewish missionary he felt had been falsely accused. Hall eventually resigned and returned to Ireland, where he died.

Hall was committed unequivocally to the inerrancy of the Scriptures, the substitutionary atonement, and the future conversion of the Jews. He delivered the Beecher Lectures at Yale in 1874 and 1875 using as his theme "God's Word Through Preaching." His stately lectures exuded great confidence in the Word of God and its power to convict of sin and change lives.[8]

Known as a slow starter in his own preaching, Hall pleaded with his listeners at Yale for consecutive book exposition. Like his friend, the distinguished lawyer Richard J. Storrs, Hall argued for preaching extempore. Homiletically, Hall stood with Hoppin of Yale and Phelps of Andover for clear division of the text and sermon along the lines of the more classical style of Claude and Simeon.[9]

This gracious preacher had "both weight as well as movement"[10] in his preaching and stood as a champion of biblical exegesis.

---

1. John Hall, *God's Word Through Preaching* (New York: Dodd, Mead, 1875), 104. The Beecher Lectures 1874–1875.
2. Alexander Carson, *The History of Providence as Explained in the Bible* (Grand Rapids: Baker, 1977). Choice.
3. James Beatty, "Memories of Evangelist W. P. Nicholson," *Banner of Truth* (June 1984): 30ff.
4. F. R. Webber, *A History of Preaching in Britain and America* (Milwaukee: Northwestern, 1957), 3:409.
5. Thomas C. Hall, *John Hall: Pastor and Preacher* (New York: Revell, 1901), 93.
6. Charles Hodge wrote a book for the Sunday School Union that treats basic doctrines so clearly that any evangelical Arminian would have no difficulty subscribing; see *The Way of Life: A Handbook of Christian Belief and Practice* (Grand Rapids: Baker, 1977). Good on sin and justification, repentance and faith.
7. Hall, *John Hall,* 185. While he was at Fifth Avenue, Hall tenderly ministered to the Theodore Roosevelt family in several of their times of need; see David McCullough, *Mornings on Horseback* (New York: Simon and Schuster, 1981), 140, 185, 284.

8. Hall, *John Hall,* 242.
9. James Hoppin, *Homiletics* (New York: Dodd, Mead, 1881); Austin Phelps, *The Theory of Preaching* (London: Richard Dickenson, 1882). Both emphasize the division of the text and the sermon.
10. T. Harwood Pattison, *The History of Christian Preaching* (Philadelphia: American Baptist, 1902), 390.

10.3.6 Theodore Cuyler—The Pulpit with a Crusading Dutchman

> "Preach my word" does not signify the clapping of a few syllables as a figure-head on a long treatise spun out of a preacher's brain. The best discourses are not manufactured; they are a growth. God's inspired and infallible Book must furnish the text. The connection between every good sermon and its text is just as vital as the connection between a peach-tree and its root.
>
> Whatever makes the Gospel or Jesus Christ more clear to the understanding, more effective in arousing sinners, in converting souls, in edifying believers and in promoting pure honest living is never out of place in the pulpit.
>
> Sometimes a sermon may produce but little impression, yet the same sermon at another time and place may deeply move an audience and yield rich spiritual results. Physical condition may have some influence on a minister's delivery; but the chief element in the eloquence that awakens and converts sinners and strengthens Christians is the unction of the Holy Spirit. Our best power is the power from on high.
>
> —Theodore L. Cuyler

An especially effervescent and sprightly Presbyterian preacher of the time was **Theodore Cuyler** (1822–1909). Born of Dutch ancestry in Aurora, New York, south of Auburn, Cuyler was reared by a widowed mother of great devotion to Christ who taught her only child the Bible and the catechism. Cuyler went on to Princeton, where he confessed Christ publicly as his Savior and then, after his call to preach, on to Princeton Seminary, where he feasted on the viands served up by the Alexanders and Hodge. A. A. Hodge was in Cuyler's graduating class of 1841. At the age of twenty Cuyler traveled to Europe and met with Wordsworth, Dickens, and Carlyle, not all of whom were easy to access.[1] Over the years, he was on intimate terms with Newman Hall, Charles Spurgeon, Beecher, John Hall, B. M. Palmer, Charles G. Finney, and many more. His impressions of his contemporaries are invaluable.

Cuyler's ministerial life began in Pennsylvania, but he served for a much longer time in Burlington, New Jersey. Then, in 1853, he began a significant pastorate at Market Street Dutch Reformed Church in New York City, where he labored and preached with distinction until 1860. He was deeply involved in the great stirring in 1859, and urged his readers:

> Every pastor ought to be constantly on the watch, with open eye and ear, for the first signs of an especial manifestation of the Spirit's presence. Elijah, on Carmel, did not only pray, he kept his eyes open to see the rising cloud. The moment that there is a manifestation of the Spirit's presence, it must be followed up promptly.[2]

In 1860 he became the first pastor of the Lafayette Street Presbyterian Church in Brooklyn, where he served for thirty years and built the membership to 3,103 souls. While he was there the Lord visited the congregation with what he called "spiritual downpour." One such revival started with the Universal Week of Prayer during the first full week of January (still observed in some communions and frequently a time of revival). At one point 320 souls were added, including one hundred heads of household. The agony of the Civil War was meaningfully reflected in his writings and preaching,[3] and his personal travail in the death of two of his children was related as part of the Lord's dealing with him. He was a gifted preacher known for his unusually effective illustrations and imagery.[4] He generally took a short text and used often startling introductions. Cuyler wrote twenty-two books and four thousand religious articles for publication. His written style reflects his lively imagination, as in his "Cedar Christians" and "The Honey of God's Word."[5]

Cuyler's lively spirit caused some to call him a Methodistical Presbyterian. He was always dutiful in his pastoral ministry, believing strongly that what a preacher does outside of his pulpit bears heavily on what he can do in his pulpit.[6] His objective was ever to preach strong gospel sermons. His splendid sermon on "Jesus Only" from Matthew 17:8 focuses clearly on Jesus' identity as Savior and sin-bearer.[7] Preaching from Joshua 10:14 on "The Pivot Battles of Life," he divided the sermon in pursuit of his big idea from the text, "And there was no day like that before it or after it."[8]

Theodore Cuyler stands as a friend of biblical preaching and the supernatural gospel.

---

1. Theodore L. Cuyler, *Recollections of a Long Life* (New York: Baker and Taylor, 1902), 12ff., 37ff., 170ff., 190ff.
2. Ibid., 84.
3. Ibid., 144.
4. Ibid., 70.
5. Theodore L. Cuyler, *Beulah-Land* (New York: American Tract Society, 1896), 34ff., 135ff.
6. Theodore L. Cuyler, *How to Be a Pastor* (London: James Nisbet, 1891), 9.
7. Theodore L. Cuyler, *The Presbyterian Pulpit: A Model Christian* (Philadelphia: Presbyterian Board, 1903), 97ff.
8. Ibid., 43ff.

10.3.7 Thomas De Witt Talmage—The Pulpit with a Trumpet Blast

> The most memorable scene in my childhood was that of father and mother at morning and evening prayers.
>
> A live church must be a soul-saving church. The Gospel of Jesus Christ must be preached in it. A church may be built around one man who shall read an essay, the church may be built around one man who shall preach something other than the Gospel, and there may be large congregation; but after a while the man dies, and the church dies.
>
> —Thomas DeWitt Talmage

He was variously called the Spurgeon of America or the cultured Billy Sunday. It was said of him that "there was no ecclesiastical starch in his collar." His sermons were in three thousand newspapers and read around the world. Yet Pattison says of him:

> He was a master of sensational rhetoric, who too easily mistook assertion for proof and illustration for argument; a scene-painter rather than an artist; a trafficker in words, who himself as much as any one of his hearers, was the victim of a florid and ill-balanced judgment.[1]

Yet the esteemed **J. Gregory Mantle** pays him high tribute for his freshness as a preacher, his fearlessness, and his fidelity to truth.[2] Who is right?

Thomas DeWitt Talmage (1832–1902) was the twelfth child of farmer folks, born in Bound Book, New Jersey. His father, though an invalid, was precentor at the local church and with his wife read the Bible daily with their children. Though very poor, young De Witt attended the University of the City of New York. He had been converted at eighteen in the revivals of the time.[3] Called to preach, he graduated from New Brunswick Seminary of the Dutch Reformed Church and served congregations at Bellville, New Jersey, Syracuse, New York, and the First Reformed Church of Philadelphia (1862–1868). He was a gospel preacher and when he was warned he wouldn't get calls from churches he replied, "If I cannot preach the gospel in America, then I will go to heathen lands and preach it."[4] The death of his first wife in a boating accident seemed almost to destroy him, but through the grace of God he rebounded from this tragedy.

Talmage was approached by the old Central Presbyterian Church in Brooklyn, now known as the Brooklyn Tabernacle, to become their pastor. Once strong and vital, the church had dwindled to nineteen members rattling around in their twenty-nine hundred seats. He accepted the task in 1869 and called for the building of a new sanctuary seating five thousand, with fine acoustics, free pews, a great organ, and only congregational singing. Two of his great tabernacles burned down, and each was rebuilt larger than the previous one. His Tabernacle in Brooklyn had the largest seating capacity of any in America. He had a theatrical style and was much criticized. On occasion he preached with police protection because of threats on his life. Yet when he traveled abroad, he was always received by great audiences.[5] His was a commanding pulpit presence:

> A tall, stalwart man, slighting stooping; broad-shouldered, long-armed, bony and spare of flesh; a massive, superbly developed head, bald on top; an expansive brow; rather small and deeply-set blue eyes, that now laughed like sunbeams and now blazed like forked lightnings; a large, mobile mouth; a square, pugnacious jaw, trimmed with spare sandy side-whiskers; the whole figure clad in plain black. He was not a handsome man, nor the miracle of ugliness the caricaturists have tried to make him. He was a commanding and intellectual figure, compelling respect and inviting confidence and affection.[6]

Talmage was anchored squarely in the authority of Holy Scripture. He preached "the old, sweet story of Christ's love and Calvary's sacrifice."[7] "I shall take all of the Bible or none," he insisted. Hicks summarizes the whole of his theology: "No theme can afford such consolation in sorrow, such hope in despondency, such strength in weakness, such light in darkness, as the Cross of Christ."[8] Talmage preached without notes for about half an hour. He testified that "to think in metaphor is natural for me."[9] He wrote best-selling books on his tour of the Holy Land,[10] and was the founding editor of *The Christian Herald* magazine. He was also chaplain of the famous Thirteenth Regiment in Brooklyn. Like Cuyler, he loved to visit notables abroad, leading a massive effort to feed the starving Russian people and dining with the Tsar. He crusaded against vice, drinking, and dissipation. Taking the First Presbyterian Church of Washington in 1895, he served "the Church of the Presidents" until 1899. He then lived in retirement until his death in 1902.

Some of Talmage's sermons do seem disorganized and use too many illustrations. Yet his message on Queen Esther in which he gives a ringing call to greater Christian aggressiveness, using the theme "The Christian for the Times,"[11] is powerful. His sermon on "Attacks on the Bible" is a masterpiece.[12] His sermon on "The Highway from Earth to Heaven," based in Isaiah 35:8–10, is choice, and his study of "Easter Joy" out of 1 Corinthians 15 is carefully divided.[13] He was not an expositor in great depth, but he was a faithful servant of the Word.

One visitor to the Brooklyn Tabernacle described the scene:

> His style of delivery and action are somewhat uncommon. He stands upon the bare platform without desk, with the small Bible in hand, and without any note whatever speaks most feelingly . . . He suits the action to the word—wriggles and twists about, starting and pausing, raising and lowering his voice in a most striking and arresting manner.[14]

Talmage preached with zeal and passion. His message was Christ and salvation, and his torrid sermons are still widely read and circulated. He made his mark for God.

1. T. Harwood Pattison, *The History of Christian Preaching* (Philadelphia: American Baptist Publication Society, 1903), 390.
2. J. Gregory Mantle, introduction to W. Percy Hicks, *Life of Dr. Talmage* (London:

Christian Herald, 1902). He was an English Methodist who later moved within the orbit of A. B. Simpson, founder of the Christian and Missionary Alliance. He was on the committee that recommended the young Campbell Morgan not enter the ministry, but some of his remarkable collections of sermons such as *The Way of Humiliation: The Way of the Cross* and *The Counterfeit Christ* are themselves rich and rewarding.

3. Hicks, *Life of Dr. Talmage,* 44.
4. Ibid., 51.
5. T. Dewitt Talmage, *The Life and Letters of Rev. T. Dewitt Talmage* (Kansas City: Topeka Book Co., 1902), 39.
6. Ibid., 40.
7. Hicks, *Life of Dr. Talmage,* 144.
8. Ibid., 146.
9. Ibid., 76.
10. T. Dewitt Talmage, *The Palestine Sermons of T. Dewitt Talmage* (Chicago: Rhodes and McClure, 1890).
11. Hicks, *Life of Dr. Talmage,* 166.
12. Ibid., 199.
13. T. Dewitt Talmage, "Easter Joy," in *Great Sermons on the Resurrection* (Murfreesboro, Tenn.: Sword of the Lord, 1984), 11.
14. Hicks, *Life of Dr. Talmage,* 70.

10.3.8 William Taylor—The Pulpit with a Scottish Gentleman

> In truth there is nothing more absurd than this clamor against doctrine, for they who raised it do not seem to see that there is beneath the cry itself a doctrine, to the effect that it makes no matter what a man believes, if he only says he is resting upon Christ . . . but the Christ that saves is the Christ that is revealed in the Gospels.
>
> Exposition is the presentation to the people, in an intelligible and forcible manner, of the meaning of the sacred writer which has been first settled by the preacher for himself, by the use of those grammatical and historical instruments with which his preparatory training has furnished him.
>
> —William M. Taylor in his Beecher Lectures of 1875–1876

In the glittering galaxy of pulpiteers in the New York City area was heard the gentle Scottish burr on the tongue of **William M. Taylor** (1829–1895). Taylor preached at the old Broadway Tabernacle where Charles G. Finney had once stood. Born in Kilmarnock in a shopkeeper's home, Taylor graduated from Glasgow University in 1849. He went on to divinity studies at the United Presbyterian Hall in Edinburgh, receiving his degree in 1852.

Taylor pastored briefly in Ayrshire and then took the call to Derby Road Church, a congregation of seafarers and their families and others in the maritime, located in a suburb of Liverpool.[1] He became very well known during his seventeen years there, and after filling Dr. Storr's Church of the Pilgrims in Brooklyn for a summer was in demand in the United States. In 1872 he accepted a call to fill the pastoral vacancy at Broadway Tabernacle at Broadway and 34th Street. Taylor preached it full morning and evening for twenty years. Although he manuscripted his sermons and wrote forty books, his preaching seemed extempore. Just after his twentieth jubilee at Broadway, he suffered a stroke. He longed to preach again but was unable to do so.

In a lectureship titled "The Ministry of the Word," Taylor laid the stakes for biblical preaching. He argued strenuously for the preacher's study and use of the original languages.[2] He also called for expository preaching of the text on five grounds:

1. It brings the preacher and hearers into immediate contact with the mind of the Spirit;
2. It secures variety in the ministrations of the preacher;
3. The preacher will be compelled to treat many subjects from which otherwise he might have shrunk;
4. Biblical intelligence among the people will be promoted;
5. In the process of preparing expository discourses the preacher will acquire a great store of resources which he can use for many other purposes.[3]

Taylor also laid bare the potential weaknesses and vulnerabilities in expository preaching. He warned against making exposition dense with content and cautioned about lack of organic unity.[4] Twice the massively built Scot was invited to deliver the Beecher Lectures, an honor extended only to Beecher himself, Washington Gladden, and C. R. Brown. His second course of Beecher Lectures was a rare historical survey on the theme "The Scottish Pulpit from the Reformation to the Present Day."[5] These are not the equal of Professor Blaikie's classic treatment, but they are a solid argument for the supremacy of the authoritative Word of God.

One of the most popular series of books at the time was his series of sermon volumes on great characters of the Bible. His twenty-six discourses on Moses, for instance, are spiced with superb background material, choice quotations and illustrations, and good practical application.[6] His more typical sermons include "Contrary Winds," from Matthew 14:24, preached November 28, 1880.[7] The sermon is divided into a two-point problem/solution outline. "Pleasures of Sin," from Hebrews 11:25, is in four divisions and is true to the text.[8]

Along with John Hall, William Taylor must be considered one of America's finest preachers out of Europe.

---

1. F. R. Webber, *A History of Preaching in Britain and America* (Milwaukee: Northwestern, 1957), 3:406.
2. William M. Taylor, *The Ministry of the Word* (New York: Anson Randolph, 1877), 160.
3. Ibid., 161ff. Taylor would preach one expository sermon and one topical sermon each Lord's Day.

4. Ibid., 178.
5. William M. Taylor, *The Scottish Pulpit* (London: Charles Burnet, 1887).
6. William M. Taylor, *Moses the Law-Giver* (London: Sampson Low, 1888).
7. William M. Taylor, *Contrary Winds* (New York: Hodder and Stoughton, 1883), 7ff.
8. Ibid., 121ff. Taylor also authored significant, meaty, and solid volumes on the parables and miracles of Jesus.

10.3.9 A. J. GORDON—THE PULPIT WITH A YANKEE CLIPPER

> Every phrase of the New Testament has a meaning definite and single—a meaning that can be accurately ascertained and clearly expressed according to fixed and settled laws of human speech. . . . [From Professor Hackett he got] that reverent regard for divine revelation which, on the one hand, brooks no mystical importation of human fancies into the sacred text and, on the other, does not permit the smallest Greek article or conjunction to be treated as an idle or ambiguous thing in that Word, which holy men of old wrote as they were moved by the Holy Ghost.
>
> The sincere milk of the Word may be dispensed from the pulpit, yet given out so frigidly and unfeelingly as to make it very hard to receive. In Siberia, the milkmen sometimes deliver their milk in chunks, not in quarts, it being frozen solid and thus carried about to the customers. Alas! is not this the way many pulpits deliver the milk of the Word?
>
> —Adoniram Judson Gordon

The ministry of **Adoniram Judson Gordon** (1836–1895) was transformed by a dream of Christ visiting his service. Gordon subsequently wrote *How Christ Came to Church.*[1] For twenty-five years he served as pastor of the Clarendon Street Baptist Church of Boston.

Born in New Hampshire and nurtured spiritually in the home of the owner of a woolen mill, he yielded to Christ after a sleepless night and went on to study at Brown University in Providence. Gordon sensed God's hand on him to preach, and at Newton Seminary he ministered to many small churches in the area. Timid in the parlor but not in the pulpit, Gordon took his first pastoral charge at Jamaica Plain, where he authored the delightful work *In Christ,* a study of the believer's position and union with the Savior.[2]

In 1869 he assumed the pastorate at Clarendon Street, a fashionable church in Boston, which he led to pristine heights. He was a prime mover in the American Baptist Missionary Union and revamped the worship and music at Clarendon until it was among the best in the Boston area. In an atmosphere of liberalism and Unitarianism, Gordon did not pull his punches. When "repent" and "sin" were not heard, his son relates in his satisfying biography of his father:

> He proclaimed without flinching the helplessness of man, the impotence of the unrenewed will, the destiny of sorrow and punishment to which

cation titled

Philadelphia:

: Moody, rev.

6), 275ff.
t and is known
gel, rev. from
ary (Chicago:

ociety, 1931).
sser: Minister

. Great preach-

3ff., 1ff.
also wrote on

's Work in Us

age.
e in 1932

ory of preach-
the supernatu-
leading up to
the war itself
sh, alienation,
mmon people
tical, and eco-

troops on both
ancipation di-
cting in a way
with the moral
d that the Civil
ure of doubt in
eving in provi-

And where the knife probed, the ointment
s no abatement of stern truths, there was in
els, no want of tenderness.[3]

ıeighboring Episcopalian rector, **William R.**
Reformed Episcopal Church,[4] and many Ply-
an intimate of **Uncle John Vasser,** the out-
was once arrested for preaching in Boston
of the Moody campaign in 1877, and so many
rch that the congregation abandoned the use
in deference. He led an important crusade
y Glover Baker Patterson Eddy, centered in
ident of Princeton, often had him to the col-
students. He traveled extensively and preached
ngland and was especially close to the great
s.

peerless. His illustrations were "palpitating
edd called "the homiletic habit" and was,
f the most faithful biblical expositors of his
and clear, his preaching clearly under "the
Gordon urged, "Let us lay down the cudgel
lilting sentences that poured from his blazing

his, "Making the cross of Christ of none
man can sweep the stars from the sky or
r efface the splendid landscape; but one
the sight and make all those things as
tonement of Christ can never pass into
ıt there is such a thing as the eclipse of
ıl so that the cross and the atonement
cant, lifeless, meaningless. O eyes that
age; blinded, but not with tears; hard
ıear the Lord speaking from heaven,
e, that thou mayest see." It is not that
gs for us, but that we should open our

e"[8] and was staunchly premillennial, as were
Spurgeon. He loved the Jewish people and
re. Pierson was "as flint to steel" in a very

for the great hymn, "My Jesus, I love Thee,
umes of collected sermons yield such gems
" from Acts 5:13, and such symmetrical
ınd Glory" from Psalm 84:11.[9] "The Two

Heredities" from John 3:6 is a masterpiece,[10] and his study of sancti "The Two-fold Life" is for the ages.[11]

---

1. A. J. Gordon, *How Christ Came to Church: A Spiritual Autobiograph* American Baptist, 1895).
2. A. J. Gordon, *In Christ: The Believer's Union with His Lord* (Chicag from 1872).
3. Ernest B. Gordon, *Adoniram Judson Gordon* (New York: Revell, 18
4. Bishop William R. Nicholson was an outstanding preacher in his own rig for his studies in Colossians, *Oneness with Christ* (Grand Rapids: K 1903) and his unique little volume of sermons, *The Six Miracles of Ca* Moody, 1927). "Revivals to Life in the Calvary Graveyard" is special
5. Thomas E. Vasser, *Uncle John Vasser* (New York: American Tract A. J. Gordon wrote the introduction to this book. See also "John E. in Homespun," Decision (August 1995): 11.
6. Gordon, *How Christ Came to Church,* xff.
7. Ibid., 292.
8. A. J. Gordon, *Ecce Venit: Behold He Cometh* (New York: Revell, 1889 ing on prophecy.
9. A. J. Gordon, *Grace and Glory* (Boston: Howard Gannett, 1880), 1
10. A. J. Gordon, *Yet Speaking* (New York: Revell, 1897), 37ff. Gordo divine healing.
11. A. J. Gordon, *The Twofold Life or Christ's Work for Us and Chri* (Chicago: Moody, rep. 1883).

10.4 THE SOUTHERN RAPIDS IN AMERICAN PREACHIN

> So face with calm that heritage and earn contempt before the
>
> —Allen T

The southern and border states have a unique heritage in the his ing, perhaps because those in the South "clung to [their] belief in ral" more stubbornly, as Richard Weaver suggests.[1] The decade the Civil War had already sundered the largest denominations, ar claimed 360,000 Union lives and 260,000 Confederates. The ang and agony were appalling. Studies of leaders and studies of the c disclose the unimaginable trauma of war in egregious social, po nomic dislocation.[2]

Even though there were deep movings of the Spirit among the sides of the fratricidal nightmare, the issues of abolition and e vided the north ideologically and became consuming and distr that had a deleterious effect on preaching. In dealing recently trauma of slavery and the Civil War, Andrew Delbanco has argu War was the great divide between the culture of faith and the cu America.[3] He shows that the United States went into the war be dence and emerged from the war with only a hope for luck. Yet biblical faith and preaching were alive in the border and Southern states before, during, and after the carnage.

---

1. George M. Curtis III and James J. Thompson Jr., eds., *The Southern Essays of Richard M. Weaver* (Indianapolis: Liberty Press, 1987), xi. Note Weaver's illuminating essay on "The Older Religiousness in the South" (134).
2. Gene Smith, *Lee and Grant: A Dual Biography* (New York: McGraw-Hill, 1984). For a further feel of the wartime and postwar situations, see Charles Bracelen Flood, *Lee: The Last Years* (Boston: Houghton-Mifflin, 1981).
3. Andrew Delbanco, *The Death of Satan: How Americans Have Lost the Sense of Evil* (New York: Farrar, Strauss, 1995), 98, 138. I am indebted to my friend and former student Dr. Dorrington Little III for this book recommendation.

10.4.1 Alexander Campbell—Preacher on the Frontier

> Imitate the Apostles and primitive preachers—preach the gospel, which, when received, produces repentance not to be repented of . . . preach Christ crucified, in whom is manifested the wrath and judgment of God against sin; and his condescending love, mercy and grace to the sinner.
>
> —Alexander Campbell

The name of **Alexander Campbell** (1788–1866) is essential to a history of preaching not only because he was an electrifying preacher but because he also played an integral role in launching the Restoration Movement, which had such an influence in the South. Campbell was born in Ireland and came to America at the age of twenty-one. His father had preached in a Seceder Presbyterian Church near the family farm, and directed Alexander in extensive learning and much memorization of Scripture. Alexander studied one year at the University of Glasgow. He had been converted in his early teens and upon coming to the United States felt called to preach. At the age of twenty-two Campbell preached his first sermon from Matthew 7:24–27. Throughout his life he often preached polemical sermons among those who wanted unity in Christ rather than in man-made ecclesiastical structures. He founded Bethany College in West Virginia, where he was president for twenty-five years. He was a member of the Virginia Constitutional Convention and preached to Congress in 1850. He labored tirelessly, writing sixty volumes, editing the *Millennial Harbinger,* and debating Baptists and Roman Catholics.

We do not have many of Campbell's sermons because he preached extempore. We do have his great sermon from Romans 8:3 in which he contrasts the law of Moses with the gospel of Christ. Campbell often preached outdoors and usually spoke for an hour or more. In 1829 he debated the Scottish infidel Robert Owen in Cincinnati and spoke for twelve hours. The first sentence of his sermons was riveting, observers said.[1] President Madison, who was often with him on various councils, said of him:

> It was my pleasure to hear him very often as a preacher of the Gospel, and I regard him as the ablest and most original expounder of the Scriptures I have ever heard.[2]

Dr. Humphrey, president of Amherst, recalled Campbell's preaching on the clauses "justified in the spirit, received into glory," and observed:

> I never remembered to have listened to or to have read a more thrilling outburst of sacred eloquence than when he came to the scene of the coronation of Christ, and quoted the sublime passage from the twenty-fourth Psalm, beginning, "Lift up your heads, O ye gates, and be ye lifted up, ye everlasting doors, that the King of Glory may come," when he represented all the angels, principalities and powers of heaven as coming together to assist, as it were, in placing the Crown on the Redeemer's head.[3]

He did not gesticulate or pound the pulpit or speak vociferously. He used language artfully. Very few of the phenomena often seen in the great revivals of Kentucky and Tennessee were to be found in his meetings. His voice was ringing and clear and at times in crescendo. McLean says of Campbell's driving purpose:

> His aim was to set forth what the Word of God taught, and not to prove that it is true, or that some notions held were true because they are supported by texts of Holy Writ . . . His familiarity with the language of the Bible enabled him to employ its glorious expressions and beautiful similes with great effect. . . . Bible themes, Bible thoughts, Bible terms, Bible facts, were his materials, and these he wrought up with consummate skill into intellectual and spiritual palaces of glorious beauty, in which every listener desired to prolong his stay.[4]

Christ was the center and the circumference of his message. We might well say of the Restoration Movement, as we might say of many of our movements, if all who followed had stayed with the basics as did our founders, we would be better off today. General Robert E. Lee paid him high tribute:

> He was a man in whom were illustriously combined all the qualities that could adorn or elevate the nature to which he belonged; knowledge of the most various and extended virtue that never loitered in her career or deviated from her course.[5]

---

1. Archibald McLean, *Alexander Campbell as a Preacher* (Nashville: Reed and Company, rev. 1973), 11. I am indebted to my former student Dr. Sellers Crain Jr. for bringing this and other material on Alexander Campbell to my attention.
2. Ibid., 11. The problem in Restoration preaching was proof-texting—it was thematic and not very often exegetical.
3. Ibid., 14–15.

4. Ibid., 34.
5. Ibid., 45. In a study of remarkable candor, Bill Love of the Churches of Christ laments: "It was our preaching which was anemic—what we preached showed little correspondence to the richness, depth and power of the New Testament core gospel." Although there have been laudable exceptions, he regrets the lack of the preaching of the cross. See Bill Love, *The Core Gospel: On Restoring the Crux of the Matter* (Abilene: Abilene Christian University, 1992), 258.

10.4.2 John A. Broadus—The Preacher Who Taught Preachers

> Deliver me, O Lord, from wrong ambitions, from every improper desire to be first among my brethren. May I be enabled to subordinate all my desires and plans and hopes to Thy will, and when I labor and strive for success and eminence and fame, may I do all for the glory of God.
>
> An expository discourse may be defined as one which is occupied mainly, or at any rate very largely, with the exposition of Scripture . . . it may be one of a series or stand by itself. We at once perceive that there is no broad line of distinction between expository preaching and common methods, but that one may pass almost insensible gradations from textual to expository sermons.
>
> The greatest privilege of earthly life is to give some fellow creature the blessed word of God, and then try by loving speech and example, to bring home to the heart and conscience . . . the truth it contains.
>
> —John A. Broadus

Truly one of the Olympians in the history of preaching, **John A. Broadus** (1827–1895) is called by some the father of American expository preaching. Broadus was born of Welsh extraction in Culpepper County, Virginia. Converted at sixteen in "a protracted meeting," he went on to study classics at the University of Virginia. Influenced by a sermon he had heard, Broadus announced, "The question is decided; I must try to be a preacher." An able student and master of detail, he was influenced much by Dr. McGuffey, a Presbyterian minister, professor of moral philosophy at the university, and author of *McGuffey's Reader.* Broadus was fluent in eleven languages. He preached in Charlottesville and tutored and taught at the university, where he could have had the chair of Greek. Instead, he was drawn to share in the formation of the Southern Baptist Seminary in Greenville, North Carolina. Always frail, his health snapped in the shock of war. The fledgling seminary closed, and during these hard years Broadus wrote his justly famous commentary on Matthew.

Stonewall Jackson urged him to come to the front and preach.[1] He did so, and sent dispatches to newspapers from the front. He continued to preach in many small churches throughout the war. After the conflict, the seminary reopened with just six students. Broadus' first course of lectures on preaching, which later became his widely used text,[2] was delivered to one blind student. Ultimately the seminary relocated to Louisville. In all, Broadus served there for thirty-six years, the last several of which were as president.

Towering even in a field of Southern Baptists where preaching has always been strong and central,[3] Broadus was never lacking in opportunities to take pastorates and teach elsewhere. He turned down invitations from Calvary Baptist, New York City, First Baptist, Richmond, and the University of Chicago, Brown University as president, Vasser, Newton Seminary, and Crozer Seminary. In 1867 he preached the baccalaureate sermon at Washington College at the insistence of the president of the school, his good friend Robert E. Lee. He read widely in all literary genre and was totally committed to the trustworthiness of Scripture, not "embracing the higher criticism of the nineteenth century."[4]

Broadus supported the long ending of Mark's gospel and was cited as a source in that position by John William Burgon, its chief exponent.[5] In 1870 he spent a year abroad to regain his health. His meetings with Spurgeon, H. P. Liddon, Lightfoot, Eadie, Alford, Westcott, and Hort are graphically recounted in his letters.[6] He coauthored 1 and 2 Samuel in the Lange commentaries with C. H. Toy of the Southern Baptist faculty[7] and gave five lectures on the history of preaching at Newton Seminary. He worked for many years on the old International Sunday School Lesson Committee and wrote for *The Sunday School Times.* Broadus turned down a call to the First Baptist Church of Chicago but spoke regularly at Northfield and Chatauqua. He gave the Beecher Lectures at Yale in 1888.[8] And in all of this, "his health trembled in the balance."[9]

Not only was Broadus a gifted homiletical theoretician, but also he was an immensely popular and able preacher. His more classical approach is derided today on many sides for his "discursive" and "conceptual" flavor, but in 1870 he spoke more about narrative than did Haddon Robinson in 1980. Broadus argued for the sermon taking its shape from the text.[10] He always preached extempore, his task being to expose the text. He used few gestures and tended to preach conversationally. His hallmark was clarity. His fine sermon on John 4:32–38 divides the text and the sermon into four parts.[11] The classic message on "The Habit of Thankfulness" from 1 Thessalonians 5:18 has two divisions and some subdivisions.[12]

E. C. Dargan came to help him in homiletics at Southern and eventually succeeded him. Broadus wrote a unique *Harmony of the Gospels,* served as a regent of the Kentucky School of Medicine, and kept up a prodigious correspondence with many, including General Lew Wallace, author of *Ben Hur.* Broadus was "always looking for the coming of Christ"[13] and strongly supported the Moody-Sankey campaigns. He declined writing on the Pastorals for the ICC series but turned down little else.

By the time of his retirement, the seminary had close to three hundred students. In his last class meeting, one of his students recalled his words, which so beautifully capture this man and his message:

> "Young gentlemen, if this were the last time I should ever be permitted to address you, I would feel amply repaid for consuming the whole hour in endeavoring to impress upon you these two things: true piety and, like

Apollos, to be men 'mighty in the Scriptures.'" Then pausing, he stood for a moment with his piercing eye fixed upon us, and repeated over and over again in that slow but wonderfully impressive style peculiar to himself, "mighty in the Scriptures," "mighty in the Scriptures," until the whole class seemed to be lifted through him into a sacred nearness to the Master. That picture of him as he stood there at that moment can never be obliterated from my mind.[14]

---

1. A. T. Robertson, *Life and Letters of John Albert Broadus* (Harrisonburg, Va.: Gano, rev. 1987), 197.
2. John A. Broadus, *A Treatise on the Preparation and Delivery of Sermons* (New York: Armstrong, 1907). Dargan revised the original on suggestions by Broadus; J. B. Weatherspoon later revised it; and Vernon L. Stanfield again revised it.
3. Al Fasol, *With a Bible in Their Hands: Baptist Preaching in the South 1679–1979* (Nashville: Broadman, 1994).
4. Raymond H. Bailey, "John A. Broadus: Man of Letters and Preacher Extraordinaire," *Preaching* (November–December 1993): 58ff. Bailey paints Broadus as the "gentleman-scholar-preacher."
5. John William Burgon (1813–1888), bishop of Chichester, born in Ixmir (Smyrna), Turkey, was himself a fine preacher. See Edward M. Goulburn, *John William Burgon: A Biography* (London: John Murray, 1892). Analyzes the textual issue.
6. Robertson, *Life and Letters of John Albert Broadus,* 243–44. Everett Gill's fine *A. T. Robertson* (1943) is invaluable because it shows how one of Broadus's students "got hold of preaching" in his class. Robertson married Ella Broadus, the youngest daughter.
7. The tragedy of C. H. Toy was seen in his drift from orthodoxy and his departure from Southern Baptist Seminary for Harvard and infidelity.
8. Bailey, "John A. Broadus," 60, on the Beecher Lectures, which were never published as such but incorporated in various books and articles by Broadus. David McCant calls them "The Lost Yale Lectures on Preaching."
9. Robertson, *Life and Letters of John Albert Broadus,* 323. Robertson's own fine sermons are in *Passing the Torch* (New York: Macmillan, 1943).
10. Steve Reagles, "One Century after the 1889 Lectures: A Reflection on Broadus' Homiletical Thought," *Preaching* (November–December 1989): 35.
11. V. L. Stanfield, ed., *Favorite Sermons of John A. Broadus* (New York: Harper, 1959), 14ff.
12. Ibid., 21ff.
13. Robertson, *Life and Letters of John Albert Broadus,* 417.
14. Ibid., 430.

10.4.3 R. L. Dabney—The Teacher Who Could Preach

My charge hangs on my hands like a growing burden, heavier and heavier continually. They listen to my preaching very attentively, and often with fixed interest; but it always feels to me like the interest of the understanding and imagination only, and not of the spiritual affections.

My preaching seems to human eyes to be utterly without effect; bad for me, and bad for them.

—R. L. Dabney of some of his early struggles at Tinkling Spring Church

You now perceive that when once the inspiration of the Scriptures is established, they become practically the great storehouse of proofs for pulpit argument. . . . The only hope for Protestants is the work of the Holy Ghost . . . to the objection that didactic preaching is dry, I answer, that if it ever seems to be so, this is the fault of the preacher and not of the truth. . . . The exact mind of the Spirit in the text must then be ascertained before you preach on it.

It is a noble thing to make the truth beautiful!

—R. L. Dabney

A notable company of Southern Presbyterian preachers came together around the time of the Civil War. Their dean, **James Henley Thornwell** (1812–1862), was called by D. Martyn Lloyd-Jones "one of the greatest preachers that America has ever produced." His teaching and pastoral work were chiefly done in Columbia, South Carolina.[1] "The glory of the Southern Pulpit" was an accolade heaped on **Benjamin M. Palmer** (1818–1902), described as "an insignificant-looking little fellow." He succeeded Thornwell in Columbia and then served First Presbyterian Church in New Orleans for forty-six years. Palmer preached free-style and knew episodic visits of the Spirit in revival.[2] His *Theology of Prayer* is in a class by itself. His tongue was "fire-tipped" and his homiletics outstanding.

The third member of this dauntless trio was **Robert Lewis Dabney** (1820–1898), who came from Louisa County near Richmond. In a revival in his home church he made his profession of faith. He was trained by Hampden-Sidney College and the University of Virginia, where he took his M.A. Dabney resolved to enter the ministry and studied at Union Seminary, then located at Hampden-Sidney.[3] The school had eighteen students at the time. After serving the Scots-Irish Church in Tinkling Spring, he accepted a call to teach at the seminary, now down to twelve students, and served concurrently as copastor of the College Church for some thirty years.

Dabney was hungry for revival in the churches.[4] He preached at Fifth Avenue Presbyterian Church in New York and at Princeton and was moderator of the Synod of Virginia in the fateful year of 1860. Stonewall Jackson wanted his services at the front as adjutant general, and out of that relationship came Dabney's biography of the great general.[5]

Dabney's outstanding sermon to Synod in 1881 from Colossians 2:8 on "A Caution Against Anti-Christian Science" left a profound impression. But controversies at Union Seminary led him to the chair of mental and moral philosophy at the University of Texas. Due to some misunderstandings, he resigned after eleven years and became one of the founders of the Austin Presbyterian Seminary.

His preaching was didactic and packed with content but also imaginative and full of word pictures. John Broadus heard his sermon from John 4:35 on "The World White to the Harvest; Reap, or It Perishes" at a large missions meeting in New York and pronounced it "one of the most powerful sermons with which he was acquainted."[6] Dabney was a staunch defender of plenary inspiration, although properly recognizing the use of phenomenal language in Scripture.[7] Dabney was cautious, as his article on "Aesthetics as a Substitute for Christianity" indicates.[8] Nonetheless, many listeners were struck by "the energy and power of his constructive imagination."[9]

His lectures on sacred rhetoric are outstanding and touch the danger of fragmentary preaching. He underscored the need for "one burning focus," division of the text, pleasing transitions, a clear announcement of the proposition, and the desirability of beginning softly![10] In this, like Hoppin and Broadus, he was Aristotelian and thus anathema to many contemporaries. Yet while emphasizing that unity implies parts and eulogizing "lucid order," he treated the narrative genre, pushed continuous application and the use of many illustrations.[11] Yet he distinguished his position from scholastic preaching[12] and emphasized imagination and preaching extempore for maximum effect. Dabney quoted a French writer who characterized American orators as "very ingenious and fluent, but his conclusion is too much like that of the pointer dog, who when he wishes to sleep turns around and around following his own tail, and at last lies down just where he began."[13]

Too much of Aristotle may indeed be problematic, but the idea of rhetoric as the application of style for the purpose of persuasion and the law of contradiction are good even if they emanate from a Greek pagan. Logical investigation and rational judgment are also Aristotelian but, like Robert Dabney's preaching, are eminently defensible.[14]

---

1. B. M. Palmer, *The Life and Letters of James Henley Thornwell* (Edinburgh: Banner of Truth, 1875, 1986).
2. Thomas C. Johnson, *The Life and Letters of Benjamin Morgan Palmer* (Edinburgh: Banner of Truth, 1987).
3. Thomas C. Johnson, *The Life and Letters of Robert Lewis Dabney* (Edinburgh: Banner of Truth, 1903, 1977), 80.
4. Ibid., 111.
5. Ibid., 261ff.
6. Ibid., 167.
7. Ibid., 342.
8. Ibid., 518.
9. Ibid., 545.
10. R. L. Dabney, *R. L. Dabney on Preaching: Lectures on Sacred Rhetoric* (Edinburgh: Banner of Truth, 1870, 1979), 310.
11. Ibid., 197, 254.
12. Ibid., 217–18.
13. Ibid., 178.

14. Jean Dietz Moss, ed., *Rhetoric and Praxis: The Contribution of Classical Rhetoric to Practical Reasoning* (Washington, D.C.: Catholic University of America Press, 1986). A thoughtful case.

10.4.4 B. H. Carroll—The Preacher on the Prairies of Texas

> I certainly understand the passage [2 Timothy 3:17] to teach the plenary inspiration of the Holy Scriptures—the Old Testament directly, the New Testament by implication. That, being inspired, they are authoritative and inerrant. That as such they constitute an all sufficient standard of human belief, conduct, and destiny.
>
> The only way to find pardon for past offenses is in Christ. Will you come to Him? Here now, press through this throng—make a way—come up here now and let us unite our prayers that God today will give you the Holy Spirit that you may be led to repentance toward Him and faith in the Lord Jesus Christ.
>
> —B. H. Carroll

The centrality of religion and the importance of preaching before, during, and after the American Civil War are abundantly clear.[1] As a young man, **Benajah Harvey Carroll** (1843–1914) was carried off the battlefield with a rifle ball in one of his legs. He went on from that close call to enjoy an especially blessed ministry.

Born in Mississippi, Carroll and his family moved to Texas when he was fifteen. He attended Baylor University, fought in the war, and then received Christ as his Savior at a Methodist camp meeting.[2] He started as assistant pastor at the First Baptist Church in Waco, Texas, and in 1871 became its pastor, a post he filled for thirty years. Carroll was the founder of the Southwestern Baptist Theological Seminary, probably to this day the largest seminary in the world and a fountainhead of the kind of preaching emphasis that has made the Southern Baptist Convention a leading influence in the United States and abroad.

Carroll wrote his *Interpretation of the English Bible* in 13 volumes. To him the preaching of the Word was of the essence in the church and the pastor's task.

> Just think of it seriously. Eternal interests hinge on every sermon. Every sentence may be freighted with eternal weal or woe. Every word may be the savor of life unto life or death unto death.[3]

Of the 241 sermons we possess from Carroll, 157 are expository, 55 topical and 24 textual. His outlines were terse and clear.[4] In a searching message on "The Conquering Word of God" from Jeremiah 23:28, Carroll faced head-on the misuse of the Word of God by the false prophets who presented a counterfeit Word which "had the semblance of wheat, in order to deceive."[5] His illustrations and quotations are sparkling and effective.

Following Carroll and shaping Southern Baptist preaching in Texas and westward was **Jefferson Davis Ray** (1860–1951), who served as professor of preaching at Southwestern from 1907 to 1944. He was known especially for his powerful reading of the Scripture, and he epitomizes the preaching Carroll modeled for his students. In arguing for expository preaching, Ray pleaded for preachers to probe the text for "the juicy inner substratum meaning of the Word of God."[6] He was clearly an advocate of what we have called the classical expository sermon, with unity and an orderly structure. Ray wrote movingly of the calling of the local pastor of a smaller church.[7] He helped fulfill the vision of B. H. Carroll in the founding of Southwestern. He wanted "knowledge on fire."

---

1. Richard J. Carwardine, *Evangelicals and Politics in Antebellum America* (New Haven, Conn.: Yale University Press, 1993).
2. Al Fasol, *With a Bible in Their Hands: Baptist Preaching in the South 1679–1979* (Nashville: Broadman, 1994), 84.
3. Ibid., 85.
4. Ibid., 87.
5. B. H. Carroll, *Revival Messages* (Nashville: Broadman, 1939), 115.
6. Jeff D. Ray, *Expository Preaching* (Grand Rapids: Zondervan, 1940), 60.
7. Jeff D. Ray, *The Country Preacher* (Nashville: Sunday School Board of the Southern Baptist Convention, 1925).

10.5 THE SCOTTISH WATERFALL

> The priestlike father reads the sacred page, How Abram was the friend of God on high;
> Or, Moses bad eternal warfare wage with Amalek's ungracious progeny . . .
> Perhaps the Christian volume is the theme, How guiltless blood for guilty man was shed;
> How He, who bore in Heaven the second name, Had not on earth whereon to lay His head.
>
> —Robert Burns in *The Cotter's Saturday Night*

Apart from the special place the Bible had in the Scottish heart and home, it is hard to understand the remarkable outcropping of biblical preaching that flourished in Scotland in the nineteenth and early twentieth centuries. The Scottish church clung tenaciously to an educated ministry, but there was tragedy in the offing that had its genesis in concessions made to higher criticism and skepticism in the centers for ministerial training. It will be our task to trace the zenith as well as the recession of biblical preaching in this small, pastoral land.

Adam Phillip (b. 1856), one of the biographers of Chalmers and a parish pastor of long experience, in his Warrack Lectures in 1930 urged preachers to make points "which like peaks, catch attention."[1] The concern of the preacher must be to know "the gales of the Spirit."[2] In a land where confidence in preaching is now low, we must look carefully at what made the Scottish pulpit soar, and at which crossroad the wrong turn was taken.

1. Adam Phillip, *Thoughts on Worship and Preaching* (London: James Clarke, 1930), 128.
2. Ibid., 154.

10.5.1 Thomas Guthrie—The Preacher Who Painted a Picture

> I am a painter . . . only I paint in words. While this faculty is not to be allowed to run away with a man, it is a telling one, and valuable for the highest ends. Mind the three P's: In every discourse the preacher should aim at proving, painting and persuading; in other words, addressing the Reason, the Fancy and the Heart.
>
> Jesus Christ is the propitiation for our sins; and not for ours only, but also for the sins of the whole world. The whole world . . . ah! some would say that is dangerous language. It is God's language; John speaking as he was moved by the Holy Ghost. It throws a zone of mercy around the world. Perish the hand that would narrow it by a hair's breadth.
>
> —Thomas Guthrie

Considered second only to Chalmers as a Scots preacher in the nineteenth century, **Thomas Guthrie** (1803–1873) was born in Brechin in Angus. He trained at Edinburgh, which he entered at twelve and from which he graduated at sixteen. Guthrie inherited a warmth for the Seceders from his mother. He tried medical studies in Paris (1826–27) but yielded to God's call to preach. His first charge was at Arbirlot and then Greyfriars in Edinburgh in 1837 and the new St. John's near Cowgate.

Guthrie was a social reformer with great compassion for the poor. His homespun manner and illustrations went straight to the hearts of the common people. He participated in the Disruption, serving afterwards at Free St. John's. He succeeded Candlish as moderator of the Free Church in 1862. Not only the poor flocked to hear him, but such as Sir James Simpson, inventor of chloroform, were his members. He worked ceaselessly for the working class "ragged schools." In the auspicious row of statues in the park along Prince's Street in Edinburgh, Guthrie's is the only one of a clergyman.

Guthrie was "not in the strictest sense of the term, a refined and intellectual preacher,"[1] but his "vivid imagination and quick sympathies" made him a magnet for the multitude.[2] He seemed to have an inexhaustible fund of anecdotes. James M'Cosh called him "the pictorial preacher of the age," very much like another Scot, Peter Marshall, in his sermons in the book *Mr. Jones, Meet the Master*. As one observed:

> The swing of the broad shoulder, the head bent forward, the look of earnestness of the flushed countenance, all tell of a man who feels he has come forth on an important errand, and is straitened till it be accomplished

> . . . an unusually tall and commanding person, with an abundance of easy and powerful gestures; a strongly expressive countenance; a powerful, clear and musical voice, the intonations of which were varied and appropriate, managed with an actor's skill, though there was not the least appearance of art.[3]

Such were Guthrie's gifts. He could have spoken impromptu, for "the oil which he brought into the sanctuary was 'beaten oil.'"[4] He was a pastoral evangelist who poured through the commentaries in his meticulous preparation.[5] His magnificent messages in *The Gospel in Ezekiel* unfold Ezekiel 36 in a painstaking but most pleasurable form. A typically effective message is "The Nature, Necessity and Power of Prayer" from Ezekiel 36:37, "I will yet for this be inquired of by the house of Israel, to do it for them." The sermon is divided under five heads.[6] Guthrie argued that our good and God's glory ever run in the same direction. His studies in Colossians were widely read, under the theme *Christ and the Inheritance of the Saints* from Colossians 1.[7] His books like *Man and the Gospel*[8] and a collection of his stories like *Out of Harness,*[9] with a most intriguing sermon on "The Rechabites" from Jeremiah 35, are eminently worthwhile.

A heart ailment finally forced Guthrie to retire. What a monumental pulpit ministry of the Word!

---

1. Thomas Guthrie, *Life of the Rev. Thomas Guthrie,* compiled mostly from his own lips (Glasgow: John S. Marr, n.d.), 105.
2. Thomas Guthrie, *Autobiography of Thomas Guthrie and Memoir by His Sons* (London: Daldy, Isbister, 1876), 188.
3. Ibid., 197ff.
4. John Edwards, *Nineteenth-Century Preachers and Their Method* (London: Charles H. Kelly, 1902), 59.
5. Lewis O. Brastow, *Representative Modern Preachers* (New York: Macmillan, 1904), 368.
6. Thomas Guthrie, *The Gospel in Ezekiel Illustrated in a Series of Discourses* (Grand Rapids: Zondervan, n.d.), 340ff. He quotes from John Wesley and uses illustrations from ancient history and from nature.
7. Thomas Guthrie, *Christ and the Inheritance of the Saints Illustrated in a Series of Discourses from the Colossians* (Edinburgh: Adam and Charles Black, 1858). Dwells minutely on each phrase from Colossians 1:12–20.
8. Thomas Guthrie, *Man and the Gospel* (New York: E. B. Treat, n.d.). Clarence Macartney in his Stone Lectures at Princeton in 1928 highlights Guthrie as a pictorial preacher who addresses himself with model effectiveness to the average person; see *Sons of Thunder* (New York: Revell, 1929).
9. Thomas Guthrie, *Out of Harness: Sketches, Narrative and Description* (New York: E. B. Treat, n.d.). His depictions of French Protestantism are most enlightening (108ff.), and his chapter on "Dr. Chalmers and the Cowgate" describes the encouragement Guthrie received from the great Chalmers in the poorest section of Edinburgh.

10.5.2 *William Cunningham—The Theologian Who Took a Stand*

> The Reformers were all led by God to give careful attention to the study of the sacred Scriptures . . . Their strength and success arose very much from their familiar and intimate acquaintance with the word of God—the whole word of God. They were familiar with the meaning and application of its statements, and they were deeply imbued with its spirit. The word of God dwelt in them richly. There is reason to fear, that, since the period of the Reformation, the careful study of the word of God itself has not received the share of time and attention which its importance deserves . . . We know but little of the word of God as it ought to be known.
>
> —William Cunningham in *The Reformers and the Theology of the Reformation*

Described by Webber as "one of the most majestic preachers of Disruption days" and one of the confidantes of Chalmers and Candlish, **William Cunningham** (1805–1861) was a key leader in the Free Church of Scotland. Born in Hamilton and trained at Edinburgh, which he entered at fifteen, he was licensed in 1828. Walker says of Cunningham, "As a student he was known as an omnivorous reader and also a vigorous thinker and effective speaker."[1]

Cunningham was apparently a moderate initially, but under Andrew Thompson (cf. 9.1.5) and the fiery evangelical preaching of **Robert Gordon** (1786–1853), he became a strong evangelical. After serving at Greenock, Cunningham went to Edinburgh in 1834 to teach at Trinity College. Although he gave up much, he was with Chalmers in the Disruption and was one of the first to march out of St. Andrew's Church that fateful May 18, 1843.[2] He was the first professor of theology at New College and then moved over to church history, succeeding Chalmers as principal. Cunningham also moderated the General Assembly in 1859.

Dealt a heavy blow in the death of their champion, Thomas Chalmers, the Free Church looked to Cunningham and Candlish, who did not see all issues alike. Cunningham was a deep-dyed Calvinist[3] but wrote significantly on the history of theology. He was unswerving in his commitment to the authority of Scripture for which he argued both on the grounds of rational evidence and the witness of the Spirit. Though holding to particular atonement, he strongly advocated the free offer of the gospel:

> It is right that these offers and invitations should be freely and indiscriminately addressed to men of all characters and in all circumstances, without exception, condition or qualification.[4]

John J. Bonar (1803–1891) said of Cunningham that "the splendour that surrounds his name was quickly eclipsed as Scottish churchmen opted for the theology of the Enlightenment in preference to that of the Reformation. If that situation is ever reversed people will again take seriously Cunningham's claim to be Scotland's greatest theologian."[5]

Cunningham visited the United States to preach and was awarded an honorary doctorate at Princeton. He traveled with Guthrie to England to interpret developments. His powerful sermon on the cross at the opening of the General Assembly in 1860 was epochal. J. W. Alexander described him:

> A stout but finely formed man . . . powerful reasoning and sound judgment . . . a walking treasury of facts, dates and ecclesiastical law. I heard him for an hour on Friday . . . indescribable Scottish intonation, but little idiom and convulsion of body, but flowing elegant language and amazing power in presenting an argument . . .[6]

The rise of higher criticism would ultimately spell disaster for Scottish preaching. The sad story is chronicled by Riesen.[7] The silence of A. B. Davidson, the radical thinking of William Robertson Smith, and the concessions of George Adam Smith were the death knell. Riesen purports to see the seeds of this sedition even in the Free Church fathers Chalmers, Cunningham, and Bannerman.[8] Nicholas Needham sets that record straight.[9] We shall return to the gloomy account of the spiritual declension that ravaged the Scottish church. In his preaching and teaching, however, Cunningham stood fast for "the faith once for all delivered to the saints."

---

1. Norman L. Walker, *Chapters from the History of the Free Church of Scotland* (Edinburgh: Oliphant, 1895), 92.
2. Henry Wellwood Moncrief, *The Free Church Principle: Its Character and History* (Edinburgh: Macniven, 1883).
3. William Cunningham, *The Reformers and the Theology of the Reformation* (London: Banner of Truth, 1862, 1967).
4. D. Macleod, "William Cunningham," in *Dictionary of Scottish Church History and Theology,* ed. Nigel M. de S. Cameron (Downers Grove, Ill.: InterVarsity Press, 1993), 230.
5. Ibid., 230. The Cunningham Lectures were in his memory and among the most prestigious in Scotland.
6. F. R. Webber, *A History of Preaching in Britain and America* (Milwaukee: Northwestern, 1955), 2:352.
7. Richard Allan Riesen, *Criticism and Faith in Late Victorian Scotland* (Lanham, Md.: University Press of America, 1985).
8. Ibid., 377.
9. Nicholas R. Needham, *The Doctrine of Holy Scripture in the Free Church Fathers* (Edinburgh: Rutherford House, 1991). Needham demonstrates that the Free Church fathers were not the unwitting precursors of Robertson Smith. Riesen seems to tar Charles Hodge himself with the same brush, which undercuts his entire case (400).

10.5.3 ROBERT CANDLISH—THE PASTOR, PROFESSOR, AND PREACHER

> Do we not need as a people, a new and fresh interposition of Divine power, to quicken and revive our spiritual life, a new outpouring of the Spirit, a

> new baptism from above! Oh! that it might please Him who, when He ascended up on high, received gifts for men . . . to shed forth His saving and unerring grace, in such manner and measure as might be seen and heard. Oh! that it were thus owned and blessed by some signal tokens of the Spirit's power, in unquestionable instances of sinners converted, backsliders reclaimed, anxious inquirers comforted and humble followers of the Saviour filled with every new joy and peace in believing.
>
> —Robert S. Candlish

At the apogee of Scottish biblical preaching, onslaughts against soundness and scripturality were mounted. **John McLeod Campbell** (1800–1872) denied scriptural authority and penal substitution. In this he was influenced by the maverick **Thomas Erskine of Linlathen.**[1] Campbell went to trial in 1831 and was deposed from his charge at Row to spend his last twenty-five years at a small, independent chapel in Glasgow. Likewise, the celebrated capitulation of the brilliant young **William Robertson Smith** (1846–1894) to the blandishments of higher criticism and the ensuing trial were a dark hour for the Free Church of Scotland.

Among the stalwart defenders of orthodoxy at this time was the able **Robert S. Candlish** (1806–1873), who was closely allied with Cunningham and Chalmers. Candlish was born in Edinburgh. His father was a teacher of medicine. Both of his parents were related to the Scottish poet Robert Burns. Candlish tutored at Eton for a time. Early on he had a reputation as a moderate and served associateships under such auspices. Then he won the call to St. George's, the largest in Edinburgh, over Cunningham. St. George's was a parish with eight thousand souls, and among his assistants there were Andrew Bonar, the famous oratorical preacher J. Oswald Dykes, and Alexander Whyte. He was offered a professorial chair at New College but canceled his acceptance when the new pastor-designate died. Candlish stayed at St. George's—known as Free St. George's after the Disruption—for the rest of his life.[2]

Thus Candlish both taught and preached for many years. In 1862 he was appointed principal of New College. Although he never had finished his theological studies, Princeton gave him a D.D. in 1841. His decorous sermons before the General Assembly were memorable, and his funeral sermon for Dr. Guthrie was a classic. His study and desk were neat, as were his sermons.[3] In appearance he was slight with a large head and "a great shock of unruly hair." Before the close of the pulpit hymn he would almost jump up and move quickly to the pulpit to unleash a tidal flow of passionate discourse.[4] Three volumes of his lectures on Genesis are still read, and his masterful studies in 1 John are peerless. His work on *Reason and Revelation* is significant and is exceeded only by Professor James Bannerman's six-hundred-page treatise on the authority of Scripture.

Alexander Whyte spoke of the exposition of Candlish in the following terms:

> He would set himself to unwind and unweave its texture, filament by

> filament, and fibre by fibre, with the most minute analysis and the most practiced exegetical skill. And then how he would address himself to the reweaving of it all again, and that into a rich web of evangelical doctrine.[5]

In his exposition of 1 John 4:4–6, "The Spirit of Christ in us greater than the Spirit of Antichrist in the world," he uses two divisions very simply—he who is in the world is great; but he who is in us is greater because he is the Lord Almighty.[6] Especially arresting in this series are the messages on "The Test of Antichrist" and "Passing Away of the World." This is solid biblical fare which wore well for many years. Today the highlight of the week at St. George's West on Shandwicke Place is the senior citizens' lunch. At St. George's, the battle over the Bible was lost and great preaching went with it.[7]

---

1. George M. Tuttle, *John McLeod Campbell on the Atonement* (Edinburgh: Handsell Press, 1986). Sympathetic.
2. Jean L. Watson, *Life of Principal Candlish* (Edinburgh: James Gemmell, 1882), 124.
3. Ibid., 163. See also the massive work by William Wilson, *Memorials of Robert Smith Candlish* (Edinburgh: Adam and Charles Black, 1880).
4. F. R. Webber, *A History of Preaching in Britain and America* (Milwaukee: Northwestern, 1955), 2:360.
5. Quoted by Wilbur M. Smith in his biographical preface to Robert S. Candlish, *1 John* (Grand Rapids: Zondervan, n.d.).
6. Ibid., 367ff.
7. "What Are We to Say?" A Church of Scotland pastor writes to his congregation of devout Highlanders about the drift away from the Word of God in our time, *Christian Heritage Magazine* (November 1977): 4ff.

10.5.4 John Eadie—The Preacher Who Taught Exegesis

> I have, as I dare say you will bear me witness, preached the Gospel, and the great central truth of the Gospel—salvation by the cross; and I have uniformly done this, I can plead to no neglect or indifference in this. This crown I will let no man take from me. I was "separated to preach the Gospel," and that Gospel I have endeavored to preach with all freedom and fullness . . . I have preached more than a thousand sermons from a thousand texts . . . and yet I mourn not the want of themes; I feel in no danger of falling into monotony. I find the riches of Christ to be unsearchable.
>
> —John Eadie on his 25th Anniversary at Cambridge Street Church, Glasgow

Times of thriving preaching are also times of the writing and publication of many sound commentaries on Scripture. A superb example of this is the preaching and writing of **John Eadie** (1810–1876) from the minuscule United Secession Church, which also gave us Orr and Cairns. Born in Sterlingshire and educated at Glasgow, Eadie entered the divinity hall at sixteen and was soon conspicuous for his gift of speech.[1] He also gained renown for his feats of memory, being able to recite all of *Paradise Lost*. Often called to lecture on temperance, he gave himself unstintingly to "the scientific exposition of Scripture."[2] In 1835 he took the call to the Cambridge Street Church in Glasgow, where he ministered for twenty-eight years to a working class audience of seven hundred. Eadie's first message was from Acts 10:39. Following that, he went through book by book with his flock. Not surprisingly, he preached from memory.

In 1843 Eadie was elected to the chair of biblical literature in Secession Hall, where his deep reverence for the text strengthened the strong tradition of exegetical preaching in his communion. His exposition had dramatic power. His aim was "a faithful attempt to unfold the real meaning of Scripture and apply it to the practical wants of daily life."[3] Along with his teaching and preaching he published prodigiously, including a biographical memoir of the deaf English scholar, **John Kitto** (1804–1854).[4] He also produced a condensation of Cruden's concordance, a biblical encyclopedia (1848), an *Analytical Concordance* (1856), an *Ecclesiastical Encyclopedia* (1861), and a family Bible. We have already referred to his *Paul the Preacher* (1854 cf. 2.3.3), and while not as strong in grammar as he was in exegesis, he wrote substantive and valuable commentaries on Ephesians, Colossians, Philippians, and the Thessalonian correspondence published after his death. His commentary on Galatians is especially strong.[5]

Not at all sectarian, Eadie loved all believers. In 1861 he planted a new church in Lansdown in Glasgow, where he sought to introduce some changes in worship, including response to prayers with an audible "amen" from the congregation. He visited the U.S. in 1871 and developed a lasting friendship with William Cullen Bryant, the American poet. Eadie also preached for John Hall and enjoyed good fellowship with Professors Schaff at Union and Charles Hodge at Princeton. He spoke at John Wanamaker's Bethany Sabbath School in Philadelphia, and was an integral part of the revision of the Scripture (RV). In 1876 his health broke, and his ministry was unexpectedly over.[6] Yet his dedication to the explication of Bible truth remained. One writer observes:

> Because Eadie held to the highest view of the New Testament text as inspired by the Holy Spirit, he also had the highest conception of the task of the biblical exegete. For the same reason he rejected the subjectivism of much of the rationalistic scholarship of his day.[7]

---

1. John Brown, *Life of John Eadie* (London: Macmillan, 1878), 38.
2. Ibid., 47.
3. Ibid., 172.
4. John Eadie, "A Critical Estimate of Dr. Kitto's Life and Writings," in J. E. Ryland, *Memoirs of John Kitto* (Edinburgh: William Oliphant, 1856), 667ff. S. P. Tregelles, the Plymouth Brother, also made contribution to this volume.

5. John Eadie, *Commentary of the Epistle of Paul to the Galatians* (Grand Rapids: Zondervan, 1869, 1894).
6. Brown, *Life of John Eadie,* 370.
7. Nigel M. de S. Cameron, ed., *Dictionary of Scottish Church History and Theology* (Downers Grove, Ill.: InterVarsity Press, 1993), 270.

10.5.5 NORMAN MACLEOD—A POPULAR PREACHER WHO WRESTLED WITH PRINCIPLE

> I was ordained here. You know what an awful thing it is. I feel as if the weight of those hands is still upon my head, crushing me with responsibility. But it was a delightful scene. I got well over my first sermon, "Now are we ambassadors." Once or twice nearly overcome; and this day I have preached twice. I have been then, in the parish a week, have been over it all, visited each day from ten till five. . . . It is in a terrible state . . . there is in all the parish an awful want of spiritual religion.
>
> —Norman Macleod in a letter, March 25, 1838

Norman Macleod (1812–1872) came from a distinguished line of clergy out of the island people of the Highlands. Known popularly as Macleod of Barony and ultimately as "the chief ecclesiastic of the Church of Scotland" (Dean Stanley), he was raised in the seaport of Campbeltown, where he learned Gaelic. Macleod loved literature and had a powerful imagination.[1] Studying at Glasgow and then at Edinburgh, he acknowledged that Chalmers made "an ineradicable impression on him." The death of his younger brother James also proved to be a spiritual turning point.

The springtime of Macleod's ministerial life was the five-year period he served his first parish in Loudoun in Ayrshire. In some respects he was Bunyan's Mr. Facing-both-ways, and the Disruption in 1843 found him in the middle. At a time when some would "peril their all for conscience sake,"[2] Macleod stayed in the Church of Scotland. He was identified with the "forty" who did not want to be identified with the moderates or the evangelicals, whom he called those "firebrands."[3] Although he loved Christ and the Word, he found it hard to maintain the middle ground.

In 1843 he transferred to Dalkeith near Edinburgh and was sent to North America with a team to interpret the Disruption to Scottish churches and immigrants. His sermons were growing elaborate by now, but his preaching was always well received.[4] Although he endeavored to restrain his descriptive bent, as he matured, his preaching developed a higher teaching component and was more "homely talk."[5]

On the death of Dr. Black, Macleod assumed the pastorate of the Barony Church in Glasgow in 1851, the same year in which he married. The population of the parish was more than 87,000, and he gave himself with great abandon to reaching them. He established Sunday schools, savings banks and a special service for the poor, and edited a periodical called *Good Words.* He assumed denominational leadership of the India Mission and became a chaplain and advisor to Queen Victoria. His stand against the traditional Scottish Sabbath involved him in a hurricane of controversy. He was active in the Evangelical Alliance and served as moderator of the General Assembly in 1869.

Although lovable and congenial, Macleod's aversion to taking a stand undercut his preaching ministry, and nowhere in his massive two-volume memoirs do we hear about a passion for conversions. Yet he was known as an able preacher who "could swing with a wide cable." He was most influenced by Thomas Arnold (the English broad churchman) and by his cousin John Macleod Campbell, with whom he walked every Saturday evening. He regarded the discipline of Campbell as "barbarous intolerance,"[6] and saw his own theological views "expanding" and moving way from any penal sense in the atonement.[7]

Macleod was increasingly uneasy about requiring any subscription to theological standards and felt this should be left to the individual.[8] He did not see the Second Coming of Christ as "objective," and though he was shocked by infidelity, he believed "the infidel is nearer the kingdom of God than many an Orthodox minister."[9] Condemnation after death was to be a process of education. In this he was with Thomas Erskine and F. D. Maurice, two of his best friends. He advocated reducing all standards to the Apostles' Creed and overlooking other differences. Webber accurately reflects Macleod's theological imprecision in his observation:

> Men who have heard him preach have said that he was inclined at times, when preaching an expository sermon, to skip from verse to verse, causing an attentive hearer to regret that certain truths had not been developed more fully.[10]

Yet despite all of this vacillation, Norman Macleod was a winsome and popular preacher.

---

1. Donald Macleod, *Memoir of Norman Macleod* (London: Daldy, Isbister, 1876), 1:100.
2. Ibid., 1:170.
3. Ibid., 2:228.
4. Ibid., 2:249.
5. Ibid., 2:231.
6. Ibid., 1:275.
7. Ibid., 2:116, 118, 138.
8. Ibid., 1:302.
9. Ibid., 1:315.
10. F. R. Webber, *A History of Preaching in Britain and America* (Milwaukee: Northwestern, 1955), 2:388.

10.5.6 *John Kennedy of Dingwall—The Preacher Who Was Firm as a Rock*

> My style of preaching has been described as antiquated, as ignoring the superior enlightenment of these bright times, as making no use of the wondrous results of recent scientific researches. . . . As I judge the position of the age, I desire my preaching to be behind it; for I think that, in

> these days, the preacher's work is to be calling back his generation to "the old paths" in which the Lord was found and followed by the fathers. Nor can I discover any difference between the men of this age and those of another as sinners, and I cannot, therefore, see how the gospel which suits the one can be unsuitable to the other.
>
> —John Kennedy of Dingwall

At this time a surge of biblical preaching was complementing an outpouring of rich theological reflection. **James Buchanan** (1804–1870) had a thriving preaching ministry in North Leith. He succeeded Chalmers, and bequeathed us masterpieces of solid theology on the Holy Spirit and on justification by faith alone.[1] Another preaching theologian in the Free Church was **George Smeaton** (1814–1889), who wrote powerful and profound works on the Holy Spirit and two magnificent tomes on the atonement. Another in this brave legion was **S. D. F. Salmond** (1837–1904), principal at Aberdeen and author of *The Christian Doctrine of Immortality,* a lucid and convincing statement of the doctrine of everlasting punishment. Another in this camp who stayed in parish ministry and was known as the prince of Highland preachers was **John Kennedy** of Dingwall (1819–1884), called by some the greatest preacher of his generation in Scotland.

Kennedy was born in a Scottish manse and studied at Aberdeen. He became serious about spiritual things and ministry upon his father's death. Up to that time he had been "clear as an icicle and equally cold."[2] He went out in the Disruption to serve his only charge, the Free Church in Dingwall, where the Lord gave him a ministry in which "He exercised a peculiar fascination over the minds of the Highland population."[3] Kennedy preached services in both Gaelic and English every Lord's Day. It was said he spoke Gaelic as if he knew no English and English as if he knew no Gaelic.[4] He became immensely popular as the speaker for the communion services in the north. Spurgeon himself came up for the dedication of the new Free Church. As early as 1869, Kennedy was troubled with diabetes and traveled extensively to regain his health. Upon visiting the United States, he bonded with Charles Hodge and shrank from Beecher, who so downplayed sin and the Atonement.[5]

Kennedy loved paintings, music, and Shakespeare. He opposed union with the United Presbyterians and had grave reservations about the Moody and Sankey meetings. He was not naturally feisty or combative, as his good friend **Hugh Martin** (1822–1885) observed: "What a pity that our brother Kennedy's modesty muzzles him on the floor of the Assembly."[6] He believed in spoken not read prayers and that preaching was central in worship. His own messages were solidly constructed and described in the *Daily Review:*

> The sermon was built up, block upon block, of granite reasoning. Each of those fundamental propositions was presented with intense and overpowering earnestness. The blocks were laid upon each other red hot. . . . As the discourse went on, and the reasoning became molten into fiery flood . . . the labouring breath struggled into voice and rang over the hillside like a clarion . . . and the whole responding multitude bent forward.[7]

Vintage Kennedy is heard in the following from his sermon "The Preaching of Christ Crucified":

> Pauline preaching is becoming, in the estimation of many, an antiquated kind of thing, which, in an age such as ours, should be quite laid as a fossil on the shelf. And what do they propose to substitute? We preach Christ crucified, and in doing so we preach peace to sinners through "the blood of His cross." O what a blessing is peace with God to a sinner condemned to die! The sinner himself can do nothing to meet the Law's claims . . . but Christ crucified hath done and suffered all that is required in order to a free and full exercise of divine mercy such as shall be to the praise of the divine glory. In preaching Christ crucified there is presented to the sinner this one ground on which he is called to take his stand before the mercy, free and infinite, of God, to receive "with money and without price" the blessing of everlasting peace with God.[8]

---

1. James Buchanan, *The Doctrine of Justification* (Grand Rapids: Baker, 1867, 1955). Included in the Cunningham Lectureship, this volume still stands as the single best treatment of this vital Reformation doctrine.
2. Maurice Roberts, "Dr. John Kennedy—A Memorial Sketch," *Banner of Truth* (August–September 1984): 4.
3. Ibid., 3.
4. Donald Beaton, *Some Noted Ministers of the Northern Highlands* (Glasgow: Free Presbyterian, 1929, 1985), 274.
5. Alan P. F. Sell, *Defending and Declaring the Faith: Some Scottish Examples 1860–1920* (Exeter: Paternoster, 1987), 19. John Kennedy is the first of eight notable defenders of the faith analyzed in this glowing work. Hugh Martin's volumes of preaching on Jonah and *The Shadow of Calvary* are among the finest of the wheat.
6. Roberts, "Dr. John Kennedy," 20.
7. Ibid., 2.
8. F. R. Webber, *A History of Preaching in Britain and America* (Milwaukee: Northwestern, 1955), 2:408–9.

10.5.7 William B. Robertson of Irvine—The Poet-Preacher

> The doctrine of the Atonement might be called the doctrine of Scripture; and woe be to them that would swerve in the least away from that. It was very sad to think that earnest, gifted men like the late Robertson of Brighton, should swerve from this soul-saving truth, and go their weeping, woeful way, in darkness.
>
> —William B. Robertson

One of the truly soaring spirits in the Scottish pulpit at this time as agreed by all hands was **William Bruce Robertson** of Irvine (1820–1886). The old-timers would often say of even a good preacher that "the vintage was not equal to the gleanings in Robertson's time." He spent his entire ministerial life in Irvine, where David Dickson (cf. 7.5.2) had such a signal ministry. Robertson was born near Stirling and educated at Glasgow, where he was deeply influenced by Candlish and Chalmers. He entered the divinity hall of the United Secession Church in Edinburgh in 1838. One of his classmates was **John Ker** (1819–1886), who was to become professor of practical training for the ministry.[1] Ker recalled the originality and imagination of young Robertson as he preached on King Ahaz and the "eerie awesomeness" of the impression.[2] Robertson also knew De Quincey and went with Ker to study at Halle under Tholuck and Neander.

Licensed in 1843, he began his preaching in the Cotton Row Church (U.P.) in Irvine, a kind of sleepy hollow of not six thousand souls. One who saw him mount the pulpit in those days was indignant that one so young should dare to preach. But that same observer reported, "[When] I heard him pray, I felt that the most aged might sit at his feet."[3] A doctrinal preacher, Robertson gave moving expository lectures as well as sermons. His lifting sermon from Exodus 24:11, "They saw God and did eat and drink," had three heads:

I. To eat and drink and not see God is sin.
II. To eat and drink and not see God because of tears is sorrow.
III. To eat and drink and see God, that is salvation.[4]

He presented an unforgettable series on "The Silences of the Bible" that gave a "sense that he spoke from immediate inspiration." He loved to preach on praise to God and was in great demand for the communion seasons. Robertson held devoutly to a view of the premillennial return of Christ. At times some felt his sermons were "a little too luscious in their ripeness and unformed in their splendor."[5] His magnificent sermon on Ephesians 4:30 on not grieving the Holy Spirit, however, is straight as an arrow:

I. A great period: "the day of Redemption";
II. A great privilege: "being sealed by the Holy Spirit of God";
III. A great practical requirement: "grieve not the Holy Spirit of God";
IV. The grand persuasion to the performance of the requirement—that which knits up the whole: "grieve not the Holy Spirit of God by whom ye are sealed."[6]

Robertson loved poetry and wrote much of it himself. Some called him the modern Jeremy Taylor. Imagination was a dominant faculty in his preaching, and his picture images were most rare. He enjoyed preaching in the open air. His congregation was rocked by the great revival of 1859, and to hold the influx of people a new building, called Trinity Church, was constructed. After a long illness, William Robertson died in Mentone, France, just as Spurgeon had.

1. John Edwards, *Nineteenth-Century Preachers and Their Methods* (London: Charles Kelly, 1902), 65ff. We have already benefited from Ker's pioneering lectures on preaching and especially on German preaching.
2. Arthur Guthrie, *Robertson of Irvine: Poet-Preacher* (Edinburgh: Menzies, 1889), 25, 209, 318.
3. Ibid., 56.
4. Ibid., 74.
5. Ibid., 122.
6. Ibid., 125ff.

10.5.8 ADOLPH SAPHIR—THE HEBREW CHRISTIAN WHO REALLY PREACHED CHRIST

> There subsists an essential and vital connection between the eternal Word of God and the written Word which testifies of Him, of His person and work, of His sufferings and glory. . . . It is impossible for us to understand the nature of Scripture unless we view it in relation to the Son of God, the Messiah of Israel, the Redeemer of God's people; for He is the centre and kernel of the inspired record.
>
> —A. A. Saphir

The background of the startling ministry of **Aaron Adolph Saphir** (1831–1891) was the Church of Scotland mission to the Jews of Budapest. This was conceived providentially in Candlish's proposal, McCheyne's trip to Palestine (cf. 9.1.3), and the ministry in Budapest opened by Rabbi "Rab" Duncan (cf. 9.1.6).

From a distinguished old Jewish family, Adolph Saphir avowed faith in Jesus the Messiah. Saphir went with Duncan and Alfred Edersheim, another convert, back to Edinburgh to perfect his English.[1] From 1844 to 1848 he studied in Berlin, where he was received by Neander and Hengstenberg. He later recalled this time: "I suffered for years from the teachings of Scheiermacher's disciples when I was about seventeen."[2]

In 1854 Saphir was ordained a Free Church missionary to the Jews and served briefly in Hamburg. Always coping with physical infirmity, he served a succession of English Presbyterian churches and launched his amazing writing ministry, out of which came such widely-read titles as *Conversion, Christ and the Scriptures* and *The Divine Unity of Scripture.* Thoroughly premillennial, Saphir watched constantly for Christ's imminent return. His expository lectures on Hebrews are classic and give a clue to the richness of his preaching.[3] Always meticulously prepared, he preached extempore. He later wrote:

> The preaching of the gospel, however legitimately allied to natural and mental acquirements, must always retain the mark of crucifixion. It does not become us to be orators. There is an element in human eloquence, which is not according to the gospel of Christ. Preaching is more than an exposition of Scripture; it is a reproduction of Scripture . . . the gospel is preached with the Holy Ghost sent down from heaven . . .[4]

Franz Delitzsch of Leipzig, a friend of evangelism to the Jews, wrote the introduction to Saphir's influential tract "Who Is an Apostate?" Saphir convened a Free Church Conference on the Jews in 1889, where Andrew Bonar also spoke. "The future of Israel is bright and glorious," Saphir proclaimed. The future restoration of Israel is a certainty.[5] A typical exposition of his is "The Christian's Hope" from 1 John 3:2. Here Saphir nicely divides the text and the sermon:

I. We shall see Christ as he is
  A. The object of our vision
  B. The manner of our vision
    1. How we have it at present
    2. How we shall have it in the future
II. We shall be like Christ
  A. We shall know him as we are known
  B. We shall be healed[6]

When Saphir's wife died, he was so frail that he could not attend the funeral. William Wingate stayed with him. A day later, Aaron Adolph Saphir was taken home also.

---

1. Gavin Carlyle, *Mighty in the Scripture: A Memoir of Adolph Saphir* (London: John Shaw, 1894), 17. The report was by the missionary, the Reverend William Wingate, grandfather of Lt. Gen. Orde Wingate, a well-known British military genius and lover of the "hope of Israel." On the Scottish mission, see David L. Larsen, *Jews, Gentiles and the Church: A New Perspective on History and Prophecy* (Grand Rapids: Discovery House, 1995), 129.
2. Ibid., 64, 251.
3. Adolph Saphir, *Epistle to the Hebrews* (Grand Rapids: Kregel, 1874, 1983). Nine of his titles are published in this series. Arno Gaebelein of *Our Hope* magazine picked up Saphir's writings and popularized them in the U.S.
4. Carlyle, *Mighty in the Scripture,* 354.
5. Ibid., 299, 303.
6. Ibid., 303.

10.5.9 John R. MacDuff—The Preacher with a Powerful Pen

> The righteousness of that law must be "fulfilled;" its requirements must be met, and its sanctities upheld, either in the person of the sinner or of his divine Surety . . . by His voluntary substitution and suretyship He has once and for ever solved the momentous problem—settled the awful alternative, condemn or not condemn.
>
> —John R. MacDuff

Here is a preacher who touched many lives through his more than seventy-five books and his preaching of the Word with effect and power. **John R. MacDuff**

(1818–1895) was born in the parish of Scone in Perthshire. He was brought to evangelical conviction and experience through Dr. Chalmers while studying at Edinburgh. MacDuff served several congregations, including the Sandyford Church in Glasgow, "where he had a large, handsome church building and a large, intelligent congregation."[1] His books are sermonic in nature but are richly biblical and devotional. Among many favorites is his series of studies on John 4 under the title *Noontide at Sychar.*[2] Sermons such as "The Gift of God and Living Water" and "The Heavenly Food and the Field of Harvest" are especially tantalizing. Also of note is his volume on *In Christo* or *The Monogram of St. Paul.*[3] These studies of the "in Christ" formula in the apostle Paul are doctrinally probing and practical.

---

1. F. R. Webber, *A History of Preaching in Britain and America* (Milwaukee: Northwestern, 1955), 2:400.
2. John R. MacDuff, *Noontide at Sychar* (London: James Nisbet, 1877).
3. John R. MacDuff, *In Christo* (London: Charles J. Thynne, n.d.).

10.5.10 Henry Drummond—The University Preacher Who Touched Students

> Evangelism was the master-passion of his life . . . He found the heart of Christianity in a personal friendship with Jesus Christ, and it was his ambition as an evangelist to introduce men to Christ. It was a simple message; but delivered with the thousand subtle influences radiating forth from his strong and rich personality, it evoked a wonderful response in the crowded meeting and in the quiet talk in the streets or in young men's lodgings.
>
> —Rev. D. M. Ross

A singular spirit among the preachers at the end of the century was **Henry Drummond** (1851–1897), who had an unusually effective outreach ministry to university men in Scotland and beyond. He touched Arthur James Balfour, later British Prime Minister and Foreign Secretary, Von Moltke of Germany, and countless others. Drummond was born in Stirling in a traditional Scottish Free Church home. After studying at the University in Edinburgh starting at age fifteen, he entered New College for the divinity course.

Drummond had been moved by F. W. Robertson's sermon on "The Loneliness of Christ" (cf. 9.3.5) and joined with classmates such as James Stalker, George Adam Smith (who later wrote a fine biography of Drummond), and John Watson (Ian Maclaren).[1] While he was somewhat influenced by A. B. Davidson's concessions to biblical criticism, Drummond was soon caught up in the Moody-Sankey mission of 1873 to 1875. He organized meetings for students with Stalker and spoke to thousands about Christ. He became a deep friend of D. L. Moody.[2] Returning to school, Drummond finished his course. Meanwhile, the Moody campaigns filled the theological halls of Scotland. While appointed as lecturer in natural science in the Free Church College in Glasgow, Drummond assisted both Hood Wilson in Barclay Church in Edinburgh early on and then Marcus Dods in Renfield Church in Glasgow.

The Free Church had come into existence in large part because the sermons of the moderates "might have been preached in a heathen temple as fitly as in St. Giles."[3] Drummond was torn, and though he had no comment on the Robertson Smith case in 1879, he did not know which way to turn. He traveled widely, visiting America several times and ministering at Northfield, where his ideas on evolution were a problem.[4] He pursued geologic and evangelistic aims in Africa and ministered in Australia and the South Seas. His sermon from 1 Corinthians 13 on "The Greatest Thing in the World" was one of Moody's favorites.[5] It is a classic of exposition and elegance. Drummond spoke in house meetings to the cream of British society. He also worked with C. T. Studd of Cambridge in the great Edinburgh Students' Revival of 1884 and 1885.[6] His distinctive style is recalled for us:

> Attired in a well-cut frock-coat . . . with a voice that reached the farthest seat in the auditorium in tones of sweet reasonableness . . . frequently lasting fifty minutes . . . his vocabulary was a rich one . . . he had read widely in belles lettres as well as in science and theology; he had traveled much; and enriched by fitting figures of speech or apt illustration, he spoke under the influence of the master-passion of his life.[7]

I can well remember the impression of reading Drummond's three great sermons on the will of God in my own early collegiate years. His majestic sermon on "Ill-Temper: The Elder Brother" is peerless, and his message on "The Eccentricity of True Religion" from Mark 3:21 is unforgettable. He preached on "The Christian's Clairvoyance" out of 2 Corinthians 4:18 and masterfully on the facts of sin and salvation.[8]

In his last years, Drummond became very ill and died of a malignant disease of the bones. He had never married. Henry Drummond was a light that burned brightly and then sadly flickered out in such physical extremity.

---

1. James Y. Simpson, *Henry Drummond in Famous Scots Series* (Edinburgh: Oliphant Anderson, 1901), 32.
2. Ibid., 43, 45.
3. W. Robertson Nicoll, *The Ideal Life* (New York: Dodd Mead, 1898), 6.
4. Cuthbert Lennox, *The Practical Life Work of Henry Drummond* (New York: James Pott, 1901), 152ff.
5. Henry Drummond, *Addresses* (Chicago: Revell, 1891), 7ff.
6. Lennox, *The Practical Life Work of Henry Drummond,* 96.
7. Ibid., 100.
8. These sermons are all found in Nicoll, *The Ideal Life.*

10.5.11 Principal Rainy—The Preacher-Professor Who Defined a Movement

> Learn to serve Christ on the great scale, and even, if the scene of your work be narrow or obscure, serve Him on the grand principles which make life strong, noble and spacious. Never look at any period of the past with a timid or a cringing heart. From the greatest and most impressive of past services and departed servants turn to your own work with the thought—I also, I too, am a servant of Christ Jesus.
>
> —Robert Rainy

Nineteenth-century Scotland saw a brilliant array of scholars and preachers. **Robert Flint** (1834–1910) was born in a shepherd's cottage, served as assistant to Norman Macleod, and followed William Milligan at Kilconquhar. While his sermons "occasionally flew over their heads like birds of paradise," Flint was indeed noteworthy.[1] **A. B. Davidson** (1831–1902) succeeded Duncan at New College, but who was "doubting at every pore."[2] Yet Stalker spoke of Davidson's gripping preaching, and many a student and congregant could testify, "His prayer revived my drooping feelings."[3] Both **Andrew Fairbairn** and **Patrick Fairbairn** were able preachers and scholars, and **George Milligan,** minister in Caputh in Perthshire, produced an outstanding commentary on 1 Thessalonians.[4]

But chief among these is **Robert Rainy** (1826–1906), who after Cunningham and Candlish presided at the defining hours of the Scottish Free Church. The son of a professor of medicine in Glasgow, Rainy was related to William E. Gladstone and the Balfours. He served the Free Church in Huntly, where George MacDonald had his roots. He attracted notice for his solid preaching at the High Free Church in Edinburgh over eight years. Still, his chief biographer acknowledges, "He did not have the exuberant oratory with which Dr. Guthrie drew a crowd of all classes, nor even the immense nervous force with which Dr. Candlish kept his great congregation at St. George's."[5] Rainy tended to be a bit heavy, but his sermons are luminous and direct.[6] My particular favorite is "Mutability and Endurance" based on 1 Peter 1:24–25.

In 1862 Rainy took Cunningham's chair in church history, which he filled for thirty-eight years. As principal he had to handle the Robertson Smith case. The brilliant young Smith had studied with Wellhausen and had given way to higher critical views, including the abolition of predictive prophecy. Salmond defended him, A. B. Davidson remained silent, and Andrew Bonar moved for Smith's suspension from teaching after a rebuke achieved no alteration. Bonar's motion carried by one vote. Although Rainy was evangelical ("I remain orthodox on the atonement," he claimed), he tried to walk both sides of the street and found himself successively defending Marcus Dods, Henry Drummond, A. B. Bruce, and George Adam Smith. The soul of the Free Church was at stake. K. R. Ross notes of Rainy, "Personally he did not find criticism a major issue and he underestimated the degree to which it provoked questions regarding biblical authority."[7]

In the ensuing discussion of preaching, Rainy distinguished between the moralistic preaching of the moderates—which was, as Lord Roseberry described it, "flat as decanted champagne"—and the evangelical preaching of the gospel.[8]

Three times Rainy was moderator of the General Assembly and finally in 1900 steered the merger of the Free Church with the United Presbyterians. Asked how he managed to maintain any semblance of equanimity in all of this conflict, Rainy's oft-quoted response rings a chord: "Oh, man, I am happy at home."[9]

Although Rainy was a successor to the fathers of the Disruption, he catalyzed the liberalization of the Free Church. Ross observed that Rainy was unduly set on building a consensus "when something more prophetic was needed. . . . The fact that his leadership was characterized by complacency and opportunism, rather than initiative and conviction, accounts in part for the loss of ground which the Free Church suffered in his time."[10]

---

1. Donald Macmillan, *The Life of Robert Flint* (London: Hodder and Stoughton, 1914). Flint went on to teach at St. Andrews, Edinburgh (where he succeeded Thomas J. Crawford, whose *Doctrine of the Atonement* was sound. Flint's Baird Lecture in 1876 on theism (Edinburgh: Blackwood, 1887) is a classic.
2. James Strahan, *A. B. Davidson* (London: Hodder and Stoughton, 1917) shows how his study with Ewald at Gottingen and the influence of Driver in the U.S. made him "a noncommittal article."
3. Richard Allan Riesen, *Criticism and Faith in Late Victorian Scotland* (Lanham, Md.: University Press of America, 1985), 322.
4. George Milligan, *St. Paul's Epistles to the Thessalonians* (Grand Rapids: Eerdmans, 1908, 1952).
5. Patrick Carnegie Simpson, *The Life of Principal Rainy* (London: Hodder and Stoughton, 1909), 1:128.
6. Robert Rainy, *Sojourning with God and Other Sermons* (London: Hodder and Stoughton, 1902).
7. K. R. Ross, "Robert Rainy" in *Dictionary of Scottish Church History and Theology,* ed. Nigel M. de S. Cameron (Downers Grove, Ill.: InterVarsity Press, 1993), 690.
8. Simpson, *The Life of Principal Rainy,* 1:417ff.
9. Ibid., 2:92.
10. Ross, "Robert Rainy," 690.

10.6 THE ENGLISH ESTUARY

> Depend on it, my friends, that there is no security whatever except in standing upon the faith of our fathers and saying with them that the Blessed olde Book is "God's Word written" from the very first syllable down to the very last, and from the last to the first.
>
> —Lord Shaftesbury

> It aimed at bringing back, on a large scale, and by an aggressive movement, the Cross, and all that the Cross essentially implies.
>
> —Prime Minister William E. Gladstone speaking of the Evangelicals

Meanwhile, the religious climate in England, Wales, and Ireland was much like that of Scotland, albeit even more fissured and fractured. Evangelicals in and out of the Church of England were burdened to stress the authority of the Word of God, clear teaching on original sin, and the necessity of conversion and justification by faith alone. Other vital doctrines included eternal punishment, millenarianism and the return of our Lord, special providence, and the assurance of salvation.[1] Strong emphasis was also placed on liturgical piety, the family and the home, missionary and philanthropic endeavor, and the response to the world. An impressive array of evangelical scholars began turning out solid commentary and theology. A magnificent host of preachers from many backgrounds entered the fray to do battle for the gospel.

Authors of fiction occasionally reflected certain of these concerns as seen in "the apocalyptic mood of late romanticism," but on the whole writers either misunderstood biblical faith or were downright hostile to it. Thackery's "wild onslaught upon sermons and preachers" is a case in point.[2] George Eliot understood the truth but mocked it, and Samuel Butler showed suspicion of emotional conversion. Trollope was generally disdainful. Dickens assaulted evangelicalism. Charlotte Yonge's novels carried the Tractarian message, and George MacDonald detested evangelicalism. Nonetheless, Gladstone endorsed Mrs. Humphrey Ward's concern about negative scholarship as seen in *Robert Elsmere*.[3]

Amid this maelstrom of confusion and religious pandemonium, God graciously raised up some of the best and most biblical preaching the British Isles ever saw.

---

1. Elizabeth Jay, *The Religion of the Heart: Anglican Evangelicals and the Nineteenth-Century Novel* (Oxford: Clarendon, 1979). She underestimates the evangelical scholarly enterprise as if T. R. Birks were the only one (40).
2. Ibid., 122.
3. Robert Lee Wolff, *Gains and Losses: Novels of Faith and Doubt in Victorian England* (New York: Garland, 1977). Cf. also my upcoming, *The Irresistible Rewards of Reading: A Theological Guide to Great Literature* (Grand Rapids: Kregel, 1999).

10.6.1 Marcus Rainsford—The Irish Anglican Who Excavated the Text

> For centuries there has not been a time of so much practical, hearty work, so much earnest preaching, so much instruction and consolation given, so much care for the poor and for the young.
>
> —Gladstone to the queen, 1874

As in the United States and Scotland, by midcentury in England a massive attack was mounted on the authority of Scripture. Rebellion against the preaching of repentance and substitutionary atonement was rampant. Benjamin Jowett at Oxford hated imputation, and the move away from teaching on hell quickened. **John William Colenso** (1814–1883), who became bishop of Natal in South Africa, attacked "penal substitution—liberating God from the charge of being a 'blood-thirsty pagan tyrant.'"[1] Prime Minister Gladstone commendably held to depravity and the cross and maintained good rapport with evangelicals. He allied with Wilberforce in reforming aspects of the Church of England.

In the face of it all, "The sermon was still an effective means of persuasion."[2] **John Bird Sumner** was the strongly evangelical archbishop of Canterbury starting in 1828 and **Archibald Campbell Tait,** conciliatory to nonconformists and evangelicals, was first bishop of London and in 1868 became archbishop of Canterbury. The son of Scottish Presbyterians, he was persuasive but not eloquent. Five of his six children died of scarlet fever in 1856. Tait was called the layman's bishop. He made many positive appointments, including the partisan evangelical, J. C. Ryle to be bishop of Liverpool. His Presbyterian low-church views were encouraging to evangelicals in the Church of England.[3]

One of the choicest examples of strong biblical preaching in the Church of England at this time was **Marcus Rainsford** (1820–1897). Rainsford had the decisive influence on **W. H. Griffith Thomas** and was much sought after by D. L. Moody, with whom he developed some remarkable "gospel dialogues."[4] Though descended from Norsemen who settled in Lancashire, Rainsford's ancestors had moved to Ireland, where he was born. At age sixteen he was startled by a dream and sought the Lord, early finding Romaine's *Life of Faith* to show him the way. He graduated from Trinity College, Dublin, and began serving in 1850 as vicar in Dundalk, a town of some ten thousand mostly Roman Catholic inhabitants.[5]

The revival of 1859 deeply touched Rainsford's ministry and his churches. In 1866 he took the call to St. John's, Belgrave Square in London, a strong and fashionable church. His biblical preaching stirred up a storm—the Prince of Wales was often there, as was Gladstone, and the Lord Chancellor became a member. After working so closely with Moody in London, Rainsford was invited to Northfield and made a memorable impression there. He preached the imminent return of Christ and sought conversions in each of his sermons.

His son William described Rainsford's "fine, carrying voice and Irish eloquence" and "his precious devotion to close and systematic study of the Holy Scriptures."[6] Sadly, William abandoned the views of his father.

Rainsford's expository studies in John 17, titled *Our Lord Prays for His Own*, exceed even Thomas Manton's glorious study.[7] His books of lectures on the believer's standing in Christ from Romans 5, 6, and 7 moved Griffith Thomas.[8] Another fine collection of his sermons shows them to be "soaked through and through with the Word of God." A glowing message on "Did I Receive the Holy Spirit When I Believed?" from Acts 19 is divided into six parts.[9] His exegesis is painstaking and rich. Marcus Rainsford offers Anglican biblical preaching at its best.

---

1. Boyd Hilton, *The Age of Atonement: The Influence of Evangelicalism, 1795–1865* (Oxford: Clarendon, 1988), 383.
2. P. T. Marsh, *The Victorian Church in Decline: Archbishop Tait 1868–1882* (Pittsburgh: University of Pittsburgh, 1969), 6. This book shows how after Newman's secession, Liddon and Stanley "exerted winning influence."
3. Sidney Dark, *Seven Archbishops* (London: Eyre and Spottiswoode, 1944), 197ff.

4. Marcus Rainsford, *Our Lord Prays for His Own* (Chicago: Moody, 1876, n.d.), 244ff.
5. S. Maxwell Coder, "Biographical Introduction" in Rainsford, *Our Lord Prays for His Own,* 13.
6. Ibid., 15.
7. Ibid. Every chapter is a gem. The first message is on "Father, the hour is come" (25).
8. Marcus Rainsford, *Lectures on Romans 5* (London: John Hoby, n.d.); *Lectures on Romans 6* (London: Charles Thynne, 1898); *Lectures on Romans 7* (London: John Hoby, n.d.).
9. Marcus Rainsford, *The Fullness of God* (London: S. W. Partridge, 1898), 62ff.

10.6.2 John Charles Ryle—The Bishop Who Preached and Built

> You preach the Gospel of Jesus Christ so fully and clearly that everybody can understand it. If Christ crucified has not His rightful place in your sermons, and sin is not exposed as it should be, and your people are not plainly told what they ought to be and do, your preaching is no use.
>
> —John Charles Ryle

With evangelicalism taking hits from rationalism, hedonism, and ritualism, one outstanding preacher and writer was the first Anglican bishop of Liverpool, **John Charles Ryle** (1816–1900). Ryle embodied the pastoral strengths important to evangelicals.[1] Millions of copies of his tracts and other writings, such as his *Expository Thoughts on the Gospels,* have made a substantial impact. As a moderate Calvinist, Ryle believed in general rather than particular atonement and was a staunch premillennialist. A bit skittish about the Keswick deeper life teaching, he also felt that the ritualism of the Tractarians was incongruous with the essentially Protestant nature of the Church of England.

Methodist by background, Ryle studied at Eton and Christ Church, Oxford. While out hunting one day, an old Eton friend rebuked him for his profanity. He was sobered by the incident, and later was converted in the face of the truth of Ephesians 2:8–9.[2] Immediately he began to gobble up books by Wilberforce, John Angell James, John Newton, and Bickersteth. Upon graduation he served as curate in Exbury and then took pastoral appointments in Winchester, Helmingham, and Stradbrooke. Although he had a somewhat antisocial disposition, his preaching filled these places to "suffocation," as he put it.[3] Again and again he was named select preacher at both Cambridge and Oxford. In 1880, this man "who lived to be missed" was named the first bishop of Liverpool, by now a teeming city of seven hundred thousand, which had come into such dominance during the surging days of empire-building.

Ryle's preaching style was increasingly plain and direct, with short sentences that allowed only one subordinate clause. He carefully divided the text and discourse with strong bridging to daily life and the adept use of telling illustrations. He was a tall, well-built man. As one reporter testified, Ryle spoke to a crowd of four thousand "with a force and earnestness which have been rarely equalled, and which riveted the attention of the vast audience from commencement to finish."[4]

His friend Tollemache, when he felt that Ryle had preached long enough, would occasionally stand up in the service and look at his watch. Ryle's style was earthy and true to his Reformed convictions; he refused to dress "in an embroidered cope and mitre and carry a pastoral staff."[5] He railed at "the enormous folly of baptismal regeneration" but purred at what he called "the unspeakable beauty and excellence of the doctrine of the Second Advent."

In 1883 he welcomed D. L. Moody and company to Liverpool. Twelve years later Ryle sponsored the Liverpool General Christian Mission with W. Hay Aitken. Among his close friends were Canon **Cyril Garbett,** who preached at his enthronement as bishop,[6] **Bishop W. Boyd Carpenter** of Ripon,[7] and **Hugh MacNeil,** the impetuous Irish flame-thrower who preached without notes and only a small pocket Bible in his hand.

Of his children only his daughter shared his views, and his favorite son Herbert, who became a bishop, went off in another theological direction, as did his descendants Martin and Gilbert Ryle, men of auspicious scientific accomplishment but no faith.

Ryle's tracts such as "Are You Converted?" and "Are You Free?" had immense circulation. A collection of his tracts on divisive matters, titled "Knots Untied," argues that controversy is a positive duty on key issues.[8] Likewise his messages on "The New Birth" and "Practical Religion" were widely read, as was his "No Uncertain Sound," earlier known as "Charges and Addresses." Vintage Ryle is *Holiness: Its Nature, Hindrances, Difficulties and Roots.* The laudatory foreword by D. Martyn Lloyd-Jones, who speaks of him as "always scriptural and expository," is worthwhile. Messages in this collection on "Sanctification" and "The Ruler of the Waves" show careful organization and faithful adherence to the text.[9]

J. C. Ryle's strength was "His steadfast theological convictions which did not perceptibly change throughout his life."[10] Here is a preacher of purpose and pertinacity.

---

1. D. N. Samuel, ed., *The Evangelical Succession in the Church of England* (Cambridge, Mass.: James Clarke, 1979), 76.
2. J. C. Ryle, *A Self-Portrait* (Swengel, Pa.: Reiner, 1975), 40.
3. Peter Toon and Michael Smout, *John Charles Ryle: Evangelical Bishop* (Swengel, Pa.: Reiner, 1976), 37.
4. Ibid., 46.
5. Ibid., 76.
6. Cyril Garbett wrote the classic defense of biblical infallibility, *God's Word Written* (New York: E. P. Dutton, 1879).
7. Bishop William Boyd Carpenter was one of the most eloquent and biblical preachers among the Victorian prelates. See H. D. A. Major, *The Life and Letters of William Boyd Carpenter* (London: John Murray, 1925), 115ff. His noted lectures on preaching given at Cambridge are worthwhile: *Lectures on Preaching* (London: Macmillan, 1895).
8. J. C. Ryle, *Knots Untied,* 31st ed. (London: James Clarke, 1954). "A man of granite with the heart of a child."

9. J. C. Ryle, *No Uncertain Sound* (Edinburgh: Banner of Truth, 1903, 1978). Ryle released his own son as examining chaplain in Liverpool because of the latter's concessions to higher criticism. J. C. Ryle, *Holiness* (Grand Rapids: Kregel, 1956). The thesis of these sermons is simply, "No holiness, no happiness."
10. Ibid., 104. The cathedral he longed to construct in Liverpool was not built until the time of Bishop F. J. Chavasse.

10.6.3 Alexander Maclaren—Expositor Without Peer

> I cannot ever recall any hesitation as to being a minister. . . . It just had to be.
>
> To efface oneself is one of a preacher's first duties.
>
> I thank God for the early days of obscurity and struggle.
>
> I have always found that my own comfort and efficiency in preaching have been in direct proportion to the depth of my daily communion with God. I know no way in which we can do our work but in fellowship with God, in keeping up the habits of the student's life, which needs some power of saying "No" and by conscientious pulpit preparation. The secret of success is trust in God and hard work.
>
> —Alexander Maclaren

Known as the prince of expositors and described as "the supreme example, the perfect type, of the classic Protestant tradition of expository preaching," **Alexander Maclaren** (1826–1910), is one of our best models in commending strong biblical preaching. Born in Glasgow of Highland stock and reared in a merchant's home, Maclaren of Manchester followed his parents under the influence of the Haldanes into the Baptist church. He was a classmate of Robert Rainy (cf. 10.5.11) at the University of Glasgow, from which he went to Stepney College in London (forerunner of Regents Park College) to study for the Baptist ministry in 1842. The tall, shy, silent Scot did not impress the examiner, but he dug into Hebrew and Greek and mastered "the holy tongues." "Binney taught me to preach," he would say later, referring to the notable preacher of the old Weigh House Chapel (cf. 9.3.2).[1]

Maclaren's dedication to exegeting the original text was a lifelong hallmark. When asked to fill in briefly at the Portland Chapel in Southampton, he found a barnlike building seating eight hundred with fifty on the roll and twenty in attendance. He began to preach and the people kept coming for the rich biblical fare for the next twelve years.

As was his habit throughout life, he gave himself much to study, refusing many invitations beyond his own flock. He would visit his own church families two nights a week. In 1858 he took the call to the Union Chapel in Manchester, where he served for forty-five years. A new church was built during his ministry that seated fifteen hundred people. The sanctuary was typically jammed with two thousand souls. Maclaren's preaching ministry had a long radius. His sermons were printed on Mondays in the *Manchester Guardian.*

Maclaren's listeners were drawn to his beautiful and faultless diction. It was said he served up the Bread of Life on a "three-pronged fork." As Robertson Nicoll exquisitely phrased it: "Maclaren touched every text with a silver hammer and it broke up into three natural and memorable divisions."[2] The sermons we read were preached extempore and transcribed as he preached them. They seldom required editing. "Burn your manuscripts," he counseled preachers. Ernest Jeffs in his *Princes of the Modern Pulpit* recalls it well:

> The charm of Maclaren's preaching was intellectual and artistic. It lay in the logical closeness and firmness of his exposition, the architectural culmination of proof and argument, the warmth and richness of his metaphor and illustration; and under all this was the stern challenge to righteousness and repentance, bringing into the sunshine, so to speak, when the emphasis changes from the God who judges to the Jesus who redeems . . .[3]

Maclaren stayed with his text. He preached for about forty minutes, his sermon delivered in a "rich, musical voice, clear and penetrating," and always with that delightful Scottish brogue.[4] He read Carlyle ravenously, as well as the English poets, Shakespeare, and the Puritans. In that inevitable introspection that follows a message delivered from the heart, Maclaren would say, "Well, I can't help it, I did my best and there I leave it."[5] His commitment was to the infallible Word, and he never "turned from the old conception of a vicarious atonement."[6]

Nicoll surmises that in some respects Maclaren's expositions have never been superseded. His thirty-two original volumes of *Expositions of Holy Scripture* are exceedingly rich—Genesis and Colossians are considered the best. He also did Psalms for the Expositor's Bible. His absolutely astonishing *The Life of David Reflected in the Psalms* is my all-time favorite. His several volumes *Sermons Preached in Manchester* were described by F. B. Meyer as: "a great cathedral, so exquisitely constructed were they, and so entirely complete in proportion." These do, however, present one problem. As some have observed, it can be dangerous to read a Maclaren outline before one preaches. The temptation to preach his outline is too great.

When Binney heard Maclaren preach on "The Lord said by the hand of Moses," he went home and wept. One of the hundreds of sermons we possess, "Mahanaim: The Two Camps" from Genesis 32 is especially recommended:

I. The angels of God meet us on the dusty road of common life.
II. The angels of God meet us punctually at the hour of need.
III. The angels of God come in the shape we need.[7]

He closed the sermon with a great illustration about Gordon of Khartoum. In preaching on "no more sea" from Revelation 21:1, he projected the sea as standing for mystery, frightening power, unrest, distance, and separation.[8] Departing from his custom of staying at home as he grew older, he was twice president of the Baptist Union (breaking with Spurgeon in the Downgrade Controversy) and first president of the Baptist World Alliance (1905), to whose delegates he addressed the following searching words:

> We are crying out for a revival. Dear friends, the revival must begin with each of us by ourselves. Power for service is second. Power for holiness and character is first, and only the man who has let the spirit of God work His will upon him, and do what He will, has a right to expect that he will be filled with the Holy Ghost and with power. Do not get on the wrong track. Your revival, Christian ministers, must begin in your study and on your knees. Your revival must be for yourselves with no thought of service. But if once we have learned where our strength is, we shall never be so foolish as to go forth in our own strength, or we shall be beaten as we deserve to be.[9]

No sermons from the nineteenth century are so thoroughly worth reading as Maclaren's.

---

1. John C. Carlile, *Alexander Maclaren: The Man and His Message* (New York: Funk and Wagnalls, 1902), 27ff.
2. Johnstone G. Patrick, "A Prince of Preachers: A Ter-Jubilee Tribute to Dr. Alexander Maclaren," *Life of Faith* (February 7, 1976): 7. Also John Bishop, "Alexander Maclaren: A Great Expositor," *Preaching* (July–August 1987): 51–52.
3. John Pitts, "Alexander Maclaren: Monarch of the Pulpit," *Christianity Today* (June 5, 1964): 8.
4. Carlile, *Alexander Maclaren,* 71.
5. E. T. McLaren, *Dr. McLaren of Manchester* (London: Hodder and Stoughton, 1911), 209. E. T. McLaren was the cousin and sister-in-law of Alexander Maclaren and explains the change in the spelling of the name.
6. Carlile, *Alexander Maclaren,* 147.
7. Alexander Maclaren, "Mahanaim: Two Camps" in *Christ in the Heart and Other Sermons* (London: Macmillan, 1887), 195. Maclaren reads well but we are assured that he spoke better than he wrote.
8. Alexander Maclaren, *Sermons Preached in Manchester* (New York: Funk and Wagnalls, 1905), 2:325.
9. McLaren, *Dr. McLaren of Manchester,* 241.

10.6.4 Charles Haddon Spurgeon—The Prince of All the Preachers

> The preaching of Christ is the whip that flogs the devil. The preaching of Christ is the thunderbolt, the sound of which makes all hell shake.
>
> I must and I will make men listen.
>
> —as a boy preacher

> The revealed Word awakened me; but it was the preached Word that saved me.
>
> —Charles Haddon Spurgeon

Spurgeon was called the people's preacher. He had preached a thousand sermons by the time he reached the age of twenty-one. His printed sermons sold twenty-five thousand copies a week. No preacher up to this time had so influenced the masses. He is unique in the history of preaching.[1] He recommended that young preachers "make the pulpit your first business." He said he would rather be a preacher of the gospel than the angel Gabriel. He called the pulpit the Thermopolyae of Christendom. He saw the Reformation as the liberation of the Bible. He added fourteen thousand members in his thirty-seven years at the Metropolitan Tabernacle. Brastow calls him "the Puritan pastoral evangelist . . . the most impressive and permanently successful evangelistic preacher of the age."[2] Prime Minister David Lloyd George called him "the greatest preacher of his age." Ruskin, Gladstone, Florence Nightingale, and General James Garfield, later president of the United States, came to his working-class church to hear him. Helmut Thielicke, the German theologian of the twentieth century, counseled: "Sell all you have and buy Spurgeon." Vincent Van Gogh, the Dutch artist, began ministry preaching in the London slums using Spurgeon's sermons.[3]

Preaching was Spurgeon's life. He claimed to have seen the devil preaching in one of his dreams. When the devil was asked how it was he preached so capably, he replied: "I cannot further mine own cause better than by preaching without unction." Charles Haddon Spurgeon was a Bible preacher with unction.

---

1. G. Holden Pike, *The Life and Work of Charles Haddon Spurgeon* (Edinburgh: Banner of Truth, 1894, 1991), 5:16. The two massive volumes by Pike, who had edited *Sword and Trowel* for Spurgeon, are the best. The single volume without peer is Lewis Drummond, *Spurgeon: Prince of Preachers* (Grand Rapids: Kregel, 1992). For a modest introduction for a beginner, Arnold Dallimore, *Spurgeon* (Chicago: Moody, 1984).
2. Lewis O. Brastow, *Representative Modern Preachers* (New York: Macmillan, 1904), 383–84.
3. Irving Stone, ed., *Dear Theo: Autobiography of Vincent Van Gogh* (New York: Signet, 1937), 16, 19, 38.

The Progress of the Pilgrim

Born in Essex, the oldest of seventeen children, **Charles Haddon Spurgeon** (1834–1892) was the son and grandson of Congregational ministers of Flemish descent. Charles spent the bulk of his childhood with his grandparents and was exposed to Puritan writers, Foxe's *Book of Martyrs,* and especially Bunyan's *Pilgrim's Progress,* which he read through twice a year over his lifetime.

Spurgeon possessed a photographic memory. He attended several schools and began to feel "the evil of sin." He did not share this churning inner turmoil with his parents, but while visiting the small Artillery Street Primitive Methodist Church in Colchester, Spurgeon heard an unidentified preacher pour out his heart to the tiny congregation. The minister spoke from Isaiah 45:22, "Look unto me and be ye saved, all the ends of the earth, for I am God and there is none else."[1] Spurgeon danced all the way home, and recalled, "I wanted to tell the cows!" He immediately began to teach Sunday school, was baptized as a Baptist, and joined the St. Andrew's Street Baptist Church in Cambridge. His mother was clearly disappointed in the latter development, saying, "We had not prayed you would be a Baptist."

For two years Spurgeon preached at the Baptist Church in Waterbeach. His preaching gifts were already in evidence, and his voice unusual. One elderly listener addressed him after a service, "You are the sauciest dog that ever barked in a pulpit."[2] Here also he began his lifelong smoking habit. Spurgeon was never ordained and had no formal training, largely through the mistake of a maid when he missed an appointment with the tutor of Stepney College, Dr. Joseph Angus. He did make a point to hear preachers like John Jay and John Angell James and modeled many things well. When he was nineteen he began his ministry at the New Park Street Baptist Church in London, following **Benjamin Keach, John Gill,** and **John Rippon.** On the south side of the river, the church neighborhood reminded Spurgeon of "the black hole of Calcutta" The congregation was down to eighty or so attendees in twelve hundred seats.[3] From the outset of the ministry, a praying nucleus and a passionately preaching pastor experienced an outpouring.

> When I came to New Park Street Chapel it was but a mere handful of people to whom I first preached, yet I could never forget how earnestly they prayed. Sometimes they seemed to plead as though they could really see the Angel of the Covenant present with them, and as if they must have a blessing from him. More than once we were all so awe-struck with the solemnity of the meeting that we sat silent for some moments while the Lord's Power appeared to overshadow us; and all I could do on such occasions was to pronounce the benediction, and say, "Dear friends, we have had the Spirit of God here very manifestly tonight; let us go home and care not to lose His gracious influence." Then down came the blessing; the house was filled with hearers, and many souls were saved.[4]

Hayden attributes the blessing to "sound doctrine" and "loving invitation." Spurgeon never gave an outward invitation, as his friend D. L. Moody did. Although he was a firm Calvinist, he was not systematic in his commitment and held tenaciously to the necessity of human response in repentance and faith. "You don't have to reconcile friends," he replied when he was asked how he handled divine sovereignty and human responsibilities. He was totally committed to evangelism and the need for making "a bee-line" for the cross and Christ's substitutionary death. Yet he was never fully accepted by the Strict Baptists.

The Pattern of the Preaching

Spurgeon knew his Bible and had a personal library of twelve thousand volumes. Although he did not come to his morning sermon until Saturday night or his evening sermon until Sunday afternoon, he was primed to preach to his great urban congregation as the result of much study, compulsive reading, and fervent prayer. "My people pray for me," was his own explanation of what took place. Soon they had to move to Exeter Hall, which seated five thousand people, while the new Metropolitan Tabernacle, which seated six thousand, was being built.

Spurgeon rejected many conventionalities in preaching; he was humorous, dramatic, used catchy titles ("Turn or Burn" on Psalm 7:12), and employed sense appeal particularly in his marvelous illustrations.[5] His voice was natural and easily reached six thousand hearers. His fresh style and forceful Anglo-Saxon discourse connected, and clearly Whitefield was his model. Craig Skinner, who has written widely on Spurgeon, sees his sermonic appeal in his fresh style, his uncommon clarity, his solid doctrine "upon which people could base their lives," and his ability to bridge to people's needs.[6] Some accused him of showmanship, and he did believe in advertising and promotion, but it was because, to use his own words, "I would preach standing on my head if I thought I could convert your souls."[7]

Strictly speaking, Spurgeon was not a classical expositor as was Maclaren. Regarding the Puritans in their eminently textual style, Spurgeon eschewed their "far-fetched similitudes and long-winded sentences."[8] He loved to break a text and was only occasionally textual-topical. Joseph Parker, who loved Henry Ward Beecher, admitted of Beecher that "I could not smell so much as a text in his velvet-collared coat." But Spurgeon regarded Beecher as an evil influence because he did not preach the gospel.[9] Spurgeon's commentary on Matthew was published posthumously, but this was as close as he ever came to expounding the natural thought unit.

Assuaging some of our concerns here is the fact, not frequently noted, that as Spurgeon read the Scripture lesson, he gave a running commentary. Some thought this was as good as the preaching.[10] He always preached without paper, and greatly admired Charles Simeon's ability to outline.[11] But Spurgeon must be read, especially in thematic anthologies, if we are to pick up his thinking on great doctrines.[12] He used to advise giving the people something worth hearing and they would listen like a woman hearing a will read or a condemned man hearing his sentence given by the judge. Spurgeon gave what was worth hearing.

The Power of the Pen

Spurgeon is epochal in the history of preaching not only because of his sermons in London and throughout the British Isles, but also because what he preached he published. Three hundred million copies of his printed works have been in circulation, chiefly his printed sermons.[13] Five hundred thousand copies of his *Lectures to My Students* have been printed, the product of his Friday afternoon lectures and visits to the Pastor's College.[14] Three hundred thousand copies of the quaint *John Ploughman's Talks* have been issued, and 150,000 sets of his massive *Treasury of David* have sat on Bible students' shelves. Two hundred churches in England were planted under the aegis of his ministry and students. Twenty social ministries were established, the chief of which was the great Stockwell Orphanage. He turned down an astronomic financial offer to come to America to preach.

Spurgeon addressed political issues widely in the pages of *Sword and Trowel,* and was a close follower of Gladstone and the Liberal Party until the issue of Irish home rule. He was an avowed pacifist, and spoke out for total abstinence from alcohol. He had a strong aversion to instrumental music but was known for his remarkable soliloquies at the Lord's Table and was a convinced premillennialist. Spurgeon spoke so vehemently against slavery that American publishers occasionally excised his comments on the subject. What an extraordinary influence and impact for the preacher—God blessed His Word as it was preached and then printed.

The Poise of the Person

Like Moody, who attended the Tabernacle and was invited to preach there, Spurgeon was physically "without angles" and very heavy.[15] He was blessed with a happy marriage to Susannah Thompson, but she became an invalid at age thirty-three and was seldom able to attend services after that. They were parents of twin boys, Thomas, who succeeded his father as pastor of the Tabernacle after serving in Auckland, New Zealand, and Charles Jr., who managed the orphanage.[16]

Often lecturing ten times a week, he spoke rapidly—140 words per minute for forty minutes at a time. He took heavy hits from such tragedies as the Royal Surrey Gardens stampede, which happened while he was praying. Seven were killed in that incident and twenty-eight hospitalized. He also suffered from "fainting fits" and depression. From 1871 he was virtually an invalid.[17] He had chronic kidney problems from early on (Bright's disease) and rheumatic gout. Sent abroad repeatedly to recover his health, he died at Mentone in southern France at the age of fifty-seven.

Spurgeon broke with Parker over some theological issues and the theater. He was embroiled in a great controversy over baptismal regeneration, which alienated him perhaps unnecessarily from some of his good friends in the Church of England. The famous Downgrade Controversy led to his resignation from both the Evangelical Alliance and the Baptist Union. He also parted ways with Angus and Maclaren. The Downgrade Controversy was a sticky affair in which he had problems with his own brother James, who was associate pastor at the Tabernacle. Spurgeon made his move essentially out of a growing concern for liberal incursions and inroads into the Baptist Union.

In a beautiful issue on Spurgeon, *Christian History* magazine properly comes to the conclusion that Charles Haddon Spurgeon was the greatest preacher in the nineteenth century. The sixty thousand people who passed his coffin after his death bore testimony to that assertion.

1. Lewis Drummond, *Spurgeon: Prince of Preachers* (Grand Rapids: Kregel, 1992), 116.
2. G. Holden Pike, *The Life and Works of Charles Haddon Spurgeon* (Edinburgh: Banner of Truth, 1894, 1991), 1:69.
3. Eric W. Hayden, *A History of Spurgeon's Tabernacle* (Pasadena, Tex.: Pilgrim Publications, 1962, 1971).
4. Eric W. Hayden, *Spurgeon on Revival: A Biblical and Theological Approach* (Grand Rapids: Zondervan, 1962), 14. See also Iain Murray, *The Forgotten Spurgeon,* 2d ed. (Edinburgh: Banner of Truth, 1973). A bit tilted.
5. Drummond, *Spurgeon,* 282. Jay Adams, *Sense Appeal in the Sermons of Charles Haddon Spurgeon* (Grand Rapids: Baker, 1975). Studies both titles and sermons. A most revealing study.
6. Craig Skinner, "The Preaching of Charles Haddon Spurgeon," *Baptist History and Heritage* (October 1984): 16–26.
7. Drummond, *Spurgeon,* 283.
8. Pike, *The Life and Works of Charles Haddon Spurgeon,* 5:83.
9. Ibid., 3:71; 5:67.
10. Ibid., 2:177; 3:37, 67.
11. Drummond, *Spurgeon,* 295.
12. Charles Haddon Spurgeon, *The Passion and Death of Christ* (Grand Rapids: Eerdmans, n.d.).
13. *The Metropolitan Tabernacle Pulpit* in 57 volumes is the most popular set; *Spurgeon's Sermons* by Funk and Wagnalls was also widely distributed.
14. C. H. Spurgeon, *Lectures to My Students* (Grand Rapids: Zondervan, 1972) has gone into many printings.
15. Pike, *The Life and Works of Charles Haddon Spurgeon,* 5:80.
16. Craig Skinner, *Spurgeon and Son* (Grand Rapids: Kregel, 1999). Traces how James Spurgeon, the brother and sometimes associate (also pastor of the Croyden Tabernacle), promoted A. T. Pierson, an American Presbyterian, and baptized him in West Croydon, but his son Thomas took the call in 1894. The Tabernacle burned in 1898, and a new building was constructed. The health of Thomas, who served for fourteen years, finally broke, and A. C. Dixon came from America to serve from 1911 to 1919.
17. Pike, *The Life and Works of Charles Haddon Spurgeon,* 5:24.

10.6.5 Joseph Parker—The Preacher with Personality

> Sunday is my festival day. I love Sunday. All the days of the week lead up to it and I hold high festival with my God and my people every Sabbath.
>
> You must study the idea of your text: try to pierce it to its very heart and, having seized the truth, expound it with all simplicity and earnestness.
>
> —Joseph Parker

To him, preaching was "dignified conversation" and a propulsive passion. When asked what his hobby was, he replied "preaching." When pressed what else beside preaching, he insisted: "Preaching, nothing but preaching. Everything with me ministers to preaching."[1] Sometimes called the "Beecher of England," **Joseph Parker** (1830–1902) came from Hexham in the far north of England, the son of a stonemason (as were Thomas Carlyle and D. L. Moody). He had only common school education but taught himself Greek in his late teens. His stalwart and stubborn father led the family from the Independent (or Congregational) church to the Methodists. Converted at the age of twelve, Parker later visualized the scene:

> I remember the Sunday night when, walking with my father and a most intelligent Sunday School teacher, I declared my love to Christ, and asked him to take my child-heart into His own gracious keeping . . . It was a summer evening, according to the reckoning of the calendar, but according to a higher calendar it was in very deed a Sunday morning, through whose white light and emblematic dew and stir of awakening life I saw the gates of the Kingdom and the face of the King.[2]

At eighteen Parker felt the call into the Lord's vineyard and preached his first sermon most unexpectedly on the text in Matthew which reads: "It shall be more tolerable for Tyre and Sidon in the judgment than for you."[3] Being a Congregationalist at heart, he wrote Dr. Campbell, pastor of the Whitefield's Tabernacle, Moorlands, for help in finding a place of service. Campbell invited him to London, took him under his wing, and force-fed him theology and exegesis for nine months.[4] From 1852 to 1859 Parker served in Banbury in Oxfordshire, grew in stature and reputation as a preacher, had a famous debate with an atheist, and dedicated a new building with R. W. Dale as preacher.

For the next eleven years Parker preached in the Cavendish Chapel, Manchester, a chief nonconformist center. The church had a congregation of 350 in a sanctuary seating 1,700. He soon filled the church, and his remarkable gift of prayer, both public and private, was a matter of notice.[5] He received a D.D. from the University of Chicago in 1862. In 1869 he moved to London, assuming the pastorate of the old Poultry Chapel where he served powerfully for thirty-three years. This was the church Thomas Goodwin (cf. 7.3.2.3) had founded and which had come on hard times in a commercial neighborhood.[6] Parker led in the building of a new City Temple in Holborn Viaduct in 1874 with the Corporation of London donating a massive white pulpit. He saw it filled to three thousand persons morning and evening on Sunday and averaging one thousand at a Thursday noon service. At the Thursday services he usually spoke, but to the rostrum he also invited such speakers as Prime Minister Gladstone, Newman Hall of Christ Church, Westminster Road, and many others. Parker read extensively and founded an Institute of Homiletics in 1871. His book *Ad Clerum* addressed aspects of preaching and pastoring. He made four trips to the United States, was close to Beecher, and became a confidant of John B. Gough, the famous temperance lecturer. Newman's sermons also influenced him.

Parker wrote many books, including a choice piece on the Holy Spirit. He also wrote verse and fiction. He was an expansive, creative soul who took a stand on prison reform and preached strongly against gambling. He was immensely dramatic in his delivery. Here he is described in action in the City Temple pulpit:

> His massive figure and leonine head at once fixed the attention and his voice, rich as an organ, held his audience spell-bound. It rose and fell in sonorous periods as he poured out his perfectly-phrased sentences. He was a superb actor and he delivered his thoughts with a dramatic force that kindled each sentence . . . the gleaming eyes, the vigorous gesture, the constantly changing inflection of his voice, now soft as a whisper, then challenging as a trumpet.[7]

Although he was close to Beecher, who gave up textual analysis in preaching, Parker gave himself to preaching through the Bible in about seven years. This resulted in the twenty-five-volume *People's Bible* and about one thousand sermons from Genesis to Revelation. Studded with his prayers, these sermons do not see the division of the text but do deliver what the passage as a whole says. A good sample is "On the Building of Babel" from Genesis 11.[8] His illustrations are more suggestions than sequential stories. He also published *The People's Family Prayer Book.* Parker was rather ecumenical and spoke repeatedly to the Scottish Free Church assemblies.[9] Yet he stood with the conservatives when he addressed the Free Church Assembly in the imbroglio over high criticism.

Parker was sound on the Bible. "It is not as many think, a mere record containing the Word of God, but the Word of God itself, speaking with a divine voice in divers manners, authoritatively and finally."[10] He was solid on the Atonement, and said that if he ever preached in Westminster or at St. Paul's he would preach nothing but salvation through the blood of Jesus.

Yet Parker had a somewhat dismissive attitude toward theology and its importance and sometimes sounded mincing and mediating.[11] His successor, R. J. Campbell, espoused the "new theology" and denatured the Atonement entirely. Campbell was finally forced out in 1915 because of his socialistic views and replaced by the liberal Joseph Fort Newton. Later incumbents were F. W. Norwood and Leslie Weatherhead, a gifted Methodist but a preacher who psychologized the gospel.

City Temple was destroyed in World War II and rebuilt. Even though Leonard Griffith served for a time (1960–66), the congregation has died. After Spurgeon's death, the succession question became ugly and divisive. Did Parker's depreciation of doctrine and Beecherish association make the succession a fatality?

Robertson Nicoll gave Joseph Parker's funeral address with Principal P. T. Forsyth joining the procession. Campbell and J. H. Jowett preached the memorial sermons at City Temple.

---

1. John Bishop, "Joseph Parker: Poet, Seer, Preacher," *Preaching* (November–December 1988): 43.
2. William Adamson, *The Life of Joseph Parker* (New York: Revell, 1902), 12–13.
3. Ibid., 23.

4. Ibid., 38.
5. Ibid., 126. He stressed preaching the meaning of the text, not the text as such.
6. Arthur Clare, *The City Temple: 1640–1940* (London: Independent Press, 1940). The tercentenary volume.
7. Bishop, "Joseph Parker," 45. This is the recollection of Alexander Gamme.
8. Joseph Parker, *The People's Bible: Discourses on Holy Scripture* (London: Richard Clarke, 1885), 1:176ff. He also wrote and published six volumes of *Studies in Texts.* Both series have been reissued by Baker.
9. Adamson, *The Life of Joseph Parker,* 255.
10. Ibid., 238.
11. Ibid., 163.

10.6.6 H .P. Liddon—Surgeon of the Soul and of the Scriptures

> Brethren, Jesus Christ has been with us Englishmen as a nation for at least some sixteen or seventeen hundred years. As a nation, do we know Him? Are our laws—our marriage laws, our poor laws, for instance—all of them, in clear agreement with His law of high and pure morality? Are our habits, our great currents of opinion, our national enthusiasms and aversions, such as become His disciples? Is He our King, not merely recognized in our temple, but honoured in our streets, in our organs of national opinion and feeling, in our great representative assemblies, in our halls of science, as well as in our sanctuaries?
>
> If we believe that He is the true Light of the world, we shall close our ears against suggestions impairing the credit of those Jewish Scriptures which have received the stamp of His Divine authority.
>
> —Henry Parry Liddon

At the three-quarter mark of the century Spurgeon was speaking to ten thousand people each Sunday, Parker to six thousand, but a great variety of others were "fatally uninteresting" or unorthodox.[1] But near Parker in majestic St. Paul's, "ministering to the wise," was **Henry Parry Liddon** (1829–1890), "whose sweet and gentle melancholy" in preaching made such a lasting impression on so many. Services had been held in the choir for a long time but then moved out into the nave, where thousands listened to sermons that invariably took an hour.

Liddon's father was an officer in the Royal Navy. When Henry went up to Oxford, he became associated with the Tractarians and wrote the life of E. B. Pusey, who led the high-church forces and authored an outstanding commentary on the Minor Prophets. Ordained in 1852 and serving as assistant curate at Wantage, Liddon was appointed by Bishop Wilberforce as vice principal of the Theological College, Cuddesdon. He never married.

Liddon had a first-rate mind and was returned to be vice principal at St. Edmund Hall, Oxford, where he gave his famous Bampton Lectures on The Divinity of Our Lord in 1866. These lectures were the bane of all Unitarians.[2] Liddon's trenchant themes of "the divine personality of the Eternal Son" and "the virtue of His atonement" pressed his hearers to acknowledge Christ as the Son of God or dismiss him as a flagrant deceiver. He railed at negative higher criticism as undercutting the Savior's infallibility. His basic argument was that Christ could not err.

Serving also as Ireland Professor of Exegesis, Liddon gave a series of popular Bible readings and expositions. In 1870 he was appointed canon of St. Paul's and came down to preach Sundays. Stanley said, "Liddon took us straight up to heaven and kept us there for an hour." Interestingly, Liddon refused to preach in Westminster because of Dean Stanley's fellowship with liberals and rationalists.[3] Donaldson describes "his appearance as striking, his voice sweet and penetrating, his influence magnetic . . . yet there was about him a holy self-restraint that kept in check the explosive forces of that sensitive physique."[4] Some said that Spurgeon was Isaiah and Liddon was Jeremiah.

Liddon in some ways emulated the French court preachers. His introduction was classic, and he usually used three heads. His magnificent sermon on "Profit and Loss" from Mark 8:36 was needed in the City of London. "The Cleansing Blood" was likewise right on the mark. His analytical outlines on Romans are unique and indispensable for the serious student.[5]

His health began to falter early on, and when Pusey died Liddon resigned his post at Oxford. He never felt strong, and on April 18, 1863, before his first sermon at St. Paul's, he characteristically wrote:

> Feel very unequal to preaching at St. Paul's tomorrow, both spiritually and physically. Oh, Lord Jesus, help me, a poor sinner.

The Bible was to him "power—the power of an Infallible Spirit teaching the souls of men from pages which have been preternaturally preserved from the taint of error, and with a living force which bridges the centuries that have passed since its latest books were written."[6] Just before his sudden death in 1890, he took a trip with his sister to Palestine and Egypt. It was to her that he dedicated his glorious magnificat which comes from his *Advent in St. Paul's.* Its twin, *Easter in St. Paul's,* is without an equal in our language.[7]

Liddon trumpeted the trustworthiness of the Old Testament, which he loved and preached. His sermon on the disobedient prophet is a treasure. He often spoke of the Holy Spirit as the "great preacher of the Godhead."[8] Such earnestness was owned of God. Dr. Bright queried of the man: "What made Liddon so vitalizing a preacher? What but his supreme devotion to a Christ alive forevermore."[9]

---

1. C. Maurice Davies, *Unorthodox London: Phases of Religious Life in the Metropolis* (London: Tinsley Bros., 1875).
2. H. P. Liddon, *The Divinity of Our Lord and Saviour Jesus Christ* (London: Rivingtons, 1885).
3. Aug. B. Donaldson, *Henry Parry Liddon* (London: Rivingtons, 1905), 38.
4. Ibid., 33. For some interesting footnotes on Liddon, see *Autobiography of Robert Gregory, Dean of St. Paul's, 1819–1911* (London: Longmans, Green, 1912). Reflects on Liddon's extraordinary prowess as a preacher.

5. H. P. Liddon, *Explanatory Analysis of St. Paul's Epistle to Romans* (Grand Rapids: Zondervan, 1876, 1961). Dr. Merrill Tenney calls this "A model of analytical work in the Greek text."
6. Donaldson, *Henry Parry Liddon,* 107.
7. H. P. Liddon, *Easter in St. Paul's* (London: Longmans, Green, 1895).
8. Donaldson, *Henry Parry Liddon,* 139.
9. Charles Smyth, *The Art of Preaching: A Practical Survey of Preaching in the Church of England 747–1939* (London: SPCK, 1940), 247.

10.6.7 Robert W. Dale—The Preacher Who Loved Doctrine

> He has his arena down at Birmingham, where he does his practice with Mr. Chamberlain and Mr. Jesse Collings and the rest of his band; and then from time to time he comes up to the metropolis, to London, and gives a public exhibition of his skill. And a very powerful exhibition it often is.
>
> —Matthew Arnold

> I advise you to read every book on preaching that you can buy or borrow, whether it is old or new, Catholic or Protestant, English, French or German. If your experience corresponds with mine, the dullest and most tedious writer on this subject will remind you of some fault that you are committing habitually, or of some element of power which you have failed to use.
>
> Exposition will do something to protect you from the desultoriness and want of method which is one of the gravest faults of modern preaching, and which is one of the chief causes that it conveys so little definite and systematic instruction. Our practice of preaching from texts has accustomed people to try what they can discover in single sentences and even single phrases, of the Bible, and to disregard the general current and structure of the argument or history.
>
> —Robert W. Dale

Robert William Dale (1829–1895) "put his pulpit first." Born and reared in London, Dale and his family were spiritually nurtured at Moorlands Tabernacle. He started teaching school at age fourteen and was captured by John Angell James' (cf. 9.3.1) *Anxious Inquirer After Salvation.* He preached his first sermon at age sixteen and attended a small college in Birmingham, taking his degree at the University of London in 1853. Dale became an assistant to James while a student. Upon James' death after fifty-six years at Carr's Lane Chapel, Dale assumed the pastorate and remained there for forty-two years. He was known above all as a fervent and effective doctrinal preacher even though he had been warned Carr's Lane would not stand for it. His reply was, "They will have to tolerate it."

Dale was not at ease with hyper-Calvinism and particularly resisted restricted grace. At first hesitant, he soon sensed when Moody and Sankey came to Birmingham in 1875 "that the work was most plainly of God."[1] He saw authentic life-change in the great after-meetings and became an ardent backer.

Dale often reflected that what drew him above all else to Moody was that he never spoke about hell and lost souls without tears in his eyes. The Moody-Sankey visit provided a year of powerful impact in the services. This was the year that Dale gave his masterful lectures on the Atonement at the Sunday evening services in which he so adroitly argued the case for objective atonement. It was also the time when Dale's ministry was quickened as he wrote his Easter sermon and realized: "Christ is alive! Alive! Alive!" An Easter hymn was sung at Carr's Lane every Sunday thereafter. Dale's sermons on *The Laws of Christ for Common Life* show Christian ethics applied. Moody's revival ministry was bearing fruit.[2]

Dale typically preached from a manuscript for about an hour. Robertson Nicoll described his style as "one of the most perfect in the whole range of English literature."[3] Edmund Burke was his model, and like Burke he made few concessions to his audience. There was little personalization but meticulous preparation. Before he preached the centenary of Wesley's death in City Road Chapel in London, he read through the complete works of Wesley.

In 1877 Dale gave the Beecher Lectures at Yale, published as *Nine Lectures on Preaching*. These are poignant and powerful lectures and were considered some of the best in the early history of the lectureship. He rewrote his lectures four or five times in order to perfect them.[4] Dale shunned fancy or clever sermons and could be intense. Close examination of his lectures on the atonement of Christ reveal the mettle of the man as a preacher. He opened up the Atonement as Turretin called it, "The chief part of our salvation, the anchor of Faith, the refuge of Hope, the rule of Charity, the true foundation of the Christian religion, and the richest treasure of the Christian Church."[5]

Dale saw the atoning sacrifice of Christ as the key, even more than Christ's teaching or His life. He intended to show in his discourses the relationship between Christ's sacrifice and the remission of sin. "The real truth is that while He came to preach the gospel, His chief object in coming was that there might be a gospel to preach,"[6] said Dale. He engaged the thinking of the clever Unitarian, James Martineau, and was unflinching in asserting that in propitiation, "His [Christ's] face is turned toward God, not toward man."[7] He tracked the substitutionary atonement through all the documents of the New Testament and through church history. As Paul deployed his message, clearly it was essentially "Christ died for our sins."

> The Death of Christ, as the objective ground of the Divine forgiveness of human sin, was the substance of Paul's preaching; it was the central idea of his theology; it was the spring of the mightiest motives by which he was animated in his apostolic work.[8]

And how did Birminghamites take such preaching? One member said, "If Dr. Dale preaches like that I shall not come to hear him, for I cannot stand it; it goes through me."[9] What a giant for God! What a spokesman for God! What a trumpeter for truth!

1. D. W. Lambert, "The Scholar and the Evangelist: R. W. Dale and D. L. Moody," *Life of Faith,* (February 15, 1975): 3.
2. Ibid.
3. John Bishop, "Robert William Dale: Interpreter of Evangelical Truth," *Preaching* (September–October 1989): 40.
4. John Edwards, *Nineteenth-Century Preachers* (London: Charles Kelly, 1902), 37.
5. R. W. Dale, *The Atonement* (London: Congregational Union, 1897), 3.
6. Ibid., 46.
7. Ibid., 165.
8. Ibid., 264.
9. Bishop, "Robert William Dale," 41.

10.6.8 F. W. Farrar—The Preacher Who Exemplified Versatility

> Thousands came to be fed by a man [Farrar] who believed in righteousness, and was not afraid of thundering against those who did not. Upon the whole I think his most helpful sermons were those which explained a book of the Bible in its broadest outlines . . . a sermon on the Book of Job haunts me today.
>
> —Bishop Montgomery

If Ryle was low church and Liddon was high church, then Dean **Frederic William Farrar** (1831–1903) was broad church. Born in Bombay, India, the son of a chaplain, Farrar was a gifted and forceful preacher in the Church of England. His voracious appetite for books was manifest early, and in 1847 he entered King's College, Cambridge, where F. D. Maurice became his mentor. Farrar taught at Marlborough and Harrow under C. J. Vaughn, a noted preacher and leader in his own right.[1] He returned to Marlborough as headmaster, and his chapel sermons there began to attract attention. In 1875 he was appointed rector of St. Margaret's, adjacent to Westminster and the church of the House of Commons. He was soon chaplain to the queen and then dean of Canterbury in 1895.

An accomplished writer of many books, Farrar was best known for his massive *Life of Christ* and *Life of St. Paul.* Although he lamentably had given up the biblical teaching of a universal flood in Noah's day and had stepped forward as a defender of Bishop Colenso, both his teaching and preaching about Christ were thoroughly orthodox.[2] As one described him:

> But the crowning impression for me that afternoon was when the time came for the second lesson, which, I believe, is always read by the Dean, when he is present, as his regular part of the service. In the same absorbed manner, as if seeing nothing around him, but wholly devoted to the thing he was doing, he went up to the reading-desk, found the lesson of the day, and began to read words which, of all Scripture, were to me the most perfect and wonderful to express what I was feeling . . . I sat spell-bound.[3]

Farrar's style was vigorous (some felt vehement at times). He loved to preach in series. Illustration was his forte. For Farrar, the purpose of preaching was always "to utter and interpret, to feel and to know that God was in Christ reconciling the world to Himself, not imputing their trespasses to them."[4] In a sermon delivered in the royal chapel in 1872, Farrar preached from Micah 6:6–8 on "What God Requires." He drew the mains from the text in its natural order and made bridges to the New Testament with skill and effect.[5] His Victorian rhetoric was at times "audacious," as when he spoke of "the luminous wand of the milky way" or "the glorious conflagration of the earth's decay."[6]

Farrar wrote *The History of Interpretation* for his Bampton Lectures of 1875. He also penned several Bible commentaries, biographical novels of giants such as Chrysostom, and more than seventy other volumes. He veered toward universalism as the years went by, a heresy that plagued the well-known American Quaker, Hannah Whitall Smith, and others. Farrar's daughter Maud married Bernard Law Montgomery, son of a bishop and later to be celebrated as General Montgomery of Alamein.[7] Scandal and sorrow among his sons and other considerations denied him preferment, but F. W. Farrar was a remarkably articulate preacher, "admired by many, intensely disliked by a few."[8]

---

1. C. J. Vaughn was a prolific and controversial schoolman and preacher. Bishop B. F. Westcott read one of Vaughn's sermons every Sunday afternoon for thirty years.
2. F. W. Farrar, *The Life of Christ* (Hartford, Conn.: S. S. Scranton, 1918), 656ff.
3. R. A. Farrar, *Life of Dean Farrar* (New York: Thomas Crowell, 1904), 320.
4. John Edwards, *Nineteenth-Century Preachers and Their Methods* (London: Kelly, 1902), 54.
5. F. W. Farrar, *The Silences and the Voices of God* (London: Macmillan, 1892), 71ff. Another volume of typical sermons is F. W. Farrar, *Sermons—The Contemporary Pulpit Library* (London: Swan, Sonnenschein, 1890).
6. F. R. Webber, *A History of British and American Preaching* (Milwaukee: Northwestern, 1952), 1:595.
7. Nigel Hamilton, *Monty: The Making of a General* (New York: McGraw-Hill, 1981), 1:3–4, 19. Montgomery was an eccentric genius but bore witness to the bodily resurrection of Christ; see *Prophetic Witness* (November 1983): 11.
8. Ibid., "Grandfather Farrar," 20ff.

10.6.9 Hugh Price Hughes and Mark Guy Pearse—The Team That Made a Mark

> Look at it. Think of it. A hundred and twenty men and women, having no patronage, no promise of earthly favor; no endowment, no wealth—a company of men and women having to get their living by common daily toil—and yet they are to begin the conquests of Christianity! To them is entrusted a work which to turn the world upside down! None so exalted but the influence of this lowly company shall reach to them, until the throne of the Caesars is claimed for Christ . . . a thing

> impossible, absurd, look at it as you will, until you admit this—they are to be filled with the Holy Ghost. Then the difficulties melt into the empty air. Their strength is as the strength of the Almighty. This is Christ's idea of Christianity; the idea not of man—it is infinitely too sublime—the idea of God.
>
> —Mark Guy Pearse

The vitalities in preaching in Britain at this time were not reserved for one theological perspective or denomination; the networking encompassed the heirs of John Wesley as well. There was huge theological defection in Methodism, as seen in the drastic concessions to higher criticism made by **A. S. Peake** (1865–1929), who taught at Manchester and himself came from the Primitive Methodists. Although he had been reared with great reverence for the Word by his godly preacher father, Peake followed Wellhausen, gave up the Virgin Birth, and clashed with James Denney on the meaning of Christ's atoning death.[1] This is the stream that led to Weatherhead and Donald Soper and extreme liberalism. Thank God there was another stream in the likes of Professor G. G. Findley and Samuel Chadwick that led to William Sangster and Alan Walker in Australia and others.

But mightily used of God in a unique preaching ministry at this time were two gifted individuals, **Hugh Price Hughes** (1847–1902), from Wales, and **Mark Guy Pearse** (1842–1930), who hailed from Cornwall. Hughes was a doctor's son who was converted and felt the call to preach. At age fourteen, on a Sunday when the preacher did not show up, young Hughes walked to the pulpit and preached a creditable sermon. After training in London, he served three years in Dover. At his first service eighteen people professed salvation.[2] Pearse was a medical student when God tabbed him to preach, and he subsequently served several pastoral charges, beginning in Leeds. In 1887 these two preachers began a copastorate in West London which met at St. James Hall in a more informal setting with music that targeted the people in Piccadilly. Spurgeon preached at the opening with the proviso that there be no instrumental music. Pearse knew Spurgeon especially well and was greatly influenced by him.

Hughes was a spellbinding preacher. His sermons in *Essential Christianity* include a moving address on "The All-Sufficiency of Christ" from John 14:6.[3] His series on *Ethical Christianity* was widely heard and read, as was his well-known sermon, "The Christian Extra" from Matthew 5:47, "What do ye more than others?"[4] Both Hughes and Pearse were essentially evangelists. The attendance at the West London Mission was consistently more than three thousand.

Charles Bradlaugh, the notorious freethinker, once challenged Hughes to a debate. Hughes accepted with a counterchallenge: I'll bring one hundred whose lives have been changed by the gospel; you bring one hundred whose lives have been changed through your testimony. Bradlaugh never showed up, and Hughes turned the occasion into a great testimony meeting.

Pearse was an aggressive, somewhat cycloid preacher, known as the apostle of good cheer. His gift was imagination in preaching that painted a picture. His messages on *The Christianity of Jesus Christ* are direct and engaging.[5] Pearse patterned himself after Billy Bray (cf. 10.1.6), whose biography he wrote.

Copastorates have not on the whole been very successful, but Pearse's ministry in West London with Hughes was outstandingly fruitful. Here is the fulfillment of the desire and dream of the Wesleys for soul-saving stations everywhere. As John Wesley insisted in the first *Methodist Discipline:* "You have nothing to do but to save souls. Therefore spend and be spent in this work."[6] To that end Pearse preached:

> I cannot consecrate myself to the Lord. My purpose falters and fails in changing circumstances; I am fickle, forgetful, false. My lofty desires of today, tomorrow cease to soar, and sink beneath the clouds again, and rest once more with wearied wings indifferent upon the earth. The only consecration possible is not with me or with my will. It is the entrance of the Lord himself, his possessing and claiming and using me; that is the only true consecration. It is not my giving so much as my receiving; not so much my surrender to him so much as my acceptance of him, on which my mind is to be stayed.[7]

---

1. John T. Wilkinson, *Arthur Samuel Peake: A Biography* (London: Epworth, 1971) 6, 115ff., 119. The primary source here is A. S. Peake's own disappointing *The Nature of Scripture* (London: Hodder and Stoughton, 1922).
2. F. R. Webber, *A History of British and American Preaching* (Milwaukee: Northwestern, 1952), 1:641.
3. Hugh Price Hughes, *Essential Christianity* (New York: Hunt and Eaton, 1894), 73ff.
4. Hugh Price Hughes, *Ethical Christianity* (New York: Dutton, 1891), 1ff.
5. Mark Guy Pearse, *The Christianity of Jesus Christ* (Cincinnati: Jennings and Pye, n.d.).
6. For an exposition of this point, see Robert E. Coleman, "Nothing to Do but Save Souls," *John Wesley's Charge to His Preachers* (Grand Rapids: Francis Asbury/Zondervan, 1990).
7. Pearse, *The Christianity of Jesus Christ,* 187.

CHAPTER ELEVEN

The Glory and Agony of Twentieth-Century Preaching

Part One: Vitality or Entropy?

It was revealed to them that they were not serving themselves but you, when they spoke of the things that have now been told you by those who have preached the gospel to you by the Holy Spirit sent from heaven.

—1 Peter 1:12

For you have been born again, not of perishable seed, but of imperishable, through the living and enduring word of God. For, "All men are like grass, and all their glory is like the flowers of the field; the grass withers and the flowers fall, but the word of the Lord stands forever." And this is the word that was preached to you.

—1 Peter 1:23–25

For certain men whose condemnation was written about long ago have secretly slipped in among you. They are godless men, who change the grace of our God into a license for immorality and deny Jesus Christ our only Sovereign and Lord. . . . "In the last times there will be scoffers who will follow their own ungodly desires." These are the men who divide you, who follow mere natural instincts and do not have the Spirit.

—Jude 4, 18–19

The Word proclaimed is a divine word and as such it is an active force which creates what it proclaims.

—G. Friedrich

True preaching from start to finish is the work of the Holy Spirit.
—John Knox

When we built Redeemer Church in Atlanta, we had carved on the front of the pulpit the cry of Jeremiah, "O earth, earth, earth, hear the word of the Lord." To preach the Word of the Lord is to preach on a text from the Bible. Like a blooming flower that opens its petals to the sun, a preacher takes a text and lets it unfold with authority and certainty. People recognize it as coming from God and respond, "You'd better believe it" or "You'd better do it!"
—John Brokhoff

How is the Kingdom of Heaven opened and shut by the preaching of the holy gospel? In this way: the Kingdom of Heaven is opened when it is proclaimed and openly testified to believers, one and all, according to the command of Christ, that as often as they accept the presence of the gospel with true faith all their sins are truly forgiven them by God for the sake of Christ's gracious work. On the contrary, the wrath of God and eternal condemnation fall upon all unbelievers and hypocrites as long as they do not repent. It is according to this witness of the gospel that God will judge the one and the other in this life and in the life to come.
—Heidelberg Catechism (1563), Lord's Day 31, Q & A 84

With the dawn of the twentieth century, humankind was awash in optimism and euphoria. The Darwinian vision was overwhelmingly positive. Science was on the way to leading the human race to utopia. As Carl F. H. Henry put it, "From Descartes to Dewey one finds the same confidence that man, apart from any reference to a special supernatural revelation, can solve his problems."[1] The underpinnings of this mindset were (1) the inevitability of human progress; (2) the inherent goodness of man; (3) the absolute uniformity of nature; (4) the ultimate reality of nature; and (5) the ultimate animality of man.[2]

But all of this was doomed as modern civilization experienced two fratricidal world wars, uncontrolled worldwide economic depression, the horror of the Holocaust, and the advent of the atomic age. Even the fall of state socialism in the former Soviet Union and her satellites has unleashed narrow new nationalisms that torment the nations. The sexual revolution and AIDS, the war in Vietnam, the insoluble challenges in the Middle East, and the increasing gulf between the "haves" and the "have nots" in the "two-thirds world" have ripped societies and stabilities asunder. In all of this the Word has been preached, and in the face of the theological turmoil and ecclesiastical tension, the gospel goes forth. To this unstable and mottled time we turn.

---

1. Carl F. H. Henry, *Remaking the Modern Mind* (Grand Rapids: Eerdmans, 1948), 22. Still the classic analysis. Note also Henry's *The Drift of Western Thought* (Grand Rapids: Eerdmans, 1951). For an astute study of the collapsing moral foundations

of Western civilization, see Donald G. Bloesch, *Crumbling Foundations: Death and Rebirth in an Age of Upheaval* (Grand Rapids: Academie Books, Zondervan, 1984).
2. Ibid., 26ff. Nothing excels Henry's massive six-volume work on *God, Revelation and Authority* (Waco, Tex.: Word, 1976).

11.1 THE PLYMOUTH BRETHREN AND DISPENSATIONAL WORTHIES

> What we are about to consider will tend to shew that, instead of permitting ourselves to hope for a continued progress of good, we must expect a progress of evil; and that the hope of the earth being filled with the knowledge of the Lord before the exercise of His judgment, and the consummation of this judgment on the earth, is delusive. We are to expect evil, until it becomes so flagrant that it will be necessary for the Lord to judge it . . . I am afraid that many a cherished feeling dear to the children of God, has been shocked; I mean, their hope that the gospel will spread by itself over the whole earth, during the actual dispensation.
>
> —J. N. Darby, "Progress of Evil on the Earth," 1840

Preaching among the so-called Plymouth Brethren is usually overlooked in the history of preaching, but this is unfortunate. The Brethren have been avid students of Scripture. Their history began with Darby and his associates and our indebtedness to them should be reviewed. These New Testament "restorationists" have some twelve hundred assemblies in North America and have been strong in Britain and Germany (the late Erich Sauer is included among them).[1]

While every believer who does not offer animal sacrifices is in a sense a dispensationalist, the seeds of an interpretive system are found in Augustine *("distingue tempora et scripturae concordabint"),* Joachim of Fiore, Cocceius, Isaac Watts, and in Thomas Bernard's Bampton Lectures for 1864 on *The Progress of the Gospel in the New Testament.*[2] Dispensationalism as a system has come more from the Brethren than from anyone else, and thus their influence extends far beyond what their actual numbers would lead us to project.

Homiletically, the Brethren generally reacted against all traditional ideas of form and tended to revert to the ancient homily with its running commentary on the text. So Edith Blumhofer has recently written of Darby and the Plymouth Brethren:

> Replacing the typical sermon with a "Bible reading," they devised a preaching form that dismayed some of the era's pulpiteers but had enormous influence on popular evangelicalism.[3]

George Needham spoke for the Brethren in presenting himself as "a plain man, telling a plain story, in a plain manner."[4] D. L. Moody and many others took this form (i.e., took "a string of related texts or passages with brief comments").[5]

Though admiring the biblicality of this kind of preaching, President Francis L. Patton of Princeton warned his homiletical students "against supposing that you have given an adequate substitute for a sermon when, with the help of

Cruden's Concordance, you have chased a word through the Bible, making a comment or two on the passages as you go along."[6] Patton well argued that a sermon is a "rhetorical organism evolved by a genetic process from the text" with careful hermeneutical discipline.[7]

---

1. Thomas Stewart Veitch, *The Story in the Brethren Movement* (London: Pickering and Inglis, n.d.); Robert Baylis, *My People: The History of Those Christians Sometimes Called Plymouth Brethren* (Wheaton, Ill.: Harold Shaw, 1995). I am indebted to my student Mark Stevenson for lending me this book—a rewarding study. For a study of present Brethren losses in Britain, cf. Peter Brierley et al, *The Christian Brethren as the Nineties Began* (Carlisle, U.K.: Partnership, 1993).
2. Thomas D. Bernard, *The Progress of Doctrine in the New Testament* (Grand Rapids: Eerdmans, 1949). Bernard argues the case for progressive revelation (i.e., the gradual process of divine self-disclosure).
3. Edith R. Blumhofer, *Restoring the Faith* (Urbana/Champaign: University of Illinois Press, 1993), 16.
4. Ernest R. Sandeen, *The Roots of Fundamentalism: British and American Millenarianism, 1800–1930* (Grand Rapids: Baker, 1970, 1978), 137.
5. J. C. Pollock, *Moody: the Biography* (Chicago: Moody, 1963, 1983), 90. Compare 10.1.7.
6. Sandeen, *The Roots of Fundamentalism,* 137. F. F. Bruce, himself a Plymouth Brother, contrasts preaching a coherence and a sequence with "a mere stringing together of gospel texts" as was common; see *In Retrospect* (Grand Rapids: Eerdmans, 1980), 15.
7. John L. Patton, *Presbyterian and Reformed Review* 1 (1890): 36–37.

11.1.1 John Nelson Darby—The Prophet among the Ruins

> Oh, the joy of having nothing and being nothing, seeing nothing but a living Christ in glory, and being careful for nothing but His interests down here.
>
> I love not only to preach, but to be in direct communication with souls as to their relation with God—saints, and sinners yet more.
>
> It is no mistake to be always expecting the Lord to return. The object of the conversion of the Thessalonians was to wait for God's Son from heaven. People fancy that the truth of the Lord's return is a bit of knowledge at the top of the tree; but instead of that, it is what the Thessalonians were converted for, and meanwhile they are to serve God.
>
> —John Nelson Darby

Born in London, the sixth son of eight children in an old English family of Leicestershire, **John Nelson Darby** (1800–1882) is considered the founder of the Plymouth Brethren movement. He was early separated from his mother when his parents parted company. Educated in Westminster Public School, in 1815 he went to Trinity College, Dublin, where he studied to become a barrister. One of his close friends was J. G. Bellett, who later joined him in the early days of the Brethren.

A series of "spiritual awakenings" led to Darby's conversion at twenty-one.[1] He was ordained a deacon and then a priest in the Church of Ireland (by Archbishop Mager), yet he was without peace.[2] Thrown from his horse in a violent accident, he came to assurance of salvation and found "deliverance" from the condemnation of the law.[3] "The absolute, divine authority and certainty of the Word" became his compass, and he began to meet with others for the breaking of bread and the exposition of Scripture.

The Brethren movement sprang from a pessimism about the organized church. The church was seen as in ruins and the assemblies were "the little flock." Christ was the focus of the exposition as the crucified and risen Savior, now ascended and seated, about to return for his bride, the church. Evangelism was primary, but prophecy was also important. The great prophetic meetings at Powerscourt and Darby's broken engagement which had such a personally shattering effect upon his life were all integral to this amazing story.

There was a shyness in Darby's public speaking; he was "original but not obtrusive."[4] He never displayed his knowledge of the original languages but continued to pour forth scriptural exposition not only in Britain but also in America, where he preached for Moody, in France, Germany, and particularly in Geneva, Switzerland. Darby was an assiduous student of the Hebrew and Greek Scriptures. His collected writings run to 34 volumes. The best of his exposition is found in his extensive *Synopsis of the Books of the Bible.*[5]

Robert Louis Stevenson wrote of Darby's influence in his *Travels with a Donkey in the Cevennes,* and Tolstoy refers to the Plymouth Brethren whom he came to know through Lord Radstock. Interestingly, Darby was a lifelong paedo-Baptist.

Darby wrote much poetry and many hymns and translated the Bible into three languages. His message was driven home again and again:

> As an external body, the Church is ruined [has drifted into apostasy]; and though much may be enjoyed of what belongs to the Church, I believe from Scripture that the ruin is without remedy, that the professing church will be cut off. I believe that there is an external professing Christendom, holding a most important and responsible place, and which will be judged and cut off for its unfaithfulness. The true body of Christ is not this. It is composed of those who are united by Christ by the Holy Ghost, who, when the professing church is cut off, will have their place with Him in heaven.[6]

---

1. Max S. Weremchuk, *John Nelson Darby* (Neptune, N.J.: Loizeaux Brothers, 1992), 33.
2. Ibid., 42.
3. Ibid., 48.

4. Ibid., 189.
5. John Nelson Darby, *Synopsis of the Books of the Bible* (London: G. Morrish, n.d.). The Word "is more immediately of God" than mere abstract truth, 3:10.
6. John Nelson Darby, *Collected Works,* 14:417. For examples of his poetry, *Spiritual Songs* (Kingston-on-Thames: Stow Hill Bible and Tract Depot, n.d.).

11.1.2 George Müller—Practitioner of Faith among the Desolate

> Immediately upon beginning to expound "Blessed are the poor in spirit . . ." I felt myself greatly assisted; and whereas in the morning my sermon had not been simple enough for the people to understand it, I now was listened to with the greatest attention, and I think I was also understood. My own peace and joy were great. I felt this was a blessed work.
>
> —George Müller

Thus is described the initial preaching experience of **George Müller** (1805–1898) in the environs of Halle, where he was studying for the ministry. He was born in Prussia and lost his mother when he was fourteen. Though reared in a religious environment and undergoing confirmation, Müller had no concept of God. He drank, played cards, and at sixteen was in jail as a libertine and a thief.[1]

Despite his dissipated lifestyle, he commenced study for the ministry at Halle. While there, he was invited to a cottage Bible study and prayer meeting where he was converted in November of 1825. The well-known Professor Tholuck was his mentor (cf. 8.2.6). To help pay his way through the university, Müller tutored Americans in German, one of whom was Charles Hodge. He went to England as a missionary to the Jews under the auspices of the Church of England, but soon sundered his ties with the established church and moved into the orbit of the rapidly growing Plymouth Brethren movement.

The Second Coming of Christ was a frequent subject of his preaching. His expositions of Romans particularly commended him to the Brethren.[2] Müller was called to minister to the congregation at Ebenezer Chapel in Teignmouth, though they were somewhat divided over him. He remained there for two and a half years, preaching with a strong German accent.

Müller became a great lover of the Word, usually reading his Bible on his knees. He spoke of learning "the preciousness of the Word of God." Soon he moved to Bristol where he shared in preaching and ministry at several chapels, chiefly Bethesda, where he reached this conclusion:

> We ought to receive all whom Christ has received, irrespective of the measure of grace or knowledge to which they have attained.[3]

Müller and **Henry Craik** alternated in the preaching. They set aside evenings when people could come to the vestry for individual conversation and counsel.[4] Deep tensions tore the movement apart when Darby and Müller broke fellowship. The split launched the Closed Brethren (Darby) and the Open Brethren (Bethesda and Müller). In all of this Müller founded the orphanages accommodating two thousand children, a ministry which continues to this day. His life of faith compelled him never to take a salary or ask for money.

Müller preached an average of three sermons a week, more than ten thousand in his lifetime. He could preach fluently in seven languages. His method is described like this:

> Expository preaching . . . instead of a solitary text detached from its context, he selects a passage, it may be of several verses, which he goes over consecutively clause by clause. His first care is to give the meaning of the passage, and then to illustrate it by other Scriptures, and afterwards apply it.[5]

Müller utilized the typical Brethren homiletic with great impact, preaching into his ninety-third year. He traveled to America several times, where he preached for Talmage in Brooklyn, met with President and Mrs. Hayes at the White House, and preached at Moody's Church in Chicago. In England he worked untiringly with the Moody-Sankey meetings and preached for Spurgeon. Shaped above all by Scripture but also by the biographies of Francke, John Newton, and George Whitefield, George Müller shook his generation for Christ. If indeed 1849 to 1914 was the great age of liberalism, this oft-divided but resilient movement of Darby, Müller, William Kelly, and F. C. Grant faithfully held forth the Word of Life.

---

1. Roger Steer, *George Müller: Delighted in God,* rev. ed. (Wheaton, Ill.: Harold Shaw, 1981), 15.
2. Basil Miller, *George Müller: Man of Faith and Miracles* (Minneapolis: Bethany, 1941), 25.
3. Thomas Stewart Veitch, *The Story of the Brethren Movement* (London: Pickering and Inglis, n.d.), 37.
4. A. T. Pierson, *George Müller of Bristol and His Witness to a Prayer-Hearing God* (New York: Revell, 1899), 88.
5. Steer, *George Müller,* 220.

11.1.3 Charles Henry Mackintosh—The Preacher Who Loved Learning

> The Word of God was rejected. . . . remember the words of the Lord Jesus Christ, how He said, "As it was in the days of Noah, so shall it be in the days of the Son of Man . . ." Some would have us believe that ere the Son of Man appears in the clouds of heaven, this earth shall be covered from pole to pole with a fair mantle of righteousness. They would teach us to look for a reign of righteousness and peace, as the result of agencies now in operation; but the brief passage just quoted cuts up by the roots, in a moment, all such vain and delusive expectations. How was it in the days of Noah?
>
> —C. H. M. (as he was known among the Brethren)

Many Plymouth Brethren Bible students were amazingly productive. They include George Wigram in *Englishman's Hebrew and Chaldee Concordance,* Samuel P. Tregelles in textual criticism,[1] F. W. Grant in his *Numerical Bible,* which influenced H. A. Ironside so decisively, and William Kelly's New Testament commentaries to which F. F. Bruce and Spurgeon paid such high compliment.[2]

Another astute Bible teacher was **Charles Henry Mackintosh** (1820–1896), born in Ireland and moved by Darby's "Operations of the Spirit," in which the case is made for our assurance on the basis of Christ's work for us. Mackintosh ran a school in Westport for ten years and then gave himself to the ministry of the Word. He was in the thick of the revival that swept over Ireland in 1859 and 1860 and is known for his *Notes on the Pentateuch.*[3] He spoke and wrote in a strong and perspicuous style, although a given interpretation may be forced. He was among those who remained totally loyal to Darby. Andrew Miller correctly said of his work:

> Man's complete ruin in sin, and God's perfect remedy in Christ are fully, clearly and often strikingly presented.[4]

---

1. George H. Fromow, *B. W. Newton and S. P. Tregelles: Teachers of the Faith and the Future* (London: Sovereign Grace Advent Testimony, 1969).
2. F. F. Bruce, *In Retrospect: Remembrance of Things Past* (Grand Rapids: Eerdmans, 1980), 293.
3. C. H. Mackintosh, *Notes on the Pentateuch* (New York: Loizeaux Brothers, 1879). My experience of delight with these five small volumes in my youth directly parallels Warren Wiersbe's *Giant Steps* (Grand Rapids: Baker, 1981), 133. C. H. M. demonstrates so vividly that there is meaning for us in "the old, old story."
4. Hy Pickering, *Chief Men among the Brethren* (London: Pickering and Inglis, 1918), 111.

11.1.4 C. I. Scofield—Doyen of the Dispensationalists

> If you're going to do it, and do it for God, there is only one way—not a smooth, easy way, but as unto the Lord.
>
> —C. I. Scofield

> We commend him to you as one who delights to hide behind the uplifted cross of Jesus; one who will preach a full and free salvation through the shed blood of God's Lamb; one who will lead you into the deep things of the Word, and one who teaches and who preaches the whole truth of God.
>
> —Letter on the occasion of Scofield's dismissal from the First Congregational Church of Dallas in 1895

Although not of the Brethren but of the dispensational family, no one is more pivotal in the progress of this movement than **Cyrus Ingersoll Scofield** (1842–1921). Born in Michigan and reared in Tennessee, Scofield served in the

Confederate Army under General Robert E. Lee. After the war he read for the law and was admitted to the bar in 1869 in Kansas, where he was then elected to the State House of Representatives. Scofield was active in politics and named U.S. Attorney for Kansas when he was thirty. Many enemies of his theological system have written scurrilously about his personal life, and much of it may be true, before his conversion.

A friend led him to Christ when he was thirty-six, and he testified, "the passion for drink was taken away."[1] Then the young lawyer living in St. Louis came under the teaching of **Dr. James H. Brookes,** Presbyterian pastor and Bible teacher.[2] Brookes led him deeply into the Scripture, and in 1882 Scofield was called to the First Congregational Church of Dallas. Scofield's solid Bible preaching was used of God to build the membership from fourteen to 551 members.

D. L. Moody had met Scofield in St. Louis and invited him to speak at Northfield and the Niagara Conferences. In 1895 he invited Scofield to come as pastor of Moody's home church in Northfield, where he labored for seven years. As early as 1888, Scofield wrote his famous *Rightly Dividing the Word of Truth* and soon after the equally well-known Scofield Correspondence Course. He also founded the Central American Mission.

Returning to Dallas in 1902, he worked on the *Scofield Reference Bible,* of which Brookes was a consulting editor. R. A. Torrey suggested the use of subheads. Oxford University Press was and is the publisher of the famous Bible study tool. Always when Scofield visited Oxford in connection with his editorial work, he and Mrs. Scofield found fellowship in a Plymouth Brethren gathering.[3]

Scofield was an energetic and effective preacher on any biblical theme but especially on the victorious Christian life.[4] His preaching style was similar to that of the Brethren in that he seldom divided the text or the sermon. His illustrations were practical and memorable. He could be aggressively evangelistic or pastorally didactic.[5]

---

1. Charles G. Trumbull, *The Life Story of C. I. Scofield* (New York: Oxford University Press, 1920), 31. Trumbull, editor of the *Sunday School Times,* was the son of Henry Clay Trumbull, who with John Wanamaker bought the *Times.* The elder Trumbull gave the Beecher Lectures at Yale on the Sunday school in 1887 and 1888. The younger Trumbull became a protégé of Scofield and himself wrote messages on the victorious life which were widely heard and read. Philip E. Howard (a son-in-law and later editor) wrote *The Life's Story of Henry Clay Trumbull* (Philadelphia: Sunday School Times, 1905).
2. Ibid., 35. Cf. David Riddle Williams, *James H. Brookes: A Memoir* (St. Louis: Presbyterian Board of Publications, 1897).
3. Ibid., 108. The linkage of Scofield to Darby via Walter Scott, Gaebelein, and Brookes is judiciously explored in David J. MacLeod, "Walter Scott, A Link in Dispensationalism Between Darby and Scofield," *Bibliotheca Sacra* 153, no. 610 (April–June, 1996): 155ff.
4. C. I. Scofield, *The New Life in Christ Jesus: Messages of Joy and Victory* (Chicago: Moody, 1915).
5. C. I. Scofield, *In Many Pulpits with C. I. Scofield* (Grand Rapids: Baker, 1922, 1966).

11.1.5 A. C. Gaebelein—Dean of the Dispensationalists

> Laodicea is all about us. It is the final state of Protestant Christendom, lukewarm, indifferent and modernistic. Yet the work of the true servant of God is not to denounce the professing Church, but to go and bear a loving, faithful testimony to those in Laodicea.
>
> One of the temptations of a busy life of ministry is the neglect of study, and especially of that which is most essential, the study of the Word of God and prayer.
>
> —Arno Clemens Gaebelein

Born in Thuringia in Germany, coming to the United States, and settling in Lawrence, Massachusetts, **Arno Clemens Gaebelein** (1861–1945) was always close to the Brethren and is certainly one of the founts of dispensational truth. He was converted at twelve, dedicated to Christ's service at eighteen, and became a preacher in the German Methodist Conference in Baltimore, Harlem, and Hoboken. He started to study Hebrew to reach the Jews for Christ.

In 1892 he preached a series of sermons on "Joseph and His Brothers" which were published and widely distributed.[1] In close touch with A. B. Simpson, founder of the Christian Missionary Alliance, James M. Gray, Rector of First Reformed Episcopal Church of Boston and later dean and president of Moody Bible Institute,[2] and C. I. Scofield, Gaebelein soon launched *Our Hope* magazine. He also began an itinerant Bible preaching ministry that crisscrossed the United States over the next forty years.

Gaebelein left the Methodist church in view of the merciless onslaughts of higher critical thought. When S. Parkes Cadman trumpeted that inerrancy was "no longer possible of belief among reasonable men" and that the New Testament "contains contradictions," Gaebelein left.[3] Gaebelein contributed to *The Fundamentals* (1910–1912) and participated in Plymouth Brethren conferences, the Niagara Bible Conference, and the great Chicago Prophecy Conference of 1914. His lucidly written commentaries on Psalms, Daniel, Joel, Zechariah, Matthew, Acts, and Revelation along with his extensive *Annotated Bible* contain the substance of his communication over the years. Speaking in his German accent, he was one of the first to foresee the Bolshevistic threat in Russia.[4]

His preaching style was clear and calm and always utilized helpful illustrations. Wilbur M. Smith recalled the impression Gaebelein made from the pulpit:

> Dr. Gaebelein spoke before about 2,000 [in Bethany Presbyterian Church of Philadelphia] on the phrase: "We wait for thy salvation O God." I do not remember five occasions in my life when I was so lifted as I was that morning. There was no desire to take notes. I did not even care to remember what he was saying. I felt my soul cleansed and refreshed and my whole being ennobled. I went out of that auditorium determined to be a different kind of preacher and student than I had ever been before.[5]

The lead editorial in *Our Hope* was always focused on the Lord Jesus. So Gaebelein in the morning service would preach Christ and then move to Bible prophecy in the evening. I believe the list of his close compatriots shows how influential he was. He wrote sixty books, including *The Christ We Know* (in answer to Bruce Barton's *The Man Nobody Knows*), *The Lord of Glory, The Conflict of the Ages, The Harmony of the Prophetic Word, Hopeless—Yet There Is Hope.* Gaebelein would speak topically on occasion and in his exposition followed the Brethren verse-by-verse style very well. How many have been converted and blessed through the faithful proclamation of the Word by this servant of Christ!

---

1. Arno Clemens Gaebelein, *Half a Century: The Autobiography of a Servant* (New York: Our Hope, 1930), 29.
2. Dr. James M. Gray was himself a gifted preacher; see *Salvation From Start to Finish* (Chicago: Moody, n.d.). In a beautiful exposition on Titus 3:3–8, Gray nicely divides the text and the sermon into three classic main points.
3. David A. Rausch, *Arno C. Gaebelein: Irenic Fundamentalist and Scholar* (Lewiston, N.Y.: Edwin Mellen Press, 1983), 60.
4. Ibid., 107. His analysis of Marxism is in *The Conflict of the Ages* (New York: Our Hope, 1933).
5. Ibid., 231. A. C. Gaebelein's gifted son, Frank E. Gaebelein, became an evangelical icon and gifted writer.

11.1.6 SIR ROBERT ANDERSON—THE SERMONIZER FROM SCOTLAND YARD

> One day soon after my conversion I received a letter from a friend telling me that he was unable to keep an engagement to address a Gospel meeting, and asking me to take his place. The messenger waited for an answer and I promptly replied that I could not take such a position. But then I fell a-thinking. I had been praying that God would give me work to do for Him; might not this be the answer? So I hurried after the messenger to tell of my change of mind. And the next day I preached my first Gospel sermon.
>
> The Coming of Christ is not some strange thing that faddists have imported into Christianity. No one has any right to call himself a Christian who denies the Coming of the Lord Jesus Christ . . . you ought not to be merely a person who holds the doctrine of the Advent; if you are a Christian you should hold it as a living hope in the heart.
>
> —Sir Robert Anderson

Representative of lay preachers who were so prominent in the Brethren ranks are such names as Dr. A. T. Schofield, the well-known Harley Street physician,[1] F. W. Baedeker, brother of the travel-book man who with Lord Radstock opened such a remarkable door to Russia, and **Sir Robert Anderson** (1841–1918), who had high office in the Metropolitan Police of London and in Scotland Yard.

Born in Dublin, Anderson called himself an "anglicised Irishman of Scottish extraction." He studied at Trinity College, Dublin, where the eminent historian of morals, W. H. E. Lecky, was his friend and classmate. He returned to Trinity to study after the law but was converted at the age of nineteen in the ripple effect of the Great Revival of 1859.[2] He soon began to preach both evangelistically in gospel meetings and in serious expositions of the deeper things of Scripture.[3] Through his long lifetime he continued to preach in many venues, frequently among the Brethren, although he fellowshiped with Adolph Saphir's ministry in Notting Hill. He took a position with the British Home Office and then became head of the Criminal Investigation Department of the London Police and Scotland Yard in the wake of the Jack the Ripper scare.

Nonetheless, Sir Robert's first love was gospel ministry. He once said he could not understand anyone standing up with the Bible in his hand and failing to be interesting.[4] Tinged with humor, his messages always exalted the grace of God in Christ. He was well received at Mildmay and other conferences, being close to A. C. Dixon, Ada Habershon (who wrote so memorably on the names and titles of the Lord of Glory), J. Stuart Holden, Professor Henry Drummond, and W. F. Moulton, the New Testament scholar. He was much influenced by F. E. Marsh and the rather idiosyncratic Church of England Bible teacher Dr. E. W. Bullinger.[5] In his large circle of friends was also the delightful Bishop Taylor Smith and Professor Hechler from Vienna, who had a great influence on Theodore Herzl, founder of Zionism.[6] None other than Horatius Bonar first interested him on the doctrine of the Second Coming.

A great stream of books and pamphlets flowed from Anderson's pen. Not least of these is his magisterial *The Coming Prince,* which treats the prophecy of the seventy sevens in Daniel 9:24–27.[7] He made the case for the accuracy and historical reliability of Daniel.[8] The Sir Robert Anderson Library Series is still in print and is well worth reading.[9] His study *The Bible and Modern Criticism* was commended by Bishop Moule in its preface, and his notable piece on *Daniel in the Critics' Den* (a reply particularly to Professor Driver at Oxford) was endorsed by Spurgeon, Gaebelein, and Griffith Thomas.

---

1. A. T. Schofield, *Behind the Brass Plate* (London: Sampson, Low, n.d.). Dr. Schofield lived 1846–1929.
2. A. P. Moore-Anderson, *Sir Robert Anderson and Lady Agnes Anderson* (London: Marshall, Morgan, 1947), 18–19.
3. Ibid., 27.
4. Ibid., 121.
5. Ibid., 82. Dr. Bullinger wrote some scholarly and searching books, particularly on *The Apocalypse* and *The Gifts and the Giver* (a masterpiece on every reference to the Holy Spirit in the New Testament), but he lurched into extreme dispensationalism. Compare H. A. Ironside, *Wrongly Dividing the Word of Truth* (New York: Loizeaux, n.d.).
6. Ibid., 98.
7. Robert Anderson, *The Coming Prince: The Marvelous Prophecy of Daniel's Seventy Weeks Concerning the Antichrist* (Grand Rapids: Kregel, 1957).

8. Robert Anderson, *Daniel in the Critics' Den* (Grand Rapids: Kregel, 1990).
9. The library published by Kregel contains such notable volumes as *The Silence of God, Forgotten Truths, The Gospel and Its Ministry,* and *Types in Hebrews.*

11.1.7 H. A. Ironside—The All-Around Bible Preacher

> "Pray for us . . ." Who can tell how much each servant of Christ is indebted to the prayers of God's hidden ones? To bear such up before Him is a wondrous ministry, the fullness of which will only be manifested in that day when every secret thing will be revealed according to his own service. Let none think it is a little thing to pray. There is no higher ministry, no more important office, than that of intercessor.
>
> —H. A. Ironside

Henry (Harry) Allan Ironside (1876–1951) was a short, rotund, bald-headed man of calm and humble bearing. Yet he was a mightily used preacher of the Word. Sometimes called the archbishop of fundamentalism, Ironside was born in Toronto, where his father was a street preacher known as the eternity man.

John Ironside died at twenty-seven, when Harry was only two years of age. Mrs. Ironside then moved with her two sons to Los Angeles, where Harry was converted at twelve following one of D. L. Moody's meetings.[1] At fifteen he left home to become a Salvation Army officer and was commissioned a lieutenant.[2] Ultimately he left the Army because of his inner struggle for perfection (as related in his *Holiness: The True and the False*). Helped by George Cutting's little book, *Safety, Certainty and Enjoyment,* H. A. I., as he was called, soon found himself among the Brethren and deeper and deeper into the Word.

He worked in evangelism for awhile with **Henry Varley,** who had given Moody the epigram, "The world has yet to see what God will do with a man who is fully yielded to him."[3] This was the Golden Age of Independent Brethren, and Ironside traveled the next thirty years preaching the Word in simple and direct ways to thousands. His sermons exuded Scripture as he preached his typically Brethren verse-by-verse exposition with stories and anecdotes.

Ironside had a long connection with Dallas Theological Seminary, where his style was appreciated early on. He was known for book-by-book studies, all of which found their way into print.[4] His favorite sermon was from Philemon and was titled "Charge That to My Account."[5]

In 1930 Ironside shocked the Brethren world by accepting the call to pastor the great Moody Memorial Church in Chicago. From that year until 1948 he preached to full houses of four thousand morning and evening. He was especially known for his studies on the Lord's return from Daniel, Revelation, and his signature volume, *The Great Parenthesis.*[6]

In his standard collections of sermons, Ironside did not divide the text, nor did he divide the sermon.[7] With their teaching charts, Brethren preachers traveled and preached, the finest of them Ironside, August Van Ryn,[8] Frederick Tatford, and Neil Fraser.

1. E. Schuyler English, *H. A. Ironside: Ordained of the Lord* (Grand Rapids: Zondervan, 1946), 33.
2. H. A. Ironside, *Random Reminiscences* (New York: Loizeaux, 1939), 9. A great story of exposition in a Pullman, (68ff.).
3. English, *H. A. Ironside,* 83.
4. H. A. Ironside's lectures on Jeremiah, Romans, Revelation, and almost every Bible book were given at schools and preached from pulpits all over the country and around the world.
5. "Charge That to My Account" is the lead sermon in a book by that title but is also found in English, *H. A. Ironside,* 181ff.
6. H. A. Ironside, *The Great Parenthesis* (Grand Rapids: Zondervan, 1943). This title has been maligned as depreciating the church in God's plan, but Ironside spoke of the interval from the standpoint of Israel.
7. Especially choice are *The Lamp of Prophecy, Great Words of the Gospel,* and *Care for God's Fruit Trees.*
8. August Van Ryn, *Sixty Years in His Service* (Waynesboro: Ga.: Christian Missions Press, n.d.).

11.1.8 ARTHUR W. PINK—THE TROUBADOUR OF GOSPEL TRUTH

> God has said in his Word, "He that believeth shall not make haste" (Isa. 28:16), and if ever there was a time when his children needed to give special heed to this admonition it is now. The children of God are infected with the spirit of the world. The mad rush which characterizes everything around us, the awful hustle and bustle of the ungodly as they rush headlong to eternal death, has affected the members of the household of faith . . . the irreverent speed with which the Holy Scriptures are read in the average pulpit; the rate at which sacred songs are commonly sung; the unholy manner in which many rush into the presence of the Most High God, and gabble off the first words that come to their lips, are so many examples of this infection . . . stand, sit, wait, tarry.
>
> —Arthur W. Pink

If a Christian can be a curmudgeon, **Arthur W. Pink** (1886–1952) was such a person. Better known through his extensive writings and his magazine, *Studies in the Scriptures*, Pink preached to large conferences and was a vigorous and effective preacher. He was born in Nottingham in England and reared in a godly home but got tangled up in Theosophy, opening a correspondence with Annie Besant.[1] His concerned father gave him Proverbs 14:12, and he stayed in his bedroom under such conviction that he was converted three days later.[2]

In 1910 he traveled to Chicago and began studies at Moody Bible Institute, but seemed bored and stayed only two months. He moved on to a brief pastorate in Silverton, Colorado, where his first recorded sermon was on "Beholding the Crucified Christ," from Matthew 27:35–36, incisive on imputed righteousness and the atonement. He moved on to California, where a man in Oakland was saved hearing a message on thanksgiving from Hebrews 13:15 because he realized he had never praised God! During ministry in a small church in Kentucky, he met and married his wife, Vera Russell, who worked with him on the editing of *Studies in the Scriptures,* which he launched in 1922.

Although of independent frame of mind, Pink was close to the Brethren and used many Brethren writers in the earlier issues of the magazine. Enduring frequent bouts of discouragement and depression, the Pinks served a Baptist Church in Spartanburg, North Carolina, but then in 1925 moved to Australia. After much reading in the Puritans, Pink began to move toward a narrow Calvinism and away from his premillennial and dispensational roots.[3] His preaching became more and more doctrinal. He was determined not to fuss over people and was very quick to rebuke.

Pink was addicted to typology, demonstrated when he developed 101 ways in which Joseph prefigures Christ.[4] Still, his rich *Gleanings from Genesis, Gleanings from Exodus, Gleanings from Joshua,* and *Gleanings from Paul* were nourishment for saints and stimulation for preachers.

The Pinks went back to England, and "cut off from visible fellowship," tried again in the United States, back to England, and then to Scotland. Their last years were in Stornoway on the Island of Lewis in the Outer Hebrides, where they did not understand Gaelic, nor did they fellowship in any church. Murray analyzes this disconsolate time when a man who had formerly preached three hundred times a year now did not preach at all. He calls him "the unwanted preacher."[5] Still the flow of rich expository materials continued, as Pink produced three incomparable volumes on John, *The Life of David,* theological tomes on the inspiration of Scripture and the attributes of God. His messages on the Seven Last Words, unlike most of his preaching, do see the division of the sermon in a more classical mode because the texts were very brief.[6] His magazine dropped in circulation to less than nine hundred in 1938, but Mrs. Pink finished several issues after his death in 1952. But here was a preacher of the Word!

---

1. Pink's ensnarement in Theosophy reminds us of the enormous influence of this pseudo-eastern religion on Yeats, James Joyce, Jack London, D. H. Lawrence, Mahler, Sibelius, and Shirley McLaine. For the best overall resource to survey the subject, see Sylvia Cranstrom, *The Extraordinary Life and Influence of Helena Blavatsky* (New York: Putnam, 1993).
2. Iain H. Murray, *The Life of Arthur W. Pink* (Edinburgh: Banner of Truth, 1981), 7.
3. A. W. Pink, *The Antichrist* (Swengel, Pa.: Bible Truth Depot, 1923). Acceptable to any dispensational interpreter.
4. A. W. Pink, *Gleanings from Genesis* (Chicago: Moody, 1922), 142ff.
5. Murray, *The Life of Arthur W. Pink,* 100ff.
6. A. W. Pink, *The Seven Sayings of the Savior on the Cross* (Grand Rapids: Zondervan, 1951).

11.2 *THE SCOTTISH GIANTS IN THE EARLY TWENTIETH CENTURY*

> The William Robertson Smith case in the Free Church of Scotland, which was of so much interest to Americans, marked the beginning of a new relationship between British evangelicals and biblical criticism. Smith freely applied the criticism of the Continent to the Old Testament, but he did so while maintaining a belief in miracles, personal divine revelation, and the supernatural. At the end of a complicated series of hearings, Smith lost his professorship in 1881, but retained his status as an ordained minister. Of this action it was said that the Free Church secured its liberty in biblical criticism by the sacrifice of one individual.
>
> —Mark A. Noll

Bible-believing Christians in Scotland won the battle but effectively lost the war. Their traditional views gave way because practitioners of the new criticism, which savaged the Bible, ultimately presented themselves as part of the community of faith and piety.[1] Cambridge scholars like H. C. G. Moule, B. F. Westcott, and J. B. Lightfoot all defended the Scripture's integrity. Preachers like Spurgeon, Liddon, Jowett, Morgan, and Meyer upheld inerrancy. James Denney defended the substitutionary atonement against Ritschl's subjective view.[2]

A parallel situation in the United States found Charles Augustus Briggs, a Presbyterian who taught Old Testament at Union Seminary in New York, under charges of wholesale concessions to modern criticism on issues like Pentateuchal authorship, the unity of Isaiah, and Daniel's authorship of the prophecy bearing his name. He was suspended from Presbyterian standing but became an Episcopalian, and Union became independent to keep him on the faculty. Briggs lost, but his views became dominant.[3] The fallout soon became all too apparent.

---

1. Mark Noll, *Between Faith and Criticism* (New York: Harper and Row, 1986), 72.
2. Ibid., 79.
3. Mark S. Massa, *Charles Augustus Briggs and the Crisis of Historical Criticism* (Minneapolis: Fortress, 1990).

11.2.1 *Alexander Whyte—The Master of the Pulpit*

> The pulpit is a jealous mistress, and will not brook a divided allegiance.
>
> Somehow a great Gospel text is always the most difficult text for me to preach on, so as to make it fresh and interesting. But difficult or easy, I must preach more on such texts, and so must you. It is for such texts, above all else, that we have our pulpits committed to us.
>
> Never think of giving up preaching. The angels around the throne envy you your great work. You say you scarcely know how or what to preach. Look into your own sinful heart, and back into your sinful life, and around

> on the world full of sin, and open your New Testament and make application of Christ to yourself and your people and you will preach more freshly and more powerfully every day.
>
> —Alexander Whyte

From the depths of obscurity to the peaks of prominence and popularity was the road that **Alexander Whyte** (1836–1921) took, but Scotland's most distinguished preacher of his time took it all with becoming humility before God and man. Whyte was born in Kirriemuir, a weaving community. His parents were never married.[1] At the time of Alexander's birth his father was not a Christian, and his mother, a believer, would not compound her disobedience. His father was later converted and died in America serving with the Union Army at Bull Run.

In the morning, young Whyte would accompany his mother to the South Free Church and in the afternoon go with his grandmother to the Relief Church (known to readers of Sir James Barrie, who wrote *The Little Minister* and who was a contemporary of Whyte). Whyte was apprenticed in a shoemaker's shop, and, according to G. F. Barbour's incomparable biography of him, he would read Milton in the kirkyard during his breaks.[2] Whyte attended King's College, Aberdeen, where he was on the debating society. In the revival of 1859, he showed great power of preaching in surrounding churches and then went on to New College, Edinburgh, for divinity, where he studied under Rainy, Candlish, and Davidson and talked theology with his friend Marcus Dods. He spent his time studying four volumes of Henry Alford and twelve volumes of Thomas Goodwin. His struggle was as much against "inward depression as it was against hindering circumstances."[3]

Here are a few milestones that mark his meteoric ascension.

- Worked as a student under Dr. Moses Stuart at Free St. Luke's.
- Preached on Ezekiel 37:1–14 which Candlish criticized, "Not a bad sermon if it had been a little more on the text."
- Was an assistant at Free St. John's (1866–1870) in Glasgow under Dr. John Roxburgh, where Chalmers had been; saw the rejuvenation of the prayer meeting; was a consistent soul-winner; explored Shorter Catechism.
- Became a colleague (1870–1873) of Dr. Candlish, who was nearing retirement at the cathedral of the Scottish Free Church, Free St. George's, Shandwicke Place. Here he first met the young William Robertson Smith.
- Took full charge at St. George's (1873) and shared in the revival of 1874 when Moody and Sankey ministered.
- In the ten-year controversy over Robertson Smith, stood loyally with Smith, who was declared "unsettling and unsafe" by the General Assembly. Yet even his biographer admits, "He was by no means satisfied that Smith had sufficiently considered the wider bearings of certain statements he had used."[4] His own preaching was sound.
- Married Jane Barbour (1881); became a total abstainer; almost died in a serious coach accident.

- Shared ministry with several associates, including Hugh Black, whose brother James succeeded Whyte and wrote the book from his Warrack Lectures which is titled *The Mystery of Preaching,* John Kelman (after Hugh Black went to Union Seminary in New York City, where he taught until 1948), and George H. Morrison of "Wellington" (N.B. 11.2.7).
- Added the duties of principal at New College when Rainy died; pushed church union; resigned the church at eighty and the principalship at eighty-two; died in his sleep in 1921.

Whyte was gregarious and a loyal friend. He interviewed and appreciated Cardinal Newman (which evoked quite a ruckus), liked Joseph Parker, and was close to Professor Henry Drummond. He was a good friend to Baron Von Hugel,[5] and was especially close to his nephew by marriage, **Hubert Simpson**. Simpson served Westborne United Free Church in Glasgow and was invited to succeed Dr. Kelman at Free St. George's but went rather to Westminster Chapel in London.[6]

In his study at 7 Charlotte Square, Whyte read extensively and had a brilliant grasp of a huge body of data, but he always complained about a proverbially bad memory. Here he prepared his five weekly presentations at St. George's, among which were his famous lectures on Bunyan, St. Teresa, William Law, Samuel Rutherford, and Tauler's sermons for Whyte's classes.[7]

Although somewhat shy, he was leonine in the pulpit. Even early in his career his preaching was described as on the highest evangelical level, "awakening, arresting, interesting, scintillating with imaginative insight."[8] His was a most extraordinary imagination, and he studied with Roget's *Thesaurus* ever at his elbow. He used a manuscript in the pulpit to pace himself but was more effective when he spoke extempore. His preaching was "personal, ethical, inward and it dealt but sparingly with speculative or social problems."[9]

Whyte preached against sin with great vehemence, but along with this preaching of righteousness "he did not heal the wound of the people slightly."[10] His trademark was "his scourging of depraved human hearts in the pulpit."[11] Barbour argues that he mellowed with the years.[12] Heart attacks slowed him down but even at seventy-eight, when Chapman and Alexander came for an Edinburgh crusade, the old war-horse filled the pulpit when Chapman became ill.

Whyte was portrayed as "a man of deep and various silences."[13] Admittedly, he was sympathetic to Christ-centered mysticism (to use Deissman's frame of reference), but his sermons were powerful expositions. His *Bible Characters*[14] is greatly loved, as are his beautiful messages on the life of our Lord and on the apostle Paul. Especially favored are his twenty-three sermons on prayer. "The Psalmist—Setting the Lord Always Before Him," from Psalm 16:9, is particularly noteworthy.[15] The last sermon which he preached was "A Study on the Swelling of the Jordan" from Jeremiah 12:5.[16]

Whyte may not have discerned all of the issues being faced by the Free Church in terms of Enlightenment biblical criticism, but he himself was a giant of a preacher—so clear on sin and the need for salvation. Whyte of St. George's had received the commission from the Lord:

What seemed to me to be a divine voice spoke with all-commanding power in my conscience, and said to me as clear as clear could be, "No, go on and flinch not! Go back and finish the work that has been given you to do. Speak out and fear not. Make them, at any cost, to see God's holy law as in a glass. Do you that, for no one else will do it. No one else will so risk his life and his reputation as to do it. And you have not much of either left to risk. Go home and spend what is left of your life in your appointed task of showing my people their sin and their need of my Salvation."[17]

---

1. G. F. Barbour, *The Life of Alexander Whyte* (London: Hodder and Stoughton, 1923), 15.
2. Ibid., 30–31.
3. Ibid., 49.
4. Ibid., 206.
5. Baron Von Hugel was a Roman Catholic mystic, though his mother was reared a Scottish Presbyterian. Von Hugel was very clear in his warnings about the dangers of subjectivity and pantheism; see Michael De La Bedoyere, *The Life of Baron Von Hugel* (New York: Scribner's, 1961). "Holiness is sanctified courtesy" was a favorite saying.
6. Hubert L. Simpson, *The Intention of His Soul* (London: Hodder and Stoughton, 1921). Note especially "Abigail Voices."
7. Alexander Whyte, *Bunyan Characters* (Edinburgh: Oliphant Anderson, n.d.); two volumes on *Pilgrim's Progress* and one on *The Holy War.* I have treasured my copies of these extraordinarily creative sermons. Spurgeon also preached on Bunyan's characters; cf. C. H. Spurgeon, *Pictures from Pilgrim's Progress* (Grand Rapids: Baker, 1982).
8. Barbour, *The Life of Alexander Whyte,* 164.
9. Ibid., 304. See Wilbur M. Smith, "Some Lesser-Known Pages from Dr. Alexander Whyte," *Chats from a Minister's Library* (Boston: W. A. Wilde, 1951), 103ff.
10. Ibid., 305.
11. Ibid., 373.
12. Ibid., 532.
13. Ibid., 371.
14. Alexander Whyte, *Bible Characters* (Grand Rapids: Zondervan, 1952).
15. Alexander Whyte, *Lord, Teach Us to Pray: Sermons on Prayer* (New York: Ray Long, 1931), 90.
16. Alexander Whyte, *In Remembrance of Me* (Grand Rapids: Baker, 1906, 1970), 83, 95.
17. Ralph G. Turnbull, *Dargan's History of Preaching* (Grand Rapids: Baker, 1974), 3:511.

11.2.2 JOHN KELMAN—THE PREACHER ASTRIDE THE ATLANTIC

The true aim of any one sermon is to be suggestive rather than exhaustive in its treatment of its subject. One great object of preaching is to startle

> men and women into thinking, to suggest even by opposition, to stimulate thought by exaggeration. There is all the difference in the world between the exaggeration which is the habit of the untruthful mind, and that which the art of a skillful master of persuasive speech.
>
> —John Kelman in the Beecher Lectures

Known for his long and loyal association with Alexander Whyte at Free St. George's (1907–19), **John Kelman** (1864–1929) became known as a influential pulpiteer in his own right. Born in a Free Church manse, he studied at New College in Edinburgh and then three years at Ormand College in Melbourne, Australia. He returned to Scotland to work under **George Adam Smith** (1856–1942) at Queen's Cross, Aberdeen.[1] Later under Whyte he achieved some visibility as a preacher and gave the Beecher Lectures at Yale on "The War and Preaching."[2]

Kelman did war work in France for the YMCA for which he received the O.B.E., but the lectures, like many of his sermons, seem a bit thin. Instead of succeeding Whyte as had been supposed, Kelman took the call to Fifth Avenue Presbyterian Church in New York City after Jowett's departure. But he came to Fifth Avenue as a "worn-out, prematurely old man of fifty-five."[3] With his health breaking, he resigned and returned to Britain to serve a Presbyterian church in Hampstead. He died in Edinburgh at the age of sixty-five.

Yet Kelman had remarkable gifts. He took pages out of Smith's book and used poetry and other literature with skill. He wrote a book on the religion of Robert Louis Stevenson, the fabled Scottish poet and novelist who had a heritage of biblical knowledge and was familiar with Bunyan. (Stevenson's defense of Father Damien was noble, but he had little spirituality himself.)[4]

Kelman's fifty-two abstracts of sermons from Fifth Avenue were published as *Things Eternal.* A reviewer at the time lamented his avoidance of controversial issues, and mused over the lack of reference to redemption.[5] The reviewer wrote, "It will leave the readers waiting for the next work before they can decide on Dr. Kelman's position and power as a preacher."[6] One of the better sermons in the collection is from 2 Kings 5:11, 15 and is titled "Opinion and Knowledge." The text contrasts "Behold I thought" with the consequent "behold now I know."[7]

Kelman's hesitancy in matters of theological commitment mirrors the effect of the general equivocation seen in the Free Church at the time. Theology filters down to the pulpit.

---

1. George Adam Smith studied under both Delitzsch and von Harnack but followed the latter in a more evolutionary approach to biblical origins. His *Historical Geography of the Holy Land* was widely used. His sermons in *Forgiveness of Sins* (1904) are poetic and strong. The sermons on the Gideon cycle from Judges are especially suggestive (London: Hodder and Stoughton, n.d.), 192ff. He also wrote *Life of Henry Drummond* and worked with John Buchan on a history of the Scottish kirk.
2. John Kelman, *The War and Preaching* (London: Hodder and Stoughton, 1919).

3. F. R. Webber, *A History of Preaching in Britain and America* (Milwaukee: Northwestern, 1955), 2:514.
4. John Kelman, *The Faith of Robert Lewis Stevenson* (Edinburgh: Oliphant Anderson, 1903), 88.
5. Anonymous, "Review of *Eternal Things*," *The Evangelical Christian* (February 1921): 34f.
6. Ibid.
7. John Kelman, *Eternal Things* (New York: George H. Doran, 1920), 157ff.

11.2.3 JAMES STALKER—THE SCHOLAR AND STATESMAN IN GOOD BALANCE

> It is no good sign of the times that controversy should be looked down upon.
>
> The preacher must be a master of human words . . . The message from God which we carry is to become a message to men, and therefore we must know how to introduce it successfully to their notice. Strong as our own conviction may be, yet it may be crude and formless; and before it can become the conviction of others, it must take a shape which will arouse their attention. It may belong to a region of thought with which they are unfamiliar, and it has to be brought near, until it enters the circle of their own ideas.
>
> —James Stalker

In the face of the howling gales of rationalistic and evolutionary thought, the divinity halls in Scotland were laid waste. Yet some preachers still stood, as did **James Orr** (1844–1913) of the United Presbyterian Church. Orr's position was conservative and effective in polemics (although he did not stand with Warfield on inerrancy).[1] With him stood **James Denney** (1856–1917) of the Cameronians or Reformed Presbyterians, who like Orr taught at the Free Church College in Glasgow. He was particularly effective in relation to the doctrine of the atonement.[2] Similar in position but more gifted as a preacher was the longtime professor at Aberdeen, **James Stalker** (1848–1928). He was born in Perthshire and studied at Edinburgh, Berlin, and Halle. Stalker pastored in Kirkaldy and then for fifteen glowing years at St. Matthew's in Glasgow. He was known as a more effective preacher than teacher, and was so steady in a time of theological vacillation. Stalker had proportion and balance in whatever he did.[3]

His beautiful study books (coedited with Alexander Whyte) on *The Life of Jesus Christ* and *The Life of St. Paul* were to be in many homes on both sides of the Atlantic. His delightful *Imago Christi: The Example of Jesus Christ* gives a sample of his style and directness. His volume titled *The Atonement* asserts emphatically that "The Bible does not speak of a limitation of the Atonement."[4] He faulted Macleod Campbell and Ritschl for being "insensible to the element in sin which we call guilt and therefore to the process by which this is put away."[5] His matchless devotional study, *The Trial and Death of Jesus Christ,* is compelling.[6] His

Beecher Lectures of 1891 are among the best of the last century. Titled *The Preacher and His Models,* even the outline is worthwhile:

I. Introductory
II. The Preacher as a Man of God
III. The Preacher as a Patriot
IV. The Preacher as Man of the World
V. The Preacher as a False Prophet
VI. The Preacher as a Man
VII. The Preacher as a Christian
VIII. The Preacher as an Apostle
IX. The Preacher as a Thinker[7]

In preaching on New Year's Day, Stalker took Psalm 73:24 and divided it as follows: (1) Thou shalt guide me; (2) Thou shalt guide me with thy counsel; and (3) Thou shalt guide me with thy counsel, and afterward . . . "[8] James Stalker knew what it was to dig into the Word of God, and his ministry of teaching and preaching was a blessing to many in a day of widespread drift and defection.

---

1. Glen D. Scorgie, *A Call for Continuity: The Theological Contribution of James Orr* (Ph.D. dissertation, St. Andrews, 1986). His outstanding work includes his article on the Virgin Birth for *The Fundamentals* as well as other articles; his editorship of *International Standard Bible Encyclopedia;* James Orr, *Revelation and Inspiration* (New York: Scribner's, 1916); James Orr, *God's Image in Man* (Grand Rapids: Eerdmans, 1948).
2. James Denney, *The Death of Christ* (London: Tyndale, 1951). This is choice. Also, *The Atonement and the Modern Mind* (London: Hodder and Stoughton, 1903) and *Studies in Theology* (New York: Armstrong, 1895). These are his lectures at the University of Chicago. Denney's wife thought his preaching needed more pathos. She introduced him to the writings of Spurgeon, and he became Christ-centered and evangelistic.
3. Ralph C. Turnbull, *Dargan's History of Preaching* (Grand Rapids: Baker, 1974), 3:479. One of Stalker's colleagues at Aberdeen, Sir William M. Ramsay (1851–1939), made a strong contribution toward the appreciation of the integrity of the Book of Acts over against the Tubingen emphasis. See W. Ward Gasque, *Sir William Ramsay: Archaeologist and New Testament Scholar* (Grand Rapids: Baker, 1966).
4. James Stalker, *The Atonement* (London: Hodder and Stoughton, 1908), 105.
5. Ibid., 122.
6. James Stalker, *The Trial and Death of Jesus Christ* (Grand Rapids: Zondervan, 1894). Well-divided sermons.
7. James Stalker, *The Preacher and His Models* (Grand Rapids: Baker, 1967). Here Stalker shares what McMillan of Ullapool gave him: "Begin low; proceed slow; rise higher; take fire."
8. James Stalker in *Sermons and Outlines for Special Occasions* (Grand Rapids: Baker, 1952), 9ff.

11.2.4 GEORGE MATHESON—THE BLIND PREACHER WHO HELPED PEOPLE SEE

> At the beginning of the week it [his sermon] was without form and void, but at the end he was always able to pronounce it very good!
>
> —of George Matheson and often said by him

Outbursts of genuinely moving preaching took place in the Church of Scotland itself,[1] and considered one of the two best preachers in Edinburgh along with Alexander Whyte was **George Matheson** (1842–1906). Born in a wealthy Glasgow merchant's home, he suffered from severely impaired vision which was congenital and progressive. His eldest sister helped him with his studies and throughout his life, though he did learn to use Braille.

At seven Matheson preached to his family.[2] In divinity hall he received honors and was drawn to Professor John Caird, who, like his brother Edward (who went on to teach at Oxford), became a stout defender of Hegelian absolute idealism.[3] This perspective tinged Matheson's thought throughout his life. Matheson preached his first homily on "Precious in the Lord's sight is the death of his saints," immediately marking him as a great preacher in embryo.[4] A born actor, Matheson was also a poet and wrote the well-known hymns "O Love That Will Not Let Me Go" and "Make Me a Captive, Lord."

His first pastoral charge was as assistant to J. R. MacDuff at Sandyford (cf. 10.5.8), where his first sermon had beauty of style but not much spirit. In 1867 he became pastor at the resort village of Innellan. Matheson had a clear, ringing voice, and for eighteen years he drew throngs to hear his striking twenty-minute sermons and original prayers. He would choose his text for the next Sunday morning on Sunday afternoon after preaching and then ponder it for a few days. Blessed with a remarkable memory, he would write it out completely and memorize it. He did this until one unforgettable day when he went blank in the pulpit and had to sit down. From then on he mastered his material more generally and preached extempore. His reading of Scripture was such that strangers had no idea he was blind. As one visitor wrote:

> There is a power of eloquence wielded by Dr. Matheson which places him on a level with any or all of them [referring to Guthrie, Caird, Macleod, and Tullock], while in originality of conception, and forcible, quaint expression, he excels them all.[5]

Matheson wrote some philosophical books and gave the Baird Lectures in 1881. He was noncommittal on evolution at this time but later came to disbelieve in it. He wrote fourteen books in all, the later of which were richly devotional messages. Tennyson was very fond of Matheson for his writings.[6]

In 1885 Matheson preached before the queen at Balmoral. Rather than her customary signed portrait, she presented the sightless Matheson with a small bust of herself as a remembrance of the occasion.

In 1886 he took the pastoral charge for St. Bernard's in Edinburgh, a congregation of some fifteen hundred members, where he served with great distinction for thirteen years. He never preached a sermon to his congregation for a second time. In addition to his pulpit work he was known for his Bible classes and addresses to teachers. For years he employed a secretary and helper with his own funds. In his prime he was an indefatigable visitor—blindness was never an excuse for him. He had a special relationship with Joseph Parker and often exchanged pulpits with Alexander Whyte from Free St. George's. Also of encouragement to Matheson was his old friend Dr. Hugh Macmillan of Greenock.[7]

Matheson's books of brief sermon summations are exceedingly rich and suggestive, though some show a tendency to overlook the essential context. His messages on "seek that you may excel" from 1 Corinthians 14:12, and "The Peaceableness After Purity" from James 3:17, "First pure, then peaceable," are powerful.[8] So too, his studies of men and women of the Bible are well worth perusing. His gripping turn of phrase and his trenchant exposition can be seen in his last book, *Rests by the River*. Favorites include "The Abuse of Noble Things" from Matthew 6:23, "If the light that is in you be darkness, how great is that darkness!"[9] Another is his remarkable "The Temporary Loss Involved in Eternal Gain," from John 4:28–29 on the woman's forgotten waterpots.

Always frank and outspoken, he was yet much loved by his parishioners. When he retired in 1899 at the age of fifty-seven, the sorrow of his people knew no bounds. He died on holiday in 1906. We are richer preachers ourselves because of the insights of the preacher who could never observe his congregation.

---

1. An outstanding example is James MacGregor, who served forty years at St. Cuthbert's in Edinburgh. Lady Frances Balfour has given us a splendid biography of this preacher who always "felt dull in the forenoon." See *Life and Letters of James MacGregor* (London: Hodder and Stoughton, 1912).
2. D. Macmillan, *The Life of George Matheson* (London: Hodder and Stoughton, 1907), 20.
3. Alan P. F. Sell, *Defending and Declaring the Faith* (Exeter: Paternoster, 1987), 64ff.
4. Macmillan, *The Life of George Matheson,* 50.
5. Ibid., 111.
6. Macmillan, *The Life of George Matheson,* 215.
7. A very choice study on John 15 is one of the legacies of Hugh Macmillan, *The True Vine* (London: Macmillan, 1879).
8. George Matheson, *Times of Retirement* (New York: Revell, 1901), 77, 143.
9. George Matheson, *Rests by the River* (Cincinnati: Jennings and Graham, 1906), 305, 356.

11.2.5 George MacDonald—The Preacher Who Wrote Fantasy and Novels

> But you can begin at once to be a disciple of the Living One—by obeying Him in the first thing you can think of in which you are not obeying Him. We must learn to obey Him in everything, and so must begin some-

> where. Let it be at once, and in the very next thing that lies at the door of our conscience! Oh fools and slow of heart, if you think of nothing but Christ, and do not set yourselves to do His words! You but build your houses on the sands.
>
> —George MacDonald

Known for his influence on C. S. Lewis and upon his circle, **George MacDonald** (1824–1905) was born in rural Aberdeenshire and studied science at Aberdeen. His mother died when he was very young. MacDonald reacted strongly against the high Calvinism of his father but retained a close and communicative relationship with him until the old man's death in 1858.[1] MacDonald became a Congregational minister and served the congregation at Arundel, in Sussex, where his denial of heathen condemnation was argued and he was ultimately starved out of the manse.[2] For a while he preached in Manchester. He started writing to supplement the income for his large family, and the widow of Lord Byron began to assist him financially. He moved to London and ultimately joined the Church of England and moved to Italy. Always sickly, he yet toured and lectured in America extensively in 1873. He was close to F. D. Maurice and John Ruskin and was acquainted with Dickens, Carlyle, and Trollope.

MacDonald's original works were not easy to read. Many had rambling sentences of 100 to 150 words in length and some in excess of 200 words. Many of his books have been rewritten and simplified and are widely read today, one of the most popular being *The Minister's Restoration,* the story of a minister's sin and the way back.[3] In all, he wrote twenty-nine realistic novels, all of which have the conventional happy ending. He also wrote books of fantasy which may have been a model for the *Chronicles of Narnia.* His imaginative fiction gave T. S. Eliot his wasteland motif.

MacDonald's preaching was Christocentric and clear. He argued that "correct opinions are no substitute for obedience,"[4] but he was unfortunately influenced by rationalistic German theology and by Blake, Swedenborg, and Boehme. MacDonald kept working to bring the focus clearly on the person of the Lord Jesus but veered off toward universalism. He taught that hell is not eternal, there is a second chance after death, and even Satan will ultimately repent. C. S. Lewis argues against this lurch to universalism in *The Great Divorce.*

George MacDonald's sermons breathe the fresh air of creativity and beauty, but his belief system eroded sadly.

---

1. Rolland Hein, ed., George MacDonald, *Life Essential: The Hope of the Gospel* (Wheaton, Ill.: Harold Shaw, 1974).
2. Richard H. Reis, *George MacDonald* (New York: Twayne, 1972).
3. George MacDonald, *The Minister's Restoration* (Minneapolis: Bethany House, 1988). The Scottish novel uses the Scottish dialect, which is a treat to read.
4. Rolland Hein, ed., George MacDonald, *Creation in Christ* (Wheaton, Ill.: Harold Shaw, 1876). Especially sermons 1, 2, and 3.

11.2.6 *John Watson (Ian Maclaren)—The Preacher Who Could Tell Great Stories*

> Of the parishioners in Logiealmond in the Highlands: I am in the ministry today because of the tenderness and charity of those country-folk, those perfect gentlemen and Christians.
>
> The critical and influential event in the religious week is the sermon . . . whenever preaching falls into low esteem, the Church becomes weak and corrupt . . . it is impossible to exaggerate the opportunity given to the preacher when he ascends the pulpit and faces his congregation.
>
> —John Watson (Ian Maclaren)

Inheriting from his mother a fiercely patriotic, Highland Jacobite, and Roman Catholic background, and from his stern father a Free Church upbringing, **John Watson** (1850–1907), or **Ian Maclaren,** as he called himself in many of his writings, carved a unique niche for his ministry.[1] He was born in England, where his father was a civil servant, but was reared in Perthshire. His minister there was the Reverend John Milne of the McCheyne school of evangelistic piety. Watson was fed on Spurgeon's sermons and learned of Henry Drummond while at Stirling High School.[2] In 1866 he began studies at Edinburgh, where he sat under the ministry of Horatius Bonar at the Grange Free Church and became a student for Free Church ministry. In his studies under A. B. Davidson and Principal Rainy, "the determined orthodoxy of the Free Church began to yield."[3]

Watson studied briefly at Tubingen under Beck and then spent three miserable months at Barclay Church in Edinburgh. The fit was just not right. This was followed by three idyllic years in Logiealmond in Perthshire, which he later memorialized in his charming books like *Beside the Bonnie Brier Bush.*[4] In 1877 he took pastoral responsibility in Free St. Matthew's in Glasgow. During this time he stood firmly in the premillennial advent camp.[5] Conservative in his instincts, he was an established churchman in theory and broad in his sympathies.

His preaching style began to embrace a wider message and appeal, and this he brought to his famous twenty-five years at Sefton Park Presbyterian Church in Liverpool. The church grew rapidly, and he soon visited America, where he gave the Beecher Lectures in 1896.[6]

Not a high Calvinist by any means, he was a sentimentalist in his characterization of rural Scottish idylls. Many loved to hear him, including Matthew Arnold, who worshiped at Sefton Park on the day that he died. Watson himself retired in 1906 and died in America on his way to deliver a lectureship at Vanderbilt University.[7]

We see in Watson the incipient dilution of the orthodox insistence on the deity of Christ and the doctrines of grace as based on the trustworthy documents of Scripture. He did not deny the doctrines but backed off from any strong assertion of biblical authority.[8] Watson believed that the Word was *contained* in the Bible and was not to be equated with it. Although he did not follow the logical consequences of his position, Watson opened the door to the trend that would gut Scottish evangelicalism and its preaching even to the present day.

1. Ian Maclaren is not to be confused with the also very able Ian Macpherson, who delivered the important lectures on preaching, *The Burden of the Lord* (Nashville: Abingdon, 1955). See Macpherson, *Kindling* (Old Tappan, N.J.: Revell, 1969).
2. W. Robertson Nicoll, *Ian Maclaren: The Life of John Watson* (London: Hodder and Stoughton, 1908), 26. Nicoll was a gifted preacher in his own right who spent his life in England as an editor and founder of *The British Weekly.* He was quite evangelical and edited both *The Expositor's Bible* and *Expositor's Greek Testament.*
3. Ibid., 49.
4. Ian Maclaren, *Beside the Bonnie Brier Bush* (Chicago: E. A. Weeks, 1894). Drumtochty is of course the Logiealmond of his own experience. The most well-known chapter is "His Mother's Sermon," in which the liberally touched young dominie is urged by his dying mother to "say a gude word for Jesus." Another book of the rural Scottish pastorate is the more recent *Highland Shepherds* by Arthur Hewitt (1939).
5. Watson's Glasgow stories are found in the delightful *St. Jude's* (London: Religious Tract Society, 1907).
6. John Watson, *The Cure of Souls* (New York: Dodd, Mead, 1896). Several chapters on preaching are convincing.
7. John Watson, *God's Message to the Human Soul* (New York: Revell, 1907). The Cole Lectures that he never delivered.
8. Ibid., 164.

11.2.7 George Morrison—Silver-Tongued Expositor of Wellington Church, Glasgow

> Young preachers will do well to guard against the tendency to rush, which is the bane of modern life. The habit of unprofitable bustle and rush, the present-day preoccupation with small affairs and engagements, is withholding many good things from us. For myself, it is essential that I have leisure to brood and meditate.
>
> I simply get my message, then I prepare my heart and mind to deliver it, sit down and write it, and on Sunday give it to my people.
>
> —George Herbert Morrison

Just as Alexander Whyte captured Edinburgh, **George Herbert Morrison** (1866–1928) took Glasgow. People lined up to get into his evening services.[1] He was born in Glasgow, the youngest of seven children in a line that traced back to the Island of Lewis. His father was a schoolman and Free Church elder, and his mother, who died when he was only five, named him George Herbert after the celebrated preacher/poet (cf. 6.2.3).

In 1883 George commenced study at Glasgow, where he was influenced by the Cairds and where C. Sylvester Horne (cf. 11.3.7) was a classmate and a confidant. Henry Drummond deeply influenced him at this time, and he worked for two years under Sir James Murray on the *Oxford English Dictionary.*[2] Both James Denney (who would later be his member at Wellington) and James Candlish (son of the great old warhorse of the faith) tilted him conservatively. Morrison strongly supported the doctrine of substitutionary atonement.

Morrison served as city missionary at Oakshaw Free Church and then as assistant to Whyte at St. George's. Here he helped develop the evening service. In 1894 he began a four-year pastorate in Thursoway in the North and first came to the attention of the General Assembly when he reported on the revival in that region. In 1898 he moved to St. John's in Dundee, where his weak voice was at great disadvantage in a sanctuary notorious for poor acoustics. His health was never robust, and he was forced to take a respite. When he returned to work, it seemed as if he was more compassionate and companionable than before. As always, he engaged in a strenuous pastoral ministry as well as a rigorous regimen for his preaching. Despite his health problems, he never took Monday off. His book of sermons titled *Flood-Tide* came out of these difficult years.[3]

The Morningside Church in Edinburgh coveted his services, and Rainy proposed him for Fifth Avenue in New York, but Morrison stayed put. He also turned down the new Stevenson Memorial Church in Glasgow, where W. M. Clow then took the call. In 1902 Morrision did accept an invitation to the Wellington Church in Glasgow, which sits like a Greek temple on the edge of the university. Here he served for twenty-six glorious years until his death at age sixty-two.

The Wellington Church was an original secession congregation but had become the largest United Free Church in the city. Morrison moved the afternoon service to the evening. The worship services were strongly Presbyterian. Morrison typically preached a traditional expository series in the morning, moving to a textual-topical style in the evening. He held a popular Bible class after the evening service, and in June gave Monday night lectures which claimed considerable attention for many years. Typical series on the life of Abraham and the Book of Nehemiah show his strengths.[4] Communion services at Wellington were memorable. His favorite hymn, "When I Survey That Wondrous Cross," was invariably sung at those services. His prayer meeting addresses were also well-remembered,[5] and Morrison was known for his children's sermons. He also had the distinction of preaching the first Scottish sermon over the radio.

Morrison had a modest and gentle spirit. He was an inveterate reader of sermons, selecting one to read each day. He had a personal library of more than six thousand volumes and possessed "great dexterity in quotation."[6] His facility with words was most attractive, but his sermons were pastoral and devotional—not the best models on how to handle a text. He had a tendency to do much with obscure texts, such as Job 5:23, "Thou shalt be in league with the stones of the field," or Revelation 12:16, "The Earth Helped the Woman," using the theme "How Science Helps Religion."[7]

In 1926 Morrison was elected moderator of the General Assembly and traveled the next year in Africa. Shortly after returning, he became critically ill and died suddenly. Gammie describes Morrison and how he appealed to the young who populated his evening services: "The man in the pulpit with the soft voice, the quiet, effortless style, and the subtle elusive charm."[8]

1. Many noted preachers were in Glasgow, including the stately W. M. Macgregor whose sermons *Scholar as Preacher* were well known, as later became the case with his Warrack Lectures on *The Making of a Preacher.*
2. Alexander Gammie, *Dr. George H. Morrison: The Man and His Work* (London: James Clarke, 1928), 34–35.
3. George H. Morrison, *Flood-Tide* (Grand Rapids: Baker, 1971). The George Morrison Library has six volumes.
4. George H. Morrison, *Morning Sermons* (Grand Rapids: Baker, 1971).
5. Gammie, *Dr. George H. Morrison,* 112.
6. Ibid., 48.
7. Examples of this abound as "The Message of the Colt," in *Wind on the Heath* (Grand Rapids: Kregel, 1994), 79ff. What should be emphasized is that Palm Sunday is about Jesus Christ not the colt.
8. Alexander Gammie, *Preachers I Have Heard* (London: Pickering and Inglis, n.d.), 180.

11.3 THE ENGLISH CHAMPIONS

Let us not give up the great principles of plenary inspiration.

—Bishop J. C. Ryle

With the death of Queen Victoria and the move into the Edwardian age, even the novelist Henry James was moved to remark, "The wild waters are upon us now."[1] **Thomas Hardy** (1840–1928), the famous novelist and poet, is an example of the currents flowing. A lifelong Anglican who early had aspiration for holy orders, he knew the Bible better than any other writer of his time. Even though he became an unbeliever and gave up the supernatural entirely, he continued communing.[2] Influenced by positivism and the indifferent God of Darwinianism, he kept going to church as a habit, interested only in a Christ without dogma. Even though he had praying Christian friends like the Baptist Henry Brastow (whom he caricatures in "A Laodicean") and Horace Moule from his Dorchester days (of the well-known Moule family from which Bishop H. C. G. Moule comes), Hardy's poems "The Funeral of God" and "God-Forsaken" say it all. Yet even in the face of massive and militant unbelief, there were preachers who stood mindful of the example of Spurgeon and the exhortation of Ryle.

---

1. After Strachey's *Eminent Victorians* (Garden City, N.Y.: Garden City Publishing Co., n.d.), cf. Piers Brendon's *Eminent Edwardians* (New York: Houghton Mifflin, 1980); also John Paterson, *Edwardians: London Life and Letters, 1901–1914* (New York: Ivan Dee, 1995).
2. Martin Seymour-Smith, *Hardy: A Biography* (New York: St. Martin's, 1994), 28, 30. Key to this distinguished writer.

11.3.1 William L. Watkinson—The Preacher with Architectonic Genius

> Preaching is a subject of which we are never weary; it has for us an abiding charm. For my own part, I love a book on homiletics as much as ever I did in my life. I read with eager expectation the last published lectures on the art of preaching, trusting to know how to do it before I die.
>
> I see no reason why our preaching should not display the same skill that is brought into the artistic world, the same power, the same delivery, the same perfection of finish. If an artist puts all the labor and pains that he does into a picture, should we put any less into our sermons?
>
> —William L. Watkinson

The spiritual heirs of the Wesleys were particularly hard hit by the tidal waves of skepticism and unbelief that pilloried the people of God at this time, but there were still resolute voices that spoke and knees that did not bow. Among these is **William L. Watkinson** (1838–1925). Watkinson was born in Hull in Yorkshire, where his father was a chapelkeeper at Kingston Methodist Church. We know little about him apart from a book of letters exchanged between him and a friend in their declining years. Watkinson started to preach at age eighteen. He was so tall and thin and frail in appearance that he was turned down for overseas service in India and narrowly approved for the itinerant Methodist ministry.[1] He spent only six weeks in training college and then was thrust into a needy vacancy. He served Methodist preaching points, most notably in Liverpool, and was then editor and president of the Wesleyan Methodist Conference. Watkinson made one extensive tour of the United States and was well received at Moody Bible Institute, where he preached from John 6.

Hugh Sinclair marks Watkinson as a preacher known for "the explicit, architectural manner of preaching, which is almost a lost art in these impressionistic days."[2] He read voraciously and crafted his massive discourses most carefully. He read Gibbon's *Decline and Fall of the Roman Empire* three times aloud to himself in order to ingest its striking lucidity and style. Watkinson loved to preach through a biblical book and distribute outline summaries. He used irony (and few have ever used it well) and occasionally allowed humor to get away from him. He was known for his illustrations and for the timeliness of his preaching.

One book of Watkinson's preaching gives a searching and scathing exploration of what sin is.[3] His oratory occasionally was a bit too florid and turgid but such was characteristic of the Edwardian Age. Especially poignant is his message on "The Plea of Evil," from the man with an unclean spirit who cried "Let us alone!" This is a thoughtful exposé of the masochistic nature of sin.[4]

Like George Morrison, he had a penchant for unusual texts and short texts. He tended to be moralistic and hortatory, which may have become the general rule in his movement rather than the exception.[5] John Bishop is accurate in his assessment:

> The chief criticism that can be made of these sermons is that there is too little of Christ in them, and too much of man, his character and conduct.

> There is a man-centeredness in his sermons as the very titles of his books suggest. They are uniformly exhortatory or didactic. Exhortation and instruction are honorable forms of preaching in the New Testament but they are definitely subordinate forms. They rise out of the Kerygma. In these sermons we are instructed about character and conduct, but rarely are we given a vision of God.[6]

What appeared as a hairline fracture in Watkinson would become a shattered bone in the movement of which he was a part.

---

1. John Bishop, "W. L. Watkinson: The Touch of Reality," *Preaching* (March–April 1990): 41.
2. F. R. Webber, *A History of Preaching in Britain and America* (Milwaukee: Northwestern, 1952), 1:621.
3. W. L. Watkinson, *The Transfigured Sackcloth* (New York: Dutton, 1906).
4. Ibid., 87ff. Watkinson wrote many volumes of published sermons.
5. W. L. Watkinson, *Frugality in the Spiritual Life* (New York: Revell, 1908). The title sermon comes from the text in John 6:12, which tells of gathering up the leftovers. This misses the aorta of the passage, which is Jesus and the great hunger.
6. Bishop, "W. L. Watkinson," 44. Another example of this type of evasion of authorial intent in a text is the famous Lenten series brought by Rev. William Havergal (father of Frances Ridley Havergal) on the Queen of Sheba.

11.3.2 Dinsdale T. Young—One of the Last of the Shouting Methodists

> Preaching as an ordinance is part of God's good pleasure. There has been no revocation of this supreme ordinance. It is the sacrament. Of all the acts of worship it is the most helpful. The churches grieve God's Spirit when they depreciate preaching.
>
> Preaching which has taken the deity out of Christ, the Atonement out of the Cross, faith out of the method of salvation, and the indwelling of the Divine Spirit out of Christian experience, is "cut down like the grass and withereth."
>
> No preacher is permanently popular if he does not make people uncomfortable. We must wound with the sword of the Spirit. We must show them all the mercy by showing them all the sin.
>
> —Dinsdale T. Young

One of London's most popular preachers in his day, but a man of direct and simple speech, **Dinsdale T. Young** (1861–1938) was born in Northumbria (as was Joseph Parker). Young's father was a prominent physician. Dinsdale was converted and called to the ministry, beginning to preach at fifteen. He was ordained in 1879, the youngest person until then ever ordained to the Methodist ministry.

Young trained at Headingley College in Leeds and served with growing reputation in places like Nicholson Square Wesleyan Methodist Church in Edinburgh. In 1906 to 1914 he served Wesley Chapel, City Road, in London, and then was assigned to Westminster Central Hall, where he preached to full houses for twenty-four years until just weeks short of his death in 1938. Young spoke to the largest congregations in London during those years, and though he was not nearly as gifted a preacher as Jowett, it was said that "Jowett gets Dinsdale Young's overflow."[1] Liberals in and out of his denomination did not think he would last because he was such a fundamentalist, but he continued to preach seven or eight times weekly and travel ten thousand miles a year. He graciously never attacked his opponents but neither did he deviate from the old gospel.

Dressed always in frock coat and silk hat, Young was increasingly picturesque as he grew old, his "white locks streaming out behind him as if he were Liszt, while two triangles of white hair flanked the high pink dome of his forehead."[2] He was a preacher of the old school and yet attracted many young people. He had a great speaking voice and was a skillful communicator. Young loved to dig into commentaries—one of his favorites was Thomas Goodwin—and he reread Bonar's diary every year. A great lover of Trollope, Young was an "inveterate homiletician."

He usually struck three mains and extolled expository and evangelistic preaching. Occasionally his predilection for unusual texts got him off track, as did his sermon on "Religious Solidity" from Song of Solomon 1:17, "The beams of our house are cedar."[3] Young did preach the gospel of sin and grace unflinchingly. One observer said that he was so orthodox that he had become a heretic.[4] Young's classic message on "The Protevangelium" from Genesis 3:15 breaks down into two sections:

I. The Savior's Injury of Satan
II. Satan's Injury to the Savior

The emphasis is strongly on redemption.[5] The reader may chafe at his use of such short snippets of texts, yet one cannot but marvel at the insights of a sermon like "The Consistency of Character and Conduct" from John 10:13, "The hireling flees because he is a hireling."[6]

Young addressed the largest audiences in Britain right up until World War II. He apparently indulged a little foray into British Israelism, but remained loyal to the everlasting gospel. In his last moments of consciousness, he sang over and over, "Just as I am without one plea." His last words were, "I triumph."[7]

---

1. John Bishop, "A Champion of Orthodoxy: Dinsdale T. Young," *Preaching* (November–December 1987): 46.
2. Alexander Gammie, *Preachers I Have Heard* (London: Pickering and Inglis, 1945), 145.
3. Dinsdale T. Young, *Sermons on Unfamiliar Texts* (Grand Rapids: Baker, 1899, 1970), 117ff.

4. F. R. Webber, *A History of Preaching in Britain and America* (Milwaukee: Northwestern, 1952), 1:679.
5. Dinsdale T. Young, *The Enthusiasm of God* (Cincinnati: Jennings and Graham, n.d.), 79ff.
6. Dinsdale T. Young, *The Crimson Book and Other Evangelical Sermons* (Grand Rapids: Baker, 1903, 1974), 206ff.
7. Bishop, "A Champion of Orthodoxy," 47.

11.3.3 G. Campbell Morgan—The Expositor of Expositors

> For two years my Bible was shut; two years of sadness and sorrow. Strange, alluring materialistic theories were in the air, and to these I turned . . . I became well-versed in the philosophies that were the vogue in England at that time, but from them I got no relief. In my despair I took all the books that I had, placed them in a cupboard, turned the key, and there they remained for seven years. I bought a new Bible, and began to read it with an open mind and a determined will. That Bible found me. The Book gave forth a glow which warmed my heart, and the Word of God which I read therein gave to my troubled soul the relief and satisfaction that I had sought for elsewhere. Since that time I have lived for one end—to preach the teachings of the Book that found me.
>
> It is my conviction that the Scriptures, as originally committed to writing, were safeguarded in every word by the Holy Spirit. . . . There is nothing I desire more in my dealing with the Bible than to lead people to a personal appreciation and understanding of it . . . We are out to storm the citadel of the will and seize it for Jesus Christ.
>
> —G. Campbell Morgan

Called the Prince of Expositors, the greatest expository preacher of his time, **George Campbell Morgan** (1863–1945) held great masses of people spellbound by his preaching for sixty years. Born in Tetbury, England, he was known on both sides of the Atlantic as "a specialist in the interpretation of God's Blessed Book." His parents reared him in Cardiff, Wales, where he was part of the Roath Road Wesleyan Methodist Church. His father was an independent Baptist of strong views who came under the influence of George Müller and the Plymouth Brethren. Young George preached sermons in his home as a boy of seven, and was deeply troubled with the death of his beloved sister, Lizzie. At thirteen he preached his first public sermon in Monmouth on salvation. The sermon had four main points:

I. A great salvation (Hebrews 2:3)
II. A common salvation (Jude 3)
III. An eternal salvation (Hebrews 5:9)
IV. A present salvation (2 Corinthians 6:2)[1]

At nineteen he had a deep crisis with respect to the authority of the Word. This was resolved in favor of faith and an unflinching confidence in the Scripture.[2] He taught for three years at a Jewish college for boys in Birmingham, an exposure that greatly enriched his understanding of the Old Testament. Yet Morgan had no formal education.

Morgan's Career

In 1888, to his great anguish, his trial sermon before the Methodist establishment in Birmingham did not meet muster.[3] He preached the sermon in a hall seating more than one thousand, but only seventy-five listeners were present. Morgan would harbor lifelong negative feelings toward small crowds. Despite this rebuff, Morgan remained close to Methodists like Dinsdale Young, William Watkinson, Samuel Chadwick, and even J. Gregory Mantle, who had been one of the examiners.

Morgan nearly joined the Salvation Army, but after a thirteen-month mission in Hull (where his lifelong friendship with Gypsy Smith began), he was ordained by the Congregationalists and entered into a distinguished and well-heard ministry.

From 1889 to 1891, Morgan pastored in Stone. His first text was Matthew 28:20, which was also used for his last sermon at Westminster. From 1891 to 1893, he served Heron Court Congregational Church in Rugeley, where his expository method began to jell. In the years 1893 to 1897, Morgan served at Westminster Road Church in Birmingham, where he enjoyed much fellowship with R. W. Dale. In 1897, Morgan took the call to New Court Church, Tollington Park North, where he served until 1899. Here also is where Manton, Baxter, and Goodwin had preached.

The great numbers of converts in the Moody-Sankey meetings both in Britain and in America needed to be built up in the Word. This was the wave which Morgan rode to such eminence. When Moody died in 1899, Morgan was invited to come to Northfield and spearhead the extension and conference ministry. In a series of farewell meetings before he left for America, Morgan was surrounded by his close friends J. D. Jones, F. B. Meyer, and Joseph Parker, who took occasion to observe:

> You may depend upon one thing, the only ministry that will last, and be as fresh at the end as it was at the beginning, is a biblical and an expository one. Mere anecdotes fail and in the long run exhaust themselves, the Word of the Lord abideth forever.[4]

Morgan traveled extensively in North America from 1901 to 1904. "The nomad in his blood" drove him to exhaustion. From 1904–1917, Morgan served at Westminster Chapel, London, "the white elephant of Congregationalism." Westminster had never filled its twenty-five hundred seats since the new building was dedicated in 1865 but was filled from Morgan's first Sunday twice every Lord's Day.

The Welsh Revival of 1904–05, in which Morgan was involved, was part of the cascading impact of his ministry. He went on to serve conjointly as president of Chestnut College, Cambridge, which unfortunately sped the collapse of his health. In 1917, Morgan was forced to resign this post due to one of his episodic health breakdowns. He then served Highbury Quadrant Church, which lost eighty of its sons in World War I. (Interestingly, Nonconformist bore disproportionate losses in both world wars.)

In 1919, Morgan returned to America for frenetic itineration. He served terms at the Bible Institute of Los Angeles (BIOLA), Gordon in Boston, and brief pastorates in Cincinnati and at Tabernacle Presbyterian in Philadelphia. He enjoyed tremendous response to his studies. Then in 1933, it was back to Westminster at age sixty-nine (though not all in the church favored it). He ministered there for a decade, endured the horrors of the blitz, and retired.

In all, Campbell Morgan made fifty-four crossings of the Atlantic and wrote seventy-two books by 1930. His first book, *Discipleship,* came in 1897; his strong book *The Ten Commandments* was issued in 1901. In 1915 came *The Living Messages of the Books of the Bible,* which shows his genius for synthesis as his commentaries demonstrate his brilliance in analysis.[5] His work on Jeremiah is one of the best, as are his commentaries on Matthew and Acts.[6]

Morgan's Communication

"He made the Bible come alive!" was the verdict on his preaching. Standing tall and slender, frail and almost gaunt in the pulpit, his voice (which may be heard on recordings) was amazingly strong and deeply resonant. John Hutton, who had a vastly influential ministry at Westminster in the 1920s, observed, "Morgan always spoke with authority."[7] Morgan felt that the grave danger for the preacher was to use scriptural fragments out of context. His method applied the contextual principle in Bible study.[8] He was dispensational from early on, seeing that Israel is different from the church.[9]

Morgan loved new translations, particularly modern-language versions like Weymouth's. "This man believes the Bible!" his listeners agreed. He built his great Friday evening Bible classes with more than fifteen hundred in attendance. The charts and analysis we have in *The Analyzed Bible* first saw the light of day in that setting.

Morgan rarely used illustrations and almost stands alone in his general disdain for application, believing that application is the work of the Holy Spirit. Painting word pictures was his special strength (as in *The Great Physician* and *The Parables and Metaphors of Our Lord*). In his Sprunt Lectures at Union Seminary in Richmond, published as *The Ministry of the Word,* he showed the close relationship between the preacher and the pastor in ministry. In "Biblical Homiletics" he put his oar into the water on the behalf of his method and called for the essentials: truth, clarity, and passion.[10]

The "one thing" for Morgan was preaching and its careful preparation. His public reading of the Scripture was momentous, and his choice of hymns was careful, though he was fond of the newer genre of music, gospel songs.[11] His monumental *Westminster Pulpit* is still well worthwhile for the expositor. He used various patterns in dividing the sermon, but his progression was always natural and logical. The text remained supreme and structure was never bony. Even to the end, when his sermons were under thirty minutes, his published works on Job, the Corinthian correspondence, and his studies in the Psalms are scintillating. "Let the text make its statement," was his plea. One of the aristocrats of the pulpit, Morgan was eloquent yet substantial. Horton Davies said of him, "He proves conclusively the varied spiritual wealth that is at the disposal of the preacher who mines the deep lodes of the Bible."[12] Even a secular journalist found himself taken with the man and his message during a memorable ministry in Baltimore.[13] Who has ever led us into Hosea as has Morgan in his *Hosea—The Heart and Holiness of God*? Most would agree that they are seldom left unmoved by this venerable practitioner of the craft.

Morgan's Commitment

Wilbur Smith described Morgan's preaching as "a mystic spell" and "the intangible atmosphere of union between teacher and taught." In probing for the secret of Morgan's extraordinarily fruitful ministry in the Word, we find both Smith and Warren Wiersbe attributing his success to hard work.[14] He truly gave himself to unremitting toil and concentration on the task of exegesis and sermonics. Those who have written about him speak of his "capacity for friendship." Although somewhat unapproachable in manner, Morgan built and sustained rich, warm friendships that ennobled his insights and inspiration. His dear friend and longtime associate Albert Swift, his soul brother Len Broughton from Atlanta, and his colleague Dr. John MacInnis, for whom he left BIOLA out of loyalty, are but samples of the breadth and depth of his relationships. His association with D. Martyn Lloyd-Jones, whom he brought from Wales to share his pulpit beginning in 1938, testifies to this particularly in view of the sharp differences between the two on Calvinism-Arminian issues. Lloyd-Jones's remarks at Morgan's memorial service demonstrate a genuine friendship.[15]

Always an impeccable dresser, Morgan was sometimes accused of being a free spender and of traveling too luxuriously. Yet he was generous and kind, self-effacing and genuinely humble. A significant testimony to Morgan is the fact that all four of his sons became preachers, three Presbyterian and one Anglican. Some have wanted him to be more doctrinal but he was never one to subordinate the text to a doctrine. His priority was ever to release the Word of God. As such a champion, he must be accorded a large place in this history.

When he preached at Moody Bible Institute, he gave the people Malachi, and when he was at Northfield one season, he gave them what we have in his work on the Minor Prophets. Oh for such a steady and solid diet today! How many would love to be so nourished.

---

1. John Harries, *G. Campbell Morgan: The Man and His Ministry* (New York: Revell, 1930), 27.
2. Jill Morgan, *A Man of the Word: Life of G. Campbell Morgan* (New York: Revell,

1951), 39. An outstanding work by his daughter-in-law. Also of great interest is Morgan's *This Was His Faith: The Expository Letters of G. Campbell Morgan* (London: Pickering and Inglis, n.d.). One of his grandsons has also written an intriguing article in which he studies three sermons delivered in Westminster Chapel in times of great crisis as examples of "holistic preaching." See Richard Lyon Morgan, "Preaching as Pastoral Moment: A New Slant on G. Campbell Morgan," *Preaching* (September–October 1987): 29ff.

3. Ibid., 58ff.
4. Harries, *G. Campbell Morgan,* 65.
5. Wilbur M. Smith, "The Life and Writings of Dr. G. Campbell Morgan," in *A Treasury of Books for Bible Study* (Grand Rapids: Baker, 1960), 133.
6. G. Campbell Morgan, *Studies in the Prophecy of Jeremiah* (Westwood, N.J.: Fleming H. Revell, 1955).
7. Jill Morgan, *A Man of the Word,* 245. Wiersbe says he tries to read this book every year.
8. Don C. Wagner, *The Expository Method of G. Campbell Morgan* (Westwood, N.J.: Revell, 1957), 69.
9. G. Campbell Morgan, *God's Methods with Man* (New York: Revell, 1898), along with a colored chart of God's plan for the ages; also *The Spirit of God* (Westwood, N.J.: Revell, 1953), 81ff.
10. G. Campbell Morgan, *Preaching* (New York: Revell, 1937), 37ff.
11. Jill Morgan, *A Man of the Word,* 251.
12. John Bishop, "George Campbell Morgan: A Man of the Word," *Preaching* (March–April 1991): 59–60.
13. William G. Shepherd, *Great Preachers as Seen by a Journalist* (New York: Revell, 1924), 173ff.
14. Smith, "Life and Writings," 131; Warren W. Wiersbe, *Living with the Giants* (Grand Rapids: Baker, 1993), 185.
15. *The Westminster Record* 19.7 (July 1945) gives the transcript of the memorial service, including the praise of Lloyd-Jones for "the wonderful campaigns of Moody and Sankey in this country" and a moving description of his close association with Morgan and "never the slightest suspicion of difference between us." Lloyd-Jones says of Morgan that "preaching was the supreme passion of his life" and that the only poor sermon he had ever heard Morgan deliver was a topical sermon (60ff.).

11.3.4 F. B. Meyer—A Baptist for All the Believers

> What we need is the old, old story preached by new, new men! Ethics by all means; but the fair temple must have its foundations set deep in the death which destroyed Him that had the power of death, and delivered them who throughout their lives had been subject to bondage.
>
> It is impossible to preach to men unless you know men.
>
> My earnest advice to all young ministers is—to mix freely with the people; to visit systematically and widely; to study men as well as books;

> to converse with all classes and conditions of men: always on the alert to learn from some fresh pages of the heart opened to the view of the sympathetic soul.
>
> —F. B. Meyer in *The Bells of Is*

The founder of Bible Study Fellowship with branches all over the world, **A. Wetherell Johnson** (1907–1984) was reared in Leicester in England and recalls Andrew Murray, Evan Roberts of the Welsh Revival, and Mrs. Jessie Penn-Lewis, but especially **Frederick Brotherton Meyer** (1847–1929), their pastor. Johnson recalls:

> A rather fragile looking man, with a very fresh complexion, clear blue eyes, a face wrinkled like a russet apple. His expression was that of a gentle radiancy. You felt that you had come into contact with a man who lived with God and who was a friend of God. His voice was quiet, yet it reached into every part of the large hall or chapel. While he spoke, there came a sense of stillness, and we seemed to hear the strong, virile voice of God which reached to the deepest part of one's being.[1]

F. B. Meyer was called the Christian cosmopolitan, the archbishop of nonconformity, the ubiquitous Dr. Meyer, and the evangelical opportunist. He was born in London—his successful great-grandfather came from Germany and worshiped at Charlotte Baptist Chapel in Edinburgh while living in that city; his mother came from staunch Quaker stock. The family attended Bloomsbury Chapel, where Dr. Brock had a strong influence on the young lad, who very early had an awareness of "the constant interchange between Him [the Lord] and me."[2] While he was yet very young, he preached to his family and the servants. He attended Brighton College and preached his first public sermon (from Psalm 84:11) at sixteen. Sensing a deep call to ministry, Meyer worked two years for a tea merchant—a positive experience for certain of his future Christian enterprises. Meyer then went on to Regent's Park College and took his B.A. from London University in 1869.

The Wellsprings of F. B. Meyer

While he was at school, in addition to enjoying a high profile in the debating society, Meyer served the nucleus that would become the Duke Street Baptist Chapel in Richmond. Turning down a call to Portland Chapel in Southampton, where Alexander Maclaren had served, he went in 1870 to be associate of Dr. C. M. Birrell of Pembroke Chapel, Liverpool. Birrell was a dedicated exegetical preacher who taught the fledgling preacher much, but Meyer had to unlearn delivery by memoriter. After two years he took the call to the Priory Street Baptist Chapel in York, where he came into contact with **James Parsons** (1799–1877) at Salem Congregational Church. Parsons was known throughout England as the barrister preacher, whose eccentric style and constantly twitching face and blinking eyes could not foreclose two passionate hours of extraordinary discourse.[3] In York, Meyer was the first English preacher to welcome D. L. Moody and Ira Sankey. It was in this stirring in 1873 that Frances Ridley Havergal, the well-known hymn writer, came to a deepening of her spiritual life. In 1874 Meyer moved on to the Victoria Road Church in Leicester, where the leadership was not in harmony with his evangelistic thrust. One well-to-do deacon protested by saying, "We cannot have this sort of thing here. This is not a Gospel shop!"[4]

Meyer went on to establish a new church in Leicester, Melbourne Hall, which would seat twelve hundred persons. Here he enjoyed a great prison ministry and preached his first character studies on Jacob and Joseph. In 1887 he accepted the call to the wealthy Regent's Park Chapel in London, then in 1892 followed the well-known Newman Hall at Christ Church, Westminster Road in Lambeth, south of the river, known as the Cathedral of Nonconformity. **Newman Hall** (1816–1902) had taken Surrey Chapel, once served by Rowland Hill, and made it into Christ Church, with a morning service like low Church of England and an evening service that was typical nonconformity.[5]

In 1909 Meyer went back to Regent's Park; in 1915 he returned to Christ Church, where John McNeill and Len Broughton had served in the meantime. Meyer became minister emeritus in 1921 and died in 1929 at the age of eighty-two. He lived at such a fast pace that some called him "St. Francis with Bradshaw's Railway Guide."[6]

The Well-Crafted Sermons of F. B. Meyer

Meyer did not have the great intellectual depth of Campbell Morgan nor the brilliant eloquence of Jowett, but his was a tireless expenditure of energy and a love affair with Scripture. Birrell had advised him that topical sermons were limited by the number of topics possible and therefore, "Become an expositor of Scripture. You will always retain your freshness and will build up a strong and healthy church."[7] He defined expository preaching as "the consecutive treatment of some book or extended portion of Scripture."[8] Meyer warned against recapitulation ("last Sunday I was saying") or any kind of forecasting. Let each sermon stand independently on its own even if it is in a series.[9]

He had a clear voice that conveyed tender compassion. Nor were there any "hammer-marks" on his sermons. While there could occasionally be a little Prussian autocracy in his manner, the Quaker softness and sweetness prevailed. He decried lack of fervor yet was known for the brevity of his public prayers. His illustrations were graphic and luminous. Hugh Sinclair's assessment reflects this:

> His preaching is expressive of his personality, suggesting spiritual fastidiousness and a sweet, sun-washed serenity of soul. So simple and intimate is his utterance that many hearers will scarcely divine the art that conceals art, but the practiced will soon realize with what consummate ease and subtle mastery of effect he handles speech and thought, and how enchantingly he plays upon an instrument whose limitations are known and accepted by him.[10]

Meyer preached some sixteen thousand sermons. Called by his intimates the Skipper, he experienced new impact on his ministry subsequent to a filling of the Holy Spirit under the tutelage of Hudson Taylor at Keswick during the time he was in Leicester.[11] One of his hearers exclaimed, "It's good just to see him!" Spurgeon said, "Meyer preaches as a man who has seen God face-to-face." His good friend Joseph Parker remarked that Meyer always brought a benediction along with him, and he called him his father confessor.

One firm sold 2,545,000 copies of his books. He was very popular in Sweden, and twenty volumes were translated into Swedish. His marvelous Bible biographies are representative of his preaching at its best. Abraham and Jeremiah are favorites.[12] His two volumes on Exodus and his two volumes on John are superb. He also produced rich studies in Hebrews and Zechariah. His sermon "Reckon on God's Faithfulness," from Mark 11:22–24, picked up the theme of his ministry. Beginning with three biblical illustrations, he proceeded to show how we need to reckon on God for forgiveness of sin, for answers to prayer, and for guidance.[13] Although he always spoke of himself as a two-talent person, he was also a man who aspired to please God and proclaim Christ.

The Works and Service of F. B. Meyer

Meyer was visible at Keswick for many years and active in its cause. He was president of the Free Church Council in 1904 and involved in the serious protest movement on educational issues thereafter. His Quaker gentility further involved him in objecting to a prize fight in London in much the same way as Telemachus challenged gladiatorial combat in the early church. He was great for holding lantern slide meetings for the poor and building a Brotherhood movement to involve men. For a brief time he was principal of All Nations Bible College and was closely tied to Regions Beyond Missionary Union led by the Guiness family. He established a children's home, as did Spurgeon, and took leadership in the Advent Testimony Movement which was especially vocal at the time of the Balfour Declaration in 1917 and which trumpeted the imminent return of Christ for his church. He even got Mrs. Emmeline Pankhurst, a militant suffragette, worked up about the Second Coming. He established the Window Cleaning Brigade for his converted convicts and put his business prowess to good use.

Christ Church had its "teetotaler corner" and its "consecration corner," and here the exposition of Scripture was at the core of all this outreach and ministry. Here he preached on "God Is Near" and "A Vision of the New Life" from Acts 26:19; "The Power of Appropriation" and "Reigning in Life" from Romans 5:17; and "Living the Life of Christ" from John 6:57.[14] Though president of the Baptist Union, Meyer's heart was in the dark alleys of Lambeth described so vividly by Somerset Maugham in '*Liza of Lambeth*. His ministry was to the conversion of the notorious Hooligan family and the like.[15] What a servant! What a preacher!

---

1. A. Wetherell Johnson, *Created for Commitment* (Wheaton, Ill.: Tyndale House, 1982), 28.

2. W. Y. Fullerton, *F. B. Meyer* (London: Marshall Morgan and Scott, 1929), 9. Fullerton also wrote a biography of Spurgeon as his longtime assistant and later followed Meyer at Melbourne Hall. Called the happy warrior of the London pulpit, his own *Sunset Sermons* (Philadelphia: Judson, 1929) are done well in the Keswick style.
3. F. R. Webber, *A History of Preaching in Britain and America* (Milwaukee: Northwestern, 1952), 1:482.
4. A. Chester Mann, *F. B. Meyer: Preacher, Teacher, Man of God* (New York: Revell, 1929), 45.
5. Newman Hall drew the plans for the striking "pile" called Christ Church, which seated twenty-three hundred people. We have a sample of his fine preaching in *The Lord's Prayer: A Practical Meditation* (Edinburgh: T & T Clark, 1883).
6. Fullerton, *F. B. Meyer,* 70. Two exquisite little books by Meyer describe his early and later city ministries, *The Bells of Is* (New York: Revell, 1894) and *Reveries and Realities: Life and Work in London* (London: Morgan and Scott, n.d.). He was heard both by the poor in London and at Northfield with rapt attention.
7. Mann, *F. B. Meyer,* 74. Some his finest expositions are in *The Directory of the Devout Life, Matthew 5–6–7.*
8. F. B. Meyer, *Expository Preaching: Plans and Methods* (London: Hodder and Stoughton, 1912), 29.
9. Ibid., 32–33. His expositions on 1 Peter, *Tried by Fire,* are particularly outstanding.
10. Mann, *F. B. Meyer,* 71.
11. The first series of sermons Meyer preached at Carnegie Hall, New York, and in Tremont Temple, Boston, are published as *The Christ-Life for the Self-Life* (Chicago: Moody, 1897). A copy of this book of sermons given to my mother by her Sunday school teacher came into my hands in my early teens and led to a deep crisis of consecration.
12. F. B. Meyer, *Jeremiah: Priest and Prophet* (New York: Revell, 1894). These are eleven Bible biographies that I regard as superior to those of either Alexander Whyte or George Matheson—much stronger exegetically and in their bridging from then to now. Meyer's study on Psalm 23, *The Shepherd Psalm,* is one of the best.
13. F. B. Meyer, *Five Musts of the Christian Life* (New York: Revell, 1927), 91ff.
14. F. B. Meyer, *Meet for the Master's Use* (New York:. Revell, n.d.).
15. Mann, *F. B. Meyer,* 60. Meyer's *Our Daily Homily* and his daily notes on each biblical chapter are superb.

11.3.5 John Henry Jowett—The Wordsmith Who Preached Grace so Gloriously

> If the pulpit is to be occupied by men with a message worth hearing, we must have time to prepare it.
>
> I have a conviction that no sermon is ready for preaching, not ready for writing out, until we can express its theme in a short, pregnant sentence as clear as crystal. I find the getting of that sentence is the hardest, the most exacting, and the most fruitful labour in my study. To compel oneself to fashion that sentence, to dismiss every word that vague, ragged, ambiguous, to think

> oneself through to a form of words which defines the theme with scrupulous exactness—this is surely one of the most essential factors in the making of a sermon: and I do not think any sermon ought to be preached or even written, until that sentence has emerged, clear and lucid as a cloudless moon. Do not confuse obscurity with profundity, and do not imagine that lucidity is necessarily shallow. Let the preacher bind himself to the pursuit of clear conceptions, and let him aid his pursuit by demanding that every sermon he preaches shall express its theme and purpose in a sentence as lucid as his powers can command.
>
> —J. H. Jowett

Called by many on both sides of the Atlantic the greatest living practitioner of the homiletic art, **John Henry Jowett** (1863–1923) was a slight, frail, bald man, and so mightily used of God. He was born in Halifax, in the north of England in the moorland country of the Bronte novels. His father was a tailor and a draper. How shall we understand his usefulness?

What Shaped Jowett?

"I was blessed with the priceless privilege of a Christian home," Jowett testified.[1] His parents were not leaders in the Square Congregational Church of Halifax, but Jowett learned to pray at his mother's knee and "she taught me to see." He also said, "When I think of a Christian man, I think of my Father."[2] Through his lifetime he started work in his study at 6 A.M. because he had seen in his youth how all the tradesmen started early. His pastor, Dr. Enoch Mellor, made a deep impression with his pulpit oratory, but they never really met. His Sunday school teacher, Mr. Dewhirst, a humble carpenter, challenged young Jowett when he was inclined to the law with the words God used to redirect his life, "I had always hoped you would go into the ministry."[3] The vivid learning experience in his Sunday school class was never effaced. Jowett preached his first sermon from 1 Samuel 3:19 during an evangelistic outreach sponsored by his Sunday school class.

He matriculated at Airedale College in Bradford, where **Dr. Andrew Fairbairn** (1838–1912) had a profound effect on his thinking.[4] When Fairbairn heard Jowett preach in class, he remarked, "Behind that sermon is a man." Jowett then moved on to Edinburgh where he often heard Alexander Whyte and George Matheson preach and where the prince, Henry Drummond, drew him ever deeper into discipleship and "many a time sent me home to my knees."[5] In his student pastorates, "He learned the necessity of interesting his congregation." In 1888 and 1889 he spent two terms at Mansfield College, Oxford, with his beloved Fairbairn, where he also met one of his dearest friends, C. Sylvester Horne, who went on to serve a significant tenure in Kensington.

What Set Jowett Apart?

Right out of school, Jowett unusually was accorded a call to the important St. James Congregational Church in Newcastle-on-Tyne. St. James was packed from the beginning of his ministry, and he spent six satisfying years here. In 1889 he was ordained here with **Charles Berry,** who was later called to succeed Beecher in Brooklyn.[6]

Immediately Jowett's "originality of thought and rhetorical power" were in evidence in his preaching. He was painstaking and methodical in his Bible study, pasting a page of text on one side of a large book and entering exegetical notes and observations on the other side.[7] He and his wife had a great ministry to children, and he strongly espoused the temperance cause. He believed in conversion and preached for a verdict.[8] He had what he called "the wooing note" as he preached grace, the center of his message.

In 1895 he was tapped to succeed R. W. Dale at Carr's Lane, Birmingham, which A. T. Pierson called "the finest church in the world." From the outset Jowett determined to be himself. The difference was well put: "Dale's congregation could pass an examination in the doctrines and Jowett's in the Scriptures."[9] Nicoll reported:

> In Dr. Jowett everything preaches. The voice preaches, and it is a voice of great range and compass, always sweet and clear through every variety of intonation. The eyes preach, for though Dr. Jowett writes every word of his sermons, he is extraordinarily independent of his manuscript. The body preaches, for Dr. Jowett has many gestures, and not one ungraceful. But above all, the heart preaches. I have heard many great sermons, but never one at any time which so completely seized and held from start to finish a great audience . . . Above all preachers I have heard, Dr. Jowett has the power of appeal . . . at times the tension of listening, the silence, and the eagerness of the crowd were almost oppressive . . . it was all very wonderful and very uplifting.[10]

Besides his two Sunday services, Jowett had a great Thursday night service and a class for the Sunday school teachers. Although he was only thirty-one when he came to Carr's Lane, he was soon in widespread demand. In 1906 he was chair of the Congregational Union, having earlier preached his famous sermon, "Apostolic Optimism" from Romans 12:12 on "rejoicing in hope" to them. In 1911 he was president of the Free Church Council after visiting America and ministering at Northfield.

Also in 1911, he faced three overtures from Fifth Avenue Presbyterian Church in New York City and finally accepted, although he never felt at home in New York. When he came to New York, he insisted on taking no more than his salary at Carr's Lane. His preaching was well received—"Yet I wish I were in England."[11] He turned down the call to Free St. George's and enjoyed his happiest season in 1913 and 1914, when he gave one of the finest series in the history of the Beecher Lectures at Yale.[12]

Finding it hard to contend with endless distraction and so many invitations, Jowett was open when City Temple, London, approached him. He did not accept the call because of his conservative stand in the furor over R. J. Campbell's views, but then took the call to Westminster Chapel in London, succeeding Campbell

Morgan. It was not easy for an Englishman to be absent from his native country during the crisis of the first world war. Even Prime Minister Lloyd George urged him to come home. His ministry in London was brief but much appreciated. Jowett suffered a total collapse of health; what seemed to be a mysterious illness turned out to be pernicious anemia. He led and spoke at the great armistice service in Albert Hall with the king and queen present and also spoke at a highly controversial interdenominational service in Durham Cathedral. Yet he was "a bird with a broken pinion," and he soon resigned.

What Sustained Jowett?

Jowett's secret was first of all his commitment to the spacious and grand themes of Scripture and of the Christian faith. As he prepared, he would ask himself how other preachers he knew would treat the text and how the people would handle it. Jowett had both heat and light. He avoided topical preaching and did not care much for apologetics from the pulpit. When he returned from England he ventured more into application for national life. But he was in fact an unashamed "old-fashioned preacher."[13] He was the stylist of preachers of his time and may have used the English language more effectively than did any other preacher in the twentieth century. He loved to read the dictionary and was committed to Saxonisms rather than Latin. He was a planner *par excellence* and was always punctual. He began preparing his sermons on Tuesday and when taking the train into Birmingham on Sunday morning, he would read Spurgeon for the atmosphere. He had a great sense of humor, and while he walked with kings, he never lost the common touch.

Jowett wrote voluminously, but it was mainly his sermons that were published. He divided sermons brilliantly. Whether it is his *The Passion for Souls, The Silver Lining,* his arresting expositions of *The Whole Armour of God,* or his *Life in the Heights: Studies in the Epistles,* this is great preaching.[14] Who but Jowett could turn a phrase like "Faith is not a safe orthodoxy but a hazardous adventure" or, in speaking of worship, see the great danger of luxuriating in our own emotion. Some favorite Jowett sermons are in *The School of Calvary.*[15] Let the reader respond to his prayer: "Open our eyes to discern the footprints of our Lord."

---

1. Arthur Porritt, *John Henry Jowett* (London: Hodder and Stoughton, 1924), 4. Introduction by Archbishop Davidson.
2. Ibid., 6.
3. Ibid., 21.
4. Andrew Fairbairn (not to be confused with Patrick Fairbairn, who wrote the great volume on typology) came out of the United Secessationists and gave the 1891–1892 Beecher Lectures, "The Place of Christ in Modern Theology." He had wrestled with issues of faith and doubt but had been much helped in Germany by Tholuck and Hengstenberg. He was brilliant but long, often preaching an hour and twenty minutes.

5. Porritt, *John Henry Jowett,* 35. It was said of Whyte and his associate Hugh Black that "in the morning Whyte painted the people black and in the evening Black painted the people white."
6. Charles M. Berry (1852–1899) declined calls to both Brooklyn and Westminster Chapel. He is known for his conversion at the bedside of a dying lady, "I got her in," he declared to Jowett, "and I got in myself." His son Dr. Sidney Berry succeeded Jowett at Carr's Lane Chapel in Birmingham.
7. Porritt, *John Henry Jowett,* 62.
8. Ibid., 63.
9. John Bishop, "John Henry Jowett: A Preacher of Grace," *Preaching* (January–February 1987): 54.
10. Porritt, *John Henry Jowett,* 76.
11. Ibid., 172.
12. J. H. Jowett, *The Preacher: His Life and Work* (New York: Hodder and Stoughton, 1912). Excellent and elegant.
13. John Pitts, "John Henry Jowett: Prince of Preachers," *Christianity Today* (December 6, 1963): 13.
14. J. H. Jowett, *The Whole Armour of God* (Grand Rapids: Baker, 1916, 1969); *Life in the Heights* (Grand Rapids: Baker, 1925, 1973).
15. J. H. Jowett, *The School of Calvary* (Grand Rapids: Baker, 1956).

11.3.6 J. D. Jones—The Welsh Preacher Who Drew Young and Old

> In the deepest sense of all a man cannot be taught to preach. The Word must be like a fire in a man's bones if he is to become an effective preacher. But a man can be taught how to put his message forcibly, he can be taught how to stand and how to speak and how to arrange his matter.
>
> Preachers often seem to me to fight shy of the big themes and to be content with secondary and subsidiary topics. Since I have had the opportunity of sitting more often in the pew, I have heard sermons on social justice, on peace, on ethical subjects, but I can't recall a single sermon on such a central theme as the Incarnation. We are never going to build strong churches that way. To make strong vigorous churches we must launch out into the deep.
>
> —J. D. Jones

Undeniably there was at this time a great swell of powerful preaching in the churches of nonconformity. Yet there was still strong preaching in the established church, such as by **Henry Scott Holland**, for twenty-six years canon of St. Paul's in London and close to Liddon.[1]

Another sparkling example from the nonconformity was **John Daniel Jones** (1865–1942), who was born in Wales, the grandson of a Wesleyan preacher and the son of a schoolman who obtained quite a name for himself in Welsh hymnody. After the early death of his father, Jones was reared in the Calvinistic Methodism of his mother. He heard much strong preaching and was a "thricer" (i.e., attended church Sunday morning and evening with Sunday school in the afternoon). He served as organist in his home church and in due time was converted and joined the church. Jones testified that the ministry really chose him rather than vice versa. When he preached his first sermon, the service was moved outdoors and the wind blew his manuscript away. This led him to his conviction that preaching without a manuscript is preferred.[2] He went on to Owen's College in Manchester and then took his B.D. at St. Andrews.

His first pastoral charge was the Congregational church at Newland, Lincoln, where he spent nine happy years. The church held twelve hundred people, and Jones filled it. Jones was known for the uniform excellence of his messages. His preaching was even and calm, in contrast to the "fiery eloquence and dramatic" power of his predecessor in the Richmond Hill Congregational Church in the seaside resort city of Bournemouth, to which he went in 1898. Jones spent thirty-nine years as pastor of this outstanding church and turned down many opportunities to move. He became a fixture in the life and affairs of the community and was greatly loved. Every Sunday there were 350 to 500 strangers in the services. His Tuesday morning studies were very popular and a four-volume devotional commentary on the Gospel of Mark affords insight into the reason for that popularity. His sermons were well designed, but his sentences were not oratorically polished. Twenty volumes of his sermons have been published, and half of the sermons are from the Old Testament. He loved Scripture and used many Scripture quotations as well as quotations from literature and biography. There were "no dramatic moments" in Jones, but part of his strength resided in the fact that he was a great pastor.[3] One observer commented on a sermon he preached in Tremont Temple in Boston:

> It was "different" from an American sermon, exegetical and expository rather than topical, quiet and simple, but holding the throng as the preacher made them sit in the heavenly places with Christ Jesus . . .[4]

Jones was active in denominational affairs in the Congregational Union of England and Wales and made many trips to the U.S. and Australia in connection with Congregationalism. In 1899 he heard D. L. Moody preach at Plymouth Church in Brooklyn (Moody himself being a Congregationalist). J. D. Jones gives his experience:

> I remember how he announced his text. "My text," he said, "is all the way from Genesis to Revelation." What he was really intent upon was to show that the idea of atonement ran through the whole Scripture. "I guess," he said at the beginning of his sermon, "I shall make some of you mad this morning." And I daresay he did—for he preached a theology to which I fancy Ward Beecher's and Dr. Hillis' people were not accustomed . . . and though he stated the old substitutionary theory in the baldest way, he got down to the quick of things and we felt the power of his speech. I am glad I got a grip of his hand.[5]

Out of his contact with Moody came invitations to speak at Northfield, which he fulfilled several times. In his own sermon at the Second International Council of Congregationalists, his message was well received. Indeed, he "dispensed with his paper," but in his own view, P. T. Forsyth's great message on the cross was the spiritual high moment. "He flamed, he burned," was Jones' vivid recollection.[6] One cannot escape the sense in Jones that already Enlightenment rationalism was driving a serious wedge in the Congregational fabric not only in America but also in Britain.[7] Jones was clearly evangelical and found Forsyth's theology of the cross preferable to George Gordon on "The Glories of Congregationalism," which he thought was "puff pastry" or "a bee buzzing about in vacuity."[8]

Jones knew the deep valley of sorrow as his wife died in 1917, and his only son was twice wounded and severely gassed in France, recovering but then dying in Africa. He retired in 1937 and moved to Wales, where his ministry continued in other forms. He was a steady biblical influence in his time. A splendid example of biblical preaching can be seen in his *The Lord of Life and Death,* a series on John 11.

Described as "a burly figure with white hair with a rich silvery voice," Jones demonstrated his careful work in the Greek text.[9] Some his messages are classic, such as "When the Half-Gods Go, the Gods Arrive," from 1 Corinthians 13:10, "The Originality of Jesus" from John 7:46, and "The Reserve of Jesus" from Matthew 12:19.[10] It was J. D. Jones who urged his friend Campbell Morgan to bring D. Martyn Lloyd-Jones to London. J. D. Jones, "the unmitred bishop of Congregationalism," urged Lloyd-Jones to step into the deepening leadership vacuum in that fellowship.[11]

---

1. Henry Scott Holland (1847–1918) was close to Liddon but not homiletically what Liddon was. He served Christ Church, Oxford, before and after his twenty-seven years at St. Paul's and later became Regius Professor at Oxford.
2. J. D. Jones, *Three Score Years and Ten* (London: The Book Club, 1940), 26–27. Arthur Porritt, a close friend, also wrote a brief memoir of Jones.
3. John Bishop, "J. D. Jones: 'Man with the Mouth of Gold,'" *Preaching* (May–June 1989): 53.
4. Jones, *Three Score Years and Ten,* 174.
5. Ibid., 126.
6. Ibid., 132.
7. Note A. E. Garvie's own view of the Bible at this time: "The Bible is not the Word of God but contains the Word of God," in *The Christian Preacher* (New York: Scribner's, 1923), 350. Garvie was Congregationalism's ecumenist.
8. Jones, *Three Score Years and Ten,* 171. George Gordon (1853–1929), born in Scotland, served Old South Church, Boston. His liberalism totally denuded Christ and the Bible of anything supernatural. In his autobiography, *My Education and Religion* (Boston: Houghton Mifflin, 1925), he shares how his friend Phillips Brooks disdained Jonathan Edwards (301). Gordon could preach, as his sermon "The Lilies on Top of the Temple" suggests, but he had no gospel message.
9. J. D. Jones, *The Lord of Life and Death* (Grand Rapids: Baker, 1972). On his grave: "Preacher of the Gospel."

10. J. D. Jones, *The Gospel of the Sovereignty* (London: Hodder and Stoughton, 1914), 44ff., 74ff., 134ff.
11. Iain H. Murray, *David Martyn Lloyd-Jones: The Fight of Faith* (Edinburgh: Banner of Truth, 1990), 61ff. J. D. Jones lamented the general loss of the great preachers, asserting that the average was raised but not the "great ones."

11.3.7 Charles Sylvester Horne—With the Sweep of a Tornado

> The one supreme qualification for the ministry is a soul of flame.
>
> Nobody ought ever to go into a pulpit who can think and talk about sin and salvation, and the Cross of Christ, which is for all true men the symbol of hope and service, without profound emotion and passion.
>
> —C. Sylvester Horne

Embodying and personifying that flame of passion of which he spoke, **Charles Sylvester Horne** (1865–1914) was a meteorite that streaked across the heavens and was too soon gone. Born in Sussex, the son of a Congregational minister, Horne was educated at Glasgow, where his radiant personality and plethora of gifts were already evident. He then went to Mansfield College, Oxford, under Fairbairn. His forensic and oratorical abilities were marked early and came into fruition in two distinct phases of pastoral ministry.

First, he spent ten years in Kensington, London, where he preached amid high society and fashion. He was an unusual preacher. Webber is right in describing him as "winsome, eager, radiant, fascinating and glowing."[1] Gammie said, "No platform speaker could excel Sylvester Horne at his best . . . grasping his coat lapels as he began quietly, he gradually gathered momentum until the sparks were flying and the whole atmosphere became electric. With shafts of humour, pungent phrases, and the glow of a burning passion, he could rouse an audience to an enthusiasm which brought them to their feet time and again."[2]

Then Horne underwent a drastic change of venue and style. For another ten years he moved to Whitefield's Tabernacle on Tottenham Court Road among the poor and the downtrodden. In this time he also served as a member of Parliament from Ipswich, and while he did not bring politics into his sermons as such, he preached to great Sunday afternoon rallies on current issues. In 1914 he sailed for America to give the Beecher Lectures at Yale, after which he died suddenly of a massive coronary while sailing with his wife into Toronto harbor. He was forty-nine.

There was a scholarly side to Horne that bespoke his fine mind and that can be seen in his splendid history of the Free Churches. In the epilogue of this work he refers to the Welsh revival of 1904, which began with prayer meetings in Newcastle Emlyn and spread like a prairie fire throughout Wales, resulting in thousands of accessions in the Free Churches.[3] One wishes that more exegetical foundation were visible in his sermons as published. His Beecher Lectures in 1914 give us a significant window into the soul of the preacher as he sought to inculcate a wondering sense of "The Romance of Preaching," as the lectures were titled.[4] The approach is historical and yet a clear call for conversion rings out in his last lecture, as he insisted, "Amid all changes of thought and phrase the wonder of conversion remains, to be the supreme joy and glory of the preacher."[5]

The theological tensions among Congregationalists over the new theology and R. J. Campbell were becoming increasingly acute (Campbell finally left for the Church of England). An important symposium on *The Old Faith and the New Theology* drew contributors who, in a gentlemanly way, spoke of Campbell's drift, among whom were Peter Forsyth, J. D. Jones, and Sylvester Horne. Horne's piece was a sermon from Romans 1:16 on "The Power Unto Salvation," in which he ranged over the entire first chapter of Romans and was clear on sin and the atonement.[6] He openly challenged Campbell on the sinlessness of Jesus and pleaded with him "to believe with the rest of us, in a sinless Saviour, a Lamb without blemish and without spot."[7] Yet others in the anthology made dangerous concessions, and the increasingly schizoid composition of nonconformity was clear.[8] More than romance or ecstatic extroversion was needed. Clear, cogent doctrinal exposition of Scripture was the need of the hour.

---

1. F. R. Webber, *A History of Preaching in Britain and America* (Milwaukee: Northwestern, 1902), 1:703.
2. Alexander Gammie, *Preachers I Have Heard* (London: Pickering and Inglis, n.d.), 69.
3. C. Sylvester Horne, *A Popular History of the Free Churches* (London: James Clarke, 1903), Epilogue.
4. C. Sylvester Horne, *The Romance of Preaching* (Boston: Pilgrim's Press, 1914).
5. Ibid., 275.
6. Charles H. Vine, ed., *The Old Faith and the New Theology: A Series of Sermons and Essays on Some of the Truths Held by Evangelical Christians and the Difficulties of Accepting Much of What is Called the "New Theology"* (New York: Eaton and Mains, 1907).
7. Ibid., 59.
8. Ibid., 220, 227.

11.3.8 John Hutton—On the Edge of Greatness

> The teachers of our new theologies are never under a greater mistake than when they imagine that it is the preaching of this old Gospel of the grace of God—old, yet ever new—which is alienating the modern world from the Churches. It is not the preaching of this Gospel which is emptying the churches, but the want of it.
>
> —James Orr

Apart from Morgan and Meyer, the tendency to take a microtext seemed to be prevailing. Jowett talked about "fat texts" but they tended to be short "fat texts." Of course there is a time for a minitext, but exposition requires a natural thought unit. Not only do we sense some decline in biblicality (with the small texts) but as well a waning of sharp, clear affirmation of biblical authority. Few of these preachers wanted to enter the lists of controversy and engage the poisonous currents which were sucking supernaturalism out of discourse.

This troubles us about **John Hutton** (1868–1947), but it was he who, in his brief pastorate at Westminster Chapel after Jowett, captivated the young Martyn Lloyd-Jones. "This man's preaching appealed to me tremendously," he recalled. Iain Murray says of him, "Hutton's preaching was uneven in effect. He was not expository, and his best efforts were occasional rather than regular . . . he believed in rebirth and regeneration."[1]

Hutton was born in Scotland and studied at Glasgow. He came out of the old United Presbyterians and served parishes in Scotland and then in the Presbyterian Church of Scotland in Newcastle. In 1923 he took the call to Westminster and "took London by storm." He was warmhearted and effective in the pulpit, filling Westminster morning and evening for the brief time he was there. When J. M. E. Ross, editor of the influential *British Weekly,* died, Hutton was called as editor and served from 1925 to 1946 in that capacity. He was often featured at Moody's Northfield Conference and at Morgan's Mundesley Conference in Norfolk. His analytic skills were described by Joseph Fort Newton, who was even thinner theologically than Hutton but who heard him in City Temple:

> The faces of the great congregation became ashen grey as Dr. Hutton described Antichrist, wearing the robes of the Christian Church and grappling with the Lord Jesus Christ. Dr. Newton declares that his sentences flashed like lightning as he crouched in the pulpit, his face livid. Then, rising triumphantly, with ringing sentences he described the incredible love of the Saviour in His death on the Cross for the sins of the world . . . he spoke without manuscript, and under the excitement of the moment there was, at times, an energetic fervor that the printed page cannot reproduce.[2]

On occasion Hutton could probe into Scripture, as in his studies titled *The Tragedy of Saul.*[3] These are among the finest studies ever done on Saul. Hutton's personal love for the poets Browning and Francis Thompson sometimes threatened to preclude anything biblical, as in his curious messages at Mundesley published as *The Winds of God.*[4] His works on Paul in *Finally* are ably strategized, but he does not seem to pull the cord.[5] Undeniably there are rich gifts here, and there were moments of effective ministry, but what might have been if Hutton had really opened Scripture?

---

1. Iain Murray, *D. Martyn Lloyd-Jones: The First Forty Years, 1899–1939* (Edinburgh: Banner of Truth, 1982), 61.
2. F. R. Webber, *A History of Preaching in Britain and America* (Milwaukee: Northwestern, 1952), 1:525–26.
3. John A. Hutton, *The Tragedy of Saul* (New York: George H. Doran, 1926).
4. John A. Hutton, *The Winds of God* (New York: Hodder and Stoughton, 1911).
5. John A. Hutton, *Finally: With Paul to the End* (New York: Harper, n.d.). My favorite

sermons, *The Fear of Things* (New York: George H. Doran, 1911), include "The Fear of the Threshold" and "The Love of God in the Embarrassments of Life."

11.4 THE AMERICAN VENTURERS

> The majestic testimony of the Church in all time is that its advances in spiritual life have always been toward and not away from the Bible, and in proportion to the reverence for, and power of realizing in practical life, the revealed Word.
>
> —Casper Wistar Hodge

The disuse of the Bible is always a scourge, and the iconic use of the Bible is a travesty, but Bible-believing preachers were now facing not only the buffetings of unbelief and skepticism but also new forms of agnosticism. Liberalism and its naive optimism about humankind were collapsing in the face of the unmitigated horrors of the so-called enlightened twentieth century. Two individuals symbolize the two extremes.

Thomas Edison (1847–1931) represents the venturesome American spirit of enterprise and energy. Born of Dutch extraction in Milan, Ohio, and reared in Port Huron, Michigan, Edison was "a singular genius" whose "Napoleonic zeal" and prodigious creativity made him famous and wealthy. Though an instance of the Puritan work ethic, he drew his philosophy from Emerson:

> If a man can write a better book, preach a better sermon or make a better mousetrap than his neighbor, though he builds his house in the woods, the world will make a beaten path to his door.[1]

An omnivorous lifelong reader, he loved Thomas Paine's *Age of Reason* and found Hume and Gibbon very much to his liking.[2] Although he recited portions of the Bible over his new phonograph, he dabbled in Theosophy and Swedenborg. He was "intoxicated by the expansive rhetoric of social Darwinianism."[3] Like his friend, John Burroughs, the New England Transcendentalist, he was "seduced by Emerson, Thoreau and Whitman."[4] Though toward the end of his incredibly productive life he was preoccupied with thoughts about existence after death, he did not turn to the Bible but rather to Blavatsky. There is something very American about Edison.

In contrast stood a small, brilliant New Testament scholar named J. Gresham Machen (1881–1937). In this time, even the sardonic H. L. Mencken saw it clearly:

> What survives under the name of Christianity, above the sub-stratum of the mob, is no more than a sort of humanism with little more supernatural in it than you will find in mathematics or political economy.[5]

Machen, whose father was an outstanding attorney and whose mother was related to the Southern poet Sydney Lanier, studied classics at Johns Hopkins. His "Uncle Henry" Van Dyke, who taught at Princeton and served the Brick

Church in New York City, turned viciously on Machen in the controversies at Princeton.[6] Machen took his stand against "the claims of the new scholarship." He supported the 1910 stand of the General Assembly of the Presbyterian church, which "reaffirmed inerrancy as an essential article of faith." He was brushed off as a "high-brow fundamentalist" but argued persuasively that liberalism was essentially dishonest in tailoring the gospel to fit the modern mood and was "nothing more than positive thinking in modern garb."[7] In his masterful *The Origin of Paul's Religion,* he went straight to the solar plexus, and in *The Virgin Birth of Christ*, published by Harper and Row, he worried over "the Christless Christianity" peddled from many pulpits.

Dismissed from Princeton because he refused to allow theology to be reduced to matters of polity, Machen saw Princeton, the bastion of Warfield and the Hodges, reorganized in 1929. The center no longer held, and uncheered by what neo-orthodoxy offered in place of a discredited liberalism, Machen went on to found Westminster Seminary. Casper Wistar Hodge called him "The greatest theologian in the English-speaking world." A portion of the evangelical resurgence after World War II must be attributed to the clarity of his vision and the doughtiness of his courage. It was in the dialectic between Edison and Machen that American preaching took place in this century.

---

1. Neil Baldwin, *Edison: Inventing the Century* (New York: Hyperion, 1995), 66.
2. Ibid., 26.
3. Ibid., 230.
4. Ibid., 327ff.
5. D. G. Hart, *Defending the Faith: J. Gresham Machen and the Crisis of Conservative Protestantism in Modern America* (Grand Rapids: Baker, 1994), 2.
6. Van Dyke resented his relative so much that when Machen was stated supply in First Presbyterian Church in Princeton, Van Dyke would not attend to hear him preach. Van Dyke's very thin Beecher Lectures in 1895 were published as *The Gospel for An Age of Doubt.* The companion volume was titled *The Gospel in an Age of Sin.* Infinitely preferable is Machen's volume, *Christianity and Liberalism* (New York: Macmillan, 1923). Walter Lippmann pays Machen high tribute in *A Preface to Morals* (New York: Macmillan, 1929), 30–32. Lippmann calls Machen a "scholar and a gentleman" and asserts that the liberals never answered Machen.
7. Hart, *Defending the Faith,* 81.

11.4.1 Arthur T. Pierson—Balanced and Biblical

> Preaching is a divine art, and therefore the finest of the fine arts. There is, about the logical structure of a true sermon, that which suggests all that is most beautiful in architecture; about the elaboration of its rhetorical features, all that is most symmetrical in sculpture; and about the use of imagination in illustration and metaphor, all that is most fascinating in painting; while oratory, itself a fine art, suggests that other kindred art of music, to which it is so closely allied in the utilization of all that is

> most attractive and persuasive, melodious and martial, in the human voice. As Paul Veronese said of painting, preaching is a "gift from God."
> —Arthur T. Pierson

The first subject in this section is a servant of Christ distinguished not only as a preacher but as a missionary statesman who held the highest view of the verbal inspiration of Scripture and therefore the highest view of preaching. His lectures on preaching at Spurgeon's College are pithy and pointed.[1] His motto was that of the Waldensian church, *Trituntur mallei, remanet incus* (the mallets or hammers are broken, but the anvil still stands).[2] The ministry of **Arthur T. Pierson** (1837–1911) was on both sides of the Atlantic and rather than inching toward accommodation, he is one who became progressively more committed to orthodox formulation.

Born in New York, Pierson was educated at boarding school, Hamilton College, and Union Seminary in New York City, which he entered in 1857 and which had 120 students and five faculty at the time. He was a student there when the revival of 1859 erupted, and this genuine moving of God's Spirit marked him for life.

Pierson's first pastorate was in First Congregational Church in Binghamton (two-and-a-half years); here his increasingly conservative ideas were attacked, and he went into a brief eclipse of confidence but emerged all the stronger after a study of Christian evidences, particularly the argument from prophecy.[3] His next pastorate was a six-year stint at the Presbyterian church in Waterford, New York. He was an intense preacher of a somewhat nervous temperament, but his preaching was truly developing, as was his lifelong commitment to the world missionary task. His Sunday afternoon Bible class usually numbered 150 to 200.[4]

In 1869 Pierson took a call to the Fort Street Presbyterian Church in Detroit. (He declined the call to the chair of systematics at McCormick Seminary in Chicago.)[5] The congregation had 238 members and met in a sanctuary which seated eight hundred. Pierson had a great evangelistic urge and saw much growth. "Always tell men the truth" was his credo.

After a brief interlude in Indianapolis in 1882, he resigned because of impatience in the situation,[6] but out of this time came his choice *Many Infallible Proofs: The Evidences of Christianity* (London: Morgan and Scott, 1882). This work has some of the best treatment of the fulfillment of prophecy in the destruction of Jerusalem in 70 A.D. of which I am aware.

At forty-six, Pierson became pastor of the Wanamaker church in Philadelphia, Bethany Presbyterian, where he had six glorious years. Active in prophetic Bible conferences, he was at times weighed down by too much introspection.[7] He began espousing the imminence of Christ's premillennial coming.

Pierson then moved on to a more international ministry and filled in for Spurgeon when the latter was ill (1891–93). He had been influenced much by George Müller, whose biography he had written. In the tensions after Spurgeon's death there were those who called for Pierson's assumption of the pastorate. Indeed, this staunch Presbyterian was baptismally immersed in that interest, but he was passed over in favor of Thomas Spurgeon. Pierson continued to travel and write in an expanding arena of usefulness and fruitfulness. He died at seventy-six, spending his last years with Brooklyn as headquarters.

Pierson was deeply involved in ministry at the Keswick Convention in the Lake Country in northern England and in the Keswick emphasis on the victorious life around the world. Some of his finest preaching was done under these auspices.[8] His preaching was always anchored in the biblical text.[9] He believed that preaching is more the discovery of what the Bible says than it is the invention of ideas for discourse. An example of his analysis of the believer's relationship to the world is set forth in his sermon on our Lord's high-priestly prayer in John 17:

1. Believers are in the world;
2. Believers are not of the world;
3. Believers are chosen out of the world;
4. Believers are sent into the world.[10]

Charles Inwood, the Methodist preacher from Ulster who gave himself full-time to the Keswick message, described services in Belfast conducted by Pierson:

> The great Grosvenor Hall, accommodating over 3,000, was crowded every night and his address on Foreign Missions was by far the most eloquent and soul-moving missionary address I ever heard. Many features of his character and work have left an indelible and sacred impression on me—his knowledge, his gifts, his warm and guileless love, his holy and blazing indignation where the honour of his Lord and His Word were at stake . . . most of all I was impressed with his absolute abandonment of his whole personality to the ministry of the moment; every cubic inch of his being was in every message, in every sentence, in every word, every tone, every look as he spoke.[11]

Pierson was close to D. L. Moody and was influential on John Mott and Robert Speer in the Student Volunteer Movement. One of his biographers, J. Kennedy Maclean, opines, "At Keswick, perhaps more than anywhere else, he possessed his kingdom and occupied the sphere fitting his great gifts. There he dominated the Convention by his spiritual and intellectual gifts and thousands hung upon his words with great eagerness for instruction and help that was never disappointed."[12]

---

1. Arthur T. Pierson, *The Divine Art of Preaching* (New York: Baker and Taylor, 1892), 84ff.
2. Ibid., 94.
3. Delaven Leonard Pierson, *Arthur T. Pierson* (New York: Revell, 1912), 81.
4. Ibid., 93.
5. To sense how such institutions shift and change, cf. George L. Robinson, *A Short Story of a Long Life* (Grand Rapids: Baker, 1957). Robinson was a distinguished and principled Old Testament scholar at McCormick.

6. Pierson, *Arthur T. Pierson,* 162.
7. Ibid., 181.
8. J. Kennedy Maclean, *Dr. Pierson and His Message* (New York: Association Press, 1911), 34ff. For a good sample of his Keswick ministry, see Arthur T. Pierson, *A Spiritual Clinique* (New York: Gospel Publishing House, 1907).
9. Pierson, *Arthur T. Pierson,* 238.
10. Ibid., 265–66.
11. In Herbert F. Stevenson, ed., *The Ministry of Keswick* (Grand Rapids: Zondervan, 1963), 1:101–2.
12. Ibid., 103ff.

11.4.2 Charles E. Jefferson—Gentleman with a Biblical Message

> How is it possible for a young man reared in the world of books to take a hearty and genuine interest at once in a world so stupid and belated? It is by no means easy for a young man to become a shepherd, and he ought not to be discouraged if he cannot become one in a day, or a year. An orator he can be without difficulty. A reformer he can become at once. In criticism of politics and society he can do a flourishing business the first Sunday. But a shepherd he can become only slowly, and by patiently traveling the way of the cross.
>
> It is surprising how stoutly and stubbornly the church insists upon preachers knowing how to preach. They will forgive almost anything else, but they will not forgive inability to preach.
>
> —Charles E. Jefferson

High praise was always given to **Charles Edward Jefferson** (1860–1937). He was typical of a growing company of able preachers who tilted toward a mediating position with reference to the historic faith. Frederick Keller Stamm speaks of him as "the greatest American preacher,"[1] and it was generally conceded that "he was always at his best."

Jefferson was born in Ohio and trained for teaching and indeed taught oratory at Ohio Wesleyan and Ohio State Universities. When he heard Phillips Brooks preach, he felt called to preach himself and prepared at Boston University School of Theology. Brooks, who claimed that F. D. Maurice, the English immanentist, influenced him as none other, shaped Jefferson. When Jefferson asked Brooks if he had to believe in the miracles and the resurrection, Brooks retorted, "I should not say you must, I should say you may."[2] After serving several smaller churches, Jefferson took the call to the Broadway Tabernacle in Manhattan, where he served for the next thirty-one years. This is the church where Finney and William Taylor served. In 1905 a new church was built at Broadway and 56th. The congregation does not now exist as such.

Some have compared Jefferson to Alexander Maclaren in his reserved and shy appearance and his "penetrating seriousness" about ministry and preaching. He was a man of the study,[3] simple and direct in his style. He felt that the sermon should be as long as necessary, which for him was about an hour.[4] He always preached extempore. His Beecher Lectures at Yale in 1910 on "The Building of the Church" sought to put the preacher's task in an ecclesiological context. In this lectureship, Jefferson resoundingly called for more personal preaching and summoned preachers to public Bible reading. He advanced the sensible idea that "It is possible to work too long on a sermon."[5]

Jefferson's twin volumes on *The Minister as Prophet* and *The Minister as Shepherd* were given as lectureships at Bangor Seminary in Maine. Perhaps no one in modern times has spoken or written as movingly about the shepherd character of ministry as has Jefferson.[6] His studies of *Cardinal Ideas of Isaiah* and *Cardinal Ideas of Jeremiah* show the range and depth of Jefferson's mind.[7] He spoke wisely and well to younger preachers and those just entering the ministry.[8] He always saw indolence and idleness as the demon for young aspiring preachers.

Although he would not get on the antidogma bandwagon, Jefferson made some painful concessions to the modern mood. He went so far as to blur the uniqueness of the Christ-event.[9] While he lamented the decline of preaching on the cross of Christ, he rejected substitutionary atonement in favor of something new and undefined. Jefferson set up a false dichotomy of options regarding the authority of Scripture and set dictation against illumination as the choice. He accepted an evolutionary account of biological and spiritual origins and clearly held to degrees of inspiration.[10] Along the same line, Jefferson gave up the idea of a literal second coming of Christ.[11] These concessions led ultimately to the mutilation of the gospel in Protestant preaching on a grand scale. Many like Jefferson had a sentimental attachment to the old paths, but little by little they jettisoned the supernatural elements of Christian faith on the alleged basis of scholarly criteria. The result was disastrous for the mainline, notwithstanding the gifted preachers. It would be disastrous for evangelicals as well.

---

1. Frederick Keller Stamm, *The Best of Charles E. Jefferson* (New York: Thomas Y. Crowell, 1960), 3.
2. Ibid., 75. Jefferson would read the Bible and Shakespeare aloud annually.
3. John Bishop, "Charles Edward Jefferson: Preaching the Great Doctrines," *Preaching* (September–October 1991): 61ff. Jefferson was part of the "preach positively" school, which wanted to flush away all negatives.
4. Stamm, *The Best of Charles E. Jefferson,* 10.
5. Charles E. Jefferson, *The Building of the Church* (New York: Macmillan, 1923), 294.
6. Charles E. Jefferson, *The Minister as Prophet* (New York: Grosset and Dunlap, 1905); *The Minister as Shepherd* (New York: Thomas Y. Crowell, 1912). The latter kindled the crisis of commitment to pastoral/preaching ministry in my life as a seminary senior. This book is warm and so alive!
7. Charles E. Jefferson, *Cardinal Ideas of Isaiah* (New York: Macmillan, 1925).
8. Charles E. Jefferson, *Quiet Talks to Growing Preachers in My Study* (New York: Thomas Y. Crowell, 1901).
9. Charles E. Jefferson, *Doctrine and Deed: Expounded and Illustrated* (New York: Thomas Y. Crowell, 1901).

10. Stamm, *The Best of Charles E. Jefferson,* 15. Jefferson goes so far as to state, "The Bible is not the only book. God has revealed himself through other men than the Jews. English literature contains a revelation" (*The Minister as Prophet,* 89). To say that the Bible contains the Word of God is to move away from the absolute uniqueness of divine revelation in Holy Scripture. Unknowingly, I believe, the store was being given away.
11. Ibid., 58.

11.4.3 George C. Lorimer—Massive Messages

> There is only one answer possible: Death, sacrifice, blood, an offering made once for all in the end of the old ages for the redemption of the world. The knowledge of it and faith in it were needed in the past; they are needed still; and impotent and faithless the Christian message whenever its significance is minimized or lost. St. Paul gloried in the cross; and it will be a bitter day for humanity when the church shall hide it, apologize for it, and explain away its only possible meaning as though it were her shame.
>
> —George C. Lorimer

Preaching in the United States was veering farther and farther away from anything exegetical. Among the conservatives, preaching was moving toward the oratorical and ornamental. A prime example is the Baptist preacher, **George C. Lorimer** (1838–1904). He was born in Edinburgh but came to the U.S. at the age of seventeen and traveled as an actor. While he was playing in Louisville, he was converted. He studied for the ministry and served churches in Harrodsville, Paducah, Walnut Street Baptist Church in Louisville, and First Baptist in Albany, New York. While serving the Shawmut Avenue Baptist Church in Boston, Lorimer came into contact with a group who purchased the old Tremont Theater across the street from Park Street Church in order to offer a vigorous evangelical ministry with free seats.[1] A magnificent structure was built, which burned down three times and was subsequently rebuilt. It stands yet today on Tremont Street, with its giant pipe organ with consoles on two levels. Here Charles Dickens gave his readings. The interior of the church is equal to the eight-story buildings beside it.

In 1873 Lorimer did his first ministry at Tremont. The thriving work bore ample testimony to his gifts as a preacher. To the disappointment of his people, he left for a successful ministry at two churches in Chicago (there is still a Lorimer Baptist Church in a southern suburb of Chicago). In 1891 he returned for a second ministry at Tremont Temple that lasted ten years. Lorimer then took a call to the old Madison Avenue Baptist Church in Manhattan, where he served until retirement.

Lorimer was dramatic, massive in content, and generally sound. His memory was exceptional; he had only to read his manuscript once and then could preach it without referring to it.[2] He wrote a noted biography of Spurgeon and penned many books. His son, George H. Lorimer, was the longtime editor-in-chief of the *Saturday Evening Post.*

But as was increasingly common, we find little exegesis in Lorimer's sermons. A text was taken almost as a pretext. At best it supplied the motif or main idea of the sermon. Is this enough?[3] No doubt Lorimer was essentially committed to Christ and the historic gospel, but where is the gospel and any appeal to sinners in these sermons?[4] They were intellectual, heavy with literary and historical quotation but desperately short of Bible truth.[5] In the absence of gospel dynamic, the tendency is to be moralistic. His heavy critiques of Harnack do not altogether assuage our anxiety because of such sentiments as "The Bible of verbal inspiration is not the true Bible."[6]

Yet even in such a prestigious Baptist theologian as A. H. Strong, we see modifications in historic orthodoxy in an attempt to accommodate evolutionary and higher critical ideas.[7] Other noted preachers were similar, including **Newell Dwight Hillis** (1858–1929), who served Plymouth Church in Brooklyn,[8] and the articulate **Cortland Myers** (1864–1941), who had notable ministries in the Baptist Temple in Brooklyn and at Tremont Temple.[9] Their thoughts were ordered and compelling but bereft of the Bible. No wonder that the Plymouth Brethren and their compatriots were drawing followers with their more exegetical preaching (cf. 11.1).

---

1. F. R. Webber, *A History of Preaching in Britain and America* (Milwaukee: Northwestern, 1957), 3:448.
2. Ibid., 3:449.
3. Defining a current trend along these lines is Harold T. Bryson, *Expository Preaching* (Nashville: Broadman and Holman, 1995), 32. Bryson seems to argue that only the point need come from the text, not the mains and subs.
4. George C. Lorimer, *The Modern Crisis in Religion* (New York: Revell, 1904); *Messages of Today to the Men of Tomorrow* (New York: George H. Doran, 1896).
5. George C. Lorimer, *Argument for Christianity* (Philadelphia: American Baptist Publication Society, 1894).
6. Lorimer, *The Modern Crisis in Religion*, 270.
7. Carl F. H. Henry, *Personal Idealism and Strong's Theology* (Wheaton, Ill.: Van Kampen, 1951), 77.
8. Newell Dwight Hillis, *A Man's Value to Society: Studies in Self-Culture and Character* (New York: Revell, 1896). These are more the essay-sermon of Tillotson, but for all their beauty they have no anchorage in Scripture.
9. Cortland Myers, *Making a Life* (New York: Revell, 1900); *Dangers of Crooked Thinking* (New York: Revell, 1924); *The Real Holy Spirit* (New York: Revell, 1909). Sound and popular but no wrestling with a text, no modeling of how Scripture is relevant. Brilliant but encouraging spectatorism.

11.4.4 Russell H. Conwell—Name It and Claim It Early On

> You must keep in mind the question, "Will Jesus come here and save souls?" You must carefully eliminate all that will show irreverence for holy things or disrespect for the church. You must carefully introduce,

> wherever you can, the direct teachings of the Gospel, and then your entertainments will be the power of God unto salvation. The entertainments of the church need to be carefully guarded; and if they are, the church of the future will control the entertainments of the world. Then the theater that has its display of low and vulgar amusement will not pay because the churches will hold the best classes and, for divine and humane purposes, will conduct the best entertainments. There will be double inducement that will draw all classes, and the institutional church of the future will be free to use any reasonable means to influence men for good.
>
> —Russell H. Conwell

The American entrepreneurial spirit and policy of manifest destiny were part of what made the U.S. the great frontier and a success story without parallel. This was reflected in preaching, especially in a charismatic figure like **Russell H. Conwell** (1843–1925). Born on a New England farm, Conwell was suckled on the sermons of Beecher and, as a young boy, did plays on *Uncle Tom's Cabin.* He would preach to the chickens.[1] He ran away from home at fifteen and worked his way to Europe. Eventually he attended a Methodist academy and entered Yale, where he did not seem to mind his shabby clothes. He took a dip into atheism but turned back to Christianity after attending a service in Plymouth Church, where Beecher auctioned off a runaway slave in a famous public-relations gambit.[2]

Enlisting in the army, Conwell fought in the Civil War and was wounded at Kenesaw Mountain. He was converted while he was in the army hospital. After the war he studied law at Albany University of New York State. (He could repeat the two volumes of Blackstone's commentaries from memory.) Admitted to the bar, he moved to Minneapolis, where he worked in legal and journalistic enterprises. He was a mover and a shaker. At thirty-seven he moved to Boston and took a position on the Boston *Traveler.* He traveled widely and interviewed Bismarck, Von Moltke, Tennyson, Garibaldi, Dickens, Gladstone, Victor Hugo, Beecher, and John Greenleaf Whittier. Conwell became popular as a lecturer on these persons and taught a large Sunday school class of two to three thousand at Tremont Temple.

With the death of his wife, Conwell turned anew to the Bible.[3] Remarried and living in Newton Centre, he ingested the influence of Newton Seminary nearby and took the pastorate of a virtually defunct little Baptist church in Lexington. His methods were sensational and highly controversial, but he averred, "Woe be to me if I preach not the Gospel!" He was an electrifying speaker who was "not limited for lung power."[4] He took a call to a floundering little church in North Philadelphia called Grace Baptist Church. He did little actual preparation of his messages, which were "simple, direct, full of homely illustrations that stayed in the memory and enabled his hearers to make the spiritual truths he preached a part of their everyday lives."[5]

A man of tremendous energy, Conwell led in breaking ground for a new church called the Baptist Temple, which seated 3,135 in the sanctuary and another 2000 in the lower Temple. Nine thousand people attended on the day the Temple was opened. Dues were charged regular attendees. The seats were soft, and Conwell had designed an uncustomarily user-friendly environment. He reiterated his conviction that "The mission of the Church is to save the souls of men."[6] The frenetic pace always threatened to distract, as Temple University was founded and then Samaritan Hospital. Gordon-Conwell Seminary represents a merging of several of these interests. Conwell did baptize more than ten thousand people in his thirty-three years as pastor at the Temple, and yet in all those years there was never a case of church discipline. The music was outstanding, with Professor David Wood, the blind organist, being a great drawing card. Prayer meetings were large and participative. Conwell was a social crusader who vigorously combatted evil. He was one of the original Chatauqua lecturers and itinerated constantly. His great lecture on "Acres of Diamonds" was given six thousand times to a total of thirteen million people and earned him eight million dollars, which he ploughed back into the work. "Only in America," one is tempted to say. This lecture is the idea that the diamonds we seek are in our own back yards, and the message is very much the "you can do it!" notion so quintessentially American, but so Pelagian.

Conwell wrote biographies prolifically, including a popular biography of Spurgeon. He claimed John Wanamaker as a close friend and was an advocate of Gladstone's "Do It Now Club." His glorification of prosperity reflected the American ethos of the time, but how biblical was it?[7] A sermon outline on Acts 16:31 focuses our concern:

1. Belief in a person means belief in his character;
2. If we believe in a man's character, we desire to be like him;
3. If we desire to be like him, we will naturally act like him [my response: reading of Christ's innocence makes us innocent?];
4. To be like him is to be saved.

Whatever Conwell might protest to the contrary, we miss the Cross and redemption entirely. He preached the spirit of the age.[8] Much American preaching at this time and on into our own day is such an amalgam of patriotism, self-help, and positive thinking. We saw this at the great Central Church in Chicago, established by **David Gram Swing** (1830–1894), who left the Presbyterian church under duress and charges of heresy and established a church which met in Orchestra Hall, seating three thousand. This influential and affluent congregation was subsequently served by Newell Dwight Hillis, who went on to Plymouth Church in Brooklyn. **Frank Gunsaulus** (1856–1921) was literally crippled by overexertion but preached brilliantly. No one answered the agnostic Robert Ingersoll as effectively as did Gunsaulus, yet there was no gospel of the grace of God in what he said.[9] Another preacher at Central Church, **Frederick Shannon** (1877–1947), was a homiletical craftsman of spectacular skill, and yet his sermons had no exegesis or biblical substance.[10] We sense something so American in this preaching, but there is so little that is biblical or theological. This pervasive tradition continues in our own time.

1. Agnes Rush Burr, *Russell H. Conwell and His Work* (Philadelphia: John Winston, 1926), 63. This is the authorized biography of Conwell and quite hagiographic.
2. Ibid., 107.
3. Ibid., 167.
4. Ibid., 176.
5. Ibid., 188.
6. Ibid., 207.
7. F. R. Webber, *A History of Preaching in Britain and America* (Milwaukee: Northwestern, 1957), 3:472.
8. Burr, *Russell H. Conwell and His Work,* 391.
9. Frank W. Gunsaulus, *Paths to Power* (New York: Revell, 1905); *Paths to the City of God* (New York: Revell, 1906). Gunsaulus admirably takes a text but its use is only to supply his motif rather than his outline. He gave the Beecher Lectures at Yale in 1911 on "The Minister and the Spiritual Life." David Swing had been converted at fifteen in a Methodist revival meeting; see Joseph Fort Newton, *David Swing* (Chicago: Unity Publishing Co., 1909).
10. Frederick F. Shannon, *A Moneyless Magnate and Other Essays* (New York: George H. Doran, 1923). The essay-type sermon is polished and brilliant but textually lacking in acuity. The Central Church has long since ceased to be.

11.4.5 A. B. Simpson—The Bible Preacher and Sweet Singer of the Gospel

> I am no good unless I can get alone with God.
>
> Every fiber in my soul was tingling with the sense of God's presence.
>
> —A. B. Simpson

> I traveled with him in conventions and what he preached he lived . . . He was the greatest heart preacher I ever listened to. He preached out of his own rich dealings with God.
>
> —Paul Rader, who followed Simpson as head of the CMA

> I count Dr. A. B. Simpson the foremost in power to reach the depths of the human soul. And his message was so bathed in love that it was always redolent of the personality of Him who having not seen we love.
>
> —C. I. Scofield

Born and raised on King Edward Island in Canada, **Albert Benjamin Simpson** (1844–1919) was a Scot by extraction. He was strongly influenced by his mother, who prayed he would enter the ministry.[1] Simpson testified that he knew from age fourteen that God wanted him to preach. During his early years he devoured Scripture with "unspeakable ecstasy."[2] He pleaded with his austerely Calvinistic father to allow him to become a preacher. At seventeen Simpson made a remarkable nine-hundred-page "Covenant with God" and then went on for thorough training at Knox College in Toronto. When he preached while he was home one Christmas, everyone realized that his was to be "the prophet's mantle."[3]

At twenty-two, Simpson took the pastoral office at Knox Presbyterian Church in Hamilton and served there eight years, seeing 750 accessions to membership. Then he moved on to the Chestnut Street Presbyterian Church in Louisville, where his vision for worldwide evangelism began to enlarge. He spearheaded an evangelistic crusade with Major Whittle and P. P. Bliss. The churches benefited greatly, but Simpson had to come to terms with his own problem of self and arrogance. He yielded to the Lord and experienced powerful fillings of the Holy Spirit. Subsequently, he founded the Christian and Missionary Alliance (CMA).

Simpson oversaw the building of an evangelistic tabernacle in Louisville, but in 1879 he moved on to the Thirteenth Street Presbyterian Church in New York City. Sharing his vision for missions was not easy in this fashionable church, and after a year he had a total health breakdown. While up at Old Orchard Conference in Maine, Simpson received a healing touch from God. Jesus as healer has remained a focus in the CMA ever since.

After an amicable parting with Thirteenth Street Church, Simpson began an independent evangelistic ministry in Caledonian Hall, which ultimately became the Gospel Tabernacle at Eighth Avenue and West Forty-forth Street, just off Time Square. Called by some the Cave of Adullum, the Tabernacle became an extraordinary center of ministry and missions in the heart of New York City. An early German service was held each Sunday, and an Episcopalian communion service was officially sanctioned.

Simpson never expected to found a denomination as such, but the conventions he promoted, the magazines he edited, the school he started (Nyack Missionary Training School), and his extensive ministry resulted in a worldwide fellowship of churches that authentically carried forth the vision of the founder. Deeply committed to premillennialism, Simpson heralded the fourfold message of Jesus as Savior, Sanctifier, Healer, and coming King.[4]

D. L. Moody said of Simpson, "No one gets at my heart like that man."[5] He was truly a man who knew and walked with God. He published more than seventy books, including his classic pair of volumes on the Holy Spirit in the Bible as well as his twenty-four-volume commentary, *Christ in the Bible*.[6] He was also the composer of many hymns, some of which are timeless.[7]

Simpson was providentially led to part company with John Alexander Dowie of Zion, Illinois, whose obsession with healing would have distracted Simpson and his movement.[8] One of his closest heart-brothers was F. E. Marsh of Bristol, with whom he had many meetings.[9]

Weariness and fatigue began to plague him, and in Simpson's final years, as Tozer described it, "He lost the sense of the presence of the well-beloved."[10] But those shadows could not eclipse the remarkable Bible preaching of this stalwart soldier of the Cross who, along with **I. M. Haldeman** at First Baptist Church at Seventy-nineth and Broadway, exemplify the soundest and most exegetical preaching being done in New York City.[11] With respect to the burgeoning ministry of the Alliance, Tozer's analysis is that "The true headquarters was the pulpit of the Gospel Tabernacle."[12] "He was a minstrel . . . preaching was melodious and musical when it fell from his lips," Leon Tucker observed.[13] Tozer describes the preacher in action:

> Mr. Simpson steps forward, pauses for a moment, and then in a low reverent tone announces his text. The tense silence is broken only by the voice of the speaker. His early training has given him a quiet reserve. His manner is relaxed and natural as he faces his hearers. Large framed, impressive and dignified, his very appearance gives promise of a great message to follow. He begins to speak with the Bible out-spread on one hand and the other hand resting lightly upon his hip. At first the words come slowly, spoken in a rich baritone of remarkable range and power. As he warms to his theme the speed of utterance increases, his voice takes on mounting degrees of emotional intensity, while his body sways back and forth rhythmically . . . his gestures are few, but when moved more than usual he lays his Bible down, places both hands on his hips and shakes his great head to emphasize a point. The lofty truth he is proclaiming, the strong, magnetic quality of his voice, the swift flow of his language, all combine to produce an impression so profound that when he is through speaking and the benediction is pronounced the listeners sit in hushed silence, unable or unwilling to break the spell of the sermon . . .[14]

A. B. Simpson's sermons were "models of structural perfection." He loved to use biblical illustrations and did so with great skill. His printed sermons glowed, and his devotional pieces are radiantly incandescent.[15] He may have been as one described him, "a cadaverous-looking minister," but he was vibrantly alive in the Spirit.

---

1. A. W. Tozer, *Wingspread: Albert B. Simpson—A Study in Spiritual Altitude* (Harrisburg, Pa.: Christian, 1943), 18.
2. Ibid., 27.
3. Ibid., 33.
4. Ibid., 105.
5. Daniel J. Evearitt, "A. B. Simpson, the Man," *Alliance Life* (November 10, 1993): 7.
6. A. B. Simpson, *The Holy Spirit or Power from on High,* 2 vols. (Harrisburg, Pa.: Christian, 1896, 1924). Powerful!
7. Tozer, *Wingspread,* 117. N.B. A. B. Simpson, *Songs of the Spirit* (Harrisburg, Pa.: Christian, 1920).
8. Ibid., 134.
9. Ibid., 137. Cf. F. E. Marsh, *Night Scenes of the Bible* (Grand Rapids: Baker, 1904, 1967), N.B. 4.2.3, note 21.
10. Ibid., 141.
11. I. M. Haldeman (1845–1933) has given some mighty scriptural studies on the Tabernacle and sacrifices of the Old Testament, against liberalism and various cults, and on prophecy; see *The Coming of Christ: Premillennial and Imminent* (New York: Charles C. Cook, 1906).

12. Tozer, *Wingspread,* 111.
13. Ibid., 114.
14. Ibid., 114f.
15. A. B. Simpson, *The Christ-Life* (New York: Alliance, 1925); *Wholly Sanctified* (New York: Alliance, 1925); *The Life of Prayer* (New York: Alliance, 1925); *Days of Heaven Upon Earth* (New York: Alliance, 1925). His daily readings.

11.4.6 David James Burrell—Bible Preacher and Homiletician

> Just here it becomes apparent why the much exploited New Theology is not adequate to the business at hand. In eliminating the divine factor from the Scriptures it undermines the only reliable authority for the fundamental facts of the Gospel and drives one to the logical conclusion that conversion is a figment of the imagination and that revivals are out of date.
>
> In all my life I have never asked a man or woman to come to church or to join the church. I have stood on my platform and told the truth to all who came. I held Him before them, because I knew that the power came from Him, not from me.
>
> I don't believe in taking Christianity half-way. If Christianity is not good for every day in the year and for every minute in the day; if it isn't good in business as well as in church; if it doesn't make a burdened man or woman happier and hopeful and a business man honest and clean-conscienced, then I don't want anything more to do with it. But it does. I know it does. For over half a century I have proved that it does.
>
> —David James Burrell

David James Burrell (1844–1926) was born in Pennsylvania but was reared in Freeport, Illinois. He attended Phillips Academy and then went on to Yale, where he lost his faith. His mother expected him to go into the ministry, and he could not admit to her that he had become an unbeliever, so he went to Union Seminary in New York City. While working among impoverished boys near Washington Square, he was called to assist a dying Scotsman who had drifted from the faith himself but who interrogated Burrell about his faith. Lying repeatedly to the dying man, Burrell at last capitulated. Having come into the room a skeptic, he left "a fanatic for Christ."[1] He went on to work with his wife for four years in the slums of Chicago and then spent eleven years as pastor of the Second Presbyterian Church in Dubuque, Iowa.

In 1887 Burrell moved to the prestigious Westminster Presbyterian Church of Minneapolis, which he brought to a strength of more than two thousand members. In 1891 he accepted a call to the Marble Collegiate Church (Reformed Church in America), which he pastored until his death in 1926. There were only 115 members left in this historic church when he arrived, but his strong biblical preaching soon built a mighty flock. Marble Collegiate was at one time a great center of gospel preaching. During four of those years he filled a vacancy in the chair of homiletics at Princeton Seminary, traveling by train to Princeton for lectures.

He gave the first of the Sprunt Lectures at Union Seminary in Richmond; they were published as *The Sermon: Its Construction and Delivery.* This distillation of his teaching and practice registers his clear preference for expository preaching.[2] Classically oriented, he devoted fifty-eight pages to the argument in the sermon (developing the body). While stressing the importance of the exordium (introduction), he is particularly pointed on the urgency of the peroration:

> The peroration winds up the argument . . . the peroration is intended to clinch it. For this reason, the preacher should devote more careful and prayerful attention to the close of the sermon than to any other portion of it. He cannot safely trust to the moment for his last words.[3]

While disliking "vulgar buffoonery" in the pulpit, his dislike for dullness was even greater. He did not entirely exclude appropriate use of humor. Burrell preached well-packaged doctrinal sermons in which he effectively argued that the Bible is not "a mingled tissue of truth and falsehood or as merely 'containing' a less or greater modicum of truth."[4] A sample of his probing expository work can be seen in his practical exposition of John 13–17 in the *Short Course Series* of T & T Clark. His message here on "The Dispensation of the Holy Ghost" from John 16:5–15 is especially noteworthy.[5] Examples of his versatility and verve in preaching are observed in splendid messages on "Watchman, What of the Night?" from Isaiah 21:11–12 and "A Sensational Gospel" from 1 Corinthians 1:21, which concludes with an impressive flourish and invitation.[6] Both the texts and body of these sermons are well-divided, and the preacher is careful to practice what he enjoins in his own lectures on the nature of preaching.

Shepherd said Burrell reminded him "of a great stone, set in a certain place to hold a burden. His square chiseled face, his broad shoulders and his medium stature gave me a sense of his solidity; the grayness that comes of his eighty years gave me an impression of the hoariness that settles through the centuries on an immovable stone."[7]

---

1. F. R. Webber, *A History of Preaching in Britain and America* (Milwaukee: Northwestern, 1957), 3:482. Though not acknowledged by Webber, these insights appear to be sourced from William G. Shepherd, *Great Preachers as Seen by a Journalist* (New York: Revell, 1924), 20–21.
2. David James Burrell, *The Sermon: Its Construction and Delivery* (New York: Revell, 1913), 63, 71.
3. Ibid., 188.
4. David James Burrell, *Why I Believe the Bible* (New York: Revell, 1917), 15.
5. David James Burrell, *In the Upper Room* (Edinburgh: T & T Clark, 1913), 87ff.

6. David James Burrell, "The Morning Cometh," in *Talks for the Times* (New York: American Tract Society, 1893), 5ff., 56ff.
7. Shepherd, *Great Preachers as Seen by a Journalist,* 16.

11.4.7 A. Z. Conrad—Preacher and Promoter in Boston

> Religiously, Boston, like other cities, has undergone a considerable change in its attitude toward the church and the spiritual activities represented by the church. A considerable indifference toward church attendance has been painfully apparent. A sense of religious responsibility has seemed to grow more and more feeble. As a corrective of these tendencies the church has been importuned to popularize its services. But the effort in this direction has not seemed to stem the tide outward. The church has been importuned to rationalize her preaching. But every added elimination of the supernatural has only accentuated the disinterestedness of the people in the church. The church has been urged to institutionalize herself and devote her attention increasingly to the material interests of the people. In Boston, as elsewhere, where an honest effort to answer the demand has been made, it is perfectly apparent that this has not solved the problem. Indeed it has been in this very period when the church has been trying all these various devices to stem the outward tide, that the decline in church attendance has been most in evidence.
>
> —A. Z. Conrad

To address the above-described need, 166 churches representing 120,000 members from many denominations united in simultaneous evangelistic crusades early in 1909, the central movement being led by Dr. J. Wilbur Chapman and Charles M. Alexander. The general chairman of this massive concerted effort was **Arcturus Zodiac Conrad** (1855–1937), for thirty-two years the pastor of historic Park Street Church at the head of Boston Common. The response was overwhelming, with hundreds professing Christ and joining the churches. The united prayer meetings were indescribably beneficial.[1] Many of the central meetings were held in Tremont Temple, which was without a pastor at this time.[2] Conrad gave revitalizing leadership to the movement in the greater Boston area as he was giving strong leadership at Park Street Church. Other revivals followed, including one in 1928 with Dr. Biederwolf.

Conrad was born in Indiana, where his father was a Presbyterian minister. He graduated from Carleton College in Minnesota and from Union Seminary in New York, where he also did doctoral study at New York University. He served congregations in Brooklyn and in Worcester, turning down a call to serve a church in London, England. In 1905 he began his ministry at Park Street. This historic church (cf. 9.2.8) was at low ebb at the time of his coming. Conrad was an activist and gave himself unsparingly to the rejuvenation of the Sunday school, the work among youth, and overseas missions. He was an able and a fighting preacher:

> We are too much afraid of open collision. We spend our time parleying about consequences. The apostles told the truth and told it straight without such adjustment as emasculates the truth declared.[3]

Conrad's sermons were thoroughly biblical and often controversial. He tackled topics like "Proven But Not Persuaded: The Word That Defies Dungeons, Demons and Death," and "When the World Slams the Door in Your Face and Goes Back to Bed." He certainly rang the changes in his sermon from Mark 4:39 and 5:8 on "Civilizing, Socializing, Christianizing the World," but the sermon is not very exegetical.[4] One obtains a similar impression from other collections of his sermons.[5] A deeper expository ministry would await the coming of Conrad's successor, Harold John Ockenga.

During the last fourteen years of Conrad's ministry, both Sunday services were broadcast over a local radio station. At age seventy-six he remarried a twenty-seven-year-old[6] and died of cancer in his eighty-second year.

---

1. A. Z. Conrad, *Boston's Awakening* (Boston: King's Business Publishing, 1909), 13ff.
2. Tremont Temple would soon be occupied by gifted preachers such as J. C. Massee (1871–1965), who was an able evangelist himself; see *Revival Sermons* (New York: Revell, 1928) and *Evangelism in the Local Church* (Philadelphia: Judson, 1939). Massee was in the forefront of those concerned about the theological drift in the Northern Baptist Convention; see L. Rush Bush and Thomas J. Nettles, *Baptists and the Bible* (Chicago: Moody, 1980), 355. Later preachers of spiritual power to preach from the Tremont pulpit were Sidney Powell and Gordon Brownville.
3. H. Crosby Englizian, *Brimstone Corner: Park Street Church* (Chicago: Moody, 1968), 221.
4. A. Z. Conrad, *Comrades of the Carpenter* (New York: Revell, 1926), 123ff.
5. A. Z. Conrad, *Radiant Religion* (New York: Harper, 1930).
6. Englizian, *Brimstone Corner: Park Street Church*, 223.

11.5 THE EVANGELISTIC WHEELHORSES

> He sends his command to the earth; his word runs swiftly.
>
> —Psalm 147:15

Evangelists have always nudged the church toward the cutting edge. If, as Archbishop William Temple insisted, "Evangelism is the winning of men to acknowledge Christ as their Savior and King, so that they may give themselves to His service in the fellowship of His Church," we must say that the evangelists in the United States (apart from B. Fay Mills) did some of the soundest and most effective biblical preaching of this time.

Kerygmatic preaching is of the essence whether it is done by the local pastor/teacher or a visiting evangelist.[1] The marks of solid evangelistic preaching, as the late Methodist preacher and editor Roy Short crystallized them so clearly, are (1) authoritative; (2) scriptural; (3) hopeful; (4) urgent; (5) far-reaching.[2]

Without the evangel, nothing can be right. As Vincent Taylor put it so well, "The test of a good theologian is—can he write a tract?"[3]

---

1. David L. Larsen, *The Evangelism Mandate: Restoring the Centrality of Gospel Preaching* (Wheaton, Ill.: Crossway, 1992). This work surveys the nature and history of evangelistic preaching.
2. Roy Short, *Evangelistic Preaching* (Nashville: Upper Room, 1946). Longtime editor of The Christian Advocate.
3. William Barclay, *Fishers of Men* (Philadelphia: Westminster, 1966), 103.

11.5.1 Sam Jones—The Gospel Voice from the South

> It is considered vulgar now, really vulgar, for a man to get up and preach hell to sinners . . . It is not polite to believe that way, and many a little fellow has scratched that out of his creed; but he won't be in hell more than fifteen minutes before he will revise his creed and having in it nothing but hell.
>
> Quit your meanness!
>
> —Sam Jones

Samuel P. Jones (1847–1906) was born in Alabama and moved about with his Southern Methodist family during the Civil War. To the great sorrow of his family, young Jones became a heavy drinker and not until he was converted in 1871 did he stop.[1]

Traveling as an itinerant evangelist for the North Georgia Conference, Jones was unimpressive in appearance. He was much influenced by Spurgeon's sermons but tended to theological weakness on sin and the atonement. He emphasized repentance more than faith. Sam Jones hated sham and pretense, and "His fiery sermons in plain, simple Anglo-Saxon, with a sprinkling of the homely colloquialisms of the common people, attracted attention."[2] He was a lifelong Methodist, but testified, "I like loose-fitting denominational garments." He was brutally blunt if not downright insulting at times—"skin 'em in rabbit-fashion" was his counsel. Yet he cautioned, if someone has a sore throat, you say "open your mouth," but you don't throw in the whole medicine case.

Jones maintained a frenetic pace, preaching at 6:00 A.M., 10:00 A.M., 3:00 P.M., and 7:00 P.M. daily. In his great Nashville crusade, fifteen hundred people confessed Christ. He went North to do a great crusade with Talmage in Brooklyn in 1885. E. O. Excell (who wrote "Since I Have Been Redeemed" and put "Count Your Blessings" and "Jesus Wants You for a Sunbeam" to music) was frequently his musician. He ventured North again for a great crusade in Chicago, but his ministry was mainly Southern. It was estimated that in 1885 and 1886 seventy thousand souls were added to the roles of the Methodist Episcopal Church South as the result of his ministry.

R. G. Lee's father said that Sam Jones was the greatest master of an audience he had ever heard. He made "sinners smell sulphur." Robert Ingersoll, the great freethinking orator, would not debate him. As Methodism increasingly became "indifferent to creed," Jones clashed with the bishops and identified with the dissidents. He did seem to become more coarse toward the end, and he was beside himself because of troubles in his family. Bishop Ivan Lee Holt heard him as a university student and recalled that "there were tears in all our eyes and hearts."[3] He was every bit as popular on the Chatauqua circuit as was William Jennings Bryan.[4] When he died, thirty thousand people passed by his casket in Atlanta, where he was buried.

"Fighting the Devil," based on Acts 17:16, is a typical sermon. Jones preached as few local pastors would dare to preach. Half of his sermons were illustrations, and he used sarcasm devastatingly, but he also used ancillary Scriptures effectively.[5] He brought the great audience in St. Louis to the Cross and closed with Wesley's moving hymn, "I saw one hanging on the tree," put to music by Excell. "Men Pay Dearly for Eternal Damnation" from Mark 8:36 is another example of his fearless preaching.[6] He excoriated people who earned money from liquor and gambling, which he called blood money. A gambler offered him five hundred to test him, and Sam took the proffered contribution. "The devil's had it long enough," was his quick retort. Jones was a highly controversial preacher but effective for God and faithful to the Word.

---

1. Kathleen Minnix, *Laughter in the Amen Corner* (Athens: University of Georgia, 1993), 7. This understanding study must be seen as the definitive biography of Sam Jones. It probes his deep depressions and instability.
2. F. R. Webber, *A History of Preaching in Britain and America* (Milwaukee: Northwestern, 1957), 3:492.
3. Ivan Lee Holt, "A Genius in the Pulpit," in *Great Pulpit Masters: Sam Jones* (Grand Rapids: Baker, 1950), 9.
4. Bryan, the perennial populist of American politics, was a gifted lay preacher and gave the tenth of the Sprunt Lectures in Richmond titled *In His Image* (New York: Revell, 1922). They have a sermonic ring.
5. Sam Jones, "Fighting the Devil" in *Sam Jones' Sermons* (Chicago: Rhodes and McClure, 1888), 68ff.
6. Ibid., 290ff.

11.5.2 Wilbur Chapman—The Gospel Voice Which Moved Men

> When the great evangelist called for an after-meeting I was one of the first to enter the room and to my great joy Mr. Moody came and sat down beside me. I confessed that I was not quite sure that I was saved. He handed me his opened Bible and asked me to read John 5:24. He said to me: "Do you believe this?" I answered: "Certainly." He said: "Are you a Christian?" I replied: "Sometimes I think I am and again I am fearful." "Read it again," he said. Then he repeated his two questions and I had to answer as before . . . he spoke sharply: "Whom are you doubting?" and

> then it came to me with startling suddenness. "Well, are you a Christian?" and I answered: "Yes, Mr. Moody, I am." From that day to this I have never questioned my acceptance with God.
>
> —J. Wilbur Chapman

An evangelist with striking appeal to men, **J. Wilbur Chapman** (1859–1917) was a choice servant of Christ and an unusual preacher. Born in Indiana, he was raised in a godly home. His mother was related to Senator Sumner and Archbishop Sumner. Chapman's earliest surrender to Christ took place in his Sunday school class in the Methodist Episcopal Church.[1] He went on to study at Oberlin and Lake Forest College, from whence he went into Chicago and heard Moody preach. (Lake Forest College is also where B. Fay Mills attended, who ultimately become the reprobate Unitarian evangelist.)

In 1879 Chapman went to Lane Seminary in Cincinnati, from which he graduated, and took with his new bride yoked parishes, a circuit of several local charges. In 1883 he answered the call to the Reformed church in Schuylerville, New York, where his emphasis on ministry to men was in clear evidence.[2] For five years he served the First Reformed Church in Albany, where a genuine evangelistic breakthrough, with Sankey's songs and inquirers' meetings, took place in the rather staid and traditional setting. Five hundred members were added. In 1890 Chapman went on to the great Bethany Presbyterian Church in Philadelphia (succeeding A. T. Pierson), where in the two years he worked with John Wanamaker more than eleven hundred members were added. In 1899 he took the pastorate of Fourth Presbyterian in New York City.[3]

In 1903 Chapman went full-time into evangelism and built the Chapman/Charles Alexander team which held numerous crusades and simultaneous evangelistic campaigns in North America, "under the Southern cross," and through the Orient and Europe. He was closely identified with summer conferences which were beginning to thrive in such places as Niagara-on-the-Lake, Winona Lake, Montreat, and Stony Brook. The ministry of "Praying Hyde," the American Presbyterian minister, was deeply intertwined with Chapman's.[4] Chapman served as moderator of the Presbyterian General Assembly in 1917 but failed in health and died on Christmas morning in 1917 at the age of fifty-eight.

His was an unbending defense of the full inspiration of the Scriptures. The imminent return of Christ for his church was a precious article of faith for Chapman.[5] He took a steadfast stand for "the full authority and integrity of God's Word," manifest in his view and practice of preaching. He created quite a stir when he advocated recalling all overseas missionaries who did not hold to inerrancy.[6]

> What was it that held such vast audiences spellbound as if eternity itself were closing round them? It was the simple story of Jesus. Never in all these meetings did Dr. Chapman or any member of the part make a single apology for the Word of God. They believed in it, in its inspiration from Genesis to Revelation, and preached it as men preach who believe themselves to be ambassadors of Christ and messengers of the Most High God to a world of sinners.[7]

Chapman was steady and even-tempered. He had "a commanding presence" and a "rich, deep and musical voice." He also had a rare sense of humor.[8] The lucidity and clarity of his prose style is apparent in "Conversion Is a Miracle."[9] His evangelistic sermons are well outlined, such as his famous "And Judas Iscariot" from Mark 3:19,[10] and his deeply moving "And Peter" from Mark 16:7.[11] One of his most effective messages was to Christians and was titled "The Power of a Surrendered Life" or "Turning Back at Kadesh-Barnea."[12] Well illustrated and deftly applied, J. Wilbur Chapman's sermons were models for many young preachers, including Billy Sunday, who got his start with him. Those sermons serve as excellent examples for us yet today.

---

1. Ford C. Ottman, *J. Wilbur Chapman: A Biography* (New York: Doubleday, 1920), 22.
2. Ibid., 47. Ottman was an American Presbyterian minister best known for his superb writings on Bible prophecy.
3. Ibid., 68ff.
4. V. Raymond Edman, *They Found the Secret* (Grand Rapids: Zondervan, 1960), 81.
5. Ottman, *J. Wilbur Chapman,* 308.
6. Ibid., 203. The associate song leader, Henry Barraclough, wrote "Ivory Palaces" from a sermon from Psalm 45:8.
7. Ibid., 256.
8. Ibid., 317.
9. J. Wilbur Chapman, *The Personal Touch* (New York: Revell, n.d.), 149.
10. J. Wilbur Chapman, *And Judas Iscariot* (New York: George H. Doran, 1906), 11ff.
11. J. Wilbur Chapman, *And Peter* (Chicago: Moody, n.d.), 38ff.
12. J. Wilbur Chapman, *The Power of a Surrendered Life* (Chicago: Moody, n.d.), 32ff.

11.5.3 Reuben Archer Torrey—The Gospel Voice to Intellectuals

> I have no dread of preaching now; preaching is the greatest joy of my life, and sometimes when I stand up to speak and realize that He [the Holy Spirit] is there, that all the responsibility is upon Him, such a joy fills my heart that I can scarce restrain myself from shouting and leaping.
>
> —R. A. Torrey

From very early in his life, **Reuben Archer Torrey** (1856–1928) was haunted by a sense of call to preach. Born in Hoboken, New Jersey, R. A. was raised in Brooklyn in a devout Congregational home of considerable means. His father made and lost several fortunes and was active in Democratic party affairs. The wife of President William Howard Taft was a Torrey.

It was his mother's prayers that were decisive for young R. A.[1] Wanting to be a lawyer, he entered Yale at fifteen in 1871. He was struggling and thought to take his own life when he decided to yield to God: "I will preach."[2] Torrey was utterly at sea at Yale Divinity School but claimed John 7:17. D. L. Moody taught him to win souls during a visit to Yale. Upon graduating, Torrey took his first pastoral charge in Garrettsville, Ohio. At this time he was not altogether clear on inerrancy, was still a universalist like his father, and was hazy on the Second Coming. Under the stimulus of Finney's revival sermons, he aggressively sought to win souls to Christ and even held revival meetings in saloons.[3]

In 1882 Torrey and his family spent a year studying in Germany, primarily with Delitzsch and Luthardt at Leipzig and with Frank and Zahn at Erlangen. In this time he came to clear focus on the inerrancy of Scripture and soon the premillennial return of Jesus Christ.[4] Torrey had a brilliant mind and wrestled with all of these issues in profound depth.

Torrey returned to the U.S. in 1883 to plant a new church in Minneapolis and a second new church as well. Soon he came to see the need for the endowment of the Holy Spirit for life and ministry, normally called "the filling of the Spirit" but which he called "the baptism of the Holy Spirit."[5] In 1889 he went to Chicago as the first superintendent of the Moody Bible Institute (as it was later called) and the pastorate of what was to be the Moody Church. His indefatigable labors in personal evangelism saw particular fruit at the World Colombian Exposition in Chicago in 1893 when he brought evangelist John McNeill for a six-month period. Torrey broke with D. L. Moody's son, Will R. Moody, over the latter's espousal of George Adam Smith's high critical views.[6] Yet the mantle of Moody fell on Torrey at the conclusion of the Kansas City Crusade, which was Moody's last. A. C. Dixon took the pastorate of Moody Church in Chicago, and R. A. Torrey went full-time into evangelism. Tremendous response to the crusades was reported around the world.

Traveling with Torrey was Charles Alexander with "the Glory Song" signature.[7] Grace Saxe was part of the team to set up follow-up Bible classes. Midday meetings were held in the grinding regimen of the campaigns. In launching the Chicago meetings, he said:

> You, who think we need a new Bible; something better than the Bible, the old Bible; an expurgated Bible; take heed to our experiences. Eighteen months of preaching its Gospel, thirty thousand men and women won to Christ, proves that the Bible, the old Bible, is what the world needs, what the twentieth century needs.[8]

One of his chief backers over the years was the Quaker Oats layman, Henry Crowell.[9] Vitriolic opposition from such as S. Parkes Cadman was only a further stamp of God's approval on the man and his message. In his great Toronto crusade, Oswald J. Smith and his brother came to Christ.

By 1908 Torrey became the founding dean of the Bible Institute of Los Angeles (BIOLA) and the first pastor of the Church of the Open Door. Among his students at BIOLA were Charles E. Fuller, Donald Gray Barnhouse, and A. A. MacRae. "Strong currents of unbelief" and apostasy in the mainline denominations continually confronted conservatives. Slashing attacks by Dean Shirley Jackson Case and Shailer Matthews of the University of Chicago Divinity School were common. Torrey repeatedly gave his great message on "Why I Believe the Bible is the Word of God."[10]

Torrey had an unusual mind. He read Scripture in five languages. His messages were solidly biblical, logical, and clear in their form and presentation. He had no great eloquence or fanciness, yet he was impressive in appearance. He is described here at age forty-six:

> His erect figure, his broad shoulders, the manly face with its massive brows give an impression of great strength . . . and his face, when seen close at hand, with its bright complexion and clear eyes and a certain radiancy of smile, has still the freshness of youth.[11]

Some his most memorable sermons were "What Are You Waiting For?" and "The Need of a Hiding Place." One of his best-selling books has been his sound and powerful work, *What the Bible Teaches.*[12] In a typical sermon on "The Great Judgment Day" from Acts 17, Torrey characterized the judgment under five headings:

I. The certainty of it
II. The universality of it
III. The basis of it
IV. The administrator of it
V. The issues of it[13]

An especially thoughtful message he shared is "God's Roadblocks on the Road to Hell" from 2 Peter 3:9 and John 3:16.[14] Torrey was also known for his magnificent preaching on the resurrection of Christ, an example of which is "Up from the Grave He Arose!" from 1 Corinthians 15.[15]

Torrey was one of the founders of the World Christian Fundamentals Association and one of the prime movers in the publication of *The Fundamentals.* In 1924 he concluded his ties in Los Angeles and went home to glory in 1928. Will Houghton of Atlanta's Baptist Tabernacle preached the funeral sermon.

---

1. Roger Martin, *R. A. Torrey: Apostle of Certainty* (Murfreesboro, Tenn.: Sword of the Lord, 1976), 25.
2. Ibid., 34. A provocative study on Torrey, the best we have.
3. Ibid., 51.
4. Ibid., 69.
5. Ibid., 118. I possess documents which seem to prove that Torrey later clarified his use of the terms.
6. Ibid., 124.
7. Helen C. Alexander and J. Kennedy Maclean, *Charles M. Alexander: A Romance of Song and Soulwinning* (London: Marshall, 1920). When Alexander went with Chapman, Homer Hammontree became songleader.
8. Martin, *R. A. Torrey,* 164.
9. Richard Ellsworth Day, *Breakfast-Table Autocrat: The Life Story of Henry Parsons Crowell* (Chicago: Moody, 1946). Crowell's anguish over the drift of his denomination is exceedingly poignant.
10. Martin, *R. A. Torrey,* 244; the content of the lecture is on 281ff.

11. Ibid., 140.
12. R. A. Torrey, *What the Bible Teaches* (New York: Revell, 1898). See page 144 on the atonement. Solid!
13. R. A. Torrey, "The Great Judgment Day," in *Great Preaching on Judgment* (Murfreesboro, Tenn.: Sword of the Lord, 1990), 159ff.
14. R. A. Torrey, "God's Roadblocks on the Road to Hell," in *Great Preaching on Hell* (Murfreesboro, Tenn.: Sword of the Lord, 1989), 195–96.
15. R. A. Torrey, "Up from the Grave He Arose!" in *Great Preaching on the Resurrection* (Murfreesboro, Tenn.: Sword of the Lord, 1984), 155ff. One of Torrey's significant books was *The Higher Criticism and the New Theology* (1911).

11.5.4 Billy Sunday—The Gospel Voice Through a Roughneck

> I am an old-fashioned preacher of the old-time religion, that has warmed this cold world for two thousand years.
>
> This Bible is God's inspired Word, and every word in it from cover to cover is God's Word. If you try to tell me that some old beer-soaked Higher Critic says otherwise, and that the consensus of "modern scholarship" says otherwise, then I can only tell you and your professor and the consensus of modern scholarship that they are going to perdition.
>
> —Billy Sunday

Such a character, so often uncouth and rough-and-tumble, Billy Sunday was a powerful preacher of the gospel of Christ! **Dr. Maitland Alexander,** pastor of First Presbyterian Church of Pittsburgh, testified how the Sunday campaign shook the whole community. Nine department stores in the city held daily prayer meetings before business. His own church seating thirty-two hundred was filled for the special services for lawyers and doctors, and the tabernacle seating twenty thousand was jammed with steel workers night after night. After the crusade, 419 joined his congregation on their profession of faith.[1]

William Ashley Sunday (1862–1935) was born in Ames, Iowa. His father died while serving with the Union Army. When he was ten, Sunday was sent by his mother with another brother to an orphanage because she was unable to provide for them. Never graduating from high school, Billy Sunday at eighteen went to work in Marshalltown, where he played baseball. In 1883, Cap Anson of the Chicago White Stockings called him up to the big city to play ball. His remarkable speed made him a valuable player.

While playing for Chicago for five years, Billy was confronted with the claims of Christ by the Gospel Wagon from the Pacific Garden Mission. Upon invitation, he went to the mission, where he went forward and gave his life to Christ.[2] Although he continued to play for Chicago and subsequently signed contracts with Pittsburgh and Philadelphia, his heart and the heart of his dear bride from Jefferson Park Presbyterian Church, where he attended, were increasingly drawn to the Lord's work. He quit baseball, giving up good money to work and speak for the YMCA.[3]

As Dorsett points out, "It was becoming voguish to question the veracity of

Scripture,"[4] but Billy Sunday was anchored to the old gospel. In a marvelous networking, he became J. Wilbur Chapman's advance man for two years and served an apprenticeship that prepared him for his own crusades on "the sawdust trail." Besides Chapman, who gave him his homiletics course, the writings of F. B. Meyer and E. M. Bounds shaped him to be the man of God he became.

When Chapman went back to Bethany Presbyterian in Philadelphia, Sunday was unemployed. He received an invitation to do his first crusade in Garner, Iowa.[5] God blessed the "baseball evangelist" with his relentless message of "get right with God!" In 1898 he was licensed by the Presbyterians to preach. The first eleven years were tough, but Billy Sunday preached on.

Sunday was quite theological in style. "Although he joked, used homey illustrations, and relied on barnyard metaphors [recall Zwingli, 5.4.1, 2], he was no buffoon. His Christology was strong and his knowledge of Scripture impressive."[6]

Billy Sunday preached to more than one hundred thousand people from 1908 to 1920. Even New York City responded to the preacher who preached with every muscle in his body. Carnegie Hall was filled and thousands milled about outside. Not even Andrew Carnegie himself could get in! Sunday's songleaders were Homer Rodeheaver and Harry Clark. He led great crusades against liquor and special interests. He preached in a time of growing urbanization and understood where so many of his hearers came from. His warnings about immorality and the dangers of the city were needed and in many cases heeded.

But Sunday's call was to salvation and forgiveness of sin through repentance and faith. He was "the midwestern storyteller," who could live out the Bible stories, enacting five-minute segments which made them vivid and alive.[7] People crowded every inch of the Moody Church at his funeral (the auditorium has 4,400 seats) with Dr. John Timothy Stone, former pastor of Fourth Presbyterian Church in Chicago, giving the funeral sermon in which he urged those present who were not Christians to repent: "Don't put off accepting Christ until the end of this funeral service."[8]

If there was a flaw in Sunday, it might be that as he become well known and a good friend of John D. Rockefeller, neither he nor his children handled money or fame well. So too, his platform gymnastics and acrobatic preaching scandalized some. But he was a born actor and remarkable in his repartee:

> You say, "Mr. Sunday, the Church is full of hypocrites." So's hell. I say to you if you don't want to go to hell and live with that bunch forever, come into the Church, where you won't have to associate with them very long. There are no hypocrites in heaven.
>
> You say, "Mr. Sunday, I can be a Christian and go to heaven without joining a church." Yes, and you can go to Europe without getting on board a steamer. The swimming's good—but the sharks are laying for fellows who take that route. I don't believe you. If a man is truly saved, he will hunt for a church right away.[9]

In some crusades the response was phenomenal. Billy had a great day at the University of Pennsylvania, with amazing fruit. In Columbus, Ohio, the eighteen thousand converts included the chief of police and all of the policemen detailed to duty at the tabernacle. Members in congregations this author has served date their conversion to a Billy Sunday meeting. Gordon H. Clark, the noted apologist and philosopher, was converted under Billy Sunday.

A typical Billy Sunday sermon is his textual-topical message on "Heaven Is a Place," in which he pulls out the stops.[10] The text is John 14:1–6 and the sermon is saturated with Scripture. One can visualize Billy Sunday preaching—

> I'm against sin. I'll kick it as long as I've got a foot, and I'll fight it as long as I've got a fist. I'll butt it as long as I've got a head. I'll bite it as long as I've got a tooth. And when I'm old and fistless and footless and toothless, I'll gum it till I go home to glory, and it goes home to perdition!

---

1. William T. Ellis, *Billy Sunday: The Man and His Message* (Philadelphia: John Winston, 1914), 174.
2. Lyle W. Dorsett, *Billy Sunday and the Redemption of Urban America* (Grand Rapids: Eerdmans, 1991), 26.
3. Ibid., 30–31.
4. Ibid., 47.
5. Ibid., 58.
6. Ibid., 77.
7. Roger Bruns, *Preacher: Billy Sunday and Big Time American Evangelism* (New York: Norton, 1992), 82.
8. Dorsett, *Billy Sunday and the Redemption of Urban America,* 145.
9. Ellis, *Billy Sunday,* 150–51.
10. Billy Sunday, "Heaven Is a Place," in *Great Preaching on Heaven* (Murfreesboro, Tenn.: Sword of the Lord, 1987), 93ff.

11.5.5 Aimee Semple McPherson—The Gospel Voice with Spiritual Static

> She was an actress whether she liked it or not.
>
> —Charlie Chaplin

Whatever one may think of **Aimee Semple McPherson** (1890–1944), and there are shadows and reproaches to be sure, two recent major works have focused attention on her ministry and on the issues it raises for our time. That she used effects and was dramatic is not unique in these annals (remember Whitefield). She was fundamental and orthodox in her doctrine. "If the Scriptures tell one lie, they lie like a sieve" she would say. Many who packed the fifty-three hundred seats night after night in Angeles Temple in Los Angeles were genuinely converted as they listened to the simple gospel message. Paul Rader, William Edward Biederwolf, and William Jennings Bryan filled her pulpit. Anthony Quinn *(Zorba the Greek)* worked closely with her for a time.[1] Charlie Chaplin and she took walks together in Marseilles.

Yet there were scandals, and her ministry was always close to "show business."[2] Angeles Temple in Echo Park resembled a theater, and Sister Aimee epitomized Hollywood stardom. She argued it was simply "being all things to all men," but the question must be raised as to whether there are not some canons of good taste which must be observed. How user-friendly can we properly become without mutilating the gospel? How much is legitimate?

She was born Aimee Kennedy in Ontario into a Methodist home, but her mother, Minnie, had joined the Salvation Army before Aimee's birth. Young Aimee was early drawn to the Pentecostals, and in 1902 she won a gold medal in the WCTU public speaking contest. In 1908 she married Robert Semple, a Pentecostal minister, and went with him to Hong Kong for missionary service. He died in 1910 just before the birth of her first child. McPherson returned to New York and began a nationwide revival ministry. In 1921 she was ordained by the First Baptist Church of San Jose just after groundbreaking for Angeles Temple. The time was ripe for evangelism as the huddled masses crowded into the cities of America and population grew by one-third.

Unlike Billy Sunday, McPherson tapped into the American tradition of preaching of love and light and joy. "Let's forget about hell," she advised.[3] There was an erotic quality to her preaching from early on, and while the morning services were more traditional in form and preaching (and healing was always handled out of the large rallies), Sunday night was showtime.[4] Hers was "a ministry of performance."[5] In the 1930s she had a series of fairy-tale sermons. Despite horrific blowups with her mother and her daughter, there was "never an empty seat on Sunday night."[6] Numbers correlated with God's favor. Certain familiar motifs surely make her a forerunner of thinking and theory today.

Sister Aimee's institutions have long survived her, and the Church of the Foursquare Gospel has immense vitality in this country and overseas. She saw Christians as "end-time people," and the gift of the Spirit entrusted to Pentecostals was to be shared with all believers. Occasionally her hermeneutic was outlandish.[7] She had a richly melodic, somewhat incantatory voice, and mixed piety with pageantry.[8] Aimee Semple McPherson brought drama into the lives of those who were bored. She adapted the use of technology to mass evangelism as did no one else up to her time. Blumhofer says in conclusion:

> That legacy involved not only presentation but content. In significant ways, Sister's user-friendly gospel anticipated Norman Vincent Peale's positive message and Robert Schuller's media extravaganzas blending the Bible, patriotism and the stage.[9]

---

1. Edith L. Blumhofer, *Aimee Semple McPherson: Everybody's Sister* (Grand Rapids: Eerdmans, 1993), 343–44.
2. Daniel Mark Epstein, *Sister Aimee: The Life of Aimee Semple McPherson* (New York: Harcourt, Brace, 1993), 383.
3. Blumhofer, *Aimee Semple McPherson*, 383.
4. Ibid., 125.
5. Ibid., 389.

6. Ibid., 422.
7. Epstein, *Sister Aimee,* 62ff.
8. Blumhofer, *Aimee Semple McPherson,* 231.
9. Ibid., 390.

11.5.6 William Edward Biederwolf—A Plain and Powerful Gospel Voice

> I am here to fight the devil tooth and nail, wherever he may be found. I am going to hunt out Satan.
>
> I'd rather be a dog with gratitude enough to wag his tail, a foul-featured orangutan of the jungle, a leather-hided rhinoceros, my jaws dripping red with the blood of slaughtered prey, a dodo, an ichthyosaurs, a big hippopotamus, or any sort of a cloven-hoofed, web-footed, sharp-clawed creature of God's earth, than to be a man with a soul so contemptibly mean as to sit down at the table three times a day and gulp down the food that God has provided and never once lift my heart in thanksgiving to God who gives it all.
>
> —William Edward Biederwolf

Almost patrician in his propriety and precision, **William Edward Biederwolf** (1867–1939) was born in Montecello, Indiana, to German emigrant parents. As a boy of fifteen he ran away but was soon converted and made public confession of his faith in Christ. He attended Wabash College and then Princeton University for his M.A.

The husky young man worked summers in mission work in the Bowery of New York City with Jerry McCauley. After finishing Princeton Seminary, he traveled a year with evangelist B. Fay Mills and then used his New Testament Greek Fellowship to study for a year in Berlin and Paris. While serving his first pastoral charge in the Broadway Presbyterian Church of Logansport, Indiana, Biederwolf spent one year as a chaplain with the U.S. Army in Cuba. In 1900 he entered evangelism, working at first with J. Wilbur Chapman and then going out on his own.[1] He used magical illusions in the early days to draw attention and illustrate biblical truth.

Biederwolf was a refined Billy Sunday and preached on sin, as did the master; he proposed to "clean up the town!" His famous sermon on "The White Life" from Psalm 119:9 appeals to people to live the overcoming life.[2] He flayed the cults, such as Christian Science, and was agile enough to do stunts to draw the students at the University of Southern California. Like others, he did shop meetings while in a local crusade. Occasionally he would do single-church crusades, as in the memorable series at Temple Baptist in Los Angeles with Dr. James Whitcomb Brougher.[3] One of the great burdens of his life was his leper project in Korea.

Like Chapman and Torrey, Biederwolf traveled widely. His erudition was reflected in his volumes *Illustrations from Mythology* and *Illustrations from Art.* His massive *Millennial Bible* is an amazing repository of data from Scripture on the Second Coming.[4] He also directed the Winona Lake Conference and the Winona Lake School of Theology. In his later years he pastored the affluent Royal Poinciana Community Chapel in Palm Beach, Florida. He also directed the Family Altar League and did a one year copastorate of the famous Cadle Tabernacle in Indianapolis.

Biederwolf was a fiery preacher. He had "a forensic style, an expressive voice and an unusually fine vocabulary."[5] He was skilled in the dramatic pause, and his illustrations were well blended and effective. His outlines are clear and memorable, reflecting Burrell's influence at Princeton.

Many of Biederwolf's evangelistic sermons had real doctrinal substance, as his mighty message on "The Atonement" from Hebrews 9:26.[6] He took full advantage of the narrative in preaching on "Determined to Find Christ" on Luke 19:1–10.[7] An impressive series of messages for believers has as its apex an unusual message on "Arrested Development and Spiritual Dwarfage" from John 15:2. This is splendidly nuanced.[8] Biederwolf is akin to Chapman and Torrey and was greatly available to the Lord, who used him mightily.

---

1. Ray E. Garrett, *William E. Biederwolf* (Grand Rapids: Zondervan, 1948), 26ff.
2. Ibid., 45.
3. Ibid., 41.
4. William Edward Biederwolf, *The Millennium Bible* (Grand Rapids: Baker, 1924, 1964). This runs to 728 pages.
5. Garrett, *William E. Biederwolf,* 40.
6. William E. Biederwolf, *Biederwolf's Evangelistic Sermons—Doctrinal Series* (Chicago: Glad Tidings, n.d.), 55ff.
7. William E. Biederwolf, *Later Evangelistic Sermons* (Chicago: Moody Colportage, 1925), 75ff.
8. William E. Biederwolf, *The Growing Christian* (Grand Rapids: Eerdmans, n.d.), 67ff.

11.5.7 GYPSY SMITH—THE GOSPEL VOICE OUT OF THE GYPSY WAGON

> Then he said to his servants, "The wedding banquet is ready, but those I invited did not deserve to come. Go to the street corners and invite to the banquet anyone you find." So the servants went out into the streets and gathered all the people they could find, both good and bad, and the wedding hall was filled with guests.
>
> —Matthew 22:8–10

To this point we have considered American evangelists who often had extensive overseas involvement. Mention must also be made of **John McNeill** (1854–1933), sometimes called "the Scottish Spurgeon."[1] Not to be omitted are the inimitable **Evan Roberts** and **Rhys Bevan Jones,** who were so used in the Welsh revival of 1904 and 1905.[2]

Born in England but with a world evangelistic ministry was **Rodney "Gypsy" Smith** (1860–1947). Even with minimal education (he taught himself to read and write), Gypsy was known as one of the finest exponents of Anglo-Saxon speech in his time.[3] He was born in a gypsy tent and lost his mother very early. His father was not converted until sometime later, but young Rodney Smith was saved when the gypsy wagon was in Bedford, where John Bunyan had lived. "By the grace of God, I will be a Christian and meet my mother in heaven!" Smith exclaimed.[4] Immediately he began to study the Bible intensively and to preach and sing to the turnip fields.[5]

At seventeen, Smith became an evangelist for William Booth and the Christian Mission, which became the Salvation Army. He was dismissed from the Army over a misunderstanding and then launched a four-year mission in Hanley, "the nearest place to the bottomless pit" in all of England.[6]

Though often scorned and ridiculed, there was a disarming charm about the little rotund gypsy. "When you sing 'Throw out the Life-line,' be sure you make more room in the boat," he liked to say. He spoke of butterflies as "God's flowers on wings."[7]

Smith preached simply but directly from Scripture, and the invitations began to pour in. He made repeated trips to America, where he was very popular. He led the great Manchester Wesleyan Mission in which F. B. Meyer and G. Campbell Morgan assisted him. In 1893 and 1894 he preached the great Glasgow Mission Campaign and then conducted a mission for Alexander Maclaren in Union Chapel, Manchester, the only special series Maclaren ever had in his long pastorate there.[8] Six hundred converts resulted. In America, Smith was a favorite at Ocean Grove and had a most fruitful ministry at Harvard University. He sang some of the compositions of the blind hymn writer Fanny Crosby to the composer herself.

Smith's messages are basic but biblical. One favorite is "The Hope of Glory" from Colossians 1:27–28 in which he contrasts the cry, "educate-educate-educate" with Christ's word, "regenerate-regenerate-regenerate."[9] "What crowd do you belong to?" he liked to ask. Often there was great joy among the angels when Gypsy Smith preached.

---

1. John McNeill was of humble origin but his sermons, like "David in the Dumps," were heard around the world. The best collection of his addresses is *The Passionate Pilgrim* (London: Pickering and Inglis, n.d.). Vivid preaching.
2. Cf. George T. B. Davis, *When the Fire Fell* (Philadelphia: Million Testaments Campaign, 1945), 63ff.; a most remarkable study is D. M. Phillips, *Evan Roberts: The Great Welsh Revivalist and His Work* (London: Marshall, 1906).
3. G. Campbell Morgan in *Gypsy Smith, An Autobiography* (New York: Revell, 1907), 6.
4. Ibid., 79. I remember hearing Gypsy Smith give his life story and preach in the Minneapolis Armory in the early 1940s. He was along in years but irrepressibly winsome. He taught us to sing, "Let the Beauty of Jesus Be Seen in Me." He radiated a Christ-like warmth which has been irrevocably etched upon my memory.
5. Ibid., 85.
6. Ibid., 142–43.
7. Ibid., 178.
8. Ibid., 285.

9. Gypsy Smith, *Evangelistic Talks* (London: Epworth, 1922). Largely given in the Nashville, Tennessee, crusade.

11.5.8 John R. Rice—The Gospel Voice That Never Swerved

Do the work of an evangelist.

—2 Timothy 4:5c

Called the Will Rogers of the pulpit and the dean of American evangelists, **John R. Rice** (1895–1980) represents those who have become independent Baptists and independent fundamentalists and have maintained a concentration on evangelistic preaching. Such would include Bob Jones Sr. (an old-fashioned Methodist by background), B. R. Lakin (who preached for years in the Cadle Tabernacle in Indianapolis, which seated ten thousand), Sam Morris, and countless others.[1]

John R. Rice was born in Gainesville, Texas, and was, as they used to say of him, "born to preach." He was saved at age nine when he went forward after hearing a sermon on the prodigal son, but nobody dealt with him. Hence, he used to say he was "saved for certain at age twelve."[2] Rice lost his mother early and taught school before going off to college. Deeply moved by R. A. Torrey's *How to Pray,* Rice went to study at Decatur Baptist College and served a brief stint in the army at the end of World War I. He taught English at Wayland Baptist College and then studied at Baylor and the University of Chicago. He surrendered for the ministry at Pacific Garden Mission in Chicago and went on to Southwestern Baptist Seminary, where he graduated in 1921.

For a while Rice served as associate pastor at First Baptist, Plainview, but then went on for two years to Shamrock, Texas, where the church under his preaching grew from 200 to 460 in two years. He loved to preach, blistering and blessing the congregation as he did. He was known for his copious weeping in his early preaching.[3]

In his early years he was close to J. Frank Norris, the controversial pastor of First Baptist in Fort Worth and at the same time, for a period of time, pastor of the Baptist Temple in Detroit, both large churches. Rice broke with Norris over Rice's insistence on a powerful Holy Spirit enduement for preaching. He soon left the Southern Baptist Convention over doctrinal deviation in some of the schools.

In 1926 Rice entered evangelism. In 1934 he founded *The Sword of the Lord* paper, which continues as an influential organ in the interest of soulwinning and great evangelistic preaching.[4] He founded several independent Baptist churches, including the great Galilee Baptist Church of Dallas, which grew to seventeen hundred members in seven years. In 1940 he moved to Wheaton, Illinois, to concentrate on the publishing ministry but continued to do citywide campaigns with J. Straton Shufeldt, Harry Clark, and others. In 1946 he joined with Bob Jones Sr. and Paul Rood of California in a great Chicago crusade which was mightily blessed.

In his earlier days, Rice did united crusades but eventually broke with Billy Graham and others over the issue of inclusivity in sponsorship and became increasingly separatistic and critical. His writing was prolific and extended to millions of copies. His little book *Soulwinner's Fire* kindled evangelistic passion in many a pastor and layman.[5] Who could ever forget his sermons on "All Satan's Apples Have Worms," or "Trailed by a Wild Beast" from "Be sure your sin will find you out," or his tender "Watching Jesus Die."

Rice fought worldliness, lodges, and wrote a book on *Bobbed Hair, Bossy Wives and Women Preachers.* The resultant fracture of fellowship with this wing of the gospel cause has been painful and the splintering has seemed endless, but we must not allow that to obscure the great biblical preaching that has often come from these brothers. Often we could wish for more exegetical care and a more rigorous hermeneutic, as in Rice's sermon that makes the gates in Nehemiah 3 representative of the steps to salvation, but here is love for Christ and for the lost. Inspection of Rice's sermons is rewarding and richly worthwhile.[6]

---

1. Dallas F. Billington, *God Is Real* (New York: David McKay, 1962). The story of Akron Baptist Temple, is very typical. The new Baptist Temple built after World War II could seat five thousand. This story has been duplicated many times over.
2. Robert L. Sumner, *Man Sent from God: A Biography of Dr. John R. Rice* (Grand Rapids: Eerdmans, 1959), 29. Viola Walden, Rice's longtime secretary, has also given us a fine biography.
3. Ibid., 69.
4. I am aware that Sumner and the Sword people parted company over another controversy later.
5. John R. Rice, *The Soulwinner's Fire* (Chicago: Moody, 1948).
6. John R. Rice, "Jesus May Come Today," in *Great Preaching on the Second Coming* (Murfreesboro, Tenn.: Sword of the Lord, 1989), 212–13. I heard Rice preach from the old Broadway Temple in North Minneapolis years ago. Excellent expostulation. Another superbly biblical evangelist, Harry Vom Bruch, *Modern Prodigals* (Mt. Morris: Kable, n.d.), 211ff. on Hebrews 12:1ff.

11.6 METHODISTIC AND HOLINESS AMBASSADORS FOR CHRIST

> How far have we gotten with our various substitutes? Look over our churches: they are full of people, who have been brought up on these substitutes, are strangers to those deeper experiences without which there had been no New Testament and no Church of Christ.
>
> —Professor Edwin Lewis

> We have acted and spoken as though our pluralism permits us to pick and choose which part of the gospel we will employ and enjoy and which part we will reject and put aside.
>
> —Bishop Roy Short

The twentieth century has seen a general spiritual and theological drift in world Methodism and the proliferation of smaller and more conservative bodies which have sought to preserve and perpetuate the biblical supernaturalism championed by John Wesley. Says one prominent Methodist leader, "Methodism so easily turned to schemes of world betterment and social uplift as a substitute for the declining evangelistic urge."[1] The theology of immanence with its antisupernatural theology of meaningfulness laid great waste to biblical preaching. "The supernatural character of the Gospel is the vital issue."[2]

Yet there are those who have cherished and treasured the everlasting gospel as encased in Holy Scripture. We now highlight several of these as well as a few representatives of those who left Methodist structures for a broader ministry in the Salvation Army.

---

1. R. P. Marshall, "Trends in Modern Methodism," *Christianity Today* (January 4, 1960): 9ff.
2. Kenneth Hamilton, *Revolt Against Heaven: An Inquiry into Anti-Supernaturalism* (Grand Rapids: Eerdmans, 1965), 181–82. How this applies to the Methodist scene is fine-lined by Ira Gallaway, *Drifted Astray* (Nashville: Abingdon, 1983); Jerry L. Walls, *The Problem of Pluralism: Recovering United Methodist Identity* (Wilmore, Ky.: Good News Books, 1986).

11.6.1 Louis Albert Banks—A Spokesman for the Living Gospel

> The stories Jesus told and the stories which are related concerning the people whom He healed and who were converted under His ministry, are a constant source of power and inspiration to Christian people today. We get faith and courage to cast out devils from men now because of the picture we have of that redeemed man of Gadara whom Christ transformed and sent forth to tell to his friends the good news of salvation.
>
> —Louis Albert Banks

Across the years there have been godly Methodist bishops who were great biblical preachers, such as Bishop Quayle of Minnesota and Bishop Moore of Georgia.[1] Pastors and evangelists loyal to the historic faith have been dwindling in number, but they have fearlessly proclaimed the Word in the face of much criticism and great opposition.[2]

One of these giants was **Louis Albert Banks** (1855–1933). He was born in Corvallis, Oregon. His roots were in the old United Brethren Church. At age eleven he entered Philomath College with grown men and ultimately went on to Boston University. In the intervening years he served as a circuit rider on the Oregon frontier and saw changed lives and the power of God capture even a city for Christ.[3] Though always engaged in evangelistic itineration, he served Methodist churches in South Boston, Kansas City, the great Trinity Methodist Church in Denver, and the huge First Methodist Church of Cleveland, Ohio, where the Spirit visited with a powerful revival. In 1893 he ran as candidate of the Prohibition Party for governor of the state of Massachusetts.

The first sermon Banks preached lasted only eight minutes. Thereafter he spoke longer and much more eloquently. The sermons of his maturity were spacious, bright, alive, and direct. Many volumes of his collected sermons were published, and they were widely disseminated. Especially impressive is a series of evangelistic messages delivered from Galatians starting with "The Key-Note of Christ's Gospel" from Galatians 1:3–4 and including such other messages as "The Tragedy of Frustrating the Grace of God" from Galatians 2:21 and a clear word on "Christ Cursed for Us" from Galatians 3:13.[4] Banks' discourse abounds with pertinent illustrations and quotes from a wide range of sources. Strong hortatory preaching can be seen in his fine sermon "The Emphatic Date in Human Life" from Hebrews 3:15, "Today if you hear his voice . . ." His passionate evangelistic message, "The Greatest Thief in the World Is Neglect," from Hebrews 2:3, "How shall we escape if we neglect to great salvation?" is equally dramatic.[5] What is so deeply satisfying in Banks' preaching is his wrestling with the text. For most preachers, the text was becoming chiefly a pretext. Banks was not a scintillating exegetical preacher, but he was strong in telling us what the text really said.

---

1. Bishop William Quayle was a gifted preacher (as in *The Hidden Shadow* [New York: Abingdon, 1923] and other works) who reflected helpfully on the craft, as in his fine *The Pastor-Preacher* (Cincinnati: Eaton and Mains, 1910). Bishop Arthur J. Moore could also deliver the evangel, as in *The Mighty Saviour* (New York: Abingdon, 1952), which he preached at First Methodist Church in Atlanta. Moore sought scripturally to stem the tide that for years had sought to humanize God, deify man, and minimize sin. His outstanding lectures on the Christian world task as given at Southern Methodist University were published as *Immortal Tidings in Mortal Hands* (New York: Abingdon, 1953).
2. An example of a truly effective preacher who had an outstanding ministry in Detroit for over twenty years was Merton S. Rice, whose magnificent sermons can be studied in *The Advantage of a Handicap* (New York: Abingdon, 1925, more biblical) and in *Diagnosing Today* (New York: Abingdon, 1932, more cultural/analytical and brilliantly developed). Rice had "Preach the Word" engraved in stone on his desk and every ten days telegraphed that message to his preacher son. Another engaging but controversial preacher was Robert P. ("Fighting Bob") Shuler who pastored the great Trinity Methodist Church at 12th and Flower in Los Angeles for twenty-six years. His sermons in *What New Doctrine Is This?* (New York: Abingdon, 1946) are stirring. Shuler ran for governor of California.
3. Louis Albert Banks, *Soulwinning Stories* (New York: George H. Doran, 1902), 95.
4. Louis Albert Banks, *The Sinner and His Friends* (New York: Funk and Wagnalls, 1907), 28ff., 82ff., 104ff.
5. Louis Albert Banks, *Paul and His Friends* (New York: Funk and Wagnalls, 1898), 150ff., 182ff. From his Cleveland days.

11.6.2 Clovis G. Chappell—A Spokesman to Reasonable People

> We ought to major on preaching because it is our job . . . because we are God's one chance at our congregation . . . because preaching is a necessity. Every great day of the Church has been a great day of preaching.

> On Jesus rescuing Peter from sinking: "That mighty hand that is always feeling for yours and mine in calm and in tempest, in the daylight and in the dark, gripped the uplifted hand of Simon and lifted him out of defeat into victory. So it may happen to us. Let us reach our hands to him in the faith that his hand is reaching to ours."
>
> —Clovis G. Chappell

Charming, biblically solid, well heard, and widely read, the sermons of **Clovis G. Chappell** (1877–1972) are among the best in Methodism.[1] Born and reared in Flatwoods, Tennesee, of farmer folk, Chappell studied only briefly at what would become Duke and then at Harvard. The youngest of six children, he had a Puritan father and a sweet Irish mother. He later testified that his father left him no worldly goods to speak of, but "He left me that kind of faith and it made all the difference in my world."[2]

Family worship each day was the center of life, and out of those homely scenes and situations came so much of the picturesque language and anecdotes that Chappell's gentle humor utilized so aptly. Called Muttonhead in his hometown, Chappell's "intellectual conversion" took place at Webb School Academy, where he carried his class by rising at 3:45 A.M. daily to study.

Chappell taught school for several years and soon began to preach in a series of pastorates which brought him to effective service in Washington, D.C., Birmingham, Memphis, Dallas (where George W. Truett was one of his best friends), Houston, Oklahoma City, Jackson, Mississippi, and finally Charlotte, North Carolina. These were downtown churches on the whole, and Chappell used the public invitation to receive Christ and come forward wherever he preached.[3] He was wed to the text of Scripture. Finney's logic was his model, but there was a winsome pleading, what one called "the gentle persuasions of Christ." Everywhere he preached he saw people coming to Christ. But the preaching was under the divine anointing, and later he pointed back to his source:

> Today was the greatest day in my life. For a long time I had been longing and praying for the Holy Spirit. He came today. What a wondrously joyous experience. I am so glad I found the secret.[4]

In lectures on preaching, which he gave at Candler School of Theology, Chappell had much to say about the techniques of crafting, but he mainly spoke to the preacher's own call and spiritual maintenance under the Spirit.[5] He used illustrations with consummate skill. He could dramatize the biblical story masterfully, as in his great sermon "The Prodigal Wife" on Gomer, the spouse of Hosea, perhaps equaled only on this text by Donald Grey Barnhouse. His outline on 2 Timothy 1:11–12 is simple but unbeatable:

I. I believe
II. I commit
III. I know[6]

Chappell's sermons on "The Lost Book" from 2 Chronicles 34 and on "A Glimpse of the After Life" from Luke 16:19–31 are especially appealing.[7] But of course he is best known for his sermons on Bible characters.[8]

A withering blast has been directed at preaching Bible biographies by Sidney Greidanus in our time. Greidanus' point is important because in preaching about humankind we can horizontalize and psychologize to the point that God is left out.[9] Yet the peril of missing the vertical exists in the preaching of any literary genre. On the whole Chappell avoided this pitfall and almost always focused sharply on the Lord, as in "The Supreme Question—the Philippian Jailer" from Acts 16:30–31.[10] The jailer in question is the point of contact, and the subject of the sermon is raised by the jailer's question.

Chappell was deemed one of the top ten in a survey on America's most popular and influential preachers. He was always thoroughly prepared and preached the Word effectively.

---

1. Ralph Sockman once said over his nationwide broadcast that he considered Clovis G. Chappell the "outstanding biblical preacher in America." Though Sockman, who pastored Christ Church (Methodist) in Manhattan for many years, and his successor, Harold A. Bosley, were well-known and published, neither had the evangelical warmth, the essential biblicality, and the unflagging burden for evangelism and conversion that Chappell had.
2. Wallace D. Chappell, *Clovis Chappell: Preacher of the Word* (Nashville: Broadman, 1978), 11. Wallace Chappell is Clovis Chappell's nephew.
3. Ibid., 31.
4. Ibid., 28.
5. Clovis G. Chappell, *Anointed to Preach* (New York: Abingdon-Cokesbury, 1951). Great on "Keeping Fit," 106ff.
6. Chappell, *Clovis Chappell,* 64.
7. Clovis G. Chappell, *The Village Tragedy and Other Sermons* (Nashville: Cokesbury, 1925), 128ff., 79ff.
8. Clovis G. Chappell, *Sermons on Biblical Characters* (New York: George H. Doran, 1922); *Faces About the Cross* (Nashville: Abingdon-Cokesbury, 1941). Chappell wrote and published some thirty different books of sermons.
9. Sidney Greidanus, *The Modern Preacher and the Ancient Text* (Grand Rapids: Eerdmans, 1988), 162ff. See also Andrew W. Blackwood, *Biographical Preaching for Today* (Nashville: Abingdon, 1954). After all, the Bible does use historical figures as models and exemplars: see Hebrews 11, James 5:11 (Job), and James 5:17 (Elijah). I wish Greidanus' concern were shared more clearly in Blackwood and Roy E. De Brand, *Guide to Biographical Preaching* (Nashville: Broadman, 1988). The whole move to emphasis on narrative needs to face the challenge of God-centeredness.
10. Chappell, *Sermons on Biblical Characters,* 129ff.

11.6.3 General William Booth—Spokesman to the Disenfranchised

Booth died blind and still by faith he trod
Eyes still dazzled by the ways of God.
Booth led boldly and he looked the chief
Eagle countenance in sharp relief,
Beard a-flying, air of high command
Unabated in that holy land.
—Nicholas Vachel Lindsay in "General Booth Enters Heaven"

A fighter against the sufficiency of religious formality and a true evangelist was **General William Booth** (1829–1912), who with his wife, Catherine, founded the Salvation Army and who with his sons and daughters spearheaded the worldwide extension "through blood and fire." Booth was born in Nottingham, England, and was apprenticed out when he was thirteen. His father died that year and left the family in grinding poverty. Trying his luck in London, William was spiritually stirred at Wesley's chapel and was moved from the premise that with regard to the Bible, it is all or nothing.[1] He made up his mind that God would have all of him, and he would argue that his conversion made him a preacher.[2] Booth began lay preaching and took a charge in Lincolnshire for eighteen months. He rejoiced to see people coming forward and testified:

> I shall always remember the week that I spent at Swineshead Bridge, because I prayed more and preached with more of the spirit of expectation and faith, and then saw more success than in any previous week of my life. I dwell upon it as, perhaps, the week which most effectually settled my conviction forever that it was God's purpose by my using the simplest means to bring souls into liberty, and to break into the cold and formal state of things to which His people only too readily settle down.[3]

Booth sought knowledge and continued campaigns so vigorously that the charge he held in Brighouse/Gateshead was called "a converting shop." He wanted to travel for the Lord, but the Liverpool Conference gave a resounding no. Deprived of Methodist backing, Booth did eventually travel and establish the Christian Mission in London's East End on Whitechapel Road amid much squalor. He had bands play in the streets and then march to the hall followed by the seekers. Booth's goal was the glory of God and the salvation of souls. His was "a perpetual motion to the Cross." He preached long sermons—sometimes an hour and a half—and expected and saw old-fashioned conversions.[4] One hearer said:

> At one moment he is full of humor and robust talk, a genial, merry, shrewd-eyed old gentleman; at the next—at the mention of real sin—his brows contract, his eyes flash, and his tongue hisses out such hatred and contempt and detestation as no sybarite could find on the tip of his tongue for anything superlatively coarse or ill-favored.[5]

Booth preached between fifty and sixty thousand times. The stringent disciplines he exacted from the soldiers and officers he more than required of himself. His wife was also an eloquent preacher, and together they fostered inner empowerment through an ever-deepening experience of the Holy Spirit.[6] His messages were biblical and direct and simple.

Booth's son and successor Bramwell recalled that his voice was not his greatest asset. He customarily began like a lamb, would project two or three points from the text, and then move with cyclonic force. "What is your Delilah?" he would ask. "What is your Delilah?"[7] All of his offspring preached, and the story of his daughter, *The Marechal,* who opened France and Switzerland for the gospel, is but one of many that could be told.[8]

No one denied that William Booth was a bit of a sensationalist, but he spoke appropriately for the needy masses. "It is as a preacher of Jesus Christ and His Salvation, with a direct and arresting message, that he will be most remembered in all the lands that he visited."[9]

---

1. George S. Railton, *General Booth* (London: Hodder and Stoughton, 1912), 13. The statement on biblical inspiration as found in the Statement of Doctrine of the Salvation Army is a strong and high statement.
2. Ibid., 17.
3. Ibid., 34.
4. Harold Begbie, *Twice-born Men: A Clinic in Regeneration* (New York: Revell, 1909). Begbie collected vivid and moving instances of transformed lives. My favorite has been "Lowest of the Low," 169ff.
5. Railton, *General Booth,* 210. Railton was Booth's first commissioner.
6. J. Gilchrist Lawson, *Deeper Experiences of Famous Christians* (Anderson, Ind.: Warner, 1911), 355ff.
7. Bramwell Booth, *Echoes and Memories* (London: Salvationist Publishing, 1925), 21.
8. James Strahan, *The Marechal* (London: Hodder and Stoughton, 1914). Strahan authored a great study of Job.
9. Booth, *Echoes and Memories*, 24.

11.6.4 Samuel Logan Brengle—The Spokesman to the Seekers

> I find Satan tempting me to seek rapid promotion—it's on the lines of my old ecclesiastical ambitions. Dear Lord, save me from it. Would you be disappointed very much, my sweet wife, if I should take a low rank in The Army? I want to be useful. God save me from wanting to be famous. He does save me from it, bless His Name.

> Did either Luther, Fox, Wesley or the Founder . . . ask what special message he should bring to his age? I hardly think so. Each one of these men first got a definite, burning experience of redeeming love and grace, that filled his own heart with peace, with flaming love to God, restful confidence in Jesus, tender compassion for his fellowmen, and then, after

> diligent searching of the Scripture, and after much prayer, he spake as he was moved by the Holy Ghost.
>
> —Samuel Logan Brengle

Sharper than a Damascene blade for Christ and his kingdom was the Lord's servant, **Samuel Logan Brengle** (1860–1936). Born in Fredrickburg, Indiana, in a family of Presbyterian and Methodist preachers, his schoolteacher father never recovered from the wounds he sustained at Vicksburg. His mother remarried, and Brengle was reared on a farm where the situation was extremely lonely for the young boy.

Brengle turned to study and reading, including an absorbing obsession with the dictionary. Although he had a reverential fear of God, he sought conversion and went five nights to the altar in a revival, but no one dealt with him. He finally received the "witness" of his personal relationship to God through Christ.[1] Going on to Indiana Asbury University (now DePauw), he gave himself to oratory studies and won prizes in that field. Although intending for the law, in one oratorical contest on the East Coast he said to the Lord: "If you let me win, I will preach!"[2] He did start to preach, memorizing his messages as he would an oration. Brengle was consumed with ambition to be a great preacher.

Going on to Boston University School of Theology, he was led into a deeper experience of death to self at the Cross through his mentor, Professor Daniel Steele (whose *Half Hours with St. Paul* and other works touched so many). Of this crisis, General Evangeline Booth later wrote, "The Christ of the Cross summoned a soldier of Salvation to His bleeding side and sent him forth."[3] Brengle was now willing to say, "Let me stammer and stutter if that be your will."[4]

In 1885 Brengle heard General Booth at Tremont Temple in Boston and was deeply stirred. In seeking the hand of Elizabeth Swift, a young Salvationist, he had to weigh the call to the prestigious Studebaker Methodist Church in South Bend against going to London to train as a cadet in the Salvation Army. His will was yielded to the Lord and he went to London. His first assignment, to clean muddy boots, tested his submission.[5]

Upon returning to the States, Brengle and his wife took officership in a series of assignments, including Boston #1, where he was violently attacked and permanently injured. Yet increasingly his powerful preaching of the gospel and of holiness moved him to strategic leadership in both District and Provincial Office in places like Chicago and San Francisco. Ultimately he was given the post of "National Spiritual Special" and traveled almost constantly, preaching within and outside the Army for the rest of his life.

Brengle was always known as a long-winded preacher.[6] His sense was that the problem he faced in preaching to the culture was "failure to believe in the vitality of the Word."[7] He was so immersed in Scripture that he was sometimes called the talking Bible. He usually read the Scriptures on his knees. As a preacher he was graphic and pictorial. "Vast things simply" was his motto.[8] Logical in his organization and with little pulpit manner in his delivery, he was known as the "psychologist of the heart." The goal in his preaching was Christ and the penitent form.

"Sanctified sanity" is the best description of Brengle and his preaching. His dear friend and confidante Professor Doremus Hayes shared with him a great thirst for the deeper things.[9] He was often assigned to troubleshoot tensions engendered by the tongues movement. In Bergen, Norway, on one occasion, he had to counteract a new theology and its onslaught against the historic faith. Brengle's famous Atonement sermon on this occasion is a classic on the substitutionary death of Jesus.[10]

In 1915 his wife died, but Brengle carried on and was made commissioner in 1926. He exerted extraordinary influence outside of the Army as well as in the case of his friendship with J. Stuart Holden, whom we shall meet in the next chapter. There was never any change in his doctrine. He held to the faith when even in the Army social concerns threatened to overmatch spiritual concerns, and was much blessed of God for it. Other sermons indicate an intellectual rigor which relied on the Holy Ghost for insight and passion. This made Brengle one of the choicest spokesmen of his time. But at core, as he put it, "The honey pots were spilled into his own heart."

---

1. Clarence W. Hall, *Samuel Logan Brengle: Portrait of a Prophet* (New York: Salvation Army, 1933), 28.
2. Ibid., 40.
3. Ibid., v.
4. Ibid., 49.
5. Ibid., 74.
6. Ibid., 127.
7. Ibid., 112.
8. Ibid., 123.
9. Professor Hayes of Garrett Biblical Institute was a New Testament scholar who has given us the exquisite *The Most Beautiful Book Ever Written* (New York: Methodist, 1913) and *Paul and His Epistles* (New York: Methodist, 1915). The former is a priceless study of the Gospel of St. Luke.
10. Samuel Logan Brengle, *The Guest of the Soul* (London: Marshall, Morgan, and Scott, 1934), 9ff. Other sermons also are included here including a searching study of the work of the Holy Spirit, "The Guest of the Soul," 58ff.

11.6.5 Samuel Chadwick—The Spokesman for True Holiness Before God

> I would rather preach than do anything else I know in this world. I have never missed a chance to preach. I would rather preach than eat my dinner, or have a holiday, or anything else the world can offer. I would rather pay to preach than be paid not to preach. It has its price in agony of sweat and tears and no calling has such joys and heartbreaks, but it is a calling an archangel might covet; and I thank God that of His grace He called me into this ministry. Is there any joy like that of saving a soul from death? Any thrill like that of opening blind eyes? Any reward like the love of little children to the second and third generation? Any treasures like the

> grateful love of hearts healed and comforted? I tell you it is a glorious privilege to share the travail and the wine of God.
>
> If this be my last word in the name of my Master, I could say with all due solemnity and earnestness, there is no other Gospel, there is no other Saviour. But if you reject this Gospel of Jesus Christ you will be lost, you will be damned, and that forever.
>
> —Samuel Chadwick

Samuel Chadwick (1860–1932) was one of English Methodism's greatest preachers. The foreword to his biography was written by former British Prime Minister D. Lloyd George, who visited at Cliff College. He heard Chadwick, whom he termed "a pulpit giant," speak at Brighton and said of him, "I never saw a man so hold his audience."[1] Chadwick preached on occasion for three hours and prayed publicly for twenty-five minutes.

Chadwick was small and slightly built and was ailing most of his life. His head was big with a prominent nose. He was known as "champion of the oppressed and advocate of revivalism."[2] Born in Burnley in a strong Methodist home, Chadwick signed the Pledge when he was eight. He worked in the cotton mill from six to six as a boy and never got much education. At ten he was converted in an anniversary service and from the start committed himself to a regimen of daily prayer. He always loved chapels and cathedrals. At sixteen he began to preach, having admired his dear pastor as "a master of exposition."[3] Chadwick visited a sick friend every Sunday afternoon and read him the sermons of Talmage.

When he was twenty-one, Chadwick became lay pastor at Stacksteads, where he formed a prayer league. He came with fifteen sermons and after preaching twelve of them still saw no revival. He stopped leaning on his sermons, entered into what he called "a crisis of obedience," and saw his first converts. In this time he took some classwork at the Methodist College, where he made some of his best lifelong friends: **Frederick Luke Wiseman** (later president of the Methodist Conference and pastor of Wesley Chapel); **W. B. Pope** (greatest Methodist theologian of the time);[4] and **Herbert B. Workman** (whose epochal work on the persecution of the early church we have already referred to early on in this book cf. 3.1.3).

Chadwick went on to serve successively the Nicholson circuit in Edinburgh, Clydebank (where he was known for his outdoor preaching), in two very powerful ministries in Leeds separated by a brief time in Shoreditch in London. He was known as the most loved and the most hated man in Leeds. At Wesley Leeds Hall, the chapel was full a half-hour before the service, and at Oxford Place on the other side of the river the crowds kept coming for thirteen years.

Chadwick loved to preach doctrine and saw conversions every Sunday and often every day.[5] He preached on subjects like "God's Lions," "Two Right Hands," "Angels and Asses," "Devil Making," and "Buried Alive." In 1907 he shared a memorable series of expositions from the Book of Revelation. He served for twenty-five years as editor of *Joyful News* magazine,[6] and at forty-seven he became tutor in biblical and theological studies at Cliff College. After a five-year interval in the coal fields he became principal of Cliff College upon the death of Thomas Cook.[7]

As an expositor, Chadwick was without a peer. His lectures on preaching were legendary. He drove his preachers into the Word and gave an exam to them on themes such as, "Write an epitome of the call of the prophet Ezekiel." In his sermon clinic, he would listen to the students preach in what they called "the inquest." In giving what he called "the canons" of preaching, he insisted on fidelity to the text, unity of discourse, and order in presentation.[8] As he would say, "In every text there is a unique feature, and the unique feature of the text becomes the subject of the sermon and unifies the whole."

His own preaching was well heard in America, which he visited seven times. Large congregations heard him at Northfield, in Atlanta where he preached for Len Broughton, and at Winona Lake. In 1917 he served as chairman of the Methodist Conference and in 1922 as president of the Free Church Council. He held a great evangelistic crusade in Edinburgh, the first service of which he preached in Free St. George's.

In a weighty book of sermons (he averaged an hour in preaching), Chadwick shared the kind of strong biblical preaching which built up the work of God. His sermon on "The Divine Servant" from Matthew 12:18–21 is a good sample:

I. The Divine Servant and His Lord
II. The Servant's equipment
III. The Servant's mission

The exegesis is rich and deep, and the application is strong.[9] His message on "The Standard Miracle" from Ephesians 1:18–20 on Christ's resurrection as the paradigm for God's power working in human life is arresting and suggestive. In Samuel Chadwick we see the godly life and powerful preaching in God-glorifying balance.

---

1. Norman G. Dunning, *Samuel Chadwick* (London: Hodder and Stoughton, 1933), 104ff.
2. Ibid., 16.
3. Ibid., 28.
4. William Burt Pope, *A Higher Catechism of Theology* (New York: Phillips and Hunt, 1884). Strong on the Atonement.
5. Dunning, *Samuel Chadwick,* 50.
6. Samuel Chadwick, *The Way to Pentecost* (London: Hodder and Stoughton, 1921). This meaty study of the person and work of the Holy Spirit consists of articles that he wrote for *Joyful News.* Good on names of the Holy Spirit.
7. E. W. Lawrence, "Samuel Chadwick: God's Servant," *The Free Methodist* no. 6 (November 22, 1960): 766.
8. Samuel Chadwick, *Humanity and God* (New York: Revell, n.d.), 92ff., 136ff.
9. Ibid., 92ff.

11.6.6 E. M. Bounds—The Spokesman for Prayer and the Life of Sanctity

> Hold fast to the old truths—double-distilled.
>
> Have a high standard and hold to it . . . we hold definitely without compromise in the least to the plenary inspiration of the Scriptures.
>
> The preaching that kills may be, and often is, orthodox . . . dogmatically, inviolably orthodox. We love orthodoxy. It is good. It is the best. It is the clean, clear-cut teaching of God's Word, the trophies won by truth in its conflict with error, the levees which faith has raised against the desolating floods of honest or reckless misbelief or unbelief; but orthodoxy, clear and hard as crystal, suspicious and militant, may be but the letter well-shaped, well-named and well-learned, the letter which kills. Nothing is so dead as dead orthodoxy, too dead to speculate, too dead to think, to study or to pray.
>
> —E. M. Bounds

A massive flow of soundly scriptural and aggressive preaching emanated from the Methodist Episcopal Church, South, in this country before and after the turn of the century. We have already identified the evangelist Sam Jones, who lodges in this category, and there are many others.[1] Not the least of these is **Edward McKendree Bounds** (1835–1913), who traced the relationship between lively Bible preaching and old-fashioned, on-your-knees praying more compellingly than did anyone in the history of preaching.

Bounds was born in Shelby County, Missouri, where he was given a middle name in honor of the first American-born Methodist bishop who was such a force for God on the frontiers of America. Even though his father died when he was fourteen, Bounds gave himself to studying the law and at nineteen was admitted to the bar in Missouri. Though converted earlier, the young and successful Bounds came to the crisis of surrender in 1859 and yielded to God's call to preach.[2] After voracious study he was licensed to preach the following year. Although two older brothers served in the Union Army, he was a chaplain with the Confederates.

Only five feet five inches tall and with a receding hairline, Bounds showed great courage with Hood's forces. In the battle of Franklin, he was captured by the Union army and spent a year and a half in a federal prison. Yet the fiery-eyed preacher was never bitter or vindictive. He served the Methodist church in Franklin, Tennessee, after the war. In one week of revival under the pastor's preaching, 150 souls were converted.[3]

Appointment was made to Selma, Alabama, and then to two different parishes in St. Louis. First Bounds served St. Paul's Methodist Episcopal and then First Methodist Episcopal, before returning to St. Paul's. His strong biblical preaching led to conversions and growth.

Bounds then took editorial responsibility for *The Christian Advocate* and itinerated widely in and beyond the St. Louis conference. His preaching on *The Resurrection and Heaven* reflect something of the Christian solace Bounds and his wife found in the experience of losing two of their sons.[4] In the face of mounting liberalism and its denial of hell and original sin and Christ as the only way, Bounds (like Sam Jones) was increasingly at odds with the ecclesiastical hierarchy. His analysis is astute:

> John Wesley said that if Methodism was ever destroyed, it would be destroyed by the love of money. He wrote his last sermons and spent his last years in warning the Methodist people against the love of money. He knew that the enterprising and hearty genius of Methodism would tend to make our people rich, and he foresaw that unsanctified wealth would corrupt.[5]

Resistance to evangelism drove Bounds to seek voluntary location, and he thus became a minister to the nation. Moving from Nashville to Georgia, he continued to rise at 4 A.M. to pray, as he did throughout his lifetime. He was so immersed in his studies that on occasion he forgot to eat. Bounds ministered at great revivals at Asbury College and Seminary in Wilmore, Kentucky, and many other places. His best-known book, originally *Preacher and Prayer* (slightly altered and issued as *Power Through Prayer*), made an immense impact. In all he wrote eight volumes on prayer.

He often said he was willing to be "crazy for God," and Bounds was confessedly eccentric. Homer Hodge, who saw to the publication of Bounds' works, said of him: "He was one of the most intense eagles of God that ever penetrated the spiritual ether."[6] His studies of Satan were notable in their time.[7] The platform for his praying and his preaching could not have been made more clear:

> The true ministry is God-touched, God-enabled, and God-made. The Spirit of God is on the preacher in anointing power, the fruit of the Spirit is in his heart, the Spirit of God has vitalized the man and the word; his preaching gives life; gives life as the spring gives life; gives life as the resurrection gives life; gives ardent life as the summer gives ardent life; gives fruitful life as the autumn gives fruitful life. The life-giving preacher is a man of God, whose heart is ever athirst for God.[8]

---

1. Representative of the vigor and vibrancy of this heritage is William Elbert Munsey (1833–1877), who preached on hell and everlasting punishment as have very few; see "The Awfulness of Eternal Punishment" from Mark 9:43–48 in Curtis Hutson, ed., *Great Preaching on Hell* (Murfreesboro, Tenn.: Sword of the Lord, 1989), 151ff.; also Henry Clay Morrison, *Some Chapters of My Life Story* (Louisville: Pentecostal Publishing Co., 1941). Morrison was an evangelist, pastor, editor, and longtime president of Asbury College in Wilmore, Kentucky.
2. Lyle Wesley Dorsett, *E. M. Bounds: Man of Prayer* (Grand Rapids: Zondervan, 1991), 16.
3. Ibid., 16.
4. E. M. Bounds, *Heaven: A Place, A City, A Home* (Grand Rapids: Baker, rep. 1966).

5. Dorsett, *E. M. Bounds,* 42.
6. Ibid., 59.
7. E. M. Bounds, *Satan: His Personality, Power and Overthrow* (Grand Rapids: Baker, rep. 1933).
8. Dorsett, *E. M. Bounds,* 66. His best-known work is *Power Through Prayer* (Chicago: Moody, n.d.). My favorite of his messages on prayer is *Purpose in Prayer* (Chicago: Moody, n.d.).

11.6.7 William E. Sangster—The Spokesman for Biblical Preaching at Its Best

> Commissioned of God to teach the Word! A herald of the great King! A witness of the eternal gospel! Could any work be more high and holy? To this supreme task God sent his only begotten Son. In all the frustration and confusion of the times, is it possible to imagine a work comparable in importance with that of proclaiming the will of God to wayward men?
>
> I believe that I was born to be a minister. I cannot recall a time in my life when I was without a sense of holy vocation. It did not derive from any conviction in the mind of my parents who had never so much as entertained the thought. But I felt the pressure of a directing hand upon me from my tenderest years.
>
> —William E. Sangster

In the forefront of English preachers in this century and an avid student of the craft of preaching was **William Edwin Sangster** (1900–1960).[1] Sangster exceeded his Methodist cohorts Leslie Weatherhead,[2] who tended more to psychology than Scripture, and Donald Soper, who was consumed in radical politics.

Though his parents were in the established church, Sangster was an unabashed evangelical, having come to Christ at the Radnor Street Mission (Methodist) in London.[3] After serving in the army at the end of World War I, he committed himself to the ministry and trained at Richmond College, Surrey, where C. Ryder Smith influenced him particularly, and where his preaching gifts were in evidence to his classmates and to the faculty.[4] He then ministered consecutively in Wales (1926–1929), in Liverpool (1929–1932), at Central Hall in Scarbourough (where he had four churches in his charge), and then succeeded Weatherhead at Brunswick in Leeds, where he had an unusual ministry.

In 1938 Dinsdale Young of Westminster Central Hall died, and after Dr. Luke Wiseman filled in for a year, Sangster came to serve in 1939, thus beginning a sixteen-year ministry of unusual depth and proportion. Westminster Central Hall, right across from the Abbey, seated three thousand people. Sangster had a five-year ministry there during the London blitz, when he virtually lived in the great bomb shelter beneath the church.

A saintly and resilient soul, Sangster was heard on both sides of the Atlantic and left Westminster reluctantly to spearhead the entire evangelistic thrust of

British Methodism as the head of home missions. He always endorsed the Billy Graham crusades and worked with Alan Redpath, Stephen Olford, and the bishop of Barking in a great evangelistic campaign.[5] His son Paul, who has given us a classic volume on the preacher's declamatory skills, wrote a biography of his father which ranks among the most candid and richly-layered preacher biographies ever written. In the chapter "Warts and All," which Dr. Sangster told his son must be written if the book were to be published at all, young Sangster sketched his father's life and manner:

> In appearance: tall, strong, manly; talked incessantly with his hands; scrupulous but old-fashioned in his dress.
>
> Of great natural dignity seeming at times pompous to some, but very kind and understanding of people in fact.
>
> Driven by a great energy and strong will, "Impatience was his greatest blemish," but he learned this in his illness.
>
> He never passed a church without going into it; tremendous enthusiasm; dramatic in all things.
>
> Tended to be Puritanical and a bit severe with regard to worldliness reflected in his great sermon "This Britain" in 1953.
>
> Possessed a keen sense of humor; a prodigious memory; people mattered much to him. Totally God-obsessed.
>
> His illness with onset in late 1957 was probably his greatest sermon although for the last year he could not speak.[6]

Young Sangster spoke of his father as "a preacher curious about the craft of preaching."[7] Not all effective preachers are reflective of their craft, but Sangster not only preached well but has given us several volumes of significant worth on preaching itself and one of the best books ever written on sermon illustration.

Those who knew him spoke of his evangelistic intensity, brief introductions and conclusions, short, staccato sentences with memorable structure.[8] One of his early books of sermons begins with a gem, "When I Survey the Wondrous Cross."[9] The richness of his preaching can be gauged by his widely-read daily devotional extracts.[10] The finest of the wheat from his Westminster days can be assayed in Sangster's *Special Day Sermons* and *Can I Know God?* which contain such capital messages as "Christ Has Double Vision" from John 1:42 and "The Homesickness of the Soul" from 2 Corinthians 5:8. One could wish he would take a bigger piece of text more frequently, but there is a lilt and scriptural practicality in his sermons, as in the three sections of "The Secret of Radiant Life":

I. The Life—the person I could be
II. The Truth—the person I am
III. The Way—the path between[11]

Sangster became ill with a progressively debilitating disease known as muscular atrophy and could not speak at all during the last year of his strenuous and productive life. To catch the flavor and the fervor of this life poured out as a drink offering for God, read the mighty memorial address given by Sangster's lifelong friend, Professor H. Cecil Pawson. Pawson pointed out that Sangster's sermon as president of the Methodist Conference was titled "Offering Christ to the People."[12] A fitting epitaph for a Spirit-filled life.

---

1. The American Methodist who most closely approximates this double-giftedness must be G. Ray Jordan, who taught at Candler in Atlanta. His most influential book was *You Can Preach* (New York: Revell, 1958), and his typical good preaching is seen in such books as *We Face Calvary and Life* (Nashville: Cokesbury, 1936).
2. Weatherhead went on to serve City Temple in London for twenty-four years and led the march toward the psychologization of preaching. He could really preach, as we see in *That Immortal Sea,* but even his Beecher Lectures in 1948 were published as *Psychology, Religion and Healing.* Yet most often he took no text.
3. Paul Sangster, *Doctor Sangster* (London: Epworth, 1962), 33.
4. W. E. Sangster, *The Path to Perfection: An Examination and Restatement of John Wesley's Doctrine of Christian Perfection* (London: Epworth, 1943). His 1954 title *The Pure in Heart* is less technical.
5. Sangster, *Doctor Sangster,* 67.
6. Ibid., 311ff.
7. W. E. Sangster, *The Craft of Sermon Construction and Illustration* (Grand Rapids: Baker, 1981) combines two books. Sangster preached forty minutes to an hour.
8. John Bishop, "William Edwin Sangster: An Evangelical Greatheart," *Preaching,* September-October 1987, 48.
9. W. E. Sangster, *He Is Able* (London: Wyvern, 1936). Dedicated to his wife, Margaret, with the lovely words, "With whom it is as easy to keep in love as fall in love."
10. Frank Cumbers, ed., *Daily Readings from W. E. Sangster* (New York: Revell, 1966).
11. W. E. Sangster, *The Secret of Radiant Life* (New York: Abingdon, 1957).
12. W. E. Sangster, *Sangster of Westminster* (London: Marshall, Morgan, and Scott, 1960), 59.

11.7 THE KESWICK CONNECTION ON THE DEEPENING OF THE SPIRITUAL LIFE

> Preaching is the art of making a sermon and delivering it? Why, no, that is not preaching. Preaching is the art of making a preacher and delivering that.
>
> —Bishop William Quayle

It is fair to say that in the face of all her foes and the swirling ideological currents which beat upon her, humanly speaking the church of Jesus Christ should have been long dead and theological orthodoxy but a corpse long since interred. As Paul Johnson has observed, "The most extraordinary thing about the twentieth century was the failure of God to die!"[1] The vaunted death-of-God theologians molder in a theological grave, while a faithful gospel preacher like Billy Graham flourishes. Noted scholars speak about "Wesley's World Revolution" in which "throughout the Third World and the former Communist bloc, a vibrant Protestant Christianity is radically remaking people's lives."[2]

A catalyst for the preservation and propagation of biblical Christianity has been the Keswick conventions, in which worship and preaching are central. Controversial since its founding in 1875 and centering on annual conventions in Keswick in the English Lake Country, Keswick has drawn from a broad span of denominational bodies and has as its theme "All One in Christ Jesus." Anglican in its inception, Keswick emphasizes on successive days the nature and holiness of God, the sin of man, redemption through Christ, the lordship of Christ, and the fullness of the Spirit.[3] Outreach and mission as inescapable concomitants are of the essence.[4] We shall examine some representative preachers in this renewal movement and see the criticality of their preaching.

---

1. Paul Johnson, *The Quest for God: A Personal Pilgrimage* (New York: Harper/Collins, 1996), 6.
2. David Martin, "Wesley's World Revolution," *National Review* (December 31, 1995): 26.
3. Of the several histories of Keswick, I think the best is J. C. Pollock, *The Keswick Story* (Chicago: Moody, 1964).
4. An instance is the legendary Anglican Temple Gairdner, who surrendered his life for missions at Keswick in 1893 and burned himself out in ministry to the Muslims in Cairo. Close to Samuel Zwemer. See Constance E. Padwick, *Temple Gairdner of Cairo* (London: SPCK, 1929). His patron saint was General Gordon of Khartoum.

11.7.1 Evan H. Hopkins—The Theologian of Keswick

> Many can give Bible expositions who are not able to help seeking souls into the fullness of the blessing. We must keep to the original lines of the Movement; in other words, we must set forth definitely Sanctification by faith.
>
> —Evan H. Hopkins

> I ask Thee not for subtle thought, for pictures exquisitely wrought,
> For speech of grand or graceful turn, for tones that thrill and words that burn;
> But let me touch Thy garment's hem, and bear the fragrance unto them.
>
> —trans. from the French of Theodore Monod,
> a very close friend of Hopkins

Keswick has been more than spiritual gourmandism. The movement arose out of a concern that orthodoxy had become "iron-cold, hard and dull." The message of full salvation in Christ was intended to be bread not confection, not a time for discussion so much as a time for decision.

Rising out of higher life meetings at Broadlands, Oxford, and Brighton, the prime mover of Keswick was Canon **Thomas Dundas Harford-Battersby** (1822–1883), who had been living in St. John's in Keswick for the last thirty-two years of his life. He presided at the first convention.[1] Although not at the first convention but at the next forty was Harford-Battersby's good friend **Evan H. Hopkins** (1837–1918). Hopkins, who spoke Spanish fluently, was born in South America, the son of a British mining engineer. After returning to England, he worked as a mining engineer in Dorset, but while there was converted and began to preach. He matriculated at King's College, London, where the strong biblical teaching of E. H. Plumptre especially moved him. He was ordained in 1865 and served a curacy at what became St. Paul's, Portman Square, and counted Lord Cairns and Lord Shaftesbury among its constituents.[2] From 1870 to 1893 Hopkins served Holy Trinity, Richmond, in Surrey. One said:

> I can see him now, in his old black gown, with the quiet manner, the well-sustained voice, the clear-cut divisions, the simple well-illustrated teachings, making the things of God real and practical to a schoolboy. I remember the hush of expectation, when all faces were turned toward the pulpit.[3]

Hopkins' messages were richly expositional.[4] In this time he not only led in the development of Keswick but also established the Church Army. He dealt with misunderstanding and criticism of Keswick in the recognition that some were puzzled, some provoked, and some were persuaded. Among these "converts" were Bishop Moule, R. W. Dale, D. L. Moody, who attended conventions, and even J. C. Ryle, who never spoke at Keswick but did seem to modify his earlier hostility.[5]

Understanding sanctification as both crisis and process, Hopkins' exposition of the Keswick message stands as the classical statement.[6] In 1893 he moved to St. Luke's in South Kensington, a church that seated twelve hundred people. He regularly used the aftermeeting for the care of souls under conviction.[7]

Whether in the tent at Keswick or elsewhere, Hopkins' ministry was astonishingly across denominational lines. He visited Sweden and held seven meetings under the aegis of Prince Oskar and Princess Ebba Bernadotte. Along with Lord Radstock, he was called to anoint Archdeacon Basil Wilberforce according to James 5.[8] He visited the Holy Land several times and, along with Alfred Eidersheim, was the prime mover in raising funds for the Jerusalem Garden Tomb Maintenance Fund.[9] He was likely the first preacher who used the differentiation of faith-fact-feeling to positive advantage.

Hopkins was dedicated to preaching not only justification but sanctification as well. Above all, in his preaching and leadership, Hopkins was the foremost exponent of full salvation in Britain at this time. He retired in 1906 and moved to Woburn Chase in Surrey. At his funeral, Prebendary Webb-Peploe, his closest associate in Keswick, and Bishop Taylor Smith spoke. The hymn that Keswick inspired Frances Ridley Havergal to write "Like a River Glorious" made an apt musical tribute.

---

1. J. Elder Cumming, *Holy Men of God* (Chicago: Moody, rev. 1961), 227–37. Cumming, a Scottish Presbyterian, was also well heard at Keswick and led the Keswick convention that was held in Glasgow.

2. Alexander Smellie, *Evan Henry Hopkins* (London: Marshall Brothers, 1920), 33. Smellie, himself from the Reformed Presbyterian Church, wrote *Men of the Covenant* and gave memorable messages at Keswick, especially his 1919 Bible readings on "We Beheld His Glory," in Herbert Stevenson, ed., *The Ministry of Keswick* (Grand Rapids: Zondervan, 1963), 1:327ff.
3. Ibid., 36.
4. Ibid., 46.
5. The most caustic onslaught of all time was led by B. B. Warfield in his *Perfectionism* (Philadelphia: Presbyterian and Reformed, rev. 1967). The attack on Keswick is largely *argumentum ad hominem* in relation to the Pearsall Smiths, though Warfield does hold out an olive branch to the "Arminian" James McConkey and his well-known work *The Three-fold Secret of the Holy Spirit* (Pittsburgh: Silver, 1897). McConkey, a graduate of Princeton University, like many other North Americans imbibed the Keswick message; see Louise Harrison McCraw, *James H. McConkey: A Man of God* (Grand Rapids: Zondervan, 1939), 46ff. The message is union with, yielding to, and abiding in Christ.
6. Evan H. Hopkins, *The Law of Liberty in the Spiritual Life* (Philadelphia: The Sunday School Times, 1952).
7. Smellie, *Evan Henry Hopkins,* 119.
8. Ibid., 192.
9. Ibid., 174.

11.7.2 H. C. G. Moule—The Compass of Keswick

> We want preachers so filled with Christ, by the Holy Ghost, that they cannot get away from Him as their theme; that they know they have in Him the Word, the Message, authentic from the throne, for every need of the human soul. We want those to preach to us who are never tired of exploring the written Word for the glories of the living Word, and who come out from their exploration to set Him forth, in all the power of faith, in the spoken Word.
>
> Let us preachers be, in a profound sense, "men of one Book," and above all, "men of one Name," and we shall never lack listeners.
>
> —H. C. G. Moule

Initially he was cautious about the Keswick message, but after he attended and experienced drastic spiritual rejuvenation, **Handley G. C. Moule** (1841–1920) became a strong leader of Keswick and one of the mainstays of the platform speakers. Moule was born into a Dorsetshire vicarage in a family which gave many clergy, scholars, and missionaries to the cause of Christ (cf. 11.3). He studied at Cambridge and served two curacies with his father.

For nineteen years Moule was dean of Ridley Hall at Cambridge, a divinity training school founded for evangelically-minded candidates for the Church of England.[1] He often preached at Simeon's old church, Holy Trinity, endeavoring "to maintain the fine evangelical traditions of that great leader."[2] He then served as Norrisian Professor of Divinity at Cambridge and in 1901 became bishop of Durham as successor to Westcott, who in turn had succeeded J. B. Lightfoot in the tradition of Bishop Butler. Both Westcott and Lightfoot were also professors at Cambridge and shone brightly in this remarkable constellation of conservative thinkers there.[3]

Moule was known for his scintillating expositions of the Greek text, which he gave nightly at Cambridge. Later he gave these expositions at an early hour in the chapel at Ridley Hall, influencing more than one thousand young men. Moule's "dark wavy hair, prominent nose and full lips" made him look like the half-Huguenot that he was.[4] He played a pivotal role in Moody's mission at Cambridge and had an insatiable hunger for holiness.

Moule became convicted that his critical attitude to Keswick involved a great deal of "mixed motive, jealousy and prejudice."[5] In response to the strong biblical preaching of Evan Hopkins, Moule and his wife were deeply stirred and both stood in surrender to Christ. Even after Moule moved into his nineteen-year bishopric in Durham and his remarkable ministry to miners during the world war, his profile at Keswick was commanding. It was said of Moule's hearers, "They came expecting to be led to the Cross and to hear of Christ, and they were never disappointed."[6]

Moule's role in the Cambridge Greek New Testament, the Cambridge Bible, and the Expositor's Bible (he did Romans) is well known. His commentary on the Greek text of Philippians, for instance, is most helpful in the CGNT,[7] and his devotional commentaries on Ephesians and Colossians are rich.[8] His messages on the Pastorals are outstanding,[9] as are his studies on the Holy Spirit.[10]

Moule's messages on ecclesiastical occasions never disappoint. He trumpets for conscientious work in the text and for intimacy with Christ as absolutely essential:

> "That they might be with Him, and that He might send them forth to preach." There is the first, the deepest, the absolutely vital qualification of the preacher who is to be true; "that he should be with Him." Personal knowledge of the Lord Jesus Christ, "nothing between," is the first requisite for the preaching apostle; and it is the first requisite assuredly for the man who, in any sense instinct with life and power, would be the preaching apostle's successor.[11]

A typical jewel is "The Cross and the Spirit," an exposition of Galatians that captured the Keswick theme so poignantly.[12] His first message at Keswick in 1886 was titled "The 'Total Abstinence' of the Gospel," from Ephesians 4:1–2, 31–32.[13] From a message to ministers out of Luke 1:19 on the subject "Essential Principles of Christian Service," he drew three mains: (1) in the presence of God; (2) standing in the presence of God; and (3) "I am sent"; words well worth weighing for the servants of Christ.[14]

At the end of Moule's long involvement at Keswick, one seasoned listener said, "In some ways, the most impressive speaker I ever heard at Keswick was Dr. Handley Moule. His very presence seemed to express the beauty of the Lord. He had a rich, cultured voice, and his spiritual intensity was so great that tiny beads of moisture covered his brow."[15] Dr. Moule left a legacy of orthodoxy and truth.

1. As evidence of his stand, see H. C. G. Moule, *The Evangelical School in the Church of England* (London: Nisbet, 1901).
2. F. R. Webber, *A History of Preaching in Britain and America* (Milwaukee: Northwestern, 1952), 1:634.
3. Arthur Westcott, *The Life and Letters of Brooke Foss Westcott* (London: Macmillan, 1903). Westcott's great commentaries on the Johannine corpus, on Hebrews, and on Ephesians are choice. He had a weak voice but took great pains in articulation. The scholarly fecundity of this circle is amazing—Westcott's domestic chaplain, Charles H. Boutflower, has given us a splendid study on the Book of Daniel. For a measured evaluation of J. B. Lightfoot's scholarly stature, see Warren W. Wiersbe, *Living with the Giants* (Grand Rapids: Baker, 1993), 47ff. Lightfoot on Galatians, Philippians, Colossians, and the Fathers is peerless.
4. J. C. Pollock, *The Keswick Story* (Chicago: Moody, 1964), 68.
5. Ibid., 69.
6. Webber, *A History of Preaching,* 1:635.
7. H. C. G. Moule, *Philippians in the Cambridge Greek Testament* (Cambridge, Mass.: Cambridge University Press, 1897).
8. H. C. G. Moule, *Ephesian Studies* (London: Pickering and Inglis, n.d.); *Colossian and Philemon Studies* (New York: Revell, n.d.). Though strong in the great text, these are in the valued genre of devotional commentaries.
9. H. C. G. Moule, *The Second Epistle to Timothy* (Grand Rapids: Baker, 1952).
10. H. C. G. Moule, *Veni Creator: Thoughts on the Person and Work of the Holy Spirit* (London: Hodder and Stoughton, 1890).
11. H. C. G. Moule, *My Brethren and Companions and Other Sermons* (London: Nisbet, 1905), 23f.
12. H. C. G. Moule, *The Cross and the Spirit* (London: Pickering and Inglis, n.d.).
13. H. C. G. Moule, "The 'Total Abstinence' of the Gospel," in *Keswick's Authentic Voice* (London: Marshall, Morgan, and Scott, 1959), 51ff.
14. Ibid., 521ff.
15. Ibid., 27.

11.7.3 W. H. Griffith Thomas—The Scripturality of Keswick

Preachers must know this Book if they are to preach acceptably. If we go to our people with "Thus saith the Lord," this Book must be in mind and heart and life. There is no Christianity worthy of the name that is not based upon this Book. By this Book we stand; on it we rest; with it we fight; through it we shall conquer, because it is the Word of God which liveth and abideth forever.

There is another criticism, the Highest Criticism. Here it is. "To this man will I look, even to him that is of a contrite spirit and trembleth at my word." I now refer to the criticism of the humble soul. You will find that text in Isaiah 66:2. Also another text: "The Word of God is a critic of the thoughts and intents of the heart" (Heb. 4:12). If the soul of man will allow God's Word to criticise it, if we will do a little more of that trem-

> bling at God's Word; that will be the Highest Criticism and it will be the criterion that will settle almost everything for us.
>
> —W. H. Griffith Thomas

The Bible-based and Christ-centered nature of Keswick preaching is seen at its quintessential best in **William Henry Griffith Thomas** (1861–1924), whose varied gifts and multiplied ministries brought great blessing to the church. Few things were positive in his early life. His father died before he was born. He was reared by Grandfather Griffith for a while, but by fourteen he had to leave school because of the financial stringencies of the family. When he was sixteen, Thomas was asked to teach Sunday school in Oswestry, Shropshire, his hometown, but was not at the time a converted person. His teaching efforts were frustrated, but through the witness of two young men he came to know Christ at eighteen. He testified:

> When I awoke the next morning, my soul was simply overflowing with joy, and since then I have never doubted that it was on that Saturday night, I was born again, converted to God.[1]

Thomas went up to London to work for an uncle and began to study Greek. Bishop Frederick Temple admonished him "never to neglect his Greek New Testament for a single day."[2] Offered a lay curacy at St. Peter's, Clerkenwell, where he attended, he was able to take studies at King's College with distinction and was ordained in 1885. From 1888 to 1896 he was curate at St. Aldgate in Oxford. With the decline of Canon Christopher, he did most of the preaching and pastoral work and was able to win the Junior Septuagint Prize and obtain his B.D. with first class honors at Christ College. He went on to be vicar of St. Paul's, Portman Square (where Sherlock Holmes and Dr. Watson of Baker Street would have attended, had they had a mind to do so, it being very close) and a congregation where later J. Stuart Holden, Bishop Goodwin-Hudson, Prebendary Colin Kerr, Canon Harry Sutton, and others have served with such distinction.

From 1905 to 1910 Thomas went back to Oxford as principal of Wycliffe Hall, an evangelical Anglican training college. He exerted an immense influence for the historic faith as "the icy blasts of Higher Criticism were blowing from Germany, and shaking the faith of many."[3] Lawrence of Arabia and his brothers attended his Sunday afternoon classes on the Greek New Testament on occasion. In 1910 he took a professorial chair at Wycliffe College, Toronto, but when he arrived it turned out not to be systematic theology but Old Testament. Still he filled the chair competently and extended his ministry on both sides of the Atlantic.

Thomas' staunch midday messages on "The Bible and the Spiritual Life" at Keswick in 1914 are deep and compelling.[4] With Lewis Sperry Chafer and A. B. Winchester of Knox Presbyterian Church in Toronto, he founded Dallas Theological Seminary, but his death in Duluth, Minnesota, in 1924 precluded his ever teaching there.

What strikes one about Thomas' preaching is his solid biblical content and his keen sense of theological construct. His Stone Lectures at Princeton in 1913 on the Holy Spirit would have to be included in any list of ten key works on the subject.[5] His prolific output has put us in his debt particularly for his devotional commentaries on Genesis,[6] the works of the apostle John,[7] and the works of the apostle Peter.[8] His writings on Hebrews formed the basis for his highly touted Keswick Bible Readings in 1922.[9] His devotional commentary on Romans is likewise "the finest of the wheat."[10]

He would say to preachers, "We cannot make up for failure in our devotional life by redoubling energy in service."[11] The breadth of his own study is seen in his delightful compendium of Christology titled *Christianity Is Christ.* Typically he makes the case for the objective reality of the resurrection of Christ.[12] Samples of his sermons show clearly outlined messages with mains and subs drawn from the text and an obvious ability to preach it home with pointed application and illustration.[13]

Although Thomas was of such size that he had to have a bicycle especially made for him, he cast a much larger spiritual shadow. In G.T., as he was called, we have a pulpit giant.

---

1. Warren W. Wiersbe, *Living with the Giants* (Grand Rapids: Baker, 1993), 168.
2. Ibid., 169. These sketches put into book form a series of articles in *Moody Monthly*.
3. Herbert F. Stevenson, *The Ministry of Keswick* (Grand Rapids: Zondervan, 1963), 1:197.
4. Ibid., 199ff. "The messages are The Bible as (1) Revelation; (2) Authority; (3) Message; (4) Power."
5. W. H. Griffith Thomas, *The Holy Spirit of God* (Grand Rapids: Kregel, 1986). Great chapter on modernism.
6. W. H. Griffith Thomas, *Genesis: A Devotional Commentary* (Grand Rapids: Eerdmans, 1946).
7. W. H. Griffith Thomas, *The Apostle John: Studies in His Life and Writings* (Grand Rapids: Eerdmans, 1946).
8. W. H. Griffith Thomas, *The Apostle Peter: A Devotional Commentary* (Grand Rapids: Kregel, 1984).
9. W. H. Griffith Thomas, *Let Us Go On: The Secret of Christian Progress in Hebrews* (Grand Rapids: Zondervan, 1944).
10. W. H. Griffith Thomas, *St. Paul's Epistle to the Romans: A Devotional Commentary* (Grand Rapids: Kregel, 1974).
11. Wiersbe, *Living with the Giants,* 172.
12. W. H. Griffith Thomas, *Christianity Is Christ* (Grand Rapids: Kregel, 1981). Impressive bibliography as always.
13. W. H. Griffith Thomas, *The Christian Life and How to Live It* (Chicago: Moody, 1919). Pay close attention to "What We Believe" from Titus 3:4–7 as a sterling example of expository preaching with finesse. A sparkling little gem is the final message in the collection on "God's Surprises" from Genesis 48:11.

11.7.4 J. Stuart Holden—The Rock of Keswick

> At the heart of all human fellowship with God is a cross. He was never so near to the heart of the world's sin and need as when Christ Himself said, "My God, why hast Thou forsaken me?" And this is the centre of faith for us; not the mount on which the Teacher stood, not even the manger in which the Brother lay, but the cross on which the Saviour hung and died. It is this fact, and this recognition which transform sin into penitence and life into glad devotion to the Lord.
>
> —J. Stuart Holden

F. B. Meyer and G. Campbell Morgan were eagerly heard at Keswick, but the dominant figure and the key leader of the movement for many years was the exceptionally able preacher **John Stuart Holden** (1874–1934). Thus while the aforementioned were Baptist and Congregational, and while there were Brethren (George Goodman) and Methodists (Charles Inwood and J. Gregory Mantle), the core of leadership at Keswick was quite consistently Anglican.

Holden was born in Liverpool and converted at sixteen. He studied at Liverpool College and worked in a bank for five years. Some patrons made it possible for him to attend Cambridge, where H. C. G. Moule took him under his wing. After graduating in 1899, Holden was ordained to a curacy at Bath. For some years he traveled with the parochial Anglican evangelist, Canon W. Hay Aitken, also a Keswick preacher in considerable demand. Holden married in 1901. In 1905 he succeeded Griffith Thomas at St. Paul's, Portman Square, where he ministered for almost thirty years. Immediately he moved evening prayers to Sunday afternoon and established a Sunday evening evangelistic service. He also organized a well-attended Bible school.

His "mellifluous voice and polished oratory" and his eminently biblical and rich preaching made him a perennial favorite at Keswick, in North America, and in his West London pulpit.[1] "Dapper little Holden" as he was called, first appeared at Keswick in 1901 and served as chairman of the council from 1924 to 1930 at a time of some innovation. At the same time he was home director of the China Inland Mission, president of the Missionary School of Medicine, one of the founders of the Evangelical Union of South America (which came into being after the World Missionary Conference at Edinburgh when a false ecumenicity refused to regard South America as a missionary continent), and editor of *The Christian* (1915–1920). His honorary D.D. was bestowed by Westminster College in Fulton, Missouri.

Strong-voiced **J. Russell Howden** was one of Holden's truest compatriots.[2] Howden had notable ministries at Tunbridge Wells and at one of the Wren churches, St. Andrews, Holborn, and gave the Bible readings at Keswick five times. **Jessie Penn-Lewis** of Wales, whose husband was a former parishioner of Evans Hopkins, was also close to Holden, who appeared with her at the first Keswick in Wales.[3]

Holden's Bible readings at the Portstewart Convention in Northern Ireland broke new ground and furnished a sample of the kind of exposition of which he was so capable.[4] In 1914, just before the war, he gave a sermon at Keswick from Daniel 3:18, "But if not," which made a profound impression and seemed almost prophetic.[5]

At times we wish Holden would expose more text than he does, though his sermon "God's Voice in the Whirlwind" on Job is superb.[6] His analysis of the enemies of the heart in Matthew 6:19–21, the moth, rust, and the thief, is truly classic.[7] Holden had a knack for titling sermons, giving us such gems as "When Nothing Seems to Happen," from 1 Kings 18:43, or "The Polestar of the New Life," from Psalm 16:8, or "The Transformation of the Unlikely" from 1 Samuel 22:2.[8]

The Holdens were independently wealthy and childless, but there were some conflicts within the council, most of them related to leadership style, during the 1920s when he was at his zenith.[9] Yet Intervarsity Fellowship was founded in large part under a Keswickian influence as Norman Grubb, nephew of Keswick stalwart George Grubb, was quick to point out.[10] The steady biblical sermons of J. Stuart Holden helped keep Keswick on course. He died just short of his sixtieth birthday.

Fascinatingly, he and Mrs. Holden had been booked on the *Titanic* for her ill-fated voyage, in earlier years, but were unable to make the trip because of illness.[11]

---

1. Herbert F. Stevenson, *The Ministry of Keswick* (Grand Rapids: Zondervan, 1963), 1:245.
2. Herbert F. Stevenson, *The Ministry of Keswick* (London: Marshall, Morgan, and Scott, 1964), 2:57–58. Holden's series on "A Man's Foes: The World, the Flesh, and the Devil; and the Way of Victory" given in 1924 may be found in this anthology. See also his unusual *Life Indeed: The Victorious Life in Four Aspects* (London: Pickering, 1933).
3. Mrs. Penn-Lewis' gifts are to be seen in her justly noted *War on the Saints* in collaboration with Evan Roberts (Parkstone, Dorset: Overcomer Literature Trust, n.d.). Some of her best expositions include *The Conquest of Canaan: Sidelights on the Spiritual Battlefield; The Story of Job;* and *The Hidden Ones: Union with Christ traced in the Song of Songs. The Overcomer* magazine she founded continues to be published by the Overcomer Trust.
4. J. Stuart Holden, *Some Old Testament Parables* (London: Pickering and Inglis, 1934). His last public utterances.
5. J. Stuart Holden, *Your Reasonable Service* (London: Marshall Brothers, 1921), 162ff. The following year (1915), Holden delivered a remarkable series, "Perplexities of the Divine Providence," in Herbert F. Stevenson, ed. *Ministry of Keswick,* 1:247ff.
6. J. Stuart Holden, "God's Voice in the Whirlwind," in *Keswick's Triumphant Voice* (Grand Rapids: Zondervan, 1963), 269.
7. J. Stuart Holden, "Life's True Values," in *Your Reasonable Service,* 97ff.
8. J. Stuart Holden, *Redeeming Vision* (London: Robert Scott, 1908), 22ff., 56ff. The latter is one of the best sermons I know on the Cave of Adullam, although J. C. Massee's is I think better; cf. *Seven Sunday Night Talks* (Chicago: Moody, 1926).
9. J. C. Pollock, *The Keswick Story* (Chicago: Moody Press, 1964), 145ff.

10. Ibid., 141. Norman Grubb married the daughter of C. T. Studd of "The Cambridge Seven." Grubb became a missionary and director of Worldwide Evangelization Crusade. He was a great teacher of the deeper life but came dangerously close to pantheism in his last years; see his life story, *Once Caught, No Escape* (Ft. Washington, Pa.: CLC, n.d.).
11. Other collections of sermons by J. Stuart Holden, *The God-lit Road* (London: Marshall Brothers, 1926); *A Voice for God* (London: Hodder and Stoughton, 1932); *The All-round Christian Life* (London: Pickering and Inglis, 1954).

11.7.5 ANDREW MURRAY—THE COMET OF KESWICK

> My first text is: "We preach Christ crucified." 1 Cor. 1:23. May it be true! But I feel it very difficult not to preach myself, by attending too much to the beauty of thought and language and feeling too little that God alone can teach me to preach.
>
> —from Andrew Murray's first sermon after returning home from study abroad

> Would that the spiritual prosperity of the Church were as encouraging as its numbers increase in my congregations. I begin to fear that the state of a great majority of members is much sadder than I at first realized, and I feel in some little measure that nothing but God's mighty Spirit is able to conquer the deep enmity of the unconverted heart. I rejoice at the proposal of a weekly concert of prayer throughout the Church.
>
> —Andrew Murray

> His weekday English services are mainly for the young. I am obliged to listen very attentively to all his sermons for he makes me his critic and always expects to know just what I think. I tell him it is good for him that he has a simple congregation for whom he must bring down his ideas to their comprehension. He is obliged to clip his wings or else . . . I think he would be in some danger if he had a clever and intellectual congregation; he would become too fanciful or too new, if I may use this expression, in his sermons. Now they must be plain and practical, and shorn of the new, varied, and perhaps a little wild interpretations and symbolic meanings that he favors me with.
>
> —Emma Murray

He visited Keswick as early as 1882 when seeking a cure for his throat, returning only once to speak in a never-to-be-forgotten appearance in 1895. The South African Dutch Reformed preacher **Andrew Murray** (1828–1917) both embodied and emblazoned the Keswick message in his preaching. He led the South African Keswick movement, and his numerous writings continue to be a blessing around the world. In his classic biography, Professor Du Plessis shows why Murray must be seen as "the mountaineer of the higher Christian life movement."[1] The story of Andrew Murray is the gripping chronicle of a mighty man of God who transcended ecclesiastical controversy and national crisis in a worldwide ministry of preaching, Christian education, writing, and the pastorate.

Murray was born in South Africa, his father being a Scottish immigrant pastor of the old-light secessionistic Presbyterians. The elder Murray served the Dutch Reformed Church in Graaf-Reinet for forty-five years. Andrew's mother was of German-Calvinistic Dutch ancestry. In this pious home, visits from Livingstone and Moffat were well remembered. Because of the paucity of good schools, Andrew and his older brother John were sent to Scotland for schooling, first to Aberdeen, where they lived with their preacher uncle, John Murray. This was a time of much reading for young Andrew, and both sons came under the influence of Chalmers, Candlish, the Bonars, and McCheyne.[2] Other discernible influences were the writings of William Law, Madame Guyon, Professor J. T. Beck (cf. 9.4.4), and Count Zinzendorf.

After receiving their M.A. degrees at Aberdeen, the Murrays went on to Utrecht in Holland for divinity studies, since they would be ministering in the Dutch language. Here Andrew was converted.[3] The Haldane influence from Scotland tended to temper his Reformed thinking and a meeting with Pastor Blumhardt left an indelible impression upon Murray. Here the seeds were planted for his continuing emphasis on the healing of the body (cf. 9.4.3).[4] The unfolding scenario of Murray's ministry follows.

At twenty-one, he was inducted as pastor in Bloemfontein and stayed eleven years. He was the first regular pastor in a parish of fifty thousand square miles. Murray made repeated trips across the Vaal to the seven thousand immigrant Dutch farmers.[5] At the end of this time, he was part of a delegation to protest the withdrawal of British sovereignty north of the Orange River. Asked to fill Surrey Chapel in the months prior to the coming of Newman Hall, Murray felt unable to do so and spent the next two years in Europe.[6]

Murray married Emma Rutherford, the daughter of Church of England immigrants. Emma transcribed all of his books.[7] The couple took their honeymoon in an oxcart journey to the field. The Anglo-Boer War isolated him, but Murray continued to write and speak and travel as he was able. The Murrays served in Worcester, one hundred miles east of Cape Town (1860–1864), and had a tremendous visit of the Spirit in revival. They were able to reach the native Africans as well, and fifty young men went into Christian service out of this one congregation.[8]

Eventually Murray took a joint pastorate in the large Dutch Reformed Church in Cape Town (1864–1871). When he retired at seventy-eight, Murray served the Wellington pastorate (1871–1906). He established here the Huguenot Seminary to train more than one thousand young women as schoolteachers (after the Mt. Holyoke, Massachusetts, model) as well as a Missionary Training Institute. Dr. Daniel Malan, later Prime Minister of South Africa, was one of his students.

Murray built a place at Wellington called Clairvaux for retirement. It was said that "meals with the Murrays were like the Holy Communion."[9] Alexander Whyte called him "a happy man."

Always physically frail, Murray lost his voice for two years. Out of this "time of silence" (particularly through the counsel of Pastor Stockmeier, the Swiss-German pastor who also spoke at Keswick; cf. 9.5.3) there came a spiritual deepening and the writing of several of his many books on prayer.[10]

Murray's preaching was steeped in Scripture. His incomparable devotional commentary on Hebrews delves deeply into the text.[11] His message at Keswick in 1895 from Mark 10:35ff. on "The Pathway to the Higher Life" had a phenomenal effect. His mains were

I. The blessing which consecration seeks
II. The mistakes that consecration makes
III. The consecration which Christ demands
IV. The consecration yielded
V. The contention of the disciples about it
VI. Their relationship to their fellow men[12]

Murray's style was intense. He was gifted with "no peculiar charm or poetry or sentiment or willing sweetness;" his words were "naked and unadorned" but "full of weight and power." He could be vehement in the pulpit, but even when he was almost deaf and quite stooped in old age, one listener remarked, "What a voice for such a body!"[13]

Murray was an evangelist who introduced D. L. Moody's aftermeeting into the very staid Dutch Calvinism. He came to this after preaching on hell and sensing such response that many needed to be counseled and prayed with.[14] He fought liberalism and rationalism with great vigor. He preached a widely chronicled series of thirteen sermons against the liberal and Unitarian ideas that were seeping in.[15]

Murray preached the holiness message of Keswick and was ablaze with missionary passion. Few have spoken so clearly to the needs of our hearts as has Andrew Murray.

---

1. J. Du Plessis, *The Life of Andrew Murray of South Africa* (London: Marshall Brothers, 1919).
2. W. M. Douglas, *Andrew Murray and His Message: One of God's Choice Saints* (New York: Revell, n.d.), 26–27.
3. Ibid., 37.
4. Leona Choy, *Andrew Murray: Apostle of Abiding Love* (Ft. Washington, Pa.: CLC, 1978), 45.
5. Douglas, *Andrew Murray and His Message,* 60.
6. Ibid., 72ff.
7. Choy, *Andrew Murray,* 63.
8. Ibid., 85.
9. Ibid., 221.
10. Ibid., 139. N.B., *The Ministry of Intercession* (New York: Revell, 1898); *With Christ in the School of Prayer* (Philadelphia: Henry Altemus, n.d.); *The Prayer Life* (London: Marshall Brothers, 1913). He wrote 240 books.
11. Andrew Murray, *The Holiest of All* (Westwood, N.J.: Revell, n.d.); also *The True*

Vine (Chicago: Moody, n.d.); *Abide in Christ* (New York: Grosset and Dunlap, n.d.); *Waiting on God* (New York: Revell, 1895).

12. Andrew Murray, "The Pathway to the Higher Life," in *Keswick's Authentic Voice* (London: Marshall, Morgan, and Scott, 1959), 292ff. Another gifted preacher who served in Johannesburg and was well heard at Keswick was Gerald B. Griffiths, who also served Spurgeon's Tabernacle, Charlotte Chapel in Edinburgh and in Toronto. His messages at Keswick in 1958 and his printed sermons are remembered: *My Brother's Keeper* (London: Marshall, Morgan, and Scott, 1962); also "Operation Uplight" from Exodus 17:8–13 in *World Vision Magazine* (October 1965): 4ff.
13. Douglas, *Andrew Murray and His Message,* 131.
14. Choy, *Andrew Murray,* 98.
15. An earlier book of great charm, *The Children for Christ: Thoughts for Christian Parents on the Consecration of the Home Life* (New York: Revell, n.d.). See also *The Lord's Table* (Chicago: Moody, n.d.); *The School of Obedience* (Chicago: Moody, 1898); *Absolute Surrender* (Chicago: Moody, n.d.). A compilation of nine typical sermons.

11.7.6 Bishop J. Taylor Smith—The Character of Keswick

> I cannot give any decisive answer until I have consulted my Lord and Master.
>
> Heaven is more real to me than earth.
>
> The stream of power comes from the enthroned Christ in Heaven and in us.
>
> Many read, few feed. . . . You cannot be noble unless you love your Bible.
>
> —Bishop J. Taylor Smith

"He became one of the most popular preachers of his day, ever keeping the conversion of souls as the centre of his theme and illustrating his sermons by incidents drawn largely from his own experience."[1] This was the thumbnail evaluation of **Bishop John Taylor Smith** (1860–1937), who came out of modest circumstances. Born in Kendal in England, his father was a coal agent who took steps to set his two sons up in the jewelry business. At age twelve young Smith was converted.[2] Immediately he set up his lifelong custom of "the morning watch"—breakfast, time in the Word, and prayer. He was very athletic, and at seventy-five still astounded friends with his ability to do a backward somersault into the water—notwithstanding his considerable girth. Smith was serious about the Christian life and, despite ridicule and scorn, knelt by his bed morning and evening in his dormitory. He was also a dedicated soulwinner.

Smith trained not at the universities but at Highbury College, vigorously Protestant and evangelical. He lived his whole life with the deep sense of God ordering his goings. "As then, so now," was his motto. He served as curate in St. Paul's in the London suburb of Upper Norwood, where he built a great Sunday school and youth work.[3] Smith ultimately became president of the Children's Special Service Mission. At first he preached extempore but was urged to seek greater cohesion.

> He never failed to realize that the sermon, carefully prepared beforehand and then preached with or without a few pulpit notes, has a much greater hold on most people than a read sermon.[4]

In 1891, after considerable trysting before God and having an almost mystical experience in the Livingstone niche in Westminster Abbey, he surrendered to become a canon-missioner in Sierra Leone, West Africa, called by some the white man's grave. He was consecrated bishop of Sierra Leone and the Canary Islands in 1897 in St. Paul's Cathedral in London under the aegis of Archbishop Frederick Temple. Through an intriguing set of providential circumstances, he became a favorite preacher of Queen Victoria and, at the urging of King Edward VII, was appointed Chaplain-General of the British military. For more than twenty-three years "this tubby, serene, approachable bachelor bishop remained a potent influence in the British Army."[5] Despite criticism, the question he always pressed was, "What would you say to a man who was fatally wounded, but conscious, and only ten minutes to live?"[6] Smith gave himself unstintingly to Scripture distribution among the forces and to the cause of total abstinence from alcohol and nicotine.

Often called "the bishop of the merry soul," Smith faced the massive postwar problems and then took retirement at sixty-five. Yet he still spoke at Swedish Keswick under the sponsorship of Prince Bernadotte and his wife,[7] and conducted children's meetings at Royal Albert Hall. He never wrote a book, but what he wrote on the wide margins of his great Bible has been published and is a veritable encyclopedia of spiritual riches.[8]

Pollock is right that Smith was more an excavator of biblical gems than a true expositor.[9] His sermon introductions were often striking and there was a freshness and an originality in his preaching.[10] He was a graphic artist in preaching and such a character! Stevenson conjures up the picture of the "portly figure in ecclesiastical garb (gaiters and apron), surmounted by a kindly, shrewd, humorous countenance, with twinkling eyes behind rimless pince-nez."[11]

Smith did much personal counseling at Keswick. His sermon on "The Blessed Life" on the Beatitudes in 1913 was long cherished by those who heard it.[12] His 1922 message on Samson, titled "How to Overcome Temptation," is typical.[13] A true Christian gentleman exuding honesty, humor, courtesy, kindness, and generosity, J. Taylor Smith made a great impact on those whom he met. While returning home from Australia, bowing his head at breakfast somewhere in the Mediterranean, he was suddenly called home.[14]

---

1. Maurice Whitlow, *J. Taylor Smith: Everybody's Bishop* (Grand Rapids: Zondervan, 1938), 35.
2. Ibid., 185. This appendix gives an address in which Smith gives his own account of his conversion and struggles.

3. Ibid., 30.
4. Ibid., 35.
5. J. C. Pollock, *The Keswick Story* (Chicago: Moody, 1964), 144.
6. Whitlow, *J. Taylor Smith,* 97.
7. Ibid., 113.
8. Percy O. Ruoff, *Gems from Bishop Taylor Smith's Bible* (London: Marshall, Morgan, and Scott, n.d.).
9. Pollock, *The Keswick Story,* 144.
10. Whitlow, *J. Taylor Smith,* 139.
11. Ibid., 141.
12. J. Taylor Smith, "The Blessed Life," in *Keswick's Authentic Voice* (London: Marshall, Morgan, and Scott, 1959), 209.
13. J. Taylor Smith, "How to Overcome Temptation," in *Keswick's Triumphant Voice* (Grand Rapids: Zondervan, 1963), 193.
14. Whitlow, *J. Taylor Smith,* 109, 184. I heard Wilbur Smith describe Bishop Smith's visit to the Moody centenary. He was so ill he could not speak, but the huge audience in Moody Church was blessed by just a look at his face.

11.7.7 W. Graham Scroggie—The Distance Carrier of Keswick

> Preachers will take for texts, phrases which convey a moral or spiritual suggestion, and will develop that thought along one or other of many lines. But one may do that kind of work for half-a-century and yet leave his audience in appalling ignorance of the Bible. Such sentences can be found by the hundred thousand in the world's literature, and a very instructive course of sermons could be preached from the dicta of Confucius; but that is not the business of the Christian preacher.[1]
>
> Is the Bible the Word of God? It seems to be—it claims to be—it proves to be.
>
> —W. Graham Scroggie

Continuous cross-pollination between Keswick and America took place as European preachers crossed the Atlantic and as strong preachers like A. T. Pierson and S. D. Gordon came from America to preach at Keswick. Still the heavy preaching load year after year was carried by the British and by no one more regularly than the Scottish Baptist who gave the Bible readings twelve times at Keswick over a forty-two-year period. **William Graham Scroggie** (1877–1958) was born in Malvern, England, of Scottish parents who ministered as evangelists. He was reared in an ambiance of rich Christian experience.[2] Scroggie took his training at Spurgeon's College and served a succession of churches, including Leytonstone Church in London (1899–1901); Trinity Church in Halifax (1902–1905); Bethesda Free Church in Sunderland (1907–1916); and a most fruitful tenure at Charlotte Chapel, Edinburgh (1916–1933).[3] He, like Campbell Morgan, gave himself first to a mastery of the English Bible and was known for his clear-cut and well-outlined expositions of Holy Scripture. After leaving Charlotte,

Scroggie traveled the world in conference ministry for several years and then served Spurgeon's Tabernacle during the war years (1938–1944).[4]

Listeners marveled at the solid Bible content of his preaching.[5] Scroggie wrote Scripture Union and Sunday school materials for *The Sunday School Times* for years, efforts that gave him a firm footing in Scripture.[6] He also took great pains in careful and appropriate application.

He had a delightful dry wit and "his measured voice and somewhat stern mien masked warmth of affection."[7] In his years at Charlotte, thirty-two men entered the ministry and fifty-one missionaries were sent overseas. In recognizing his effectiveness as a preacher and missioner in bestowing an honorary doctorate, the University of Edinburgh paid tribute to him for his "devotion to the study and teaching of the Bible in its two-fold character of a Divine Revelation and great Literature."[8]

Scroggie led thousands through a Bible correspondence course. He was a strong premillennialist and looked for a special work of God among the Jews at the end of the age.[9] He was equally adept at analysis and synthesis. Several of his favorite Bible readings at Keswick show his gifts as an expositor and preacher. Especially memorable were his studies on *Paul's Prison Prayers, Paul's Hymn of Love, Christ in the Creed,* and *Salvation and Behavior* (Romans). A favorite is *The Land and Life of Rest* (Canaan and the Heavenlies). Scroggie was neat and concise in his layout.[10] His skill in arrangement is in clear evidence:

I. Contemplating the Land
II. Entering the Land
III. Conquering the Land
IV. Possessing the Land
V. Interpreting the Land

The Keswick movement has seen a theological and a methodological ripple effect around the world. W. Graham Scroggie personifies the best aspects of that legacy.

---

1. W. Graham Scroggie, "The Preparation of Addresses," in Ralph Turnbull, ed., *A Treasury of W. Graham Scroggie* (Grand Rapids: Baker, 1974), 192ff. Scroggie agonized over how Phillips Brooks and G. H. Morrison use the cubic dimensions of the Holy City in Revelation 21:16 to speak of Christian character, or Brooks' use of Matthew 24:27, "the lightning out of the East and West," to speak of the spread of the gospel westward. Well-taken cautions.
2. Mrs. James J. Scroggie, *The Story of a Life in the Love of God* (Edinburgh: Pickering and Inglis, 1938).
3. Charlotte Chapel was bathed in revival under the ministry of Joseph Kemp. When he came in 1902, only thirty-five members attended his induction; by 1907 the membership was 609 and 830 by 1914. The chapel was enlarged in 1912 to seat one thousand. In 1915 Kemp went on to a ministry in New York and then on to the Auckland Tabernacle in New Zealand. Described in Brian H. Edwards, *Revival: A People*

Saturated with God (Durham, N.C.: Evangelical Press, 1990), 204–5. Pastors like Kemp, Scroggie, Gerald Griffiths, Sidlow Baxter, Alan Redpath, and Derek Prime have all contributed to the strength of Charlotte Chapel as a preaching center.

4. Eric W. Hayden, *A History of Spurgeon's Tabernacle* (Pasadena, Calif.: Pilgrim, 1971), 46ff.
5. Of great substance is W. Graham Scroggie, *A Guide to the Gospels* (Grand Rapids: Kregel, 1995).
6. The two volumes of his notes on the gospels were published by Ark Publishing in London in 1981.
7. J. C. Pollock, *The Keswick Story* (Chicago: Moody, 1964), 142.
8. Nigel M. de S. Cameron, ed., *Dictionary of Scottish Church History and Theology* (Downers Grove, Ill.: InterVarsity Press, 1993), 763–64.
9. W. Graham Scroggie, *The Great Unveiling: An Analytical Study of Revelation* (Grand Rapids: Zondervan, 1979); his work, *What About Heaven?* (London: Pickering and Inglis, 1940) is most comforting. His analysis of the Psalter is choice (*A Guide to the Psalms,* 4 volumes in one, Grand Rapids: Kregel, 1995).
10. W. Graham Scroggie, *The Land and Life of Rest* (London: Pickering and Inglis, 1950).

Chapter Twelve

The Glory and Agony of Twentieth-Century Preaching

Part Two: Resurgence or Senescence?

How may we have within ourselves that which shall impart to our preaching the right sort of authority, the conviction and confidence which lacks neither a proper respect for the hearer nor the humility of a sinful man, which is neither overridingly dogmatic nor weakly diffident? I suppose in the end the secret lies in the quality of our own spiritual life and the extent to which we are ourselves walking humbly with God in Christ.

—H. H. Farmer

But Micaiah said, "As surely as the Lord lives, I can tell him only what the Lord tells me."

—1 Kings 22:14

I saw under the altar the souls of those who had been slain because of the word of God and the testimony they had maintained.

—Revelation 6:9

Then I saw another angel flying in midair, and he had the eternal gospel to proclaim to those who live on the earth—to every nation, tribe, language and people.

—Revelation 14:6

> He who was seated on the throne said, "I am making everything new!" Then he said, "Write this down, for these words are trustworthy and true."
>
> —Revelation 21:5

> The angel said to me, "These words are trustworthy and true. The Lord, the God of the spirits of the prophets, sent his angel to show his servants the things that must soon take place."
>
> —Revelation 22:6

> There is a false belief abroad that only gentle, tender, loving persuasions are in harmony with the New Testament times. It is all a mistake! Never in the world's history were fearless, resolute, whole-souled prophets called for and needed more than today. This age needs Jeremiahs to tell the truth, the whole truth, please or displease, dungeon or no dungeon, mire or no mire!
>
> —General William Booth

> Unless he has spent the week with God, and received Divine communications, it would be better not to enter the pulpit or open his mouth on Sunday at all.
>
> —James Stalker

Coming down the stretch of the tumultuous twentieth century, the tensions of the Cold War yielded to the reassertion of old tribalisms and state terrorism; the growing affluence and deepening materialism of a very small segment of the West and parts of Asia; the reinvigoration of radical Islam and Hinduism; the continued decline of mainline Protestantism and the cultural erosion of evangelicalism; as well as the increasing theological confusion of Roman Catholicism. Evangelicals seem to be victimized by the pervasive shift toward "self-seeking, self-indulgence and self-gratification" as profoundly as any.[1] Religion generally is trivialized and marginalized in American law and politics.[2] Christian exclusivity is increasingly seen as the one untenable and unacceptable position on the spectrum. Exaggerated individualism continues unabated at century's end even as Bellah and associates diagnosed it earlier.[3] The Europeanization of American Christianity is in mounting evidence.

The biblical message is proclaimed not simply in a post-Christian age but in an anti-Christian age. In the postmodern pluralistic climate, fact and opinion are seen as no different. D. A. Carson brilliantly traces the modern turn to subjectivity (remember Kierkegaard's steadfast refusal to define revelation as communication of doctrine) and what he characterizes as "the drift into intellectual nihilism."[4] This proceeds through the domestication of Scripture through higher criticism or the substitution of "spirituality" for theological construct as in "new age" and higher types of neo-gnostic hubris. The ground which must be maintained if we are to be true to "the word of our testimony" (Rev. 12:11) was articulated by Max Warren shortly before he died:

> It is all too easy . . . to talk of different roads to the summit, as if Jesus were in no particular and distinctive sense "the Way, the Truth and the Life." Of course where this point is reached, the Great Commission is tacitly, if not explicitly, held to be indefinitely in suspense if not quite otiose. This is the view forcefully propounded by some Christians holding professorial chairs in Britain and across the Atlantic. Are they right? Is courtesy always to preclude contradiction? Is choice now just a matter of taste, no longer a response to an absolute demand? Is the Cross on Calvary really no more than a confusing roundabout sign pointing in every direction, or is it still the place where *all* men are meant to kneel?[5]

This is the context and milieu of biblical preaching as the twentieth century concludes.

---

1. James Lincoln Collier, *The Rise of Selfishness in the United States* (Oxford: Oxford University Press, 1991).
2. Stephen L. Carter, *The Culture of Disbelief* (New York: Basic Books, 1993). America spinning out of control.
3. Robert N. Bellah et al., *Habits of the Heart* (New York: Harper, 1985). Bellah's latest study indicates that the pathologies he identified earlier on are more pronounced today; see "Individualism and the Crisis of Civic Membership," *The Christian Century* (May 8, 1996): 510ff.
4. D. A. Carson, *The Gagging of God: Christianity Confronts Pluralism* (Grand Rapids: Zondervan, 1996).
5. Ibid., 94–95.

12.1 EMISSARIES IN THE WORLDWIDE EXPANSION OF THE GOSPEL

> I still see the cross of Jesus as the one place in all the history of human culture where there is a final dealing with the ultimate mysteries of sin and forgiveness, of bondage and freedom, of conflict and peace, of death and life . . . I find here a point from which one can take one's bearings and a light in which one can walk, however stumblingly. I know that guiding star will remain and that that light will shine till death and in the end. And that is enough.
>
> —Bishop Lesslie Newbigin[1]

Despite the dilution of the mandate to preach the gospel to every creature through an epidemic of universalism and theological relativism, there were those like Newbigin who stayed with the historic gospel. Andrew Murray wrote a burning response to one of the early conferences. His focus was on prayer and the ministry of the Word:

> I know that it is no easy task to speak humbly, wisely, lovingly and yet faithfully and effectually, of what appears lacking or sinful in the Church.

> And yet I am sure that there are many who would welcome help in answering the questions: Is there any real possibility of such a revival in the Church that in every congregation where the full gospel is preached, her most important aim will be to carry the gospel to every creature? What is the path that will lead to this change? And what steps should be taken by those who lead the missions of the church?[2]

In response to the modernistic book by Hocking, *Rethinking Missions,* and its endorsement by Pearl S. Buck, J. Gresham Machen led in setting up the Independent Board for Presbyterian Foreign Missions in 1933.[3] The battle was over the uniqueness of Christ and his Cross for salvation.

---

1. Lesslie Newbigin, *Unfinished Agenda: An Autobiography* (Grand Rapids: Eerdmans, 1985), 254. Newbigin relates how the vision of Christ crucified changed his life (11) and how a careful study of Romans brought him to clarity on the objective nature of Christ's atoning work on the Cross (30).
2. Andrew Murray, *A Key to the Missionary Problem* (Ft. Washington, Pa.: CLC, 1979), 27.
3. D. G. Hart, *Defending the Faith: J. Gresham Machen and the Crisis of Conservative Protestantism in Modern America* (Grand Rapids: Baker, 1994), 149.

12.1.1 Samuel M. Zwemer—The Mission to Muslims

> If the Cross of Christ is anything to the mind, it is surely everything—the most profound reality and the sublimest mystery. One comes to realize that literally all the wealth and glory of the gospel centres here. The Cross is the pivot as well as the centre of New Testament thought. It is the exclusive mark of the Christian faith, the symbol of Christianity and its cynosure.
>
> —Samuel M. Zwemer

Kenneth Scott Latourette speaks of him as "frankly a conservative evangelical" and saw something of the Old Testament prophet's fearlessness and forthrightness in him. He was part of the Student Volunteer Movement which rose in dedication to "the evangelization of the world in this generation."[1] **Samuel Marinus Zwemer** (1867–1938) was born the third of fifteen children in a Dutch Reformed manse in Vriesland, Michigan. He was the descendent of French Huguenots who had fled to the Netherlands. Four of the five Zwemer brothers became ministers.

Zwemer trained at Hope College and the New Brunswick Seminary (RCA), preaching his first sermon in 1888 to a small African-American congregation.[2] He felt the call to missions and especially to follow the great missionary to the Muslims, Raymond Lull. Zwemer and his friend Cantine founded the Arabian Mission and went to Beirut to learn Arabic and explore Muslim lands.[3]

Establishing work in Bahrain, Zwemer traveled for three years on behalf of the Student Volunteer Movement. In 1912 the United Presbyterians and the Church Missionary Society jointly called Zwemer to Cairo, where his "acquisitive and inventive mind" quickly catapulted him to become the "leading authority on Islamics from a Christian perspective."[4] He traveled to every Islamic nation and blanketed the world with conference ministry. In Cairo he received the young William Borden of Yale, a wealthy visionary who had targeted Tibet for his service but who shortly died of spinal meningitis. Zwemer conducted the funeral.

Increasingly he became a platform crusader for Christ and the missionary cause. A staunch champion of verbal inspiration, Zwemer took a strong stand against Hocking's *Rethinking Missions* and published a rejoinder titled *Thinking Missions with Christ.*[5] "He had little patience for the higher critics of Scripture," his biographer says.[6]

Zwemer was a strong and insightful preacher who spoke at Northfield, Winona Lake, and three times at Keswick in England. A ravenous reader and disciplined student, he published a trilogy of books on the birth, death, and resurrection of Christ.[7] Joining the Princeton Seminary faculty in 1929, he became a popular teacher. His Smyth Lectures from Columbia Seminary in Decatur, Georgia, are a measure of his scholarly bent.[8]

Interestingly, with all his lifelong dedication to Muslim missions, Zwemer had an absorbing burden for the Jews as well.[9] Twice widowed, he retired in 1938 and then taught at Biblical Seminary in New York City and at the Alliance Missionary Training Institute (Nyack). In advanced years he continued to preach even to the convalescents in the nursing home where he died at eighty-four.[10]

What influence and impact he had and how grateful we are for the flame of concern for the Muslim world which he kindled. Over a billion Muslims in our time! How many will hear of our Savior?

---

1. Kenneth Scott Latourette, Introduction to J. Christy Wilson, *Apostle to Islam* (Grand Rapids: Baker, 1952).
2. Ibid., 31.
3. Samuel M. Zwemer and James Cantine, *The Golden Milestone: Reminiscences of Pioneer Days Fifty Years Ago in Arabia* (New York: Revell, 1938).
4. Wilson, *Apostle to Islam,* 84, 92. Cf. Zwemer's classic, *The Moslem Doctrine of God* (Edinburgh: Oliphant, Anderson and Ferrier, 1905). This book is dedicated to his minister father, Adrian Zwemer.
5. Ibid., 67, 199.
6. Ibid., 241.
7. His 1937 messages at Keswick are charming and challenging; see *No Solitary Throne* (London: Pickering and Inglis, 1937), in response to Gandhi's comment: "I am unable to place Jesus Christ on a solitary throne." The trilogy consists of *The Glory of the Manger* (New York: American Tract Society, 1940); *The Glory of the Cross* (London: Oliphants, 1954); *The Glory of the Empty Tomb* (New York: Revell, 1947).
8. Samuel M. Zwemer, *The Origin of Religion* (New York: Loizeaux Brothers, 1945). These lectures are dedicated to Professor Wilhelm Schmidt of Vienna to whom

Zwemer was indebted for his anthropological case for primitive monotheism. For a more recent assessment, see Ernest Brandewie, *Wilhelm Schmidt and the Origin of the Idea of God* (Lanham, Md.: University Press of America, 1983).

9. Wilson, *Apostle to Islam,* 241.
10. Beside J. Christy Wilson and J. Dudley Woodberry, the other great evangelical scholar in Islamic law and custom in our time has been Sir Norman Anderson, *An Adopted Son: The Story of My Life* (Leicester: Inter-Varsity, 1985).

12.1.2 E. Stanley Jones—Mission to India and the World

> I'm only a Christian in the making.
>
> But when you ask us to accept the basis that all religions are equally true, we are sorry, but we cannot. For we believe that there is something unique in Jesus Christ. And that uniqueness is the Person himself!
>
> On Hebrews 9:26: "'At the climax of history . . .' All history moved on to this climactic moment when we saw God sacrificing himself on a cross. That was the climax of history and the climax of revelation . . . this is the climax; this is the Voice, all else is echo. . . . So my contact as a Christian missionary with a non-Christian nation has led me more and more to the cross."
>
> —E. Stanley Jones

Listening to **Eli Stanley Jones** (1884–1973) was like trying to drink from a fire hydrant. The hyperenergetic preacher delivered more than sixty thousand sermons and always pressed himself to the limit—with a series of nervous breakdowns as a consequence. Born in Baltimore, Jones' home situation was difficult. But he had a praying mother and was converted at the age of fifteen in an evangelistic crusade at Memorial Methodist Church:

> I had him—Jesus—and he had me. We had each other. I belonged. My estrangement, my sense of orphanage were gone. I was reconciled. As I rose from my knees, I felt I wanted to put my arms around the world and share this with everybody.[1]

Immediately Jones got into the Wesleyan class meetings and began to grow. He had leanings to the law but went on to Asbury College after hearing Henry Clay Morrison preach. At Asbury he surrendered to missionary service. Hannah Whithall Smith's *The Christian's Secret of a Happy Life* brought him to yield all to Christ and to be filled with the Holy Spirit.[2] He had several very shaky starts in his preaching. In his first sermon, he drew a complete blank but then recovered sufficiently to give his testimony of new life in Christ, and his ministry was launched.[3] Jones went to India.

Arriving in Bombay in 1907, Jones served as pastor in Lucknow during language study, but it soon became clear that evangelism was his calling. At first he reached out to the outcasts in his district of one million souls but then gave himself to a ministry to the intellectuals. He used roundtables with Hindus and Muslims and he started Christian ashrams (spiritual retreats) where the Bible hour was central. Early on he became a bit taken with some Marxist ideas and ruefully acknowledged later how mistaken he was.[4] Jones was an evangelist and an unashamed supernaturalist, Christocentric in an almost radical sense. He preached "Jesus Christ and him crucified," and his book *Conversion* stands as a classic.[5] Often in his assertion that "Jesus is Lord!" he stressed the importance of living out the sermon. Yet his obsession with experience and his lack of training led him to a systematic de-emphasis on theology and a unfortunate turn away from the Old Testament and a strong view of biblical inspiration.[6]

Jones traveled the world as an evangelist with especially great meetings in Japan. Twenty thousand people heard him in Madison Square Garden and eighty-two hundred stayed afterward for surrender. He became a champion of racial reconciliation and federal union among churches and yet would not be deterred from his main evangelistic purpose. In 1928 he was elected a bishop of the Methodist church but resigned twenty-four hours later because he felt he was a missionary and an evangelist and not a bishop!

Jones wrote twenty-nine books and several times was nominated for the Nobel Prize for peace.[7] His glowing personality was contagious. After a serious stroke, E. Stanley Jones insisted on going back to India where he died. His sermon "The Divine Yes" from 2 Corinthians 1:19–20 effectively brings out Christ as the "yea and amen" and emphasizes spiritual rebirth, cleansing from sin, and the fullness of the Holy Spirit.[8]

---

1. E. Stanley Jones, *A Song of Ascents: A Spiritual Autobiography* (Nashville: Abingdon, 1968), 26ff., 28.
2. Ibid., 52. Another great preacher out of Asbury was J. C. McPheeters, who served as president. Note his strong expositions on Corinthians in the Proclaiming the New Testament series (Grand Rapids: Baker, 1964).
3. Ibid., 65.
4. Ibid., 148.
5. E. Stanley Jones, *Conversion* (Nashville: Abingdon, 1949). He argues here that liberals know everything but change nothing.
6. E. Stanley Jones, *The Divine Yes* (Nashville: Abingdon, 1975), 39.
7. Books of daily reading like *Abundant Living* (Nashville: Abingdon, 1942) and *Growing Spiritually* (Nashville: Abingdon, 1953) have been immensely popular and are very Scripture-driven.
8. Many missionaries to India have become great preachers (as we hark back to Carey and Duff) even into this century with Bishop J. Waskom Pickett and Donald McGavran, who founded the Church Growth Movement. Jones is true to this text without going over the edge like Henry Ward Beecher who was critiqued by an English Wesleyan "for giving too little prominence in his teaching to redemption in the blood of Christ," cf. David Bebbington in George A. Rawlyk and Mark Noll, *Amazing Grace* (Grand Rapids: Baker, 1993), 85; or without suffering total shipwreck

like Norman Vincent Peale, cf. his *The True Joy of Positive Living* (New York: William Morrow, 198); or the maceration of Pauline theology in Robert Schuller's *Self-Esteem: The New Reformation* (Waco: Word, 1982). Where is the gospel in all of this? Jesus vs. Paul is a wrong-headed false dichotomy.

12.1.3 Rowland V. Bingham—Mission to Africa and Canada

> Not to create a sentiment of peace in a world that is in rebellion against God, but to secure the acceptance of the One who made peace through the blood of His cross, is the business of the preacher.
>
> The normal life of the Christian is a triumphant life. The provision made for triumph is such that it is disloyal to consider defeat. We are "always" to triumph; to be more than conquerors.
>
> —Rowland V. Bingham

Founder of Canadian Keswick, longtime editor of *The Evangelical Christian* in Canada, **Rowland V. Bingham** (1872–1942), was the prime mover in the Sudan Interior Mission. Bingham was born in Sussex in England, the second of eight children who were financially devastated by their father's death when Rowland was thirteen. The family was nominally Anglican, but Rowland was soundly converted in a Salvation Army Hall under the ministry of a believing Jew.[1]

Bingham soon lost his meager teaching position because of his dissenting loyalties. Immediately he began to win souls.[2] Because he did not feel he could sell smoking materials in his mother's shop, he decided to migrate to Canada.[3] "God made it clear that he wanted me to preach the Gospel," he wrote, and surrendered for missionary service. With two friends he visited the Sudan in Africa, and though he was shaken by their deaths, he went on to study medicine and then Bible at Simpson's school in New York City.

Facing seemingly insurmountable odds, Bingham and his associates launched beachheads of gospel advance in hard places. Dr. Thomas Lambie led out in Ethiopia, as did the remarkable Dr. Andrew Stirrett among the Hausas in Nigeria.[4] Bingham was not only a missionary statesman and leader but also an able preacher, itinerating widely. He was a student of doctrine. His concentration on spiritual warfare and what the Bible says about demons and divine healing was salutary. He was "a man of one Book" who was "unflinchingly loyal to the sacred Word."[5] His lecture on "Prophecy Proved by Photography" strengthened the faith of many.[6]

Bingham's love for the deeper recesses of Christian experience led to the founding of Canadian Keswick at Muskoka. Here he expounded Scripture with others like Griffith Thomas, Graham Scroggie, Charles Trumbull, Canon Dyson Hague, and Gordon Watt from England.[7] Many did not agree with Bingham's eschatological positions, but his spirit was kind and genial, and he wrestled with the issues in depth.[8]

At the heart of the great Sudan Interior Mission (currently with more than thirteen hundred missionaries on the field) is the steady biblical preaching and vision of a man who sought after the Lord and reveled in the presence of the mighty God.

1. J. H. Hunter, *A Flame of Fire: The Life and Work of Rowland V. Bingham* (Toronto: Sudan Interior, 1961), 43.
2. Ibid., 46.
3. Ibid., 48.
4. Douglas C. Percy, *Stirrett of the Sudan* (Toronto: Sudan Interior, 1948). A truly remarkable saga.
5. Hunter, *A Flame of Fire,* 275.
6. Ibid., 276.
7. Ibid., 259. For a good sample of this English preacher, cf. Gordon Watt, *The Cross in Faith and Conduct* (Philadelphia: The Sunday School Times Company, 1924).
8. Rowland V. Bingham, *Matthew the Publican and His Gospel* (London: Marshall, Morgan, and Scott, n.d.). Bingham tends to build straw men in prosecuting his case. He is persuaded that all dispensationalists end up with Bullinger. To recognize that Matthew's gospel has a particular appeal to the Jew does not make it unusable by others.

12.1.4 Jonathan Goforth—Mission to China

> Like his Master, Goforth had a great compassion for the needy and helpless and a two-edged flashing sword for the self-satisfied Christian Pharisee. It was probably this searching penetrating method of preaching to bodies of even Christian workers that caused opposition to his being sent, as was urged years later, on a Mission tour in India as he had in China.
>
> —Dr. John Buchanan of India

> This I can say that on no occasion where we stood with our backs to a wall and used the Word of God did we fail ultimately in gaining a victory.
>
> —Jonathan Goforth

Adjudged to be "China's most outstanding evangelist" by Dr. J. Herbert Kane, **Jonathan Goforth** (1859–1936) was one of our time's most adept China hands, mightily used of God in China, Manchuria, and Korea.[1] Born in Thorndale, Ontario, he was the seventh child of eleven.

Goforth was converted in the local Presbyterian church under the ministry of a pastor who called for decisions at the end of every service.[2] Life was hard for the young farm boy. Many times in his life he miraculously escaped death.[3] But the lessons of sowing and reaping were never lost on him, and Goforth's love for the mission field is not surprising. He was raised on Scripture, and as a lad stood fascinated before maps.[4] After reading Robert Murray McCheyne, Goforth laid his life on the altar of missionary service.

Tutored by his pastor, he began to serve and preach. Again, his life was touched for missions.[5] He went on to study at Knox College in Toronto, where he was ridiculed and humiliated but was unswerving in his commitment. He worked in the slums, jails, and missions of the city. Soon he was walking sixteen to eighteen miles every Sunday, preaching three times. Eventually he shared the platform at the Niagara-on-the-Lake Conference with William E. Blackstone, author of *Jesus Is Coming!* with whom Goforth shared a strong premillennial conviction.

Then he met his beloved Rosalind. Rosalind saw that the shabby man was a sharp arrow for the Lord, and they made a great team. The Goforths would be the first North Americans to volunteer for the China Inland Mission. Ironically it was the students of Knox who helped raise the money enabling the Goforths to leave for China. They were commissioned at historic Knox Presbyterian Church in Toronto, where a plaque commemorating the occasion still can be seen on the wall.[6]

Taking Hudson Taylor's watchword to go forward on their knees, the Goforths endured unspeakable adversity. They narrowly escaped death in the Boxer Rebellion. Their personal effects were burned, and they lost several of their children in death. Yet Goforth continued his endless preaching tours. He had a great passion for preaching and often took as his theme "The Sacrifice of Christ."[7] His dedication was to preach Christ with an open Bible even though his cohorts warned him against so direct an approach. Sinners came to Christ from the very first.[8]

After the Boxer Rebellion, the Goforths returned to do family evangelism with great effectiveness. Meanwhile, under the influence of Finney's *Lectures on Revival,* Goforth began the revival ministry that God was opening for him. Preaching on the text from 1 Peter, "He bore our sins in His own body on the tree," he enjoyed an extraordinary response.[9] Returning for a furlough, Goforth preached in this vein at Keswick in England in 1910. He was invited to stay and itinerate for Keswick for a year, but he had to return to China.[10]

Goforth was also in the center of the spiritual conflagration that ignited in Korea. His book *By My Spirit* gives the full story. The text he used in the breakthrough service in Shansi Province in China was Revelation 3:15, the words to the church in Laodicea.[11] In 1918 he preached to General Feng's army and saw many conversions, ultimately seeing the general himself take up preaching.[12]

Goforth had considerable conflict with Roman Catholic incursion in his areas, and he fought the incessant growth of higher critical ideas and the resultant waning authority of Scripture in the lives of many of the new missionaries arriving on the field. His wife relates, "He felt powerless to stem the tide and resolved to preach, as never before, salvation through the Cross of Calvary and demonstrate its power in his own life."[13]

On their furlough in 1916, Mrs. Goforth was led into a deeper experience of the Holy Spirit through Dr. Charles G. Trumbull of *The Sunday School Times.* This opened new doors of ministry at the American Keswick in New Jersey and other places.[14]

As the years passed, Dr. Goforth lost the sight of both of his eyes and Mrs. Goforth lost her hearing. Up to that time he had his Scofield Bible in English and his Chinese Bible always before him. Rosalind Goforth testified:

> Jonathan Goforth *loved* the Word. To him the simple reading of it was a delight. It was sacred, divine. How often have I seen him, when taking up his Bible to read, first uncover his head and in an attitude of deepest

> reverence remain so a few moments before beginning his reading. In this simple act we see the secret of his life. Before he crossed the Borderland he stated that he had read the Bible seventy-three times from cover to cover.[15]

At long last the Goforths had to come home to stay in 1935. In the last eighteen months of his life he spoke more than five hundred times, including American Keswick and Ben Lippen conferences. The fiery preacher went home to glory in October of 1936.

---

1. Ruth A. Tucker, *From Jerusalem to Irian Jaya* (Grand Rapids: Zondervan, 1983), 188.
2. Rosalind Goforth, *Goforth of China* (Grand Rapids: Zondervan, 1937), 24. Her book *How I Know God Answers Prayer* is a missionary and devotional classic.
3. Ibid., 19.
4. Ibid., 21.
5. Ibid., 28.
6. Knox Presbyterian Church in Toronto is adjacent to the campus of the University of Toronto and has been a great center of biblical exposition, most signally in this century by Dr. William Fitch.
7. Goforth, *Goforth of China,* 105.
8. Ibid., 83.
9. Ibid., 181.
10. Jonathan Goforth, "Power from on High" from Acts 1:14 in *Keswick's Triumphant Voice* (Grand Rapids: Zondervan 1963), 364ff. "Revival is no pleasant process; it just means Gethsemane and Calvary," 368.
11. Goforth, *Goforth of China,* 194.
12. Ibid., 253.
13. Ibid., 214.
14. Ibid., 230.
15. Ibid., 315.

12.1.5 Robert E. Speer—Mission to North and South America

> Work without prayer is ashes; prayer without work is a dream.
>
> —Robert E. Speer

> At Northfield Dr. Speer would stand before us on the high platform in the auditorium, straight as a spruce tree against the sky, usually grave but frequently smiling too, never talking down, never given to colloquialisms, an intellectual making simple the deep things of the spirit, his fine voice matching the eloquent flow of his ordered thought. Echoes come back across the years: "The Gospel is either true for all or it is not true at all."
>
> —W. Reginald Wheeler

A pivotal missions strategist, **Robert E. Speer** (1867–1947), for forty-six years the secretary of the Board of Foreign Missions for the PCUSA, was possibly the greatest motivational preacher missions has ever had. John Mackay heard him at Edinburgh in 1910 and concluded that Speer "was the greatest personality I have ever known."[1]

Speer was born into a staunchly Presbyterian home in Huntingdon, Pennsylvania, one of five children, where the father was an attorney and two-term Democratic congressman. His mother died when he was nine, but she had elicited from him the promise that he would never use alcohol. His upbringing was Puritan, and his Bible-teaching father required that his children learn both the Shorter and Larger Catechism. Young Speer attended Andover Academy (he remembered Principal Fairbairn's ministry) and then Princeton University, where he was valedictorian of his class and played football for four years.

Speer was caught up in the Student Volunteer Movement and often visited Northfield to hear Moody and others. He became known as a forceful speaker on purity of life and character at student meetings.[2] He often traveled with John Mott, who came from Cornell.[3] Speer attended Princeton Seminary, but left in his middle year when he was invited to become secretary of the Board of Foreign Missions. Only twenty-four, he took on the large responsibility of an enterprise with 598 missionaries and 28,000 native workers. He traveled constantly, married in 1893, traveled to Mexico, and the next year to Keswick in England.

Speer was a great storyteller. He had a grave earnestness about him, but this was tempered by a sense of humor as well. He was a top administrator and promoter and a powerful preacher with immense appeal to students. Reading from his "tiny, well-worn New Testament," he would open the Scripture. He was considered "tops in exposition and application."[4]

Speer was a man who read constantly and expressed himself expertly and clearly.[5] His instincts were sound and doctrinally conservative. "He believed with Chrysostom that the cause of all our evils lies in our not knowing the Scriptures."[6] He was unreservedly a supernaturalist and at length defended the Virgin Birth of our Lord. His well-known Stone Lectures on *The Finality of Jesus Christ* are classic.[7]

He wrote scathingly of the liberally tilted Laymen's Foreign Missions Inquiry Report of 1932. He contributed several key articles to *The Fundamentals.* In all, Speer wrote and edited sixty-seven books. He profoundly influenced so many who in turn exerted great influence, such as Samuel Shoemaker, the Episcopalian missionary to China who then served parishes in New York City and Pittsburgh.[8] Speer was prophetic in his interest and vision for Latin America and in his "Brazil Plan" for the indigenization of Hispanic missions.

The center of Robert Speer's life and ministry was biblical preaching. Thus, when he was elected moderator of the General Assembly in 1927, conservatives were encouraged. The church was in turmoil and the inroads of modernism and liberal theology were gnawing away at the vitals of the communion. Here Speer failed. Was it lack of training in theology or was it the congeniality of the man or was it the bias of the organization man? Speer did not see the dangers of the Barthian denial of propositional revelation.[9] He believed he could unite the liberals and the conservatives. J. Gresham Machen felt that Speer betrayed the missionary cause and Princeton Seminary.[10] When Speer died of leukemia near eighty years of age, his lifelong friend Henry Sloan Coffin of Union Seminary in New York conducted the funeral service.[11]

At what point does the man in the middle need to take the plunge? Machen and Speer believed alike doctrinally but drew sharply different ecclesiological conclusions. We remember Robert Speer as a layman whose Christlike personality and preaching made a vast difference for many.

---

1. W. Reginald Wheeler, *A Man Sent from God: A Biography of Robert E. Speer* (New York: Revell, 1956), 9.
2. Ibid., 49.
3. John R. Mott (1865–1955) was, like Speer, a consecrated layman. He did not contribute to *The Fundamentals,* and his biographer develops the thesis that while Speer remained theologically steady, Mott accommodated. See C. Howard Hopkins, *John R. Mott* (Grand Rapids: Eerdmans, 1979). President Wilson wanted Mott to become U.S. ambassador to China. He also won the Nobel Peace Prize.
4. Wheeler, *A Man Sent from God,* 127. Speer's *John's Gospel: The Greatest Book in the World* (New York: Revell, 1915) was a widely used study book and is typical of his rich Bible study. His book of sermons from Northfield gives typical fare; see *Remember Jesus Christ* (New York: Revell, 1899). These are beautiful and moving sermons.
5. Robert E. Speer, *How to Speak Effectively Without Notes* (New York: Revell, 1918). With this little gem, Speer addresses the issue of the advantages of extempore preaching in a manner similar to such heavies as Richard S. Storrs (who served Brooklyn's Church of the Pilgrims for fifty-three years); Clarence E. Macartney; and Charles W. Koller, whose *Expository Preaching Without Notes* (Grand Rapids: Baker, 1962) has influenced so many.
6. Wheeler, *A Man Sent from God,* 143.
7. Robert E. Speer, *The Finality of Jesus Christ* (New York: Revell, 1933). These are the Stone Lectures from Princeton given in 1932 and 1933 and the Gay Lectures from Southern Baptist Seminary delivered in the same year.
8. Wheeler, *A Man Sent from God,* 138–39.
9. Ibid., 97.
10. D. G. Hart seems to feel that Speer "bore the brunt of the Board's lubricity." See *Defending the Faith: J. Gresham Machen and the Crisis of Conservative Protestantism in Modern America* (Grand Rapids: Baker, 1994), 149; Ned B. Stonehouse, *J. Gresham Machen: A Biographical Memoir* (Grand Rapids: Eerdmans, 1954) expresses much stronger disappointment in Speer's unwillingness to draw the line in the Pearl Buck case and to speak out (469ff.).
11. Henry Sloan Coffin (1843–1929) was baptized by Pastor John Hall at Fifth Avenue Church. His father was treasurer of Moody's New York campaign. In his long pastorate at Madison Avenue Church in New York City (1905–1926) and his presidency at Union Seminary, he moved steadily left. He disavowed the work of Billy Sunday and was a prime mover in the Auburn Affirmation of 1923–1924. See Morgan Phelps

Notes, *Henry Sloan Coffin* (New York: Scribner's, 1964). The Robert Speer story dramatically demonstrates the dilemmas of the organization man.

12.1.6 Frank Laubach—Mission to the Illiterates

> Oh, if we only let God have His full chance He will break our hearts with the glory of His revelation. That is the privilege which the preacher can have above others. It is his business to look into the very face of God until he aches with bliss.
>
> Deeper yet, O Christ, deeper, deeper, yet into Thy broken heart let me bury my will, that from Thy heart I may draw the power of Pentecost. Help me stay. Help me abide. Nothing else in the world matters but that.
>
> —Frank Laubach

Sometimes called the apostle of literacy, **Frank C. Laubach** (1884–1970) was born and reared in Benton, Pennsylvania. He trained at Princeton University and Colombia University as well as Union Seminary in New York City. He was a missionary educator and preacher among the Muslim Moros on Mindanao in the Philippine Islands and served as dean of Union College in Manilla.

While handling the tough assignment among half a million hostile Moros, Laubach experienced a most extraordinary breakthrough of the sense of the Lord's presence as he prayed.[1] Prayer was for him "the mightiest force in the world." Laubach went on to lead the "Each one reach one" campaign of winning the world for Christ. This involved using his method for teaching people to read the Word of God.[2]

He had a doctorate in sociology from Colombia but soon realized that people needed the transformation that only God can give through his Word. But what is the Bible for those who cannot read? Laubach saw the answer. He wrote or co-authored more than two hundred primers for illiterate adults in more than 165 languages in fifty-one countries.

Laubach was more of an exhorter than an expositor. A dynamic preacher in his own right, he was deep into the Scriptures.[3] His delivery was rapid-fire, and he seemed to sweep over all resistance as he poured forth his heart and the great need. Pieces of his sermons show the biblical thrust from the launching pad and his artistic arc to application for life.[4]

---

1. Frank Laubach, *Practicing His Presence* (Auburn, Me.: Christian Books, 1973); *Letters by a Modern Mystic* (New York: Revell, 1937).
2. Frank Laubach, *How to Teach One and Win One for Christ* (Grand Rapids: Zondervan, 1964).
3. Frank Laubach, *Frank Laubach's Prayer Diary* (New York: Revell, 1964). Each day is anchored in a Bible portion.
4. Frank Laubach, *Living Words* (Grand Rapids: Zondervan, 1967); *Wake Up or Blow Up* (New York: Revell, 1951).

12.1.7 F. J. Huegel—Mission to Mexico

> There has been now for some years a decided turning away from the Cross on the part of these ambassadors of Christ. They are going to most every source, biblical and extra-biblical, for their sermon material. But in the main they are not going to Calvary's Cross. This has been outmoded. The bloody Cross of the Crucified Redeemer for them is hardly a fit thing for exaltation in our churches.
>
> Calvary is the greatest moment in the moral history of God.
>
> —F. J. Huegel

Many able missionary preachers have been primarily exhorters, but there are those who have sought after and preached the "deep things of the Spirit of God." Among these is **F. J. Huegel** (1889–1971).[1] His brilliant mind led him to stray in philosophy, although he was reared in a Christian home. At the University of Wisconsin he was converted while reading F. W. Farrar's *Life of Christ.*

Huegel ministered within the Christian Church, or the Disciples of Christ as they have been called. In World War I, he was a chaplain to the American Expeditionary Force in France and then for twenty-five years was a missionary to Mexico. He taught on the faculty of Union Seminary in Mexico City and had a remarkable evangelistic ministry in the prisons of Mexico. In the anguish of a great trial, the Lord showed him the centrality of the Cross as the means of victory over Satan and sin.[2]

Huegel also acknowledged a great debt to the teaching of Jessie Penn-Lewis.[3] Known on both sides of the Atlantic for his preaching on the Cross and the victorious life, Huegel also had a great influence on L. E. Maxwell and Eugenia Price, to name but two. His language is colorful, his illustrations pungent, and his preaching drips with nourishment. Few preachers have probed so painfully but used the Balm of Gilead so generously.[4]

---

1. Another example would be L. L. Legters, cofounder with W. Cameron Townsend of Wycliffe Bible Translators; see *Partakers* (Philadelphia: Pioneer, 1936); *Freedom Through the Cross* (Philadelphia: Pioneer, 1937).
2. F. J. Huegel, *The Cross of Christ—The Throne of God* (Minneapolis: Bethany Fellowship, 1935), 137ff.
3. Jessie Penn-Lewis, *The Centrality of the Cross* (Parkstone, Dorset: Overcomer Trust, n.d.). Messages from the Swanwick "Message of the Cross Conference," April 19–24, 1920.
4. Huegel's messages are in *Bone of His Bone* (Grand Rapids: Zondervan, n.d.); *That Old Serpent, the Devil* (Edinburgh: Marshal, Morgan and Scott, 1954); *Calvary's Wonderful Cross* (Grand Rapids: Zondervan, 1949); *The Cross Through the Scriptures* (Grand Rapids: Zondervan, 1966); *John Looks at the Cross* (Grand Rapids: Zondervan, 1957); *Forever Triumphant* (Minneapolis: Bethany, 1955); *Prayer's*

Deepest Secrets (Minneapolis: Bethany, 1959). My dear friend, Dr. Gordon Johnson, president emeritus of Rio Grande Bible Institute in Edinburgh, Texas, possesses an unpublished biographical memoir of Huegel by his son.

12.1.8 Amy Carmichael of Dohnavur—Mission to South India

> If I am afraid to speak the truth, lest I lose affection, or lest the one concerned should say, "You do not understand," or because I fear to lose my reputation for kindness; if I put my own good name before the other's highest good, then I know nothing of Calvary love.

> Pour through me now: I yield myself to Thee,
> Love, blessed Love, do as Thou wilt with me.
>
> —Amy Carmichael

"Still climbing!" was the description she wanted of her life and ministry. "We have heard the preaching, but can you show us the life of your Lord Jesus?" a Hindu asked. **Amy Carmichael** (1867–1951) both taught and wrote (thirty-six books), but above all she exemplified and embodied the reality of the living Christ.

Born in Northern Ireland, Carmichael was early touched by the gospel and by the Keswick message. She became the adopted daughter of Robert Wilson, one of the early leaders of Keswick. She held children's meetings in Belfast and then reached out to working girls and required a hall seating more than five hundred, which the Lord miraculously provided.[1] A similar ministry followed in Manchester. She became the first missionary sent out by Keswick and visited Japan and Ceylon before sensing God's call to work among the Tamils in South India, particularly among the temple prostitutes.

"Amma" (Tamil for mother), as she was called in the Dohnavur Fellowship, went through incredible trials in her fifty-five years without a furlough, but she was confident:

> I think God wants to make me pure gold, so He is burning out the dross, teaching me the meaning of the fire, the burnt offering, the death of the self-part of me.[2]

Hers was not fashionable Christianity. The rich maturity of her insight and utterance did not derive from the lowering of the threshold but from "the ordination of the pierced hands." Hers was the Order of Epaphroditus (Phil. 2:30). In the last twenty years of her ministry she was an invalid, having fallen into a pit in the dark. In this time she was "climbing unawares."

Both Elizabeth Elliot and Bishop Houghton have given us invaluable studies of this woman of God. Sherwood Eddy, who knew her, spoke of the "beauty of her character," as "the most Christlike character I ever met. . . . Her life was the most fragrant, the most joyously sacrificial, that I ever knew."[3] When she left Keswick in 1895, her theme was "Nothing Too Precious for Jesus." The Fellowship still thrives at Dohnavur (now under Indian leadership entirely), and the goal is still the same: "We preach Jesus Christ as Lord and ourselves as your servants for Jesus sake."[4] Her books are still in extensive circulation.

---

1. Frank Houghton, *Amy Carmichael of Dohnavur: The Story of a Lover and Her Beloved* (Ft. Washington, Pa.: CLC, n.d.), 25ff.
2. Elizabeth Elliot, *A Chance to Die: The Life and Legacy of Amy Carmichael* (Grand Rapids: Revell, 1987), 145.
3. Ruth Tucker, *From Jerusalem to Irian Jaya* (Grand Rapids: Zondervan, 1983), 239.
4. Elliot, *Chance to Die,* 382.

12.1.9 Ruth Paxson—Mission to China and the World

> How should you and I begin the day? From a position of victory. Where should we begin each day? Yonder seated with Christ in the heavenlies, far above all principality and power and might and dominion. "All things are under his feet." What does that mean? Whose feet are they? Whose body? We can have all things under our feet too, if we will; instead of that, we go through each day with everything on top of us: we are underneath most of the time. Can you get higher up than "far above all principality and power and might and dominion"?
>
> —Ruth Paxson

A disproportionate amount of gospel proclamation on the mission fields of earth has been done by single women missionaries. Another who is representative of these is the American **Ruth Paxson,** who served as a missionary to China under the China Inland Mission for many years. Her base of ministry was Shanghai.

Paxson often spoke at the Pei Tai Ho Convention in North China and gave a noted series to women at Keswick in England in 1936. Like her beautiful *Rivers of Living Water,* the Keswick series is so clearly and logically outlined:

I. Oneness with Christ
II. Likeness to Christ
III. Fullness of Christ
IV. Wrestlers for Christ[1]

This reminds us of her most renowned series of messages on Ephesians, *The Wealth, Walk and Warfare of the Christian,* which she subtitles "The Grand Canyon of Scripture." Her ability to chart and visualize, her lucid and clear style, her "comparing spiritual things with spiritual" are most engaging.[2]

But of course her masterpiece is the three-volume work *Life on the Highest Plane,* which she gave to "pastors, evangelists, teachers and other Christian leaders in Conferences held in China."[3] R. A. Torrey paid her high tribute when he said, "Her knowledge of Scripture I have rarely seen paralleled." Upon returning to this country, she had a fruitful ministry in boys' and girls' schools and conferences. Dr. Clarence S. Roddy, in his renown sermon on Romans 6, acknowledged his great indebtedness to Ruth Paxson. Here is biblical exposition of a high order.

---

1. Ruth Paxson, *Called Unto Holiness* (London: Marshall, Morgan, and Scott, 1936).
2. Ruth Paxson, *The Wealth, Walk and Warfare of the Christian* (New York: Revell, 1939).
3. Ruth Paxson, *Life on the Highest Plane* (Grand Rapids: Kregel, 1996).

12.2 BAPTIST STALWARTS WHO TAKE A STAND AGAINST SECULARISM

> Essentially I mean the moment you consider man's real need, and also the nature of the salvation announced and proclaimed in the Scriptures, you are driven to the conclusion that the primary task of the Church is to preach and to proclaim this, to show man's real need, and to show the only remedy, the only cure for it.
>
> —D. Martyn Lloyd-Jones

The decomposition of the Judeo-Christian foundations of Western culture has gained momentum as the century has advanced. Peter Berger describes believers as a "'cognitive minority' whose standards of knowledge deviate from what is publicly taken for granted."[1] As P. T. Forsyth foresaw earlier, the critical issue in the twentieth century is the issue of authority. In postmodernism, the very idea of truth has dissolved. Man has become his own god, and in thus conforming truth to desire, he has bankrupted modern culture.[2] Some within the ranks of orthodoxy have given way to "the cultural relativizing of revelation."[3] Others saw in the evolutionary vision and in the concessions to antisupernaturalistic premises a dangerous threat to the historic Christian faith. We shall see the spokesmen for a vigorous biblical apologetic emerging from many quarters, but at this point, we want to shift the spotlight to some Baptist preachers who model for us clarity of conviction and great courage.

---

1. Wolfhart Pannenberg, "How to Think About Secularism," *First Things* (June/July 1996): 27.
2. E. Michael Jones, *Degenerate Moderns: Modernity as Rationalized Sexual Misbehavior* (San Francisco: Ignatius, 1993). Jones makes essentially the same point as Paul Johnson makes in *Intellectuals* (New York: Harper, 1988).
3. Carl F. H. Henry, "The Cultural Relativizing of Revelation: A Review of Charles Kraft's Christianity in Culture," *Trinity Journal* 1 n.s. (1980): 153–64. Kraft asserts that even "biblically informed believers have no universally valid information about God." Kraft follows the neo-orthodox notion that revelation is personal rather than informational. Not both?

12.2.1 *John Roach Straton—Taking a Stand in the Heart of New York City*

> While many Protestant churches in this city—literally scores of them—have died in recent years because of unbelief and unbiblical methods of work, and while other modernist churches are fanatically striving "to hold the young people" by having dances, theatricals, etc. and are straining to keep up attendance on Sundays by introducing into their services "dramatics," movie "stars" speaking in the pulpits and such other novelties, and even by having bare-legged girls dancing in the sanctuary on the Lord's Day with vari-colored lights playing on them, Calvary Church has prospered and built up on the Old Gospel and spiritual methods of work. The "novelties" finally play out—and have no power even while they are playing in—but the "word of God endureth forever."
>
> —John Roach Straton

One of the central citadels of biblical preaching in New York City for one hundred fifty years has been Calvary Baptist Church in two locations, on Twenty-third Street and in two buildings on Fifty-seventh Street.[1] The seventh pastor at Calvary was a crusader and a communicator. **John Roach Straton** (1875–1929) served Calvary for twelve years. He was a preacher's son and was raised in the South, though he was born in Evansville, Indiana.

Backsliding into skepticism, Straton was soundly converted in a revival meeting in the First Baptist Church of Atlanta. He went on to study at Mercer University in Macon and Southern Baptist Seminary in Louisville. So outstanding were his oratorical gifts that he took further study at the Boston School of Oratory and then taught oratory and literature at Mercer and at Baylor University in Waco, Texas.

But the call to preach was incessant, and he served successively Second Baptist Church of Chicago, Seventh-Immanuel Baptist Church of Baltimore, and First Baptist Church of Norfolk, Virginia. At age forty-three he came to New York, "slender, handsome, dynamic and an orator who immediately attracted attention."[2] Straton crusaded against white slavery, the liquor industry, gambling, pornography, and prize fighting. His somewhat sensational methods brought him great attention; then he moved in with the gospel message with all of his might. Unable to obtain radio time, he established the first church-owned radio station in the nation. He cried:

> The Church of God is not a hospital to nurse sick saints into heaven. The church is rather an armory for the training of soldiers to fight for righteousness and to strive for the salvation of souls. . . . Christianity means heroic self-renunciation, or it means nothing at all.[3]

The Sunday school trebled and the evening service attendance soared to two thousand. In the summer he toured the streets with his portable automobile pulpit. He was a flaming evangelist and invited William Biederwolf, George Truett, and Mordecai Ham (the Southern Baptist under whose preaching Billy Graham came to Christ) to hold great crusades at Calvary. He championed the cause of historic orthodoxy against evolution and higher criticism and took the case into a series of public debates at Carnegie Hall. Straton also went after the Ku Klux Klan.

In all of this, Calvary flourished, and Straton led in the demolition of the old church and the building of a combination church and hotel which still stands on the Fifty-seventh Street location. His lecturing and preaching reached their zenith in the 1928 presidential campaign, when he focused his shot against Al Smith and Tammany Hall. He was struck down with a heart attack and then a stroke that took him from the battles of this life at the early age of fifty-four.[4]

After interviewing the liberal Harry Emerson Fosdick, a New York journalist then interviewed Straton. If the former spoke to his head, the latter spoke to his heart. He told the newspaper man "the old, old story of Jesus and His love."[5] The journalist concluded that Straton had a religion for men and women who were troubled in a troubled world.

The sermonic strategy of Straton (who bore a striking resemblance to Woodrow Wilson) was to burrow down in a great text. His message on "The Modern Need of a Great God" from Isaiah 6 is exegetically weak, but the progression of thought in the passage prevails.[6] The sermon on "How the Fisherman Captured Rome," based in Acts 2:46–47, is more loosely strung but delineates the message, the method, and the might of the early church.[7] The sermon on "The Empty Place" from 1 Samuel 20:18 is moving, but builds a temple where the Scripture only has a tent.[8] His illustrations are crisply developed and his style is not florid. Straton clearly loved to preach on the Second Coming of Christ and on the Cross of Christ and its meaning. His vibrant and enthusiastic delivery was doubtless a potent factor in the great impact this preacher of the Word made upon the city.

---

1. William R. De Plata, *Tell It from Calvary* (New York: Calvary Baptist, 1972). This study traces the growing years under Dr. Robert S. MacArthur (1870–1911); the call to Joseph Kemp of Charlotte Chapel, Edinburgh, and his brief ministry before going to New Zealand; the great ministry of Will Houghton, who followed Straton (cf. Wilbur M. Smith, *A Watchman on the Wall: Life Story of Will H. Houghton* (Grand Rapids: Eerdmans, 1951); and the pulpit eloquence of William Ward Ayer, who served Calvary from 1936 to 1949 (see his sermons, *Marked Men* [Grand Rapids; Eerdmans, 1947] and his lectures on evangelism at Bob Jones University, *Flame on the Altar* [Grand Rapids: Zondervan, 1952]).
2. F. R. Webber, *A History of Preaching in Britain and America* (Milwaukee: Northwestern, 1957), 3:577.
3. De Plata, *Tell It from Calvary,* 47.
4. Ibid., 53.
5. William G. Shepherd, *Great Preachers as Seen by a Journalist* (New York: Revell, 1924), 72.
6. John Roach Straton, *The Old Gospel at the Heart of the Metropolis* (New York: George H. Doran, 1925), 17ff.
7. Ibid., 36ff.
8. Ibid., 201ff.

12.2.2 *William Bell Riley—Taking a Stand in the Midwest for the Bible and the Supernatural*

> The reason there are so many poor preachers is because there are so few who are willing to put gray matter into the preparation of sermons.
>
> When we remember these mighty conflicts and see that the ultimate issue has ever been on the side of truth, we wonder at the arrogance of that heterodoxy which under many forms of liberalism is today disturbing the evangelical creeds of Europe, England and America. We are also surprised that the religious age should seem alarmed at these freaks of faith! Why not remember, and so remind them, that the procession of orthodoxy has left buried in its triumphal track greater names than even theirs, and still sweeps on, conquering and to conquer, till the time shall come when the paean of eternal triumph shall be shouted once for all?
>
> —W. B. Riley

Standing tall and straight as an arrow with his shock of snow-white hair, he was an unforgettable figure in the pulpit. William Jennings Bryan called him "the greatest Christian statesman in the American pulpit." **William Bell Riley** (1861–1947) was reared in Boone County, Kentucky, where he worked hard as a young lad on his father's farm. Of Irish-Scotch, English, and Dutch pedigree, Riley had early impressions of the nation torn and divided and earned his first substantial money as a tobacco trader.

In August of 1878, Riley was converted in a revival, followed the Lord in baptism, and made public profession of his newfound faith.[1] He was driven by a motivation he could not understand to seek education. He enrolled at the Normal School in Valparaiso, Indiana, where he paid $1.45 per week for food and owned but a $13.00 suit for school. By 1880 he had his teaching certificate and was set to go in Possum Ridge, Owen County, Kentucky. A wealthy farmer wanted to pay his way through Hanover College at this time, and to help with expenses, Riley traveled by horse and buggy to fill preaching places. He did not want to be a preacher—debate and oratory were his obsessions—but God would not let him go.[2] Riley served a string of congregations while he studied at Southern Baptist Seminary in Louisville under the great John Broadus and John Sampey.

It was while Riley was at Louisville that the higher critical views of the promising young Crawford H. Toy compelled his leaving school. Riley became part of D. L. Moody's Louisville crusade and early on was an evangelist himself.

In 1888 Riley gave the ringing graduation address at Southern Seminary on "The Triumph of Orthodoxy." One senses in reading it that the sail is set.[3] Dr. George Lorimer of Chicago preached his installation sermon at New Albany, Indiana, from whence young Riley went to serve a successful pastorate in Lafayette, Indiana. Here he met and married a young Methodist. Riley went on to Bloomington, Illinois, and then to Calvary Baptist Church on the south side of Chicago. Here he bumped into the liberalism of President William Harper at the University of Chicago and became a thorn in the side of those who denied the gospel. Along with his high-profile activism in the community, he evolved a dream of building something like the Tremont Temple at the heart of a great city, but by then Chicago was too vast and sprawling.[4]

The opening of opportunity came remarkably in 1897, when he accepted the call to the First Baptist Church of Minneapolis. There he was to be the pastor for the next forty-five years and the pastor emeritus for three years. Immediately a power bloc in the church was antagonized by Riley's outspoken opposition to pew rents, church fairs, and bazaars. His enemies hired a private detective, but after five years of struggle, 146 of them left to found their own congregation on Lowrey Hill. Riley led into battle the Bible-believing forces of the Twin Cities against evolution, liquor interests, and gambling. Able and articulate, his debates spread around the country. He was one of the prime movers with A. C. Dixon and William Jennings Bryan in founding the World Christian Fundamentals Association.[5] In all of this time, he gave himself to the rebuilding of the First Baptist Church, which had 2,640 seats. He also founded Northwestern Schools (Bible School and Seminary), where Billy Graham succeeded him as president.

Riley held evangelistic crusades and Bible conferences around the world and always brought in the finest of biblical preachers to fill his pulpit when he was absent. He believed that if a sermon is worth preaching, it should be printed. He preached through the entire Bible from 1923 until 1933, and these sermons can be found in the forty-volume *Bible of the Expositor and the Evangelist*. The more expositional messages for Sunday morning are here along with the evangelistic addresses from Sunday night (remember that the "seekers' services" were then held on Sunday night). His sermons are well researched and well illustrated. He clipped from his reading and pasted into scrapbooks. In all, Riley had seventy volumes of these three-hundred-page scrapbooks and drew upon them freely. Almost all of his sermons have a respectable set of mains and subs. Listeners were seldom aware that the preacher was working from a fully written manuscript.

Riley was in the middle of the tensions and turmoil in the Northern Baptist Convention, from which he withdrew near the end of his life. His good friend and colleague, Earle V. Pierce, chose the more mediating way and served as president of the convention. (Pierce performed the wedding of Riley and his second wife.)[6] Even with the huge responsibilities of church and school and the broader ministry, Dr. and Mrs. Riley paid pastoral calls and never lost sight of the people.

Although usually he exposed a good piece of text, Riley once preached a series on "The Seven Things God Hates" from Proverbs 6:16ff.[7] He was a preacher's preacher who fitted strong content to appropriate form. Perhaps he pursued issues like evolution too far, too much, but he was always on the cutting edge of a society and culture cast loose from their moorings. He was a great preacher of Bible prophecy, and his books, though dated, are well worth obtaining and reading.

---

1. Marie Acomb Riley, *The Dynamic of a Dream: The Life Story of W. B. Riley* (Grand Rapids: Eerdmans, 1938), 43.

2. Ibid., 31.
3. Ibid., 53ff.
4. Ibid., 63.
5. Riley was succeeded in the presidency of the WCFA by the founder of the Bryan Bible League and his close friend Dr. Paul Rood, pastor of Beulah Covenant Church, Turlock, California, and later pastor of the Church of the Open Door and President of BIOLA. Rood was a mighty preacher in his own right; see *When the Fire Fell* (Grand Rapids: Zondervan, 1939). I heard Rood preach the memorial address at the Minnesota Fundamentals Conference following the homegoing of W. B. Riley in 1947.
6. Earle V. Pierce served Lake Harriet Baptist Church in Minneapolis and was a most engaging preacher; see *The Conflict Within Myself* (New York: Revell, 1942). "A Kiss That Did Not Count" from Ruth 1:14 is exceptional; also see *The Church and World Conditions* (New York: Revell, 1943); *The Supreme Beatitude* (New York: Revell, 1947). The latter is one of the best books of sermons preached on stewardship.
7. W. B. Riley, *The Bible of the Expositor and the Evangelist,* 40 vols. (Cleveland: Union Gospel Press, 1926 and on). I came into possession of the entire set through the kindness of the late Mr. and Mrs. Dan Bren; *Youth's Victory Lies This Way* (Grand Rapids: Zondervan, 1936); *Christ the Incomparable* (New York: Revell, 1924); *The Seven Churches of Asia* (New York: Christian Alliance, 1900); *Seven New Testament Converts* (Grand Rapids: Eerdmans, 1940); *Re-Thinking the Church* (New York: Revell, 1940). These are my favorite titles.

12.2.3 A. C. Dixon—Taking a Stand for the Saving Gospel on Both Sides of the Atlantic

> God's work in God's way with God's power to God's glory.
>
> My delight is in the Lord, and not in what man may think or say about me. My constant prayer is that my heart may be perfect toward God. . . . I desire to be Christ's in body and mind and heart and time and purse.
>
> How I do long to preach Jesus to the lost, and to see them saved! May God prepare us for our future work. We are in His hands for success or failure, and it is blessed to rest just there. I have a vision of my own selfish, sinful soul, which has crushed me into the dust, but I have also the glorious vision of Christ and His Word.
>
> —A. C. Dixon

The motto of **Amzi Clarence Dixon** (1854–1925) was "The whole Christ in the whole Bible for the whole world." He had a commanding love and loyalty for Scripture. It was said of his preaching, "He quoted Scripture with the readiness and alacrity of a lover quoting poetry."

This confidence in the Word seemed to be in his blood, born as he was in Shelby, North Carolina, the son of a farmer-lay preacher. His early years were caught up in the maelstrom of the Civil War, but Dixon was converted in a revival at nearby Old Buffalo Church under his father's preaching from Acts 16:31. Ninety-seven others were baptized the day he was.[1]

Dixon attended Wake Forest College and on one occasion was forced to preach when the assigned speaker failed to come. Out of this experience came his sense of call to preach and an insatiable desire to master the Greek New Testament.[2] He wrote to Charles Spurgeon in London about the feasibility of taking his seminary work at the College in London, but Spurgeon counseled that Dixon study at home. He began seminary studies at the Baptist Seminary in Greenville, South Carolina (since moved to Louisville), and particularly benefited from John Broadus as a teacher.

Dixon was a pastor-evangelist by calling. He never finished seminary but took the pastorate of First Baptist in Chapel Hill, North Carolina, where he launched his ministry with a series of protracted meetings in which revival fell upon the congregation. On one occasion when he was ill, he recovered dramatically when a country lad was saved.[3] He moved on to Asheville, North Carolina, where there was almost continual revival for the two-and-a-half years he was there. One young carpenter whom Dixon led to Christ in turn led a lad to Christ of whom we shall hear much—George W. Truett.

Systematic visitation was a key thrust in Dixon's strategization. He moved on to the Immanuel Baptist Church of Baltimore, where he had a gracious ministry. Crusading against liquor was important to Dixon, and he dealt much with "the dangerous lure of some popular amusements." In Baltimore he led in the building of a new tabernacle seating twelve hundred and began to visit Northfield and other venues of biblical preaching.

"The trend away from biblical authority" was very apparent and grievous to Dixon.[4] He spoke out against Roman Catholic heresy even in Baltimore. While speaking at the World Sunday School Convention in 1889, Dixon became well-acquainted with Spurgeon, who invited him to speak at the Metropolitan Tabernacle. Dixon analyzed Spurgeon's strength as "The fact that he has the anointing of the Holy Spirit, and preaches God's Word, relying on Him to bless it."[5]

Dixon's next charge was the Hanson Place Baptist Church in Brooklyn (1890–1901). Its second pastor, Dr. Robert Lowry, wrote such hymns as "Up From the Grave He Arose," "Shall We Gather at the River?" and "I Need Thee Every Hour." Dixon brought Fanny Crosby in to speak to the youth. He promoted large prophetic conferences and a training institute at which Dr. Nathaniel West spoke effectively on "The Pentateuch and Higher Criticism." Dixon was so outspoken against the forces of unbelief that the famous skeptic Robert Ingersoll sued him. Although Beecher was gone, Dixon had to face the legacy of his equivocation on Scripture, the Atonement, and future punishment.[6] Clearly apostasy was spreading.[7]

In 1893 he was invited to be part of the evangelical pulpit team that ministered at the Chicago World's Fair. The team consisted also of David Burrell (cf. 11.4.6) and Theodore Cuyler (cf. 10.3.6). After resistance to expansion, Dixon took the call to Ruggles Street Baptist Church in Boston. Here he entered into an ongoing sparring match with Christian Science. He spoke at the first Baptist World Congress in London in 1905, as did F. B. Meyer, and preached for Campbell Morgan at Westminster Chapel and for Thomas Spurgeon at the Metropolitan

Tabernacle. He had fine opportunity for fellowship with his dear friend Sir Robert Anderson of Scotland Yard (cf. 11.1.6). Dixon also made the first of two visits to preach at Keswick on this visit abroad.

In 1906 he began an eventful five-and-a-half year ministry at the Chicago Avenue Church, which later became the Moody Church. During this time he played a vital role in the writing of *The Fundamentals.* In 1911 he began his ministry at the Metropolitan Tabernacle in London, a ministry he continued until 1919. The ministry at Elephant and Castle more than held its own during these trying years, and Dixon ministered in Norway, Scotland (preaching for Joseph Kemp at Charlotee Square in Edinburgh), and elsewhere with great energy. In one twelve-month period, seven hundred souls were converted at the Tabernacle.

Dixon, together with Campbell Morgan, F. B. Meyer, Dinsdale Young, and Stuart Holden, hailed the signing of the Balfour Declaration in 1917 as having prophetic significance.[8] Upon returning to the United States after the war, he traveled in conference ministry and taught at the Bible Institute of Los Angeles. He returned to Baltimore and a ministry at the new University Baptist Church near John Hopkins University.

He and Mrs. Dixon then went to China. While ministering there, she suddenly died. He came back to Baltimore for a last shot, challenging high criticism, Bolshevism, and evolution. He brought such scholars as Robert Dick Wilson from Princeton (who worked in twenty-six languages)[9] and Melvin Grove Kyle from Xenia Seminary in Pittsburgh to defend historic Christianity.[10]

Early in his ministry in London, Dixon held a three-week evangelistic crusade, and his sermons from that effort were published as *The Glories of the Cross.* These sermons are biblically based, some expository and some textual, imagistic, and pictorial. He illustrated extensively and well. Several of the messages are like the Plymouth Brethren and F. E. Marsh Bible readings.[11]

Dixon had a simple and direct style. On occasion, we wish he would probe further into the passage, yet he divided a text well, sometimes with as many as seven or eight mains. Truly a man of great humility and one who was indifferent to popular approval, Dixon's life text was, "Worthy is the Lamb that was slain to receive power and riches and wisdom and strength and honor and glory and blessing." A. C. Dixon was plain but powerful, and he was always biblical![12]

---

1. Helen C. A. Dixon, *A. C. Dixon: A Romance of Preaching* (New York: Putnam's, 1931), 31.
2. Ibid., 38. The second Mrs. Dixon was the widow of Torrey's song leader, Mrs. Charles Alexander.
3. Ibid., 41.
4. Ibid., 95.
5. Ibid., 107.
6. Ibid., 127.
7. Ibid., 181.
8. See my book *Jews, Gentiles and the Church* (Grand Rapids: Discovery House, 1995), 169ff.

9. Robert Dick Wilson, *A Scientific Investigation of the Old Testament* (Chicago: Moody, 1959).
10. Melvin Grove Kyle, *Mooring Masts of Revelation* (New York: Revell, 1933). Dixon's successor at University Baptist was Russell Bradley Jones, whose sermons *Gold from Golgotha* on the seven last words are a classic series.
11. A. C. Dixon, *The Glories of the Cross* (Grand Rapids: Eerdmans, 1962), 69ff.
12. A. C. Dixon, *Through Night to Morning* (Grand Rapids: Baker, 1969); *The Bright Side of Life* (New York: George H. Doran, n.d.); *Heaven on Earth* (Greenville, S.C.: Gospel Hour, n.d.).

12.2.4 Len G. Broughton—Taking a Stand for Christ in Atlanta and on the Thames

> But there is coming a time when the Gentile dispensation is coming to an end; when the church shall have done its work in proclaiming Jesus Christ as the Savior of the world; and when the Gentile period, or church period of the world is at an end, then Israel will be restored, and she will take her rightful place as the favorite of God, proclaiming the Messiah to a lost and ruined world . . . the Jew as a nation is going to receive Jesus Christ.
>
> —Len G. Broughton

One of the most eagerly awaited preachers of the Word at this time was the six-foot, 118-pound physician-evangelist **Leonard G. Broughton** (1864–1936). Born in Wake County, North Carolina, Broughton received his medical education at the University of Kentucky. He was practicing medicine in Reidsville, North Carolina, when the call of God to be a physician of souls took priority above all else. He studied theology, was ordained in 1893, and then pastored successfully in Knoxville, Tennessee, and in the Grove Avenue Baptist Church of Richmond, Virginia.

In 1898 Broughton came to Atlanta, then a city of sixty-five thousand, and founded the Baptist Tabernacle. It would ultimately become the largest Southern Baptist church of its time. Broughton's vision came to fruition in a great sanctuary seating thirty-three hundred. He also established the Tabernacle Hospital and Training School for Christian Nurses.[1] In 1914 he went to Christ Church, Westminster Road, in London (cf. 11.3.4), where he enjoyed an astounding ministry until his health collapsed. Webber gets to the heart and soul of Broughton's preaching:

> Dr. Broughton was not the first American who filled a London pulpit, but few have attracted the attention he did. In a day when it was customary for the majority of London's clergymen to take at least a neutral attitude toward biblical criticism and the New Theology, later known as Modernism, Dr. Broughton did not hesitate for a moment to make his theological position clear. He took it for granted that Genesis is of Mosaic authorship, that the world was created as the Bible states, that the

> Book of Isaiah was written by Isaiah. . . . He believed in eternal life for the true believer and endless punishment for the wicked and the unbelieving. Once more the people of London flocked across Westminster Bridge, almost as they had done in the days of Spurgeon, whose Metropolitan Tabernacle was not far from Dr. Broughton's church.[2]

Broughton preached the Second Coming of the Messiah and an end-time scenario in which the Jews return to Palestine and come to Christ (Romans 11).[3] His style was electrifying and explosive. He preached the old-time religion with great charm and warmth. "Possessed of a ringing voice of pleasant quality, he won men instantly by his preaching . . . His eloquence had a note of the Southern grandiloquence now and then."[4] Clear outlines were not his forte; rather, he made use of the dramatic story, "the American anecdote."

Analysis of his sermons shows them to be no models of tight organization, but the great personal magnetism of the preacher leaps off the printed page. Contagious warmth and pastoral tenderness radiate from "He Lifted Him Up" from Mark 9:26–27 and from "The Cup of Cold Water" from Matthew 10:42.[5] Pungent address to practical issues emanates from "Forgiveness" out of Matthew 18:21; genuine exegetical analysis is evident in "The Things That Defile" from Mark 7:15.[6] He argued emphatically that great preaching and great practice must be in parallel. Loved at Northfield as much as in the Bible belt in the deep South, Leonard Broughton was an unusual preacher who made a remarkable impact.

---

1. Among the strong preachers who led the Baptist Tabernacle on to even greater heights was John W. Ham, whose unusually fine preaching is reflected in his *Present-Tense Salvation* (Chicago: Moody, 1927) and in *Good News for All Men* (New York: Doubleday, Doran, 1928). These sermons are well outlined and illustrate what became the dominating type of sermon in Southern Baptist preaching—the stirring evangelistic or kerygmatic sermon.
2. F. R. Webber, *A History of Preaching in Britain and America* (Milwaukee: Northwestern, 1957), 3:565.
3. Len G. Broughton, *Where Are the Dead?* (Atlanta: Phillips-Boyd, n.d.). His *Revival of a Dead Church* is famous.
4. Webber, *A History of Preaching,* 3:566.
5. Len G. Broughton, *Christianity and the Common Place* (London: Hodder and Stoughton, 1914), 23ff., 41ff.
6. Ibid., 105ff., 119ff.

12.2.5 GEORGE W. TRUETT—TAKING A STAND IN THE OPEN SPACES OF TEXAS

> When I see the varied temperaments and relative needs of my church members, sermons come to me like birds in flocks. [Yet "His preaching always leaves the impression that it is founded on and fortified by the Word of God."—Powhatan W. James]

> I have sought and found the shepherd's heart.
>
> Think of a preacher being a moral coward! We are to be willing to pay the price for spiritual power. It is a great price. We must be crucified with Christ. We must die to self. We must live unto the Lord without evasion or reservation, if we are to be the witnesses, the prophets, the advocates of the Gospel of Christ that we ought to be . . . What manner of men preachers should be! Good men. Not goody good men. Good men. God's men, impassioned and empowered by the living Spirit. What manner of men we ought to be!
>
> —George W. Truett

The distinguished historian Douglas Southall Freeman wrote of **George W. Truett** (1867–1944), "It would be difficult to exaggerate the influence of Dr. Truett's positive preaching on American ministers in a critical age."[1] Truett was born in Clay County in the rugged blue hills of North Carolina, the seventh child of a farmer, Charles Truett and his wife, Mary. He and his siblings attended Hayesville Academy because the parents desperately wanted their progeny well educated. Because his brother Spurgeon was deaf and was taught to lip-read, young George developed unusually good enunciation.[2]

In his childhood, "the big-faced boy of Charlie Truett," as he was known, gave an eloquent oration on the death of a pet squirrel.[3] He was converted in a revival meeting. He started to teach school and established a successful academy but moved with his parents when they emigrated to Texas. Folk frequently asked him, "Oughtn't you to be preaching?" The church in Whitewright, Texas, moved to ordain him. At first he objected, but finally yielded when he realized that God was indeed calling him to preach.

In 1890, B. H. Carroll (cf. 10.4.4) approached him to raise funds for the almost defunct Baylor College. Young Truett virtually lived with the Carrolls during this time and indeed saved Baylor (and the seminary, which moved to Fort Worth and is now known as Southwestern Baptist Seminary). From 1893 to 1897, he studied at Baylor and served as a student pastor in East Waco. When he graduated from Baylor, the First Baptist Church of Dallas (with 715 members) called him. He served that great church for forty-four years, leading them to seven thousand members and an enlarged auditorium seating four thousand persons.

Accidentally killing his best friend, the sheriff of Dallas County, in a hunting mishap, almost drove Truett from the ministry. He went on with the support of God, his wife and family, and strong friends like the gifted preacher and executive of Texas Baptists, J. B. Gumbrell.[4] He preached to cowboys and in evangelistic crusades around the world. Three times he was president of the Southern Baptist Convention (1927–1929) and of the Baptist World Alliance (1934). Still, First Baptist of Dallas was his home and haven.

Known as the "devout dogmatist," Truett always preached Christ crucified. Books were his hobby. He averaged one sermon or lecture per day for forty years. The tall, raw-boned preacher was popular on college and seminary campuses. His preaching was like a cavalry charge; his "short, smashing sentences" were well suited to Texas. His eyes were "blue-gray . . . his voice was pleading and clear as a bell."[5] Yet the Bible in its perfection and power was basic to everything he did.

Truett preached to the troops in Europe both before and after the armistice. He preached an annual two-week revival in his own church, and the noon services in a theater broke new ground in evangelism and outreach. Together with Merton Rice of Detroit (cf. 11.6.1 note 2) Truett was among the leaders in "America's Preaching Mission" in 1936 and 1937.

Yet unlike his successor, W. A. Criswell, Truett was not expository. He preached the main thought of his text but did little exegesis. His biographer explains:

> He will be accorded this place in the Hall of Fame, not for profundity of thought, nor brilliance of rhetoric, or originality of exegesis, nor cleverness of homiletics, but for his simplicity of language, his singleness of purpose, force of delivery, depth of compassion, ability to reach humanity's heart and will, and power to exalt Christ as Savior and Lord. It will be said of him as he said of Spurgeon: "The pulpit was his throne and he occupied it like a king."[6]

Truett's gestures were limited. His titles were simple and seldom announced beforehand. He put his notes for preaching on the back of envelopes with his personal abbreviations. "He trusts his memory and it seldom betrays him. He prefers to stumble a bit, if need be, with repetitions and inverted sentences, rather than to fall back on his written notations."[7] Yet he could be dazzlingly eloquent, as when he spoke to fifteen thousand on the steps of the United States Capitol on "Baptists and Religious Liberty."[8]

Truett's pastoral prayers were especially powerful. His outlines were sound, but his written sermons cannot begin to match the charm of what was preached. His basic pattern was to prompt the audience to think, move them to feel, and motivate them to choose.[9] Explanation and argumentation were not large parts of his style. Yet the George W. Truett Library, with its 108 sermons and fifteen hundred pages of his preaching, is well worth owning and perusing. He never preached in series, but his messages on the person and work of Christ in *Who Is Jesus?* are typical.[10] In sample Old Testament sermons as found in *On Eagle Wings,* two messages on the Word are particularly moving—"The Bible Lost and Found" from 2 Kings 22:8 and "Mutilating God's Word" from Jeremiah 36:23.[11]

All of these sermons are replete with strong, winning illustrations and good application. The focus always shifts to commitment to Christ before bridging to the public invitation. His son-in-law biographer phrased it well: "He was gifted with access to the human heart."[12]

---

1. Powhatan W. James, *George W. Truett* (Nashville: Broadman, 1939), viii.
2. Ibid., 17–18.
3. Ibid., 22.
4. Al Fasol, *With a Bible in Their Hands: Baptist Preaching in the South 1679–1979* (Nashville: Broadman, 1994), 102ff.

5. James, *George W. Truett,* 105.
6. Ibid., 235.
7. Ibid., 249.
8. Ibid., 1.
9. Ibid., 255.
10. George W. Truett, *Who Is Jesus?* (Grand Rapids: Baker, 1952).
11. George W. Truett, *On Eagle Wings* (Grand Rapids: Baker, 1953), 65ff., 77ff.
12. James, *George W. Truett,* 246.

12.2.6 Robert G. Lee—Taking a Stand for the Bible in the Mid-South and Border States

> The Bible is our greatest national asset—that supreme Book, supernatural in its origin, divine in authorship, human in penmanship, infallible in authority, inexhaustive in its adequacy, a miracle book of diversity in unity, infinite in scope, universal in interest, eternal in duration, personal in application, inspired in totality, regenerative in power, inestimable in value, immeasurable in power, unsurpassed in literary beauty, unequalled in simplicity of expression, immortal in its hopes, the masterpiece of God.
>
> —Robert G. Lee

Preaching has always enjoyed primacy in the Southern Baptist Convention.[1] No one exemplifies the old-time Southern Baptist preacher better than **Robert G. Lee** (1886–1978). Lee was born in a log cabin where his devout parents were sharecroppers who earned an annual wage of $250. He was educated in a one-room school and was converted in a protracted revival meeting in 1898.[2] He had a passion for reading but was obsessed with the Book of all books. When Lee heard Dr. Edwin Poteat, president of Furman University, preach, he sensed God's call.[3] Attempting to raise funds to go to college, he went to work on the Panama Canal and almost died of black fever. Returning to graduate from Furman in 1913, he served twelve student pastorates and grew in his reputation as a preacher. Studying further at Tulane, Lee was offered the Latin chair at Furman but declined it because the school stipulated he could not pastor and teach.

In 1918 Lee took the call to First Baptist Church in Edgefield, South Carolina, where Senator Strom Thurmond's father, the district attorney, was a member. Here for the first time he gave his famous sermon, "Pay Day, Some Day," which he preached one thousand times. It is the narrative of Ahab and Naboth's vineyard in eight scenes. At this time he completed a doctoral degree in law by correspondence at the Chicago Law School. Starting in 1921, he spent sixteen months at First Baptist in Chester, South Carolina, where he introduced tent revivals and many other innovations. Four hundred and fifteen members were added to the church while he preached there. On one day alone, five thousand people saw him baptize 120 converts.

In 1922 Lee began a ministry at First Baptist Church, New Orleans (where Dr. J. D. Grey and others were to have such distinguished ministries). But he worked himself into a breakdown of health and needed a ten-week reprieve in which to recover. In 1925 he took the Citadel Square Baptist Church of Charleston, where E. C. Dargan had served. Despite a struggle with the church's debt, a revival broke out.[4]

By 1927 he began what would be a thirty-two-year pastorate at the Belleview Baptist Church in Memphis, Tennessee. The church took in 600 new members in his first year, and he built the membership to 6,106 by 1942. Lee was a dutiful pastor and visited constantly to win souls. He taught the men's Bible class forty-four Sundays of the year, wrote thirty books, traveled widely, and served as president of the Southern Baptist Convention for three terms.

Yet with all of this, preaching had priority for Robert G. Lee. He was at his best when he was preaching about Jesus Christ![5] Twenty-five percent of his sermons were about the atoning work of Christ on Calvary; two-thirds were textual-topical. The sermons of Talmage and Edwin Poteat shaped his style. His forty-five-minute sermons were ornate, much like Halford Luccock's "confectioner's sermon." He had a vast vocabulary and used alliteration adeptly, speaking about 110 words per minute.[6] As Paul Gericke observes in his study of Lee's preaching, Lee was "attracted to the English language—he gave special attention to the meaning of words and the construction of sentences." His titles were unique like "A Grand Canyon of Resurrection Realities"; "Glory Today for Conquest Tomorrow" (from Matt. 17:1–7, 14–18); "The Menace of Mediocrity"; "When We Bleed, We Bless"; "Chasing Fleas and Dead Dogs" (from 1 Sam. 24:14); and "Boo!" (from Ezek. 25:3–4).

A typical sermon is "Christ Above All," which he based on the thought of John 3:32. His outline was:

I. Christ is above all as to His Source;
II. Christ is above all in relation to Creation;
III. Christ is above all in the way he made entrance into the world;
IV. Christ is above all as to his revelation of God;
V. Christ is above all in his supernatural power;
VI. Christ is above all in his teaching;
VII. Christ is above all in his sacrificial suffering;
VIII. Christ is above all in his relation to death;
IX. Christ is above all as to his promised return.[7]

What is missed in Lee and some other Southern Baptist preaching is suggested by Gericke: "Lee understood New Testament Greek but not Hebrew. However, he did not use it much in his study. . . . He did not study commentaries much, but when he did, he favored the commentaries of Matthew Henry and Jamieson, Fausset and Brown."[8]

What Lee did read was sermons, endless sermons, and literature generally, which tended to inflate his style. Neither was his style sufficiently enriched with strong exegesis. After considerable "picturizing" of the sermon, Lee preached it without notes. Gericke characterizes Lee's strong points as being clarity, energy, elegance, imagination, and humor.[9]

Robert G. Lee was a powerful influence for the historic gospel, but there is little digging into Scripture in this preaching.[10] We read Lee not as a model but as an example of a period piece.

---

1. O. Eugene Mims, "The Importance of Biblical Preaching in Southern Baptist Churches," *Proclaim,* 1994, 4ff. There was some poison in the water even after the Toy affair. Fasol shows how E. Y. Mullins, longtime president of Southern Baptist Seminary, Louisville, was influenced by Schleiermacher (see *With a Bible in Their Hands,* Nashville: Broadman, 1994), 99; cf. E. Y. Mullins, *Why Is Christianity True?* (Philadelphia: American Baptist Publication Society, 1905); for a study of the Mullins Preaching Lectures at Southern Seminary, see Don M. Aycock, *The E. Y. Mullins Lectures on Preaching with Reference to the Aristotelian Triad* (Washington, D.C.: University Press of America, 1980).
2. John E. Huss, *Robert G. Lee* (Grand Rapids: Zondervan, 1967), 29. E. Schuyler English wrote an earlier study.
3. Al Fasol, *With a Bible in Their Hands: Baptist Preaching in the South 1679–1979* (Nashville: Broadman, 1994), 116.
4. Huss, *Robert G. Lee,* 123.
5. Ibid., 141, 144.
6. Paul Gericke, *The Preaching of Robert G. Lee* (Orlando: Christ for the World Publishers, 1967), 98ff.
7. Clarence S. Roddy, ed., *We Prepare and Preach* (Chicago: Moody, 1959), 86ff.
8. Gericke, *The Preaching of Robert G. Lee,* 119.
9. Ibid., 140ff. One of Lee's successors, Adrian Rogers, is more exegetical; see *The Secret of Supernatural Living* (Nashville: Thomas Nelson, 1982). Belleview has relocated and has more than thirteen thousand members.
10. For sample collections of sermons, see Robert G. Lee, *This Critical Hour* (Grand Rapids: Zondervan, 1942); *Great Is the Lord* (New York: Revell, 1955). Doctrinally sound preaching on justification and the return of our Lord—but there is little exegesis.

12.2.7 Robert Thomas Ketcham—Warrior for Christ

> The scriptural injunction is, "Be ready to give an answer to everyone that asketh for the hope that lies in you"; and when a man is asked in all Christian courtesy if he believes that Jesus Christ is God, pre-existent with the Father and born of a virgin, and that His death upon the cross bore the wrath of God against our sins, and he refuses to answer, he cannot blame his questioner if he assumes that his reason for silence is due to the fact that he does not believe it.
>
> —R. T. Ketcham

All of the mainline denominations were facing the massive inroads of liberalism. Nowhere was the battle hotter than in the Northern Baptist Convention as W. B. Riley, J. C. Masse, and Cortland Myers led the champions of the fundamentals. Leading for the liberals were Cornelius Woelfkin and Harry Emerson Fosdick.[1]

Coming up out of the trenches as point man for the conservatives was **Robert Thomas Ketcham** (1889–1978). Ketcham was born in modest circumstances in a Methodist home in Nelson, Pennsylvania. His mother died when he was seven, and his father married a Baptist widow. Hence, in the providence of God, the children were raised Baptist. Leaving home as a rebel when he was sixteen, young Ketcham nonetheless yielded to Christ in meetings at Galeton Baptist when he became enamored with messages by W. W. Rugh on the types in the tabernacle in the Old Testament.[2]

Surrendering his life to Christ, at age twenty-three Ketcham took a call to pastor the Roulette Baptist Church, comprised of twenty-eight women and five old men. His first message was out of Matthew 1 in which he found an extra virgin birth.[3] He had only two books in his library: his Scofield Bible and a volume of sermons for special occasions. Ketcham gave himself to a study of the cults which were thriving about him and started correspondence courses at Crozer, a Baptist seminary. Quickly he learned of liberal advances in the convention and saw them even at his own ordination council.[4]

In the thirty-four months he was at Roulette, six hundred percent growth occurred as the membership moved up to two hundred. Yet already his chronic eye problems, which would finally leave him blind, were apparent. Throughout his ministry, he memorized his text and the hymns and then pretended to read. Occasionally he held his Bible upside-down.

In 1915 Ketcham moved to First Baptist, Brookeville, Pennsylvania, where he had a fine ministry and wrote a pamphlet challenging the New World Movement, a unified budget program of the convention. W. B. Riley was so impressed he ordered twenty thousand copies. Taking the call to First Baptist in Butler, Pennsylvania, Ketcham became more and more embroiled in the liberal/fundamentalist controversy. About this time his first wife died, leaving him with two daughters. He later remarried, and to that union one son was born.

In one convention after another, the conservatives were outfoxed or defeated. Serving in Niles, Ohio, and then at First Baptist in Elyria, Ohio, following R. E. Neighbor, Ketcham was increasingly recognized as an able spokesman for historic Christianity. After the 1927 convention in Chicago, Ketcham saw the handwriting on the wall and told Riley, "I am never coming back."[5] He left the convention.

In 1932 the Ketchams took up a new ministry at Central Baptist Church in Gary, Indiana, following William Ward Ayer. Here he was part of the leadership of the new General Association of Regular Baptists (GARB). Total separatism did not end the turmoil, as Ketcham and J. Frank Norris (who pastored First Baptist, Fort Worth, and Temple Baptist, Detroit, simultaneously) continued to feud for many years. In 1939, when young Pastor P. B. Chenault was killed, Ketcham became pastor of the Walnut Street Baptist Church of Waterloo, Iowa, where God mightily blessed the Word. In 1948, though virtually blind, he was appointed national representative of the GARB. For his remaining years he sustained an amazing profile of activity and ministry even in seriously declining health, preaching as much as 283 times a year.

R. T. Ketcham was a preacher of unusual charm and effectiveness. He could be tender but was always tough-minded. He was hard-hitting but from the heart. His famous series on the Twenty-third Psalm titled "I Shall Not Want" must stand among the classic sermons preached on the shepherd psalm. His illustrations were riveting and revealing. But like some other gifted preachers, Ketcham was not always reflective on the preaching process—indeed, he occasionally disparaged homiletics.[6] When he stayed with a text he was outstanding, but occasionally he rambled, speaking the truth but not supporting it with sound hermeneutics. Several of his published sermons show this weakness.[7] Yet anyone who heard him preach could only concede that he was eminently able.

---

1. Harry Emerson Fosdick (1878–1969) was unusually gifted as a preacher but was in no sense biblical. He testified: "The stereotyped routine into which old-fashioned expository preaching had fallen was impossible to me, i.e. the elucidation of a scriptural text, its application and then exhortation." See Lionel Crocker, *Harry Emerson Fosdick's Art of Preaching: An Anthology* (Springfield: Charles C. Thomas, 1971). His espousal of "life-situation preaching," which does not begin with the Bible, is a method not unpopular among evangelicals today. The theoretical base for this approach can best be traced in the works of Charles F. Kemp; see *The Preaching Pastor* (St. Louis: Bethany Press, 1966). Kemp's example sermons have two sermons by Fosdick.
2. J. Murray Murdoch, *Portrait of Obedience* (Schaumburg, Ill.: Regular Baptist Press, 1979), 24f. I am indebted to my doctoral student Gilbert Parker for this book.
3. Ibid., 31.
4. Ibid., 47.
5. Ibid., 117.
6. Ibid., 248.
7. R. T. Ketcham, "Did You Leave Something on the Stairs?" in Murdoch, *Portrait of Obedience,* 301ff. This is an allegorization of the Song of Solomon every bit equal to that of Bernard of Clairvaux; see also "The Course and End of Satan's World System," in Warren W. Wiersbe, *Classic Sermons on Spiritual Warfare* (Peabody, Mass.: Hendrickson, 1992), 29ff. This is a powerful statement of truth, but when a sermon is not text-driven, we sacrifice the clear advantage of the most effective demonstration of biblical truth; see Walter C. Kaiser Jr., "The Crisis in Expository Preaching Today," *Preaching* (September/October 1995): 4ff.

12.3 SCHOLARS AND TEACHERS WHO STOOD IN THE BREACH

> The postmodernist rejection of objectivity pervades the evangelical Church . . . This downplaying of doctrine and objective thinking . . . This openness to personal feelings and experience is a point of contact with postmodernism, which has gone on to exaggerate the role of subjectivity beyond anything that a "hot gospeler" of the nineteenth century would ever recognize.
>
> —Gene Edward Veith Jr.

Subjectivity is in vogue as we head into the new millennium. A. E. Garvie had protested, "In view of many tendencies towards an excessive subjectivity, what needs to be asserted is that the Christ of the faith of the Church is a constant objective reality, and that the preacher is Christian only as he recognizes and respects the distinctiveness of the faith he preaches as historical."[1] Likewise, the patriarch of American evangelical theologians, Carl F. H. Henry, laments "the loss of the objective reality of God and the objective truth of His revelation, which has been replaced in our society by a looming skepticism and a despairing hedonism."[2]

The emphasis today is mood, not mind. We have opinions but not facts. In the face of this drift, many scholars and teachers among conservatives have stood steadfastly and resolutely for the truth, often taking their stand along the lines of the Lausanne Covenant:

> We affirm the divine inspiration, truthfulness and authority of both Old and New Testament Scriptures in their entirety as the only written word of God, without error in all that it affirms and the only infallible rule of faith and practice.

Few wrote more cogently or compellingly than did Francis Schaeffer of L'Abri Fellowship in words that point to the watershed issue for biblical preaching:

> There is the danger of evangelicalism becoming less than evangelical, of its not really holding to the Bible as being without error in all that it affirms. We are then left with the victory of the existential methodology under the name of evangelicalism. Holding to a strong view of Scripture or not holding to it is the watershed of the evangelical world.[3]

We now look at several representatives of the learned academy who used the pulpit as well as the classroom for the articulation of "the faith once for all delivered."

---

1. A. E. Garvie, *The Christian Preacher* (New York: Scribner's, 1923), 278. Garvie's own call came while he was reading Stalker's *Life of Paul,* "and there came home to me the world's need of the preacher. As though I heard a voice, the words possessed my mind—'Woe be to me if I preach not the Gospel'—I sat down and wrote my decision to my Father." From Ralph G. Turnbull, *A Minister's Obstacles* (Grand Rapids: Baker, 1946).
2. Carl F. H. Henry, *Chicago Tribune,* November 20, 1982, 17.
3. Francis A. Schaeffer, *No Final Conflict: The Bible Without Error in All that It Affirms* (Downers Grove, Ill.: InterVarsity Press, 1975), 48. Schaeffer himself came to Christ in a tent meeting where he went forward; see Louis Gifford Parkhurst, *Francis Schaeffer: The Man and the Message* (Wheaton, Ill.: Tyndale House, 1985). He was an able preacher, and a selection of his sermons, *No Little People* (Downers Grove, Ill.: InterVarsity Press, 1974) shows he is biblical but not text-driven.

12.3.1 Peter Taylor Forsyth—Contending for the Bible and Its Authority

> The key to history is the historic Christ above history, and in command of it, and there is no other.
>
> Preaching is the Gospel prolonging and declaring itself. The gift of God's grace was, and is, his work of Gospel. And it is this Act which is prolonged in the word of the preacher and not merely declared.
>
> There is penalty and curse for sin, and Christ consented to enter that region . . . Christianity is not the sacrifice we make but the sacrifice we trust. An undogmatic Christianity is a contradiction in terms.
>
> —P. T. Forsyth

The brilliant **Peter Taylor Forsyth** (1848–1921) has a slot in the history of preaching not only as a fine preacher and a theorist of preaching (in his Beecher Lectures at Yale in 1907 titled *Positive Preaching and the Modern Mind*) but also as a liberal who turned back to Christ and the Bible. He became a pillar and a rock for the faith. Listen to him lamenting the "lost note of authority" in the contemporary church:

> Without a real authority Protestantism is not only a blunder but deserves to be a failure. We need an authority more than anything else . . . There is only one thing greater than liberty, and that is authority.[1]

Forsyth was notoriously reticent about his personal life, but we know he was born in Aberdeen, Scotland, the son of very poor people. He never knew birthdays or presents in his upbringing but was brought up devoutly and joined the Blackfriars Street Congregational Church. Always physically precarious, he was a brilliant student at Aberdeen, where he studied under Andrew Fairbairn, and he went to Germany to study under Ritschl at Gottingen. He lapped up Ritschl's subjectivity in doctrine and returned to England to serve several churches.[2] While he was at Leicester he realized the bankruptcy of liberalism and moved from "being a Christian to being a believer, from being a lover of love to an object of grace."[3] He then served Emmanuel Congregational Church in Cambridge, a low ebb time for him with the death of his wife, and was made principal of Hackney College in 1901, teaching at the University of London at the same time.

His theological conversion was profound. He returned to orthodoxy and defended the gospel against R. J. Campbell and the New Theology. His critique of liberalism was devastating. As a liberal he had denied substitution in the Atonement, but now stressing the centrality of the cross, he insisted on "the need of an objective expiatory idea of the Atonement."[4] He felt that the pulpit in nonconformity had lost its power "because it has lost intimacy with the Cross, immersion in the Cross."[5] Forsyth asserted the radicality of evil and felt that Americans tended to a Pelagian superficiality in thinking about sin. His ripest work was probably his masterpiece on *The Person and Place of Jesus Christ.*[6]

Basic in all of this was his insistence on the priority and authority of the Word of God. Conservative German scholars such as Adolph Schlatter now weighed heavily with Forsyth. Coupled with his resurgent orthodoxy was the conviction that "a man's life is seen at the level of his prayer life."[7] Yet Forsyth still retained some vestiges of liberal thinking, most especially his universalism. Soren Kierkegaard also influenced him.

Forsyth wrote twenty-five books. Always epigrammatic in his writing and preaching, he was sharp-featured with a "fine forehead, with a large moustache and deep piercing eyes."[8] Donald Miller says that trying to follow the majestic stream of Forsyth's thought is like standing beside Niagara with a tin cup.[9] Forsyth felt that the great danger of the preacher was in so preaching *to* their age they might well *preach* their age. He urged preachers to take a substantial piece of text for their expository sermons. We possess few of Forsyth's sermons, and so it is difficult to know how well he practiced his own counsel.[10] Of this we are sure: his stand for Christ and Scripture was unexpected and is still influential. He said:

> How can we hope to regain the influence the pulpit has lost until we come with the surest Word in all the world to the guesses of science, the maxims of ethics, and the instincts of art.[11]

---

1. Robert McAfee Brown, *P. T. Forsyth: Prophet for Today* (Philadelphia: Westminster, 1952), 94. Archbishop Donald Coggan's intriguing endorsement of Forsyth's lectures, "Under-estimated Theological Books" in his *Christian Priorities* (New York: Harper and Row, 1963), 149ff. Coggan's ringing conservatism is a great encouragement.
2. To assay this, see Albrecht Ritschl, *The Christian Doctrine of Justification and Reconciliation* (Edinburgh: T & T Clarke, 1900); for a sympathetic view, see Albert T. Swing, *The Theology of Albrecht Ritschl* (New York: Longmans, 1901).
3. Robert S. Paul, "P. T. Forsyth: Prophet for the Twentieth Century," in *P. T. Forsyth* (Pittsburgh: Pickwick, 1981), 63. He traces this radical move from liberalism in *Positive Preaching and the Modern Mood* (281–85).
4. Ibid., 57. A. M. Hunter also shows how Forsyth retained the penal idea; see *P. T. Forsyth* (London: SCM, 1974), 120.
5. P. T. Forsyth, *The Cruciality of the Cross* (Grand Rapids: Eerdmans, 1909). The issue: sympathy or salvation?
6. P. T. Forsyth, *The Person and Place of Jesus Christ* (Grand Rapids: Eerdmans, 1909). A sad example of a Scottish professor who went to more liberal and concessive thinking would be the prolific and often helpful William Barclay (1907–1978). N.B. Clive L. Rawlins, *William Barclay* (Grand Rapids: Eerdmans, 1984); also William Barclay, *A Spiritual Autobiography* (Grand Rapids: Eerdmans, 1975). His commentaries are homiletically pregnant but antisupernatural (he holds the "little brown paper bag theory" on feeding the five thousand and denies the Virgin Birth).
7. P. T. Forsyth, *The Soul of Prayer* (Grand Rapids: Eerdmans, 1916). Some have waxed eloquent that Forsyth was "Barth before Barth," but while they both rediscovered sin, Barth would never have extolled biblical authority like this.

8. Hunter, *P. T. Forsyth,* 21.
9. Donald G. Miller, *P. T. Forsyth: The Man* (Pittsburgh: Pickwick, 1981), 16.
10. P. T. Forsyth, *Revelation Old and New: Sermons and Addresses* (London: Independent Press, 1962).
11. P. T. Forsyth, *Positive Preaching and the Modern Mind* (Pittsburgh: Pickwick, repr. 1981), 184.

12.3.2 J. Gresham Machen—Contending for Historic Orthodoxy

> The Bible is not a ladder; it is a foundation. It is buttressed, indeed, by experience; if you have the present Christ, then you know that the Bible account is true. But if the Bible were false, your faith would go. You cannot, therefore, be indifferent to biblical criticism. Let us not deceive ourselves. The Bible is at the foundation of the Church. Undermine that foundation and the Church will fall. Two conceptions of Christianity are struggling for the ascendancy; the question that we have been discussing is part of a still larger problem. The Bible against the modern preacher. . . . The Church is in perplexity. She is trying to compromise. God grant that she may choose aright. God grant she may decide for the Bible!
>
> —J. Gresham Machen

We have already introduced **J. Gresham Machen** (1881–1937) as one of the key figures in the pitched battle between modernism and historic orthodoxy (cf. 11.4). He belongs in the body of this study not only because of his immense and impressive scholarship, but also because he was a believer in preaching.

Machen was a brilliant teacher who was early stirred by the preaching of Dr. Hoge and later by Dr. Harris Kirk at his home church, Franklin Street Presbyterian Church in Baltimore. Hesitating over his vocation, he felt called to go to Princeton, where he learned preaching under David J. Burrell and was grounded in the Word under B. B. Warfield and Francis Patton (who had prosecuted David G. Swing in 1874).[1] He went on to study at Gottingen and Marburg in Germany and felt the attraction of the liberalism of Julicher at the former and William Hermann's Ritschlianism at the latter, but he held his ground.[2] He hoped to do more study in Germany, but his mother was worried he would lose his faith. He therefore took the opportunity at Princeton Seminary to be the junior colleague of Professor William Park Armstrong in New Testament. His earliest efforts at preaching put his listeners to sleep, but he was soon infected with a great love for preaching, particularly the Old Testament.[3]

Machen early on took a strong stand for inerrancy, and his brilliant scholarship earned him widespread respect. He used Galatians in exegesis, and his classic text in beginning Greek has been the guide for thousands of expositors over the years.[4] Unafraid to take on the hard questions, Machen was yet sensitive to the cultural issues. He observed, "The great questions may easily be avoided . . . many preachers are avoiding them."[5]

As early as 1914 signs of Princeton being on the slippery slope were discernible, but by and large the church was indifferent to this bold prophet's warnings.

His detractors spoke of his "high-brow fundamentalism." He did associate with W. B. Riley and the WCFA and spoke to them, though he was not a member.[6] He spoke also at Northfield and had a sympathetic view of Billy Sunday even though a greater contrast between two servants of Christ can hardly be imagined.[7]

Machen began to want to preach more widely. He appreciated Jowett in New York City but blanched at what Parkhurst, Coffin, and Fosdick were doing with Scripture. Around the time of World War I, he left Princeton to work for the YMCA in France. In 1924 he returned to the battle for the soul of Princeton and stood with Clarence Macartney of Arch Street Presbyterian Church in Philadelphia in the General Assembly. The fundamentalists faced Fosdick, who had just put forth his nasty sermon, "Shall the Fundamentalists Win?" and the thirteen hundred signers of the Auburn Affirmation, which attacked inerrancy and viewed all doctrinal formulation as theorization.[8]

In the inevitable reorganization of the seminary, Machen was out. With others he founded Westminster Seminary and the Independent Board of Foreign Missions, which ultimately led to his ecclesiastical trial in 1936 and his expulsion. He was never given a chance to defend his views. In the following year he died of pneumonia at the untimely age of fifty-six while on a preaching tour in Bismarck, North Dakota.

A steady stream of his powerful books, published chiefly by mainline secular houses, kept coming through all of those difficult years. His *What Is Faith?* (1925) argued effectively against the separation of religious experience from theology.[9] A sparkling series of radio addresses show how serious theology can be communicated.[10] The collection of his major addresses has many treasures.[11] Dr. Stonehouse has done all of us a great service in gathering some of the choice sermons together, including significant messages on such subjects as "God Transcendent" from Isaiah 40:22, "The Gospel and Modern Substitutes" from Romans 1:16, and "The Separateness of the Church" from Matthew 5:13. The sermons are not long and show a simple organizational schema.[12] When Machen left Princeton, he encapsulated his experience:

> If you decide to stand for Christ, you will not have an easy life in the ministry . . . You will graciously be permitted to believe in supernatural Christianity all you please if you will only act as though you did not believe in it, if you will only make common cause with its opponents. Such is the program that will win the favor of the church. A man may believe what he pleases, provided he does not believe anything strongly enough to risk his life on it and fight for it. "Tolerance" is the great word. Men may ask for tolerance when they look to God in prayer. But how can any Christian possibly pray such a prayer as that? What a terrible prayer it is, how full of disloyalty to the Lord Jesus Christ.[13]

---

1. Ned B. Stonehouse, *J. Gresham Machen: A Biographical Memoir* (Grand Rapids: Eerdmans, 1954), 64.
2. Ibid., 105.

3. D. G. Hart, *Defending the Faith: J. Gresham Machen and the Crisis of Conservative Protestantism in Modern America 1881–1937* (Grand Rapids: Baker, 1994), 30.
4. J. Gresham Machen, *New Testament Greek for Beginners* (New York: Macmillan, 1923, 1952). In its twenty-fifth printing.
5. Stonehouse, *J. Gresham Machen,* 188.
6. Hart, *Defending the Faith,* 66. Cf. Mark Noll, ed., *The Princeton Theology 1812–1921* (Grand Rapids: Baker, 1983).
7. Stonehouse, *J. Gresham Machen,* 223. Another strong spokesman for the faith is T. J. McCrossan, *The Bible: Its Christ and Modernism* (New York: Alliance, 1925). He was examiner in Greek and Hebrew for the Presbytery of Minneapolis.
8. Stonehouse, *J. Gresham Machen,* 364. Unaccountably this dastardly sermon is held up as "a model sermon for today's preachers" in Long and Plantinga, *A Chorus of Witnesses* (Grand Rapids: Eerdmans, 1994), 243.
9. Hart, *Defending the Faith,* 91. N.B. J. Gresham Machen, *What Is Faith?* (Grand Rapids: Eerdmans, 1925).
10. J. Gresham Machen, *The Christian Faith in the Modern World* (Grand Rapids: Eerdmans, 1936).
11. J. Gresham Machen, *What Is Christianity?* (Grand Rapids: Eerdmans, 1951). Compare this with von Harnack's *What Is Christianity?* (New York: Putnam's, 1904) and its pabulum of the fatherhood of God and brotherhood of man.
12. J. Gresham Machen, *God Transcendent and Other Sermons* (Grand Rapids: Eerdmans, 1949).
13. David Otis Fuller, *Valiant for Truth: A Treasury of Evangelical Writings* (New York: Lippincot, 1961), 450.

12.3.3 Walter A. Maier—Contending for Grace and Mercy

> Culinary clatter and dramatic razzle-dazzle called "church work" are drowning out the testimony of the saving Gospel.
>
> Picture the cancerous growth of modern infidelity as ego-complexed pulpiteers, disguising the breed of the wolf beneath silk cassocks . . . read from the Scriptures with crossed thumbs, tongues in cheek and with mental reservations, who place the Bible on the level with heathen philosophies . . . Think of the smooth, oily surrender of the deity of our Savior . . . I still repeat the cry, "Back to Luther!"
>
> —Walter A. Maier

Time called him "the Chrysostom of American Lutheranism." Billy Graham labeled him the greatest evangelist of this century. Daniel Poling spoke of him as "the preeminent voice of Protestant faith and practice." We know **Walter A. Maier** (1893–1950) as the speaker on "Bringing Christ to the Nations." He was the founder and preacher of this broadcast, which aired on 1,236 stations in 120 countries in thirty-six languages with some twenty million hearers. He was "a preacher of the old-fashioned religion."[1] He also held a doctorate in philosophy in Old Testament and Semitics from Harvard and was a professor at Concordia Seminary in St. Louis.

Maier defended the reliability and trustworthiness of Scripture and preached it with power. He was born in Boston of German immigrant parents. His father was an organ builder. He attended Concordia Collegiate Institute in Westchester County, New York, where he early on loved Latin, Greek, Hebrew, and German.[2] Graduating as valedictorian of his class, he went on to finish his B.A. at Boston University. Maier continued on to Concordia Seminary in St. Louis, where such giants as Franz Pieper and J. Theodore Mueller defended the old gospel, and then on to Harvard Divinity School and Graduate School for his doctoral studies. At this time he won the Billings Prize in Oratory.[3] Imbued with a great heart for missions and evangelism, Maier served for two years as executive secretary of the Walther League, the youth branch of the Missouri Synod.

In 1922 he became professor of Old Testament at Concordia Seminary in St. Louis. There he trumpeted the genuine gospel and the need for a forthright facing of the problem of human sinfulness. He found that his message was in high demand all over the country. Holy Week in 1922, he preached to great throngs in the American Theater Noonday Services and so contemporized the events of the first Holy Week that he spoke "as if he had witnessed them himself."[4]

Maier had a vision for the inner city and helped found St. Stephen's in a blighted area of St. Louis. Then he became the leader of the Lutheran Hour broadcast, which received two hundred thousand letters per week. He filled Soldier's Field in Chicago for a great Lutheran Hour rally and similarly the Hollywood Bowl in 1948. Maier was Lutherlike and potent in his biblical citation. With rapid-fire delivery and vehemence, he opened Scripture and fearlessly applied it. He believed "firmly in a verbally inspired Bible . . . Gifted with an exceptionally keen mind, he had weighed the arguments of the Higher Critics and the Modernists and had come to the conclusion that these men are religious mountebanks."[5] He was a creationist (and we are indebted to the Missouri Synod for such preceptors as Rehwinkel, Zimmerman, and Klotz for scholarship in this area). He challenged the efforts of the modernist Federal Council of Churches to obtain a monopoly on the religious airwaves.[6]

Ordinarily Maier's sermons were two points, problem and solution. His introductions were brief and direct. He used all of the rhetorical tools available to the skilled communicator.[7] He was the author of thirty-one books, including an influential study of marriage, *For Better Not For Worse.* Of his Lutheran Hour sermons, 509 have been published in twenty volumes. "Jesus Christ Is Your God" from John 14 divides into two parts: (1) Believe in God; (2) Believe also in Christ.[8] "Join the Jury Trying Jesus" and "Follow Christ on the Calvary Road" are sterling examples of his preaching. His commentary on Nahum is the best ever done on that great Old Testament book.[9]

This is the heart of a preacher from a liturgical tradition who in the onslaught of liberal and neo-orthodox challenges did not lower the flag. He had defended his doctoral dissertation in a citadel of unbelief before the likes of Robert Pfeiffer and Paul Foot Moore. No wonder both Machen and Maier died at fifty-six! They poured forth their all in loyalty to the historic gospel. Successors like Oswald C. J. Hoffmann would carry on the ministry of the Lutheran Hour.

1. F. R. Webber, *A History of Preaching in Britain and America* (Milwaukee: Northwestern, 1957), 3:594.
2. Paul L. Maier, *A Man Spoke, A World Listened: The Story of Walter Maier* (New York: McGraw, 1963), 17.
3. Ibid., 25.
4. Ibid., 75.
5. Webber, *A History of Preaching,* 3:594.
6. Maier, *A Man Spoke, A World Listened,* 188. Other great radio preachers were Charles E. Fuller, M. R. DeHaan, and Theodore Epp.
7. Ibid., 206–7. Kenneth Hartley Sulston, "A Rhetorical Criticism of the Radio Preaching of Walter Arthur Maier" (doctoral dissertation, Northwestern University, 1958); Lester Erwin Zeitler, "An Investigation of the Factors of Persuasion in the Sermons of Dr. Walter A. Maier" (St. Louis: M.S.T. dissertation, Concordia Seminary, 1956). For a recent sample of Missouri Synod homiletics, see Francis Rossow, *Preaching the Creative Gospel Creatively* (St. Louis: Concordia, 1983).
8. Walter A. Maier, *Global Broadcasting of His Grace* (St. Louis: Concordia, 1949), 88ff.
9. Walter A. Maier, *The Book of Nahum: A Commentary* (St. Louis: Concordia, 1959). A masterpiece. He shows twenty-two respects in which the prophetic predictions of Nahum were historically and actually fulfilled, 114ff.

12.3.4 A. T. Robertson—Contending for the Bible and Its Accuracy

> Some people appear to rest their minds when they preach.
>
> What on earth can I do that I haven't done to inspire those men to learn this book? What are they thinking about? Why do they not master it? How can they expect to preach the book unless they know it?
>
> The greatest proof that the Bible is inspired is that it has stood so much bad preaching.
>
> Never get out of a text what was never in it.
>
> —A. T. Robertson

For twelve seasons a favorite preacher at the Northfield Conference, whose preaching sent F. B. Meyer into "ecstasies," was **Archibald Thomas Robertson** (1863–1934), or Dr. Bob as he was called. He was a key figure who, as Machen argued, combined "scholarship and popular power" in a trenchant way.[1] Well received at Winona Lake as well, Robertson was a teacher of six thousand students at Southern Baptist Seminary and the author of forty-five books. He preached with his Greek New Testament in his hand—and wore out a dozen of them in the process. In this he resembled the English Quaker, Dr. J. Rendal Harris of Birmingham, who was so scintillating in his expositions.[2]

Robertson was born in Pittsylvania, Virginia, the son of a doctor whose fortune was broken. Young "Archie" moved with his family to North Carolina when he was twelve. He sensed a change of heart in 1876 and was greatly influenced by his pastor, J. B. Boon, who wondered if he had not thought of preaching.[3] Enrolling at Wake Forest College, Robertson tried to overcome a speech impediment. "I am like Demosthenes," he said, "in that I have a hesitation in my speech when I grow nervous." But he entered into debating societies and other activities and became "an impressive speaker." He developed great prowess in Greek, though he tended to overwork himself and was through his lifetime subject to infection and exhaustion.[4]

"He wanted to be a preacher and he became one of the great expository preachers of his day."[5] Entering Southern Baptist Seminary in Louisville in 1885, he "got hold of preaching," and became the much appreciated supply preacher at First Baptist in Covington, Kentucky. Upon his graduation, he was made assistant to John Broadus (cf. 10.4.2) in Greek and homiletics and stayed on at Southern for forty-six years.

Preaching was a vital part of his ongoing ministry. While he deliberately avoided denominational office, Robertson was one of the founders of the Baptist World Alliance. He made several trips to Europe and knew Maclaren, Spurgeon, and Professor Zahn in Leipzig.[6] Although demanding, Robertson was a great teacher with whom "The New Testament became a new and glowing book."[7] In academic circles his work was highly respected, but it was thought he talked too fast and was hyperorthodox. His most significant scholarship was as a philologist and textual critic.

His first writings were the critical notes for Broadus' *Harmony.* He challenged the radical notions of President Harper of the University of Chicago, a fellow Baptist. In 1894 Robertson married the youngest daughter of Dr. John Broadus. Upon the death of Broadus four months later, he was made full professor of New Testament Greek at Southern. Robertson eventually wrote the definitive biography of John A. Broadus.

He advanced from the premise that the Bible is true. In the face of the massive doses of negative higher criticism, the cause of classical biblical Christianity needed scholars who would give their genius to the state of the biblical text as received. This Robertson did in *An Introduction to the Textual Criticism of the New Testament* and his twenty-six-year project, a fifteen-hundred-page "big grammar," *A Grammar of the Greek New Testament in the Light of Historical Research.* Here he argues conclusively, as Rendal Harris had earlier, that the Greek of the New Testament is the koine of the average person and the papyri. His work was praised by Warfield, Zahn, Stalker, Souter, and many others. He knew and worked with Sir William Ramsay, A. H. Sayce, Principal Fairbairn, and Walter Lock. His six-volume work, *Word Pictures in the New Testament,* has assisted many expositors. Twice he gave the Stone Lectures at Princeton, the last of which in 1926 was his splendid *Paul and the Intellectuals: The Epistle to the Colossians.*[8] When he died, he was working on a new translation of the New Testament.

Robertson's written and spoken style befits his ancestral Scottish trait of economy in words, and he never lost his passion for preaching. Early on he tended to be subject-centered, but he became increasingly text-driven. His sermons were described as "spritely" and thus quite consistent with his character. He hated "sham and pretense" and confessed on one occasion that "I have been too ambitious for personal fame."

The death of his daughter, Charlotte, left Robertson devastated with the question as to why the Lord who raised the daughter of Jairus would not raise his daughter, but he yielded, "Not my will but Thine be done." He loved to preach revivals and do evangelism. Some thought him a bit severe because he was so blunt and direct, but he had a delightful sense of humor as he described Deacon Skinflint and Sister Sharp-tongue and Rabbi Smell-fungus and Pastor Dry-as-dust. He exulted in *The Glory of the Ministry* and skillfully delineated *Types of Preachers in the New Testament.* The collection of his sermons demonstrates his ability to use appealing illustration.[9]

Robertson loved to hear great preaching, and he listened with appreciation to Mark Guy Pearse in England and Hugh Black in Scotland. He compared notes with Ellicott, Lightfoot, Alford, Westcott, and Hort at a luncheon it would have been marvelous to attend. Here was a man of valor and virtue who stood steadfastly in a culture on the brink.

---

1. Everett Gill, *A. T. Robertson: A Biography* (New York: Macmillan, 1943), 132.
2. For a sample of J. Rendel Harris' preaching, see *As the Hart Pants* (London: Hodder and Stoughton, 1924).
3. Gill, *A. T. Robertson,* 31.
4. Ibid., 49.
5. Ibid., 50.
6. Ibid., 70.
7. Ibid., 116. A typical book by Robertson, *The Mother of Jesus: Her Problems and Her Glory* (Grand Rapids: Baker, 1963).
8. A. T. Robertson, *Paul and the Intellectuals: The Epistle to the Colossians* (Nashville: Broadman, 1956). In his *Studies in the Text of the New Testament* (New York: George H. Doran, 1969 rep. College Press, Joplin, Mo.), Robertson makes a strong case for the preacher's ongoing reading and studying, 106.
9. A. T. Robertson, *Passing on the Torch and Other Sermons* (New York: Revell, 1934). Particularly impressive are the sermons titled "The One Talent Man" from Matthew 25:13–30 and "Buying Up the Opportunity" from Colossians 4:5 and Ephesians 5:16. Another significant Baptist scholar and preacher was H. Wheeler Robinson (1872–1945), long associated with Regent's Park College in London and Oxford. His works on *The Cross of Job, The Cross of the Servant, The Cross of Jeremiah*, and *The Christian Experience of the Holy Spirit* make some concessions but are homiletically rich. Note Ernest A. Payne, *Henry Wheeler Robinson* (London: Nisbet, 1946). Robinson points out the perennial danger for the preacher when the introduction and exegesis take all of his time and he never "gets to the real sermon" (40).

12.3.5 Wilbur M. Smith—Contender for the Supernatural Gospel

Wilbur Smith believes that Christians have a supernatural gospel, that it can transform lives through the work of the Holy Spirit, that we learn

> about it in the inerrant Scriptures, and that it ought to be constantly preached and taught . . . He is a man who tried to apply these principles and has been successful in doing so.
>
> —Paul Woolley

> The pulpit was the one place for which I really lived.
>
> —Wilbur Moorehead Smith

One of the century's foremost bibliographers and a bibliophile of the first order, **Wilbur Moorehead Smith** (1894–1977) was a special gift to Bible-believing Christians. As a man of encyclopedic knowledge on many religious subjects and an honored professor at three prestigious evangelical institutions, Smith was a powerful preacher in his own right. His indefatigable reading uncovered a gem by a biographer of E. W. Hengstenberg, who wrote:

> [Hengstenberg] saw that the entire literature of religion stands or falls with the early documents which are its elements and alphabet: that if these individual books were not written by the men to whom the later Scriptures ascribe them—if they do not record facts that are historical—if the New Testament inspiration is not really an approval and guarantee of an Old Testament inspiration—if the Scriptures of the old and new covenants contradict each other—if, in short, there is not a perfect unity in the grand and complete record, then Christianity is undermined and ready to fall, bringing down with it the hopes of mankind.[1]

Smith was born into a wealthy Chicago home. His parents were active in the Moody Church. His father was called the apple king because of his large orchards in Michigan. Yet young Smith had little formal education apart from a brief stint at Moody Bible Institute and a short tenure at Wooster College in Ohio. Upon his marriage, he assumed the pulpit in a series of Presbyterian churches in Wilmington, Delaware; Ocean City and Baltimore, Maryland; Covington, Virginia; and the large Presbyterian church in Coatsville, Pennsylvania (1930–1937). Coatsville was a church of more than eighteen hundred members, where he followed the fine incumbency of Dr. Roy Brumbaugh.[2] In 1933 he preached at Moody Founder's Week in Chicago, the first of seventeen appearances over the years. His gifts as an expositor were increasingly recognized, and he began to write and review for the *Sunday School Times* and to write the commentary on the International Sunday School lesson, which he maintained for thirty-five years. Pastors built their libraries on the bibliographies in *Peloubet's Notes.* His years of teaching at Moody Bible Institute, Fuller Theological Seminary (in English Bible and apologetics), and later at Trinity Evangelical Divinity School were exceedingly positive.[3]

Smith built a personal library of more than thirty thousand volumes and was "tireless" in his reading, writing, and preaching. His burden was what he perceived to be "terrible errors menacing evangelical Christianity today."[4] His primary focus was:

1. The effect of the Bible on history, translations of the Bible, and Bible dictionaries.
2. The defense of the bodily resurrection of Christ. His *Therefore Stand* was a great encouragement in its day.[5]
3. The historicity of Christ's nativity. *The Supernaturalness of Christ: Can We Still Believe in It?* was most timely.[6]
4. The literal interpretation of biblical prophecy. His works on *Egypt in Biblical Prophecy, World Crises and the Prophetic Scriptures,* and *Israeli/Arab Conflict and the Bible* are balanced contributions.[7] His widely praised *The Biblical Doctrine of Heaven* is in a unique category.[8] He owned 284 commentaries on Revelation.
5. The impact of science on Christian faith as in his 1945 study, *The Atomic Bomb and the Word of God.*[9]
6. Preaching and sermons in his editing of the "Great Sermons on" series and his invaluable radio talks for pastors as published cannot conceal his great excitement and enthusiasm for the Word of God and its infinite treasures.[10]
7. The subject of revival, particularly his fine study on the revival in the days of King Hezekiah.[11]

Roger Phillips assesses Smith as a bibliographer, and Smith's own memoirs afford many insights into his friendships and involvements over the years. The close association between Smith and Machen is fascinating.[12] Smith served on the Scofield Bible Revision Committee and was offered the post as first editor of *Christianity Today.*

Always fresh and prepared in the lecture hall or pulpit, Smith impressed some as abrupt and a bit fussy. His "excessive use of superlatives" became a trademark and for some a hindrance. Yet those who got past the somewhat crusty veneer found a wondrously gentle and generous follower of Christ. His wit and humor, his passion in preaching, his rich content impress us with the hard work he put into preaching.[13] Tributes by his colleagues and contemporaries put him into scale.[14] Typical sermons are those he preached at Keswick in England in 1952 on *The Word of God and the Life of Holiness.*[15] These sermons follow no set rules but both burn and bless their readers as they did the listeners who first hung on the words as spoken. In many ways Smith is not to be a model for preachers, but he was always a motivator.

---

1. Wilbur M. Smith, *A Treasury of Books for Bible Study* (Grand Rapids: Baker, 1960), 202. One of the most popular of all Smith's writings and still read is his *Profitable Bible Study* (Boston: W. A. Wilde, 1939).
2. Roger Wendell Phillips, *Wilbur Moorehead Smith: A Profile and Bibliography* (thesis for the M.L.S. degree at Emporia Kansas State College, 1976), 18ff., 84.
3. Smith was one of the four original faculty (the others being Harold Lindsell, Carl F. H. Henry, and Everett F. Harrison). The story of why he left Fuller and one point of view on the changes in Pasadena is given by George Marsden, *Reforming Fundamentalism: Fuller Seminary and the New Evangelicals* (Grand Rapids: Eerdmans, 1987).

4. Phillips, *Wilbur Moorehead Smith,* 6.
5. Wilbur M. Smith, *Therefore Stand: A Plea for a Vigorous Apologetic in This Critical Hour of the Christian Faith* (Boston: W. A. Wilde, 1945). Josh McDowell, in his popular work on the resurrection, quotes this book twenty-three times.
6. Wilbur M. Smith, *The Supernaturalness of Christ: Can We Still Believe in It?* (Boston: W. A. Wilde, 1940).
7. Wilbur M. Smith, *Egypt in Biblical Prophecy* (Boston: W. A. Wilde, 1957); *World Crises and the Prophetic Scriptures* (Chicago: Moody, 1952); *Israeli/Arab Conflict and the Bible* (Glendale, Calif.: Gospel Light, 1967).
8. Wilbur M. Smith, *The Biblical Doctrine of Heaven* (Chicago: Moody, 1968). All of Smith's writing are quite homiletical.
9. Wilbur M. Smith, *The Atomic Bomb and the Word of God* (Chicago: Moody, 1945).
10. Wilbur M. Smith, *Chats from a Minister's Library* (Grand Rapids: Baker, 1951); *The Minister in His Study* (Chicago: Moody, 1973). The latter work is a series of lectures given at Trinity Evangelical Divinity School in 1972.
11. Wilbur M. Smith, *The Glorious Revival under King Hezekiah* (Grand Rapids: Zondervan, 1937).
12. Wilbur M. Smith, *Before I Forget: Memoirs* (Chicago: Moody, 1971). Some remarkable byways in memory lane.
13. Wilbur M. Smith, "No Set Rules," in *We Prepare and Preach,* ed. Clarence S. Roddy (Chicago: Moody, 1959), 160ff.
14. Kenneth Kantzer, ed., *Evangelical Roots: A Tribute to Wilbur Smith* (Nashville: Thomas Nelson, 1979).
15. Wilbur M. Smith, *The Word of God and the Life of Holiness* (Grand Rapids: Zondervan, 1957). I recall hearing Wilbur Smith speak at a seminary convocation in the fall of 1953 on "Preach the Word" from 2 Timothy 4:2, a sermon which will always be for me one of the most dynamic and inspirational expositions I have ever heard.

12.3.6 THEODOR ZAHN—CONTENDER FOR THE INTEGRITY OF THE WORD OF GOD

> Men may receive much grace, and yet go forth empty. It is the undeserved grace of reconciliation itself that we have to accept aright. The one gracious Word of God, the love of God, revealed on the Cross, must do all for us; we must accept it again and again, and allow it to work in us that for which it has the power. Then our lives will also show forth the fruits of grace.
>
> —Theodor Zahn

The providential networking of Bible-believing servants of Christ took place all over the world, even in the den of German rationalism (cf. 9.4). An important link in the defense of the gospel was the distinguished New Testament and patristics scholar, **Theodor Zahn** (1838–1933).

Zahn's grandmother, Anna Schlatter, came out of the pietistic "awakening" *(Erweckung)* in St. Gallen, Switzerland.[1] It is interesting to note that the Iron Chancellor himself, Otto Van Bismarck, though caught in the coils of pantheism, professed conversion and read the Bible morning and evening through the influence of his first wife, a Lutheran fundamentalist.[2]

Zahn taught at several universities but chiefly at Erlangen (1892–1909), Leipzig, and Berlin, where A. T. Robertson heard him.[3] Their friendship ripened, and Zahn paid tribute to Robertson's range of knowledge of German literature.[4] Wilbur Smith called Zahn "One of the greatest New Testament scholars of our time," and paid special tribute to his three-volume *Introduction to the New Testament.*[5] Few of his magnificent commentaries have been translated.

In his widely used work, *Introduction to the New Testament,* Henry Clarence Thiessen of Wheaton makes thirty-five references to Zahn. His work on the Greek text and his strong defense of Lucan authorship of the third Gospel and the Book of Acts and Paul's authorship of the Pastorals have been like a guiding star for conservatives.[6] His multivolume history of the canon is superb.

Zahn was university preacher at Gottingen and was eagerly heard at the other universities where he taught. One volume of these sermons has been translated. As a "loyal Lutheran" he used the pericope; the lucidity of his discourse is marvelous. His sermon for Palm Sunday, "The Beauty of Praise," is well divided and does not dodge the difficult issues.[7] His Lenten sermon on "Death in Sin or Death in Grace" is built on the expression found three times on the lips of Jesus in John 8:21–30, "dying in your sins." He admonishes:

> I know well that this is a hard saying, but it is the word of my Lord, who is Lord of us all. Let philosophers philosophize, let poets romance, let fine orators speak of what they do not know and do not believe! But woe be to the Christian preacher, who here in the pulpit, or by the sick-bed, or at the grave, speaks otherwise than he has heard the Lord speak . . . The great alternative: either we die in faith in the Vanquisher of death or we die in our sins.[8]

God has never been without his witness. His faithful messengers have spoken for him even in the greatest of difficulty. May we be so faithful in our time.[9]

---

1. Another influential conservative scholar with the same grandmother was Adolph Schlatter (1852–1938), whose chief goal was "the opening of Scripture" and whose Tubingen sermons were a high priority. He has given us four hundred publications. He appreciated Karl Barth's attention to Romans but lamented his "ahistorical tone, subjectiveness, and irrationality." Werner Neuer, *Adolph Schlatter* (Grand Rapids: Baker, 1995), 135.
2. Edward Crankshaw, *Bismarck* (New York: Viking, 1981), 30.
3. Everett Gill, *A. T. Robertson: A Biography* (New York: Macmillan, 1943), 70.
4. Ibid., 208.
5. Wilbur M. Smith, *Chats from a Minister's Library* (Grand Rapids: Baker, 1951), 134.
6. Henry Clarence Thiessen, *Introduction to the New Testament* (Grand Rapids: Eerdmans, 1954), 35, 149–52, 256–57.

7. Theodor Zahn, *Bread and Salt from the Word of God* (Edinburgh: T & T Clark, 1905), 93ff. Another striking book of published sermons by Zahn is *The Apostle's Creed* (London: Hodder and Stoughton, 1899).
8. Ibid., 59.
9. Another significant German teacher and preacher is Erich Sauer of the Bible School in Wiedenest, Rhineland, Germany. His works include *The Dawn of World Redemption* (commended by F. F. Bruce), *The Triumph of the Crucified, From Eternity to Eternity,* and *The King of the Earth*, translated by G. L. Lang. His sermons on Hebrews 12 titled *In the Arena of Faith: A Call to the Consecrated Life* (Grand Rapids: Eerdmans, 1956) are the highest quality exposition with careful divisions of the text. A prominent French-speaking Swiss preacher was Rene Pache of Emmaus Bible School in Lausanne; his major works, *The Inspiration and Authority of Scripture, The Return of Jesus Christ, The Future Life* and *The Person and Work of the Holy Spirit,* have been circulated in ten languages.

12.3.7 C. S. Lewis—Contender for the Skeptical Mind

> It would seem that Our Lord finds our desires not too strong, but too weak. We are half-hearted creatures, fooling around with drink and sex and ambition when infinite joy is offered us, like an ignorant child who wants to go on making mud pies in a slum because he cannot imagine what is meant by the offer of a holiday at sea. We are far too easily pleased.
>
> —C. S. Lewis

What an extraordinary gift to classical biblical Christianity was given in the person and genius of **Clive Staples Lewis** (1898–1963). Emanating from the halls of Oxford and Cambridge through his inimitable prose and his often forgotten preaching was "a voice for old-fashioned Christian orthodoxy." Born and reared in Northern Ireland, sent to England at the age of nine after his mother's death, Lewis has been the subject of numerous biographical probings. His life as represented in the film *Shadowlands* has spoken deeply to millions. Even a secular biographer like A. N. Wilson has to face the conversion experience of Lewis: first his move to theism in 1929 ("It really happened!") and then his personal commitment to Christ two years later.[1]

Lewis' personal testimony is this: When he started for Whipsnade Zoo in the sidecar of his brother's motorcycle, he "did not believe that Jesus Christ is the Son of God and when [they] reached the zoo [he] did."[2] His full conversion "released literary flow," as the torrent of his brilliant works of fiction and nonfiction bear striking witness. His discovery of George MacDonald and his friendship with Tolkien and the Inklings are all part of the mysterious mix which made the man. We would be in his immense debt only for the works on literature, the Narnia stories, *Till We Have Faces, The Screwtape Letters, The Problem of Pain, Miracles, The Pilgrim's Regress, The Great Divorce,* and on and on. C. S. Lewis was such an encouragement to persons of faith in the supernatural in a time of increasing denial and drift from orthodox positions and formulation.

As a lay theologian, his *Reflections on the Psalms* are especially helpful with a section on the imprecatory psalms. His magnificent piece on prayer titled *Letters to Malcolm* and *A Grief Observed* are classics. His poignant work on the illness and loss of his wife, Joy Davidman (whose work on the Ten Commandments, *Smoke on the Mountain,* is special), is timeless. What is less frequently recognized is that Lewis was a preacher, not only on the broadcast talks which launched him into prominence during the war (and were published as *Mere Christianity*) but also in churches and gatherings as time and schedule allowed. He so ably addressed what he called "the inconsolable longings" of humanity. Lewis was wounded in the First World War and loved to preach to the troops in the Second.

George Sayer's truly fine biography of Lewis has a chapter on him as "Preacher and Broadcaster." Here Sayer traces not only those aided by Lewis in toddling steps of faith but also those—especially among his colleagues—who were offended by his apologetic efforts.[3] Lewis was gifted in being personal and good at expressing emotion, yet "he strongly admonished preachers to not 'accommodate to the world' and preach a watered-down gospel."[4]

Usually when he spoke, he wore clericals but with a regular suit to let the audience know "he was one of them."[5] His major collection of sermons is given its title by the first sermon that Lewis preached in an Oxford church in 1941, "The Weight of Glory," from 1 Corinthians 4:16–18. The sermon is biblical, theologically sound, and aptly and personally applied.[6] Another sermon in this brief anthology is called "Transposition" and was preached on Whitsunday 1944 in Magdalen College Chapel, Oxford, on the subject of spirituality. Lewis was so moved that he stopped preaching. A hymn was sung while the preacher collected himself, and then he resumed and concluded. Eric Routley, the theologian and hymnologist, heard him often and described his preaching as not only showing "superb delivery and wonderful command of language but also the ability to capture his hearer's hearts by his love of Christ and his obvious enjoyment of preaching."[7] C. S. Lewis wrote and spoke as one who was raised up to protest the relativization of Christ and promote the supernatural Christ of the historically reliable and trustworthy New Testament documents.[8]

---

1. A. N. Wilson, *C. S. Lewis: A Biography* (New York: Fawcett Columbine, 1990), 133.
2. C. S. Lewis, *Surprised by Joy: The Shape of My Early Life* (London: Fontana, 1955), 189.
3. George Sayer, *Jack: C. S. Lewis and His Times* (San Francisco: Harper and Row, 1988), 168–74.
4. Perry Bramlett, "The Weight of Glory: C. S. Lewis as Preacher," *Preaching* (September–October 1994): 45.
5. Ibid., 45.
6. C. S. Lewis, *The Weight of Glory* (Grand Rapids: Eerdmans, 1949), 1ff.
7. Bramlett, "The Weight of Glory," 45.
8. Another English man of letters who created a stir in roughly the same time frame was J. B. Phillips, whose *New Testament in Modern English* and *Four Prophets,* as well as his *Your God Is Too Small* and his sermons *Making Men Whole* (London: Fontana, 1952) had considerable impact. His impressions of the power of the text and the "historicity

and reliability of the New Testament" are given in his fine piece, *The Ring of Truth* (New York: Macmillan, 1967). Phillips' personal struggle with depression is reflected in his autobiographical *The Price of Success* (Wheaton, Ill.: Harold Shaw, 1984).

12.4 BRITISH PRACTITIONERS OF CREATIVITY AND CAPABILITY

> The archbishop of Canterbury at the coronation of a British monarch in the presentation of a Bible: "Our gracious King [or Queen]: we present you with this Book, the most valuable thing that this world affords. Here is wisdom; this is the Royal Law; these are the oracles of God."

For centuries the Word of God was respected and revered in Britain as it was in most of the Western world.[1] How do we account for "the almost incredible disappearance of the knowledge of the Bible," as Sir Charles Marston spoke of it, not only in Britain but also in America? The diminution of the preaching and teaching of the Word of God in the churches is simultaneously symptom and cause of the secularizing of a shrunken Christianity.

The twentieth century has been traumatic for the once mighty and proud British Isles with its massive wars, loss of empire, moral decline, and naturalistic temper. Sporadic glimmers of the old faith surface, as when Margaret Thatcher gave unequivocal witness to her belief in the Bible and Christianity to the General Assembly of the Church of Scotland.[2] We now identify some of the preachers who have stood firmly for classical biblical Christianity through this turbulent century. For a good backdrop on the mood and movements of this relativistic period, I refer the reader to Johnson's *Modern Times*.[3]

---

1. For a fascinating documentation of this thesis, see Barbara W. Tuchman, *Bible and Sword: England and Palestine from the Bronze Age to Balfour* (New York: Ballentine, 1956). Chapter 5, "The Bible in English," is key.
2. Margaret Thatcher, "Sow and Ye Shall Reap for All," *The Wall Street Journal,* 31 May 1988, and Paul Johnson's insightful commentary on it, "Thatcher Captures Moral Initiative," 9 June 1988.
3. Paul Johnson, *Modern Times: The World from the Twenties to the Eighties* (New York: Harper, 1983).

12.4.1 ARTHUR JOHN GOSSIP—THE PREACHER WITH RARE SKILL

> Always it has been through preaching that revivals have come and always by preaching that the Spirit has made the tired Church young again.
>
> Preach to your own heart, and many startled passers-by will stop to listen, feeling you are addressing them. Draw anonymously on the story of your life, and they will sit astonished in the pews, asking, "Who has been telling him about me?"
>
> —Arthur John Gossip

He did not have a very good voice; he did have a heavy accent; his gestures were "often ungainly"; he was not strong in outlining his sermons; and he clearly needed to be more exegetical. Nonetheless, **Arthur John Gossip** (1873–1954) belongs in Britain's Westminster Abbey of preachers. He was born and reared in Glasgow, educated at Edinburgh University where he sat under the ministry of Alexander Whyte, and served four Free Churches with distinction (Liverpool, Forfar, St. Matthew's in Glasgow, and Beechgrove, Aberdeen). He was a military chaplain with the Glasgow Highlanders in the First World War. In 1928 he was chosen to be professor of practical theology and ethics at Trinity College, Glasgow, until his retirement in 1945.

Gossip was as intense and "headlong as a Highland torrent."[1] One memorial tribute put it this way:

> He often spoke in breathless sentences in which clause was piled on clause, and the bonds of syntax were strained in a way no grammarian would have allowed; and yet each clause added its own quota to fan the fires of eloquence until every heart in a congregation was warmed to a generous glow.[2]

He was a master of illustration and the apt quotation. Four books of his choice sermons have been published and are eminently readable.[3] Pastoral and caring in his preaching, Gossip could write titles and topics such as "How to Face Life with Steady Eyes," "On the Art of Thinking in Terms of the Cross," and "What Christ Hates Most." His "A Peep at the Last Page" is a message on Moffat's translation of Romans 10:11–12, "No one who believes in Him, the Scripture says, will ever be disappointed. No one." Gossip practiced preaching without notes and was known for his children's sermons, which were published in *The Expository Times.*

Gossip loved to quote Pere Didon, "Your influence over a soul is conditioned by the depth of your love for it." He made his listeners feel the genuineness of his caring. When his dear wife was suddenly snatched from his side by death, he preached his famous sermon from Jeremiah 12:5: "But When Life Tumbles In, What Then?" He begins the sermon:

> Here is a man who, musing upon the bewilderments of life, has burst into God's presence, hot, angry, stunned by His ordering of things, with a loud babble of clamorous protest. It is unfair, he cries, unfair! And frowningly he looks into the face of the Almighty. It is unfair! And then suddenly he checks himself, and putting this blunt question to it, feels his heart grow very still and very cold.[4]

Rounding out his remarkably versatile ministry as a teacher of young preachers, he gave a memorable course of the Warrack Lectures in 1925, published as *In Christ's Stead.*[5] In his lectures, he admits us into the nooks and crannies of his own soul. He is like Chalmers "slowly catching fire." We wince as he gives us James I on his court preacher, "It is not preaching, it is playing with his subject." It was said of Arthur John Gossip, "Never has preaching been more full of Christ."[6]

---

1. John Bishop, "Arthur John Gossip: A Passion for Preaching," *Preaching* (May–June 1988): 52.
2. Ibid., 52.
3. Arthur John Gossip, *The Galilean Accept* (Edinburgh: T & T Clark, 1926); *From the Edge of the Crowd* (New York: Scribner's, n.d.). Gossip is epigrammatic as when he says "Novelty and progress are not necessarily synonymous." His last book of sermons is titled *Experience Worketh Hope* (New York: Scribner's, 1945).
4. Arthur John Gossip, *The Hero in Thy Soul: Being an Attempt to Face Life Gallantly* (New York: Scribner's, 1933), 106.
5. Arthur John Gossip, *In Christ's Stead* (Grand Rapids: Baker, 1925). Other notable Warrack lectureships must include James Black's *The Mystery of Preaching* (1923); R. E. McIntyre's *The Ministry of the Word* (1949); and David MacLennan's *Entrusted with the Gospel* (1955). J. Paterson Smyth's *The Preacher and His Sermon,* given at Trinity College, Dublin, in 1922 is also most helpful. The renowned Warrack lectureship has fallen into leaner times.
6. Bishop, "Arthur John Gossip," 51.

12.4.2 William M. Clow—The Preacher with a Relentless Theme

> The missing note in the preaching of today is the note of persuasive urgency . . . a sociological message is being delivered . . . Yet it sometimes suggests that Christianity is little more than a movement for the social betterment of the people . . . There has been a neglect of the counsel to "do the work of an evangelist."
>
> —William M. Clow

Of one preacher it was said, "He went down deeper, stayed down longer and came up drier than anyone else," but this could never be said of **William McCallum Clow** (1853–1930).

Born and reared in Glasgow, Clow was educated at the University of Glasgow and the United Free Church College. He had a significant pastoral ministry in Aberdeen at the South Church, in Edinburgh at the Barclay Church in Glasgow, from which he was called in 1911 to serve as professor of practical theology and ethics at the United Free Church College. Here he was closely associated with A. B. Bruce, its principal, to whom we are indebted for his seminal *The Training of the Twelve.*[1] Clow later became principal of the college and continued his unusually effective preaching ministry in many locales.

Though he is not usually considered in the ranks of Scotland's foremost preachers, Clow is compelling for two reasons: he was more exegetical than Alexander Whyte or George Morrison and works in a text without abandoning serious application; he was dedicated to the centrality of Christ's atoning work. "The atonement was the primary message of Clow."[2] His preaching can be described as "beautiful" but substantive.

Clow's series of messages titled *The Idylls of Bethany* is an unparalleled study of the Bethany household where "the light always falls on the figure of Jesus."[3] His sermons on Matthew 16–17, beside being singular in their attention to the transfiguration of our Lord, are profound and gripping.[4] A splendid sample of his evangelistic preaching is found in his bracing collection of sermons, *The Evangel of the Strait Gate.* These twenty-six messages are divided into five sections:

I. The Parable of the Gate
II. Led into the Way
III. Passing Through the Gate
IV. Finding Life
V. End of the Broad Way

His quotes are from Augustine, Bunyan, Tennyson, John Bright, Matthew Arnold, Robert Burns, Henry Martyn, George Whitefield, and Frances Ridley Havergal, to name a few.[5] His outlines are exemplary. But his priceless masterpieces are his two volumes of sermons on the cross of Christ, which vie with those of Krummacher and Schilder. This ranks his preaching on the Cross with the best in English in several centuries. The first volume is "a course of sermons on the men and women and some of the notable things of the day of the crucifixion of Jesus," published as *The Day of the Cross.*[6] Unlike some treatments of this type, Clow avoids being distracted from the cross of Christ and the Christ of the cross.

Preeminent among Clow's preaching is his companion volume of twenty-five sermons coming out of his Glasgow pastorate. These he called *The Cross in Christian Experience.*[7] The forewording sermon is "Simply to Thy Cross I Cling," based on Romans 5:1; the afterwording sermon is "The Primacy of the Atonement," built on 1 Corinthians 15:3. The meat in the sandwich between these two delicious morsels include such striking studies as "The Dark Line in God's Face," "Love in Four Dimensions," "Receiving the Atonement," and "Christ's Last Gospel Message"—something unique from Acts 26:18. His guiding thesis is, "The Cross is never out of sight of the Christian soul."[8]

---

1. Alan P. F. Sell, *Defending and Declaring the Faith: Some Scottish Examples 1860–1920* (Exeter: Paternoster, 1987), 89, 92. Bear in mind that the Church of Scotland and the United Free Church merged in 1929.
2. Ralph G. Turnbull, *A History of Preaching* (Grand Rapids: Baker, 1974), 524. The updating of Dargan's work.
3. W. M. Clow, *The Idylls of Bethany* (London: Hodder and Stoughton, 1919; repr. 1969).
4. W. M. Clow, *The Secret of the Lord* (London: Hodder and Stoughton, n.d.)
5. W. M. Clow, *The Evangel of the Strait Gate* (New York: George H. Doran, 1916). Another Scot burdened for evangelism tells his story from his experience at North Kelvinside in Glasgow. See Tom Allan, *The Face of My Parish* (London: SCM, 1954). He inveighs strongly against "the acceptable sermon."
6. W. M. Clow, *The Day of the Cross* (London: Hodder and Stoughton, 1909).

7. W. M. Clow, *The Cross in Christian Experience* (London: Hodder and Stoughton, 1908).
8. Ibid., 11. Clow also edited *The Bible Reader's Encyclopedia and Concordance* (London: Collins, 1930).

12.4.3 John Macbeath—The Preacher with a Robust Word

> The Bible is the preacher's warrant and first reference library. There is no book that takes so much knowing, and there is no book that is so rewarding to the questing mind. Out of its fullness it is the preacher's prerogative to bring things new and old.
>
> —John Macbeath

Another engaging Scottish Baptist preacher on the order of Graham Scroggie and J. Sidlow Baxter was **John Macbeath** (1881–1967). Born in Edinburgh and schooled at Glasgow University and the Baptist Theological College of Glasgow, he served congregations in St. Andrews, Cambuslang, Fillebrook Church in London, Hillhead Church in Glasgow, and Haven Green Church in Ealing, London. His preaching was biblical, his delivery winsome. As Turnbull observes, "His literary bent was unmistakable and all the riches of his literary knowledge shone through in allusion, quotation, and interpretation of themes expounded."[1] Macbeath broke loose from his manuscript.[2] He was widely heard in training schools, on broadcasts, and on nine visits to preach in the U.S. and Canada.

Sane and sound exposition can be sampled in a brief series of sermons on Ephesians. Here we see his ability to divide and outline the text well and move that registration of truth efficiently to an appetizing sermon outline.[3] Evidence of his charm and creativity is clear in an extended series in which he preaches sermons on twenty-four hills or mounts in Scripture under four headings:

I. Hills of Testimony
II. Hills of Trial
III. Hills of Tragedy
IV. Hills of Triumph[4]

---

1. Ralph G. Turnbull, *A History of Preaching* (Grand Rapids: Baker, 1974), 450.
2. Turnbull is not right on this point; cf. John Macbeath in *My Way of Preaching* (London: Pickering and Inglis, n.d.), 106. This symposium, edited by Robert J. Smithson, is like those edited by Donald MacCleod (1952), Clarence Roddy (1959), and Richard Bodey (1992).
3. John Macbeath, *The Life of a Christian* (London: Marshall, Morgan, and Scott, n.d.).
4. John Macbeath, *The Hills of God* (London: The Religious Tract Society, 1930). A touch of revival struck the Hebrides Islands off the west coast of Scotland after World War II under the ministry of Duncan Campbell. His strong biblical preaching is found in *God's Standard* and *God's Answer* (Ft. Washington, Pa.: CLC, 1964, 1960).

12.4.4 Oswald Chambers—The Preacher with a Radiant Testimony

> All He wants from me is unconditional surrender.
>
> After I was born again as a lad I enjoyed the presence of Jesus Christ wonderfully, but years passed before I gave myself up thoroughly to His work. I was in Dunoon College as tutor of Philosophy when Dr. F. B. Meyer came and spoke about the Holy Spirit. I determined to have all that was going, and went to my room and asked God simply and definitely for the baptism of the Holy Spirit, whatever that meant.
>
> My mind still grows impatient at much of the success-lusting desire of Christian workers. How many patrons had Jeremiah or the apostles! Alone for God is the greater calling of a man.
>
> —Oswald Chambers

If only for his devotional classic, *My Utmost for His Highest,* he would be a household word among Western Christians! **Oswald Chambers'** (1874–1917) extensive writings and preaching were posthumously compiled and guarantee him a portico in this temple of biblical preaching.

Many find Chambers hard to understand, while others find him so fresh and fragrant in his utterance as to be without peer.[1] His life was cut short while he was with the British military in Egypt in 1917. However, Chambers lived to the hilt.

- 1874–1889, born in Aberdeen; his father was a Baptist minister and raised his family there and in Perth. Both of his parents were baptized by Charles Haddon Spurgeon. His father's economizing ways grated upon young Oswald.[2]
- 1889–1895, left home at fifteen, already an accomplished musician; studied art; active in Rye Lane Baptist Church.
- 1895–1897, studied at the University of Edinburgh; enjoyed the preaching of Matheson and Whyte. He was destitute. His lodgings in Edinburgh had just been vacated by John Henry Jowett. He was a gifted painter.[3]
- 1897–1905, tutor in philosophy at Dunoon College. He struggled much with the "dark night of the soul," but in a "crisis of self-surrender" yielded to the Lord's call to ministry. He became a much sought-after preacher. Dinsdale T. Young discovered him and greatly influenced him "toward a more evangelical attitude."[4]
- 1906–1907, associated with the Japanese holiness evangelist Nakada, he traveled and taught in both America (God's Bible School in Cincinnati) and in Japan. His ties in Japan were with the Cowmans, the Oriental Missionary Society, and Dr. James Cuthbertson's Japan Evangelistic Band.[5] (Cuthbertson has given some of the finest expositions on the Song of Solomon ever heard.)
- 1907–1911, associated with the Pentecostal Prayer League. Met Gertrude (Biddy) Hobbs onboard ship to the U.S. in 1908; married in 1910. He traveled much in preaching missions to Ireland and all about.

- 1911–1915, founded the Bible Training College in Clapham, London. Many of his books were developed out of the lecture notes his wife took at this time (which accounts for their highly condensed form). His famous *Biblical Psychology* shows the influence of J. T. Beck's work on psychology; (see 9.4.4).
- 1915–1917, accepted by the YMCA (much as J. Gresham Machen was in Europe) for work in the desert camps in Egypt as survivors of Gallipoli and the British disaster in the Dardenelles fell back upon Egypt. His family was permitted to join him.

Although he was somewhat mystical and at times imprecise, Chambers' basic theological stance was this:

> The true pattern for the experience of the Christian, is the life of Christ. The Christian ideal is not the outward and literal imitation of Jesus, but the living out of the Christ life implanted within by the Holy Spirit.[6]

Both P. T. Forsyth and James Denney shaped Chambers' thinking on the meaning of Christ's death. Forsyth wrote the foreword to one of his books. Rendel Harris was in Egypt after being torpedoed and found much in common with him. Archbishop Donald Coggan payed him eloquent tribute as truly "a man of one book."[7] Samuel Zwemer preached his funeral.

His preaching was exceedingly idiosyncratic and creative. A report from Egypt indicated:

> Mr. Oswald Chambers' address on the subject "Has History Disproved the Song of the Angels?" was a convincing defense of Christianity; he was listened to with rapt attention and much appreciation by the audience, soldiers and civilians alike.[8]

Two favorite books of his messages are built on the schema of the believer's life in parallel with the life of Jesus. They are *Bringing Sons Unto Glory* and *The Psychology of Redemption,* prolific and productive to the end. His messages on the life of Abraham are highly condensed but show his penchant for the alliterative outline, tight structure, meaty exposition, and memorable application.[9] As a poet of some ability he was used to compressing language, and this shows in his prose style.

Chambers had just finished his talks on Job and was beginning his studies in Ecclesiastes when his health crisis came.[10] "Drench us with humility" was the lifelong prayer of this servant of Christ whose life and work in the Scriptures have made so many of us his beneficiaries.

---

1. Some of Chambers' opaqueness could be due to his early dabbling in Swedenborg, the cultic Swedish mystic; see David McCasland, *Oswald Chambers: Abandoned to God* (Grand Rapids: Discovery House, 1993), 88. Also, Biddy Chambers, *Oswald*

Chambers: His Life and Work (London: Simpkin, Marshall, 1933), 62. The deleterious influence of Swedenborg on William Blake is traced at length in Peter Ackroyd's *Blake: A Biography* (New York: Knopf, 1996).
2. McCasland, *Oswald Chambers.* This is a magnificent study. Highly recommended.
3. D. W. Lambert, *Oswald Chambers: An Unbribed Soul* (Ft. Washington, Pa.: CLC, 1968), 14.
4. Chambers, *Oswald Chambers,* 63.
5. For a fine study of the Cowmans and their work, see B. H. Pearson, *The Vision Lives On* (Los Angeles: Cowman, 1961). Mrs. Cowman will always be remembered as the author of the widely used *Streams in the Desert.*
6. Lambert, *Oswald Chambers,* 59.
7. F. D. Coggan, *Stewards of Grace* (quoted in Lambert, ibid., 45–46). Coggan's careful and inspiring study on *The Ministry of the Word* (London: Canterbury Press, 1945) is a solid and substantial piece.
8. McCasland, *Oswald Chambers,* 242.
9. Oswald Chambers, *Not Knowing Whither: The Steps of Abraham's Faith* (London: Marshall, Morgan, and Scott, 1957). "God's call is a command that asks us, that means there is always a possibility of refusal on our part" (11).
10. Oswald Chambers, *Baffled to Fight Better* (London: Marshall, Morgan, and Scott, 1955); *Shade of His Hand* (London: Simpkin, Marshall, 1947). Both series were given in the YMCA Hut in Zeitoun, Egypt, in 1917.

12.4.5 James S. Stewart—The Preacher with a Remarkably Rich Endowment

> There are rich rewards of human gratitude waiting for the man who can make the Bible come alive.
>
> Stint no toil to achieve clear thought, fit language, true construction, decisive appeal.
>
> Imagination is one of the preacher's essential weapons. Put yourself and your people into the heart of what you are preaching about. Imagination is a living quality. Its place is among the attributes of God.
>
> —James S. Stewart

The waning of biblical Christianity in Scotland is tragical and lamentable. At the present rate of attrition the Church of Scotland will virtually cease to exist in the next century. Yet there has been a movement in the interest of expository preaching through whole books of Scripture led by William Still of Gilcomston South Church in Aberdeen.[1] Certainly Scotland's "premier preacher" of the last half of the twentieth century has been "thoroughly orthodox" and an extraordinarily gifted Bible preacher.[2] We refer to **James S. Stewart** (1896–1990), who was born in Dundee.

Stewart received M.A. and B.D. degrees from St. Andrews and did postgraduate study at Bonn. His father was converted under D. L. Moody, sold his business, and became a well-known Bible teacher for the YMCA. Stewart pastored at

Auchterarder in Perthshire, the Beechgrove Church in Aberdeen, and then with such conspicuous favor at the North Morningside Church in Edinburgh.[3] For the next twenty-two years, he was professor of New Testament at New College, Edinburgh. His best-selling book, *The Life and Teaching of Jesus Christ,* sold more than one hundred thousand copies in the United States. His serious study of *A Man in Christ: The Vital Elements of St. Paul's Religion* (his Cunningham Lectures) continue to be well worth reading, as he argues that "Paul's is a conversion theology." His Warrack Lectures on preaching in 1945, published as *Heralds of God,* ranks as one of the finest in that prestigious series and displays a great acuity and sensitivity to the preaching task.[4] His Beecher Lectures in 1952 focus on the great doctrines of the gospel and come to us under the title *A Faith to Proclaim.* They are rich and show no signs of what has become an increasing aversion to doctrine and the cognitive in our time.

It has been Stewart's published sermons that have vaulted him into such an exclusive circle of admiration. Always grounded deeply in the text, his sermons are those of a preacher's preacher. Festooned with choice titles ("Hearsay or Experience," "Sport of Fate or Plan of God?" and "Rumor or Reality?"), they are outlined with such memorable divisions, applied with fine illustrations, and facilitated with skillful transitions. Longenecker underscores his brilliant blending of "rigorous scholarship, reverential reading of Scripture and effective communication of the gospel."[5] He recalls vividly when Professor Stewart—who tended to be "unimposing and shy"—would "start expounding on a subject in a pedantic and discreet manner, then get so carried away with his subject that it began to take control of him, so that, without any rise in pitch or volume, there would be an increase in emotional intensity and a crescendo of descriptive detail and lyrical expression, and finally, when he had exhausted his subject, he would drop back to his discreet manner. His hearers often experienced that buildup and drop—sometimes inadvertently expressing their empathy in a gasp."[6]

Stewart's printed sermons, titled *The Strong Name, The Gates of New Life, The Wind of the Spirit,* and *River of Life,* are worth owning, reading, rereading, and digesting thoroughly. His lectures on *Thine Is the Kingdom: The Church's Mission in Our Time* clearly indicate his commitment to the evangel around the world.[7] Here is a preacher who preaches out of the overflow.

Bishop expresses special joy over Stewart's sermon, "The Strengthening Angel," from Luke 22:43.[8] The text is a bit meager, but the outline is magnificent:

I. The strengthening angel today is often some shining word out of the Book of God
II. The strengthening angel today may be some fellow creature
III. The strengthening angel today may be the Lord himself[9]

Even more are we drawn to his regal "The Triumphant Adequacy of Christ" from Romans 15:29:

I. I am coming to you with Christ
II. I am coming to you with the gospel of Christ

III. I am coming to you with the blessing of the gospel of Christ
IV. I am coming to you with the fullness of the blessing of the gospel of Christ[10]

Stewart models an effective preacher who could serve as chaplain to a local professional soccer club, preach regularly at the rescue mission, or lecture around the world.[11] His was not an "intellectual isolation" but a powerful engagement with the Word of God and with the times in which he lived.

---

1. Douglas F. Kelly, "The Recovery of Christian Realism in the Scottish Expository Ministry Movement," in *Pulpit and People: Essays in Honour of William Still on His 75th Birthday*, ed. Nigel M. de S. Cameron and Sinclair B. Ferguson (Edinburgh: Rutherford House, 1986), 17ff. Also, *Evangelicals Now*, June 1995, "William Still—A Modern Simeon."
2. Richard Longenecker, "Missing One of Scotland's Best," *Christianity Today* (July 22, 1991): 11.
3. John Bishop, "James S. Stewart: Passionate Intensity, Evangelical Fervor," *Preaching* (January–February 1988): 61.
4. James S. Stewart, *Heralds of God* (New York: Scribner's, 1946).
5. Longenecker, "Missing One of Scotland's Best," 61.
6. Ibid., 61.
7. James S. Stewart, *Thine Is the Kingdom: The Church's Mission in Our Time* (New York: Scribner's, 1959).
8. Another intriguing sermon on this text by Clarence Macartney's successor at Arch Street Presbyterian Church in Philadelphia, G. Hall Todd, *O Angel of the Garden* (Grand Rapids: Baker, 1961), 11ff.
9. James S. Stewart, *The Wind of the Spirit* (Nashville: Abingdon, 1968), 103ff.
10. James S. Stewart, *The Strong Name* (Grand Rapids: Baker, 1972), 90ff.
11. Longenecker, "Missing One of Scotland's Best," 61.

12.4.6 William Temple—The Preacher with Rare Acumen

> To worship is to quicken the conscience by the holiness of God, to feed the mind with the truth of God, to purge the imagination by the beauty of God, to devote the will to the purpose of God.
>
> —William Temple

> Lunch-hour talks! In church! During August Bank Holiday Week! In Blackpool! On the Revelation! Most of us felt he was batting on a sticky wicket, and despite extensive postering not more than forty or fifty people turned up. The next day there were over two hundred, and for the remaining days the church was packed, a queue outside stretching almost down to the Front, waiting to get in—a wonderful example of his judgment and an amazing testimony to his power of exposition!
>
> —A missioner from the Blackpool mission of 1922
> (conducted along "rather old-fashioned evangelical lines")

The desperate plight and sad state of the Church of England are well known to us. Yet in the Stott-Lucas wing of the church there has been vigorous biblical preaching.[1] Even in the broad church, or centrist branch, we have the intellectual and spiritual giant **William Temple** (1881–1944). His father, **Frederick Temple,** was also a schoolman who became archbishop of Canterbury in his seventy-sixth year.

Frederick Temple lived with his mother until he was fifty-five and then married as the bishop of Exeter. He had two sons, one of whom followed in his footsteps. William eventually served as headmaster of Repton, rector of St. James in Picadilly, bishop of Manchester in 1921, and then successively archbishop of York after Cosmo Lang and archbishop of Canterbury. William was a large, rotund man, and a spokesman for religion in both world wars. He was unforgettable in his preaching and could preach to scholars and the common people with equal effectiveness and seeming effortlessness. This "Pickwickian figure," was without pretension. Even though he was the primate of England, he could be seen queuing up for a bus after addressing meetings at Royal Albert Hall.[2]

Of course Temple was a Rugby man, where his father and Thomas Arnold had been headmasters, and went to Balliol at Oxford. Here he was tutored by Benjamin Jowett and shaped by Edward Caird, the Scottish Hegelian. Temple was never well, suffering his first attack of gout when he was two years of age.[3] His eight Sunday evenings at Oxford in 1931 became the spiritual crossroad for many a soul.[4] From 1932 to 1934, he gave the Gifford Lectures in Edinburgh, published as *Nature, Man and God.* In them he argued for the transcendence of immanence and the immanence of transcendence.

Temple was supremely a preacher and a teacher and served as president of the Oxford Union.[5] He took a strong stand for the Virgin Birth of Christ and the bodily resurrection of our Lord.[6] His favorite preaching portion was John's gospel, which he attributed to the disciple of Jesus. His incomparable *Readings in John's Gospel* came out of his years at St. James, Picadilly.[7] Iremonger, his chief biographer, calls this "the greatest devotional treatise since William Law's *A Serious Call to a Devout and Holy Life.*[8]

He enjoyed facing off with H. G. Wells on the issue of a finite God and joined with Dick Sheppard in heading up the Life and Liberty Movement, which concerned life in the Church of England rather than secular confinement.[9] While he was canon at Westminster and bishop of Manchester (with six hundred parishes), he preached incessantly and had particular effect with his great university missions.[10] As early as 1931, he warned of the danger of Marxist communism[11] and always felt Pelagianism was damnable.[12] Still he was adamant in maintaining that Christianity had immense implication for society and culture.[13]

Temple's speaking voice was not outstanding, nor was his oratory finished, but he had a presence and an ability to think on his feet. Even with only fifty percent vision, he read constantly and wrote thirty-five books. It was said of him that "he spoke pamphlets." He had great spontaneity but prepared well, though he never prepared the words he would use. Dean W. R. Matthews of St. Paul's described "the believing quality of his mind."[14] Iremonger was of the opinion that "he moved more and more to the right during his later years."[15] His sermons were not startling compositionally, but they were direct, biblical, and steeped in an honesty and a practicality that consistently made their mark.[16] His friend, A. E. Baker, said of his preaching:

> He combined, in a quite unique way, the knowledge of the student of ideas and affairs, the understanding of the thinker, and the prophet's power to speak to and move the spirit of the nation.[17]

---

1. A superb example of strong biblical exposition was Canon Guy H. King of Christ Church, Beckenham, successor to the Reverend Harrington Lees, who went on to be archbishop of Melbourne. King's sermons are meticulous with the text and appear in such volumes as *A Belief That Behaves* (James), *Joy Way* (Philippians), *Crossing the Border* (Colossians), and *A Leader Led* (1 Timothy). An American Episcopalian of great evangelical influence was the celebrated Dr. Sam Shoemaker, who served parishes in New York and Pittsburgh; see his *Extraordinary Living for Ordinary Men* (Grand Rapids: Zondervan, 1965). Paul Rees said he had fireball not mothball theology.
2. Alexander Gammie, *Preachers I Have Heard* (London: Pickering and Inglis, n.d.), 188ff.
3. Charles W. Lowry, *William Temple: An Archbishop for All Seasons* (Washington, D.C.: University Press of America, 1982), 18.
4. Lowry, *William Temple,* 48–49.
5. Ibid., 22.
6. Ibid., 24.
7. William Temple, *Readings in John's Gospel* (Wilton, Conn.: Morehouse Barlow, 1985 ed.).
8. F. A. Iremonger, *William Temple: Archbishop of Canterbury, His Life and Letters* (London: Oxford, 1948), 176. This is the official biography of Temple, who was often called the people's archbishop.
9. Lowry, *William Temple,* 35. Sheppard was quite a preacher in his own right; see R. J. Northcott, *Dick Sheppard and St. Martin's* (London: Longmans Green, 1937); another friend of Temple was G. A. Studdert-Kennedy, whose sermons on the Apostles' Creed, *I Believe,* were widely heard but tended to be weak and vague.
10. Iremonger, *William Temple,* 377.
11. Ibid., 82.
12. Joseph Fletcher, *William Temple: Twentieth-Century Christian* (New York: Seabury, 1963). Lowry correctly feels that Fletcher is "too eager to show the modernity of Temple" (146).
13. William Temple, *Christianity and the Social Order* (London: Penguin, 1942). N.B. Robert Craig, *Social Concern in the Thought of William Temple* (London: Gollancz, 1963); Owen C. Thomas, *William Temple's Philosophy of Religion* (London: SPCK; New York: Seabury, 1961); W. R. Rinne, *The Kingdom of God in the Thought of William Temple* (Abo, Finland: Abo Akademi, 1966).
14. Craig, *Social Concern in the Thought of William Temple,* 12.
15. Iremonger, *William Temple,* 512.
16. William Temple, *Fellowship with God* (London: Macmillan, 1920), preached in Westminster; *Studies in the Spirit and Truth of Christianity: University and School*

Sermons (London: Macmillan, 1914). Particularly moving is his sermon on "Faith and Doubt" based in 2 Timothy 4:6–8 and Mark 15:34, 17ff. This last book is dedicated to Charles Gore, who had an unusual influence on Temple. Gore was bishop of Oxford and the force behind the Lux Mundi volume.

17. A. E. Baker, *William Temple: An Estimate and an Appreciation* (London: James Clarke, 1946), 100.

12.4.7 David Martyn Lloyd-Jones—The Preacher with a Resounding Message

> To me the work of preaching is the highest and greatest and the most glorious calling to which anyone can ever be called.
>
> Every preacher should believe strongly in his own method . . . I can say quite honestly that I would not cross the road to listen to myself preaching, and the preachers whom I have enjoyed most have been very different indeed in their method and style. But my business is not to describe them but to state what I believe to be right, however imperfectly I have put my own precepts into practice. I can only hope that the result will be of some help, and especially to young preachers called to this greatest of all tasks, and especially in these sad and evil days.
>
> —D. Martyn Lloyd-Jones

He was called by Wilbur M. Smith "the greatest Bible expositor in the English-speaking world." The Doctor, as he was often referred to, exerted a powerful and profound influence at the heart of London with reverberations all around the world. His ministry was essentially the opening of Scripture to a vast congregation three times a week. **David Martyn Lloyd-Jones** (1899–1981) and his preaching silence those who claim that the preaching of historic orthodoxy under the unction of the Spirit makes no impact in postmodern times. The current panic to market-driven preaching and abandonment of text-driven preaching needs to come to terms with how God used Lloyd-Jones.

The Building of the Preacher

Lloyd-Jones was a Welshman born in Cardiff, the middle son of three born to Henry and Maggie Lloyd-Jones. Part of the Calvinistic Methodist (or Presbyterian) Church, he narrowly escaped death as a boy when his father's general store burned down. When his father went bankrupt, they moved to London. Here they attended the Welsh Chapel, although Lloyd-Jones often heard Campbell Morgan or John Hutton at Westminster Chapel.

Lloyd-Jones was reluctant to speak about himself or his own conversion in public.[1] He began to study medicine at St. Bart's Hospital Medical School and became a protégé of the world-famous Lord Horder. Soon he married a fellow medical student, Bethan Phillips. Yet his practice of medicine after his graduation in 1921 did not satisfy him, and he increasingly struggled with what seemed to be God's hand on him to preach. The newlyweds left Harley Street to take the pastorate of the Bethlehem Forward Movement Mission Church in Sandfields, Aberavon, a congregation of miners, dockworkers, and metalworkers, which numbered ninety-three when he came. In just over eleven years, Aberavon grew to a membership of 530, with attendance at 850. Many came as new converts.[2]

Though not theologically trained, Lloyd-Jones was a student and a logician of the first magnitude, using Horder's Socratic method.[3] In 1938 he accepted Campbell Morgan's invitation to come as associate pastor at Westminster. Though they were so different, the two men worked together harmoniously. They alternated morning and evening services monthly until Morgan retired in 1943 under the acute strains of old age and war.[4] After the war, attendance began to build and soon twenty-five hundred people filled Westminster morning and evening with twelve hundred for the Friday night Bible study. Westminster was one of the largest congregations in London. The lofty attendance continued until the Doctor retired in 1968.

The Burden of the Preacher

In the early days at Westminster, Lloyd-Jones did not always follow consecutive book exposition but developed series like "God's Plan for World Unity" and "A Preview of History" from Revelation 4–5. He early on did a series on 2 Peter, followed by his famous extended series, *Studies in the Sermon on the Mount.*[5]

While Campbell Morgan tended to be Arminian, Lloyd-Jones was staunchly a Calvinist and a great admirer and student of the Puritans, who were models for him in many respects. He decried "concessions made to so-called scholarship" and the "slide toward a liberal view of the Scriptures."[6] He saw clearly that what was at stake was "the loss of a doctrine of the full inspiration and inerrance of Scripture." During the war years, Lloyd-Jones was president of Inter-Varsity in Britain and was a part of the vital leadership the movement took in pointing the way back to classical biblical Christianity. The need for revival was a lifelong burden of his.[7] Although he was an amillennialist, Lloyd-Jones was of the conviction that God had something special for the Jews at the end of the age. He said, "I feel increasingly that we may be in the last times."

Lloyd-Jones established the Westminster Library and the Westminster Ministers' Fraternal, which made a great impact.[8] His pneumatology was a bit of a strain on his followers since he held that a believer "could have more than one baptism of the Spirit" and that the sealing of the Spirit was subsequent to conversion.[9] He was quite a separatist and did not support the Graham crusades. He broke with Stott, insisting that Anglican evangelicals leave the Church of England.[10] He was always waspish with regard to Keswick and probably misunderstood the movement. His critique of S. D. Gordon's preaching was unfair.[11] Yet having pointed out the flyspecks in the marble of the Parthenon, we can only rejoice that this preacher stood so stalwartly and strongly for the historic Christian faith. He was eminently theological in his mindset and in this sets an important standard.

The Brilliance of the Preacher

Lloyd-Jones loved to preach; the circulation of his sermons in print and by tape is without parallel in our time. His multivolume series on Romans is epochal; his eight volumes of Sunday morning preaching from Ephesians is equally impressive. His sermons on *Spiritual Depression* have aided and assisted thousands.[12] His expository studies from Psalm 73 under the title *Faith on Trial* are spectacular.[13] His Sunday morning sermons on *The Kingdom of God* during the Profumo scandal show the startling relevance of the Word to the contemporary situation.[14]

In the strict sense Lloyd-Jones's preaching was almost always textual-topical because he exposed such a small piece of text (like the Puritans, whom he emulated in so many ways). He used an inverted pyramid, moving from a small piece of text to what the Scripture as a whole taught on the subject and what its theological ramifications were. Lloyd-Jones could pray publicly for thirty-five minutes at a time. He was not expository in the sense of taking a natural thought unit and modeling how one moves through the thought of the author in the sermon. Occasionally, as in his famous sermon on Peter healing Aeneas (based on Acts 9:33–34), in which he made the miracle a parable about what must happen in the church, he moved to a kind of odd allegorization.[15] Neither has his idiosyncratic interpretation of Romans 7 found many followers. At times his views of preaching and worship are a bit cranky; he sounds like he is death on illustration and quotation in the sermon and would not have a choir or special music. Yet he used more methodological aids than he was willing to concede. But nothing can obscure the driving passion of his soul for preaching the Word of God. Who could more trustworthily be our guide in considering the vexed issue of the phenomena of revival than Lloyd-Jones? Who could preach on grace as he could? Something in the sober, serious manner of the Doctor captivated multitudes in a response that, humanly speaking, should not have taken place. But it did. God spoke through his servant.

The Blessing of God on the Preacher

Although he is an Anglican, J. I. Packer was greatly shaped as a young listener in Westminster Chapel. R. V. G. Tasker, the brilliant New Testament lecturer at King's College, University of London, came under Lloyd-Jones's message Sunday evenings at Westminster Chapel and forsook liberalism because he became convinced of original sin and the wrath of God.[16] Sunday night was the evangelistic service, and the Doctor at Westminster as at Aberavon would be available to talk to seekers afterward as he was indeed available Sunday morning. (Who says being seeker-focused is new?) An Indian journalist, Sunder-Rao, reported:

> What impressed me was not the personal aspect of the great preacher, though that made no uncertain impact. It was that as the preacher unfolded the theme he seemed to have been possessed, or to be discreet, motivated by One greater than himself, in Whom he lived, moved and

> had his being. All great preaching becomes a sacrament, nay, a miracle, when in and through it, it holds forth the indications and intimations of the presence of God.[17]

In D. Martyn Lloyd-Jones we have described the imparting of the Spirit, "the sacred anointing," a spiritual work much needed today.[18]

---

1. Iain H. Murray, *D. Martyn Lloyd-Jones: The First Forty Years 1899–1939* (Edinburgh: Banner of Truth, 1982), xiii. Murray's two massive biographical volumes are pure gold. Reading almost every page is a spiritual experience.
2. Bethan Lloyd-Jones, *Memories of Sandfields 1927–1938* (Edinburgh: Banner of Truth, 1983). His glorious messages from this period are found in *Evangelistic Sermons* (Edinburgh: Banner of Truth, 1983).
3. Christopher Catherwood, *Five Evangelical Leaders* (Wheaton, Ill.: Harold Shaw, 1985), 61.
4. *The Westminster Record,* vol. 17, no. 7 through vol. 25, no. 2 with the G. Campbell Morgan Memorial Issue.
5. D. Martyn Lloyd-Jones, *Expository Sermons on 2 Peter* (Edinburgh: Banner of Truth, 1983); *Studies in the Sermon on the Mount* (Grand Rapids: Eerdmans, 1959) in two volumes.
6. Interview with Carl F. H. Henry, "Martyn Lloyd-Jones: From Buckingham to Westminster," *Christianity Today* (February 8, 1980): 17ff. Reprinted in Christopher Catherwood, ed., *Martyn Lloyd-Jones: Chosen of God* (Wheaton, Ill.: Crossway, 1986), 95ff.
7. D. Martyn Lloyd-Jones, *Revival* (Wheaton, Ill.: Crossway, 1987). Sermons on the one hundredth anniversary of the British revival.
8. D. Martyn Lloyd-Jones, *The Puritans: Their Origins and Successors* (Edinburgh: Banner of Truth, 1987).
9. D. Martyn Lloyd-Jones, *Preachers and Preaching* (Grand Rapids: Zondervan, 1971), 308. Lectures at Westminster Theological Seminary in Philadelphia.
10. Iain H. Murray, *D. Martyn Lloyd-Jones: The Fight of Faith 1939–1981* (Edinburgh: Banner of Truth, 1990), 535ff.
11. D. Martyn Lloyd-Jones, *Knowing the Times: Addresses 1942–1977* (Edinburgh: Banner of Truth, 1989), 264. Cf. 12.7.4
12. D. Martyn Lloyd-Jones, *Spiritual Depression: Its Causes and Cure* (Grand Rapids: Eerdmans, 1965).
13. D. Martyn Lloyd-Jones, *Faith on Trial* (Grand Rapids: Eerdmans, 1965).
14. D. Martyn Lloyd-Jones, *The Kingdom of God* (Wheaton, Ill.: Crossway, 1992). The more standard homiletical form is seen in Geoffrey King, who for twenty years served West Croydon Tabernacle in London; see *The Forty Days* (Grand Rapids: Eerdmans, 1949), recommended by James Stewart; *Truth for Our Time* (Grand Rapids: Eerdmans, 1957), especially a sermon like "The Sterner Side of the Twenty-Third Psalm" (89).
15. Murray, *The First Forty Years,* 328, 334.
16. Interview with Carl F. H. Henry, "Martyn Lloyd-Jones," 29.

17. Murray, *The Fight of Faith,* 198.
18. Tony Sargent, *The Sacred Anointing: The Preaching of Dr. Martyn Lloyd-Jones* (Wheaton, Ill.: Crossway, 1994).

12.5 AFRICANS, AFRICAN-AMERICANS, NATIVE AMERICANS, AND ASIANS PREACHING THE WORD OF HIS GRACE

> It has always been my ambition to preach the gospel where Christ was not known, so that I would not be building on someone else's foundation.
>
> —Romans 15:20

The devastating and erosive effects of Enlightenment rationalism have been seen not only in the centers of Western Christendom but also in all parts of the earth. The viciousness of this plague can be seen even in Judaism, within which a perceptive scholar like Eugene Borowitz bemoans Judaism's "love affair with modernity." He sees that "modernization has become our Messiah," that is, liberal religion with its deification of the self has accommodated itself to culture.[1] With Abraham Heschel, Borowitz he accepts the accuracy of the biblical record—its content is accurate and binding. On this basis he believes that the covenant between God and Israel continues in full force.[2] He sees the Documentary Hypothesis in shambles and finds liberalism wanting in its notions that revelation is discovery, sin is error, judgment is self-criticism, and atonement is self-sacrifice. He asserts on the basis of Scripture that Israel is a nation covenanted with God and therefore will survive in historic continuity until messianic days and "the culmination of the Covenant in the days of the Messiah."[3] Similar confidence in the Bible has given impetus to the worldwide proclamation of the gospel with amazing fruit among the nations. Yet Western fads and theological bypaths have made deep inroads into the growing churches of the two-thirds world, the part of the world that is non-Western. We now sample some of the vitalities in other ethnic settings.

---

1. Eugene B. Borowitz, *Renewing the Covenant* (New York: Jewish Publication Society, 1991), 19.
2. Ibid., 45.
3. Ibid., 298.

12.5.1 JOHN JASPER—THE ROOTS OF AFRICAN-AMERICAN PREACHING

> In the black church, if you do not have a Jesus Punch Line, you have not preached.
>
> —T. Hoyt

> On the power of proclamation: "It is not in the tone of voice. It is not in the eloquence of the preacher. It is not in the gracefulness of his gestures. It is not in the magnificence of his congregation. It is in a heart broken, and put together, by the eternal God!"
>
> —Gardner C. Taylor

Black Christianity in the United States rose among slaves who found the theme of liberation in the exodus from Egypt and in the gospel story. The African-American pulpit tradition reflects the centrality of the church in the black community. Preaching is critical for leadership in the black church.[1] The rhythms of black worship and the exhortations of the preacher in sync with the congregation make us realize that the cultural roots of this remarkably vibrant people are deep in Africa.[2] The penchant for narrative in the black sermon is reflected in African-American preaching today.[3] Preachers like Henry Mitchell, Gardner Taylor, and others have helped us understand the genius of black preaching as well as its susceptibilities.[4] All of this can be seen in the preaching of a remarkable pioneer, **John Jasper** (1812–1901).

John Jasper was the twenty-fourth and last child born to slaves named Philip and Tina Jasper. His father was "an exhorter" and died before his birth. His mother called him John after John the Baptist. Working as a slave in a tobacco factory, he was gloriously converted. His master, Sam Hardgrave, a deacon at First Baptist Church in Richmond, Virginia, sent him on his way to preach the Good News with the advice to "Fly like an angel, John!"[5] He soon became pastor of the Sixth Mount Zion Baptist Church in Richmond, where he drew large audiences. Without education, he was tutored in the Word and in preaching by the Reverend William E. Hatcher of Grace Street Baptist Church, who said of Jasper:

> He was a theater within himself, with the stage crowded with actors. He was a battlefield—himself the general, the staff, the officers, the common soldiery, the thundering artillery and the rattling musketry. He was the preacher.[6]

White people as well as black came to hear Jasper preach. He could tell a story and paint a picture. In his sermon "The Stone Cut Out of the Mountain," based on Daniel 2:45, he depicts Nebuchadnezzar troubled by his dream and the imagery of the great stone not cut out with human hands rolling and rolling and rolling.[7] His most famous sermon, which he preached about the country 250 times, was "The Sun Do Move" from Joshua 10:12–14. His message on "Frogs, Frogs, Frogs" from Exodus 8 is graphic beyond imagination. These are not homiletically polished expositions, but we can imagine the postwar Richmond audience hearing these sermons built off the dynamic storyline of Scripture. He concluded his sermon out of Joshua 10 unforgettably:

> The chariot that will come to take us to our Father's mansion will sweep out by them flickerin' lights and never halt till it brings us to clear view of the throne of the Lamb. Don't hitch your hopes to no sun nor stars; your home has got Jesus for its light, and your hopes must travel up that way![8]

---

1. C. Eric Lincoln and Lawrence H. Mamiya, *The Black Church in the African-American Experience* (Durham, N.C.: Duke University Press, 1990). For beautiful insight into a typical, more rural local black church experience, see Alex Haley, *Easter in Henning*

(New York: Doubleday, 1985), about the New Hope Colored Methodist Episcopal Church.
2. Bengt Sundkler, *Zulu Zion* (New York: Oxford University Press, 1976). A fascinating study of how this now independent church in Swaziland owes its origins to John Alexander Dowie (1847–1907) and the Christian Catholic Church of Zion, Illinois. The ministry of Simon Kimbangu, the African prophet, is also fascinating. He died in 1951 as a martyr.
3. Brad Hill, "Preaching the Word in the CEUM: Toward a Theology of Obedience," *The Covenant Quarterly* (February 1987): 37–44. Hill analyzes such varied narrative forms as "the diminishing spiral model; the pin-cushion model; the sunburst model; the linear-progression model."
4. Henry Mitchell, *Black Preaching* (San Francisco: Harper, 1979); Gardner C. Taylor, *How Shall They Preach* (Elgin, Ill.: Progressive Baptist Publishing, 1977). His 1976 Beecher Lectures. See the interview, "The Pulpit King," *Christianity Today* (December 11, 1995): 25ff. For his sermons, see *The Scarlet Thread* (Elgin, Ill.: Progressive Baptist Publishing, 1981).
5. Al Fasol, *With a Bible in Their Hands: Baptist Preaching in the South 1679–1979* (Nashville: Broadman, 1994), 74–75.
6. William E. Hatcher, *John Jasper: The Unmatched Negro Philosopher and Preacher* (Chicago: Revell, 1908), 9.
7. Fasol, *With a Bible in Their Hands,* 74.
8. Quoted in Richard Lischer, "John Jasper," in *Concise Encyclopedia of Preaching* (Louisville: Westminster John Knox, 1995), 279. Richard Ellsworth Day also has a lovely book, *Rhapsody in Black: The Life Story of John Jasper* (Philadelphia: Judson, 1953).

12.5.2 Martin Luther King Jr.—The Rage of African-American Preaching

> Our ultimate allegiance is not to this nation. Our ultimate allegiance is to the Almighty God and this is where we get our authority . . . When God speaks, who can but prophesy?
>
> There are two aspects of the world which we must never forget. One is that this is God's world and He is active in the forces of history and the affairs of men. The second is that Jesus Christ gave his life for the redemption of this world and as his followers we are called to give our lives continuing the reconciling work of Christ in this world.
>
> I'm a Baptist preacher and that means I am in the heart-changing business.
>
> —Martin Luther King Jr.

James Welldon Johnson's great poem, "God's Trombones," affords us insight into the amazing imaginative skills of the African-American preacher. Very few such sermons are in print, and even if they were available, the printed page cannot convey the electrifying aliveness of the preaching situation. In a day of dismal oratorical performance generally, we need to consider the arousing effectiveness of a Jesse Jackson or a Malcolm X. Rhetorical skill is not dead.

We see this in a Christian context in the preaching of **Martin Luther King Jr.** (1929–1968). His father had been a country preacher. At the age of fifteen, the elder King had put himself through school and became pastor of Ebenezer Baptist Church in Atlanta after the death of his father-in-law, who was its second pastor. Martin Sr. was known for his "hard preaching" and "sulfurous evangelism," and he would on occasion "walk the benches" when the poetic and musical crescendo mounted into an almost unbearable climax.[1]

Martin Luther King had unusual gifts as a preacher—we mark his rage, his tremendous sense of climax, his rhetorical genius, his near-hypnotic rhythm, his masterful use of irony, his use of the focal instance, his instinct for symbolic action. But he is included in this narrative because, unlike many, he came back from liberalism to his roots as a Christian and as a Bible preacher.

The younger King was schooled by theological liberals but was strongly influenced by Gardner Taylor, who held to "an explicitly evangelical doctrine of salvation centered in the substitutionary atonement of Christ."[2] King preached his trial sermon and was ordained when he was eighteen. Successive scholarships allowed him to study at Morehouse College in Atlanta, Crozer Seminary near Philadelphia, and at Boston University, where he did his doctoral work. Although embracing much of Enlightenment liberalism's vocabulary, Lischer argues, King did not become a liberal.[3] He learned the love ethic from Beecher and Brooks out of the previous century, but toward the end of his ministry that liberal optimism was blown away, "exposing once again the bedrock of black eschatology," which insists that not human idealism but God's mighty power will accomplish what needs to be done.[4] But at this time King was dipping heavily into Fosdick, Wallace Hamilton (the Methodist),[5] Howard Thurman of the Church of All Nations in San Francisco, Paul Tillich, and Chuck Templeton.[6] His failure to acknowledge his sources was a lifelong problem.

In 1954 he became pastor of the prestigious Dexter Avenue Baptist Church of Montgomery, Alabama. His intern, J. T. Porter, characterized King's early preaching at Dexter Avenue as a "very positive, Schuller type thing."[7] The boycott battles pushed King back into the more confrontational "smite 'em" style of his outstanding predecessor, Vernon Johns, who had "vanquished the power of positive thinking."[8] This was more the style of Jonathan Edwards than of Phillips Brooks. His seminary education had turned him away from the Bible, and he had lapped up the BOMFOG (brotherhood of man and fatherhood of God) thinking.[9] Lischer astutely observes:

> He did not notice that the historical criticism he was learning stifled the Christian impulse to get close to the Scripture, to live it, and did nothing to bridge the gap between the cultures. In fact, higher criticism only magnified the distance between the Book and its modern readers.[10]

In 1960 King moved to a one-hundred-month copastorate with his father at Ebenezer, where he preached what Lischer calls "the Ebenezer gospel." Churches without a sense of mission he called "entertainment centers." Increasingly his reference was to the supernatural, the Christological foundation, the meaning of the cross. His 1966 sermon on "the acceptable year of our Lord" from Luke 4 is explosively eschatological.[11]

King believed in original sin and that only God's pardon can rectify the human predicament.[12] The base of all is the nature and character of God, who is the Father of the Lord Jesus Christ. He was clearly evangelical on Jesus and salvation,[13] and used the altar call as an invitation to accept Christ.[14] He and his staff consulted with the Billy Graham crusade.[15]

We must see King in the cultural and social trauma of the racial revolution of the 1960s. Certainly there are aspects of his life and ministry that we cannot understand, but here was a man who preached Christ. His was a tragic loss for all Americans and in a very particular sense for all Christians in America, black or white, when he was killed in his thirty-ninth year. "But the Word of our God stands forever."

---

1. Richard Lischer, *The Preacher King: Martin Luther King, Jr. and the Word that Moved America* (New York: Oxford University Press, 1995), 45. An important study. See also Paul Scott Wilson, *A Concise History of Preaching* (Nashville: Abingdon, 1992), 170ff.
2. Lischer, *The Preacher King,* 51.
3. Ibid., 53.
4. Ibid., 57.
5. J. Wallace Hamilton is in the Peale-Schuller genre; see his sermons in *Where Now Is Thy God?* (New York: Revell, 1969); *What About Tomorrow?* (New York: Revell, 1972). He told good stories, but the well was dry.
6. Lischer, *The Preacher King,* 104. Templeton was a tragic cul-de-sac with his abandonment of friendship with Billy Graham, abandonment of the ministry, and abandonment of the faith; see Charles Templeton, *An Anecdotal Memoir* (Toronto: McClelland and Stewart, 1983). Paul Tillich likewise could put thoughts together memorably (although when I heard him his heavy accent made him somewhat difficult to follow), but he was not even a theist. See his popular books of sermons, *The Shaking of the Foundations* (New York: Scribner's, 1943); *The Eternal Now* (New York: Scribner's, 1956). Tillich was also a notorious philanderer. Lischer faces this issue in *The Preacher King,* 168ff.
7. Lischer, *The Preacher King,* 81.
8. Ibid., 85.
9. Ibid., 199, 148.
10. Ibid., 199.
11. Ibid., 235.
12. Ibid., 224.
13. Ibid., 226.
14. Ibid., 240. Lischer speaks of his "reversion from the philosophical method he learned in graduate school to his native theological assumptions" (202). His was a growing disillusionment with white liberals.
15. Ibid., 243.

12.5.3 Toyohiko Kagawa—The Reach of Asian Preaching

> By the truth as man thinks of it, we cannot come to understand the redeeming blood of Christ. Even by means of the philosophy of the eighteenth and nineteenth centuries, it could not be understood. When we come to have the feeling of the God of the whole universe, that is, the heart of the suffering Christ, only then can we come to comprehend the atonement.
>
> The theology of the nineteenth century left out the atonement . . . a certain church almost entirely left out the atonement . . . But in the Bible it is not so. If we ask why the doctrine of the atonement is left in many chapters of the Bible, it is because of the existence of the great problem of sin.
>
> When one man is converted there flows out a river of influence by which many people receive life. By the conversion of Jerry McCauley, Bradley was saved. By this influence, Merle [sic] Trotter, who had served ten sentences in prison, was saved.[1] Then Billy Sunday was saved and by his influence tens of thousands were converted. That is what it means for rivers of living water to flow from us. It is not merely influence. It is the influence of the Holy Spirit which draws the lineage to one after another, until it is wonderful to trace.
>
> —T. Kagawa

The twentieth century has seen the modernization of Japan, the breaking of Japan on the wheel of World War II, and its postwar rejuvenation into a mighty economic and political power. The Christian minority is minuscule here, but exerts a significant influence. Japan's greatest biblical preacher beyond question has been **Toyohiko Kagawa** (1888–1960). Kagawa was born in Kobe to a wealthy and politically significant Samurai and his geisha concubine.[2] When he was four years of age both of his parents died, and he was sent to live with his father's legal wife and a foster grandmother. Here he knew only abuse. Kagawa studied in the Buddhist temple and was forced to work very hard in the Kagawa enterprises. He was often taunted as the "concubine child."[3] While he was a student, he came under the influence of American missionaries, H. W. Myers and C. A. Logan, who led him to Christ. He went on to the Presbyterian College in Tokyo and ultimately took his B.D. at Princeton. Frail in health and tubercular, Kagawa spent fifteen years living and ministering in the infamous Shinkawa slums of Kobe. Always "a flaming evangel," he had to take a year off in "a rendezvous with death."[4]

Some scholars have questioned aspects of Kagawa's theology. He was well read in both Asian and Western classics, and his faith was so contextualized that the mode of his expression seems a bit strange to us. Yet his favorite hymn was "Jesus, Keep Me Near the Cross," and his *Meditations on the Cross* (1935) are sound. He preached vigorously against sin in all of its forms and the blood of

Christ as the antidote.[5] Clearly he was a Trinitarian and Nicaean in his Christology and was strong on the divinity of our Lord and Christian experience through the Holy Spirit.[6] Kagawa was part of the Kingdom of God Movement and its simultaneous evangelistic crusades in six major Japanese cities in which verbal proclamation loomed large. Of his preaching:

> His addresses are characterized by quiet fervor and moving power. He sways the multitudes who everywhere gather to hear him. Himself a man of action, his addresses lead men to action. Throughout his messages there are the delicate touches of a poet and the telling action and gestures of an actor. However, the most vivid and abiding impression left with the listeners is that of a mind alert, a soul on fire, an overwhelming passion in possession of the disease-riddled body all dedicated to one high, unselfish purpose and working together in absolute harmony toward its realization.[7]

Even when Kagawa was studying at Princeton (imagine him listening to Warfield), he worked in the Bowery among the needy in New York City. His wife, Haru, would join him after he returned to Japan in preaching to beggars and gamblers in the alleys of the slums.[8] His book *Psychology of the Poor* made a deep impression. He was imprisoned for siding with the oppressed workers. The great earthquake of 1923 gave him great opportunity for ministry, but the darkness of Pearl Harbor and World War II and imprisonment brought him to desolation. He spent much of the conflict consigned to a tubercular colony he had founded on the Inland Sea. After the war, he had opportunity to preach before the emperor and the empress. Indeed the first public appearance of the emperor after the war was a visit to the center where Kagawa established a ministry to twenty thousand refugees.[9] The life and message of the man can be summed up:

> As in a single Word, Christ's Love-Moment
> Is summed up in the Cross. The Cross is
> The whole of Christ, the whole of love . . .[10]

---

1. I think Kagawa means Melvin Trotter, a trophy of grace who founded a Grand Rapids rescue mission and represents all of these faithful preachers in this setting. See Melvin Trotter, *These Forty Years* (Grand Rapids: Zondervan, 1939). Campbell Morgan and H. A. Ironside write appreciative forewords to this volume.
2. Charlie May Simon, *A Seed Shall Serve: The Story of the Spiritual Leader of Modern Japan* (London: Hodder and Stoughton, 1959), 8.
3. Ibid., 26.
4. William Axling, *Kagawa* (New York: London, 1932), 19–23.
5. Ibid., 123.
6. Toyohiko Kagawa, *Meditations on the Holy Spirit* (Nashville: Cokesbury, 1939), 111ff.
7. Axling, *Kagawa,* 119.

8. Simon, *A Seed Shall Serve,* 114.
9. Ibid., 147. Kagawa wrote more than one hundred fifty books.
10. Ralph G. Turnbull, *A History of Preaching* (Grand Rapids: Baker, 1974), 401. Turnbull indicates "To Kagawa there was never any doubt concerning the validity of the scriptural records" (403).

12.5.4 Watchman Nee—The Richness of Asian Preaching

> What matters is the effectiveness of the word proclaimed.
>
> No servant of Christ should be satisfied with present attainment. Anyone who is content with what is, is a loser of opportunities. I believe those God is now giving us are far beyond anything we can conceive. Every day God is giving us opportunities and the aggregate who can assess? To redeem the time is to seize today the opportunities God has appointed for us today. When the church buries a talent there is serious loss.
>
> —Watchman Nee, after the Communist takeover of China
>
> Whether shackled by foes or hampered by circumstances, whether totally paralyzed or walled up in solitary darkness, we can pray, we can appeal to Him, we can ask. We shall surely receive. God will act again. If we will go on asking, our sorrow will be turned to surpassing joy.
>
> —Watchman Nee

The long history of missionary preaching in China has been touched at several points in this narrative, but it is important to see that part of the fruit of missionary enterprise has been the multiplication of gifted and able Chinese preachers. These include Leland Wang, Andrew Gih,[1] Marcus Cheng,[2] and most signally, **Watchman Nee** (1903–1972).

Nee was born in Swatow, the third of nine children; his father was a soft-spoken man, a cloth merchant, and his mother was very strong-willed. She became a forceful Methodist preacher in her own right. Nee's parents were converted under the ministry of evangelist Dora Yu. When in the aftermath of her conversion, his mother confessed to Watchman that she had beaten him unjustly (an unheard-of loss of face in China), he too was converted at the age of eighteen and attended Yu's Bible school.[3]

Missionary Margaret E. Barber, who was supported by Pastor D. M. Panton's Surrey Chapel in Norwich, had an immense influence on him. Under her counsel he was baptized.[4] She introduced him to the writings of Madame Guyon, the French mystic who had a marked influence on the home meetings in which young Nee was now increasingly involved. These gatherings evolved into the Little Flock Movement. Barber also initiated him into the thinking of Mrs. Jessie Penn-Lewis on the Cross, who came out of the Calvinistic Methodists of Wales and the Welsh revival. He traveled with his mother in special services in Malaysia after graduating from Anglican Trinity College in Foochow. His insightful biblical preaching and his work as editor of *Revival* (later *The Christian*) brought him into prominence and usefulness. Although he had a brief Presbyterian connection, he moved more and more to the practice of local assemblies independent of mission societies and unsalaried ministers.

He was diagnosed as having tuberculosis but left the issue of his healing in the discovery of the truth that Christ is victor![5] He spoke ceaselessly in Overcomer Conferences along the Keswick line. Kinnear describes Watchman Nee's strength:

> The appeal of Watchman's own preaching lay first of all in his gift of making so plain the way to God that relies solely upon Christ's finished work. All too many Christians were striving after a salvation based on good works of their own, a way little removed in principle from Buddhism. They had been told it was presumptuous to say confidently that they were saved. The preaching of new life as God's free gift startled them therefore with its novelty. Nor did Watchman stop with the good news of righteousness by faith. He was finding now much personal help from the writings of Andrew Murray and F. B. Meyer on the practical life of holiness and deliverance from sin. He read, too, all he could of Charles G. Finney and of Evan Roberts and the Welsh spiritual awaking of 1904–5, and he delved into Otto Stockmeier [cf. 9.5.3] and Jessie Penn-Lewis on the questions of soul and spirit and triumph over Satanic power.[6]

Many of us would have a problem with his ecclesiology. But Nee had an incredible knowledge of the biblical text. He walked back and forth as he spoke with "his hands behind his back, just speaking from his heart."[7] Yet again:

> Standing there in his dark-blue cotton gown he held their attention with his gentle manner, his simple but thorough reasoning and his apt analogies. No one ever saw him use any notes for he could reproduce anything he read. To illustrate a thing visually he could draw a swift imaginary sketch in the air (which a young worker might reproduce on poster paper afterwards) and if to illumine some point he told a personal anecdote it was nearly always a story against himself. His keen sense of humour sent frequent ripples of laughter round the hall and "you never got sleepy in his meetings." But from start to finish he never strayed from his subject.[8]

He visited Britain and America in both 1933 and 1938. Unable to fit easily into the coils and complexities of Western polities, he nonetheless enjoyed his contacts with George Cutting in England, the author of *Safety, Certainty and Enjoyment,* which at that time had run to thirty million copies. Nee also found a soul brother in T. Austin Sparks, a former Baptist preacher whose ministry at Honor Oaks Farm and through the printed page were a tonic to Nee.[9] He visited Keswick in 1938, where both his prayers and his presence made a deep impression. On his way back to China, Nee delivered a memorable set of messages in Denmark.[10]

During this time, in harmony with his conviction on ministerial compensation, Nee managed the family chemical enterprise.[11] In 1947 he came to a new emphasis on brokenness of heart and spirit.[12] He enjoyed good fellowship with two young pioneers, Geoffrey Bull and George Patterson, who were going to the Tibetan frontier.[13]

With the Chinese communist takeover in 1949, the Little Flock Movement was under strong pressure to become part of the Three Self Movement sanctioned by the government. In resisting, Nee was first arrested in 1952. In anticipation of the situation, he had sent his somewhat authoritarian colleague Witness Lee to Taiwan.[14] He visited there himself but chose to return to mainland China. Accused of being "a running dog of the imperialists," criminal charges were preferred in 1956. With a great flow of invective, he was found guilty and was sentenced to fifteen years of hard labor. Amid cruelty and persecution, Watchman Nee yet worked for the Lord in the prison and won men to Christ. In 1972 he died in prison at the age of sixty-nine, five years beyond the sentence given to him. The martyr's seed has given much fruit; the church in China, numbering one million when the missionaries were expelled in 1949, may now number seventy million. And Nee is read everywhere.

---

1. Andrew Gih, *Launch Out Into the Deep* (London: Marshall, Morgan, and Scott, 1938). Gih is highly commended by J. Edwin Orr, whose revival and preaching ministry have been crucial. See Newman Watts, *Edwin Orr: The Ubiquitous Ulsterman* (Croydon, England: Uplift Books, 1947). Orr not only wrote the history of revival but also preached revival mightily.
2. Edla Matson, *Peter Matson: Covenant Pathfinder in China* (Chicago: Covenant, 1951), 157ff. Cheng was the gifted professor at Kingchow Seminary.
3. Angus I. Kinnear, *Watchman Nee: Against the Tide* (Ft. Washington, Pa.: CLC, 1973), 18, 37.
4. Ibid., 42–43. See *The Autobiography of Madam Guyon* (Chicago: Moody, n.d.). There is a strain of Christ-mysticism (to use Deissman's phrase) in Watchman Nee, and we sense the same in Guyon, whose work he valued.
5. Ibid., 73–75. Cf. Dana Roberts, *Understanding Watchman Nee* (Plainfield, N.J.: Haven, 1980). Quite critical. He uses the word *pietism* pejoratively and tars Watchman Nee. This is to misrepresent historic pietism.
6. Ibid., 64.
7. Ibid., 141. Nee's studies on Ephesians are gripping, *Sit, Walk and Stand* (Bombay: Witness and Testimony, 1957); *The Normal Christian Life* is his best-known work (London: Witness and Testimony, 1958); *What Shall This Man Do?* (Ft. Washington, Pa.: CLC, 1961); *The Latent Power of the Soul,* in which he contrasts the spiritual with the soulish (New York: Christian Fellowship, 1972); *Love Not the World* (Ft. Washington, Pa.: CLC, 1968); *Twelve Baskets Full* (Hong Kong: Church Book Room, 1966). In these multiple text sermons we see artistic and aesthetic Asian logic in full force.
8. Ibid., 118. Roberts alleges that some of his close followers made sounds in prayer like Nee's clicking dentures.
9. The works of T. Austin Sparks are many. Some of the best, in my opinion: *The Stewardship of the Mystery* in two volumes (London: Witness and Testimony, 1939);

Rivers of Living Water (London: Witness and Testimony, n.d.); *God's Reactions to Man's Defections* (London: Witness and Testimony, 1956); *Fundamental Questions of the Christian Life* (London: Witness and Testimony, n.d.). The publication of *Toward the Mark* has recently ceased.

10. At the invitation of Pastor Fjord Christensen of Copenhagen, where he gave The Normal Christian Life studies for the first time, Kinnear *(Watchman Nee,* 113).
11. Ibid., 126–27, 140.
12. A similar message was preached in the West by Roy and Revel Hession. See his books, *The Calvary Road* (Ft. Washington, Pa.: CLC, 1950); *We Would See Jesus; Be Filled Now.* I shall never forget sermons I heard Hession deliver many years ago. See his autobiography, *My Calvary Road* (Grand Rapids: Zondervan, 1978).
13. Kinnear, *Watchman Nee,* 140. Geoffrey Bull's magnificent *When Iron Gates Yield* (Chicago: Moody, 1955) and *The City and the Sign: An Interpretation of the Book of Jonah* (Grand Rapids: Baker, 1970) are "must" reading.
14. Charges of doctrinal irregularity against Witness Lee have been reconsidered by many critics. See J. Gordon Melton, *An Open Letter Concerning the Local Church, Witness Lee and the God-Men Controversy* (Santa Barbara: Institute for the Study of American Religion, 1985). For a thoughtful survey of the ministry situation in Taiwan after 1949, see Allen J. Swanson, *Taiwan: Mainline Versus Independent Church Growth* (South Pasadena, Calif.: William Carey Library, 1970).

12.5.5 THE KOREAN PULPIT—THE REVIVAL AND PREACHING

> The Bible is the Word of God. Therefore, when we understand the truth of the Bible through the Holy Spirit, we can feel the power of life in the Bible. Preaching is not a lecture or an apologetic speech. Preaching is the product of a spiritual life. It is the fruit of the Holy Spirit through prayer, study of the Bible and obedience to the Word.
>
> —Yune-Sun Park

This has been a turbulent century for Korea, once called the hermit kingdom. Within the Chinese family of nations, Korea remained tightly closed until the arrival of Christian missionaries.

Korea has been called "the banner mission field in the world." We have already spoken of Nevius and Goforth and the revival that came early in the century. The spiritual resurgence there has been largely Presbyterian, with strong Baptist, Holiness, and Pentecostal work as well. In fact, the largest Presbyterian, Methodist, and Pentecostal local church congregations are in Korea. Yet Japanese occupation and cruelty (1910–1945) saw many martyrs and intensified purity in the church. Then came the Korean War with all of its suffering. The postwar years brought the partition of the peninsula, the communization of the North, and a hodgepodge American policy, termed by the late Sumner Wells as "one of the most serious crimes of the twentieth century." Despite all the turmoil, the urbanization and industrialization of the nation have taken root.[1] But prosperity does not bode well for the church. The life of prayer, which had been so striking in the Korean church, does not easily survive Western influence.

Under governmental encouragement, many Koreans have emigrated around the world. Two million Koreans still reside in China, and many are flocking to the U.S. The Korean church in America is facing some serious issues, many related to generational tensions.[2]

Koreans have been known as good speakers and preachers. Very little sermonic literature has been translated, but a new study of Korean preaching has just been published in this country, and several leading preachers can be identified.

Sun-Joo Kil (1869–1935) preached in the revivals of 1907, when converts increased by thirty percent. Strongly evangelistic and tending toward allegorization, Kil was strongly dispensational and premillennial.[3] He established sixty churches despite becoming blind.

Ihk-Doo Kim (1874–1950) was a notorious hoodlum who was converted and read the Bible one hundred times before his baptism. Signs of the Spirit often accompanied his powerful preaching.[4] His main themes were the Cross, the blood, and repentance.

Sung-Bong Lee (1900–1965) was often called the D. L. Moody of Korea. He was an evangelist for the Holiness Church of Korea. Persecuted by the communists, he was faithful in a ministry that was owned of the Spirit and saw many converts. He often sang a hymn while preaching.[5] Lee provided strong preaching on the Second Advent.

Hwa-Sik Kim (1894–1947) was imprisoned by both the Japanese and the communists. Although frail in health, he was an unusually gifted preacher, sometimes called the Spurgeon of Korea. Dr. Chung remarks, "We can feel a mother's warm hand in his preaching."[6] He used lively introductions and was a poet. Kim loved John Bunyan and often quoted him. In 1947 he was killed in prison.

Ki-Chul Choo (1897–1944) preached fearlessly when Shinto shrine worship was an issue (1930–1945). The Japanese required all citizens to participate in shrine ceremonies. Many Christians complied, but others led by Choo felt that participating was idolatrous. His sermons were God-centered.[7] He died in prison.

Yang-Won Sohn (1902–1951) was incarcerated for six years by the Japanese over the shrine issue, and saw two of his sons martyred in the communist revolt of 1948. He was captured by the communists and was shot three years later. His ministry had a great focus on lepers. He was called "Korea's atom bomb of love."[8] Sohn led Korean Christians by his life and example but also through his penetrating biblical preaching. Clearly the historic biblical faith and its faithful proclamation are at the heart of this dear people.

---

1. In my opinion the best history is Robert T. Oliver, *A History of the Korean People in Modern Times* (Newark, N.J.: University of Delaware Press, 1993). The postwar Korean president, Syngman Rhee, was a Methodist.
2. For interesting insight into émigré mentality, see K. Connie Kang, *Home Was the Land of the Morning Calm* (New York: Addison/Wesley, 1995) The danger for the émigré is allowing the church to be the celebration of ethnicity.
3. Sung-Kuh Chung, *The Korean Church and Reformed Faith: Focusing on the Historical Study of Preaching in the Korean Church* (Seattle: Times Publishing, 1996),

45, 51. Dr. Chung is the former president of Chongshin College and is now a professor at Chongshin Theological Seminary. The publication of Chung's study makes an inestimable contribution.
4. Ibid., 56.
5. Ibid., 66.
6. Ibid., 75.
7. Ibid., 106.
8. Ibid., 120.

12.5.6 SADHU SUNDAR SINGH—THE RISKS OF INDIAN PREACHING

> We shall never get a second opportunity of bearing the Cross after our life on earth . . . so now is the time to bear the Cross joyfully. Never again will an opportunity be given us of bearing this sweet burden.
>
> Other religions say, "Do good and you will become good." Christianity says, "Be in Christ and you will do good." The meaning of the Atonement and the Blood that washes away our sins is that we are grafted into Christ.
>
> I don't sit down and write out my sermons. As I pray, I get texts, subjects and illustrations. Preachers ought to get their message from God. If they get it from books instead, they do not preach their own gospel; they preach the gospel of others. They sit on other people's eggs and hatch them and think they are their own.
>
> —Sundar Singh

The masses of the subcontinent of India (India, Pakistan, and Bangladesh), buffeted by the renewal of native religions, tribal and religious warfare, precarious economies, and population explosion, desperately need the gospel. We have noted some of the early missionaries who have been augmented by gifted indigenous preachers, and in some areas there has been a remarkable response. Yet the teeming millions seem relatively impervious to the gospel of Christ.

One of the gifted and able preachers in this century for all too brief a time was **Sadhu Sundar Singh** (1889–1933?). He was born in a devout Sikh family in Rampur in the Punjab. Sikhism was founded by Nanak (1469–1538) as a conscious compromise between Hinduism and Islam. Their holy book, the Granth, a collection of poems, is virtually worshiped at the central shrine in Amritsar.[1] Many lawyers, military men, and police officers in India are Sikhs. Young Sundar was very religious and in fact memorized the Gita of the Hindus by the age of seven. He was searching: "I wanted to save myself! But I could not achieve it for myself."[2] Both his mother and his older brother died, and he became desperate for meaning. He had contact with an American Presbyterian mission school and had the New Testament, but he burned it publicly and became a ringleader of those who pelted the village preachers with stones.[3] Determined to take his own life, Singh had a vision of Jesus coming into his room and asking him in Hindustani, "Why do you persecute me?"[4] He became a Christian even though this meant being disowned by his father and excommunicated by the Sikhs. He was baptized at sixteen and became a sadhu, a homeless wanderer, suffering and proclaiming Christ.

There is something quintessentially Indian about this Christian mystic. Archbishop Soderholm of Sweden observed, "Sundar is the first to show the whole world how the Gospel of Jesus Christ is reflected in unchanged purity in an Indian soul."[5] Singh did spend some time studying at St. John's Divinity College in Lahore, but the lure of the road was too strong. He traveled over the whole world but was especially burdened to capture the great Buddhist strongholds in Tibet and Burma. Making several trips to the West, he was deeply disillusioned by the materialism and disunity in the church. Singh made repeated forays over the Himalayas to Tibet and was often persecuted. Even when his funds were wiped out in a bank failure, he was determined to return to preach in Tibet. In 1929 he moved out in quest for converts in Tibet and beyond and was never seen again. In 1933 the Indian government, assuming him dead, probated his will.

Sundar Singh was a great lover of the Bible, professing that "the Bible, like a lump of sugar, is sweet to me at whatever point I taste it."[6] He particularly treasured the Gospel of John and loved to share it. Repelled by modern rationalistic criticism of the Bible, Singh called it "spiritual influenza" resulting in denigration of Christ as Lord and God.[7] He had problems with any mechanistic theory of inspiration and knew and felt the power of the Holy Spirit in and through the Word. One report had it as follows:

> A few weeks ago a Christian Sadhu by name Sundar Singh came about preaching the Gospel in the villages round about Narkanda and suffered a great deal of persecution. We were sitting and chatting . . . when a farmer by name Nandi came up and said: "A very strange thing has happened in our village. We were reaping the corn in a field and a Sadhu came up to us and began to preach religion. We all felt very annoyed at this interference in our work and showered curses on him; but little heeding our curses and threats the man went on with his talk. At this my brother took up a stone and hit the man on the head. But this good man, unmindful of the insult, closed his eyes and said, 'O God, forgive them.' After awhile my brother who had flung the stone was suddenly caught with a splitting headache and had to give up reaping. At this the Sadhu took my brother's scythe and started reaping the corn. We all marveled and said, 'What manner of man is this Sadhu, that, instead of abusing and cursing us in return, he prays in our favor.' Then we took him to our house where he told us many nice things. After he had gone, we noticed an amazing thing. The field where this good man had reaped has never yielded so much corn as it has this year; we have gathered two maunds above the average this time."[8]

He knew the philosopher Tagore and he knew Gandhi, but Sadhu Sundar Singh's consuming passion was to be known as "a witness to the saving power of God in Jesus Christ."

1. Robert E. Hume, *The World's Living Religions* (New York: Scribner's, 1955), 94ff.
2. C. F. Andrews, *Sadhu Sundar Singh: A Personal Memoir* (London: Hodder and Stoughton, 1934), 64.
3. Ibid., 68.
4. Cyril J. Davey, *Sadhu Sundar Singh* (Bromley, Kent: STL Books, 1950), 32ff.
5. Andrews, *Sadhu Sundar Singh,* 131. He attended the Keswick Convention in 1922.
6. B. H. Streeter and A. J. Appasamy, *The Sadhu* (London: Macmillan, 1927), 196.
7. Ibid., 200.
8. Ibid., 209. A maund is an Indian unit of weight measuring about 82.28 pounds.

12.5.7 Black Elk—The Resilience of Native American Preaching

> Without an adequate sermon, no clue is given to the moral purpose at the heart of the mystery, and reverence remains without ethical content.
> —Reinhold Niebuhr

In recent centuries, the Roman Catholic church and Eastern Orthodoxy have been so involved in liturgy that preaching of substance has been eclipsed. The unmatched television effectiveness of Bishop Fulton J. Sheen in the 1950s (who can forget his piercing blue eyes?) held millions spellbound, but his message was practical not biblical, relational not salvific. Since Vatican II, there has come a renaissance of interest in preaching in Catholicism both stateside and abroad.[1] In areas where Catholicism has been dominant, preaching has been recessive, but with the Protestant explosion in Latin America, for instance, a rising new generation of Roman Catholic preachers of ability and skill is coming into view.

A true gospel preacher who came out of the Jesuit outreach at the St. Francis Mission in Rosebud, South Dakota, and the Holy Rosary Mission in Pine Ridge, South Dakota, was the Native American known as **Black Elk** (d. 1950). Black Elk was known technically as a catechist.[2] He lived in the world of the Lakota Sioux Indians, where for many years he was "a kind of preacher" who preached the Bible and Christian doctrine to his people for the greater part of his life.

Government Indian policy has been one of the great scandals of our national history. In 1868 the American government signed the Laramie Treaty, giving all of South Dakota west of the Missouri River to the Sioux. This treaty was broken by General George Custer in 1874 in connection with the gold rush in Deadwood and Lead, South Dakota. Uprisings led by Black Elk's cousin, Crazy Horse, and Sitting Bull resulted. At the Battle of Wounded Knee, two hundred Indians—men, women, and children—were massacred. In these years, Black Elk was a native medicine man and was partially blinded at Wounded Knee.

After these years of warfare, Black Elk was converted by the "blackrobes," as contrasted with the Episcopalians, who were called "whiterobes," or the Presbyterians, who were called "shortrobes." Black Elk's Christianity did not compromise or stultify his Indianness. Of his conversion it was said, "The Son of God called him to lead a new life."[3] He sensed God's call to "instruct the people out of the Scriptures."[4] His forte was Bible stories, and his own reading of the

Bible was legendary.[5] Black Elk faced many obstacles, including the American Indian Movement, whose members would tear down the signs advertising Black Elk's meetings. In his missionary work, he challenged the use of peyote in Native American worship, and "he converted a lot of those people."[6]

It was said of Black Elk that "on any occasion he can arise and deliver a flood of oratory." His heart was full of Christ. Literally hundreds came to the Lord through his preaching ministry. His favorite theme was the two-road map. We must remember that in Indian religion, no personal relationship exists with a personal Savior.[7] But Black Elk relentlessly hammered away with the message, "Believe in Jesus Christ."[8] We recall him with the tribute, "He practiced a Christian life."

---

1. For a European sample, see Otto Semmelroth, *The Preaching Word: On the Theology of Proclamation* (New York: Herder and Herder, 1965). The significant American work is Walter J. Burghardt, *Preaching: The Art and the Craft* (New York: Paulist, 1987). The approach of some Roman Catholic preachers is more conservative, such as Cardinal Lustiger of Paris or Joseph Cardinal Ratzinger, *Dogma and Preaching* (Chicago: Franciscan Herald Press, 1985), or more radical and liberal, such as John Dominic Crossan of Chicago, *Jesus: A Revolutionary Biography* (New York: Harper/Collins, 1994), in which he argues that dogs ate the body of Jesus (154). In contrast, the late Henri Nouwen was one of the most captivating preachers I have ever heard.
2. Michael F. Steltenkamp, *Black Elk: Holy Man of the Oglala* (Norman: University of Oklahoma, 1993), xvii.
3. Ibid., 36.
4. Ibid., 47.
5. Ibid., 47.
6. Ibid., 62. For a thoughtful statement on the issue here, see Samuel Shangchi Pan, *Some General Principles for Sermon Preparation in Cross-Cultural Preaching* (Th.M. thesis, Trinity Evangelical Divinity School, 1986).
7. Ibid., 145.
8. Ibid., 74.

12.6 GERMAN, DUTCH, SWEDISH, AND SWEDISH-AMERICAN PREACHERS IN A TUMULTUOUS TIME

> From the beginning, then, Christianity, being concerned with the Event which by definition has no parallel, God being agent in it as He is not in other happenings, was committed to preaching, to proclamation. Whoso said Christianity said preaching. There was no choice between that and absolutely ceasing to be, with not the least chance of ever occurring again.
>
> —H. H. Farmer

Western Europe in the twentieth century has become more and more a "spiritual ice-belt." The savage assaults of Enlightenment unbelief have been succeeded by postmodern "radical relativism and skepticism that rejects any idea of truth, knowledge or objectivity" (Gertrude Himmelfarb). The catastrophic loss of Christian understanding and influence in recent years has left church attendance at between two and three percent. Authority was lost when authoritarianism was dismissed by autonomous man, with no willingness to recognize the critical difference. Even so fine a preacher as F. W. Dillistone became so enamored with Lloyd Morgan's emergent evolution that he concluded we must embrace the modern scientific worldview posthaste.[1] Whether or not there is any real difference between Karl Barth's neo-orthodoxy and Jacques Derrida's deconstructionism may be argued, but there were preachers who, even in the Sahara of subjectivity, had a message from God.[2] This is what we need now even in the United States, where pragmatism is the potentate.[3]

---

1. Charles Raven, *F. W. Dillistone* (Grand Rapids: Eerdmans, 1975). He did reject "the robots of modern behaviorism."
2. Graham Ward, *Barth, Derrida and the Language of Theology* (Cambridge, Mass.: Cambridge University Press, 1996).
3. Marva J. Dawn, *Reaching Out Without Dumbing Down: A Theology of Worship for the Turn-of-the-Century Culture* (Grand Rapids: Eerdmans, 1995). She argues that there is "normative truth" which calls the community into being.

   The fierce struggle among the Jesuits against total horizontalization in which unbelief is assumed to be an option is almost paradigmatic in our time. See Malachi Martin, *The Jesuits: The Society of Jesus and the Betrayal of the Roman Catholic Church* (New York: Simon and Schuster, 1987). The whole notion of "salvation" is virtually lost as meaning is sought in the world, not from Scripture; the "new fabric" does not involve preaching "Christ crucified" (429).

12.6.1 Martin Niemoller—Preaching in the Belly of the Beast

> We can see how God's Word is being put into chains and imprisoned from the list of undesirable books on which figures nearly all the desirable Christian literature, to the prison-cells which close behind the messengers of Jesus Christ, even to the prayers . . . that God may give our people back the free and unimpeded preaching of the gospel.
>
> The gospel must remain the gospel; the church must remain the church; the creed must remain the creed; Protestant Christianity must remain Protestant Christianity.
>
> —Martin Niemoller

That ours is a spiritual battle against demon hordes is especially clear when we consider preachers who engaged in defiance of totalitarian regimes, such as **Martin Niemoller** (1892–1984). Born in Westphalia, the son of a Lutheran pastor with some Reformed proclivities, Niemoller early had a childlike devotion to Jesus.[1] His father was strong follower of Pastor Johan Wichern's Inner Mission movement, which aimed at the spiritual renewal of Germany through the huge Kirchentags and other approaches. This was a movement with which the younger Niemoller was closely associated for many years. He graduated from the German Naval Academy at Kiel and served as a U-boat commander in World War I. His exploits and adventures in sinking and destroying shipping earned him the Iron Cross.[2] Yet his thoughts were more and more turning to God. For a while after the war he farmed, but he was not content. God was calling him to preach.

Niemoller was terrified at the thought of standing before a congregation and speaking.[3] Still he could not escape the divine compunction:

> I had been taught as a child that belief in Christ as Lord and Saviour and diligent attention to God's Word can transform men and give them freedom and strength. That lesson I had never forgotten, for my own experience had proved it to be true. I now became convinced that the best and most effective help I could give to my countrymen in the national calamity would be to share that knowledge with them.[4]

He took up studies at Munster and was chiefly taken with Professor Karl Heim. Here he overcame his fears of speaking and did a curacy. He worked in Westphalian home missions from 1923 to 1931. From 1931 to 1936, he served the strategic Dahlem Church in a well-to-do suburb of Berlin and developed a deep friendship with Gerhard Jacobi, the Jewish Christian who served the Kaiser Wilhelm Church. With the advent of Hitler and the National Socialists, Niemoller found that he was one of the earliest opponents of Nazism and Hitler's dedication to create a "positive Christianity."[5] He spearheaded the formation of the Pastor's Emergency Union and quickly became the spokesman of the German churches in opposition to Hitler.

Not all clergy were so disposed. Some became Nazis, or at least strong advocates of Hitler's policies, such as Heidegger, Althaus, Kittel, and Hirsch. But the thrust of Niemoller's preaching was "God is my Fuehrer!" Not surprisingly, he had a personal confrontation with Hitler.[6] Dr. Hjalmer Schacht, the Nazi economic csar acquitted at Nuremburg, was a member of Niemoller's congregation, and the von Ribbentrops attended, but Niemoller refused to baptize their children. In 1936 he was arrested by the Gestapo and removed from his charge, but he would not be muzzled. During the war, he spent time in a number of prisons, including Sachsenhausen and Dachau. We have in printed form his letters from Moabit Prison and sermons which he preached at Dachau.[7] That any preaching at all was allowed at Dachau during the four years he was kept there is a remarkable story in itself. These strongly biblical messages are deeply moving considering the circumstances in which they were delivered.[8]

After the war, Niemoller acted as representative of the German churches, and he traveled widely in England, the United States, and Russia. He was also president of the Protestant church (Lutheran/Reformed) in Hessen, Nassau, and Frankfurt-am-Main. His wife Else was killed in an automobile accident. Nihilism was threatening to devour the populace. Writers like Gunter Grass and Herman Hesse tried to find something to say to the questions and guilt of the

German people. He remarried and continued significant ministry in the vacuum of postwar Germany until his death in 1984.

The main collection of his sermons from Dahlem days (where he had ten thousand members) shows that, while grounded firmly in a biblical text, Niemoller seldom divided the text carefully. As good Lutheran sermons, they certainly are Christ-centered and emphasize the grace of God.[9]

When his father had been deposed from his pulpit, he preached in a dance hall, filling it to the rafters for the proclamation of the gospel of Christ.[10] "The Bible is not bound," said the elder Niemoller. Martin Niemoller learned that lesson well.

---

1. James Bentley, *Martin Niemoller: 1892–1984* (New York: Free Press, 1984), 3.
2. Basil Miller, *Martin Niemoller* (Grand Rapids: Zondervan, 1942), 22–73. The truth is stranger than fiction!
3. Bentley, *Martin Niemoller,* 22.
4. Quoted in Dietmar Schmidt, *Pastor Niemoller* (Garden City, N.Y.: Doubleday, 1959), 65.
5. Bentley, *Martin Niemoller,* 237.
6. Ibid., 85. Cf. Robert P. Ericksen, *Theologians Under Hitler* (New Haven, Conn.: Yale University Press, 1985).
7. Hubert G. Locke, ed., *Exile in the Fatherland: Martin Niemoller's Letters from Moabit Prison* (Grand Rapids: Eerdmans, 1986). The life of another typical wartime hero-preacher is chronicled in Yerasmus Zervopoulos, *Kostas Metallinos: God's Messenger to Greece* (Chicago: Wordsmith, 1983). Dr. Metallinos was director of the Government Office of Accounting and led the Free Evangelical Church movement. He was the greatest preacher in Greece in this century and a dedicated student of the Scripture. He translated Godet and was an especially avid student of eschatology.
8. Martin Niemoller, *Dachau Sermons* (New York: Harper, 1946), 1ff.
9. Martin Niemoller, *Here Stand I!* (Chicago: Willet, Clark, 1937). Great preaching on the suffering and death of Jesus.
10. Miller, *Martin Niemoller,* 14.

12.6.2 KARL BARTH—PREACHING IN THE SHAMBLES OF WAR AND IN THE SUNLIGHT OF PEACE

> Preaching is the Word of God which he himself speaks, claiming for the purpose the exposition of a biblical text in free human words that are relevant to contemporaries by those who are called to do this in the church that is obedient to its commission.
>
> Theology as a church discipline ought in all its branches to be nothing other than sermon preparation in the broadest sense.
>
> If a sermon is biblical it will not be boring.

> The need is not so much to get to the people as to come from Christ . . . then one automatically gets to the people.
>
> —Karl Barth

Appropriately called the theological titan of this century, **Karl Barth** (1886–1968) shows us both the appealing strengths and the grave weaknesses of neo-orthodoxy, one of the primary theological movements of our time. The son of Fritz Barth, a theologian from Basel, Karl Barth was reared largely in Bern and was, like so many, very liberal in his theology. He studied under Wilhelm Herrmann at Marburg and von Harnack at Berlin.

Old liberalism was built on Immanuel Kant's denial of any intellectual comprehension of objective truth. Usually the alternative was Schleiermacher's theology of experience and subjectivity. The utter bankruptcy of liberalism became apparent to Barth as he served two industrial parishes in the German Reformed Church before and after the First World War.[1] He then turned to Scripture itself:

> I sat under an apple tree and began to apply myself to Romans with all the resources that were available to me at the time. I had already learnt in my confirmation instruction that this book was of crucial importance. I began to read it as though I had never read it before. I wrote down carefully what I discovered . . . point by point . . . I read and read.[2]

Aided especially by the writings of J. T. Beck (more than by Schlatter), Barth began to develop his dialectical theology, the theology of crisis or the theology of the Word, as it came to be known. Always exercised about the preaching task, he began to preach about the sinfulness of humanity and the grace of God. He shed his former liberalism and socialism and wrote his famous *Romans.* "The mighty voice of Paul was new to me," he exclaimed and found the rest of Scripture likewise new to him. Barth's rediscovery of sin and the Word have been refreshing and salutary for many. As he went on to a teaching career at Basel and shared his *Church Dogmatics* and other works, he extended his influence widely to capture evangelical institutions and thinkers, as well as others (Bernard Ramm and Donald Bloesch are two examples).[3]

Barth's neo-orthodoxy hoped to blend enough orthodoxy with Enlightenment thinking on the Bible as to make effective appeal to contemporary culture, but it is Barth's faulty and deficient view of scriptural authority that aborts his overall objective. Barth retained his critical view of Scripture. The Word of God is not to be equated with the words of Scripture in the orthodox sense. The Word is found in Christ, in the Scripture, and in preaching. "The Word is not per se Scripture, but rather what Scripture has to communicate to man from God."[4] The Bible becomes God's Word as it speaks to us, as Barth sees it, but nothing preserves Scripture from the "pick-and-choose" approach as to what is reliable and factual.[5] Barth and Bultmann parted company, but in terms of Barth's system, what can he say to Bultmann's radical antisupernaturalism?

Clearly Barth has a high view of preaching in this schema and argues strongly that "the task of the sermon is to create space for the Word of God."[6] But the

Word of God for Barth is not Scripture as such but what Scripture becomes in the divine/human encounter. In seminars held at Bonn in 1932 and 1933, before he was sacked by Hitler, Barth vigorously critiqued homiletical practice in his time. He was particularly critical of Bauer, who did not insist on a biblical text in preaching. Barth scoffed at deciding what is to be preached in terms of what attracts and what repels (hear! hear!) and summoned the preacher to preach not *about* the Bible but *from* the Bible.[7] He spoke of regard for the text, confidence in the text, and the relevance of the text in searching and challenging words. Yet the contention that the Bible is a record of divine self-disclosure and not the revelation itself perpetuates the false dichotomy between the personal and the propositional. The Bible is certainly both.

Barth in his own preaching always used the pericope, though as he grew older he often trimmed the preaching portion. Earlier on he stayed closer to the text. Because he did not accept natural revelation, he did not believe a sermon should have an introduction or a conclusion. Since there was no point of contact between God and people (a view not unlike that of Cornelius Van Til but hardly in line with Romans 1:18–32), the sermon could never serve an apologetic purpose.

Barth's preaching was Christocentric.[8] After 1954 he did most of his preaching in the Basel prison. Many of these sermons are remarkable reading, as are *Deliverance to the Captives* (1961) and *Call for God* (1965). Yet Barth was critical of Billy Graham's preaching and bemoaned what he heard at St. Jacob Stadium as "heating up hell."[9] This perhaps reflected his own strong "move toward universalism," which really stemmed from his reservations on scriptural authority.[10]

Lovers of preaching can only adulate the high place Karl Barth and many of his followers have given to preaching. They do preach! But their rejection of "objective intelligible revelation" causes them to founder at key places in doctrinal formulation (no Satan in his theology) and practical ministration (no real evangelism and no "conversion").[11] For Barth, "revelation is revelation only if it is recognized, acknowledged and accepted by man."[12]

---

1. Karl Barth, *Protestant Thought: From Rousseau to Ritschl* (New York: Harper, 1959). Barth's own critique.
2. Eberhard Bush, *Karl Barth: His Life from Letters and Autobiographical Texts* (Grand Rapids: Eerdmans, 1976), 97ff.
3. Bruce L. McCormack, *Karl Barth's Critically Realistic Dialectical Theology: Its Genesis and Development 1909–1936* (Oxford: Clarendon, 1995). Argues for the essential continuity of Barth's postliberal theology.
4. John Wick Bowman, "The Barthian Theology and the Word of God," *The Presbyterian* (September 3, 1936): 1ff. For another early analysis, see H. R. Mackintosh, *Types of Modern Theology: Schleiermacher to Barth* (New York: Scribner's, 1937). Major evangelical critiques are found in Van Til, Gordon Haddon Clark, Carl Henry, Klaas Runia.
5. Emil Brunner veered even further in doctrinal deviation and denied the Virgin Birth. Brunner was very popular in the U.S. and taught at Zurich. His sermons are of interest;

see *The Great Invitation and Other Sermons* (Philadelphia: Westminster, 1955). The flagrant and bizarre results of "our deciding" what is to be believed in Scripture can be seen in Hans Kung, *Judaism: Between Yesterday and Tomorrow* (New York: Crossroad, 1992). In eagerness for Jewish/Christian dialogue, Kung urges us to come without "trinitarian presuppositions," without a preexistent Savior, and without expiatory sacrifice. So ultimately nothing will be held back from concession to modernity.

6. Karl Barth, *Homiletics* (Louisville: Westminster/John Knox, 1991), 122.
7. Ibid., 49. An incisive analysis of Barth is in Addison H. Leitch, *Winds of Doctrine* (Westwood, N.J.: Revell, 1966), 20ff.
8. Karl Barth, *Come Holy Spirit* (New York: Round Table, 1933).
9. Bush, *Karl Barth,* 446. Bush faces the sad situation in Barth's home over the years, 185ff.
10. Well analyzed by D. A. Carson, *The Gagging of God* (Grand Rapids: Zondervan, 1995), 143f.
11. Carl F. H. Henry, *God, Revelation and Authority* (Waco, Tex.: Word, 1976), 2:158ff.
12. Herbert Hartwell, *The Theology of Karl Barth: An Introduction* (Philadelphia: Westminster, 1964), 69.

12.6.3 Helmut Thielicke—Preaching in the Nightmare of a Nation

> Having its origin in oral proclamation, Scripture presses back to its origin, i.e. to the presentation of its message by the spoken word. It seeks to be preached . . . to preach it is to understand it. Sermons are not just recitation but exposition. Exposition is possible only when the scope and emphases of what is to be expounded are taken from the text and hermeneutically evaluated.
>
> As a preacher I am involved in an unending dialogue with those to whom I must deliver my message. Every conversation I engage in becomes at bottom a meditation, a preparation, a gathering of material for my preaching. I can no longer listen disinterestedly even to a play in a theater without relating it to my pulpit . . . Thus life in all its daily involvements becomes for me a thesaurus in which I keep rummaging, because it is full of relevant material for my message.
>
> —Helmut Thielicke

Strongly drawn to Karl Barth when he was young, **Helmut Thielicke** (1908–1985) was thoroughly tinged with Barthian thought, especially on Scripture.[1] He was a theologian who loved to preach and was heard appreciatively in a wide circle. Born in Wuppertal-Barmen, Thielicke attended the famous gymnasium there. He then went on to Griefwald, where he was seriously ill, then on to Marburg, Erlangan, and Bonn for his training.[2] From 1936 to 1940, he taught at Heidelberg until he was dismissed for criticism of Nazi policies. He was then ordained and served in Ravensburg and then in Stuttgart.

Thielicke was Lutheran, and law/gospel was central in his message. After the war, he held the chair of systematic theology at Tubingen and in 1954 became the first Protestant rector of the University of Hamburg. As dean of the theological school, he saw the enrollment quickly move from 90 to 260 students. The essential charm and good sense of the man is seen in his delightful *A Little Exercise for Young Theologians.*[3] Evangelicals have always purred that he was so taken with Spurgeon.[4]

Through a unique arrangement, for many years Thielicke preached to four yearly services which he arranged from the high pulpit of the great S. Michaeliskirche in Hamburg. Even in the peak of the tourist season, the attendance here averages 150 to 400, but in his services Thielicke packed the 2,550 seats and the great galleries. Many were converted to Christ.[5] This success was somewhat controversial, as may be imagined, and those who attended were called "Thielicke Christians."

The sermons that we have from Genesis in *How the World Began*[6] and his messages on the Sermon on the Mount titled *Life Can Begin Again* are samples of what he did in the cathedral.[7] His famous sermons on the Lord's Prayer in shattered Stuttgart in the closing days of the war have been widely circulated under the title *The Prayer That Spans the World.*[8]

There is a strong biblicality in these sermons. We treasure what must be one of the finest sermons ever preached from Luke 15:11ff., "The Waiting Father," which truly captures the meaning of the text. It is in a volume of masterful sermons on the parables of Jesus.[9] The sermons are not exegetical but must be called textual-topical, or textual-thematic. Dirks has analyzed his lay appeal and found that he ranked very high in personality, originality, and use of illustrations. He was lower in credibility, confrontation with decision, and thought-provoking quality.[10] His titles are unusually arresting, and he uses questions very adeptly. He even has a book of sermons on difficult texts.[11] At so many key points we can identify with this able preacher who drew more listeners than did any other in postwar West Germany, not least when he says:

> Where is the man who can accomplish all this and who among those who are faced with this enormous assignment does not despair of accomplishing it? The only man who can assume such a bold and hazardous task is one who convinced that he need not beware the responsibility for its success and that Another is there interceding for him. He knows that not he but only the Spirit of God himself is able to reach and open the hearts of his hearers.[12]

---

1. Helmut Thielicke, *The Evangelical Faith* (Grand Rapids: Eerdmans, 1982) 3:191ff.; *Between Heaven and Earth* (Greenwood, S.C.: Attic, 1967). N.B. "Historical Criticism of the Bible," 14ff.
2. Marvin J. Dirks, *Laymen Look at Preaching: Lay Expectation Factors in Relation to the Preaching of Helmut Thielicke* (North Quincy, Mass.: Christopher, 1972), 73.
3. Helmut Thielicke, *A Little Exercise for Young Theologians* (Grand Rapids: Eerdmans, 1962).
4. Helmut Thielicke, *Encounter with Spurgeon* (Philadelphia: Fortress, 1963). The essence of his lectures.
5. Dirks, *Laymen Look at Preaching,* 59.

6. Helmut Thielicke, *How the World Began* (Philadelphia: Muhlenberg, 1961). Dirks analyzes the sermon on Cain (206).
7. Helmut Thielicke, *Life Can Begin Again: Sermons on the Sermon on the Mount* (Philadelphia: Fortress, 1963).
8. Helmut Thielicke, *The Prayer That Spans the World* (Greenwood, S.C.: Attic, 1953). From the Stuttgart years.
9. Helmut Thielicke, *The Waiting Father: Sermons on the Parables of Jesus* (New York: Harper, 1959). Strongly endorsed by Paul Scherer, another Lutheran, who taught homiletics at Union and preached brilliantly. His Yale Lectures in 1942 and 1943, *For We Have This Treasure,* are outstanding. His lectures/sermons on Isaiah are likewise remarkable but are vitiated by higher critical presuppositions; see *Event in Eternity* (New York: Harper, 1945).
10. Dirks, *Laymen Look at Preaching,* 284.
11. Helmut Thielicke, *Faith the Great Adventure* (Philadelphia: Fortress, 1985).
12. Dirks, *Laymen Look at Preaching,* 191.

12.6.4 Dietrich Bonhoeffer—Preaching in a Time of Testing

> Preaching was the great event in his life; the hard theologizing and all the critical love of his church were all for its sake, for in it the message of Christ, the bringer of peace was proclaimed. To Bonhoeffer, nothing in his calling competed in importance with preaching.
>
> —Eberhard Bethge

> A truly evangelical sermon must be like offering a child a beautiful red apple or holding out a glass of water to a thirsty man and asking, "Wouldn't you like it?"
>
> —Dietrich Bonhoeffer

Dietrich Bonhoeffer (1906–1945) loved to preach, and he preached the night before the Nazis hanged him in Flossenburg Prison just hours before Allied liberation. He was born into an upper-class German family where religion was perfunctory. He began his study at the University of Berlin, where his father was a professor of psychiatry, and his dissertation on "The Communion of Saints" was acclaimed by Karl Barth as "a miracle." Serving the German church in Barcelona briefly, Bonhoeffer returned to teach in Berlin at the age of twenty-six. He spent the year 1930 on a study fellowship at Union Seminary in New York City and taught Sunday school in Harlem. As early as 1933, he denounced Hitler over the radio and pressed hard the issue of "The Church and the Jewish Question."[1] In 1935 he took the leadership of the Confessing church seminary at Finkenwalde on the Baltic, during which time he finished his classic *The Cost of Discipleship.*[2] By late 1937, Hitler had closed down the seminary and arrested twenty-seven students.

Visiting the U.S. at the time the war began, Bonhoeffer could have stayed in safety but was determined to return home to become part of the struggle against Hitler. While in New York City, he longed to hear a sermon that was truly biblical.

At several prestigious churches he heard "quite unbearable rubbish, forced application, no exposition of a text." Then he visited Broadway Presbyterian Church and heard Dr. John McComb preach a solid biblical message.[3] He reacted with a passionate desire, "I eagerly want to preach once again!"[4] He returned to Germany and was incarcerated by Hitler in 1943 and eventually martyred.[5] Despite his pacifism, Bonhoeffer was part of the bomb plot to kill the Fuehrer.

Theologically Bonhoeffer has been claimed by "the death of God" theologians and radicals, and some evangelicals have been overzealous in making him one of their own.[6] The fact is he was quite thoroughly Barthian and did not disclaim higher critical thinking. But he was at the same time sufficiently Lutheran and pietistic—especially through Schlatter's commentaries—as to be Christ-centered and personally devout.[7]

Our special interest in Bonhoeffer stems from his great commitment to the preaching of the Word as the instrument of the Spirit's renewal of the church. He often said the importance of preaching the Bible cannot be overestimated.[8] American preaching he felt was sugared water with too much personal experience and "marginal notes on current events."[9] He saw the only answer to the increasing desecration and secularization of the Lord's day to be the renewal of preaching.[10] To him the preaching office was supreme.

Early on Bonhoeffer was long-winded and preached over the people's heads. His docent in homiletics urged him "to cultivate plain, noble simplicity from time to time in the presentation of the most important idea in the text."[11] Later he taught preaching at Finkenwalde and grappled with the issue of the necessity of preaching for the life of the church. He was an advocate of *lectio continua* (preaching in series) and greater use of the Old Testament. "The goal of the individual sermon is that the text must be orally expressed," he said.[12]

Bonhoeffer greatly stressed the work of Andrew Hyperius as the first Protestant homiletician (cf. 6.1.1). His reflections on the restlessness of the preacher after he has preached and his "sense of total emptiness" are classic and seldom verbalized. His challenges to "cheap grace" and "easy Christianity" were at the heart of his preaching and are themes greatly needed in pulpit communication in our time.

---

1. David P. Gushee, "Following Jesus to the Gallows," *Christianity Today* (April 3, 1995): 29.
2. Dietrich Bonhoeffer, *The Cost of Discipleship* (New York: Macmillan, 1949). "When Christ calls a man, he bids him come and die." This book and *Life Together* were published just before his leaving Germany and explain his discomfiture in both Hitler's Germany and materialistic America. His *Temptation* and *Ethics* are also important.
3. Clyde E. Fant, ed. and trans., *Bonhoeffer: Worldly Preaching* (Nashville: Thomas Nelson, 1975). Lectures at Finkenwalde. John Hess McComb (1898–1981) was a dear friend of mine. He wrote several books of biblical exposition, the last of which was privately published: *Reborn to a Living Hope: Peter's Message to God's Pilgrim Band* (1983). McComb served Broadway Presbyterian Church from 1935 to 1959.

4. Ibid., 23.
5. Dietrich Bonhoeffer, *Letters and Papers from Prison* (London: Fontana, 1953). Bethge edited a larger edition.
6. Georg Huntemann, *The Other Bonhoeffer: An Evangelical Reassessment* (Grand Rapids: Baker, 1993). The author has taught at Lovain and Basel and certainly makes a good if somewhat overstated case.
7. Bruce A. Demarest, "Devotion, Doctrine and Duty in Dietrich Bonhoeffer," *Bibliotheca Sacra* 148, no. 592 (October–December 1991): 399ff. Another good analysis is that of Klaas Runia, "Dietrich Bonhoeffer: The Man and His Beliefs," *Eternity* (December 1965): 11ff. It is important to see that Bonhoeffer did not hold to inerrancy or verbal inspiration.
8. Fant, *Bonhoeffer*, 3.
9. Ibid., 14.
10. Ibid., 31.
11. "A Translation of the Evaluation of D. Bonhoeffer's Examination Sermon," *Dietrich Bonhoeffer Verke* (Munich: Ch. Kaiser Velag, 1986), 9:183–6 (Nr. 114). (*Collected Works of Dietrich Bonhoeffer.*)
12. Fant, *Bonhoeffer*, 157.

12.6.5 Klaas Schilder—Preaching in a Political Cauldron

> There is not an inch of human life about which Christ, who is Sovereign over all, does not proclaim, "Mine."
>
> —Klaas Schilder

Rationalism and the ravages of higher criticism took a heavy toll on Christian witness in the Netherlands, and gospel preaching was at low ebb in the nineteenth century. Counteracting this abysmal situation were the establishment of the new theological school at Kampen and the ministry of Abraham Kuyper (cf. 9.4.7). Kuyper led those who longed to hear the Word of God proclaimed. The splinter he founded, the De Gereformeerde Kerken (GKN), was weakened not only by Kuyper's death in 1920 but also by the departure of Herman Bavinck from Kampen in favor of the Free University.[1] Challenges were raised about the historicity of the early chapters of Genesis, and the doughty champion of full scriptural integrity was the brilliantly endowed **Klaas Schilder** (1890–1952). Always a man of controversy, he was a popular preacher who served six congregations.

> Both in his preaching and in his lectures on diverse topics, he always showed that he was well prepared. No one opened the Word of God to the people of that day as K. Schilder did. His knowledge of literature and philosophy staggered the imagination of both friend and foe.[2]

Schilder's preaching voice was problematic, and he did vocal exercises "all of his adult life."[3] From the 1920s, he helped edit key periodicals and was often supported by Dr. F. Grosheide of the Free University and author of the commentary on 1 Corinthians in the New International Critical Commentary. Schilder early on saw the dangers of Barthianism. He wrote his doctoral dissertation at Erlangen in German on the use of paradox in theology, a matter dear to Karl Barth. In 1934 Schilder was installed as professor at Kampen.

Even his friends conceded that Schilder was overly polemical at times, but that his burden was the weakening of doctrine under Barthian influence. His redemptive-historical teaching and his strong emphasis on expounding the text had wide effect.

> With this type of preaching, of which Schilder was a master, the minister in the pulpit would do justice to the text and to its place in the long process of revelation. As a result of Schilder's emphasis on these matters, preaching was rejuvenated in many of the churches.[4]

He also wrote bitingly about the development of Hitler's National Socialism in Germany. He traveled in the U.S. and found much common ground with Cornelius Van Til at Westminster Seminary and Geerhardus Vos at Princeton. Those who observed him in America noticed how profusely he perspired as he preached.

During the war years of the 1940s, he was arrested by the Nazis and kept in a prison cell in Arnhem. Because of his adamant and uncompromising stand on doctrinal issues, his own synod deposed him as minister and professor. Dr. G. C. Berkouwer presided over these actions.[5] Two hundred churches and ten thousand members separated from the GKN at this time, and Schilder took the lead in founding a new school in Kampen. Ultimately the GKN acknowledged its error in suspending him. He died in 1952.

The most enduring monument to the remarkable preaching of Klaas Schilder is his massive three-volume work on the suffering and passion of Jesus, translated by Henry Zylstra. These volumes of sermonic literature, *Christ in His Suffering, Christ on Trial,* and *Christ Crucified,* must stand as the most extensive work of its kind and surely rank close to Krummacher and Clow as the most outstanding in terms of quality and depth. Such a message as "Satan at the Pulpit of the Passion" from Matthew 16:23 is striking.[6] There are great moments in his sermon "The Unimpaired Majesty of Jesus" of the mocking of Christ.

Although Schilder's style is typically Dutch and quite heavy, he offered some fresh insights as he reflected on how "Christ had already prepared the wood for the sacrifice" and how Satan "threw Christ a life-line," in the matter of Barabbas. In his message on "Christ's Last Ministration of the Word," from Luke 23:27–31, Schilder did not divide the text in the traditional manner but depicted our Lord on his way to "the dunghill of the world," faithful in presenting God's Word until the last.[7]

---

1. Henry Vander Kam, *Schilder: Preserver of the Faith* (New York: Vantage, 1996), 17.
2. Ibid., 23. J. Geertsema has also edited a volume of essays of Schilder, *Always Obedient* (Phillipsburg, NJ: Presbyterian and Reformed, 1996), on his life and thought.

3. Ibid., 23.
4. Ibid., 45.
5. Ibid., 76.
6. K. Schilder, *Christ in His Suffering* (Grand Rapids: Eerdmans, 1938), 15ff.
7. K. Schilder, *Christ Crucified* (Grand Rapids: Eerdmans, 1944), 55ff.

12.6.6 Frank Mangs—Preaching in the Maelstrom of Scandinavian Secularism

> The expositor is only to provide mouth and lips for the passage itself so that the Word may advance . . . The really great preachers are in fact only the servants of the Scripture. When they have spoken for a time—the Word gleams within the passage itself and is listened to: the voice makes itself heard . . . the passage itself is the voice, the speech of God; the preacher is the mouth and the lips and the congregation the ear in which the voice sounds.
>
> —Gustaf Wingren

Even secular writers in Scandinavia recognized how higher critical ideas had displaced biblical authority, as when the young Danish novelist Peter Hoeg relates of a certain distinguished professor of theology:

> He established on scientific grounds the falsity of the biblical texts while at the same time testifying to their profundity.[1]

Of course there were defenders of classical biblical faith. Professor Olav Valen-Sendstad was closely associated with O. Hallesby and Olaf E. Moe at the Independent Seminary in Oslo.[2] Professor Gustaf Wingren critiqued Barth for "employing the language of Scripture in a system which is totally foreign to the Bible."[3] But the typical Swedish attitude toward spiritual things was that of the inventor Alfred Nobel, who came from "the barren and God-fearing province of Smaland." Nobel inherited "high standards of right and wrong," but his ties with the church were nominal and only formal. Archbishop Soderblom preached his funeral.[4] "My life is woven out of torment," Nobel bemoaned. Fittingly, his favorite poet was Lord Byron.[5]

Certainly there were Bible preachers who moved multitudes. One of them was Lewi Pethrus, who preached in the great Filadelfia Church in Stockholm which seated five thousand. Pethrus also edited a daily newspaper in Stockholm. Another solid preacher was Knut Svensson, president of the Swedish Alliance Mission (1953–1968), whose sermons published as *En for Alla (One for All)* are exemplary. Trygve Holm-Glad of the Norwegian Mission Covenant was also a biblical preacher of moving power. But without question, the towering giant of the Swedish pulpit in this century was **Frank Mangs** (1897–1994).

Mangs was born a part of the ten percent Swedish minority on the West coast of Finland, a residue from the years that Sweden was one with the Finns. (General Mannerheim and the composer Sibelius were also Swedish Finns). Mangs served congregations in the Mission Covenant Church of Sweden, for many years the largest Free Church body in Sweden. He was a large man with a strong and commanding voice. He turned to evangelism and traveled extensively throughout Scandinavia. The existence of the Norwegian Mission Covenant and the once-great Bethlehem Church of Oslo were due to revival fires kindled through Mangs' preaching.[6] He visited the United States many times and held unforgettable midnight meetings in the old Lyceum Theater in Minneapolis with large numbers seeking after the Lord.[7] He used English passably, and after preaching under great fervor he would sit down at the piano and sing "Have You Forgotten God?" with great effect. Even until late in his life he was heard at the great summer gathering place at Torp in the interest of revival and renewal in the Christian life and in the Swedish churches.

Mang's three-volume autobiography is a commentary on a century of religious decline in Scandinavia, with but occasional and sporadic outbursts of renewal.[8] Most of his books of sermons have not been translated, but we do have his *The Master's Way* and a series of studies from Luke 5 titled *Out of Dismal Failure into Glorious Success.* The sermons are not structurally complicated. In the former volume he pursues the general order of the life of Jesus and continually urges his hearers to heed the Savior's words, "Follow me."[9] These messages are intensely personal in tone. His illustrations are apt.[10] This preaching was owned by the Spirit of God on several continents.

Frank Mangs was something of a maverick, but his great voice, now silenced, is sorely missed.

---

1. Peter Hoeg, *The History of Danish Dreams* (New York: Farrar, Strauss and Giroux, 1995), 59.
2. Olav Valen-Sendstad, *The Word That Can Never Die* (St. Louis: Concordia, 1949); O. Moe, *The Apostle Paul: His Life and His Work* (Minneapolis: Augsburg, 1950). One-third of the ministers of the Church of Norway are trained at the Independent Seminary in Oslo founded by O. Hallesby, noted devotional author and gifted preacher.
3. Gustaf Wingren, *Theology in Conflict* (Philadelphia: Muhlenberg, 1958), 125. See also his *The Living Word* (Philadelphia: Fortress, 1965), 201–3. Wingren was professor of systematic theology at Lund.
4. Charles J. Curtis, *Nathan Soderblom: Theologian of Revelation* (Chicago: Covenant, 1966); in another treatment of Soderblom, *Soderblom: Ecumenical Pioneer* (Minneapolis: Augsburg, 1967), Curtis faults Soderblom for what he calls "the sentimental, almost-sick, blood-of-Jesus piety of nineteenth-century evangelical revivalism" (132). At this point it would seem the archbishop is reflecting historic Christianity.
5. Kenne Fant, *Alfred Nobel* (New York: Arcade, 1991). This wealthy man never escaped melancholy or misanthropy.
6. "An Interview with Frank Mangs on His 90th Birthday," *Betlehem Misjonskirkes Menighetsblad,* July/August 1987, nr. 7/8, side 9ff. Mangs retained close ties to the Oslo congregation which rose out of the revival.
7. I heard Mangs preach both in Swedish and English in Sweden and in the United States. Powerful! Mangs had close ties with A. B. Simpson.

8. Frank Mangs, *Hogst Personlicht,* 3 vols. (Stockholm: Harrier, 1980). "Highly personal."
9. Frank Mangs, *The Master's Way* (London: Marshall, Morgan, and Scott, n.d.).
10. Frank Mangs, *Out of Dismal Failure into Glorious Success* (Chicago: privately published, n.d.).

12.6.7 Gustaf F. Johnson—Preaching in the Ambiguity of Immigration and Integration

> Preaching was seen as the very heart of the mission of the fathers. Their sermons were both Bible-centered and man-centered. The Bible was the trustworthy Word of God. Its message had to do with what God had done in Jesus Christ for man's salvation. It was for man—when he saw what God had done—to accept this grace and believe. The texts were as often chosen from the Old Testament as the New. The Bible was one book and spoke of one grace. The burden was to discover what the Bible had to say to man.
>
> —Eric G. Hawkinson

The masses of immigrants from countless cultures largely replicated the religious situation of their homelands. Sometimes disruption and privation made the newcomers more open to the gospel. Many Swedish migrants came out of the revival fires of the old country (cf. 9.5.3) and planted Mission Covenant congregations in the United States. The pioneer preachers of this movement were a sturdy lot who loved Scripture and continually asked, "Where is it written?"[1]

Erik August Skogsbergh (1850–1939), known as the Swedish Moody, had tremendous preaching ministries at the Chicago Tabernacle and in both the large Minneapolis and Seattle tabernacles, the latter two of which he saw built.[2] The Evangelical Free Church, the sister denomination and in a sense daughter of the Covenant, had some exceedingly able preachers such as its longtime president, **E. A. Halleen,** and its foremost evangelist, **A. J. Thorwall.**[3] Though largely contained within the Scandinavian evangelical movement, perhaps the best-known of these immigrant preachers was the always controversial but always impactful **Gustaf F. Johnson** (1873–1959).

"Texas" Johnson, as he was known early in his ministry, was born in Nasjo in Smaland in Sweden but migrated with his parents to Texas when he was nine years of age. He was converted in a Methodist church in Brushy, Texas, where his parents were members, but he soon joined the Swedish Free Church in Austin. He was ordained by Pastor C. O. Sahlstrom in Deckar, Texas, and at the age of eighteen went to Japan in the first contingent of missionaries sent by Fredrik Franson (cf. 10.2.7).[4] While he was in transit on the Pacific going to and returning from Japan, Johnson mastered the plays of Shakespeare, a fact that in part explains his excellent English diction. He served several Swedish Free Churches and was responsible under God for the rapid growth of the Free Church in Rockford, Illinois, an important center of Swedish immigration, where he served from 1901 to 1913. In 1914 he moved to the Swedish Tabernacle of Minneapolis, where he preached to huge throngs for twenty-five years. He then served thirteen years as the founding pastor of the Park Avenue Covenant Church until his retirement in 1952.

Johnson was a deep student of Scripture and was mightily used in evangelism and in the exposition of the prophetic word particularly. Many of the immigrant preachers were exhorters and devotional in their approach to the text, but Johnson opened a text with care, as did others in the movement.[5] He was pictorial and vivid, alternating humor and the sense of the incongruous with scathing jeremiads. His titles were artful: "Spiritual Geography," "A Select Band of Vagabonds" on the cave of Adullam, and "Light Burdens for Weak Shoulders" on Acts 15. One listener recorded his reaction to Johnson's preaching:

> When sixteen, I can remember attending a Sunday evening service in the First Covenant Church of Duluth to hear the Rev. Gustaf F. Johnson conclude an evangelistic series. The impact on me was not only moving; it was frightening. My hair stood up stiff on my head. Yet as much as I would not dream of another encounter of that kind, I knew I would have to return if such an event recurred.[6]

Even in translation the sermons have a tang, a colorful flow, and strong personal application.[7] In his well-known study of Luke 24, "Hearts Aflame," Johnson calls preachers:

> Many a beautiful sermon containing wonderful truth and dressed in eloquent language falls to the ground like a bird shot down in flight. What is lacking? No heart! Nothing is wrong with its theology. The teaching is correct, and truth is spoken. Scripture after Scripture is quoted. The presentation is quiet and orderly, and the language is dignified and stately. Despite all this, not a soul is gripped by the message. Why is this? Simply because the preacher has neglected to make what he says a vital issue for himself. He is like a record player which grinds out what has been cut into the record of the memory during the previous week. This is not preaching. This is merely making a speech.[8]

Johnson was both loved and hated, but no listener was ever indifferent to the message.

---

1. Eric G. Hawkinson, *Images in Covenant Beginnings* (Chicago: Covenant, 1968), 130ff.; Erik Wallgren, *A Swedish-American Preacher's Own Story* (Chicago: Covenant, 1963); A. H. Jacobson, *Adventures of a Prairie Preacher* (Chicago: Covenant, 1960).
2. Erik Dahlhielm, *A Burning Heart: Erik August Skogsbergh* (Chicago: Covenant, 1951). He was an orator (196).
3. E. A. Halleen, *The Wonders of the Cross* (Chicago: Chicago Bladet, 1929); LaReau Thorwall, *And Light New Fires: The Life of A. J. Thorwall* (Minneapolis: Free Church Press, 1969).
4. John Carlstig, *Gustaf F. Johnson: mannen med det brinnande hjartat* (Jonkoping,

Sweden: SAM Forlaget, 1965). We need a strong and reflective biography of this preacher's preacher.

5. Erik Dahlhielm, "The Value of Expository Preaching," *The Covenant Quarterly* (August 1943): 3ff.
6. Arthur W. Anderson in Glen V. Wiberg, "Is There a Covenant Way of Preaching?" *The Covenant Quarterly* (August 1996): 10.
7. Gustaf F. Johnson, *Hearts Aflame,* trans. Paul R. Johnson (Chicago: Covenant, 1970); *From a Shepherd's Heart* (Minneapolis: Free Church Publications, 1960). The latter is a collection of brief meditations.
8. Gustaf F. Johnson, *The Word Is Near You,* ed. Herbert E. Palmquist (Chicago: Covenant, 1974), 163.

12.7 EVANGELICAL HEADLINERS IN A CULTURE OF DECOMPOSITION

> The crisis is here in all its stark and unquestionable reality. We are in the midst of an enormous conflagration burning everything into ashes. In a few weeks millions of human lives are uprooted; in a few hours century-old cities are demolished in a few days, kingdoms are erased. Red human blood flows in broad streams from one end of the earth to another. Ever-expanding misery spreads its gloomy shadow over larger and larger areas. The fortunes, happiness, and comfort of untold millions have disappeared. Peace, security and safety have vanished. Prosperity and well-being have become in many countries but a memory; freedom, a mere myth. Western culture is covered by a blackout. A great tornado sweeps over the whole of mankind.
>
> —Pitirim A. Sorokin

Oswald Spengler in his *Decline of the West* and Sorokin in *The Crisis of Our Age* have meaningfully sketched "the agony of the West." This has increasingly become the milieu of preaching in our time. Along with Allan Bloom, Harold O. J. Brown has analyzed "the degenerative phase of the sensate culture" in which there is mounting challenge to "the objective meaning of any text."[1] Religion is shunted to the fringes of culture, and a chaotic syncretism has led to the general breakdown of authority.[2] Yet the Word of God is still being blessed by the Holy Spirit.

---

1. Harold O. J. Brown, *The Sensate Culture: Western Civilization Between Chaos and Transformation* (Dallas: Word, 1996), 54. Involved in the decline is "the gradual abandonment of Christian heritage" in the West.
2. Ibid., 70. This study of "late second millennium culture" is most critical for gospel communicators in our time.

12.7.1 Mark A. Matthews—The Preacher as Builder

> Hide me behind the Cross; lift me out of self; teach me to speak the truth as He taught it.
>
> —the prayer Mark Matthews prayed just before his exposition of the Word of God

> The country is in its present condition—to some extent at least—because the ministers were not firm, fundamental and persistent in preaching the great truths necessary to lead an individual to Christ and stabilize a nation . . . If we are to have a revival it must begin in the pulpit . . . Let us get back to the business of preaching, to the technique of preaching, to the art and power of preaching, to the mastery of preaching . . . The way to cure it [dullness in the pulpit] is for ministers to study the Bible and learn how to do expository preaching . . . Let us master the technique of expository preaching . . . The revival will follow and sinners will be saved and the saints revived.
>
> —Mark A. Matthews

"Preacher of the Word of God and Friend to Man" is embossed on the statue of **Mark A. Matthews** (1867–1940) in Denny Park in Seattle, Washington. Like that of Thomas Guthrie in Edinburgh (cf. 10.5.1), the ministry of Matthews shook an entire city. Of Scotch-Irish extraction and Presbyterian-Methodist roots, Matthews was born in a poor home in Calhoun, Georgia. Converted at the age of thirteen, he never graduated from high school, college, or seminary but was from childhood an avid student and reader.

He preached his first sermon at seventeen, doing constant supply preaching while working at a dry-goods store. At twenty he was ordained and served in Dalton, Georgia, and then Jackson, Tennessee, where the membership doubled.[1] In 1900 he passed the bar in Tennessee in an examination conducted by William Howard Taft.[2] He was a gangling youth and grew to six feet six inches in height, had long, flowing hair, and publicly appeared in top hat and morning coat.

In 1902, at the age of thirty-four, Matthews was called to be the pastor of First Presbyterian Church in Seattle, Washington. At that time, the sparkling city on Puget Sound had a population of eighty thousand. Matthews began with four hundred members and served the church for thirty-eight years until his death at seventy-two. In that time, he received more than twenty-five thousand new members, the majority of them new converts. The church grew to nine thousand members, the largest in the world at that time.

In 1906 a new edifice was constructed at Seventh and Spring, seating more than three thousand, the largest capacity of any church in the city. Even with these large numbers of constituents, he was known for his amazing memory for names and faces. With his 107 elders and 60 deacons he not only served his large membership but also reached out through the city in various crusades of civic righteousness. He brought his "Nineteen Symptoms of Graft" before the city council and gave his temperance lectures around the country.[3]

Matthews' church was the first to own a radio station. He established twenty-eight branch churches and Sunday schools around Seattle in a pattern many imitated as "The Mark Matthews Plan." He was active in the conservative strategy in the Presbyterian church struggles and was moderator of the General Assembly in 1912. With youth from all the branches pouring downtown for the great Sunday evening service, Matthews had a Sunday evening ministry every bit as dynamic as his Sunday morning expositions. He fought the so-called New Era program (an official denominational program of the Presbyterian Church) and stood shoulder to shoulder with the fundamentalists in the battle of the 1920s. He was one of the founders of the Day Care Movement for the weekday care of children.[4]

Like Spurgeon, Matthews did not use a pulpit when he preached but paced back and forth during his forty-five-minute message. Often called the "Tall Pine of the Sierras," he had a "pleasing and flexible voice."[5] He used no notes and was often thematic with strong reliance on the texts of Scripture. He could use "pulpit pyrotechnics" in the oratorical tradition of his day.

Matthews did not shrink from preaching the great doctrines of the Bible, particularly the doctrines of the Holy Trinity, the Atonement, and the Second Coming.[6] His sermon on "The Great Foundation" from 1 Corinthians 3 is well outlined and meaty.[7] In a prize-winning book on the church, we see the depth of his thinking and the soundness of his theological method.[8] He was truly a pastor-evangelist with a great commitment to making the way of salvation plain in every sermon. This focus is explained:

> The minister must teach absolute loyalty to the Bible, the Infallible Word of God, the only text-book of the church, the court of last resort. The minister must also present the full Gospel of Jesus Christ as the only means of salvation. The minister must determine to know only one thing, namely—the Blood of Jesus Christ. He must present the cross of Christ on which the Son of God was sacrificed for the redemption of the world, by which sacrifice His Blood was shed for the regeneration of a soul. It is the eternal purpose of that sacrifice that must be preached if the full Gospel of Christ is to be presented.[9]

After suffering a massive heart attack, Mark Matthews died in the hospital while dictating the next Sunday's sermon to his secretary. The company of the preachers was richly enhanced by the gifts and endeavors of this greatly used servant of Christ.

---

1. Ezra P. Giboney and Agnes M. Potter, *The Life of Mark A. Matthews* (Grand Rapids: Eerdmans, 1948), 19ff.
2. Ibid., 21.
3. Ibid., 31.
4. Ralph G. Turnbull, *A History of Preaching* (Grand Rapids: Baker, 1974), 242. Turnbull, a delightful Scottish preacher, was a later pastor of First Presbyterian

Church, Seattle, and oversaw the building of a new structure after an earthquake severely damaged the old building. Turnbull's work was an effort to update and complete Dargan.

5. Giboney and Potter, *The Life of Mark A. Matthews,* 44.
6. Mark A. Matthews, *Gospel Sword Thrusts* (New York: Revell, 1824). Matthews carried on a great battle against the liberals at Union Theological Seminary in New York prior to World War I; N.B. Lisa S. Nolland, "The Uniqueness of Mark Matthews, Fundamentalist: A Study of His Social Concerns," (M.C.S. thesis at Regent College, Vancouver, 1984, 53–54); also *Amazing Grace: Evangelicals in Australia, Britain, Canada and the United States,* ed. George A. Rawlyk and Mark A. Noll (Grand Rapids: Baker, 1993).
7. Giboney and Potter, *The Life of Mark A. Matthews,* 107.
8. Mark A. Matthews, *Building the Church* (New York: American Tract Society, 1940).
9. Ibid., 159.

12.7.2 Frank W. Boreham—The Preacher as Storyteller

> A man is naturally fluent or he is not. If he is not, the constant creation of manuscript will overcome his handicap. In the act of writing, the mind is ceaselessly groping for words. Every word that it captures becomes from that moment part of its stock in trade. The word, never employed before, remains within easy reach, and when he is speaking or preaching, it will be ready to his hand. A halting and hesitating speaker will, if he takes it in time, cure this slovenly and repulsive habit by persistent writing.
>
> Dr. Parker and Dr. Meyer taught me that the only remedy for this kind of thing [people not comprehending the message] lies in sane and judicious repetition. It is the duty of the pulpit to say the same things over and over again. They must be clothed in different phraseology, and illumined by fresh illustration, and approached by a new line of thought, but the things that are really worth saying must be said repeatedly.
>
> —Frank W. Boreham

The moderator of the Church of Scotland once introduced this preacher as "the man whose name is on all our lips, whose books are on all our shelves, and whose illustrations are in all our sermons."[1] That is quite a bit to say about any preacher, but it certainly was true of **Frank W. Boreham** (1871–1959). Although he was born in Tunbridge Wells, Kent, England, the greater part of his unusual ministry was in Australia. He was born into an old Anglican family that moved into the nonconformity of Emmanuel Church on Mount Ephraim of the Countess of Huntingdon's Connection.

The visit of Moody had made quite an impression on the family, but young Boreham focused on a secular future until a serious accident in the brickyard where he was working consigned him to hospital for an extended stay. He was left with a lifelong limp. The call of God took hold of him when he went up to

London and sat under the ministry of such as Newman Hall, Marcus Rainsford, Joseph Parker, and F. B. Meyer.[2] Boreham conferred at length with Hudson Taylor about his suitability for missionary work in China, but his injury led Taylor to urge upon him a ministry in the homeland.[3] He became a Baptist and graduated from Spurgeon's College, where he was much influenced by Arthur T. Pierson (cf. 11.4.1) and by D. L. Moody on his last visit to England in 1893.[4]

Boreham did much street preaching under the Open Air Mission and in several student pastorates. When Thomas Spurgeon came back from New Zealand in 1894, Boreham responded to the call to pastor a congregation of Scottish settlers in Mosgiel, New Zealand. Just as John Watson (Ian Maclaren) shared Scottish church life in *Beside the Bonnie Brier Bush* (cf. 11.2.6), so Boreham described his ministry and the people whom he pastored in essays and articles he wrote as the editor of *The New Zealand Baptist.*

Here is another preacher who could really tell a story.[5] Boreham's books of essays are dotted with choice exegetical insights and beautiful word pictures. His famous Sunday evening preaching on "Texts That Made History" have a freshness about them.[6] He wrestled with making a public appeal for decision at the end of the service and finally opted to do so.[7]

In 1970 Boreham moved to Hobart, Tasmania, where he spent nine years. Eventually he experienced a serious breakdown in his health and "spasms of lassitude." His last pastorate was for ten years with the Armdale Baptist Church in Melbourne. After thirty-four years in parish ministry, he turned to an international ministry or "gypsying," as he called it. Often he occupied significant pulpits for an extended period of time, such as Methodist Central Hall in Melbourne for six months. In 1931, Boreham delivered the Bevan Lectures on Preaching in Australia.

While at times we might wish Boreham grappled more with a text, we find his insights and structure engaging. His more than forty books never leave the reader feeling cheated. His Christmas materials catalyzed some breakthroughs toward saying the old truth in a new way.[8] Titles like "The Danger of Diffusion" on worship or "Consolation for the Disillusioned" came from Boreham. No one offers more help with Lamentations 3:27 and "Bearing the Yoke in Youth" than does Boreham.[9] His message for young preachers titled "On Frightening Timothy" from 1 Corinthians 16:10 is a classic.[10] Some of his illustrations are usable today. His lucid style, literary breadth, absolute soundness, and warmth of heart draw us to him. In our time when so much interest is attaching to narrative, we would do well to take another look at Boreham.

---

1. F. W. Boreham, *My Pilgrimage* (London: Epworth, 1940), 251. The last milestone almost up to his death.
2. Ibid., 61ff. Happily, Kregel Publications of Grand Rapids is reissuing many of Boreham's titles.
3. Ibid., 79.
4. Ibid., 95.
5. F. W. Boreham, *The Luggage of Life* (Grand Rapids: Kregel, 1995).

6. F. W. Boreham, *A Bunch of Everlastings* (Grand Rapids: Kregel, 1994) expounds Chalmer's text and those of Luther, Latimer, Bunyan, Knox, etc. In *A Casket of Cameos* (Grand Rapids: Kregel, 1994) he tackles Brainerd, Shackleton, John Bright, Melancthon, R. W. Dale, and a host of others. Different!
7. Boreham, *My Pilgrimage,* 212ff. His sermons on the Beatitudes are outstanding: *The Heavenly Octave* (New York: Abingdon, 1936), reprinted by Baker in 1968.
8. F. W. Boreham, *My Christmas Book: A Handful of Myrrh, Aloes and Cassia* (Grand Rapids: Zondervan, 1953).
9. F. W. Boreham, *The Crystal Pointers* (New York: Abingdon, 1925), 99ff.
10. F. W. Boreham, *Mountains in the Mist* (Grand Rapids: Kregel, 1995), 21ff.

12.7.3 Alan Walker—The Preacher as Soulwinner

> God-sent men never fail.
>
> —Alan Walker's father's word to him

> Proclamation by preaching was Christ's chosen method. Here is the supreme reason why preaching is central to the strategy of mission. "Jesus came preaching." In the communication of truth, nothing is so powerful as a human personality incandescent with the love and power of God. Unpredictable, wonderful things happen when a man stands up to preach. This has been shown a thousand times through the history of the Christian church. . . . Preaching sets people marching!
>
> Effective worship requires the vigor and thrust of preaching. History is stained with unethical religion. Religious practices and ritualistic services can easily lack ethical challenge. They can communicate a sense of the holy, yet become escapist and irrelevant. Religious worship without effective preaching can be so general and vague that it fails to thrust the gospel with any sharpness into the mind and conscience of those who worship. Preaching completes an act of public worship.
>
> —Alan Walker

Preaching in Australia has always been supported by the solid bedrock of evangelical Anglicanism such as is represented by the archbishops of Sidney—men like Howard Mowll, Harrington Lees, and Marcus Loane, and scholars like Leon Morris.[1]

Another Aussie whose preaching ministry encompassed the whole world came out of Methodism, **Alan Walker,** born in 1911 in Sidney. He stood thirteenth in a succession of Methodist ministers in his family. His two sons also entered the ranks. Walker was a descendant of John Joseph Walker of Hull, England, who was sent to the penal colony established in Australia in 1806.

Walker was converted under his father's preaching.[2] He saw much poverty and privation in places where his father ministered. In 1928, Alan went with his father to visit Gypsy Smith, who was conducting a crusade in the area. In this encounter and a time of prayer, Walker sensed the call to preach.[3] He entered theological college in 1930 and worked his way through by operating a fruit and vegetable run, all the time handling the Hornsby preaching circuit. With his wife, Walker spent a year in England. There he was much influenced by William Sangster, who shared with him his excellent filing system, and Norman Dunning. Dunning was "an evangelist of the old school, pietistic rather than prophetic, calling people to commitment to Christ more in personal than in social terms."[4] He tended to balance off Donald Soper, who convinced Walker of pacifism, and William Temple, whose studies on John were key to his warm, devotional approach to Scripture.

Back home, Walker took up the ministry at Cessnock, a mining town, and there started a radio broadcast called "The Friendly Road" which attracted considerable attention. While in something of a personal funk, Walker discovered Vincent Taylor's trilogy on the death of Christ while he was preparing Holy Week sermons in 1941.[5] This was a turning point in his ministry. Among his many books of lecture-sermons, a perennial favorite has been his choice work *The Many-Sided Cross of Christ.*[6] Walker and his wife faced many struggles, both ecclesiastically and with their deaf daughter, Lynette. He moved on to the Waverley Church in a suburb of Sydney, where great growth ensued and revival came. On one night, fifty came to Christ.[7]

Walker was at the forefront of crusades against liquor, gambling, and the nuclear threat. He served as advisor to the Australian delegation to the United Nations, headed up the Mission to the Nation in Australia, and did many university crusades in the U.S. and Britain. From 1958 to 1978, he served as superintendent of the great Central Methodist Mission in Sidney, where his emphasis on the priority of preaching and resultant public witness by those seeking Christ became lasting hallmarks of a significant urban ministry. His earlier work on preaching, now published under the title *Evangelistic Preaching,* well encapsulates his conviction that "the preacher's theme is the whole gospel of Jesus Christ."[8] He gave a ringing call to preach for a verdict. Walker became a strong supporter and friend of Billy Graham in his remarkable crusades "down under."

A fine book of his typical sermons is included in the American "Preaching for Today" series and contains a well-divided study of Romans 7 under the title "The Conquest of Inner Space."[9] His sermons are artfully illustrated and always practical and well applied. Walker came into increasing prominence as a preacher and was knighted by the queen in 1981, but characteristically said, "I prefer still to be known by the sufficient title of Reverend Alan Walker. For a Christian there can be no greater title than that of a minister."[10] Walker was director of evangelism for the World Methodist Council, preached in over sixty countries and was the first to hold evangelistic crusades in the Soviet Union.

---

1. Certainly one of the critical books for evangelicals after midcentury was Leon Morris, *The Apostolic Preaching of the Cross* (Grand Rapids: Eerdmans, 1955) with its vigorous defense of the substitutionary atonement. John Stott's later work on *The Cross of Christ* (Downers Grove, Ill.: InterVarsity Press, 1986) is similarly strong and substantive on this theme.

2. Harold R. Henderson, *Reach for the World: The Alan Walker Story* (London: Collins, 1981), 7.
3. Ibid., 12.
4. Ibid., 30.
5. Vincent Taylor, *Jesus and His Sacrifice: A Study of the Passion-Sayings in the Gospels* (London: Macmillan, 1951). Taylor gives us rich studies in his three volumes, but his emphasis on Christ as our representative tends to crowd out Christ as our substitute. See H. D. McDonald, *The Atonement of the Death of Christ* (Grand Rapids: Baker, 1985), in which a thoughtful critique of Taylor is made (329–30).
6. Alan Walker, *The Many-Sided Cross of Christ* (Nashville: Abingdon, 1962). Christ is victim and victor! Occasionally Walker speaks with some theological imprecision, but in the main he follows James Denney (40ff.).
7. Henderson, *Reach for the World,* 63, 68. How the Spirit of God was "very near" all day and then came the "break."
8. Alan Walker, *Evangelistic Preaching* (Grand Rapids: Francis Asbury/Zondervan, 1988).
9. Alan Walker, *God Is Where You Are* (Grand Rapids: Eerdmans, 1962). The title sermon is from Psalm 139:7–10.
10. Henderson, *Reach for the World,* 215.

12.7.4 S. D. Gordon—The Preacher as Empathizer

> A great sorrow has come into the heart of God. Let it be told only in hushed voice—one of his words is "a prodigal." Hush your voice yet more—ours is that prodigal world. Let your voice soften down still more—we have consented to the prodigal part of the story. But, in softest tones yet, He has won some of us back with His strong tender love. And now let the voice ring out with great gladness—we won ones may be the pathway back to God for the others. That is His earnest desire. That should be our dominant ambition. For that purpose He has endowed us with peculiar power.
>
> —S. D. Gordon

One of the most underrated and neglected preachers of modern times is **Samuel Dickey Gordon** (1860–1936). He was often called "Quiet Talk Gordon" because he deliberately spoke softly, believing that people listened better if they had to strain a bit. Some have spoken derisively and unfairly of his preaching because his sermons were put in a series of volumes called "Quiet Talks."[1] In fact, his trademark was the question, "Are you listening?"

While Mr. Gordon, as he liked to be called, was not a classical expositor, he was deeply into the text of the Word as his inimitable *Quiet Talks on John's Gospel* and *Quiet Talks on the Crowned Christ of Revelation* conclusively prove. One of his books of messages that had a searing effect on my soul in my early years was his *Quiet Talks on Power.* He was a layman and not trained for ministerial work but was a YMCA worker like others in this saga, including Moody and Machen.

Gordon served in Philadelphia and spent nine years as YMCA secretary for Ohio before beginning an itinerant ministry of preaching. There was a certain charm and power in his more reserved manner, and the Spirit mightily blessed his preaching and his writings. He traveled extensively in Europe and spent a year in the Far East. His two visits to Keswick were well remembered, as in 1910 and again in 1931 he "captured the hearts of his hearers" by his informal and intimate style. His "quiet talk" on "The Incoming of Power" was especially blessed.[2]

He had a gentle spirit, and his "quaint phrases" stuck in the mind so that Pollock observes that he "remains one of the very few pre-1914 speakers widely read."[3] In 1895, Gordon gave a notable series of lectures at Moody Bible Institute. About this time his first "Quiet Talk" book was published. *Quiet Talks on Prayer* has become one of the classics on that subject and is drenched with the Word. Gordon properly sees prayer as "The Greatest Outlet of Power."[4]

Gordon touched the heart. He drew people to himself and the truth he shared with deft skill. He could image a biblical text like John 7:37–39, where we sense the liquidity of "the rivers of living water."[5] His message on "The Price of Power," expounding Matthew 16:24, is among the finest ever preached on this text.[6] His depiction of "Phil," a person of an illustration he develops, and his dad tug at the heart.[7] The richness of his pictures is particularly evident in *Quiet Talks on Following the Christ,* in which he began with "The Lone Man Who Went Before" and went on to trace "What Following Means" in terms of "A Look Ahead," "The Main Road," "The Valleys," and "The Hilltops."[8]

Gordon was especially gifted in reaching youth.[9] He did not dodge the relevance of the gospel to modern issues.[10] He spoke helpfully to eschatological concerns, and has given us a marvelous study on life after death.[11] S. D. Gordon is more than a period piece in the history of preaching. He modeled pastoral and preaching strengths convincingly. He died at his home in Winston-Salem, North Carolina, on June 26, 1936.

---

1. D. M. Lloyd-Jones, *Knowing the Times* (Edinburgh: Banner of Truth, 1989), 264. Lloyd-Jones judges Gordon by the titles of his books which he says "did great harm." Lloyd-Jones completely misunderstands.
2. Herbert F. Stevenson, ed., *Keswick's Triumphant Voice* (Grand Rapids: Zondervan, 1963), 321, 379ff.
3. J. C. Pollock, *The Keswick Story* (Chicago: Moody, 1964), 131–32.
4. S. D. Gordon, *Quiet Talks on Prayer* (Westwood, N.J.: The Christian Library, 1984 Revell). A truly stimulating treatment. Other smaller works on prayer include his *Prayer Changes Things* and *Five Laws That Govern Prayer.*
5. S. D. Gordon, *Quiet Talks on Power* (New York: Revell, 1903), 21. Great on "Making and Breaking Connections."
6. Ibid., 87.
7. S. D. Gordon, *Quiet Talks with World Winners* (New York: Revell, 1908), 24ff.
8. S. D. Gordon, *Quiet Talks on Following the Christ* (New York: Revell, 1913). Messages from his travels.

9. S. D. Gordon, *Quiet Talks with Eager Youth* (New York: Revell, 1935). One of his last books.
10. S. D. Gordon, *Quiet Talks on the Crisis and Afterwards* (New York: Revell, 1926); *Quiet Talks on Personal Problems* (New York: Revell, 1906). Especially fine on "The Problem of Self-Mastery."
11. S. D. Gordon, *Quiet Talks on Life After Death* (Chicago: Moody, n.d.). Exceedingly tender.

12.7.5 Clarence E. Macartney—The Preacher as Conservator

> Put all the Bible you can into it!
> —Clarence Macartney to his brother, who was going out to preach
>
> Before I preach I must irrigate my soul with the joys and sorrows of my people.
>
> As the years go by, we think less about preaching a good sermon, and more about preaching a sermon that will do good.
> —Clarence E. Macartney

When he was to be installed as pastor of the First Presbyterian Church of Pittsburgh to succeed Dr. Maitland Alexander, who had served for twenty-nine years, the church received a letter from Dr. Francis L. Patton, longtime president of Princeton, which read:

> The new minister of your church will come with a message and not a query, and will be fully conscious that zeal in the pulpit will never grow out of doubt in the study.[1]

Well said of **Clarence E. Macartney** (1879–1957). He was the youngest of seven children and one of four preacher brothers born to a Scot-Irish immigrant minister of the Covenanters, John Longfellow Macartney, and his Huguenot wife, Catherine Robertson.

Born in Northfield, Ohio, but reared on the campus of Geneva College in Beaver Falls, Pennsylvania, of which his father was one of the founders, Macartney was raised in the Reformed Presbyterian Church with its twenty-three-minute-long prayers and one-hour sermons. He never forgot the solemnity of the semiannual communion services and his praying to receive Christ at eleven years of age and then joining the church.[2]

Moving west with his family when his father sought renewal of health, Macartney was trained at Pomona College. Here a lecturer turned him on to the fascination of biography.[3] Macartney then attended the University of Denver and the University of Wisconsin, where he majored in English and was distinguished for his achievements as a debater. After a year's break of travel, he began his studies at Princeton Seminary. Macartney was particularly drawn to B. B. Warfield in theology and Robert Dick Wilson in Old Testament. He served several summer pastorates in Prairie du Sac, Wisconsin, and out of these years traced deep and lasting friendships with Woodrow Wilson of Princeton and the LaFollette brothers of Wisconsin politics. His homiletician was David J. Burrell (cf. 11.4.6), who was just at his peak at the Marble Collegiate Church in New York City and would come over to Princeton each Monday to teach preaching. He advised Macartney to have a clear outline and to preach without notes.[4]

Macartney served three congregations:

- First Presbyterian Church, Paterson, New Jersey (1905–1914). The downtown property of this historic church was on the market when young Macartney came. God blessed the Word and the whole direction changed.
- Arch Street Presbyterian Church, Philadelphia (1914–1927). "He is digging his grave," it was said when Macartney took the call to this downtown hulk, but "the old church began to show signs of life . . ."[5]
- First Presbyterian Church, Pittsburgh (1927–1953). Here he was known above all for his Tuesday Noon Club for men and his great Sunday evening services. He filled five regular preaching and teaching preparations each week.

Macartney never married but traveled extensively and read voraciously, especially history, in which he concentrated on the American Civil War and Abraham Lincoln. In this field he wrote a number of significant works.

Macartney was pivotal as moderator of the General Assembly in 1924, to which post he was nominated by William Jennings Bryan. This was the crucial action that led to the withdrawal of Harry Emerson Fosdick from the pulpit of First Presbyterian Church of New York City. Macartney was a champion of orthodoxy, as his vigorously doctrinal sermons indicate.[6] When Fosdick's famous sermon, "Will the Fundamentalists Win?" shook the denomination, Macartney replied with "Will Unbelief Win?" Macartney backed Machen in the founding of Westminster. His ripened thought on preaching may be found in *Preaching Without Notes*. His volume of printed illustrations, though now archaic, display his wide reading and erudition.[7]

Macartney is at his biblical best in his series on the Lamb in Revelation and in his sermons on the blood of Christ.[8] He often used four points in his sermons. No one can use another preacher's method, but his steps in sermon preparation are as instructive as any. From early on he exploited the interest in preaching Bible characters.

"Biographical preaching strikes a popular chord," he asserted.[9] We have already noted some of the dangers in biographical preaching (cf. 11.6.2, note 9), and some of that concern must register with Macartney's tendency to fixate on a minor matter in the text and enlarge it beyond any sense of the author's intention.[10] In his famous sermon on "Come Before Winter," from 2 Timothy 4:21, a poignant evangelistic appeal, he makes a somewhat incidental request into the fulcrum for a strong gospel appeal. Is there not a platform text for a sermon on working together with God better suited than Acts 9:25, "and let him down in a basket?"[11] Notwithstanding this caveat, we must heartily underscore the strength and soundness of Macartney, particularly when he takes a more spacious text.[12]

Frank Gaebelein speaks of a certain grandeur in his preaching: "High seriousness, powerful directness, intentive conviction, mastery of the Scriptures, and knowledge of the human heart marked his sermons. In his imaginative illustrations and in his ability to reach the minds of his listeners, he had few equals."[13]

---

1. Clarence E. Macartney, *The Making of a Minister* (Great Neck, N.Y.: Channel, 1961). A posthumous work.
2. Ibid., 66, 68.
3. Ibid., 91.
4. Ibid., 129.
5. Ibid., 173. His Stone Lectures, *Sons of Thunder,* describe certain eminent preachers who were much used of God.
6. Clarence E. Macartney, *Twelve Great Questions About Christ* (Grand Rapids: Baker, 1956). A clarion call!
7. Clarence E. Macartney, *Preaching Without Notes* (Nashville: Abingdon, 1946); *Macartney's Illustrations* (Nashville: Abingdon, 1945) includes fifteen hundred classified stories, anecdotes, and quotes for sermons.
8. Clarence E. Macartney, compiled by Richard Allen Bodey, *The Lamb of God* (Grand Rapids: Kregel, 1994).
9. Macartney, *The Making of a Minister,* 150.
10. Clarence E. Macartney, *Peter and His Lord* (Nashville: Abingdon, 1937).
11. Donald Macleod, *Here Is My Method* (Westwood, N.J.: Revell, 1952), 113ff.
12. Clarence E. Macartney, *The Greatest Questions of the Bible and of Life* (Grand Rapids: Kregel, 1995); *Great Interviews of Jesus* (Grand Rapids: Kregel, 1996); "Christian Giving" (a sermon from 1 Corinthians 16:1); "Now Concerning the Collection" (Grand Rapids: Zondervan, 1936). Takes off on Jowett's great idea from this text.
13. John Bishop, "Clarence E. Macartney: Evangelize or Perish," *Preaching* (September–October 1990): 51.

12.7.6 ANDREW W. BLACKWOOD—THE PREACHER AS INTERPRETER

> What busy preacher does not need to keep up his study of preaching as an art? Many of us approached homiletics in school as a science. Now we know that our work was too theoretical. The way to study an art is through its choicest products.
>
> The best way to improve one's pulpit work is through the study of sermons. At some early stage almost every master preacher has made a study of printed sermons by former divines. In the classroom I have felt the need of some one volume of sermons for use in "laboratory work" . . . Men will learn more about preaching if they dig down into each sermon and discover the secrets of its effectiveness . . . Instead of admiring sweeping surveys by distant critics, why not get down and dig?
>
> —Andrew Watterson Blackwood

He was called Mr. Homiletician! One teacher of preaching said of him, "For the years of his service in Princeton Seminary he probably had as much influence as any teacher of homiletics has had."[1] **Andrew W. Blackwood** (1882–1966) "was the best-known and most widely published homiletician in America in the twentieth century," and he was an excellent preacher as well.[2] He was born into a physician's family in Clay Center, Kansas, of Reformed Presbyterian (Covenanters) stock. Moving about with his family, he then took baccalaureate degrees from both Franklin College in Ohio, with a background in classics and humanities, and Harvard, where he was active in debating and where he was negatively influenced by prevailing Unitarian ideas.

Sensing nonetheless a call to ministry, Blackwood enrolled at Princeton in 1905. Under the aegis of B. B. Warfield and John Davis, he became staunch in his orthodoxy. Taught to preach by David Burrell, he was largely unimpressed by the pure lecture method in teaching preaching and in Burrell's independent spirit as shown by his disdain of preaching from a pulpit.[3] After his first year, Blackwood had the first of several physical and emotional breakdowns and transferred to Xenia Seminary in Ohio, closer to home. He was ordained in 1908 under the United Presbyterians and took some early charges in Kansas. Preaching his first sermon in "a clear, resonant voice," he took the text in John 12:32 on "The Magnetic Christ."[4] His ministerial career prepared him well for the teaching of preaching:

- Sixth United Presbyterian Church, Pittsburgh (1911–1914). He did substitute teaching at Xenia Seminary.
- First Presbyterian Church, Columbia, South Carolina (1914–1921). He began his deep study of classical preachers and sermons.
- Indianola Avenue Presbyterian Church, Columbus, Ohio (1921–1925). He continued to produce articles, believing it was important to write.
- Chairman of English Bible at Louisville Presbyterian Seminary (1925–1930). He taught the Bible homiletically.
- Professor of preaching, Princeton Theological Seminary (1930–1950). He used the "coach method" in teaching.
- Professor of homiletics, Temple University School of Theology (1950–1958). He had *carte blanche* to effect change.

Blackwood's homiletic was built on a sound rhetorical foundation and tended to be quite traditional in its taxonomy of sermons. He insisted on the distinction between a textual and an expository sermon in which the natural thought unit is considered rather than a microtext. Yet, as Jay Adams shows, he was innovative in adding many new courses.[5] In his avid study of preachers and preaching, Blackwood introduced a highly personalized one-on-one approach to teaching—even though the classes at Princeton included more than one hundred students.[6] While at Princeton, the Blackwoods were neighbors of the Albert Einsteins; they had little spiritual success with the scientific genius but led Mrs. Einstein to Christ on her deathbed.[7]

Feeling increasingly isolated theologically at Princeton, Blackwood moved on to Temple, where he continued to develop his theory of imagination.[8] Even after retiring, he continued to preach and lecture and write for *Christianity Today* and did five more books. He advocated strong use of active verbs and avoidance of "excessive Latinization" in speaking.[9] His strong biblicality is manifested in *Preaching from Samuel.* Here we have probing insights into the biblical text and choice samples of splendid application.[10]

Not as exegetically or theologically nuanced as we might sometimes desire, Blackwood still is a champion of expository preaching that is more than explaining the passage.[11] His studies of doctrinal and biographical preaching were blazing new trails.[12] One of the most influential of his works was his unmatched work on planning our preaching.[13] No one has given us as helpful a guide on the difficult matter of public prayer.[14] Blackwood as a preacher or as a teacher was no dynamo, but he was steady and sound. As Matthew Arnold said of Sophocles, "He saw life steadily and he saw it whole," also applies to Andrew Blackwood. Fewer and fewer of his students are still actively preaching, but we are all beneficiaries of his legacy and patrimony. He must take an honored place in this chronicle.

---

1. Jay E. Adams, *The Homiletical Innovations of Andrew W. Blackwood* (Grand Rapids: Baker, 1975), 101.
2. William H. Willimon and Richard Lischer, eds., *Concise Encyclopedia of Preaching* (Louisville: Westminster/John Knox, 1995), 37.
3. Adams, *Homiletical Innovations,* 108ff.
4. Ibid., 46.
5. Ibid., 84.
6. Ibid., 61. Note his collection of master sermons in *The Protestant Pulpit* (Nashville: Abingdon, 1947).
7. Ibid., 85.
8. Ibid., 124ff.
9. Ibid., 114ff. I think Dr. Lloyd M. Perry of Northern, Gordon, and Trinity succeeded Blackwood as doyen of homiletics.
10. Andrew W. Blackwood, *Preaching from Samuel* (Nashville: Abingdon, 1946). Titles were never his strong suit.
11. Andrew W. Blackwood, *Expository Preaching for Today* (Nashville: Abingdon, 1953).
12. Andrew W. Blackwood, *Doctrinal Preaching for Today* (Grand Rapids: Baker, 1956); *Biographical Preaching for Today* (Nashville: Abingdon, 1954). We have already noted a caution on the latter; cf. 11.6.2, note 9).
13. Andrew W. Blackwood, *Planning a Year's Pulpit Work* (Grand Rapids: Baker, 1942, 1975).
14. Andrew W. Blackwood, *Leading in Public Prayer* (Nashville: Abingdon, 1958). One of several pastoral works.

12.7.7 DONALD GREY BARNHOUSE—THE PREACHER AS EXPOSITORY TEACHER

> Expository preaching is the art of explaining the text of the Word of God, using all the experiences of life and learning to illuminate the exposition.

> The prime factor in expository preaching is the belief that the Bible is the Word of God. When I take the Bible into my hands I think of it as originating with God, given by Him to every man in the very order, terms, phrases and words in which He wanted us to have it.
>
> I glory in all that scholarship has accomplished in lower criticism, establishing an ever more accurate text of the original languages. I give practically no consideration to anything that has been done in the field of higher criticism, although I have spent hundreds of weary hours plowing through the critics, trying to find out what they are driving at, and finally rejecting their conclusions because they proceed on the false premise that the Bible originated with man and that it is the record of man's thoughts about God.
>
> —Donald Grey Barnhouse

Reflective of a genuine resurgence of classical expository preaching in the last half of the twentieth century is the strikingly effective preaching of **Donald Grey Barnhouse** (1895–1960). A large and gravelly-voiced man, Barnhouse combined high-density exposition of the text with the most remarkable illustrations and a blunt, almost overbearing manner with a most delightful sense of humor and the incongruous.[1] He was born in Watsonville, California, and came under the influence of R. A. Torrey at the Bible Institute of Los Angeles (BIOLA). Exceedingly intelligent and probing as a student, he went to study at Princeton Seminary, the University of Grenoble in France, the University of Chicago, and the University of Pennsylvania, where he was a faculty assistant. He had a Th.M. from Eastern Baptist Seminary and a Th.D. from the seminary in Aix-en-Provence in France. After World War I, he had a positive ministry in war-torn Belgium and France.[2]

In 1918 Barnhouse was ordained into the Presbyterian ministry. In 1927 he began a thirty-three-year ministry at Tenth Presbyterian Church in Philadelphia, a congregation which was never huge but which had a most extraordinary influence on students and leaders in the city. From 1928 on, he had a radio ministry called the "Bible Study Hour" and later a television outreach. He edited *Revelation* and *Eternity* magazines successively and wrote prolifically. He began his ministry with three and a half years of close exposition of Romans and later expanded these messages to the radio congregation, now published in ten magnificent volumes.[3] By special arrangement, Barnhouse preached twenty-six Sundays a year at Tenth and then traveled the nation in popular Bible conferences the rest of the year. He also had a weekly New York Bible class for many years.

Staunchly Calvinistic and almost gruff in his manner, he yet enjoyed close fellowship with Billy Graham and was passionately evangelistic to the point that his appeals seemed inconsistent with his doctrine. His wife's biography documents the mellowing of Barnhouse over the years if not some softening in doctrinal precision.

Barnhouse's first book was a guide for instructing young Christians and consisted of eighty lessons on doctrine accompanied with visual sketches. This work has been translated into many languages and shows the visual tilt of Barnhouse's wonderful mind.[4] His steps in preparation of sermons are helpful because we see the importance of outline for his preaching even if he never formally emphasized structure as such in presentation.[5] He often made extensive comments on points in the scriptural text as he read it, not unlike Spurgeon.[6] Barnhouse was very much aware of the reality of spiritual warfare in the preaching process from beginning to end.[7]

His great strength was his biblical content. After all, the elaboration of a triviality is still trivial. Barnhouse was so rich in the text, as is shown in his unique devotional expositions in Genesis.[8] His creative work in John's gospel is outstanding.[9] And who else ever thought of using 1 John as a commentary on the Upper Room Discourse?[10]

Despite his "inexhaustible energy" and "pugnacious controversialism," Barnhouse became an all-time favorite at Keswick in England starting in 1935.[11] From his BIOLA days, he was an outspoken dispensationalist and pretribulation rapturist.[12] Illustrations from yesterday are often not worth reading, but Barnhouse's knack for the startling story makes his collected illustrations still valuable.[13] His tool for evangelism, *Your Right to Heaven,* was instrumental in the conversion of Dr. D. James Kennedy and is at the core of his Evangelism Explosion approach so used of God and owned of the Spirit in our time.[14] To hear Barnhouse was never to forget the experience!

---

1. The only preacher I ever heard who was more adept at this than Barnhouse was the Scottish pulpiteer, Dr. James McGinlay, who served Central Baptist Church in London, Ontario, and the Baptist Temple in Brooklyn; see *The Birthday of Souls and Other Sermons* (Grand Rapids: Eerdmans, 1939). Also, John W. Drakeford, *Humor in Preaching* (Grand Rapids: Zondervan, 1986).
2. Margaret N. Barnhouse, *That Man Barnhouse* (Wheaton, Ill.: Tyndale House, 1983), 104. This volume is written in the spirit of candor and openness which started with Elizabeth Elliot's *Who Shall Ascend: The Life of R. Kenneth Strachan of Costa Rica* (New York: 1968). A strategy of concealment and cover-up is invariably self-defeating.
3. Donald Grey Barnhouse, *God's Wrath: Expository Messages on the Whole Bible Taking the Epistle to the Romans as a Point of Departure* (Wheaton, Ill.: Van Kampen, 1952). There are ten volumes in this series.
4. Donald Grey Barnhouse, *Teaching the Word of Truth* (Grand Rapids: Eerdmans, 1940). A most useful piece.
5. Clarence S. Roddy, ed., *We Prepare and Preach: The Practice of Sermon Construction and Delivery* (Chicago: Moody, 1959), 33ff. Roddy was himself a great preacher, pastor of the Baptist Temple in Brooklyn at one time, professor at both Eastern Baptist in Philadelphia and Fuller in Pasadena. He was "my homiletician."
6. Barnhouse, *That Man Barnhouse,* 154. Both Mariano di Gangi and James Montgomery Boice, his successors at Tenth Presbyterian Church, have been strong expositors of the Word. Boice has been strongly in his mold.
7. Ibid., 369. Barnhouse's best book in my opinion and his last, *The Invisible War* (Grand

Rapids: Zondervan, 1966).

8. Donald Grey Barnhouse, *Genesis: A Devotional Exposition,* 2 vols. (Grand Rapids: Zondervan, 1970, 1971).
9. Donald Grey Barnhouse, *The Love Life* (Glendale, Calif.: Regal/Gospel Light, 1973). Vintage Barnhouse.
10. Barnhouse, *That Man Barnhouse,* 257.
11. J. C. Pollock, *The Keswick Story* (Chicago: Moody, 1964), 161ff.; see *The Ministry of Keswick: Second Series,* ed. Herbert F. Stevenson (London: Marshall, Morgan, and Scott, 1964), 155ff. A most searching series given in 1948 on "Baptized into Christ." Called "the most controversial speaker in Keswick's history," but a "genius" who drew great crowds. He loved repartee and debate. Bishop Houghton spoke of him as "a man mighty in the Scriptures." His superlative afternoon studies at Keswick in 1938 are *God's Methods for Holy Living* (Grand Rapids: Eerdmans, 1951).
12. Especially drawn out in his work *His Own Received Him Not and Revelation* (Grand Rapids: Zondervan, 1971).
13. Donald Grey Barnhouse, *Bible Truth Illustrated* (New Canaan, Conn.: Keats, 1979); *Words Fitly Spoken* (Wheaton, Ill.: Tyndale House, 1969). Barnhouse used simple everyday matters to illustrate great truth.
14. Donald Grey Barnhouse, *Your Right to Heaven* (Grand Rapids: Baker, 1977). "What right do you have to enter my heaven?" The incisive issue for everyone of us is addressed in the justifying work of Christ through Calvary.

12.7.8 Harold John Ockenga—The Preacher as Visionary Leader

> You can't stand and converse with people from the pulpit; you'll lose them. If you have a strong pulpit ministry, you're going to have a strong church, no matter what else is lacking. If you have a strong counseling church without a strong pulpit, you'll have a weak church. Preaching has got to be there, or people are not going to come. It has to be enlightening, interesting and challenging. Conversational preaching is a mistake. You've got to develop certain points, like a syllogism. You have to develop something people can follow, an outline with alliteration. When you get through, people can say, "That's what he said about this and that's what he said about that."
>
> —Harold John Ockenga

Continued strong emphasis on expository preaching continued among evangelicals in the last half of the twentieth century. One of the conspicuously excellent practitioners of the craft was **Harold John Ockenga.**[1] Ockenga was born in 1905 in Chicago and reared in the Methodist Church by a godly mother. His father was not converted until later in life. Always sickly and frail as a child but aggressive and enterprising (establishing a monopoly on box kites in his neighborhood), he announced at age nine, "I'm going to be a preacher and see the world."[2] Through the interest of a consecrated woman in his Olivet Methodist Church, Ockenga made his commitment to Christ and dedicated himself to the Christian ministry.[3] He worked his way though Methodistic Taylor University, where he excelled in forensics. Because he loved to preach, he preached four hundred times during college days and saw souls come to the Savior.[4]

From 1927 to 1929, he was at Princeton Seminary but finished at the new Westminster, where he met Macartney. After serving several Methodist charges, he became Macartney's assistant. With this pedigree, he became a strong Calvinist. Eventually he moderated his views, coming to believe in the freedom of human response to the gospel while also retaining his Methodistic emphasis on the deeper spiritual life. Ockenga eschewed any kind of perfectionism.[5] At his Presbyterian ordination in 1931, Macartney gave the charge and Machen preached.[6] From 1931 to 1936, he served Point Breeze Presbyterian Church in Pittsburgh and earned a doctorate in philosophy at the University of Pittsburgh.

In 1936, upon the recommendation of Macartney and Machen, Ockenga was called to pastor the historic Park Street Church in Boston, succeeding the venerable A. Z. Conrad, who had just died (cf. 11.4.6). This congregation had stood firmly against "the Unitarian landslide" that had almost engulfed New England. Ockenga's ministry was needed. For thirty-three years the pulpit was primary in the steady growth and expanding influence of this great congregation.[7]

Ockenga was a man of the Book, with a keenly logical mind, clear outlines, and long introductions. Deeply committed to evangelism, he witnessed on Boston Common and preached from the outdoor Geneva pulpit. "He loses himself in his preaching," it was often said for he had tremendous driving force and flow as he preached. Ockenga had a great missions emphasis and brought Oswald J. Smith from Toronto for six years to advance it (cf. 12.8.2).

Ockenga founded Boston Evening School of the Bible with Dr. Howard Ferrin of Providence Bible Institute, and he was one of the prime movers and first president of the National Association of Evangelicals founded in 1942. He was one of the minds behind *Christianity Today* and cofounder of Fuller Seminary with Charles E. Fuller, of which he was president in absentia for many years. Fuller's early conservative stand was one of Ockenga's contributions.

Ockenga catalyzed and envisioned the Billy Graham Crusade in Boston in 1949, which saw so many converts. The fruit was quickly seen; in 1950, 186 converts of the crusade joined Park Street Church.

Ockenga was heard morning and evening over a fifty-thousand-watt Boston radio station. He fully manuscripted and memorized his messages. The story of God's blessing reaching out from the ministry of Park Street Church is an exciting reinforcement of the insistence on the primacy of preaching.[8] Many churches sought to secure his services, but he turned them down. He nearly went to Seattle First Presbyterian Church to succeed Mark Matthews, but declined.[9]

His published expositions are meaty messages. His books on 2 Corinthians, Ephesians, and 1 Thessalonians were enormously popular. His expository addresses on Romans are typically superb samples of taking a good piece of text. He did not use a microtext, as did Lloyd-Jones or Barnhouse, but he took the larger natural thought unit. Ockenga covered Romans in twenty-four sermons. His message on Romans 1:1–17 is titled "The Gospel of which to be Proud":

I. The gospel of God makes us debtors;
II. The gospel of God makes us bold and daring;

III. The gospel of God brings us salvation.[10]

This is Harold Ockenga in his prime, and he was one of the best.

---

1. The move to exposition was led by William Evans of Moody and James Braga at Multnomah, by Faris Whitesell of Northern Baptist and Lloyd Perry at Trinity, and by the Dallas succession of Haddon Robinson, Donald Sunukjian, and Timothy Warren. We have already seen that strong support came from Andrew Blackwood at Princeton.
2. Harold Lindsell, *Park Street Prophet: The Story of Harold Ockenga* (Wheaton, Ill.: Van Kampen, 1951), 15.
3. Ibid., 20–21.
4. Ibid., 25. At this time he had what he called "a personal appropriation of the Pentecostal gift." See Clarence S. Roddy, *We Prepare and Preach* (Chicago: Moody, 1959), 114. Always a strong emphasis for him.
5. Ibid., 93. "The Calvinism of the classroom has been probably molded to a degree by the experiences of the pastorate and by intimate contacts with people."
6. Ibid., 33. A towering intellectual, he later became president of Gordon College and Gordon-Conwell Divinity School.
7. Cf. Earl V. Comfort, "Is the Pulpit a Factor in Church Growth?" *Bibliotheca Sacra* 140, no. 560 (January–March 1983): 64–70. This research concludes that sermons, with high biblical content, are the most significant factor in growth.
8. H. Crosby Englizian, *Brimstone Corner: Park Street Church Boston* (Chicago: Moody, 1968), 228ff. The novelist Henry James spoke of Park Street Church as "The most impressive mass of brick and mortar in the United States."
9. Lindsell, *Park Street Prophet,* 60–61.
10. Harold John Ockenga, *Every One That Believeth* (New York: Revell, 1942), 11ff.

12.8 EVANGELICAL POINT MEN AMID THE COLLAPSE OF CIVILIZATION

> The remnant . . . will know whose word will stand, Mine or theirs. My words will surely stand against you.
>
> —Jeremiah 44:28b, 29b (NASB)

The Christian communicator has always confronted enormous challenges, making the supernaturalism of the task essential. But as the century draws to a close, he or she now faces the death of truth in a spiritual and moral free-fall of staggering proportions. Even secular diehards have lamented the loss of "the common culture" of the Bible in the rush toward nihilism and relativism.[1] Judge Bork traces "the descent of popular culture into vulgarity and obscenity," into "gleeful sadism," in which "narcissistic nihilism" and "the resistance to restraints" have triumphed.[2] He was not the first to identify radical individualism and radical egalitarianism as twin demons in our time.[3] The Canadian philosopher Mark Kingwell documents the "brink culture" of which we are a part and how rationality is totally out of fashion.[4] But the "net-culture" is also beset with an "extraordinary rise in anxiety" and much fear of the future. So the stage is set again and again for "the ministry of the word and prayer."

---

1. Allan Bloom, *The Closing of the American Mind* (New York: Simon and Schuster, 1987), 58.
2. Robert H. Bork, *Slouching Toward Gomorrah: Modern Liberalism and American Decline* (New York: HarperCollins, 1996). Also weighty, Stephen L. Carter, *The Culture of Disbelief: How American Law and Politics Trivialize Religion* (New York: Basic Books, 1993). Quotes Martin Marty, "The public sphere does not welcome particularized witness."
3. On the former especially, Robert N. Bellah et al., *Habits of the Heart: Individualism and Commitment in American Life* (New York: Perennial Library, Harper and Row, 1985). Bellah's updates show that the situation has gotten worse.
4. Mark Kingwell, *Dreams of Millennium: Report from a Culture on the Brink* (Toronto: Viking/Penguin, 1996). I am indebted to my friend and former teaching fellow, the Reverend Timothy Callaway, for this invaluable source.

12.8.1 T. T. Shields—The Preacher as Fighter for the Truth

> Preaching is the biggest business I know. It is a far bigger job than being Prime Minister. I don't believe there is any occupation in the world that makes a bigger demand upon all that a man has or may become, than preaching.
>
> After a disappointing Sunday morning experience in London, but then hearing Dinsdale Young at Westminster Central Hall: "The service began with an invocation, and he put the cross right in the center. He spoke of the Mercy Seat, of Christ, of his imputed righteousness, His blood, and I just heaved a sigh and said, 'Thank the Lord, I have come to church!'"
>
> I have a vivid recollection, even now, of an experience I had more than thirty years ago. I was working on a sermon, and the bush burned with fire. I can think of nothing this side of heaven, unless it be the actual delivery of the sermon, than to be shut up with one's Bible in one's study, no extra duties calling, feeling that you are just in the proper place to await God, and let God speak to you, and just prayerfully to work out some great theme of the gospel. I would not change places with any king upon his throne when I have that really ecstatic experience.
>
> —T. T. Shields

Some saw clearly the situation developing in the flight from authority in our culture, and their baleful warnings were not always appreciated or heeded. Such a preacher was the often feisty and combative **Thomas Todhunter Shields** (1873–1955), who pastored the premier Baptist church in Canada, the great Jarvis Street Baptist Church in Toronto, for forty-five years.

Some called him the Canadian Spurgeon, and there are striking similarities between the two. Others called him the John Bunyan of Canada. Shields's was born in Bristol, the fifth of eight children. His father was a Primitive Methodist clergyman who became a Baptist and emigrated to Canada. The elder Shields was his teacher of Latin and Greek but especially of proper English usage.[1]

Shields was converted in 1891 under the preaching of a visiting speaker who pressed 1 John 1:9 on his hearers, and young T. T. "rested in the Word of God."[2] He was a tall, stately man who often carried a walking stick. Shy and reserved, he could not resist the call to the ministry. He preached his first sermon in 1894 and served several smaller Baptist churches until he enjoyed significant ministries in Hamilton and at the Adelaide Baptist Church of London, Ontario (1904–1910). Here he sought to implement the pattern of Ephesians 4:11 and saw a considerable spiritual impact.[3]

Although he could have gone to the Hanson Place Baptist Church in Brooklyn (where A. C. Dixon had served, cf. 12.2.3), Shields took the call to Jarvis Street Baptist Church in Toronto, whose fifteen hundred seats he filled morning and evening. On his regular visits to England, he filled the pulpit at Spurgeon's Tabernacle, and his reputation for strong biblical preaching was growing. He was approached at one time to take the pastoral leadership in Spurgeon's Tabernacle, but he declined. About this time, Shields received honorary doctorates both from McMaster (the Baptist school) and Temple University from Russell Conwell.

Like W. B. Riley and R. T. Ketcham in the U.S., Shields fought heavy battles in the drift toward liberalism. A considerable disruption over his views took place at Jarvis Street in 1921, but "great years" followed under his "solid Bible exposition and evangelism" Sunday by Sunday.[4] In 1924 revival came in a summer series of meetings with J. Frank Norris in which the vast Massey Hall was filled. He soon built the largest Sunday school in Canada.

Shields' preaching was first and foremost biblical and always Christ-centered. His "Christ in the Old Testament series" was one of most intently followed series he ever gave. He said:

> Take the Bible as a whole, learn the Book. Fill your mind with the Book. Whatever else you read, be sure that you master the Bible. Learn the whole Bible so that you know your way about.[5]

This he did himself, and when a storm cut off the power just as he started to read his text in a service, he recited the balance of the passage from memory in the darkened auditorium. His sermons were well outlined and abounded with effective illustration. He was frank in his speech and could never be accused of being "Mr. Facing-both-ways."[6] He preached for a verdict and was known for being pastoral.

Shields founded the Toronto Baptist Seminary and often insisted to his students that above all the preacher must be "a good man."[7] He had a striking way about him, as when he preached from John 1:29, "Behold the Lamb of God who takes away the sin of the world," and used as his title, "Jesus Christ, the Scavenger of the World." His sermons appeared every two weeks in the sixteen pages of the *Gospel Witness,* which he edited throughout his ministry.

One of the sermons in Tarr's biography reflects Shields's leadership of the Canadian Protestant League. Titled "One Sacrifice Forever," it is based on Hebrews 10:11–13.[8] His book of sermons on *The Prodigal and His Brother, or The Adventures of a Modern Young Man* present a high level of well-structured preaching.[9] His sermon on "Songs in the House of My Pilgrimage" from Psalm 119:54 for New Year's shows his skill in the appropriate use of hymn stanzas and poetry.[10] His Christmas message on Galatians 4:4–7 confirms the sound patterns of rich content, sound form, and engaging points of contact in illustration and allusion.[11] His ecclesiology and separatism distract some, but here is a preacher who did evangelism with dignity and fostered reverence toward God and His Word faithfully in a time when many veered on to the steep slippery slopes of concession.

---

1. Leslie K. Tarr, *Shields of Canada: T. T. Shields 1873–1955* (Grand Rapids: Baker, 1967), 19.
2. Ibid., 27.
3. Ibid., 46.
4. Ibid., 86.
5. Ibid., 152.
6. Ibid., 162.
7. Ibid., 183.
8. Ibid., 194ff. Shields is assessed in *Amazing Grace: Evangelicals in Australia, Britain, Canada and the United States,* ed. George Rawlyk and Mark A. Noll (Grand Rapids: Baker, 1993), 364ff.
9. T. T. Shields, *The Prodigal and His Brother, or The Adventures of a Modern Young Man* (Toronto: Gospel Witness, n.d.). Shields analyzes the Oxford Group Movement and Russellism, among others.
10. T. T. Shields, "Songs in the House of My Pilgrimage," *Sword of the Lord* (December 19, 1995): 1ff.
11. T. T. Shields, "A Christmas Message," in *Great Preaching on Christmas,* ed. Curtis Hutson (Murfreesboro, Tenn.: Sword of the Lord, 1988), 143ff. This is volume 10 of the worthwhile "Great Preaching" series.

12.8.2 Oswald J. Smith—The Preacher as Promoter of Missions

> God has laid on me a burden for revival, and in order to accomplish this I must have His blessed Spirit. Oh, God, strip me of all that hinders the filling of Thy Holy Spirit.

> God is giving me sermons by His Holy Spirit. When least expected they flash before me; I grab my notebook and take down the headings as fast as I can, all within about three or four minutes. This morning as I was

> reading in John 3, within ten minutes I had the outline for three new addresses.
>
> The Bible is becoming the Book of books to me; the message that I have to proclaim is clearer, more definite and more glorious than ever before, but I am fully conscious that unless I have the Unction, the Enduement of Power, my message will be unavailing and profitless. . . . But I must first experience it myself.
>
> —Oswald J. Smith

One of the foremost proponents of worldwide evangelization in the twentieth century was **Oswald J. Smith** (1889–1986). He was born into modest means on an Ontario farm. Very sickly as a child and a poor scholar, he nonetheless read constantly, devouring all of Henty's books of historical fiction for boys. He began to sense a call to preach even before he was converted.[1]

The death of one of his sisters, in addition to the conversion of the community drunk and the good influence of an aunt in Toronto, led him and his brother to travel to Toronto to attend the Torrey-Alexander meetings in Massey Hall, where they were both saved.[2] He began to study the Bible in earnest and prepared sermons to preach to the birds.

Smith felt called to foreign missionary service and began to take night classes at the Toronto Bible Training Institute. He was at the farewell service for the Goforths as they ventured forth to China (cf. 12.1.4). Turned down again and again for overseas ministry because of lack of preparation, he entered into colportage work with the Bible society and traveled extensively in British Columbia, especially among the Indians and the loggers. His preaching was in demand, and he conducted his first evangelistic campaign at age twenty-one. He then went on to study at McCormick Seminary in Chicago. Always a writer of poetry and verse and a gifted musician, Smith wrote more than a thousand hymns in his lifetime, including "Then Jesus Came," "The Savior Can Solve Every Problem," "With Thy Spirit, Fill Me," and "The Song of the Soul Set Free."

The thin, gangling preacher did a stint in the Kentucky hills and served First Presbyterian in South Chicago while finishing seminary. At the advice of Dr. Henry Hepburn of Buena Memorial Presbyterian Church, he returned to Toronto, where he served as associate to J. D. Morrow at Dale Presbyterian Church and met a young deaconess who became his wife. Fired with a great missionary passion, he was influenced much by Charles Finney and John Fletcher.[3] Warring factions at Dale closed that door for him after three and a half years, although revival touched the church profoundly but not the core leadership.

Smith preached for a while at Beulah Tabernacle just off Yonge Street downtown in Toronto. At this time he was much under the writings of Charles Trumbull (cf. 11.1.4, note 1) and William R. Newell. He took his stand on Romans 6:11 and on Galatians 2:20.[4] He then went with Shantyman's Mission, working especially among lumberjacks. He worked part-time for Roland Bingham as an editor for *The Evangelical Christian* but broke with Bingham over the nature of his poetry.

Smith set up his own church in the needy Dovercourt area and merged with Parkside Tabernacle of the CMA. He was close to Paul Rader, who was president of the CMA at this time. Smith was then called to the mother church, the Gospel Tabernacle in New York City. Because he felt his preaching would not carry the challenge of the work, he brought in much outside talent, like the famous Cleveland Colored Quintet.

He traveled incessantly and had a blessed ministry in Latvia and Russia, but had problems in the local church because so much money was flowing out of the treasury into non-Alliance causes.[5] For a while he served as superintendent of the central and eastern CMA churches. He was on the road all the time, and his little family suffered.

In 1927 he took the call to be pastor of the Los Angeles Gospel Tabernacle and had an unusual ministry there, but the next year he resigned and went back to Toronto. He had resigned three thriving pastorates; what was next?[6] In this time frame, both he and Rader left the Alliance, a decision he subsequently regretted.

In 1928 Smith started the Cosmopolitan Tabernacle in Toronto in a great series of meetings in Massey Hall, which seated thirty-four hundred people. Later called the Toronto Gospel Tabernacle and ultimately the People's Church, this was the church that missions built. With Rader's bankruptcy, Smith had to move into missionary management. The church grew, but often had to use rented quarters. Gypsy Smith was a personal friend and held great crusades with many saved. His son Paul worked with him, ultimately succeeded him, and built a great new church in 1962.

Oswald Smith was not an imposing presence. Thin as a rail with a birdlike physique, he was a nervous but powerful preacher. Of a frugal lifestyle, he poured everything into missions. He introduced the faith promise challenge in Toronto and around the world.[7] He preached more than twelve thousand sermons and kept at it up into his nineties. He was disciplined to take a two-hour rest each afternoon, which doubtless kept him going notwithstanding a lifelong pattern of much illness. Perhaps his frequent traveling and relentless schedule kept him from digging deeper into the Scripture.

Smith's books of sermons have had huge circulation. His message on saving faith was given many times and in many forms.[8] Tending to be a bit thin, the messages are still sound and Scripture-based, if not Scripture-shaped, and they reverberate with passion.[9] His messages on prophecy show satisfying familiarity with the relevant texts, although in the 1930s he ventured too far in speculative identification.[10]

His 1954 lectures at Bob Jones University on "The Consuming Fire" capture the man and his preaching.[11] No one has wrestled more thoroughly with the relationship between evangelism and revival than did Oswald J. Smith. I heard him over many years and up almost to the last and never failed to be deeply stirred by the singleness of his vision and the vitality of his preaching. A news report from his ministry in South Australia said:

> Let him open his mouth to speak and the outward frailty vanishes. Smith becomes a man of robust spirit, bursting with life and energy, a man on

fire. The flame of his zeal reaches you, then your neighbor, and presently the whole congregation is engulfed in a spiritual conflagration.[12]

---

1. Lois Neely, *Fire in His Bones: The Official Biography of Oswald J. Smith* (Wheaton, Ill.: Tyndale House, 1982), 24.
2. Ibid., 26.
3. Ibid., 95ff.
4. Ibid., 103.
5. Ibid., 147.
6. Ibid., 155.
7. Ibid., 231ff.
8. Oswald J. Smith, *From Death to Life* (New York: Christian Alliance Publishing, 1925), 67ff.
9. Oswald J. Smith, *The Enduement of Power* (London: Marshall, Morgan, and Scott, 1933); *The Man God Uses; The Work God Blesses; The Battle for Truth* (London: Marshall, Morgan, and Scott, 1953). He also wrote books for children. He was well read and felt at liberty to return to the enjoyment of the classics.
10. Oswald J. Smith, *Prophecy—What Lies Ahead?* (London: Marshall, Morgan, and Scott, n.d.).
11. Oswald J. Smith, *The Consuming Fire* (London: Marshall, Morgan, and Scott, 1954).
12. Neely, *Fire in His Bones,* 277. Smith's congregation at the People's Church was about two thousand for each service.

12.8.3 J. Vernon McGee—The Preacher as Communicator to the Common People

> It was fortunate for me that during my college days I met a very scholarly minister who had the knack of taking the profound truths of theology and translating them into the simple language of the ordinary person. I asked him for his secret. He assured me that this priceless gift was one that needed to be developed and cultivated. His formula went something like this: In the preparation of the sermon every effort should be made to attain simplicity—then go over the sermon the second time to reduce it to the simplest common denominator. Go over the sermon again and again until you are ashamed of its simplicity, then preach the sermon so the children can understand it. Afterward, one of the spiritual saints will come up to remark about the depth and profundity of the message.
>
> —J. Vernon McGee

No preacher has had such an avid following in a through-the-Bible exposition of Scripture over radio as did **J. Vernon McGee** (1904–1988). His broadcasts continue today, long after his homegoing. He was a great preacher and student of the Word.

McGee was a quaint, colloquial preacher who seemed to cultivate his Texas-Oklahoma twang as the years passed. Born in Hillsboro, Texas, he graduated from

Southwestern University in Memphis and Columbia Theological Seminary, taking both his Th.M. and his Th.D. from Dallas Theological Seminary. A staunch Southern Presbyterian in his early days, he served pastorates in Nashville, Tennessee, and in Cleburne, Texas. For over eight years, he pastored the Lincoln Avenue Presbyterian Church in Pasadena, where he followed Oscar Raymond Lowery. In 1949 he became pastor of the great Church of the Open Door at Sixth and Hope in downtown Los Angeles, succeeding Dr. Louis T. Talbot.

McGee consistently drew great audiences but was especially known for the thousands who came to follow his Thursday night through-the-Bible expositions, Genesis to Revelation.[1] He was much in demand at Bible conferences around the country and the world, and continued three weekly and daily radio programs through his long tenure at Church of the Open Door.

Not advocating simply verse-by-verse progression but insisting on "a logical division and method of presentation in each message," McGee captivated audiences with his unusually rich content and uncanny ability to apply the text to world conditions and everyday life. Hundreds of thousands were McGee addicts and needed the daily "fix" this gifted expositor could furnish. His marvelous studies in the Book of Ruth are peerless, as one could also say of his work on Esther.[2]

His printed sermons have tang and pop to them, uncommon when a character as colorful as McGee puts the spoken message into printed form.[3] Such sermons as "'Twas the Prayer Before Christmas" from Luke 1:5–17 or "The Power of Negative Thinking" from Proverbs 3:5–7 show McGee at his best.[4] The danger for one who is so down-home and so chatty is of course occasional demagoguery. McGee had special skill and ability in handling biblical prophecy, and his collected sermons contain such gems as "From the Top of the Mount of Olives You Can See Forever" from the Olivet Discourse of Matthew 24–25 or his "The Amazing, Alarming and Awful Apostasy" from Jude 1–4 are superb examples.[5] Any open-minded listener always got the Word of God from J. Vernon McGee. There may have been a little cornpone with it, but it was delicious and always deeply satisfying.

---

1. J. Vernon McGee's "Thru-the-Bible" books span all of Scripture. His *Moving Through Matthew* and *Reveling Through Revelation* are typical. These have enjoyed incredible circulation. W. A. Criswell of First Baptist Church, Dallas, also used the consecutive through-the-Bible approach over most of his many years in Dallas.
2. J. Vernon McGee, *Ruth: The Romance of Redemption* (Wheaton, Ill.: Van Kampen, 1954). Other fine sermon series on Ruth include Philip Mauro, *Ruth: The Satisfied Stranger* (Swengel, Pa.: Bible Truth, 1963); Charles E. Fuller, *Ruth: A Life of Love and Loyalty* (Westwood, N.J.: Revell, 1969); M. R. DeHaan, *The Romance of Redemption* (Grand Rapids: Zondervan, 1958); Carl McIntire, *Better Than Seven Sons* (Collingswood, N.J.: Christian Beacon, 1954). McIntire's classmates at Princeton were agreed that he was one of their most gifted preachers.
3. J. Vernon McGee, *The Fruit of the Sycamore Tree and Other Sermons* (Wheaton, Ill.: Van Kampen, 1952).
4. J. Vernon McGee, *The Best of J. Vernon McGee* (Nashville: Thomas Nelson, 1988), 107ff., 81ff.

5. J. Vernon McGee, *On Prophecy: Man's Fascination with the Future* (Nashville: Thomas Nelson, 1993), 111ff., 143ff.

12.8.4 Paul S. Rees—The Preacher as Ambassador of Holiness

> On consulting other preachers who have published sermons on the text, or, at any rate, the subject one has chosen: "Manifestly, this is not for the purpose of imitating them but rather of catching inspiration from them. I have met a few ministers who say they never read other men's sermons. I find it impossible to share their feeling. Currently I have between seven and eight hundred volumes of sermons in my library. My incurable interest in expository preaching leads me, understandably enough, to the works of men who are saturated with the Word of God and endowed with the ability to expound it."
>
> —Paul S. Rees

He has been described as "a mind aflame," in recognition of both the brilliance of his preaching in its content and form and the warmth and passion of his heart. **Paul Stromberg Rees** (1900–1991) was nurtured in the arms of the Holiness movement. His father, Seth Rees, was first a Quaker and then prominent in the Church of the Nazarene and finally one of the founders of the Pilgrim Holiness Church.[1]

Young Rees had an inquiring mind and compiled an outstanding record as an undergraduate at the University of Southern California. But he did not pursue doctoral studies at the request of his father because of the negative spiritual effects of doctoral studies on a brother. The unusual preaching skills of the young preacher were in conspicuous evidence as at first he helped his father at the Pilgrim Tabernacle in Pasadena, California. He then served as ministerial superintendent of the Detroit Holiness Tabernacle, an enterprise sponsored by Methodistic laymen who were burdened about spiritual decline. Rees preached at the Tabernacle and then in an increasingly wide circle of camp meetings, conferences, and evangelistic series. From 1938 to 1958, he served as pastor of the great First Covenant Church in downtown Minneapolis with an amazing outreach to college and university students and people of all denominations. In 1958 he became preacher at large for World Vision and continued to travel around the world in effective ministry almost up until his death at nearly ninety-one years of age. He was widely used in the Billy Graham crusades with the ministers, and his written products were many and highly valued everywhere.

Paul Rees was a preacher's preacher. His reading was varied, and he was quite literary in his style. He wrote full manuscripts and largely memorized his material. His reproduction was so precise that a secretary transcribing his sermon from tape found virtually no difference between the original manuscript and the ultimate delivery.[2] His vocabulary, use of illustration, appropriate literary allusion, and exegetical conscience combine to make him a memorable preacher. Popular at Keswick conventions around the world (he was featured at the Japan convention many years in a row), he visited English Keswick again and again. His Bible readings there beginning in 1956 show him at his expository best (e.g., his series on the prayers of Paul in 1956, which he titled "Prayer and Life's Highest";[3] his superb expositions from Philippians in 1958 called "The Gospel and Humanities";[4] and his careful exegetical work in 1 Peter under the theme "Triumphant in Trouble,"[5] which he did in 1961). Rees was a Christian gentleman, a gracious and godly man. It was not hard to hear him preach about holy things. Occasionally his voice had a little sob in it, but he was genuine.

Probably his most famous sermons were textual, in which genre he specialized. A typical example would be his sermon "The Rain of Righteousness," from Hosea 10:12, which reads, "It is time to seek the Lord, till he comes and rains righteousness upon you." His outline aids us in seeing his special capability:

I. Spiritual recovery and revival require man's response to God's call;
II. Spiritual recovery and revival require man's reception of God's gift;
III. Spiritual recovery and revival require man's recognition of God's time.[6]

Rees seldom preached in series, but one he did do was particularly outstanding. The series focused on "The Radiant Cross" and consisted of studies of ten brief texts related to the Cross.[7] Heavier theologically is his Trinitarian approach in *Stand Up in Praise to God* with its multiplied triads.[8] In structure, alliterative outline, and polished components, Rees had few equals. At times there seemed to be overcontrol. His Bob Jones Lectures in 1951 on *Stir Up the Gift* allowed vent for the more scholarly Rees to express himself, in connection with which he has a stirring lecture on *The Re-Validation of the Sermon.*[9] His strength in application can be appreciated especially in his sermons on *Christian: Commit Yourself!* projected in a year of denominational mobilization for evangelism.[10]

Broadcasting his morning sermons live for many years, Rees touched thinking people through the upper Midwest and around the country in his itinerant ministry. Such masterpieces as "The Hallowing of the Heart" from 1 Peter 3:15[11] or "The Victor Unveiled" from Hebrews 2:9 explain his appeal.[12]

Paul Rees did his homework. His preparation was disciplined. He stands for us as the personification of pulpit effectiveness and prowess.

---

1. Paul S. Rees, *Seth Cook Rees: The Warrior-Saint* (Indianapolis: Pilgrim, 1934). A beautiful study. See also Carl Bangs, *Phineas F. Bresee: His Life in Methodism, the Holiness Movement and the Church of the Nazarene* (Kansas City: Beacon Hill, 1995). Also, Frank Bartleman, *Azusa Street* (South Plainfield, N.J.: Bridge, 1980).
2. Clarence S. Roddy, ed., *We Prepare and Preach* (Chicago: Moody, 1959), 147.
3. Paul S. Rees, *Prayer and Life's Highest* (Grand Rapids: Eerdmans, 1956). Rees knew the literature.
4. Herbert F. Stevenson, ed., *The Keswick Week,* 1958 (London: Marshall, Morgan, and Scott, 1958) 33ff.
5. Herbert F. Stevenson, ed., *The Keswick Week,* 1961 (London: Marshall, Morgan, and Scott, n.d.), 31ff.

6. Paul S. Rees, *Things Unshakable and Other Sermons* (Grand Rapids: Eerdmans, 1947), 45ff.
7. Paul S. Rees, *The Radiant Cross* (Grand Rapids: Eerdmans, 1955).
8. Paul S. Rees, *Stand Up in Praise to God* (Grand Rapids: Eerdmans, 1960).
9. Paul S. Rees, *Stir Up the Gift* (Grand Rapids: Zondervan, 1962), 131ff.
10. Paul S. Rees, *Christian: Commit Yourself!* (Chicago: Covenant Press, 1957).
11. Paul S. Rees, *Heart Throbs from a City Pulpit* (Minneapolis: Covenant Tabernacle Church, 1945), 39ff.
12. Paul S. Rees, *The Hope That Hallows* (Louisville: Pentecostal Publishing Company, n.d.), 22ff.

12.8.5 Walter L. Wilson—The Preacher as Encourager

> If there is a definitive characteristic of his [Wilson's] ministry, it has been its remarkable simplicity. Every message he preached, every book he wrote, every class he taught—all were geared for complete understanding and digestion by any member of his audience. This is not to imply that he dealt only with the elementary milk of the Word. On the contrary, he had the remarkable gift of making the most meaty portions of scripture palatable for the untrained spiritual appetite. He could, as Spurgeon admonished his students to do, "put the cookies on the lower shelf where the children can reach them."
>
> —Kenneth O. Gangel

Walter L. Wilson (1881–1969) was a unique and singular force for God. He was born in Aurora, Indiana, into a strong Christian home. His father was a Methodist minister and a practicing physician. His mother died in 1882, and Wilson was reared by his grandparents in Ft. Smith, Arkansas.

He wanted to become a preacher and a doctor like his father.[1] Later he was taken to Kansas City by his father and his new mother. Here he joined a church but by then had been a member of two churches and was not yet converted. His employer and future father-in-law took him to a Plymouth Brethren Tent on Ninth and Agnes Streets in Kansas City, where the evangelist John Moffat preached clearly night after night successively on Romans 4:5, Titus 3:5, Ephesians 2:8–9, and on Isaiah 64:6. Wilson was under deep conviction and six months later gave in. He was converted![2] When he was sixteen, a dying Scottish preacher named Donald Ross placed his hands on him to anoint him to take his place.

Wilson began to do street preaching, faithfully attending the Gospel Hall and studying the Word deeply and constantly. He went to University Medical School in Kansas City and he and his new bride began to practice in Webb City, Missouri. He worked also with his father-in-law in the tent manufacturing business. He sold the big tops to Ringling Brothers Circus.

His great love was for preaching, and he had legendary gifts as a personal soulwinner. In 1920 he established the Central Bible Church in Kansas City. The first meetings were in a tent, but the work flourished. Under Wilson's evangelistic and expository ministries, Central Bible Church became a powerful center of

Christian witness and testimony. Many conversions took place. He began radio ministry as early as 1924 over WOQ, and he founded the Flagstaff Indian Mission to the Navajos. In 1932 he founded Kansas City Bible Institute, which later merged with Midwest Bible College of St. Louis to become Calvary Bible College in Kansas City.

Wilson was unusually gifted in doing object lessons. He was interested in nature and the relationship of science to biblical Christianity. In his teaching he made a strong emphasis on knowing the Holy Spirit personally.[3] He was excellent in repartee and was a popular youth and children's speaker.[4] His evangelistic preaching tingles with spiritual passion and warmth and is solidly based on the great texts of Scripture.[5] His expositions were rich in biblical insight, as his series of pocket commentaries indicates.

Wilson's major contribution to biblical scholarship is his famous *Dictionary of Bible Types.* Given the tendency we have noted in some Bible preachers to overdo typology, it is of interest to sense the return to consider a proper biblical typology under such scholars as Leonard Goppelt and others. Wilson classified his lengthy survey of typological material under three headings: (1) the overtly typical as indicated by Scripture itself, about which there is no question; (2) those materials which seem appropriate as types, such as Noah's ark or the cities of refuge in the Old Testament, although they are not identified as such in Scripture; (3) those material about which there is considerable doubt.[6]

Almost eighty-eight years of a life wholly given to the Lord in the midsection of America—the name of Walter Wilson is synonymous with an irenic Bible teaching ministry and aggressive evangelism that touched many.

---

1. Kenneth O. Gangel, *Walter L. Wilson: The Beloved Physician* (Chicago: Moody, 1970), 18.
2. Ibid., 23ff.
3. Ibid., 89.
4. Walter L. Wilson, "There Is a Double Need," *In Green Pastures: Ten Messages to Young People* (Findlay, Ohio: Fundamental Truth Publishers, 1937), 13ff. Here he joins others such as Dan Gilbert, Percy Crawford, and Paul Rood.
5. Walter L. Wilson, *The Doctor's Best Love Story* (Chicago: Moody, 1936). Like Moorhouse on John 3:16.
6. Walter L. Wilson, *Wilson's Dictionary of Bible Types* (Grand Rapids: Eerdmans, 1957). A compendium.

12.8.6 Alan Redpath—The Preacher as Motivator

> It is my conviction that the message, which lives and burns as a fire in the heart of the preacher, is that which he has received from the Lord Himself in his own personal quiet time and waiting upon God. Commentaries and other textbooks may be useful additions, but this surely is the supreme thing in all ministry. We are not intended to be copies of other people in the truth we present, but rather to be original. God has

> an individual pattern of ministry for every one of us. For that reason I find that a "Seed-Thought Notebook" is a most valuable part of the equipment of my personal devotional life. As the Word of God speaks in a quiet time, I register in the book some verse or promise which has stood out and then leave it there, remembering that our devotional life is not the time for the preparation of sermons but rather the time for feeding our own hearts. To return to the "Seed-Thought Notebook" for further study and to work at the text as the carpenter works among the shavings on his bench is to find the material beginning to burn and take fire in one's own heart. Complete dependence on the Holy Spirit is essential.
>
> —Alan Redpath

Over the years there has been much pulpit exchange between the United States and Britain. Certainly one of the more vibrant instances was the significant tenure of **Alan Redpath** (1907–1988) in historic Moody Church on Chicago's near north side.

He was born in Newcastle-on-Tyne in England and was a chartered accountant at Imperial Industries, the largest industrial combine in Britain.[1] Redpath obtained training at Durham University and later at Wycliffe Hall, Oxford, and increasingly felt the call of God upon his life for ministry and the preaching of the Word. He spent four years in itinerant ministry with Christian Youth Movement and then took the pastorate for thirteen years at Duke Street Baptist Church in Richmond, Surrey (where Stephen Olford followed him and had such a significant ministry). In 1953 Redpath took the call to the Moody Church, where he labored into the 1960s until returning to Britain. His proximity to Moody Bible Institute and other training schools brought large audiences to his passionate pulpit ministry.[2] His ministry was worldwide, and he was eagerly received at Keswick in England.[3] Redpath followed J. Sidlow Baxter as pastor of Charlotte Baptist Chapel in Edinburgh. Even after a serious stroke, he continued a remarkably diffuse ministry with special emphasis on the deeper things of the Spirit and the victorious Christian life.[4]

Alan Redpath was always disciplined to bring a hot coal out of each biblical text. His discourse was like a lava flow and sizzled with fire from deep within the preacher. At times his intensity was overmastering, but his moral earnestness was radioactive and seismic. One senses this in a collection of sermons preached in a particularly difficult time in this urban church, especially in the messages on forgiveness and powerlessness.[5]

The biblicality of Redpath's preaching can be seen in his marvelous expositions from Joshua; no one has ever preached this book more adeptly. His outlines are helpful and not obtrusive.[6] Likewise his studies in Nehemiah, such as "Building and Battling" from Nehemiah 4:11–23, are sparkling.[7] His illustrative material is in good blend and does not overshadow his work in the text. Most attractive are his courageous messages from First Corinthians in which he faces all of the issues head-on.[8]

Most typical of Redpath are his studies on the Lord's Prayer in which we sense the secret to his immense spiritual passion.[9] The severe acculturation of the North American and British churches was hard on such a sensitive follower of Christ as Alan Redpath. But the sheer consistency of his devotion to the Word and to

Christ was itself part of the very great legacy and gift he left to us who follow and carry on.

---

1. Clarence S. Roddy, *We Prepare and Preach* (Chicago: Moody, 1959), 134, on Alan Redpath.
2. The president of MBI during these years was Dr. William Culbertson, earlier a bishop of the Reformed Episcopal Church and a preacher of great insight and pastoral sensitivity. His Keswick messages from 1957 titled *God's Provision for Holy Living* (Chicago: Moody, 1957) and his keynote sermons from Founder's Week called *The Faith Once Delivered* (Chicago: Moody, 1972) are outstanding. See also Warren Wiersbe, *William Culbertson: A Man of God* (Chicago: Moody, 1974). Laid back in comparison with Redpath, he yet had a quiet, compelling word.
3. Alan Redpath, "When Jesus is Enthroned," in *Keswick's Triumphant Voice,* ed. Herbert F. Stevenson (Grand Rapids: Zondervan, 1963), 401ff. A thoughtful exposition of 2 Samuel 5.
4. Herbert F. Stevenson, ed. *The Keswick Week: 1975—Centenary Year* (London: Marshall, Morgan, and Scott, 1975), 75ff. A typical Redpath sermon titled "The Christian Revolution" is based on a probing exposition of Colossians 3:1ff.
5. Alan Redpath, *Learning to Live* in the Preaching for Today series (Grand Rapids: Eerdmans, 1961), 77ff., 39ff.
6. Alan Redpath, *Victorious Christian Living: Studies in the Book of Joshua* (Westwood, N.J.: Revell, 1955).
7. Alan Redpath, *Victorious Christian Service: Studies in the Book of Nehemiah* (Westwood, N.J.: Revell, 1958), 94ff.
8. Alan Redpath, *The Royal Route to Heaven: Studies in 1 Corinthians* (Westwood, N.J.: Revell, 1960).
9. Alan Redpath, *Victorious Praying: Studies in the Family Prayer* (Westwood, N.J.: Revell, 1957).

12.8.7 VANCE HAVNER—THE PREACHER AS EXHORTER

> What kind of preaching do we need today? We need the same kind we've always needed. Nothing important has changed. Just because we've split the atom and sent a man to the moon doesn't mean we need a new kind of Christianity. We have a new kind of preacher in some quarters, but we don't need him. . . . You can't preach it like it is if you don't believe it like it was. If you don't believe that the Scriptures are God-breathed and that Jesus Christ was virgin born, that he died for our sins and rose bodily from the grave and is coming again, you can't preach it like it is. You can't preach "Jesus Christ the same yesterday" today, if you don't believe what He was yesterday. For what He was then He is now.
>
> —Vance Havner

A revivalist and an itinerant exhorter to the churches, he was sometimes called the Will Rogers of the American pulpit. **Vance Havner** (1901–1986) filled a unique niche among biblical preachers for a generation, and he has no successor. Billy Graham said of him, "He knew how to preach" and labeled Havner "The most quoted preacher in America."[1]

Havner's Tarheel drawl and his "sanctified sarcasm" are as unforgettable for those who heard him as his piercing, probing soul surgery. He was born in 1901 in Jugtown in Catawba County in the Blue Ridge Mountains of North Carolina. His godly parents had three sons, all of whom became preachers. Havner was converted at age ten, when after a revival meeting he went into the woods and sought after the Lord.[2] He began to study the Bible and at age twelve was a preacher. He stood on a chair behind the pulpit. As the years went by he had a foray into "the marshlands of liberalism," but through reading Machen's *Christianity and Liberalism* he saw the futility of a desupernaturalized gospel and came back to the old faith.[3]

Spending brief periods at Catawba College near home, at Wake Forest College, and one year at Moody Bible Institute, Havner took his first pastorate at Weeksville, North Carolina. In 1934 he took the pastorate of the oldest Baptist church in the south, the historic First Baptist Church of Charleston, South Carolina. He had an effective ministry to this run-down congregation and while there had his first of fifteen invitations to address Moody Founder's Week. He also found his stride as an effective writer. His *Rest Awhile* essays were written after a vicious bout with insomnia, and through his life he alternated essays with volumes of sermons.[4]

In 1940 Havner began an itinerant ministry of awakening and renewal in the churches, and the following year he was married. He headquartered at first in Minneapolis and then later and permanently in Greensboro, North Carolina. He was especially close to Donald Grey Barnhouse, W. B. Riley, and Will Houghton at Moody during these years. The great burden of his heart was for revival in the churches.

His sermons were not structured traditionally but were anchored in a text which the preacher developed in his creative and pictorial manner. He painted the picture. He made it come alive. His study of the need for fire from heaven is movingly developed in "Road to Revival" from 1 Kings 18.[5] Havner's sermon on the man from Matthew 22:1–14 who came but went to hell can never be erased from the hearer's mind. "And he stood speechless . . ."[6] The pithy, tangy discourse and his ability as a semanticist to find the arresting epigram are part of what made people listen and say, "He can really keep people awake."[7] He could be more expository and exegetical as in his famous sermon on the Book of Amos in one message. He was persuaded along with Finney that "We must have exciting and powerful preaching or the devil will have the people."[8]

Havner could be very tender as well as searing.[9] He was designated Preacher of the Year by *Decision* magazine in 1973. Over his lifetime, he conducted more than one thousand revival campaigns and conferences and preached more than thirteen thousand times. Half a million of his books were sold to untold blessing. The homegoing of his wife left him devastated, and the sermon he preached on the day she died and then afterward is on a par with Arthur John Gossip's similar message (cf. 12.4.1).[10]

But there is more here than a theology of nostalgia. Havner's rapid-fire, blunt, severe call for repentance is exactly what the contemporary church and all Christians today need. He is right that for many congregations the pastor's preaching time could be described as "how tedious and tasteless the hours." He is correct that while we sing "Throw out the Lifeline" we don't seem to have enough pep to hang out the clothes.

Vance Havner's own testimony was steady: "I just love to point Him out!"[11] He wanted his epitaph to be, "Just a preacher."

---

1. Douglas M. White, *Vance Havner: Journey from Jugtown* (Old Tappan, N.J.: Revell, 1977), 164.
2. Ibid., 25.
3. Ibid., 51, 68.
4. Vance Havner, *Rest Awhile* (New York: Revell, 1941). A great chapter on "Country Preaching," 13ff.
5. Vance Havner, *Road to Revival* (New York: Revell, 1940), 9ff. See also *It Is Time* (New York: Revell, 1943).
6. Vance Havner, *Blood, Bread and Fire* (Grand Rapids: Zondervan, 1939), 70ff.
7. White, *Vance Havner*, 124.
8. Havner, *Blood, Bread and Fire*, 124.
9. Vance Havner, *Peace Like a River* (New York: Revell, 1942); *Rest for the Weary* (New York: Revell, 1946).
10. Vance Havner, *Just a Preacher: Selected Messages from a Doctor of Souls* (Chicago: Moody, 1981), 17ff.
11. Vance Havner, *The Best of Vance Havner* (Old Tappan, N.J.: Revell, 1969), 43.

12.8.8 A. W. Tozer—The Preacher as Disturber

> But for the searching of the Scripture and true knowledge of them, an honorable life is needed, and a pure soul, and that virtue which is according to Christ; so that the intellect guiding its path by it, may be able to attain what it desires and to comprehend it, in so far as it is accessible to human nature to learn concerning the word of God. For without a pure mind and a modeling of the life after the saints, a man could not possibly comprehend the words of the saints. He that would comprehend the mind of those who speak of God needs begin by washing and cleansing his soul.
>
> The best rule is: Go to God first about the meaning of any text. Then consult the teachers.
>
> A church can wither as surely under the ministry of soulless Bible exposition as it can where no Bible is given at all.
>
> Many a splendid church has drifted into modernism because its leaders

> would not insist on the everlasting importance of the basic doctrines of the faith; and many a church split has resulted from an undue attachment to nonessentials.
>
> —A. W. Tozer

Known variously as oracle, seer, sage, gadfly, Christian mystic, and the conscience of American evangelicalism, **A. W. Tozer** (1897–1963) called himself a minor prophet. He was born the third of six children on a farm near what is now called Newburg in the hills of western Pennsylvania. His paternal grandmother, a Scotch-Irish Presbyterian, was God's chief voice to young Tozer. The family moved to Akron, Ohio, where at eighteen he was converted and joined the Methodist church, though he was immersed in the Brethren Church.[1] He had the joy of leading his mother and sisters to Christ.[2]

Almost at once he began open-air preaching. Becoming *persona non grata* with the Methodists, Tozer joined the Christian and Missionary Alliance Church. For two summers he traveled through West Virginia preaching in schoolhouses with his sister's husband. During World War I, Tozer served in the army.

In 1919 Tozer took appointment as pastor in Nutter Fort, West Virginia. Subsequently he had good charges in Morgantown, West Virginia; Toledo, Ohio; and Indianapolis, Indiana. He and his wife, Ada, prayed for the filling of the Holy Spirit, and the clear touch of God was on his ministry.[3]

In 1928 he was recommended by R. R. Brown, then superintendent of the western district, to become pastor of the relatively new Southside Alliance Church in Chicago.[4] The church met in a remodeled garage and grew considerably during the thirty-one years of his remarkable preaching ministry. A new church seating eight hundred was eventually built, but he never drew huge crowds—his Sunday morning attendance averaged between four and five hundred.

Tozer did not do pastoral work at all and was rather antisocial except to a small group of friends. He cherished solitude and really quite neglected his wife and seven children.[5] He disliked organizations, though he served on the CMA board of managers for many years. In 1950 he began his celebrated editorship of the *Alliance Weekly,* later the *Alliance Witness* and now *Alliance Life.* Many subscribed to the magazine just to read his editorials. One of his last editorials was titled "The Waning Authority of Christ in the Churches."[6]

Leonard Ravenhill was not sure that Tozer was the greatest preacher he had ever heard, but he did believe Tozer had greater intimacy with God than any other person he had known.[7] For Tozer "the exaltation of the Triune God" was primary. His works on *The Pursuit of God* and his more theological *The Knowledge of the Holy* are classics.[8] He boasted that he never took a vacation or a day off, but he did seek the solitudes.[9] He never owned or drove a car—instead he bought books.[10] He loved the classics and read deeply in the mystics. He read *Paradise Lost* through four times aloud in order to strengthen his voice since it was not a strong preaching voice. Tozer wrote poetry and his song-leader, Raymond McAfee, put some of his verse to song.

Tozer was concerned about sound doctrine.[11] He correctly saw that figures of speech and metaphors can illustrate truth but not originate it.[12] He claimed that he was a Calvinist when he prayed and an Arminian when he preached.[13] Curiously he did seem to believe in the indefectible ability of a person even as a sinner to obey God's commandments (like Finney).[14] He was a maverick and a character. Slightly built and spare, he stood on his toes when preaching, holding his Bible in his left hand when he got going in the sermon. He used much humor (more when he was tired) and was "an incurable tease," though his humor and his illustrations are for the most part edited out of his printed sermons.

Having studied cartooning when young, Tozer's "lively imagination and eloquent descriptive powers" were striking. "Get the idea clear" was his consuming drive, and he always seemed to have just the right word. He was a great storyteller, loved music and nature, and had a long radio ministry. But as a result of overextending himself, he had a heart attack in 1952.

When the Southside Alliance Church faced the issue of relocation, Tozer felt they needed another type of leader. He resigned and took the pastorate of the large central city Avenue Road Church in Toronto, continuing with his writing and editorial duties. This was a hard decision for him, but he had good years in this pulpit. Interestingly he and D. Martyn Lloyd-Jones in London were good friends in the kind of exemplary evangelical networking that is needed today.

Tozer lambasted book digests, religious movies, gospel choruses, "hillbillyism in religion," social climbing, and a host of other issues which tended to make people uncomfortable and which, he reported to Lloyd-Jones, had preached him right off most stateside conference platforms.[15] His critics found him insufficiently loyal to the Alliance and spearheaded an effort to depose him from his editorship. They accused him of being overly cynical, too negative, hypercritical, severe, and aloof. His answer was always, "Everything is wrong until God sets it right."[16]

Yet whatever is said, Tozer preached with a laser, as Warren Wiersbe has said. He spent three years leading his congregation through John's gospel. His expositions from Hebrews in two volumes are outstanding.[17] His sermons on the Holy Spirit (edited by Gerald B. Smith) are a tonic.[18] Many of his forty books were edited after his passing. He had the burden for the shallowness of evangelical worship long before the present resurgence.[19] His love for the mystics adumbrated the current renewal of interest of classic devotional works.[20] Tozer is always good for us and works us over instead of serving up self-esteem pablum.[21] His analysis of the cult of entertainment, the cult of imitation, and the cult of celebrity are even more current and relevant than when he first shared it. Although he has been many years dead, thousands still read the preaching and writing of A. W. Tozer. The Word speaks the truth of it: "Those who impart wisdom will shine like the brightness of the heavens, and those who lead many to righteousness, like the stars for ever and ever" (Dan. 12:3).

---

1. David J. Fant Jr., *A. W. Tozer: A Twentieth-Century Prophet* (Harrisburg, Pa: Christian Publications, 1964), 14.
2. James L. Snyder, *The Pursuit of God: The Life of A. W. Tozer* (Camp Hill, Pa.: Christian Publications, 1991), 41.
3. Ibid., 44.

4. Ibid., 208. R. R. Brown, who pastored the Omaha Gospel Tabernacle for many years, had an early and effective radio ministry. He was himself an unusually gifted and lively preacher with a great sense of humor.
5. Ibid., 8.
6. Fant, *A. W. Tozer,* 88.
7. Ibid., 1.
8. A. W. Tozer, *The Pursuit of God* (Harrisburg, Pa.: Christian Publications, 1948); *The Knowledge of the Holy* (New York: Harpers, 1961). Under family pressure, Tozer published "his crowning literary achievement" with a secular house. See Snyder, *The Pursuit of God,* 127. This is a study of the attributes of God suffused with the spirit of true worship and awe.
9. Fant, *A. W. Tozer,* 63, 80.
10. Snyder, *The Pursuit of God,* 182.
11. A. W. Tozer, *A Treasury of A. W. Tozer* (Grand Rapids: Baker, 1980), 174ff.
12. Fant, *A. W. Tozer,* 81.
13. Ibid., 67. To hold to man's moral ability is to deny human depravity. Even Reinhold Niebuhr saw "the relevance of an impossible ethical ideal"; see *An Interpretation of Christian Ethics* (New York: Living Age Books, 1956), 97ff.
14. A. W. Tozer, *Paths to Power* (Harrisburg, Pa.: Christian Publications, n.d.), 29ff.
15. Snyder, *The Pursuit of God,* 112.
16. Fant, *A. W. Tozer,* 24. Another preacher very much like Tozer was L. E. Maxwell, longtime head of Prairie Bible Institute, Three Hills, Alberta, Canada. To have both Tozer and Maxwell on the same platform was a heavy dose. Maxwell's works, *Born Crucified, Crowded to Christ,* and *Abandoned to Christ,* are incendiary.
17. A. W. Tozer, *Jesus, Our Man in Glory* and *Jesus, Author of Our Faith* (Camp Hill, Pa.: Christian Publications, 1988).
18. A. W. Tozer, *Ten Sermons on the Ministry of the Holy Spirit* (Harrisburg, Pa.: Christian Publications, 1968).
19. A. W. Tozer, *Worship—The Missing Jewel of the Evangelical Church* (Harrisburg, Pa.: Christian Publications, 1961).
20. A. W. Tozer, *The Christian Handbook of Mystical Verse* (Harrisburg, Pa.: Christian Publications, 1963).
21. Snyder, *The Pursuit of God,* 122.

The history of faithful and effective biblical preaching continues on to this hour. The record is unfinished until Christ completes his chosen bride and translates her from this earth to heaven. Our preaching of this week may be part of the chronicle as we treasure God's Word and trust his Spirit.

EPILOGUE

The Prospects for Preaching

Look in the scroll of the LORD and read.

—Isaiah 34:16

On what are you basing this confidence of yours?

—Isaiah 36:4b

The word of our God stands forever.

—Isaiah 40:8b

From Whence We Have Come

Preaching is to be taken seriously as proclamation of the living Word of the regnant Christ . . . In its essence it is nothing less than an eschatological event, an act in which, for a moment, the kingly Christ stands revealed among men, and He is shown forth before them as indeed Christus Victor. It is altogether proper to speak of the pulpit as the throne of the Word of God and of the sermon as the "Monstrance of the Evangel."

—Daniel Jenkins

Certain general principles can fairly be drawn from our extended historical inquiry.

1. When preaching has been strong in the Christian church, the church has been strong; when preaching has been weak, the church has been weak. Preaching is by no means the only factor, but it is an obvious and a critical one.
2. A high view of scriptural authority leads to and sustains a high view of preaching. What we believe about the Bible and its authority will shape our view of preaching.
3. Only a high view of Scripture and of preaching focuses on and sustains the

proclamation of the *kerygma* (i.e., the saving death and resurrection of Jesus Christ). Liturgy may contain the gospel, but the gospel must be supported by preaching.

4. Rhetorical forms used in preaching are many and diverse and are culturally conditioned, but as in all contextualization of truth, assiduous care must be taken to avoid distortion. "The author (or preacher) cannot choose to avoid rhetoric; we can only choose the kind of rhetoric we shall employ."[1] Rhetoric is how we speak. Among the various rhetorical forms used in the history of preaching, the chief are the classical homily and its derivative, the Bible reading; the essay sermon of neoclassicism; the university or scholastic sermon; the modified modern sermon; and the Puritan sermon (please note appendix 3).
5. Many shoals and reefs loom before preachers, threatening disaster. These obstacles may be doctrinal, spiritual, moral, or relational. The history of preaching lays bare our human frailty and our unceasing need for dependence on the Holy Spirit in every aspect of our lives and endeavors. Much wreckage is strewn along the way.
6. At the most unexpected times and in the most unpromising of circumstances, the rediscovery of the power of the Word of God and its proclamation have been blessed of God to the renewal and the reviving of the Christian church.
7. The centers of ecclesiastical power have often been indifferent to the primacy of the preached Word and have been seduced to a fixation on other programmatic emphases, but frequently the despised and disparaged have risen with the anointing of God upon their preaching and have been catalytic in spiritual renaissance and transformation.
8. The history of preaching discloses an amazing and unpredictable networking of the Spirit, like Tozer and Lloyd-Jones. God brings it about!

Where We Are

> This hearing of the Word of God, hearing what the Lord of the Church wants to say to His Church in its actual situation, is the primary task of the Church, the basic human action in worship.
>
> —C. E. B. Cranfield

> The most effective preachers, those whose preaching is life-changing, are expository preachers. They tell and interpret the biblical story.
>
> —Lyle Schaller

With the complete collapse of the dream of the secular city, our society is in a mood of perpetual crisis. The West is in moral and spiritual crisis. While elements of the religious core of our culture remain, Woody West is correct that consensual truth, agreed-upon standards, and institutions that demand and deserve allegiance have largely disappeared. He quotes David Gelernter's re-creation of the United States in 1939 to the effect that "The most marked difference from this country today, nearly sixty years down the slope, is the absence of authority."[2] Before he died, Norman Cousins lamented the disrespect for coherent thought process and the resultant "communication collapse."[3]

Many in the homiletics of the left have capitulated to the new hermeneutic and abandoned any serious effort to break the lock of the original meaning of the biblical text.[4] Evangelicals, conversely, have been tempted by user-friendly and market-driven considerations to give up on a truly serious effort to transmit a biblical passage in its context with strong application for life. Taking the thought out of a text and preaching it rather than preaching the biblical text is now passing for expository preaching.[5] In either case, the danger is a cultural accommodation which is at best a mutation of the gospel. Even H. Richard Niebuhr saw this danger for preaching in the "Christ of culture" approach:

> The point of contact they seek to find with their hearers dominates the whole sermon; and in many instances the resultant portrait of Christ is little more than a personification of an abstraction. Jesus stands for the idea of spiritual knowledge; or of logical reason; or of the sense of the infinite; or of the moral law within; or of brotherly love.[6]

Others stand somewhat defensively, echoing the existentialist and neo-orthodox insistence that reality not ideas must be our primary concern and that the personal must be stressed over the propositional. This presents something of a challenge to the pulpit communicator. Clearly a false dichotomy is being advanced, since our choice is not between reality and ideas nor between the personal and the propositional. Yet many earnest preachers feel torn between teaching the Bible and addressing the hurts and manifest needs of humankind. Many practitioners are laid low by doubts about the craft and are confused in the face of conflicting counsel. The history of preaching shows that while these dilemmas have particular poignancy in our time, they are not new issues or concerns. Again and again, in its ministry in local parishes or around the world in a missionary context, these tensions have been felt acutely. Our study has repeatedly rehearsed God's faithfulness to bless his Word.

Anthony Trollope in 1875 spoke the truth when he averred in *Barchester Towers* that "There is, perhaps, no greater hardship at present inflicted on mankind in civilized and free countries, than the necessity of listening to sermons." This must be seen as a reflection not upon the craft but upon the craftsmen. The problems in preaching are not the problem of the Word but of those who work with the Word. In a time of massive societal, intellectual, and religious change, preachers find themselves awash in discussions about preaching and its future. Shifting paradigms on every side raise crucial questions about the craft. One leader insists that "Jesus never preached an expository sermon or a doctrinal sermon" with lamentable and dangerous conclusions. This is to cave in to the "feel-good factor" and the "look-good factor." The result is country-club Christianity with lavender-water theology. This is where we are today.

Whither Shall We Go?

> The supreme work of the Christian minister is the work of preaching. This is a day in which one of our great perils is that of doing a thousand little things to the neglect of one thing, which is preaching.
>
> —G. Campbell Morgan

> Preaching in America is not going to improve until the preachers once again believe in preaching, both in its content and its method.
>
> —John R. Brokhoff

Of course we cannot enter the new century and the new millennium (should our Lord tarry) by looking through the back mirror. The study of any past era or the vain attempt to recapture a bygone time will not suffice—an insight missed by some of our neo-Puritan enthusiasts. How then shall we face what one news commentator described as "a new form of popular religion, the rock-and-roll church with its nocturnal, narcissistic, mischievous anti-authoritarian creed"?[7] The history of biblical preaching leaves us with some clear directives. Our duty is to:

1. Stand staunchly with classical biblical faith and its worldview, espousing confidence in the Scriptures through its positive proclamation and a vigorous apologetic.
2. Uphold the cruciality of systematic biblical exposition with a strong dedication to modeling the study of a passage in its context with appropriate application.
3. Loyally practice the necessary wedding of sound exegesis to lively exposition.
4. Increasingly become devotees of the most careful and responsible hermeneutic with its relentless commitment to finding the original meaning of the text with the help of all available tools and resources.
5. Continue to seek to know the filling of the Holy Spirit, the divine author of Scripture, upon whom we must totally rely at every stage of sermon preparation and delivery.
6. Remain avid students of the craft of preaching, seeking to grow in every aspect of its practice.
7. Be open to cultivate skills in new forms, as in the present renewal of interest in the narrative portions of Scripture and their more effective presentation.
8. Be unwavering in our conviction of the essential Christ-centeredness of preaching and to neglect no portion of revealed truth and to avoid no doctrine, for all is profitable.
9. Never step back from the quest for excellence as those called by God to preach.
10. Conscientiously and wholeheartedly seek that integrity and uprightness of character and conduct which will never bring the gospel or our Lord into disrepute.[8]
11. Remember humbly that we are heirs of faithful heralds through the ages and that we stand on their shoulders as we fulfill the task of our time.

12. Rest in the power of Almighty God, our divine sovereign, whose we are and whom we serve. "The battle is the Lord's," and he will have the victory over all principalities and powers through the blood of our Lord Jesus Christ and "the word of our testimony" (Rev. 12:11). The outcome is not in doubt. Thus preaching has a great and glorious future.

> Now to him who is able to establish you by my gospel and the proclamation of Jesus Christ, according to the revelation of the mystery hidden for long ages past, but now revealed and made known through the prophetic writings by the command of the eternal God, so that all nations might believe and obey him—to the only wise God be glory forever through Jesus Christ! Amen.
>
> —Romans 16:25–26

---

1. Wayne C. Booth, *The Rhetoric of Fiction* (Chicago: University of Chicago Press, 1961, 1983), 149.
2. Woody West, "Decline in Authority . . . Demise of Democracy," *Insight* (November 18, 1996): 48.
3. Norman Cousins, "The Communication Collapse," *Time* (December 17, 1990): 114.
4. Craig A. Loscalzo, in *Hermeneutics for Preaching,* ed. Raymond Bailey (Nashville: Broadman, 1992). He shows that David Buttrick rejects the idea that biblical texts "are locked up tight in a vault labeled 'Original Meaning' . . . The world assembled before the cross is ever different, and patterns of being-saved-in-the-world are thus ever-changing" (116). Thomas Long's abandonment of classical exegesis is similar; see "The Use of Scripture in Contemporary Preaching," *Interpretation* (October 1990): 341ff.
5. As an example, Harold T. Bryson, *Expository Preaching* (Nashville: Broadman, 1995), 32.
6. H. Richard Niebuhr, *Christ and Culture* (New York: Harper, 1951), 109. Niebuhr asserts, "It seems impossible to remove the offense of Christ and his cross even by means of these accommodations; and cultural Christians share in the general limitation all Christianity encounters whether it fights or allies itself with the 'world'" (108).
7. Tom Brokaw in John Howard, *A Sure Compass* (Rockford, Ill.: Rockford Institute, 1992), 5. We have seen the stubborn persistence of moralistic and at times Pelagian preaching in the American pulpit. Kurt Hamsum, the Norwegian Nobel Prize winner of some years ago, observed that the sermons he heard in the U.S. "did not contain theology but morality . . . they do not develop the mind, though they are entertaining." God help us.
8. Billy Graham, quoted in Craig A. Loscalzo, *Evangelistic Preaching That Connects* (Downers Grove, Ill.: InterVarsity Press, 1995), 12. Graham's most timely word is "Our world today is looking primarily for men and women of integrity, communicators who back up their ministry with their lives." Graham's own unflinching stand for biblical inerrancy and the centrality of the cross of Christ in preaching is well known. See Stephen F. Olford, *A Passion for Preaching: Reflections on the Art of Preaching* (Nashville: Thomas Nelson, 1989), 126.

Appendix One

Nominations for the Fifteen Most Significant Sermons in Church History

1. Jesus Christ, The Sermon on the Mount (Matthew 5–7).
2. The apostle Peter, Sermon on the Day of Pentecost (Acts 2).
3. The apostle Paul, Sermon on the Areopagus in Athens (Acts 17).
4. Chrysostom (John of Antioch), "Homily Concerning the Statues" (Genesis 3).
5. Bernard of Clairvaux, "On Conversion: A Sermon to Clerics" (Acts 13:44; Luke 19:10).
6. Martin Luther, "The Gift of God" (John 3:16–21).
7. John Wesley, "The New Birth" (John 3:7).
8. George Whitefield, "Christ the Believer's Wisdom, Righteousness, Sanctification and Redemption" (1 Corinthians 1:30).
9. Jonathan Edwards, "Sinners in the Hands of an Angry God" (Deuteronomy 32:35).
10. William Carey, "Sermon to the Association at Nottingham" (Isaiah 54:2–3; see 8.4.3).
11. Charles Haddon Spurgeon, "Christ the Cure of Troubled Hearts" (Luke 24:38).
12. Lyman Beecher, "The Bible as a Code of Laws" (see 9.2.6).
13. J. Stuart Holden, "But if not . . ." (Daniel 3:18, preached just before World War I; see 11.7.4).
14. William E. Sangster, "This Britain: What Would a Revival Do for Britain?" (This sermon hit front-page headlines in big type at a particularly vexing time for Britain; see 11.6.7).
15. Robert G. Lee, "Pay Day, Some Day" (1 Kings 21; preached one thousand times; see 12.2.6).

APPENDIX TWO

Nominations for the Greatest Sermons in Literature

Many writers, among them Charles Dickens, Anthony Trollope, and Susan Howatch have written insightfully about preachers, but in some literature preaching itself is highlighted:

1. Father Mapple's sermon from Jonah 1 in Herman Melville's *Moby Dick.* Something of the range of diverse interpretation of the sermon is reflected in D. Bruce Lockerbie, "The Greatest Sermon in History," *Christianity Today* (November 8, 1963): 9ff.
2. Dr. Primrose's unusual sermon "On Providence," preached in prison where he is incarcerated because of debt in Oliver Goldsmith's *The Vicar of Wakefield.*
3. Father Zossima's sermon on John 12:24 from Dostoevsky's *The Brothers Karamazov.* For an appreciation of this sermon, see Eugene H. Peterson, *Under the Unpredictable Plant: An Exploration of Vocational Holiness* (Grand Rapids: Eerdmans, 1992) 49, 66–67.
4. The Reverend Cyril Maitland's two sermons in Maxwell Gray's *The Silence of Dean Maitland,* the first where under his guilt he is unable to finish his sermon (an experience Arthur Dimsdale in *The Scarlet Letter* never had), and his later sermon (and his last) in the little church at Malbourne, where he confesses his sin.
5. The Reverend Robert Elsmere's sermon on Jesus' first sermon from Luke 4:14ff. in Mrs. Humphry Ward's novel, *Robert Elsmere.* The story traces the inward spiritual and intellectual struggle of this Oxford clergyman in the Victorian/Edwardian tensions between faith and reason. The author describes his preaching on this occasion: "The preacher forgot all but his Master and his people."

6. The ambitious Pastor Theron Ware's magnificently well-received conference sermon in Harold Frederic's *The Damnation of Theron Ware* did not get him the big church he had hoped for and indeed only hastened his downfall.
7. The army chaplain preached a great sermon from Ezekiel 37, on the resurrection of dry bones, in Anthony Powell's gripping *The Valley of the Bones,* volume 7 in his twelve-volume Music of Time series. This sermon was preached to the troops facing the oppression of the German initiative. With Kipling and Proust as his models, Powell magnificently traces one hundred characters in slow motion.
8. Most unexpectedly, in A. N. Wilson's *Gentlemen in England,* Father Cuthbert preaches on "the old, old story of Jesus and his love" and confronts his audience with the contemporary Christ. Lionel Netttleship "realized he had never accepted Jesus Christ, God and Man, as his personal Savior. He had never opened his heart to Jesus and let him in, to change and purify his whole life. And now during the singing of the hymn he did so, and he felt his whole being suffused with a glow which he knew to be the sure token of our Lord's presence with him" (61, 63).
9. In William Faulkner's *The Sound and the Fury,* which traces the incredible confusion in the Compson family in Yoknapatawpha, Mississippi. The one stable figure appears to be the black servant, Dilsey, whose poise and perspective on Easter Sunday of 1928 are guided and enlightened by an Easter sermon she heard preached in St. Louis. She shares it.
10. Archbishop Thomas Becket's sermon preached on Christmas morning in Canterbury Cathedral, 1170, from Luke 2:10–11. The sermon in T. S. Eliot's play *Murder in the Cathedral* serves as an interlude between Act I and Act II. It centers on Christ's birth and the implication of his death.
11. George MacDonald treats several sermons in his clergy novels from Scotland including the Reverend James Blatherwick preaching before Isy in *The Minister's Restoration* and more notably the young cleric's sermon in *The Curate's Awakening*.
12. Corporal Trim reads the sermon by the Rev. Yorick from Hebrews 13:18 at York in Laurence Stern's pioneering novel *Tristam Shandy* (1759).
13. In the American poet Sidney Lanier's great early poem, "Jacquerie," a Franciscan father, Friar John, preaches a memorable sermon out of Revelation 6 on the seals of the Apocalypse, in which he indicts war, praises the martyrs (like Savonarola), and calls for a "vast undoing of things" (Book 2).
14. In George Eliot's *Adam Bede,* the woman Methodist preacher, the Rev. Dinah Morris, preaches a sermon on the village green and the entire chapter is given up to it (chapter 11).
15. In *The Portrait of an Artist as a Young Man,* James Joyce shares the rebellion of the young Stephen Daedalus and what is doubtless the greatest sermon on hell ever recorded in fictive literature.

Appendix Three

The Basic Taxonomy of Sermonic Form Through Church History

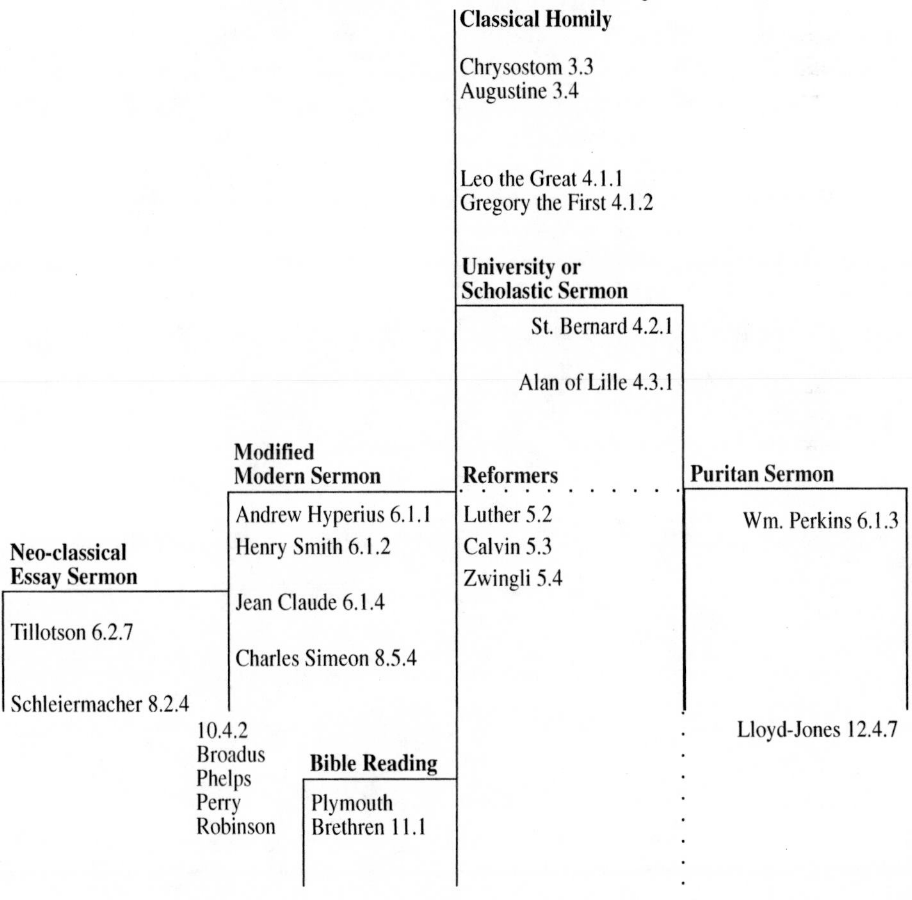

Scripture Index

Genesis

1:16 20
3 853
3:8, 10, 24 21
3:15 630
4:21–24 23
6:3 55
6:9 23
11 589
11:7 20
18:17ff 23
20:7 23
32 581
39:2 184
44 24
48:11 702

Exodus

6:12 24
7:1ff 24
8 780
17 314
20:1 23
24:11 569
31:18 23
34:27–28 23

Numbers

22–24 24
22:28 24
28:9 266
31:8, 16 24

Deuteronomy

5:5 12
18:15 23
18:18 23
19:16 25
32:35 853
33:27 21

Joshua

10 780
10:12–14 780
10:14 541

Judges

3 116
9 24

Ruth

1:14 735

1 Samuel

1:22 205
3:1 . . . . 25, 354
3:19 640
10:5–10 31
10:10 31
19:10 31
19:23 31
20:18 732
22:2 704
24:14 743

2 Samuel

22:31 199
23:2 199

1 Kings

8:27–30 34
8:65 471
18 842
18:43 704
21 853
22:14 . . . . 31, 713

2 Kings

2:3–7, 15–18 31
4:23 34
4:38 31
5:11, 15 618
6:1–2 31
22:8 741

2 Chronicles

6:18 439
15:1ff 31
17:9 22
20:14 31

24 . . . 447
29 . . . 447
34 . . . 684
34:14 . . . 24
34:15, 22–23 . . . 22
35:18 . . . 29
36:14–21 . . . 24
36:15 . . . 25

Ezra

5:1 . . . 30
6:14 . . . 30
7:10 . . . 33
8:21 . . . 267

Nehemiah

3 . . . 680
4:11–23 . . . 840
8:3b–5, 7–8 . . . 33
9:30 . . . 31

Job

5:23 . . . 626
22:21 . . . 503

Psalms

7:12 . . . 585
7:14 . . . 281
16:8 . . . 704
16:9 . . . 616
19:7–11 . . . 63
22 . . . 154
23 . . . 746
24 . . . 550
29:4 . . . 12
31:15 . . . 537
39:3 . . . 22
42:10 . . . 281
50:1–3a . . . 12
68:11 . . . 9
73 . . . 777
84:11 . . . 636
85:6 . . . 358
89:14 . . . 343
96:10 . . . 67
99:6 . . . 34
100 . . . 334
105:15 . . . 23
110:1 . . . 313
119 . . . 286, 391
119:9 . . . 141, 676
119:11 . . . 141
119:18 . . . 141
119:28 . . . 141
119:42 . . . 141
119:54 . . . 831
119:89 . . . 19
119:89–96 . . . 467
119:103 . . . 141
119:105 . . . 141
119:107b . . . 358
119:160 . . . 141
126:6 . . . 383
138:2b . . . 12
145:11 . . . 412
145:13b . . . 19
147:15 . . . 665

Proverbs

3:5–7 . . . 835
6:14 . . . 25
6:16ff. . . . 734
10 . . . 90
12:17 . . . 25
14:5 . . . 25
14:12 . . . 612
15:23 . . . 249
19:5, 28 . . . 25
21:28 . . . 25
30:5–6 . . . 19

Ecclesiastes

12:9–12a . . . 25

Song of Solomon

1:17 . . . 630

Isaiah

1–39 . . . 28
2:5–6 . . . 85
6 . . . 28, 732
8:3 . . . 28
9:6 . . . 136
12:3–5 . . . 287
21:11–12 . . . 663
24:9 . . . 184
26:4 . . . 503
34:16 . . . 847
35:8–10 . . . 543
36:4b . . . 847
40–66 . . . 28
40:3 . . . 38
40:8b . . . 847
40:22 . . . 751
44:3–4 . . . 422
45:20–22 . . . 23
45:22 . . . 584
50:4 . . . 278
51:7 . . . 377
51:16 . . . 12
52:7 . . . 417
53 . . . 424
54:1 . . . 66
54:2–3 . . . 388, 853
55:10–11 . . . 12, 21, 383
61 . . . 41
64:6 . . . 838
66:2 . . . 20, 700

Jeremiah

1 . . . 29
1:4–5 . . . 26
1:7 . . . 440
6:10 . . . 26
7 . . . 29, 32
8:20 . . . 432, 442
9:24 . . . 11
12:5 . . . 616, 764
15:9 . . . 412
15:19d–20 . . . 272
20 . . . 29
20:9 . . . 26
23:28 . . . 556
23:29 . . . 135
27 . . . 32
28:15 . . . 33
31 . . . 29
35 . . . 559
36:23 . . . 741
44:28b, 29b . . . 828

Lamentations

3:27 . . . 814

Ezekiel

1–3 . . . 29
1:1 . . . 29
2:2 . . . 31
3:12, 14 . . . 31
8 . . . 29

8:1 34
9:3 296
11:16 34
14:1 34
18 29
20:1 34
25:3–4 743
25:15–24 29
33:11 284
33:32 199
34 29
35–36 29
36 559
36:25–26 318
36:37 559
37 . . . . 29, 397, 856
37:1ff 31
37:1–14 615
38–39 29
40–48 29
47 536

Daniel

1–6 29
1:8 29
2 29
2:45 780
3:18 . . . . 704, 853
6 29
7 29
7–12 29
9:24–27 610
12:3 . . . . 525, 845

Hosea

1:2 27
8:14 27
10:12 837
14:1–3 27
14:4–8 27

Joel

1 27
2:12–17 27

Amos

3:8 . . . . 27, 32
4:12 397
7:10–17 27
8:11 . . . . 12, 98

9 49
9:11–14 27
50:1–3a 12
68:11 9
73 777
84:11 636
85:6 358
89:14 343
96:10 67
99:6 34

Obadiah

1 27
17 27

Jonah

1 855

Micah

1:1 28
1:8–9 28
2:6–7 28
3:8 . . . . 28, 31
5:2–4 28
6:6–8 595
6:8 28
7:19 28

Nahum

1:1 28
1:7 28

Habakkuk

1:5 53
1:13 28
2:1 28
2:4 28
3:1 358
3:1–19 28
3:16–19 28

Zephaniah

1:1 29
3:17 29

Haggai

1–2 30
1:12 12

Zechariah

1–8 30
1:14 30
3–4 30
4:6–9 271
4:12 31
7:1 31
7:6 30
9–14 30
9:1–10 30
11:2 401
11:4–17 30
12:1 30
12:10 30
14:1–15 30

Malachi

1:1 30
3:1 38
3:13–4:3 30
4:5 196

Matthew

1 745
1:22 42
2:15 42
3:1 38
3:5–6 39
3:7 341
3:13–17 72
4:4 . . . . 235, 249
4:14 42
4:17 41
4:23 52
5–7 . . . . 41, 853
5 42
5:12–14 110
5:13 . . . . 44, 751
5:17–18 42
5:47 596
6:19–21 704
6:23 622
6:27 44
7:3–5 44
7:7–11 118
7:24–27 . . . . 41, 549
7:29 41
8:17 42
9:35 . . . . 41, 52
10:7 41

10:10 498
10:16 44
10:27 41
10:40–41 41
10:42 739
11:2 40
11:4–6 42
11:5 . . . . 40, 52
11:7–19 45
11:7–15 39
11:7 44
11:12 503
11:20–24 45
11:27 46
11:28–30 45
11:28 137
12:18–21 690
12:19 645
12:28 42
12:40 27
12:41 . . . . 27, 32
13 . . . . 44, 55
13:36 53
14:24 545
15:15 53
16–17 766
16 29
16:12 43
16:14 32
16:18 47
16:23 805
16:24 818
17:1–7 743
17:8 541
17:14–18 743
18:12 44
18:21 739
19:24 44
21:22 118
21:33–46 84
21:33–41 74
22:1–14 842
22:8–10 677
22:29 44
22:33 43
23:24 44
24–25 835
24 29
24:14 103
24:17 505
24:36–42 475
25:13–30 756
27:20 118
27:35–36 613
28:18–20 44
28:19–20 514
28:20 632

Mark

1:14 44
1:27 43
1:38 44
3:19 669
3:21 573
4:39 665
5:8 665
5:16 53
6:2b 45
6:20 40
6:34 380
7:15 739
8:11 53
8:36 . . . . 591, 667
9:26–27 739
9:43–48 692
10:17–31 68
10:35ff. 707
10:45 . . . . 41, 56
11:18 43
11:22–24 638
12:37b 44
15:34, 17 775
16:7 669
16:15 514
16:20 64

Luke

1:1–4 63
1:2 48
1:5–17 835
1:17 38
1:19 699
1:29 53
2:10–11 856
2:15 53
2:34–35 356
3:2 39
3:3 39
3:10–14 39
4:1–13 486
4:14 855
4:14–30 41
4:16–20 35
4:18 52
4:21 42
4:32 42
5 807
5:1 42
5:21 53
6:30 118
6:32 44
7:22 52
7:37 234
7:44 53
8–23 522
8:11 . . . . 44, 383
8:34 52
8:39 53
9:10 53
9:26 350
9:60 52
11:30 27
12:8 350
13:1–5 445
15 278
15:7 412
15:11 801
16:2 501
16:19–31 . . . . . . 275, 514, 684
17:26–27 23
19:1–10 677
19:10 . . . . 41, 853
22:42 434
22:43 771
23:26–31 356
23:27–31 805
23:47–49 439
24:14 52
24:15 53
24:17 52
24:19 95
24:25–27 95
24:27 . . . . 43, 156
24:32 95
24:35 53
24:38 853
24:46–47 95

John

1:1 40
1:7–8 52
1:14 534
1:15 52
1:18 53
1:23 235
1:29 . . . . 39, 341, 831
1:32, 34 52
1:35, 39 412
1:42 694
3 . . . . 368, 832
3:1–16 243
3:3, 5 268
3:6 277
3:7 853
3:14–15 439
3:16 . . . . 68, 511, 671
3:16–21 853
3:26 52
3:27 39
3:29 39
3:30 38
3:31 . . . . 40, 46
3:32 743
3:34 46
4 572
4:9–10 118
4:21–24 34
4:28–29 622
4:29 445
4:32–38 552
4:35 555
4:48 437
5:1–24 524
5:19–20 46
5:24 667
5:33 52
5:39 156
6 628
6:12 629
6:37 275
6:57 . . . . 46, 638
6:63 42
7:16–17 43
7:17 669
7:37–39 818
7:46 . . . . 40, 645
8:18 46
8:21–30 760
8:26 46
8:28b 46
8:32 312
8:55 46
9:39 316
10:1 313
10:13 630
10:34–36 12
10:35 42
10:41 39
11 645
11:31 53
12 55
12:24 855
12:32 822
12:37–41 55
13–17 . . . . 59, 663
14 753
14:1–6 674
14:6 596
14:21 440
14:24 46
14:27 335
15 74
15:1 84
15:2 677
15:10 46
15:15 . . . . 47, 53
15:20 498
15:26–27 51
16:5–15 663
16:8–11 54
16:13–15 51–52
16:15 47
16:19 53
16:31–32 461
17 . . . . 190, 286, 577, 652
17:3 190
17:6 47
17:8, 14, 20 40
17:15 105
17:17b 12, 313
17:26 53
18:19 43
19 107
19:30 221
20:8 529
20:21–23 120

Acts

1:8 . . . . 48, 109
1:14 723
1:16–22 49
1:22b 109
2 . . . . 13, 853
2:3 101
2:14–36 49
2:14 54
2:36 54
2:37 . . . . 54, 306
2:38–39 54
2:40 54
2:42 43
2:46–47 732
3:12–26 49
3:14 118
3:20, 24 52
3:25–26 23
3:26 54
4:4 54
4:8–12, 19–20 49
4:12 50
4:15–17 54
4:20 51
5:13 547
5:29–32 49
5:33 54–55
5:42 55
6:3–4 47
6:7 48
6:10 55
6:15 55
7 34
7:2–53 49
7:22 24
7:37 23
7:55–56 55
7:59–60 55
8:1 69
8:4–8 49
8:4 . . . . 47, 69
8:25 52
8:26–40 49
8:33 53
9:20 49
9:25 820
9:27 . . . . 52, 53
9:29 52
9:33–34 777

10:8 53
10:28 53
10:34–43 49
10:39 564
10:43 52
11:5–17 49
11:15a 318
11:26 85
11:29 53
12:17 53
12:24 50
13:5 52
13:13–47 49
13:22 49
13:23 49
13:24 52
13:33 49
13:41 53
13:43 53
13:44 853
13:46 52
14:8–18 49
14:21 55
14:27 52
15:3 53
15:7–11 49
15:12 53
15:13–21 49
16:1 53
16:6 50
16:30–31 684
16:31 . . . . 658, 736
16:38 52
17 . . . . 671, 853
17:1–3 55
17:2 53
17:2–4 53
17:13 52
17:15–34 49
17:16 667
17:17 53
17:32–34 55
18:4 53
18:5 58
18:9–10 58
18:26 52
19 577
19:4 40
19:8 . . . . 52, 53
19:20 54
19:26 53
20:2 52
20:7 53
20:9 53
20:11 52
20:15–38 49
20:24 536
20:31 53
21:12 52
21:19 53
21:26 52
21:27–23:10 49
23:11 52
24 49
24:12 53
24:26 52
25:1–12 49
25:2 52
25:13–26:32 49
26:17b–18 384
26:18 766
26:19 638
26:20 52
26:26 52
26:28 53
26:29 118
26:32 53
27:9, 22 53
28:20 53
28:27 53
28:29 53
28:30 60
28:30–31 55

Romans

1–11 86
1:1–17 827
1:15 . . . . 52, 57
1:16 . . . . 647, 751
1:16–17 57
1:18–32 799
3:2 24
4 518
4:5 838
4:12 306
5–7 577
5:1 766
5:12–21 257
5:12–19 439
6:11 832
6:13 277
7 . . . . 777, 816
8 277
8:3 549
8:11 524
9 194
9:6 199
9:17 52
9:22 53
10:10 475
10:11–12 764
10:13–14 56
10:15 52
10:17 . . . . 21, 56
11 739
12:2 105
12:7 52
12:8 52
12:12 641
13:13–14 88
14:10 365
15:14 53
15:19 53
15:20 . . . . 52, 249, 779
15:21 52
15:29 771
16:25–27 249
16:25–26 851
16:25 43

1 Corinthians

1–4 59
1:11 53
1:17–25 57
1:17 . . . . 52, 57, 346
1:21 . . . . 52, 59, 663
1:23–24 59
1:23 . . . . 52, 705
1:30 853
1:31 488
2:1–5 60
2:1 . . . . 52, 59
2:2 287
2:4 59
2:13 61
3 812
3:13 53
4:14 53
4:16–18 762
4:17 52

5:11 192
7:29–31 422
9:16 . . . . 52, 57
10:12 289
10:15, 19 53
11:4–5 . . . . 52, 60
11:26 . . . . 51, 164
13 . . . . 60, 573
13:1–3 60
13:9 52
13:10 645
14:1, 3–5 52
14:5 59
14:9 132
14:12 622
14:20 365
14:24 52
14:26 60
14:26 51
14:29 60
14:31 60
14:31, 39 52
15 . . . . 543, 671
15:1–12 57
15:1–3 50
15:1–2 61
15:3 . . . . 58, 766
15:11b 320
15:15 52
16:10 814
16:12 52

2 Corinthians

1:18–19 249
1:19–20 719
2:12, 17 249
2:12–4:6 61
2:14 61
2:15 61
2:16 61
2:17 . . . . 61, 249
3:5b 61
4:1–6 57
4:2 61
4:3–4 61
4:5 . . . . 52, 61
4:6 61
4:13 435
4:18 573
5:8 694
5:18 57
5:19–20 . . . . 57, 189
6:2 631
6:7 60
6:17–18 105
7:7 52
8:8 53
10:10 . . . . 53, 58
13:2 53

Galatians

1:3–4 682
1:8–9 470
1:9 57
1:11 57
1:15–16 57
1:16 278
2 63
2:20 . . . . 135, 832
2:21 682
3:1 207
3:8 52
3:13 682
4:4–7 831
4:21–31 . . . . 74, 84
5:21 53
6:14 436

Ephesians

1 60
1:18–20 690
2:3–5 462
2:8–9 . . . . 578, 838
2:8 365
2:17 40
2:20 47
3:5 53
3:8 327
3:10 53
4:1–2 699
4:10–11 499
4:11 830
4:30 569
4:31–32 699
5:16 756
6:19–20 327
6:20 52
6:21 53

Philippians

1:18 95
2:15 358
2:30 728
3:16 309

Colossians

1 559
1:5b–6 327
1:8 53
1:9 118
1:23b 327
1:25 53
1:27–28 678
1:28 53
2:8 554
3:16 . . . . 53, 199
4:3–4 327
4:5 756
4:17 133

1 Thessalonians

1:5 . . . . 61, 415
1:8 415
1:9 52
2:2 . . . . 61, 415
2:4 415
2:8 61
2:9 61
2:12 . . . . 53, 434
2:13 . . . . 13, 415
3:4 53
4:17 84
5:12, 14 53
5:18 552

2 Thessalonians

1:10 337
2:13–14 55
3:1 . . . . 12, 189, 498

1 Timothy

1:15 177
2:5 508
2:12 52
3:16 415
4:11 52

2 Timothy

1:11–12 683

2:8b–10a 415
2:9 498
2:15 . . . . . . 128, 165, 207
3:16–17 . . . . 12, 258
3:16 309
3:17 556
4:2 . . . . . 13, 52, 331, 759
4:5c 679
4:6–8 775
4:16–17 281
4:17 . . . . 53, 416
4:21 820

Titus

1:3 497
2:1, 5b 497
2:14 303
3:3–8 609
3:4–7 702
3:5 838

Hebrews

1:1 61
1:1a 20
2:1 . . . . 354, 389
2:3 . . . . 631, 682
2:9 837
2:12 52
3:15 682
4:2 . . . . 53, 389, 497
4:12 . . . . 497, 700
5:9 631
6:5 . . . . 42, 199
9:26 . . . . 677, 718
10:9 81
10:11–13 831
10:22 503
11 . . . . 314, 684
11:5 23
11:13 30
11:25 545
11:32 53
12 761
12:5 53
12:25 497
12:27 53
13:15 613
13:18 856
13:22 57

James

1:5 118
1:18 . . . . 311, 498
1:21–22 498
1:21b 390
3 522–23
3:17 622
5:11 684
5:17 684

1 Peter

1:10–12 85
1:10 52
1:11 53
1:12 599
1:23–25 599
1:24–25 574
2:3 399
2:9 51
2:24 508
3:15 837
3:19b–20a 40
4:11 . . . . . . 56, 186, 481

2 Peter

1:14 53
1:19–21 84
2:5 23
2:15–16 24
3:9 671

1 John

1:1–3 37
1:1–2 58
1:2 52
1:3 58
1:5 . . . . 52, 58
1:9 830
2:24 149
2:26–27 84
3:2 571
4:4–6 563
4:20 277
5:4 537

2 John

2 5

Jude

1–4 835
3 . . . . 354, 631
4 599
11b 24
14 52
14–15 23
18–19 599

Revelation

1:5 25
2–3 422
2 522–23
3:14 25
3:15 722
4–5 776
6 856
6:9 713
9:13–21 242
11:3 52
12:11 . . . . . 498, 714, 851
12:16 626
14 125
14:6 . . . . 25, 713
21:1 581
21:5 714
21:16 711
22:6 714

Subject Index

Abbott, Lyman 532–33
Abelard 107, 109, 119
abortion 81
Abraham 23
Adams, John 440
Adams, Thomas 262, 264
Addison, Joseph 331
Aelfric 115, 117
Agricola 490
Aidan 111
Aitken, W. Hay 579, 703
Alan of Lille 130, 167, 201, 226, 857
Alban 102
Albert the Great 120
Albert, Prince 458
Albertano of Brescia 119
Alcock, Simon 201
Alcuin 106, 114
Alexander, Archibald 439–41, 522, 540
Alexander, Charles M. 664, 668, 670
Alexander, Maitland 672, 819
Alexander of Ashby 131
Alexandrian School 85
Alford, Henry 464, 552, 615, 756
Alfred, King 114
allegorization 84, 107
Alleine, Joseph 291–92, 344
Alline, Henry 430
Althaus, Paul 796
Ambrose 77–78, 88, 96
Ambrose, Isaac 223
American Bible Society 438
American Revolution 434
American Sunday School Union 539
Ames, William 205, 207, 239, 251, 266
Amos 27, 29
Amyraut, Moses 230
analogia fidei 175
Anderson, Robert 609–10, 737
Andrew of St. Victor 105, 116
Andrewes, Lancelot 193, 211–13
Angus, Joseph 584
Anselm of Canterbury 83, 115, 119
Anselm of Laon 105, 115
Ansgar 112, 494
Anthony of Egypt 105
Anthony of Padua 122, 125
antinomianism 265, 275, 279, 295, 324, 369, 397, 457
Antiochene School 85
Apostle's Creed 72
apostolic preaching 49, 54–55
application, perpetual 209
Aristotle 58–59, 85, 92, 115, 119, 121, 193, 555
Arminianism 212
Arminius, Jacob 164, 193
Armstrong, William Park 750
Arnauld, Antoine 226
Arndt, Johann 237–39, 242–43, 358, 488
Arnold, Gottfried 244–45
Arnold, Matthew 200, 449, 498, 592, 624, 766, 823

Arnold, Thomas 499, 566, 773
Asbury, Francis 195, 366, 373, 435, 437, 503, 507, 597, 817
Athanasius 76, 102, 105
Augustine 86–94, 110, 857
  Ambrose and 78
  Binney and 453
  conversion of 88
  Jerome and 77
  Jonathan Edwards and 376
  Pelagius and 102
  Perkins and 206
  preaching of 90, 93, 114, 130
  rhetoric of 87, 91, 93
  Roman Empire and 96
  rule of 120, 133
Augustine of Canterbury 110
Austen, Jane 449
Austin-Sparks, T. 475, 787–88
awakening. See also revivals.
  First Great 359
  Second Great 430, 435, 437, 446, 503
  "Third" 506
Ayer, William Ward 732, 745

Bach, J. S. 124, 336, 385–86, 477, 525
Bacon, Francis 211, 281
Baedeker, F. W. 609
Balfour, Arthur James 572, 574
Balfour Declaration 638, 737
Banks, Louis Albert 681
Barber, Margaret E. 786
Barebones, Praisegod 253
Baring Gould, S. 142
Barnabas, Epistle of 68, 74
Barnes, Albert 443
Barnhouse, Donald Grey 337, 683, 823–26, 842
Barrie, James 615
Barrow, Isaac 290
Barrowists 134, 204
Barth, Karl 57, 143, 165, 475, 760, 795, 797–800, 802, 805
Basevorn, Robert 131
Basil of Caesarea 106
Basil the Great 75
Baur, F. C. 80, 346–47, 350, 477
Bavinck, Herman 804
Baxter, J. Sidlow 712, 767, 840
Baxter, Richard 240, 282–85
Bayly, Lewis 274
Bayne, Peter 280–81
Beauvais, Charles de 230
Beck, Johan Tobias 476, 490, 706, 769, 798
Beck, Vilhelm 495
Bede 106, 109, 114
Beecher Lectures 532, 535, 617–18
  in 1874/1875 (Hall) 539
  in 1878/1879 (Simpson) 537
  in 1877 (Dale) 593
  in 1887/1888 (Broadus) 552, 607
  in 1895 (Brown) 293
  in 1907 (Forsyth) 748
  in 1910 (Jefferson) 654
  in 1911 (Gunsalus) 659
  in 1913/1914 (Jowett/Horne) 641, 646
  in 1952 (Stewart) 771
Beecher, Henry Ward 530–32, 585
Beecher, Lyman 432, 442–44, 446, 501, 853
Bellett, J. G. 603
Benedetto, Don 246
Benedict of Nursia 106
Bengel, Ernst Gottlieb 240, 244, 348–50, 357, 359, 476
Bengel, Johan Albrecht 240, 244, 348–50, 357
Berengar of Tours 115
Berkouwer, G. C. 805
Bernadotte, Ebba 697
Bernard of Clairvaux 107, 109, 281
Bernard, Thomas D. 601–2
Berridge, John 400, 406–7
Berry, Charles 641
Berry, Sidney 643
Bersier, Eugene 486
Berthold of Regensburg 122, 125
Bertrand de la Tour 124
Besant, Annie 612
Beveridge, William 400, 454, 507
Beza, Theodore 193
Bible
  authority 10, 12–13, 100, 121, 200
  exposition 601, 605
  translation 145
Bickersteth, Edward Henry 419, 462–64
Bickersteth, Montagu Cyril 464
Biederwolf, William Edward 664, 674, 676–77, 731
Bilderdikj, Willem 480
Bilney, Thomas 177, 179
Bingham, Rowland V. 720–21

Binney, Thomas 452–54, 580–81
Black, Hugh 616, 643, 756
Black Death 128
Black Elk 793–94
Blackstone, William E. 338, 359, 657, 722
Blackwood, Andrew W. 821–23
Blair, Hugh 329, 341, 343, 352, 441
Blair, Robert 315
Blair, Samuel 302
Blake, William 133, 261, 465, 623, 770
Blavatsky, Elena Petrovna 613, 649
Bliss, P. P. 660
Blumhard, Christian Gottlieb 472
Blumhardt, Christoph 474, 476
Blumhardt, Johan Christoph 474, 476, 706
Boehm, Anton Wilhelm 134, 237, 384, 623
Boehme, Jacob 134
Boethius, Ancius 106
Bohler, Peter 368
Boice, James Montgomery 825
Bolingbroke, Henry St. John 372
Bonar, Andrew 289, 317, 419, 420–22, 446, 562, 571, 574
Bonar, Horatius 420, 610, 624
Bonar, John J. 382, 420–21, 561
Bonar, Marjory 420
Bonaventure 116, 122
Bonhoeffer, Dietrich 802–4
Booth, Bramwell 686
Booth, Catherine 506
Booth, Evangeline 687
Booth, William 678, 685–86, 714
Boreham, Frank W. 160–61, 813–14
Borromeo, Charles 226
Borrow, George 482
Bosley, Harold A. 684
Bossuet, Jacques Benigne 228–29
Boston, Thomas 341, 343, 345
Boucher, Jean 228
Bounds, Edward McKendree 673, 691–93
Bourdaloue, Louis 233
Bourne, William 258
Boutflower, Charles H. 700
Bradford, John 181–82, 201, 269
Bradshaw, William 263
Brainerd, David 385, 387, 421
Bray, Billy 508–10, 596
Bremer, Frederica 466
Brengle, Samuel Logan 686–88
Brethren of the Common Life 133
Brewster, William 251, 267
Briggs, Charles Augustus 539, 614
Bright, John 416, 766, 815
Brightman, Edgar 212, 298
British and Foreign Bible Society 356, 401, 482
Brokhoff, John R. 600, 850
Bromyard, John 120, 126
Bronte, Patrick 406, 408
Brookes, James H. 607
Brooks, Phillips 446, 533–35, 653, 782
Brooks, Thomas 256
Brougher, James Whitcomb 676
Broughton, Leonard G. 634, 637, 690, 738
Brown, C. R. 545
Brown, R. R. 844, 846
Browne, Robert 194, 251
Browning, Robert 348, 449
Brownists 134, 204, 251
Brownville, Gordon 665
Bruce, A. B. 535, 574, 765
Bruce, Robert 192, 312–13
Brumbaugh, Roy 757
Bryan, William Jennings 667, 674, 734, 820
Bryant, William Cullen 467, 564
Bucer, Martin 134, 162, 178, 181–82, 186
Buchanan, Claudius 520
Buchanan, James 567–68
Bull, Geoffrey 788–89
Bullinger, Heinrich 171, 183, 186, 189–90, 251, 610
Bunyan, John 242, 256, 273–75, 490, 507, 790, 830
Burgon, John William 150, 463, 552–53
Burke, Edmund 329–30, 593
Burnet, Gilbert 322
Burns, Robert 311, 557, 562, 766
Burns, William C. 421, 428
Burr, Aaron 377, 434, 443
Burrell, David James 662–64
Burroughs, John 649
Bushnell, Horace 529–31
Butler, Joseph 331–32, 359, 411, 576, 699, 745

Cadman, S. Parkes 608, 670
Caesarius of Arles 101
Calamy, Edmund 223, 282
Calvin, John 20, 23, 82, 134, 160–63, 166–69, 191
Cambridge method of translation 34

Camisards 481
Campbell, Alexander 549–50
Campbell, Duncan 767
Campbell, John Macleod 426, 562–63, 566
Campbell, Macleod 619
Campbell, R. J. 589, 641, 647, 748
Campion, Edmund 213–14
Camus, Jean-Pierre 228
Candidius, George 384
Candlish, James 626
Candlish, Robert S. 562–63
Cappadose 480
Carey, William 386–89, 410, 520, 527, 789, 853
Carlyle, Thomas 251, 345, 423–24, 429–30, 449, 466, 498, 588
Carmichael, Amy 728–29
Carnegie, Andrew 673
Carnell, E. J. 495
Carolingian Renaissance 114
Carolinian underground 252
Carpenter, Alexander 125
Carpenter, W. Boyd 579
Carroll, Benajah Harvey 556–57, 740
Carson, Alexander 538–39
Carstares, William 311–12
Cartright, Thomas 187, 200, 264
Cartwright, Peter 502–4
Cassiodorus 105–6
Catherine of Sienna 120, 123
Cecil, Richard 132, 515
Cele, John 134
Cennick, John 382
Chaderton, Laurence 263
Chadwick, Samuel 596, 632, 688–90
Chafer, Lewis Sperry 701
Chalmers, Thomas 343, 374, 382, 390, 401, 410, 423–25, 560
Chambers, Oswald 768–70
Chancey, Charles 297
Channing, William Ellery 443
Chaplin, Charlie 674
Chapman, J. Wilbur 664, 668–69, 673, 676
Chappell, Clovis G. 682–84
Charles VIII of France 137
Charles the Hammer 110
Charnock, Stephen 285–88, 453
Chase, Salmon P. 443, 536
Chaucer 118, 123, 127–28
Chenault, P. B. 745
Cheng, Marcus 786
chiasm 31
Christensen, Fjord 789
Christian ashrams 719
Christrian Zionism 463
Christlieb, Theodor 153, 478–79
Chrodegang of Metz 107
Chrysologus, Peter 101
Chrysostom 79–87, 92–93, 161, 853, 857
Church, Richard William 460
Chytraeus, David 242
Cicero 35, 92, 96, 121, 168, 338
Clark, Gordon Haddon 799
Clark, Harry 673, 679
Clarke, Adam 392, 451, 506
Claude, Jean 208–9, 230, 403, 857
Clausen, H. N. 494
Clement, Books of
  First 65, 67
  Second 66
Clement of Alexandria 67, 69, 72
Clifton, Richard 264
cloistral preaching 106
Cocceius, Johannes 257, 311–12, 350
Coffin, Henry Sloan 511, 725–26
Coke, Thomas 366, 386, 436
Colenso, John William 454, 516–17, 576, 594
Coleridge, Samuel Taylor 347, 430, 529, 465, 534
Colet, John 149, 201
Columba 110
Columban 111
Comenius, Jan Amos 149
Common Sense (Scottish) Realism 324, 440
Comte, Auguste 498
Conrad of Waldhausen 147
Conrad, Arcturus Zodiac 664–65
Contarini, Gasparo 245
Conwell, Russell H. 656–57, 659
Cook, Thomas 690
Cooper, Anthony Ashley 463
Cop, Nicolas 162
Copernican revolution 129
Copernicus 324
Costa, Isaac da 480
Cotton, John 269–70, 281, 293–96, 307, 309
Coverdale, Miles 183
Cowper, William 338–40, 409
Craik, Henry 604
Cranfield, C. E. B. 199, 848

Cranmer, Thomas 178–79
Crashaw, Richard 217
Crazy Horse 793
Criswell, W. A. 146, 741, 835
Cromwell, Henry 287
Cromwell, Oliver 210, 257, 261, 263, 274, 276, 316
Cromwell, Thomas 176
Crosby, Fanny 678, 736
Cross, preaching on 233, 246, 333, 448, 568, 645, 654, 687, 699, 766
centrality of 59, 439, 612, 727, 748
English 338
Hall 412
Krummacher 471
missionary theme in 722
Puritan 287
Scottish 319
substitutionary atonement in 566, 593
Crowell, Henry 670
Cudworth, Ralph 207, 224, 276
Culverwell, Ezekiel 263
Cumberland revival 503
Cunningham, William 426, 560–61
Custer, George 793
Cuthbertson, James 768
Cyril of Alexandria 98
Cyril of Jerusalem 76

d'Ailly, Jean 230–31
Dabney, Robert Lewis 202, 553–55
Dale, Robert W. 451, 511, 592–93, 641, 697
Damien 618
Dante 83, 121, 193
Darby, John Nelson 511, 602–4
Davenport, John 293, 297, 307, 309
David of Wales 110
Davidman, Joy 762
Davidson, A. B. 215, 561, 572, 574–75, 624, 642
Davies, Horton 219, 221, 223–24, 263, 265–66, 271, 634
Davies, Samuel 380
Davis, John 822
Defoe, Daniel 256
DeHaan, M. R. 754, 835
Deissman, Gustav A. 135, 237, 616, 788
Delitzsch, Franz 476, 478, 571, 618, 670
Demosthenes 351, 370, 465, 755
Denney, James 596, 614, 619–20, 625, 769, 817
Dent, Arthur 274
Descartes, René 225
devotio moderna 133–34
Dickens, Charles 449, 540, 576, 623, 655, 657, 855
Dickenson, Jonathan 379
Dickinson, Emily 324
Dickson, David 314–15, 569
didache 41, 43, 50–51, 66
Diodorus 85
Diognetus, Epistle to 68
Dippel, Johan 244
Disruption, Scottish 560, 565
Dixon, Amzi Clarence 587, 610, 670, 734–35, 737–38, 830
Doddridge, Philip 223, 244, 284, 332–35, 338, 360, 372, 418, 454, 487
Dods, Marcus 16, 420, 573–74, 615
Donne, John 210–11, 213–16, 218, 227
Dorner, Isaac 355, 468
Dow, Lorenzo 504–6
Dowie, John Alexander 660, 781
downgrade controversy 582, 586
Driver, Samuel 610
Drummond, Henry 572–74, 610, 616, 624–25, 640
Dryden, John 224
Du Bosc, Pierre 231
Duff, Alexander 325, 390, 424
Duncan, John 421, 427–28
Duncan, "Rab" 410, 570
Dwight, Timothy 431–34, 442, 445
Dykes, J. Oswald 526, 562

Eames, Jacob 520
Eastern Orthodoxy 87
Eck, Johann Maier 149, 151, 155, 158
Eckhart, Meister 120, 135
Eco, Umberto 124
Edersheim, Alfred 36, 39, 428, 570
Edwards, Jonathan 257–58, 374–77, 385–86, 853
influences on 289, 302, 375, 376
Locke and 375
others influenced by 421, 424, 443, 500
Edwards, Jonathan, Jr. 438
Eichorn, Johann Gottfried 347
electronics age, and preaching 16
Elijah 25, 30, 38, 84, 471, 541, 684

Eliot, George 139, 449, 468, 498, 576, 856
Eliot, John 254, 302, 305
Elisha 25, 471
Ellicott, Charles J. 463
Elliott, Charlotte 483
Emerson, Ralph Waldo 324, 441, 528, 531, 649, 732, 744, 746, 820
Emmons, Nathanael 440
English Civil War 218
Enlightenment 12, 129, 227–28, 243, 324, 416, 488, 561
  biblical criticism of 12, 616
  preaching 160–61, 329, 536
  rationalism 324, 329, 347, 349, 494, 498, 528, 645, 779, 798
  unbelief 328–29, 346, 794
  vocabulary of 782
Enoch, Book of 23
Epictetus 36
Epp, Theodore 754
Erasmus 133–34, 149–52, 182, 190, 201, 206
  rhetoric of 151
Erdman, Charles R. 357, 512–13
Erigena, John Scotus 114
Erskine, Ann 401–2
Erskine, Ebenezer 343, 345
Erskine, Henry 341, 343
Erskine, John 382, 387, 418, 427, 434
Erskine, Ralph 342–43
Erskine, Thomas, of Linlathen 427, 562
Evangelical Alliance 479
Evangelical Anglicanism 402
Evangelical Patriotic Society 492
Evans, Christmas 360–61, 507–8
Evans, William 828
Ewald, Georg, H. A. 441, 472, 476–77, 575
exempla 122, 125, 145, 180
expository preaching. *See* preaching.
Fairbairn, Andrew 574, 640, 642, 748
Fairbairn, Patrick 574, 724, 755
Farel, William 162, 164
Farwell, John 511
Fasol, Al 553, 557, 741, 744, 781
Fawcett, John 406
Fenelon, Francois de 229, 234–35
Fermin, Giles 302
Ferrer, Vincent 120, 123
Ferrin, Howard 827
Ferry, Paul 229
Feuerbach, Ludwig 468
Finney, Charles Grandison 443, 446, 499–502, 540, 544, 683, 722, 787
Fitch, William 723
Fitzmyer, Joseph A. 50
Flavel, John 288–89, 399, 440
Flechere, John William de la 369
Fletcher, John 244, 369, 372, 400, 404, 506, 832
Flint, Robert 574–75
florilegium 119
Ford, Henry 14
Forsyth, Peter Taylor 13, 37, 589, 645, 730, 748–49, 769
Fosdick, Harry Emerson 531, 732, 744, 746, 820
Foster, Stephen 253
Fox, George 261, 274
Fox, Matthew 136
Foxe, John 181, 202, 583
Francis of Assisi 121, 124, 133
Francis of Sales 225–28, 230, 232
Francke, August Hermann 243, 245, 299, 356, 370, 384
Franklin, Benjamin 371–72
Franson, Fredrik 526–27, 808
Fraser, James 319
Fraser, Neil 611
Freeman, Douglas Southall 740
Freylinghuysen, Theodore 379
Froude, J. A. 454, 468
Fulbert of Chartres 115
Fuller, Andrew 387, 409–10, 419
Fuller, Charles E. 670, 754, 827, 835
Fuller, Thomas 204, 221–22, 250

Gaebelein, Arno Clemens 571, 608–9
Gairdner, Temple 696
Gale, George 500
Gallicanism 229
Gangi, Mariano di 825
Gansfort, Wessel 133–34
Garbett, Cyril 463, 579
Garfield, James 583
Garrick, David 371, 396, 418
Gaudentius of Brescia 91
Gaussen, Louis 165, 232, 418, 483
George, David Lloyd 583, 642
Gerhard, John 238
Gerhard, Paul 238
Gerson, John 143

Gesenius, Heinrich 356, 469, 472
Gifford, John 274
Gih, Andrew 786, 788
Gilbert of Poitiers 130
Gilkey, Langdon 522
Gill, John 395, 584
Gillespie, Thomas W. 59–60, 345
Gilpin, Bernard 188, 396
Girdlestone, R. B. 482
Gladden, Washington 545
Gladstone, William E. 416, 424, 458, 574–76, 588
Godet, Frederick L. 485
Goethe, Johann Wolfgang von 353, 477
Goforth, Jonathan 721–23, 832
Goforth, Rosalind 722–23, 832
Goodwin, Thomas 207, 261, 270–71, 282, 291, 298, 302, 588, 615, 630
Gordon, Adoniram Judson 546–48
Gordon, George 645
Gordon, Robert 560
Gordon, Samuel Dickey 710, 776, 817–19
Gordon of Khartoum 581, 696
Gore, Charles 457, 775
Gossip, Arthur John 763–65, 843
Gough, John B. 588
Graham, Billy 679, 695, 731, 734, 799, 816, 824, 851
crusades 694, 776, 783, 827, 836
Graham, William 440
Grant, F. C. 605
Grass, Gunter 796–97
Great Awakening. See awakenings.
Great Commission 44, 383–84, 517, 537, 715
Greco-Roman rhetoric 48
Green, David 280
Greenhill, William 335, 339, 405
Gregory I 97, 100, 113, 857
Gregory of Nazianzen 75–76
Gregory of Nyssa 76
Gregory of Thaumaturgus 75
Grenfell, Wilfred 512
Grey, J. D. 742–43
Griffin, Edward D. 438–39, 520
Griffith Thomas, William Henry 448, 577, 700–2
Griffith, Leonard 589
Griffiths, Gerald B. 708
Grindal, Edmund 175, 185, 263
Groote, Gerard 133–34
Grosheide, F. 804
Grosseteste, Richard 143
Grotius, Hugo 193, 384
Grubb, Nils 487
Grubb, Norman 704–5
Grundler, Johan 384
Grundtvig, N. F. S. 493–94
Guibert 130
Guiness, H. Grattan 519
Gumbrell, J. B. 740
Gunsaulus, Frank 658
Gurnall, William 223
Guthrie, James 317, 320
Guthrie, Thomas 469, 558–60, 811
Guthrie, William 317, 320, 344
Guyon, Madam 229, 234, 706, 786
Guyse, John 337

Habershon, Ada 610
Haggai 12, 30, 32, 137
Hague, Dyson 720
Haldane, James Alexander 410, 417–19, 450, 487, 706
Haldane, Robert 410, 417–19, 427, 450, 482–83, 487, 706
Haldeman, I. M. 660–61
Hales, Alexander 122
Haley, Alex 780
Hall, Gordon 438
Hall, John 526, 538–40, 545, 564, 725
Hall, Joseph 207, 219–20, 239, 264
Hall, Newman 540, 588, 637, 639, 706, 814
Hall, Robert 277, 387, 410–12, 423, 425
Halleen, E. A. 808–9
Hallesby, Ole 489, 806–7
Halyburton, Thomas 319
Ham, John W. 739
Ham, Mordecai 731–32
Hamann, J. G. 20, 355–56
Hamilton, Alexander 443
Hamilton, Patrick 190, 440
Hamilton, Wallace 782–83
Hammarskjold, Dag 133
Handel, Georg 372
Hardey, Richard 518
Harford-Battersby, Thomas Dundas 696–97
Harms, Claus 354
Harnack, Adolph 88, 202, 476, 495, 618, 656, 752, 798
Harris, Howell 362–63

Harris, J. Rendal 754, 756, 769
Haslam, William 509
Haslebach, John 280
Hastings, Selina. *See* Huntingdon, countess of.
Hatch, Nathan O. 437
Hauge, Hans Nielsen 487–89
Havergal, Frances Ridley 629, 637, 697, 766
Havergal, William 629
Havner, Vance 841–43
Hawthorne, Nathaniel 324, 435
Hayes, Doremus 688
Hayes, Rutherford 605
Hedberg, F. G. 490
Hegel, Georg 468, 476
Heidegger, Martin 353, 796
Heidelberg Catechism 194, 200, 600
Heiric of Auxerre 114
Henderson, Alexander 312–14
Hengstenberg, E. W. 329–30, 441, 468, 474, 476, 570, 642, 757
Henry II 119
Henry, Matthew 278, 283, 289, 334–35, 743
Henry, Philip 272, 277–79
Henry of Navarre 225
Hepburn, Henry 832
Herbert, George 133, 187, 207, 216–18, 625
Herbert of Bosham 105, 116
Herder, Johann 324, 794
hermeneutics 17, 75, 84–86, 746, 851
Herrick, Robert 217
Herrmann, Wilhelm 798
hertzpunkt 158
Herzl, Theodore 610
Hesse, Herman 796–97
Hieron, Samuel 252, 258
Higden, Ranulph 201
Hildebrand 119
Hill, Rowland 397, 399, 400–2, 407–8, 418, 637
Hillis, Newell Dwight 656, 658
Hilton, Walter 135, 206
Hippolytus 71–72, 74
Hodge, A. A. 441, 448, 540
Hodge, Casper Wistar 649–50
Hodge, Charles 440, 442, 474, 522, 529, 539, 564, 567, 604
Hofacker, Wilhelm 476
Hoffmann, Oswald C. J. 753
Hog, Thomas 319
Holden, John Stuart 519, 610, 688, 701, 703–5, 853
Holland, Henry Scott 643, 645
Holm-Glad, Trygve 806
Holmes, Oliver Wendell 374, 474
Holy Spirit
  Acts movement of 54
  preaching in 47
  revelation through 31
  striving of 55
  Torrey view of 670
homiletics, meaning of the term 35
Hoof, Jacob Otto 487
Hooker, Richard 187–88, 201, 207, 264
Hooker, Thomas 293, 304–7, 309
Hooper, John 183, 201, 251, 263
Hopkins, Evan H. 696–98
Hopkins, Gerard Manley 466
Hopkins, Samuel 440
Hoppin, James 539, 555
Horneck, Antony 360
Horsch, John 197
Hort, Fenton 150, 552, 756
Houghton, Will 671, 732, 842
Howard, John 531, 851
Howden, J. Russell 703
Howe, John 276–77, 334
Howson, John Saul 466
Hubmeier, Balthaser 195
Hügel, Friedrich von 616–17, 727
Hugh of St. Cher 120
Hugh of St. Victor 116
Hughes, Hugh Price 595–97
Huguenots 206, 225, 227, 230
Hull, Hope 505
Hult, Adolf 492–93
Humbert de Romanis 120, 131–32, 201
Hume, David 324, 328, 345, 372, 498
Huntingdon, countess of 244, 345, 361, 369, 372, 374, 380, 397–98, 407, 813
Huss, John 146–49
Hutchinson, Anne 294, 307–9
Hutchinsonianism 397
Hutterian Brothers 475
Hutton, John 633, 647–48, 775
Huxley, Thomas H. 458
Hwa-Sik Kim 790
Hyde, Praying 668
Hyperius, Andrew 185, 201–4, 206, 230, 237, 445, 803, 857

Ignatius Loyola 66, 108, 134, 247–48, 330, 456, 730
Ihk-Doo Kim 790
Illyricus 126
inclusio 31
Ingersoll, Robert 658, 667, 736
Inner Mission Movement 468, 489, 495, 795–96
Innocent III 119
inspiration of Scripture, Luther's view 155
Intertestamental Period 34
invitation 707
Inwood, Charles 652, 703
Ireland, evangelization of 102
Irenaeus 68–69, 71–72
Ironside, H. A. 606, 610–12, 785
Irving, Edward 392, 424, 428–30, 464
Isaurian Dynasty 86-87
Isidore 107
Islam 97

Jackson, Stonewall 551, 554
Jacobi, Gerhard 796
James 49
James, John Angell 446, 450, 452, 463, 487, 578, 584, 592
Jansen, Cornelius 226
Jansenism 227
Jasper, John 779–81
Jay, John 584
Jay, William 338, 340, 398–401, 446, 452
Jefferson, Charles Edward 653–54
Jennings, David 339
Jerome 77, 89, 151
Jerome of Prague 147–48
Jerusalem Garden Tomb Maintenance Fund 697
Jesus Christ
  atonement of 593
  disciples of 41
  preaching of 40–47
  Scripture and 12, 42, 44
Jewel, John 186, 193, 201
Joachim of Fiore 108–9, 149, 242, 601
John Cassian 105
John of Salisbury 119, 123
John of the Cross 213
John the Baptist 14, 38–42, 133, 229, 299, 373, 471, 513, 780
Johns, Vernon 782
Johnson, A. Wetherell 636, 638
Johnson, Edward 302
Johnson, Gisle 489
Johnson, Gustaf F. 808–10
Johnson, James Welldon 781
Johnson, Samuel 331, 336, 370, 412, 418
Johnson, Stephen 434
Jones, Bob, Sr., 679
Jones, Eli Stanley 718–19
Jones, Griffith 360–62
Jones, John Daniel 632, 643–47
Jones, Rhys Bevan 677
Jones, Russell Bradley 738
Jones, Samuel P. 666
Josiah, King 24, 29
Jowett, Benjamin 272, 468, 576, 773
Jowett, John Henry 450–51, 589, 639–43, 768
Joyce, James 613, 856
Judson, Adoniram 386, 438, 519–22, 546, 548
Jukes, Andrew 519
Julian of Norwich 135
Julicher, Gustav A. 750
Justification, forensic 154

Kagawa, Toyohiko 784–85
Kant, Immanuel 240, 324, 328, 346, 798
Keach, Benjamin 395, 547, 584
Keble, John 454, 463–64
Keil, Karl Friedrich 476
Keller, Helen 20
Kelly, William 605–6
Kelman, John 616–19
Kemp, Joseph 711, 732, 737
Kennedy, Bishop James 190
Kennedy, D. James 825
Kennedy, John 428, 566–68
Kepler, Thomas S. 160, 213, 219
Kerr, Colin 701
kerygma 41, 43, 50, 53, 59, 64, 629, 848
Keswick convention 696
Ketcham, Robert Thomas 744–46
Ki-Chul Choo 790
Kierkegaard, Søren 494–95, 749
Kimball, Edward 510
Kimbangu, Simon 781
King, Geoffrey 778
King, Guy H. 774
King, Martin Luther, Jr. 781–83
Kingsley, Fanny 467
Kirk, Harris 750

Kittel, Gerhard 79, 498, 796
Kitto, John 564
Knapp, Jacob 507
Knill, Richard 451
Knox, John 168, 186, 189–92, 251, 311, 313, 316, 345, 381, 423, 600
Krummacher, Friedrich Wilhelm 232, 441, 468–71, 486, 766, 805
Kuenen, Abraham 480
Kuyper, Abraham 480–81, 804

Labadie, Jean de 239, 242, 244
Lacordaire, Henri Dominique 120, 235, 453, 482
Lambie, Thomas 720
Lanfranc 115
Langland, William 126
Langton, Stephen 104–5, 116
Lanier, Sydney 649
Latimer, Hugh 176–77, 179–81, 201, 210, 250
Laubach, Frank C. 726
Laud, William 210, 218, 252, 265, 305
Law, William 360, 370, 407, 616, 706, 773
Lawrence, D. H. 613, 701
Leander 107
Lecky, William 332, 405, 610
Lee, Ann 431
Lee, Robert E. 550, 607
Leibniz, Gottfried W. 229, 239, 243, 329, 477
Leighton, Alexander 252
Leighton, Robert 322
Leo the Great 98–100, 857
Lessing, Gotthold, Ephraim 324, 328
Lewis, C. S. 284, 623, 761–62
Libanius 76, 80, 92
Liddon, Henry Parry 552, 590–92
Liefeld, Walter L. 416
Lightfoot, J. B. 219–20, 552, 614, 756
Liguori, Alphonsus 248
Lincoln, Abraham 503, 511, 528, 534, 536, 820
Lindsell, Harold 758
Lippmann, Walter 650
Lischer, Richard 92, 245, 781, 783, 823
Liudprand of Cremona 115, 117
Livingstone, David 515, 517
Livingstone, John 318
Lloyd-Jones, D. Martyn 251, 375, 634, 645, 648, 775–78, 845
Lock, Walter 755
Locke, John 272, 324, 374–75
Logan, C. A. 784
Lollards 145–46, 177, 250
Lombard, Peter 119
London, Jack 613
London Missionary Society 340, 392–93, 399, 401, 453, 515–16
Long, Thomas 851
Longfellow, Henry Wadsworth 119, 123
Lorenzo the Magnificent, 138
Lowell, James Russell 218
Lowery, Oscar Raymond 835
Lowry, Robert 736
Luccock, Halford 743
Lull, Raymond 130, 716
Luthardt, Christoph Ernst 478
Luther, Martin 133, 136, 152–59, 487, 853, 857
  Calvin and 162
  conversion of 153–54
  Groote and 134
  hermeneutic of 156
  Huss and 148
  rhetoric of 159
  Scripture and 155
Lutkens, Franz Julius 384
Lyte, Francis 457

McAfee, Raymond 844
McAll, Robert W. 486
McArthur, Annabel Douglas 435
Macbeath, John 767
M'Caul, Alexander 463
McCauley, Jerry 676, 784
McCheyne, Robert Murray 289, 386, 390, 420–22, 446, 721
McComb, John 803
McConkey, James 698
McCosh, James 547
McCulloch, William 381–82
MacDonald, George 574, 576, 622–23, 761, 856
MacDuff, John R. 571–72, 621
McGavran, Donald 719
McGee, J. Vernon 834–35
MacGregor, James 622
Macgregor, W. M. 627
McGuffey, William 551
Machen, J. Gresham 649–50, 716, 725, 750–52, 769
MacInnis, John 634

McIntire, Carl 835
McIntosh, C. H. 511
Mackay, John 724
Mackintosh, Charles Henry 605–6
McLaine, Shirley 613
Maclaren, Alexander 453, 580, 582, 636, 653, 678
Maclaren, Ian 572, 624–25, 814
Macleod, Norman 565–66, 574
McLuhan, Marshall 142
McMillan of Ullapool, 620
MacNeil, Hugh 579
McNeile, Hugh 464
McNeill, John 637, 670, 677–78
McPheeters, J. C. 719
McPherson, Aimee Semple 674–76
MacRae, A. A. 670
Madan, Martin 397
Madison, James 416–17, 434, 550
Magee, W. C. 416
Mahan, Asa 443
Mahler, Gustav 613
Maier, Walter A. 752–53
Maitland Alexander 672, 819
Malan, Cesar 418, 427, 482–84
Malan, Daniel 706
Mangs, Frank 806–7
Manichaeism 88, 99
Mannerheim, Carl von 490
Manning, Henry 458–59
Mantle, J. Gregory 632, 703
Manton, Thomas 273, 280–81, 285–86, 577
Marcionism 19
Mark Matthews Plan 812
Marsden, Samuel 386
Marsh, F. E. 118, 610, 660, 737
Marshall, Gordian 42
Marshall, Peter 558
Marshall, Stephen 255, 262, 265
Martensen, H. L. 494
Martin of Tours 105
Martyn, Henry 356, 386, 388–90, 404, 766
Martyr, Justin 67, 73
Martyr, Peter 120, 178, 186, 188, 246
Marxism 609
Massilon, Jean Baptiste 234
Mather, Cotton 239, 294, 298–301, 304, 306, 337, 384
Mather, Increase 295–98, 306, 308–10
Mather, Nathaniel 325
Mather, Richard 268–70, 310
Matheson, George 621–22, 640
Matthews, Mark A. 811–12
Matthews, Shailer 670
Matthews, W. R. 773
Matthias of Janow 147–48
Maugham, W. Somerset 638
Maurice, Frederick Denison 457–58, 465, 468, 566, 594, 623, 653
Maurus, Rabanus 130
Maximus of Turin 101
Mayers, Walter 454
Mede, Joseph 271, 298
Melito of Sardis 67
Mellor, Enoch 640
Melvill, Henry 465
Melville, Andrew 191, 217, 311, 313, 324, 855
Mencken, H. L. 649
Mendelssohn, Felix 477
Meyer, Frederick Brotherton 519, 635–38, 673, 678, 703, 736–37, 768
Micaiah, the son of Imlah 31, 232
Middle Ages 96
Militz of Kremsier 147–48
Mill, John Stuart 498
Milligan, George 574
Milligan, William 574
Milne, William 392
Milton, John 100, 128, 256, 272, 281, 316, 534, 615
Mission Seminary of Basle 472
Moe, Olaf E. 806
Moffat, Robert 393, 395, 516
Moltmann, Jürgen 475
Monasteries 98
Monod, Adolphe 485–86
Monod, Frederic 418, 441
Montanus 70
Montesquieu, Charles de Secondat 331
Moody, Dwight Lyman 510–12, 526, 577, 601, 607, 611, 644, 670
  missions/campaigns of 547, 567, 572, 632, 699, 707, 733
  supporters of 420, 547, 579, 637
Moore, Arthur J. 681–82
Moore, Paul Foot 753
Moorhouse, Henry 511
Moralism, its peril 169
Moravian Brethren 352, 356–57, 483, 491
More, Hannah 340, 418

More, Thomas 149, 213
Morell, Thomas 452
Morgan, G. Campbell 631–34, 678, 703
Morris, Leon 13, 246, 816
Morris, Sam 679
Morrison, Robert 391–93
Morrow, J. D. 832
Moses 12, 23–24, 41
Mosheim, Johann Lorenz 347–48
Mott, John R. 512, 652, 724–25
Moule, George 518
Moule, Handley G. C. 405, 610, 614, 627, 697–98, 700, 703
Moule, Horace C. G. 627
Moulin, Pierre du 230
Moulton, W. F. 610
Mowll, Howard 815
Muesslin, Wolfgang 208
Muggleton, Lodowick 261
Mühlenberg, William 244
Müller, George 475
Muller, Julius 474
Mullins Preaching Lectures 744
Munsey, William Elbert 692
Muntzer, Thomas 195
Murbeck, Peter 491
Murray, Andrew 527, 636, 705–8, 715, 787
Murray, James 625
Mynster, J. P. 494

Neander, Joachim 147, 239, 353, 355, 441, 472, 569–70
Neighbor, R. E. 745
neo-Platonism 88
neo-Puritan enthusiasts 850
Netherlands and the preaching of Kuyper 481
    progress of the gospel 133
    theological storms 804
Nettleton, Asahel 370, 444, 446–47
networking 845
    across denominational lines 608
    evangelical 418
    widespread and impressive 596
Nevius, Helen S. 522–23
Nevius, John Livingstone 521–23
Nevius method 523
New England Theology 446
new hermeneutics 85
New Theology 443, 501, 589, 647, 662, 672, 688, 738, 748
Newell, Samuel 438
Newman, Frank 465, 468
Newman, John Henry 226, 454–56, 458, 466, 616
Newton, George 291
Newton, Isaac 290, 324, 328, 330, 374
Newton, John 28, 338, 340, 372, 387, 397, 418, 578, 605
Newton, Joseph Fort 589, 648, 659
Nicholas of Cusa 134
Nicholson, William P. 538
Nicholson, William R. 547–48
Niemoller, Martin 795–97
Nightingale, Florence 464, 583
Nihilism, and modernity 20
Ninian 110
Nitszche, K. I. 472
Noah 23, 29
Nobel, Alfred 806–7
Norris, J. Frank 679, 745, 830
North, Brownlow 513–14
Norton, John 310
Norwood, F. W. 589
Nott, Samuel 438
Novatian 78, 87
Noyes, J. H. 501

Obadiah 27, 32
Oecolampadius 151, 189
Old Testament, neglect of 353
Oratory, Chrysostom on 81
Origen 66–67, 72–75, 85–86
Osiander, Andrew 178, 237
Oskar, Prince 697
Owen, John 254, 258, 262, 271–73, 287, 291, 321, 336, 399
Owen, Robert 549
Oxford method of translation 34

Pachomius 105
Pacianus, bishop of Barcelona 91
Paine, Thomas 431, 649
Palmer, Benjamin M. 540, 554–55
Palmer, Herbert 223
Palmer, Phoebe 506–7
Pancratius, Andreas 237
Pankhurst, Emmeline 638
Pannenberg, Wolfhart 730
Panton, D. M. 786
Papias of Hierapolis 68

Parker, Joseph 587–90
Parker, Matthew 184–85
Parker, T. H. L. 143, 164–65, 168, 170
Parsons, James 636
Pascal, Blaise 226–27, 229, 424, 484
Paton, John G. 525–26
Patrick of Ireland 102–4
Patton, Francis L. 601, 819
Paul 27–28, 36, 40, 60, 74, 156, 760
  Athens sermon 59
  Corinth ministry 58
  gospel teaching 43
  preaching 48–51, 55–62
  Rome ministry 60
Paul the Deacon 119
Paulinianism 99
Pawson, H. Cecil 695
Paxson, Ruth 729–30
Peake, A. S. 596
Pearse, Mark Guy 509, 595–97, 756
Pearson, John 223
Pecham of Canterbury 124
Pelagianism 81, 99, 773
Pelagius 77, 102
Pemberton, Ebenezer 385
Penn, William 272
Penn-Lewis, Jessie 475, 636, 703, 727, 786–87
Pepin, Guillaume 126
Pepys, Samuel 210
Perkins, William 193, 201, 205–8, 239, 251, 253, 260, 263–64, 266–68
Peter 48–49, 54
Peter the Chanter, 116
Peter the Comestor, 116
Peter the Hermit, 119
Pethrus, Lewi 806
Petri, Olaus 487
Pfeiffer, Robert 753
Philip 49
Philips, Obbe 196
Philo 33, 35, 70, 74
Pickett, J. Waskom 719
Pieper, Franz 753
Pierce, Earle V. 734–35
Pierrepont, Sarah 375
Pietism 237, 240, 242
Pink, Arthur W. 612–13
Pitt, William 407, 410
Plato 20, 85
Plumptre, E. H. 697
Plutschau, Henry 384
Polycarp 66, 71
Pontoppidan, Erik 488, 490, 494
Pope, Alexander 359
Poteat, Edwin 742
Prayer Meeting Revival of 1857–58 500
preaching 11, 19, 201, 209, 221, 441
  apostolic 48–50, 54–62
  European 225, 236
  expository 14, 682
  Greek influence on 67
  "prophetic" 26
  "pulpit pedantry" in 247
  theology of 56, 143
Preparationists 269
Preston, John 261–62, 281, 294, 302, 308, 342
Price, Eugenia 727
Priestly, Joseph 411, 440
Prime, Derek 712
Princeton Seminary 431, 441, 540, 663, 676, 717, 724–25, 750, 819, 822, 824, 827
prophecy 23, 31, 59
prophets, school of 31–32
Protestant preaching 158
Prynne, William 252
Psellus, Michael 130
Puritan Lectureships 204
Puritan Triumvirate 252–53
Puritans 183, 250, 254
  Carolinian underground 252
  decline 323
  English 264
  parties 279
  spirituality 261
  worship 267
Pusey, E. B. 454, 590

Quakers 261, 325
Quayle, William 681–82, 695
Quinisext, Council of 98
Quintillianus, Marcus Fabius 92
Qumran community 36, 74
Quodvultdeus, bishop of Carthage 96

Rachmaninoff, Sergei 81
Radbertus, Paschasius 114
Rader, Paul 659, 674, 833
Radstock, Lord 451, 519, 526, 603, 609, 697
Raikes, Robert 395

Rainsford, Marcus 576–78, 814
Rainy, Robert 311, 328, 574–75, 580, 624
Ramus, Peter 193, 201, 206, 208, 256
Randolph, John 440–41
Raulin, Jean 201
Ravenhill, Leonard 844
Ray, Jefferson Davis 557
Redpath, Alan 694, 712, 839–41
Rees, Paul Stromberg 836–38
Reformation
  effects of 142, 189
  England's 175
  Scotland's 189
Reid, Thomas 431, 440
Reinhard, Franz Volkmar 350–52
Remigius 114
Renaissance 128
Renqvist, Henry 490
Renwick, James 318
Reuchlin, Johannes 155, 244
revivals 359, 377, 501
  First Great Awakening 359–60
  hymns of 368
  Korea 523
  of 1859 518, 541, 569, 606, 610
  Second Great 430, 435, 437, 446, 503
  Wales and Ireland 513
Rhee, Syngman 790
rhetoric 34, 58, 555, 822, 848
  history of 76–77, 87, 151, 159, 255, 455
  New 24
  revival and 380
  Spirit and 255
Rhetorical Criticism 31
Ribbentrop, Joachim von 796
Ricci, Matteo 248
Rice, John R. 679–80
Rice, Luther 438
Richard of Thetford 121, 131
Richelieu 225
Ridley, Jasper 179, 181
Ridley, Nicholas 180–81
Rieger, Georg Conrad 349
Riley, William Bell 733–35, 744–45, 751, 830, 842
Rippon, John 584
Ritschl, Albrecht 239, 240, 244, 300, 476–77, 614, 619, 748
Ritschlianism 750
Robe, James 382
Robert of Basevorn 201
Robert of Holyard 125
Roberts, Evan 636, 677–78, 704, 787
Robertson, Archibald Thomas 754–56, 760
Robertson, Catherine 819
Robertson, Frederick W. 455, 460–62, 572
Robertson, William Bruce 568–70
Robertson, William, of Edinburgh 329, 343, 427
Robinson, John 207, 260, 263–64, 267–68
Robinson, Robert 209, 411
Roby, William 393
Rockefeller, John D. 673
Rodeheaver, Homer 673
Rogers, John 177–78
Rogers, Will 679, 842
Rolle, Richard 135
Romaine, William 335, 372, 396–400, 402, 406–7, 577
Rood, Paul 679, 735, 839
Ross, Donald 838
Ross, J. M. E. 648
Rous, Frances 281
Rousseau, Jean-Jacques 324, 346–47, 353 483, 799
Roussel, Gerard 166
Routley, Eric 762
Rowland, Daniel 361–62
Rowse, A. L. 509–10
Roxburgh, John 615
Ruotsalainen, Paavo 490
Ruskin, John 460–61, 465, 498, 534, 583, 623
Rutherford, Emma 706
Rutherford, Samuel 269, 315–17, 319–21, 420–22, 616
Ruysbroeck, Jan van 133
Ryken, Leland 255, 266, 325
Ryland, John, Sr. 387
Ryle, John Charles 359, 396, 398, 402, 408, 577, 579–80, 627, 697

Sahlstrom, C. O. 808
Salmond, S. D. F. 567, 574
Sampey, John 733
Sandemanianism 397, 508
Sandys, Edwin 204
Sangster, William Edwin 596, 693, 695, 816
Sankey, Ira D. 511–12, 637
Santayana, George 14
Sargent, John 457

Sasse, Herman 156
Saurin, Jacques 231
Savonarola, Girolamo 136
Savoy Conference 223, 284
Saxe, Grace 670
Sayce, A. H. 755
Scandinavia, evangelization of 112, 487
Schaff, Philip 470, 528
Schartau, Henric 357–58
Scherer, Paul 802
Schilder, Klaas 804–6
Schlatter, Adolph 749, 760, 798, 803
Schleiermacher, Friedrich 240, 352–54, 470, 472, 533–34, 744
  preaching theory of 152, 353, 857
  school of 465, 798
  Scripture and 353, 478
Schmidt, Wilhelm 717–18
Schofield, A. T. 609
Schumann, Robert 477
Schweitzer, Albert 237
Schwenckfeld, Casper 195
Scofield, C. I. 606–8, 659
Scots Confession 191, 311
Scott, George 487, 492
Scott, Walter 112, 382, 392, 424, 429
Scougal, Henry 322, 370
Scrivner, Christian 357
Scroggie, William Graham 710–12, 720, 767
Second Great Awakening. *See* awakenings.
Second Helvetic Confession 19
Selina, countess of Huntingdon. *See* Huntingdon, countess of.
Semler, J. S. 240, 346, 349, 352, 469
Seneca 35–36, 69, 162, 221, 522
sensus plenior 85
sermons 13, 131, 479
  essay 224
  history of 21, 70, 130, 256
  modified modern 201, 212
Shaftesbury Anthony, Lord 416, 463–64, 466, 575, 697
Shakers 261, 431–32, 503
Shedd, W. G. T. 547
Sheen, Fulton J. 793
Shenk, Wilbert R. 409
Shepard, Thomas 293, 299, 301–4, 319
Shepherd of Hermas 66
Sheppard, Dick 773–74
Shields, Thomas Todhunter 829–31
Shoemaker, Samuel 724
Short, Roy 665
Shufeldt, J. Straton 679
Shuler, Robert P. 682
Sibbes, Richard 239, 250, 260–61, 269, 271, 279–82, 294
Sibelius, Jean 613, 806
Simeon, Charles 209, 389, 402–4, 857
Simon, Richard 229
Simons, Menno 195–97
Simpson, Albert Benjamin 527, 544, 608, 659, 661–62, 807
Simpson, Hubert 616
Simpson, Matthew 506, 536–38
Singh, Sundar 791–93
Sitting Bull 793
Skogsbergh, Erik August 808–9
Slessor, Mary 523–24
Smeaton, George 567
Smith, C. Ryder 693
Smith, Gypsy 632, 677–79, 815, 833
Smith, Hannah Whithall 718
Smith, Henry 201, 203–6, 239, 264, 445, 857
Smith, J. Taylor 610, 697, 708–10
Smith, Oswald J. 670, 827, 831–34
Smith, Preserved 150
Smith, Robertson 573–74, 614
Smith, William Robertson 561–62, 574, 614–15
Sockman, Ralph 684
Soderblom, Nathan 381, 792, 806
Soper, Donald 596, 693, 816
South, Robert 224, 331
Spanish Succession, War of 225
Speer, Robert 652, 723–26
Spencer, Herbert 498, 532
Spener, Philipp Jacob 241
Spengler, Oswald 810
Spring, Gardiner 447–49
Spurgeon, Charles Haddon 257, 465, 582–87
  Beecher and 585
  conversion of 584
  early ministry of 452, 584
  humor of 585
  influences on 284, 335
  late ministry of 586, 590
  Moody and 511
  Scripture and 614
  temperance work 586
  The Metropolitan Tabernacle Pulpit 587
  theological themes 154, 257

Spurgeon, Thomas 651, 736, 814
Spurgeon's College 710
St. Bartholomew's Day Massacre 206
Stalker, James 572, 619–20, 714
Stanley, Arthur 283, 312, 565, 591
Stanley, Henry M. 516
Staupitz, Johann von 153
Steele, Daniel 687
Stephen 49, 55
Stephen, James 465
Stevenson, Robert Louis 603, 618
Stewart, James S. 770–72
Stier, Ewald Rudolf 55, 468, 472–74
Still, William 770
Stillingfleet, Edward 334
Stirrett, Andrew 720
Stockmeier, Otto 485, 707
Stoddard, Solomon 256, 309, 375–76, 500
Stoic diatribe 35
Stone Lectures 480, 559, 702, 724–25, 755, 821
Stone, John Timothy 673
Storrs, Richard J. 539, 545
Stowe, Calvin 443, 474
Stowe, Harriet Beecher 444, 466, 474
Strabo, Walafrid 104–5
Straton, John Roach 731–32
Strauss, David 346, 466
Strong, Augustus Hopkins 410, 656
Stuart, Moses 615
Studd, C. T. 511, 573, 705
Studdert-Kennedy, G. A. 774
Stylites, Simon 81
Sumner, C. R. 457
Sumner, John Bird 457, 577
Sunday, William Ashley (Billy) 542, 669, 672–76, 725, 751, 784
Sung-Bong Lee 790
Sun-Joo Kil 790
Sunukjian, Donald 828
Suso, Heinrich 136
Sutton, Harry 701
Svensson, Knut 806
Swedenborg, Emanuel 491, 504, 623, 649, 769–70
Swift, Albert 634
Swing, David Gram 658
Switzerland 483
synagogue worship 34–35

Tacitus 69
Taft, William Howard 669, 811
Tait, Archibald Campbell 577
Talbot, Louis T. 835
Talmage, Thomas De Witt 542, 544, 689, 743
Tatford, Frederick 611
Tauler, Johannes 120, 133, 135–36, 139, 160, 201, 237, 616
Taylor, James Hudson 421, 517, 519, 522, 527, 638, 722, 814
Taylor, Jeremy 217–19, 220, 226, 237, 273, 280, 429, 569
Teelinck, William 239
temperance 442, 564, 586, 641, 673, 709
Temple, Frederick 701, 709, 773
Temple, William 665, 772–75, 816
Templeton, Chuck 782
Tennent, Gilbert 376, 378–81
Tennent, John 376, 379
Tennent, William, Jr. 376, 379
Tennent, William, Sr. 376, 379
Tennyson, Alfred 449, 460, 498, 534, 621, 657, 766
Teresa of Avila 213, 229
Tersteegen, Gerhard 239, 244, 474
Thackeray, William Makepeace 331
Thatcher, Margaret 763
Theodore of Mopsuestia 85, 98
Theodoret of Cyprus 98
Theodulf of Orleans 114
theosophy 237, 612–13, 649
Thielicke, Helmut 583, 800–2
Tholuck, Friedrich August 355–56, 441, 469, 472, 474, 569, 604, 642
Thomas, John 388
Thomas Aquinas 108, 113, 120, 121, 122, 124, 129
Thomas of Brandwardine 144
Thomas of Cobham 124
Thomas of Salisbury 124
Thompson, Andrew 419, 560
Thompson, Francis 648
Thomson, Andrew 425–27
Thoreau, Henry David 649
Thornwell, James Henley 554–55
Thorwall, A. J. 808–9
Thurman, Howard 782
Thurneysen, Eduard 165, 475
Tillich, Paul 782–83
Tillotson, John 221, 223–25, 282, 291, 329, 334, 339, 348, 656, 857

Tocqueville, Alexis de 235, 528
Tode, Thomas 131
Toplady, Augustus M. 395
Torrey, Reuben Archer 607, 669–72, 679, 729, 824
  Holy Spirit and 670
Townsend, W. Cameron 727
Toy, C. H. 552–53
Tozer, A. W. 661, 843–46
Travers, Walter 187
Tregelles, Samuel 501, 565, 606
Trollope, Anthony 449, 460, 462, 849, 855
Truett, George W. 683, 736, 739–42
Trumbull, Henry Clay 607
Tübingen, University of 477
Twain, Mark 222, 374
Tyndale, William 177–78
typology 79, 298, 305, 613, 642, 839

Urban II 119
Ussher, James 207, 223, 281, 284–85, 316

Valdes, Juan de 246–47
Valiero, Agostino 226, 245
Van Bismarck, Otto 759–60
Van Gogh, Vincent 583
Van Til, Cornelius 799, 805
Varley, Henry 511, 611
Vasser, John 547
Vaughn, C. J. 594–95
Veitch, Thomas Stewart 602, 605
Venn, Henry 397, 403, 405, 407–9
Vestiarian controversy 251
Victor 105, 116, 142
Victoria, Queen 449, 509, 566, 627, 709
Vieyra, Antonio 247
Vincent de Paul 229
Vinet, Alexandre 231–32, 481, 484–85, 515
Viret, Pierre 162
Vitrier, Jean 126
Voetius 226, 297
Voltaire 234, 324, 329, 483
Von Moltke of Germany, 572

Waldo, Peter 124, 128
Wales, the spiritual quickening 362
Waleys, Thomas 201
Walker, Alan 596, 815–17
Wallace, Lew 552
Walton, Izaak 214, 280–81
Wang, Leland 786
Ward, Graham 795
Warfield, B. B. 88, 456, 502, 698, 750, 819, 822
Warrack Lectures 557, 616, 627, 764, 771
Warren, Timothy 828
Washington, George 434
Watchman Nee 475, 786–89
Watson, Philip 156
Watson, Thomas 250, 254, 266, 279–80, 287
Watts, Isaac 284, 289, 335–36, 338–39, 372, 453, 601
Wayland, Francis 444–45, 521
Weatherhead, Leslie 589, 693
Weld, Theodore 443
Wellhausen, Julius 476, 574, 596
Wells, Algernon 453
Welsh revival 632, 636, 646, 677, 786
Welsh, John 312, 316
Wesley, Charles 362, 367–70, 372
Wesley, John 218, 239, 244, 360, 363–68, 597, 681, 692, 853
Wesley, Samuel 332, 337, 360, 364
Wesley, Susanna 363–64, 368
West, Nathaniel 736
Westcott, Brooke Foss 150, 552, 595, 614, 699–700, 756
Westminster Confession of Faith 254
Whatley, Richard 455
Wheelwright, John 293, 307
White, John 262, 264
Whitefield, George 370–71
Whitehead, Alfred North 329, 498
Whitesell, Faris 828
Whitman, Walter 649
Whittier, John Greenleaf 139, 372, 466, 657
Whyte, Alexander 562–63, 614–17
Wichern, Johan 795–96
Wilberforce, Basil 697
Wilberforce, Samuel 456–59, 465–66, 468, 590
Wilberforce, William 340, 416, 457, 576–77
Wilfrid of Northumbria 111
Wilhelmina, Queen 480
Willard, Frances E. 537
Willard, Samuel 308
William Borden of Yale 717
William of Auvergne 201
William of Champeaux 116
William of Occam 144

William of Orange 311
William Thierry of Chartres 131
William, Frederick, III 468
Williams, John 525
Williams, Roger 294–95, 325
Williams, William 362
Willibrord 111–12
Wilson, Daniel 403
Wilson, J. Christy 717–18
Wilson, J. Hood 526, 573
Wilson, Robert Dick 728, 737–38, 819
Wilson, Walter L. 838–39
Wilson, Woodrow 732, 820
Winchester, A. B. 701
Winfrid 112
Winthrop, John 263, 294
Wiseman, Frederick Luke 689
Wishart, George 190
Witherspoon, John 416, 433–35
Witness Lee 788–89
Woelfkin, Cornelius 744
Wolsey, Thomas 176
Wood, David 658
Wordsworth, William 347
Workman, Herbert B. 689
World Missionary Conference, Edinburgh 703
Wulfstan, 115
Wycliffe, John 144–47, 176, 250

Xavier, Francis 247

Yale, Elihu 299
Yang-Won Sohn 790
Young, Dinsdale T. 629–31, 768
Yu, Dora 786

Zahn, Theodore 670, 755, 759–61
Zeno of Verona 91, 456
Ziegenbalg, Bartholomew 300, 383–84
Ziegler, Clement 195–96
Zinzendorf, Nicholas Ludwig Count von 240, 242, 244, 337, 350, 380, 384, 706
Zwemer, Samuel Marinus 696, 716, 769
Zwickau Prophets 195
Zwingli, Uhlrich 134, 150–52, 169–75, 183, 189, 196, 673, 857

Author Index

Achtemeier, Elizabeth 65
Ackroyd, Peter 770
Adams, Jay E. 180, 373, 378, 823
Adamson, William 589
Addison, Daniel Dulany 533, 535
Affleck, Bert 282
Alan of Lille 132
Aland, Kurt 73, 143, 152, 155, 173, 228, 236, 238, 241, 330, 468, 471
Albright, Raymond W. 535
Aldridge, John William 152
Alexander, Helen C. 671
Alexander, J. W. 561
Alexander, James A. 441
Allan, Tom 766
Allen, M. C. 217
Allen, Roland 48, 523
Allison, C. F. 268, 325
Ambrose, Stephen E. 504
Anderson, Arthur W. 810
Anderson, Charles S. 117
Anderson, Courtney 521
Anderson, Duncan 310–12, 315, 317
Anderson, Norman 718
Andersson, Ingvar 493
Andrea, Jacob 237
Andrews, C. F. 793
Appasamy, A. J. 793
Arden, G. Everett 489, 491, 493, 495
Arminius, Jacob 195
Armstrong, B. G. 232
Asbury, Herbert 437
Ashwell, A. R. 459
Atiya, Aziz S. 87
Atkinson, James 157, 163, 168, 177, 184–85, 192
Auerbach, Erich 94
Autrey, C. E. 359
Auxier, John Wheeler 441
Axling, William 785
Aycock, Don M. 744

Baab, Otto J. 33
Bach, T. J. 124, 385–86, 525
Bailey, Raymond H. 44–45, 50, 553, 851
Baillie, John 240–41
Bailyn, Bernard 434
Bainton, Roland H. 151–52, 154–55, 160
Baird, J. Arthur 44, 45
Baird, Robert 487
Baker, A. E. 774–75
Baker, J. Wayne 257
Baldwin, Neil 650
Balfour, Frances 622
Balleine, G. R. 459, 464
Bangs, Carl 195, 837
Banks, Louis Albert 682
Bannerman, James 561–62
Barbour, G. F. 615, 617
Barclay, William 666, 749
Bark, William Carroll 97–98
Barnes, Howard A. 530
Barnes, Timothy David 71
Barnhouse, Donald Grey 825–26
Barnhouse, Margaret N. 825
Barrett, C. K. 48, 50
Barth, Karl 58, 353, 430, 476, 799, 800
Bartleman, Frank 837
Baskerville, Stephen 252–53
Baxter, Batsell B. 535
Bayley, Peter 209–10, 227–28, 230, 232
Baylis, Charles P. 58
Baylis, Robert 602
Beach, Harlan P. 521
Beaton, Donald 568
Beatty, James 539
Beaudean, William, Jr. 58
Bebbington, David W. 329, 331, 413, 418–19, 431, 719
Beck, Johan Tobias 477
Becket, Thomas 116, 119, 856
Bedoyere, Michael De La 617

Begbie, Harold 686
Bellah, Robert N. 430, 715, 829
Benedetto, Don 247
Benne, Robert 405
Bennett, Arthur 261
Bennett, Robert 363
Benson, Bruce Ellis 151
Benson, Joseph 369
Bentley, James 797
Beougher, Timothy K. 284
Bergendoff, Conrad 491
Berger, Peter L. 17, 730
Berkouwer, G. C. 51
Berlin, Isaiah 22
Bertraut, Jean 228
Bethge, Eberhard 802
Billington, Dallas F. 680
Birch, J. H. S. 495
Birkerts, Sven 17
Birks, Thomas 463
Birrell, C. M. 452, 636
Bishop, John 168, 175, 192, 460, 582, 589, 594, 628–30, 635, 643, 645, 654, 695, 765, 772, 821
Black, James 765
Blackwood, Andrew W. 33, 684, 823
Blackwood, James R. 462
Blaikie, W. G. 318, 320, 322–23, 342, 344, 346, 423, 425, 517
Blaiklock, E. M. 62, 83
Blench, J. W. 179–82, 186–88, 203, 205, 208, 213
Blickle, Peter 172–73
Bloesch, Donald G. 601, 798
Bloom, Allan 810, 829
Blowers, Paul M. 98
Blumhofer, Edith 602, 675
Bodey, Richard Allen 135, 767, 821
Bonhoeffer, Dietrich 202, 475
Boorstin, Daniel J. 254
Booth, Wayne C. 851
Boreham, Frank W. 161, 192, 410–11, 517, 814–15
Borgen, Ole E. 367
Bork, Robert H. 828–29
Borowitz, Eugene 779
Boshold, Frank S. 475
Boston, Thomas 342
Bourne, F. W. 510
Bouwsma, William J. 161, 163
Bowman, John Wick 799
Boyle, Marjorie O'Rourke 151
Bradlaugh, Charles 596
Bramlett, Perry 762
Brandewie, Ernest 718
Brastow, Lewis O. 352–54, 456, 462, 529–30, 532–33, 535, 559, 583, 627
Brauer, Jerald C. 263
Brendon, Piers 627
Breward, Ian 206, 208, 382
Brierley, Peter 602
Bright, John 51
Bright, William 100
Brinsley, John 253
Brinton, Crane 330
Broadus, John A. 14, 26, 47, 484–85, 551, 553, 555, 733, 736, 755
Bromiley, G. W. 179
Brooke, Stopford 462
Broomhall, Marshall 392
Brown, Ira V. 533
Brown, Dale 239, 241–42
Brown, Harold O. J. 69, 810
Brown, John 104, 180, 182, 258–59, 261, 265, 271, 276, 284, 293, 306, 308, 343–45, 419, 564
Brown, Peter 78–79, 88, 90–91, 93–94
Brown, Robert McAfee 749
Brown, Stewart J. 425
Brown, W. J. 219
Browne, G. F. 107, 109
Bruce, F. F. 36, 51, 54–55, 57–58, 72, 79, 103, 113, 200, 602, 606, 761
Bruch, Harry Vom 680
Bruner, F. Dale 50
Brunner, Emil 238, 350, 799
Bruns, Roger 674
Bryson, Harold T. 169, 656, 851
Buchan, John 618
Bulkeley, Peter 293, 307
Bullmore, Michael 60
Bulloch, James 103
Bulwer-Lytton, William Henry 498
Burg, B. R. 269
Burghardt, Walter J. 794
Burkhart, Jacob 129
Burleigh, J. H. S. 314
Burns, James 360
Burr, Agnes Rush 659
Burtchaell, James 330
Burton, E. D. 166
Burton, Henry 252
Burtt, E. A. 330
Bush, Eberhard 799
Bush, L. Rush 665
Bush, Sargent, Jr. 306
Buttrick, David 851
Byrum, Bessie L. 526

Cadbury, H. J. 50–51
Cahill, Thomas 103
Cailliet, Emile 227
Caird, John 331, 621
Cairns, Earle E. 360, 386, 409, 506, 508, 697
Cameron, Nigel M. de S. 312, 344, 425, 427, 430, 561, 565, 575, 712, 772
Campbell, John 452
Campbell, Ted A. 262, 373
Campenhausen, Hans von 76, 96–97
Cannon, William Ragsdale 117, 130
Cantine, James 717
Cantor, Norman F. 98, 101, 123, 129
Carden, Allen 255
Carey, John 214, 216
Carey, S. Pearce 388
Carlile, John C. 582
Carlstig, John 809
Carlyle, Gavin 571
Carrithers, Gale H., Jr. 216
Carroll, Benajah Harvey 557
Carroll, Thomas K. 67–68, 71, 73, 75, 83–84, 94, 102
Carson, D. A. 714–15, 800
Carter, Stephen L. 715, 829
Carus, William 405
Carwardine, Richard J. 557
Case, Shirley Jackson 670

Catherwood, Christopher 778
Chadwick, Owen 108
Chambers, Biddy 769–70
Chandos, John 280
Chappell, Wallace D. 684
Cheetham, S. 241
Cheney, Mary Bushnell 530
Chesterton, G. K. 124
Chillingworth, William 223, 262
Chisholm, Robert B., Jr. 33
Choy, Leona 707
Clare, Arthur 590
Clark, Clifford E., Jr., 532
Clark, Robert D. 537
Clow, William McCallum 626, 765–67
Coder, S. Maxwell 338, 578
Coggan, F. Donald 749, 769–70
Coleman, Robert E. 597
Collier, James Lincoln 715
Collins, Varnum Lansing 435
Collinson, Patrick 286
Collis, Louise 113
Colson, Charles W. 109, 459
Come, Donald R. 295
Comfort, Earl V. 828
Conforti, Joseph 433
Conkin, Paul K. 381
Copeland, Aaron 15
Cottingham, Stephen K. 295
Coulton, G. G. 117
Cousins, Norman 849, 851
Cowan, Henry 192
Craddock, Fred 495
Cragg, George G. 408
Craig, Robert 774
Crankshaw, Edward 760
Crawford, Thomas J. 575
Crocker, Lionel 746
Crooks, George R. 538
Cross, Barbara M. 530
Crossan, John Dominic 794
Crowther, M. A. 468
Cumbers, Frank 695
Cumming, J. Elder 697
Cunningham, Charles 433
Curtis, Charles J. 807
Curtis, George M., III 549
Cusack, Pearse 102
Cutting, George 611, 787
Cuyler, Theodore 540–41, 736
d'Aubigne, Merle 232, 418, 483, 485–86
d'Avray, D. L. 123
Dabney, Robert Lewis 202
Dallimore, Arnold A. 369, 373
Daniel, Greg K. 286
Daniel-Rops, H. 484–85
Daniell, David 178
Darby, Harold S. 180
Dargan, E. C. 14, 92, 109, 113, 178, 180–83, 187–89, 209, 221, 232, 235, 238, 273, 277, 346, 352, 355, 357, 412, 478, 481, 484, 486, 552, 743
Dark, Sidney 211, 219, 577
Darlow, T. H. 482
Davey, Cyril J. 793
Davies, C. Maurice 591
Davies, Robertson 215–16
Davis, Donald Gordon 398
Davis, George T. B. 678
Dawn, Marva J. 795
Day, Gwynn McLendon 200
Day, Richard Ellsworth 671, 781
Dayton, Donald W. 502
De Brand, Roy E. 684
De Koster, Lester 93
De Plata, William R. 732
De Quincy, Thomas 429
DeJong, Peter Y. 298
Delbanco, Andrew 293, 303, 308, 310, 548–49
Demarest, Bruce A. 804
Derickson, Gary 58
Derry, T. K. 489
Devor, Richard C. 32
Dibelius, Martin 50
Diduit, Michael 22
Dillenberger, Jane 238
Dirks, Marvin J. 801
Dixon, Helen C. A. 737
Doan, Gilbert E. 462
Dockery, David S. 86
Dodd, C. H. 43, 50, 64, 512
Donaldson, August B. 591
Dorsett, Lyle Wesley 692
Dorsey, Gary 306
Doughty, W. L. 367
Douglas, W. M. 707
Drakeford, John W. 223, 825
Drummond, Andrew L. 475, 477
Drummond, Lewis A. 502
Du Plessis, J. 707
Duckett, Eleanor 113
Dunning, Norman G. 690
Dupanloup, Felix 482
Durant, Ariel 347
Durant, Will 347

Eadie, John 50, 55–56, 552, 563–65
Ebeling, Gerhard 37
Echlin, Edward P. 73, 153
Eddy, Sherwood 728
Edman, V. Raymond 103, 385, 502, 669
Edwards, Brian H. 373, 711
Edwards, John 479, 559, 570, 594–95
Edwards, O. C. 9, 456, 530
Eidsmoe, John 435
Eliot, T. S. 187, 211, 213, 623, 856
Ella, George M. 340
Eller, Vernard 476
Elliot, Elizabeth 728–29, 825
Elliott, Emory 256–57, 295–96, 298, 301
Elliott-Binns, L. 176, 179, 181, 185–86
Ellis, J. J. 526
Ellis, William T. 674
Ellul, Jacques 21–22, 475
Emerson, Everett H. 295, 298, 303, 308
English, E. Schuyler 612, 744
Englizian, H. Crosby 439, 665, 828
Eno, Robert B. 97
Ensor, R. C. K. 449
Epstein, Daniel Mark 675
Erb, Peter C. 238, 245
Ericksen, Robert P. 797
Eucken, Rudolph 88
Eusebius 65–66, 68, 72, 85, 96
Evans, Efion 514
Evearitt, Daniel J. 661

Fairweather, William 36

Fant Clyde, Jr. 66
Fant David J., Jr. 845
Fant, Clyde E. 803
Fant, Kenne 807
Farmer, H. H. 713, 794
Farrar, F. W. 74, 80, 594–95, 727
Farrar, R. A. 595
Fast, Howard 417
Faulkner, Robert K. 188
Fausett, Hugh l'Anson 340
Fawcett, Arthur 382
Faye, Eugene de 75
Fea, John 432
Fenelon, Francois de 83, 235
Ferguson, Charles W. 177
Ferguson, Everett 64, 66
Ferguson, Sinclair B. 273, 772
Findlay, James F. 510, 513, 839
Findley, G. G. 596
Finger, Charles J. 517
Finkelstein, Louis 36
Fish, Henry C. 486, 507–8
Fletcher, Joseph 774
Flood, Charles Bracelen 549
Forbes, James 47, 213
Foster, John 68, 412
Foster, R. F. 514
Foy, Matilda 487
Fraser, Antonia 261
Fraser, Elouise Renich 32
Friedrich, Gerhard 79, 498–99, 599
Froehlich, Karlfried 86
Fromow, George H. 606
Frye, Northrop 24–25, 41
Fuchs, Ernst 61–62
Fuhrmann, Paul T. 240–41, 485
Fukuyama, Francis 259
Fuller, Charles 22
Fuller, David Otis 752
Fullerton, W. Y. 639
Furcha, E. J. 173, 175

Gabler, Ulrich 170, 173, 175
Gallaway, Ira 681
Gammie, Alexander 627, 630, 647, 774
Gangel, Kenneth O. 60, 838–39
Garrett, Ray E. 677
Garvie, Alfred Earnest 203, 232, 235, 238, 241, 271, 342, 344, 348, 373, 427, 430, 484–85, 645, 747
Gasque, W. Ward 48, 620
Gaukroger, Stephen 227
Gaustad, Edwin S. 295
Gay, Peter 416–17
Geertsema, J. 805
Gelernter, David 848–49
George, Timothy 155, 166, 169, 197, 268, 388
Gericke, Paul 743–44
German, James 378
Gerstner, John H. 378
Gibbon, Edward 79
Giboney, Ezra P. 812
Gill, Everett 395, 412, 547, 553, 584, 756, 760
Gillispie, Charles Coulston 459
Glendinning, Victoria 462
Godet, Frederick L. 486
Goodman, George 703
Goppelt, Leonard 79, 839
Gorday, Peter 86
Gordon, Ernest B. 548
Gordon, Lyndall 408
Goulburn, Edward M. 553
Graham, Stephen R. 528
Grant, F. W. 606
Grauer, O. C. 527
Gray, James M. 608–9
Green, Michael 50–51
Green, Vivian 155
Gregory, Olinthus 412
Greidanus, Sidney 684
Grosart, Alexander B. 282
Grudem, Wayne A. 60
Guelzo, Allen C. 502
Guest, John 33
Guibert 130
Gundry, Stanley N. 510, 512
Gushee, David P. 803
Guthrie, Arthur 570
Gutman, Joseph 36

Hagglund, Henrik 358
Hagman, Harvey 22
Hale, John 129
Hall, Clarence W. 688
Hall, David L. 257, 306
Hall, Edward H. 68
Hall, John 539
Hall, Michael G. 298, 310
Hall, Thomas C. 539
Haller, William 257, 294–95
Hambrick-Stowe, Charles 502
Hamilton, Kenneth 681
Hamilton, Nigel 595
Hamilton-Williams, David 417
Handy, Francis J. 45
Haney, John Louis 459
Hannah, John D. 117, 507
Hanson, R. P. C. 75, 103
Harman, Allan 422
Harper, Ralph M. 535
Harries, John 634
Harris, Horton 347, 350, 477
Harris, William 286
Harrison, Everett F. 48, 51, 758
Harrison, J. F. C. 464
Hart, A. Tindal 185
Hart, D. G. 650, 716, 725, 752
Hartwell, Herbert 800
Hatch, Edwin 66, 92–93, 104
Hawkinson, Eric G. 493, 808–9
Hayden, Eric W. 587, 712
Hayward, Edward F. 444
Heath, Peter 127
Hedrick, Joan D. 444
Hein, Rolland 623
Heitzenrater, Richard P. 367
Henderson, G. D. 312, 315, 317, 323, 425
Henderson, Harold R. 817
Henderson, Henry F. 344, 427
Hennell, Michael 464, 467
Henry, Carl F. H. 15, 44–45, 600, 656, 730, 747, 758, 778, 800
Henry, Stuart C. 444
Herr, Alan Fager 185–86
Hesselgrave, David J. 385
Hession, Roy and Revel 789
Hethcock, William 535–36
Hewlett, J. P. 277
Hicks, W. Percy 544
Hill, Brad 781
Hill, Christopher 200
Hill, Ninian 312, 330

Hilton, Boyd 425, 459, 577
Hilton, Michael 42
Himmelfarb, Gertrude 416–17, 795
Hodge, Homer 692
Hoeg, Peter 806–7
Hoffman, Daniel 347
Hollister, C. Warren 118, 129
Holmes, Richard 347
Holt, Ivan Lee 667
Hood, E. Paxton 235, 247, 280, 454
Hoogenboom, Ari 533
Hopkins, Hugh Evan 405
Hoppin, James 540
Horne, C. Sylvester 370, 625, 640, 646–47
Horne, Herman Harrell 45
Houghton, Frank 729
Houghton, Walter E. 499
Houston, James 374, 378
Houston, James M. 109, 247
Howard, David M., Jr. 25
Howard, Philip E., Jr. 386–87, 607
Howden, William D. 66
Hubbard, Ethel Daniels 395
Huehns, Gertrude 295
Hughes, Edward J. 91
Hughes, H. Trevor 219
Hughes, Kathleen 103
Huizinga, Johan 124, 128, 151
Hull, J. Mervin 521
Hume, Robert E. 793
Huntemann, Georg 804
Hunter, A. H. 43
Hunter, J. H. 721
Hunter, Leslie Stannard 487, 489, 491
Huntley, Frank Livingstone 219
Huss, John E. 744
Hut, John 195
Hutson, Curtis 513, 692, 831
Huxley, Elspeth 517
Hyde, T. Alexander 45
Hyma, Albert 134

Innis, George S. 146
Iremonger, F. A. 774
Irvine, William 459

Jacobson, A. H. 809
Jalland, Trevor 99
James, Henry 438, 627, 828
James, Powhatan W. 739, 741
Jay, Elizabeth 576
Jeal, Tim 517
Jeffrey, David Lyle 340
Jenkins, Claude 109
Jenkins, Daniel 847
Jenkins, Elizabeth 177
Jenkins, R. B. 205
Johnson, James E. 502
Johnson, Elliott E. 17
Johnson, Paul 64–65, 329–30, 416–17, 695–96, 730, 763
Johnson, Thomas C. 555
Johnson, Thomas H. 257
Johnson, William Alexander 354
Johnston, Mark D. 132
Jones, Cheslyn 139, 227, 262
Jones, E. Michael 330, 730
Jones, Edgar Dewitt 535
Jones, Maurice 50
Jordan, G. Ray 15, 17, 695
Josephus 40, 116

Kaiser, Walter C., Jr. 30, 349–50, 746, 796, 804
Kane, J. Herbert 721
Kang, K. Connie 790
Kantzer, Kenneth 164, 759
Karl, Frederick R. 449
Keane, John 431
Keeble, N. H. 285
Kelly, Douglas F. 168, 772
Kelly, J. N. D. 10
Kemp, Charles F. 284, 746
Kendall, R. T. 162, 208, 373
Kennedy, George A. 59–60, 92
Kennedy, James Hardee 25
Ker, John 65, 113, 158, 160, 203, 236, 238, 241, 244, 330, 348, 350, 352, 355, 357, 469, 471, 473–74, 477–78, 569
Kerr, David W. 91
Kielland, Alexander 489
Kingsley, Charles 139, 465, 467, 476, 498
Kingwell, Mark 829

Kinlaw, Dennis 47
Kinnear, Angus I. 788
Kirk, Russell 213, 330, 441
Kirwan, William Blake 465
Kjaer, Jens Christian 495
Kleeberger, Jessie 517
Klein, Walter Conrad 25
Knight, Janice 265, 280, 293
Kohl, Manfred Waldemar 244
Koller, Charles W. 725
Kooienga, William H. 93–94, 208
Korner, S. 353
Kraehling, Carl H. 39
Krupp, R. A. 80, 82–83
Kuhns, Oscar 149
Kustra, George L. 36
Kyle, Melvin Grove 737–38
Kyle, Richard G. 192

Lachman, David C. 320, 342
Lacroix, John P. 473
Lake, Kirsop 50–51, 455
Lambert, D. W. 594, 770
Lambert, Frank 373
Lamont, William M. 285
Langan, Thomas 353
Lange, Johan Peter 479
Larsen, David L. 43, 241, 259, 571, 666
LaSor, William S. 36
Latourette, Kenneth Scott 15, 66, 103, 113, 117, 162, 245, 385, 391, 393, 395, 475, 486, 515, 716–17
Lavater, Hans Fredrich 476
Lawrence, William 534–35
Laws, Gilbert 410
Lawson, J. Gilchrist 502, 506, 508, 512, 686
Lear, H. L. Sidney 230, 235, 482
Lears, T. J. Jackson 534
Leclercq, Jean 109
Lee, Robert G. 742–44, 666, 853
Leith, John H. 168–69
Lejeune, R. 474, 476
Lennox, Cuthbert 573
Leonard, Bill J. 367
Leuenberger, Samuel 179
Levine, Raphael 36

Levy, Isaac 64
Lewis, Edwin 680
Lewis, James 437
Lewis, Peter 257
Leyser, Karl 117
Lienhard, Joseph T. 75
Lightfoot, J. B. 35–36, 68
Lincoln, C. Eric 780
Lindsay, Nicholas Vachel 685
Lindsay, T. F. 108
Lindsell, Harold 828
Lindstrom, Harald 367
Linnemann, Eta 45
Litfin, Duane 59–60
Livingstone, W. P. 524
Lloyd-Jones, Bethan 778
Loane, Marcus L. 39, 314, 317, 409
Locke, Hubert G. 797
Loeschen, John R. 197
Loetscher, Lefferts A. 441
Longenecker, Richard 772
Lorimer, George C. 655–56, 733
Loscalzo, Craig A. 851
Lossky, Nicholas 213
Love, Bill 551
Lovelace, Richard F. 299, 301, 306, 375–78
Lowance, Mason I. 298
Lowrie, Ernest Benson 309
Lowry, Charles W. 774
Ludwig, Charles 437
Lundbom, Jack R. 32
Lundin, Roger 535–36
Luscombe, David 118
Luz, Ulrich 161

MacArthur, Robert S. 732
Macaulay, J. C. 357
M'Cosh, James 558
MacDuff, John R. 572
MacIntyre, Alasdair 109
Mackenzie, Robert 345
Mackintosh, H. R. 353, 799
Maclean, J. Kennedy 652–53, 671
MacLennan, David 765
Macleod, Donald 561, 566, 821
Maclure, Millar 268
Macmillan, Donald 575
MacMullen, Ramsay 66
Macpherson, Hector 312
Maier, Walter A. 754
Major, H. D. A. 579
Malherbe, Abraham J. 51
Malzer, Gottfried 350
Mamiya, Lawrence H. 780
Mangs, Frank 807–8
Mann, A. Chester 639
Mantle, J. Gregory 542, 544
Marrat, J. 369
Marsden, George 373, 535–36, 758
Marsh, F. E. 661
Marsh, P. T. 577
Marshall, R. P. 681
Marston, Charles 763
Martin, Bernard 340
Martin, Brian 456
Martin, David 260, 696
Martin, Hugh 567–68
Martin, Malachi 795
Martin, Roger 671
Marty, Martin 239, 829
Massa, Mark S. 614
Massee, J. C. 665, 704
Mather, P. Boyd 367
Matheson, Ann 319, 330, 344
Matheson, George 622, 639
Matson, Edla 788
Matthews, Mark A. 813
Mauro, Philip 835
Maxwell, L. E. 727, 846
May, James M. 92
May, Sherry Pierpont 446
McCasland, David 769
McCloskey, Mark 217
McClure, Judith 109
McConica, James 151
McCormack, Bruce L. 799
McCoy, Charles S. 257, 312, 350
McCraw, Louise Harrison 698
McCrossan, T. J. 752
McCulloh, Gerald O. 195
McCullough, David 540
McDonald, H. D. 530, 817
McFarland, K. B. 146
McGee, J. Vernon 835–36
McGinlay, James 825
McGinn, Bernard 17
McGinness, Frederick J. 247
McGrath, Alister 154
McGraw, James 174
McIntyre, R. E. 765
McKinley, David J. 273
McLaren, E. T. 582
McLean, Archibald 550
McLoughlin, William G. 502, 510, 512, 532
McLynn, Neil B. 79
McNeil, John T. 241
Mead, Frank S. 373
Mead, Sidney 301, 510
Meadows, Denis 109
Mecklenburg, George 431
Meek, Donald E. 103
Meeks, Wayne A. 66
Meinhold, Peter 157
Meissner, W. W. 248
Melton, J. Gordon 789
Metzgar, Bruce M. 136
Meuser, Fred W. 157, 160
Meyer, Frederick Brotherton 639
Meyer, H. A. W. 479
Mezezers, Valdis 240
Middlekauff, Robert 269, 298, 301, 310
Middleton, R. D. 456
Miller, Basil 605, 797
Miller, Donald 749
Miller, Perry 208, 256–57, 262, 294, 305, 308, 374, 500
Miller, William Lee 417
Milligan, George 575
Milman, Henry H. 97
Milner, Isaac 401
Mims, O. Eugene 744
Minnix, Kathleen 667
Mitchell, Henry 780–81
Mitchell, W. Fraser 221, 223, 282, 291
Moffat, James 224
Moffat, John S. 395, 838
Moloney, Michael Francis 216
Moltmann, Jürgen 108–9
Moncrief, Henry Wellwood 561
Monod, Theodore 696
Montgomery, John Warwick 244

Moody, William R. 512, 670
Moody-Stuart, K. 514
Moore, Arthur J. 682
Moore-Anderson, A. P. 610
Moorman, John R. H. 124
Morgan, Edmund S. 308
Morgan, Jill 634–35
Morgan, Richard Lyon 635
Morimoto, Anri 378
Morris, Leon 13, 246, 815–16
Morrison, Henry Clay 692, 718
Moss, Jean Dietz 556
Mott, Wesley T. 325
Mounce, Robert H. 50–51
Mouw, Richard J. 25
Mudge, James 235
Mueller, J. Theodore 156–57, 392, 753
Mueller, William R. 213, 216
Muilenberg, James 31
Muller, Richard A. 195, 275
Mullins, E. Y. 744
Munch, Alo 476
Murdoch, J. Murray 746
Murphy, James J. 99, 101, 109, 201
Murphy, Paul R. 217
Murphy-O'Connor, Jerome 56
Murray, Andrew 707–8, 716
Murray, Iain H. 303, 378, 437, 512, 613, 646, 778
Myers, Cortland 160, 656, 744
Myrc, John 126–27

Nassif, Bradley L. 86
Nazzarino, Santo 97
Needham, Nicholas R. 427, 561
Neely, Lois 834
Neill, Stephen 83
Nelson, Gerald L. 17
Nelson, Lawrence E. 200
Nettles, Thomas J. 665
Neve, J. L. 241
Nevius, Helen S. 523
Newbigin, J. Leslie 110
Newman, A. H. 75, 485
Newsome, David 456, 459, 462
Nicholson, William R. 548
Nicoll, W. Robertson 420, 573, 581, 589, 593, 625
Niebuhr, Reinhold 793, 846
Niebuhr, Richard R. 354
Niemoller, Martin 797
Nixon, Leroy 163, 168
Njus, Joel M. 489
Noll, Mark 374–75, 377–78, 512, 614, 719, 752, 813, 831
Nolland, Lisa S. 813
North, Brownlow 514
Northcott, Cecil 395
Northcott, R. J. 774
Nuttall, Geoffrey F. 260–61, 282, 284
Nyvall, David 527

Oberman, Heiko A. 154
Ockenga, Harold John 665, 826, 828
Oden, Thomas 495, 507
Olford, Stephen F. 694, 840, 851
Olin, John C. 151
Oliver, Robert T. 790
Oliver, W. H. 464
Olivier, D. 160
Olson, A. T. 419
Olsson, Karl A. 358, 487, 493
O'Malley, John W. 248
Oman, John 201–2
Ong, Walter 21–22
Oosterzee, Van 239, 480
Orr, James Edwin 374, 619–20, 647, 788
Otten, Willemien 117
Ottley, R. L. 88
Ottman, Ford C. 669
Owst, G. R. 125, 127

Pache, Rene 761
Packer, J. I. 16, 21–22, 255, 261, 272–73, 284, 777
Padwick, Constance E. 696
Painter, Sidney 117
Painter, William Edward 374
Palmer, R. R. 417
Palmquist, Herbert E. 493, 810
Pan, Samuel S. 45
Parkhurst, Louis Gifford, Jr. 502, 747
Paterson, John 627
Paton, John G. 526
Patterson, Bob 97
Pattison, T. Harwood 82, 84, 91, 127, 180, 182, 200, 211, 216, 224, 227, 232, 235, 265, 277, 291, 316–17, 323, 332–33, 338, 340, 367, 410, 425, 427, 430, 433, 444, 467, 486, 540, 544
Patton, John L. 602
Paul, Robert S. 749
Paxson, Ruth 730
Payne, Ernest A. 756
Payne, J. Barton 71
Payne, Robert 70–71, 77, 91, 101
Peake, A. S. 597
Peale, Norman Vincent 719–20
Pearson, B. H. 770
Pelikan, Jaroslav 157
Pennington, M. Basil 109
Percy, Douglas C. 721
Percy, L. Helen 521
Perry, Lloyd M. 132, 203, 447, 823
Petersen, Rodney L. 56
Peterson, Robert A. 422
Pettit, Norman 270
Phelps, Morgan 725, 857
Phelps, Austin 484–85, 539–40
Phelps, William Lyon 200
Philip, Adam 425, 427, 557–58
Phillips, D. M. 678
Phillips, J. B. 762
Phillips, Roger Wendell 758
Pickering, Hy 606
Pierson, A. T. 123, 475, 526, 547, 587, 605, 641, 650–53, 668, 710, 814
Pierson, Delaven Leonard 652
Piggin, Stuart 391, 483
Pike, Eunice 521
Pike, G. Holden 453, 532, 583, 587
Pink, Arthur W. 613
Pinker, Stephen 22
Pinson, Koppel S. 241

Pinson, William M. 66
Piper, John 11, 378
Pipkin, H. Wayne 173, 175
Pitts, John 582, 643
Pletsch, Carl 499
Plumstead, A. W. 306
Poling, Daniel 752
Polizzotto, Lorenzo 139
Pollock, John C. 340, 464, 512, 519, 602, 696, 700, 705, 710, 712, 818, 826
Polman, A. D. 91
Poor, D. W. 486
Pope, William B. 474, 689
Porritt, Arthur 450–51, 642, 645
Postman, Neil 17, 142
Potter, Agnes M. 812
Potter, George R. 172, 175, 215
Powicke, F. M. 104
Prenter, Regin 157
Princell, J. G. 493, 527

Railton, George S. 686
Rainy, Robert 575
Raitt, Jill 139
Ramm, Bernard 165, 798
Ramsay, William 48, 620, 755
Ratzinger, Joseph 794
Rausch, David A. 609
Raven, Charles 795
Rawlins, Clive L. 749
Rawlyk, George 831
Ray, Jefferson Davis 557
Reagles, Steve 553
Redpath, Alan 841
Reed, Kevin 192
Rees, Paul Stromberg 837–38
Reeves, Marjorie 109
Reicke, Bo 36
Reid, W. Stanford 192
Reinhardt, Kurt F. 499
Reis, Richard H. 623
Renwick, A. M. 192
Reston, James, Jr. 227
Reu, J. Michael 156
Rice, John R. 680
Rice, Merton S. 682
Richard, Ramesh 201
Richardson, Caroline Francis 211, 219, 275, 284, 286, 292
Richardson, Robert D., Jr. 325
Rickert, Edith 123
Ridderbos, J. 24–25
Riesen, Richard Allan 428, 561, 575
Riley, Marie Acomb 734
Rinne, W. R. 774
Robbins, William 456
Roberts, Dana 788
Roberts, Maurice 568
Robertson, Archibald Thomas 39, 57, 64, 151, 553, 756
Robertson, Darrel M. 513
Robinson, George L. 652
Robinson, H. Wheeler 756
Robinson, William Childs 331
Roddy, Clarence S. 730, 744, 759, 825, 828, 837, 841
Roeder, Ralph 139
Rogal, Samuel J. 367
Rogers, Adrian 744
Rohr, John von 270
Rosenius, Carl Olof 486, 491, 493
Ross, D. M. 572
Ross, John S. 428
Ross, K. R. 574–75
Rossow, Francis 754
Rouse, M. A. 123
Rouse, R. H. 123
Roxborough, John 391
Rudolph, L. C. 437
Rugoff, Milton 444
Runia, Klaas 156, 799, 804
Ruoff, Percy O. 710
Rushton, William 410
Ryan, Halford R. 532
Rygh, G. T. 493

Sachs, William L. 373
Safire, William 21
Samuel, D. N. 405, 464, 579
Sandeen, Ernest R. 602
Sandmel, Samuel 36
Sandoz, Ellis 431
Sangster, Paul 695
Santillana, Giorgio de 227
Sargent, Tony 47, 213, 779
Sattler, Gary R. 245
Sayer, George 762
Schaeffer, Francis 129, 747
Schaff, David 147–48
Schaller, Lyle 848
Schleiner, Winfreid 216
Schmidt, Dietmar 797
Schmidt, Josef 139
Schmidt, Martin 238
Schrenk, G. 350
Schuller, Robert 720
Scobbie, Charles H. H. 40
Scorgie, Glen D. 620
Seaver, Paul S. 253
Sedgewick, Adam 411
Seeberg, Reinhold 156, 238
Segal, Alan F. 378
Sell, Alan P. F. 568, 622, 766
Sellers, Charles Coleman 505
Selwyn, E. G. 58
Semmelroth, Otto 794
Seymour-Smith, Martin 627
Shannon, Frederick 658
Shaw, Robert B. 216–17
Shearer, Roy E. 523
Sheehan, James J. 468
Shelly, Harold Palton 282
Shepherd, William G. 635, 663, 732
Sheridan, Richard 399, 401
Sherley-Price, Leo 124
Shields, Thomas Todhunter 831
Short, Roy 666, 680
Shuffelton, Frank 306
Sidney, Edwin 400, 402, 408
Sider, Robert D. 127
Silverman, Kenneth 301
Simeon, Charles 210
Simon, Charlie May 785
Simon, John S. 396
Simonson, Harold 376, 378
Simpson, Evelyn M. 215
Simpson, James Y. 573
Simpson, Patrick Carnegie 575
Simpson, W. J. Sparrow 230
Sinclair, Merle 435
Skillen, James W. 481
Skinner, Craig 585, 587
Smalley, Beryl 99, 104–5, 109, 113, 117
Smart, James D. 17
Smellie, Alexander 314–15, 317, 319–20, 322–23, 422, 698

Smith, Arthur H. 98
Smith, Charles 460
Smith, David L. 530
Smith, Gary V. 33
Smith, Gene 549
Smith, George Adam 389, 561, 572, 574, 618, 670
Smith, Hilary Dansey 247
Smith, J. Taylor 710
Smith, Jay E. 502
Smith, Michael 65–66
Smith, Timothy L. 367, 373, 507
Smith, Wilbur M. 47, 213, 275, 360, 471, 513, 563, 608, 617, 634–35, 710, 732, 756, 758–60, 775
Smout, Michael 579
Smyth, Charles 143, 216, 224, 403, 405, 462, 592
Smyth, J. Paterson 765
Snyder, Howard 367
Snyder, James L. 845
Sosland, Henry Adler 36
Souter, Alexander 88, 755
Southern, R. W. 105
Southey, Robert 218
Southgate, W. M. 187
Spencer, H. Leith 127
Sprague, William B. 439
Stackhouse, Max 381
Stalker, James 32
Stamm, Frederick Keller 653–54
Stanfield, Vernon L. 553
Stanford, Charles 291–92
Stapfer, Paul 485
Starkey, Marion L. 301
Steer, Roger 605
Steere, Douglas V. 495
Stein, K. James 244
Stein, Stephen J. 432
Steltenkamp, Michael F. 794
Stephens, W. P. 173, 175
Stevenson, Dwight 32
Stevenson, Herbert F. 486, 653, 702, 704, 818, 826, 837, 841
Stewart, James A. 378
Stewart, James S. 772
Stibbs, A. M. 405
Stier, Ewald Rudolf 474
Stock, Eugene 462
Stoeffler, F. Ernest 241, 282
Stone, Irving 583
Stonehouse, Ned B. 45, 60, 725, 751
Stott, John R. W. 13, 17, 52, 328, 498, 816
Stoughton, John 280, 333
Stout, Harry S. 254–55, 303, 308, 363, 373, 383
Strachan, Gordon 430
Strachey, Lytton 498–99
Strahan, James 575, 686
Straton, John Roach 732
Streeter, B. H. 793
Strickland, W. P. 504
Stuart, A. Moody 428
Stump, Joseph 182
Sugden, Edward H. 367
Sugden, Howard 132
Sullivan, Richard E. 97
Sulston, Kenneth Hartley 754
Sumner, Robert L. 680
Sunder-Rao 777–78
Sunderland, Ronald 32
Sundkler, Bengt 781
Sung-Kuh Chung 790
Swanson, Allen J. 789
Sweet, Leonard I. 380
Swing, Albert T. 749
Symington, William 288

Tallach, John 510
Tarr, Leslie K. 831
Tasker, R. V. G. 240–41, 777
Tawney, R. H. 259–60
Taylor, Gardner C. 779, 781
Taylor, Howard 519
Taylor, Larissa 126–27
Taylor, Vincent 666, 816–17
Taylor, William M. 319, 544, 546
Temko, Allan 127
Tenney, Merrill 45, 592
Terry, Milton S. 75, 86
Thielicke, Helmut 801–2
Thiessen, Henry Clarence 760
Tholuck, Friedrich August 357
Thomas, Owen C. 774
Thomas, Robert L. 60
Thompson, Augustine 127, 139
Thompson, James G. S. S. 22
Thompson, James J., Jr. 549
Thornbury, J. F. 446
Thornton, L. S. 188
Thorwall, LaReau 809
Tierney, Brian 117
Tindall, William York 275
Todd, G. Hall 772
Tomson, Ragnar 493
Toon, Peter 257, 273, 285, 579
Torjesen, Edvard 527
Tranter, Nigel 192
Trench, Richard 459
Trevelyan, G. M. 449
Trevor-Roper, Hugh 97, 248
Troeltsch, Ernst 239
Trotter, Melvin 785
Trueblood, Elton 261, 528
Truett, George W. 742
Tuchman, Barbara W. 763
Tucker, Ruth A. 515, 723
Tugwell, Simon 123
Turnbull, Ralph G. 36, 254, 259, 481, 617, 747, 766–67, 786, 812
Turner, George A. 367
Turner, H. E. W. 68–69
Tuttle, George M. 563
Tyler, Bennet 445–46

Vadian 163
Valen-Sendstad, Olav 489, 806–7
Vandenberg, Frank 481
Vander Kam, Henry 805
Vasser, Thomas E. 548
Veith, Gene Edward, Jr. 746
Vidler, A. R. 449
Vine, Charles H. 647
Vischer, Wilhelm 50–51
Volz, Carl A. 66, 77, 82

Wagner, Don C. 635
Wagner, Walter H. 68
Wainwright, Geoffrey 139, 227, 262
Wakefield, Gordon S. 262, 275
Walker, Alan 817
Walker, G. S. M. 101, 117, 123, 129, 132

Walker, Norman L. 561
Wallace, Dewey D., Jr. 286, 292
Wallace, Ronald S. 163, 166, 168
Waller, Altina L. 533
Walls, Jerry L. 681
Walters, Ronald G. 444
Walvoord, John 91, 157, 367
Ward, W. R. 242, 244, 359
Ware, Kallistos 80
Warneck, Johannes 523
Watkinson, William L. 144, 146, 628–29
Watson, Jean L. 563
Watson, Nigel 161
Watt, Gordon 721
Watt, Hugh 425
Watts, Newman 788
Weatherspoon, Jesse Burton 51, 553
Weaver, Richard M. 22, 548
Webb, Robert L. 40
Webber, F. R. 144, 177, 180–86, 188, 205, 208, 219, 221, 224, 241, 256–57, 259, 265, 268, 271, 277, 279, 288, 291, 306, 310, 314–15, 317, 319–21, 334, 342, 344–45, 363, 367, 369, 383, 387, 389, 391, 400, 409, 423, 428, 433, 439, 441, 451, 504, 510, 530, 533, 539, 545, 561, 563, 566, 568, 572, 595, 597, 619, 629, 631, 639, 647–48, 656, 659, 663, 667, 700, 732, 739, 754
Weber, Donald 257, 380
Weber, Jacques 475
Weber, Max 259
Weborg, C. John 350
Wedgewood, C. V. 211
Weidner, R. F. 478
Weinstein, Donald 139
Wells, David F. 16–17, 44–49
Wendell, Barrett 299, 301
Wenger, J. C. 197
Wenham, John W. 42–43
Weremchuk, Max S. 603
Wertenbaker, Thomas Jefferson 301, 303, 306, 308
West, Woody 848, 851
Westcott, Arthur 700
Westfall, Richard S. 330
Westin, Gunnar 419, 487
Wheeler, W. Reginald 723, 725
White, Charles Edward 507
White, Douglas M. 843
Whitgift, John 185
Whitlow, Maurice 709
Wiersbe, Warren W. 132, 203, 317, 635, 700, 702, 746
Wigram, George 606
Wilberforce, Reginald G. 459
Wilberforce, Robert 459
Wilberforce, Samuel 459
Wilder, Amos N. 60
Wilken, Robert L. 66, 82
Wilkinson, John T. 597
Willey, John Heston 82
Williams, David Riddle 607
Williams, George Huntston 197
Williams, J. B. 335
Williams, Roy Walter 262
Willimon, William H. 823
Willison, George F. 253, 268
Wills, Garry 336, 528
Wilson, A. N. 761–62, 856
Wilson, John F. 263, 265, 271, 273
Wilson, Paul Scott 9, 84, 248, 783
Wilson, William 73, 76, 563
Windelband, Wilhelm 325
Wingren, Gustaf 806–7
Winkworth, Susanna 139
Winte, David 69
Witten, Marsha G. 17
Wohl, Louis de 108, 248
Wolff, Robert Lee 576
Wood, A. Skevington 156–57, 160, 195, 330, 338, 360, 362, 367, 380, 383
Wood, Douglas C. 146
Wood, Leon J. 32
Woodbridge, John D. 482
Woodham-Smith, Cecil 464
Woolley, Paul 756–57
Woolverton, John V. 535
Wordsworth, John 493
Workman, Herbert B. 69, 146, 149
Worley, Robert C. 51
Wright, G. Ernest 33
Wuorinen, John H. 491

Yarnold, Edward 139, 227, 262
Yonge, Charlotte 480, 576, 832
Young, Dinsdale T. 630–31
Young, Edward J. 33
Yune-Sun Park 789

Zacharias, Ravi 347
Zahn, Theodore 761
Zaret, David 263
Zeitler, Lester Erwin 754
Zervopoulos, Yerasmus 797
Zylstra, Henry 805

Printed in the United States
63910LVS00002B/139-168

9 780825 430862